# THE ATHEIST'S BIBLE

# The Atheist's Bible

Diderot's *Éléments de physiologie*

Caroline Warman

https://www.openbookpublishers.com

© 2020 Caroline Warman

This work is licensed under a Creative Commons Attribution 4.0 International license (CC BY 4.0). This license allows you to share, copy, distribute and transmit the text; to adapt the text and to make commercial use of the text providing attribution is made to the authors (but not in any way that suggests that they endorse you or your use of the work). Attribution should include the following information:

Caroline Warman, *The Atheist's Bible: Diderot's 'Éléments de physiologie'*. Cambridge, UK: Open Book Publishers, 2020, https://doi.org/10.11647/OBP.0199

In order to access detailed and updated information on the license, please visit, https://doi.org/10.11647/OBP.0199#copyright

Further details about CC BY licenses are available at https://creativecommons.org/licenses/by/4.0/

All external links were active at the time of publication unless otherwise stated and have been archived via the Internet Archive Wayback Machine at https://archive.org/web

Updated digital material and resources associated with this volume are available at https://doi.org/10.11647/OBP.0199#resources

Every effort has been made to identify and contact copyright holders and any omission or error will be corrected if notification is made to the publisher.

ISBN Paperback: 9781783748969
ISBN Hardback: 9781783748976
ISBN Digital (PDF): 9781783748983
ISBN Digital ebook (epub): 9781783748990
ISBN Digital ebook (mobi): 9781783749003
ISBN XML: 9781783749010
DOI: 10.11647/OBP.0199

Cover image and design by Cressida Bell, all rights reserved.

# The Atheist's Bible

Diderot's *Éléments de physiologie*

*Caroline Warman*

https://www.openbookpublishers.com

© 2020 Caroline Warman

This work is licensed under a Creative Commons Attribution 4.0 International license (CC BY 4.0). This license allows you to share, copy, distribute and transmit the text; to adapt the text and to make commercial use of the text providing attribution is made to the authors (but not in any way that suggests that they endorse you or your use of the work). Attribution should include the following information:

Caroline Warman, *The Atheist's Bible: Diderot's 'Éléments de physiologie'*. Cambridge, UK: Open Book Publishers, 2020, https://doi.org/10.11647/OBP.0199

In order to access detailed and updated information on the license, please visit, https://doi.org/10.11647/OBP.0199#copyright

Further details about CC BY licenses are available at https://creativecommons.org/licenses/by/4.0/

All external links were active at the time of publication unless otherwise stated and have been archived via the Internet Archive Wayback Machine at https://archive.org/web

Updated digital material and resources associated with this volume are available at https://doi.org/10.11647/OBP.0199#resources

Every effort has been made to identify and contact copyright holders and any omission or error will be corrected if notification is made to the publisher.

ISBN Paperback: 9781783748969
ISBN Hardback: 9781783748976
ISBN Digital (PDF): 9781783748983
ISBN Digital ebook (epub): 9781783748990
ISBN Digital ebook (mobi): 9781783749003
ISBN XML: 9781783749010
DOI: 10.11647/OBP.0199

Cover image and design by Cressida Bell, all rights reserved.

# Contents

| | |
|---|---|
| Dedication | vii |
| Preface | ix |

PART ONE: The *Éléments de physiologie* Generally, Philosophically, and Physiologically

| | |
|---|---|
| 1. Introduction: The Curious Materialist | 3 |
| 2. 'Toutes les imperfections de l'inachèvement': The Mystification about the Manuscript Fragments | 17 |
| 3. Material World and Embodied Mind | 61 |
| 4. Diderot the Physiologist | 137 |

PART TWO: The *Éléments de physiologie*, 1790–1823

| | |
|---|---|
| 5. 1790: Naigeon and the *Adresse à l'Assemblée nationale* | 179 |
| 6. 1792: Naigeon's Article on 'Diderot' in the *Encyclopédie méthodique: Philosophie ancienne et moderne* | 207 |
| 7. 1794: 'Le citoyen Garron', the Comité d'instruction publique, and the Lost Manuscript of the *Éléments de physiologie* | 213 |
| 8. 1794–95: Garat and the École normale | 231 |
| 9. 1796–97: Cabanis and Destutt de Tracy at the Institut national | 271 |
| 10. 1798, 1802: Naigeon, the *Œuvres de Diderot*, and the Censored Preface to Montaigne's *Essais* | 319 |
| 11. 1820: Garat's *Mémoires historiques sur la vie de M. Suard, sur ses écrits, et sur le XVIIIe siècle* | 335 |
| 12. 1823: Naigeon's *Mémoires historiques et philosophiques sur la vie et les ouvrages de Denis Diderot* | 355 |

| | |
|---|---|
| 13. Conclusion | 393 |
| Acknowledgements | 399 |
| Bibliography | 403 |
| Index | 421 |

*For Leo and Viola*

# Preface

This book is about Denis Diderot's late work, the *Éléments de physiologie*. It argues, against the prevailing view, that this treatise made a substantial contribution to materialist thought, offering ways of explaining a human being without recourse to the divine and also without reducing human complexity or doing away with awe and wonder. These ways were physiological. The prevailing view accepts that Diderot planned to do something like this, but considers that unfortunately he did not complete his project. I argue that he did, and I explain not only why I think this, but also what led to the prevailing view that he did not, and why that particular story is illuminating in itself. Another aspect of the prevailing view is that it is accepted that even in its unfinished form, this work would have been of importance and interest to readers of the time, if only it had circulated and been read instead of being hidden away in two copies in the inaccessible private archives of Diderot's daughter and Catherine II of Russia, his patron. I argue that it did circulate, was read, and did have a decisive influence as early as the 1790s, and also that it was published, in an admittedly slightly odd form, in 1823. To help this rather argumentative study make its case, I offer a connected digital edition of this first publication, Jacques-André Naigeon's *Mémoires historiques et philosophiques sur la vie et les ouvrages de Denis Diderot*, which can be accessed here: https://naigeons-diderot.mml.ox.ac.uk/index.htm.

A quick word on the translations: every quoted text is followed by an English translation, with both languages equal on the page. This is to make it as accessible as possible to any interested reader, whether francophone or anglophone or somewhere in between. The translations are drawn from published works where possible, but in the many cases where there is none, I keep the translated text as close to the original as possible (while hopefully still making sense), specifically to facilitate access to the French for those who wish to toggle between the two.

# PART ONE

# THE *ÉLÉMENTS DE PHYSIOLOGIE* GENERALLY, PHILOSOPHICALLY, AND PHYSIOLOGICALLY

# 1. Introduction
## The Curious Materialist

L'amour est plus difficile à expliquer que la faim: car le fruit n'éprouve pas le désir d'être mangé.[1]

Love is harder to explain than hunger, for a piece of fruit does not feel the desire to be eaten.

Love is more difficult to explain than hunger, or so says the eighteenth-century *philosophe* and explainer of difficult things, Denis Diderot. How could we disagree? Hunger is probably a more fundamental physiological need than the complex set of feelings called love. Even if the comparison nudges us to see love in terms of another physiological need, lust and the drive to procreate, we would probably still agree that it is harder to explain than hunger. And that is where we suppose

---

[1] Throughout this book, I will give page references to the three current critical editions, in order of publication, in part to facilitate ease of reference for readers with access to only one of them, and in part because the most recent edition massively expands our understanding of the sources Diderot used when composing this work, and is therefore immediately a crucial referent. First, Jean Mayer's 1987 edition: Denis Diderot, *Éléments de physiologie*, ed. by Jean Mayer, vol. 17 (Paris: Hermann, 1987). This constitutes volume 17 of the ongoing *Œuvres complètes* of Diderot, known as DPV, after three of its founding editors, Herbert Dieckmann, Jacques Proust, and Jean Varloot. Second, Paolo Quintili's stand-alone edition: Denis Diderot, *Éléments de physiologie*, ed. by Paolo Quintili (Paris: Champion, 2004). Third, Motoichi Terada's edition: Denis Diderot, *Éléments de physiologie*, ed. by Motoichi Terada (Paris: Éditions Matériologiques, 2019). This makes available Terada's immense work on Diderot's sources, which very helpfully appeared as I was revising this manuscript. I will always signal when his indication of a source should be taken into account in our understanding of any given passage. Thus: DPV 494/PQ 328/ MT 307.

© Caroline Warman, CC BY 4.0   https://doi.org/10.11647/OBP.0199.01

Diderot is taking us, towards an analysis of hunger and love as appetites of different but recognisable sorts. But that is not where the sentence goes! The reason he gives for love being harder to explain than hunger is that a piece of fruit does not feel the desire to be eaten. What? We suddenly halt.

The perspective has switched, from the person who feels appetites to the object of their appetite, be that a piece of fruit or, implicitly, the desired person. Does a piece of fruit feel anything at all? By stating that the fruit has no desire to be eaten, Diderot raises the possibility that it might indeed have feelings of some sort, even desires, even if this particular one, not to be eaten, is negative. Furthermore, in saying that the piece of fruit does not want to be eaten, the proposed self-protective position of the piece of fruit sounds perfectly reasonable. So here we are, in agreement with the imaginary point of view of a piece of fruit. Look what he has reduced us to! We are obliged to pause and take stock; and although we do not really think that a piece of fruit has sensation or feeling, we are wondering about the relationship between an eater and an eaten thing, and seeing that it raises questions about reciprocity that might need further thought. These same questions about reciprocity return us to the other factor in this equation: love, or rather, those feeling the love, the lovers. Does a lover pulsate with the desire to be eaten? We appear to be bordering on the sexually explicit. Certainly, Diderot is presenting us with a complex knot that brings together and literally equates not only bodily urges, emotions, and feelings, but also fruitly feelings. And this all feels rather challenging, to put it no more strongly than that.

The *Éléments de physiologie* quite frequently exerts a sort of *Alice in Wonderland* pressure on the reader, inverting proportions, shaking assumptions, making bizarre comparisons, asserting relationships between phenomena we would never have thought of associating. For instance, we read that blood flows round the body faster than the fastest river.[2] That is not just an analogy to make us understand the point more quickly, not just an image that evokes coursing water only to project an internal picture of our rivery arteries, it's also an exact statement about the relative speeds of fluids in nature which requires us to think

---

2   DPV 376/PQ 195/MT 196.

*For Leo and Viola*

# 1. Introduction
## The Curious Materialist

L'amour est plus difficile à expliquer que la faim: car le fruit n'éprouve pas le désir d'être mangé.[1]

Love is harder to explain than hunger, for a piece of fruit does not feel the desire to be eaten.

Love is more difficult to explain than hunger, or so says the eighteenth-century *philosophe* and explainer of difficult things, Denis Diderot. How could we disagree? Hunger is probably a more fundamental physiological need than the complex set of feelings called love. Even if the comparison nudges us to see love in terms of another physiological need, lust and the drive to procreate, we would probably still agree that it is harder to explain than hunger. And that is where we suppose

---

[1] Throughout this book, I will give page references to the three current critical editions, in order of publication, in part to facilitate ease of reference for readers with access to only one of them, and in part because the most recent edition massively expands our understanding of the sources Diderot used when composing this work, and is therefore immediately a crucial referent. First, Jean Mayer's 1987 edition: Denis Diderot, *Éléments de physiologie*, ed. by Jean Mayer, vol. 17 (Paris: Hermann, 1987). This constitutes volume 17 of the ongoing *Œuvres complètes* of Diderot, known as DPV, after three of its founding editors, Herbert Dieckmann, Jacques Proust, and Jean Varloot. Second, Paolo Quintili's stand-alone edition: Denis Diderot, *Éléments de physiologie*, ed. by Paolo Quintili (Paris: Champion, 2004). Third, Motoichi Terada's edition: Denis Diderot, *Éléments de physiologie*, ed. by Motoichi Terada (Paris: Éditions Matériologiques, 2019). This makes available Terada's immense work on Diderot's sources, which very helpfully appeared as I was revising this manuscript. I will always signal when his indication of a source should be taken into account in our understanding of any given passage. Thus: DPV 494/PQ 328/MT 307.

© Caroline Warman, CC BY 4.0   https://doi.org/10.11647/OBP.0199.01

Diderot is taking us, towards an analysis of hunger and love as appetites of different but recognisable sorts. But that is not where the sentence goes! The reason he gives for love being harder to explain than hunger is that a piece of fruit does not feel the desire to be eaten. What? We suddenly halt.

The perspective has switched, from the person who feels appetites to the object of their appetite, be that a piece of fruit or, implicitly, the desired person. Does a piece of fruit feel anything at all? By stating that the fruit has no desire to be eaten, Diderot raises the possibility that it might indeed have feelings of some sort, even desires, even if this particular one, not to be eaten, is negative. Furthermore, in saying that the piece of fruit does not want to be eaten, the proposed self-protective position of the piece of fruit sounds perfectly reasonable. So here we are, in agreement with the imaginary point of view of a piece of fruit. Look what he has reduced us to! We are obliged to pause and take stock; and although we do not really think that a piece of fruit has sensation or feeling, we are wondering about the relationship between an eater and an eaten thing, and seeing that it raises questions about reciprocity that might need further thought. These same questions about reciprocity return us to the other factor in this equation: love, or rather, those feeling the love, the lovers. Does a lover pulsate with the desire to be eaten? We appear to be bordering on the sexually explicit. Certainly, Diderot is presenting us with a complex knot that brings together and literally equates not only bodily urges, emotions, and feelings, but also fruitly feelings. And this all feels rather challenging, to put it no more strongly than that.

The *Éléments de physiologie* quite frequently exerts a sort of *Alice in Wonderland* pressure on the reader, inverting proportions, shaking assumptions, making bizarre comparisons, asserting relationships between phenomena we would never have thought of associating. For instance, we read that blood flows round the body faster than the fastest river.[2] That is not just an analogy to make us understand the point more quickly, not just an image that evokes coursing water only to project an internal picture of our rivery arteries, it's also an exact statement about the relative speeds of fluids in nature which requires us to think

---

2   DPV 376/PQ 195/MT 196.

about them comparatively. Or, as we find on another page, 'un œil se fait comme une anémone' [an eye grows like an anemone] and 'un homme se fait comme un œil' [a man grows like an eye].³ Here, rather than moving progressively from simple to complex and thus from an anemone to an eye and thence to a human being, Diderot criss-crosses the different organisms so that we never settle into some complacent supremacist hierarchy. In fact, he is more likely to do the exact opposite, as here:

> Les animaux carnassiers sont plus sujets au vomissement que les frugivores.
> Les ruminants ne vomissent point.
> L'huître n'a point de bouche.⁴

> Carnivorous animals are more subject to vomiting than herbivores.
> Ruminants don't vomit at all.
> The oyster has no mouth.

There is a visible sequence to the order in which Diderot presents digestion here: he moves from the top of the food chain to the bottom; from complex meat-eater to simple oyster (oysters are the typical example of a crude life form in writing of the period).⁵ And yet the bodily function he chooses, the ability to vomit, might not be the normal way of establishing a top-down hierarchy. Furthermore, the mouthless oyster somehow seems seriously incapacitated in this series: it is not that the oyster does not vomit because it never needs to, but that it has no mouth so it cannot.

Diderot's human being is not a supreme life form, but a composite of life forms in all their stages: 'l'homme a toutes les sortes d'existence: l'inertie, la sensibilité, la vie végétale, la vie polypeuse, la vie humaine' [man has every kind of existence: inertia, feeling, vegetable life, polypous life, human life].⁶ Thus, analogies whereby the nervous system is like 'une écrevisse' [a crayfish],⁷ or the blood vessels around the heart

---

3  DPV 432/PQ 253/MT 250.
4  DPV 402/PQ 202/MT 220.
5  See Caroline Jacot-Grapa, 'Des huîtres aux grands animaux', *Dix-huitième siècle*, 42.1 (2010), 99–117 (pp. 107–08), https://doi.org/10.3917/dhs.042.0099.
6  DPV 337/PQ 154/MT 157.
7  DPV 355/PQ 175/MT 174.

are like its 'pattes' [paws],⁸ are not just imaginative comparisons that draw the reader in by giving them a rapid and vivid visualisation, but also genuine investigations into the cohabitation of different life systems within one complex organism. The *Éléments de physiologie* is as much about the elements as it is about the physiology: it looks at the shifting forms and patterns of matter and it considers humans in their material embodiment, as an expression thereof. It asks how the being and behaviour of any given person express that material identity, in sickness and in health. Bodily sensation, emotion, and perception are thus directly connected, as Diderot shows, using himself as an example:

> Je suis heureux, tout ce qui m'entoure s'embellit. Je souffre, tout ce qui m'entoure s'obscurcit.⁹
>
> I am happy, and everything around me grows beautiful. I am in pain, and everything around me is plunged in gloom.

And he asks what, in a context whereby physiological embodiment is all-determining, selfhood might be? The answer is that self is memory:

> La mémoire constitue le soi. La conscience du soi et la conscience de son existence sont différentes. Des sensations continues sans mémoire donneraient la conscience ininterrompue de son existence: elles ne produiraient nulle conscience de soi.¹⁰
>
> Memory constitutes the self. The consciousness of self and the consciousness of one's existence are different. What continuous sensation without any memory would impart would be the uninterrupted sense of existence, not any consciousness of self.

Selfhood is not a given, and its lack or loss have to be envisaged. It may exist for only part of life, between childhood and old age. The processes of growth and decline cannot be controlled, but are impelled forward naturally, passively. Change and flux are constant:

> Nul état fixe dans le corps animal: il décroît quand il ne croît plus.¹¹

---

8   DPV 373/PQ 192/MT 192.
9   DPV 461/PQ 287/MT 277.
10  DPV 471/PQ 298/MT 286.
11  DPV 312/PQ 127/MT 135.

> There is no fixed state in the animal body: it starts shrinking once it stops growing.

There is always movement and variation: this is a premise of materialist thought. In the context of human physiology, that means growth, age, illness, and also, inevitably, malformation. The curious materialist will be fascinated by all these variations in bodily condition, and will want to know what effect they have on perception, experience, and happiness. Diderot is this curious materialist, and while one could no doubt argue that all of his works explore aspects of human embodiment and experience in some way, it is in the *Éléments de physiologie* that he focuses on it most directly, thoroughly and systematically. Furthermore, written at the end of his life, it contains and distills aspects of everything he has hitherto engaged with; it has great range and depth of allusion, and great writerly control, such that images, phrases, stories, and subjects work their way into the reading mind and stick there. As Diderot comments with a witty and virtuoso command of rhythm and onomatopeia, 'un plat ouvrage nous endort comme le murmure monotone d'un ruisseau' [a flat piece of work sends us to sleep like the monotonous murmur of a stream].[12] This work is one long series of jolts. The chapter opened with one such, and indeed it is woven through with bizarre one-liners that specialise in startling juxtapositions.

Diderot probably started working on the *Éléments* soon after he completed the first draft of his experimental poetico-materialist dialogue *Le Rêve de d'Alembert* [*D'Alembert's Dream*] in 1769, with its quartet of truly existing but fictionalised speakers, *philosophe* Diderot, mathematician Jean le Rond d'Alembert, doctor Théophile de Bordeu, female Julie de Lespinasse. *D'Alembert's Dream* in fact serves as an imaginative introduction to the substantial materialist treatise that is the *Éléments de physiologie*, which Diderot probably continued to work on until relatively close to his death in 1784.[13] In terms of genre it is quite unlike his earlier writings in this area, be they the allusive *Lettres* (on

---

12 DPV 506/PQ 345/MT 320.
13 We know this because there are references to it in his *Réfutation d'Helvétius* and *Observations sur Hemsterhuis*, from 1773–74, and within the *Éléments* itself he remarks that he was more than 66 years old when he was working on a particular section, which would date that part to after October 1779 [DPV 313/PQ 129/MT 136], and finally, the most developed manuscript version we have, from his daughter's archive the *Fonds Vandeul*, has additions that could not have been made before 1782. So, this

the blind or on the deaf and dumb), the aphoristic *Pensées* or indeed the audacious dialogues that form *Le Rêve de d'Alembert*.¹⁴ It advertises its claim to seriousness overtly. This is obvious from the title itself, whether that title is indeed the *Éléments de physiologie* or simply *Physiologie* (there is some dispute about this).¹⁵ And despite the many startling one-liners, cunningly designed to jolt the sleepy and passive reader into wakefulness, its attentive approach to the thorough but succinct description of the human body aligns it more with the knowledge-disseminating *Encyclopédie* he edited for more than twenty years than with the rest of his generally elliptical writings, with the crucial difference that here he presents his highly contentious theories about matter, life, thought, and the human mind unmasked, and step by censorable step. As Diderot puts it, while nonetheless admitting that this method is not infallible, 'il n'y a qu'un moyen de connaître la vérité, c'est de ne procéder que par partie et de ne conclure qu'après une énumération exacte et entière' [there's only one way of getting to the truth, to proceed from one part to the next and to conclude only after an exact and total enumeration].¹⁶ His earlier text, the *Rêve de d'Alembert*, for all its playful

---

gives us periodic reference points that suggest that he was working on it across the final fifteen years of his life.

14 *Pensées philosophiques,* published in 1746, *Lettre sur les aveugles*, published in 1749 and the *Lettre sur les sourds et muets*, published in 1751, the *Principes sur l'interprétation de la nature* published in 1753, and the *Principes philosophiques sur la matière et le mouvement*, written but not published, in 1770.

15 The (early draft) St Petersburg manuscript is entitled *Élémen[t]s de physiologie*; the (mature draft) Fonds Vandeul manuscript also has *Élémens de physiologie* on the title page; Hippolyte Walferdin, describing a lost manuscript copy in 1837, gives its title as *Physiologie* (see DPV 270–71, discussed below, in the chapter entitled '1823: Naigeon's *Mémoires historiques et philosophiques sur la vie et les ouvrages de Denis Diderot*'); Gerhardt Stenger considers that 'l'ouvrage fini devait s'intituler "*Physiologie*" tout court' [the finished work was supposed simply to be called *Physiology*] (*Diderot, le combattant de la liberté* (Paris: Perrin, 2013), p. 740, n. 144); Naigeon confuses matters by alluding to it as Diderot's 'système particulier de physiologie' [his particular system of physiology] and also as 'une nouvelle théorie, ou plutôt une histoire naturelle et expérimentale de l'homme' [a new theory, or rather, a natural and experimental history of man] (*Mémoires historiques et philosophiques sur la vie et les ouvrages de Denis Diderot* (Paris: J. L. L. Brière, '1821' [1823]; repr. Geneva: Slatkine Reprints, 1970), p. 291); Terada, presumably on the basis of Naigeon's description, also calls it by the name *Histoire naturelle et expérimentale de l'homme* (MT 54, 57). It seems most probable, given that both manuscript versions carry the full title of *Éléments de physiologie* and that the 'Avertissement' of the Vandeul version explicitly names the title 'Éléments de physiologie', that this was indeed the proposed title.

16 DPV 464/PQ 290/MT 280.

profundity and exploratory discussion, was not 'an exact and total enumeration', and nor does it proceed systematically, but the *Éléments de physiologie* is and does. In the *Rêve*, Diderot has the fictionalised Bordeu offer the thought that 'la fibre est un animal simple; l'homme est un animal composé. Mais gardons ce texte pour une autre fois' [the fibre is a simple animal; man is a composite animal. But let's keep that thought for another time], and in so doing, he plants an allusion to a more systematic treatment of this idea. That more systematic treatment is to be found in the *Éléments de physiologie*.[17] We have already quoted the passage proposing that 'l'homme a toutes les sortes d'existence';[18] this is a recurrent theme which is repeatedly revisited, and later we read that 'l'homme est un assemblage d'animaux où chacun garde sa fonction' [man is an assemblage of animals, each one with its own function].[19]

The *Éléments de physiologie* is organised into three parts, each of which is subdivided into numerous chapters. It has a beginning, a middle, and an end, in the most traditional way possible, and let it be said, in a more traditional way than we normally find in Diderot's works. The first part, simply entitled 'Des Etres' [On Beings], opens with a tableau of nature in general, looking at the links in a chain of being organised according to complexity of organism. It is divided into three chapters on, in order of increasing complexity, the 'végéto-animal', the 'animal' and 'homme'. In these, he rapidly sketches the classification of living beings according to their differences and similarities, repeatedly enquiring about the ability to feel sensation across nature. What is original about this part is perhaps more than anything the way in which it fuses philosophy

---

17 Denis Diderot, *Le Rêve de d'Alembert*, ed. by Colas Duflo (Paris: GF Flammarion, 2002), p. 138; or DPV 17, p. 166. Duflo supplies a footnote reference to a slightly different passage of the *Éléments*, 'Il y a certainement dans un même animal trois vies distinctes [etc]' [there are certainly three distinct life forms in a single animal], although his reference is in fact to a very early draft of the *Éléments de physiologie*, called the *Fragments dont on n'a pu trouver la véritable place*, DPV 17, p. 226. In the *Éléments de physiologie* proper, this passage is DPV 310/PQ 126/MT 134. I discuss the relationship of these drafts to each other below, see the section in Chapter 2 titled 'From Elements to Fragments'.

18 DPV 337/PQ 154/MT 157.

19 DPV 501/PQ 338/MT 314. Terada points out that Diderot's source here is Bordeu's *Recherches sur les maladies chroniques* (1775), in which he variously writes that 'le corps vivant' [the living body] is an 'assemblage de divers organes' [assemblage of different organs] and an 'assemblage de plusieurs organes' [assemblage of many organs]. *Éléments*, ed. by Terada, p. 496, Source XI.

and natural history so totally, that it does it so briefly, and that it is so explicit in its views. Others such as the famous and successful author of the *Histoire naturelle générale et particulière* (1749–89) in 36 volumes, Georges-Louis Leclerc, comte de Buffon, or the Swiss naturalist Charles Bonnet might be diffusely, ever so cautiously, hovering on the point of suggesting similar sorts of points, but apart from needing to penetrate their actual meaning, first of all you'd have to find the passage, buried somewhere in volume 12. This is not even a joke: that is where Buffon first gets round to defining Nature, in volume 12 of 36.[20] In the *Éléments de physiologie*, it's line 1.

The second part, entitled the 'Éléments et parties du corps humain' [Elements and parts of the human body], focuses on human physiology. It displays a remarkable synthesis of disciplinary erudition, this time very specifically from the field of physiology and much bolstered by the work of the pre-eminent Swiss physiologist Albrecht von Haller, and made comprehensible and meaningful thanks to Diderot's extraordinary style, consisting at once in concise lucidity of description and in the ability to know when to puncture the description, pause, and start asking questions or drawing strange and destabilising analogies which breathe new meaning into the text. This second part does not attempt a complete synthesis of existing accounts of the workings of the human body and of its elements. There is nothing about the skeleton, for example. Instead, it focuses its attention on the basic material of the human body (fibres, cellular tissues) and on how it functions (blood, muscles, reproduction, the separate organs). Diderot repeatedly returns to two groups of questions: firstly, what is the difference between organised beings and an animal or what we'd now call an organism (can an organ be considered an animal in itself, for example?), and secondly, how is sensation communicated from one part of the body to another, what happens when that communication is interrupted, and what is the significance of that interruption?

The third and final part contains a detailed discussion of the senses and the mind, memory, imagination, thought, what it terms 'les phénomènes du cerveau' [the phenomena of the brain]. It proposes

---

20 Buffon, 'De la nature. Première vue' [On Nature. First view], in *Œuvres*, ed. by Stéphane Schmitt and Cédric Crémière (Paris: Gallimard Pléiade, 2007), p. 985, https://doi.org/10.5962/bhl.title.53421.

that human experience of self and other is first and last the product of relational material organisation in time and space, entirely determined by it, yet no less conscious and lived for all that it is determined. Thus there is no soul, no supernatural element, and also no place for the faculty supposedly exclusive to man, 'reason'. Reason is replaced with 'instinct' on the one hand, and 'understanding' on the other. Diderot rounds off the *Éléments de physiologie* with an extraordinary meditation on death in the Stoic tradition—in Montaigne's version, 'que philosopher c'est apprendre à mourir' [to philosophise is to learn to die] and in Diderot's chiastic mirroring: 'un autre apprentissage de la mort est la philosophie' [another apprenticeship of death is what philosophy is].[21]

In sum, the *Éléments de physiologie* is overtly atheist and materialist. Materialism refers to the view that the universe and everything in it is made entirely from matter in different shapes and forms; in this eighteenth-century context, it is also automatically understood to be an atheist position, and therefore dangerous, both for the person who holds it and might be imprisoned because of it (as Diderot was in 1749, for the suspect views about the existence of God expressed in his *Letter on the Blind*), and for the general population, who, the (ecclesiastical) authorities considered, would be at risk of contamination.

It is a substantial materialist treatise and there is nothing else of its time like it (and nor would there be for at least another century), nothing else that places a detailed physiological account of humans and human consciousness within an overtly materialist presentation of nature. It draws on the work of physiologists like Haller and others, and on the work of naturalists like Buffon or Bonnet. It dialogues with philosophers like the polemical Julien Offray de La Mettrie and the more mainstream Étienne Bonnot de Condillac, and re-visits many of the same examples and topoi that we find across all these writers, and which Diderot had also treated in earlier works, examples such as the man plunged in thought and perfectly unaware of his surroundings who nonetheless unhesitatingly navigates obstacles as he paces along, or the abilities of the imbecile or the mad, or the surprising strength ill men discover in themselves when rescuing possessions from fire, and so on. It extends all this into an open investigation of conscious and unconscious states

---

21  DPV 516/PQ 361/MT 328.

in all their bizarre variety. In 1759, Théophile de Bordeu (the real one, and Diderot's friend, not the loquacious fictionalised version we meet in the *Rêve de d'Alembert*) had implored some great philosopher to come forward and help make sense of what he called the 'animal economy', that is to say, the human being in both physical and moral aspects.[22]

> Il faudroit enfin un Descartes ou un Leibniz, pour débrouiller ce qui concerne les causes, l'ordre, le rapport, les variations, l'harmonie, et les lois des fonctions de l'économie animale.[23]

> Ultimately what is needed is a Descartes or a Leibniz to disentangle everything concerning the causes, the order, the relationship, the variations, the harmony, and the laws governing the functions of the animal economy.

It seems that the *Éléments de physiologie* is Diderot's answer to that challenge.

And yet, for all its manifest stature, both within Diderot's own œuvre and beyond it, as a bravely explicit exploration of what it is to be human in the absence of the soul, and also as a response to the need expressed by vitalist doctors like Bordeu for some new ways of understanding how the body, in its physical and emotional aspects, connects up, the *Éléments de physiologie* is little known and little studied. It is really only the third part, with its discussions of thought and memory, its bravura set pieces about sensation and recall which prefigure the writings of Henri Bergson or Marcel Proust, that have interested Diderot scholars. Indeed two mainstream editions of Diderot's philosophical works do not consider it worth including the first two parts, and only print the last one; they abridge no other work by so much as a paragraph, let alone

---

[22] For a discussion of the term 'animal economy', see Philippe Huneman, 'Les théories de l'économie animale et l'émergence de la psychiatrie de l'Éncyclopédie à l'aliénisme', *Psychiatrie Sciences Humaines Neurosciences*, 2.2 (2004), 47–60 (p. 47), https://doi.org/10.1007/BF03006001.

[23] Théophile de Bordeu, 'Recherches sur les glandes' (1759), in *Œuvres complètes de Bordeu: précédées d'une notice sur sa vie et sur ses ouvrages*, ed. by Anthelme Richerand (Paris: Caille et Ravier, 1818), vol. 1, p. 208. We discuss this claim and its implications below, in the section titled 'Major Debates in Physiology: Mechanism and Vitalism', in Chapter 4.

two thirds of the whole text.²⁴ The current book is, for all its faults, the only monograph devoted to it thus far.²⁵ How could this be?

There seem to be a number of rather fascinating reasons for this bizarre neglect, as we will see. This book falls into two parts: the first looks at how Diderot's *Éléments de physiologie* makes an intervention in the philosophy and physiology of his time (part of the intervention in the former, having been misunderstood, is part of the reason for the neglect), deepening our understanding of what is at stake beyond what has been sketched out thus far. The second part looks at what would normally be called its dissemination and reception, but cannot yet be, seeing as scholarship as it currently stands does not think that it was disseminated in the first place. Perhaps we can say instead that the second part presents its reasons for supposing that the *Éléments de physiologie* was being read at least to some extent in the 1790s, those turbulent and unstable years of frequent régime change, and furthermore, its reasons for thinking that it exerted influence almost immediately. The book ends with a study of what I will argue is the first publication of the *Éléments de physiologie* in 1823, in a form which is almost but not quite unrecognisable, thanks to a substantial reorganisation operation carried out on it by Diderot's intellectual disciple and literary executor, the industrious Jacques-André Naigeon.²⁶

---

24 Laurent Versini's five-volume edition of Diderot's work only contains this last part: Denis Diderot, *Œuvres*, ed. by Laurent Versini, 5 vols (Paris: R. Laffont, 1994–97). More recently, Michel Delon and Barbara de Negroni's edition of Diderot's *Œuvres philosophiques* reproduces very short extracts from parts 1 and 2, and slightly longer extracts (although also cut) from part 3, and downgrades it to an Appendix to the *Rêve*. Denis Diderot, *Œuvres philosophiques*, ed. by Michel Delon and Barbara de Negroni (Paris: Gallimard, 2010), pp. 411–44. We discuss this further below, see Chapter 2.

25 Monographs on Diderot which do substantially engage with or quote from the *Éléments de physiologie* are: Kurt Ballstadt, *Diderot: Natural Philosopher*, SVEC 2008:09 (Oxford: Voltaire Foundation, 2008); Andrew Clark, *Diderot's Part* (Ashgate: Aldershot, 2008), https://doi.org/10.4324/9781315257853; Colas Duflo, *Diderot Philosophe* (Paris: Champion, 2003); Caroline Jacot-Grapa, *Dans le vif du sujet: Diderot, corps et âme* (Paris: Classiques Garnier, 2009); Jean Mayer, *Diderot, homme de science* (Rennes: Imprimerie Bretonne, 1959).

26 Naigeon's *Mémoires* came out as the twenty-second volume of the Brière edition of Diderot's *Œuvres*; all are date-stamped as having been published in 1821, but in fact they came out gradually between 1821–23. See David Adams, *Bibliographie des œuvres de Diderot, 1739–1900*, 2 vols (Ferney-Voltaire: Centre international d'étude du XVIIIe siècle, 2000), vol. 2, p. 141. Naigeon's *Mémoires* therefore came out in 1823, and I will consistently refer to them in that way, despite the prevailing dating

Perhaps this is the moment therefore to mention that the *Éléments de physiologie* was not published during Diderot's lifetime. Those who already frequent the works of Diderot know that this puts it in good company, and indeed in the same camp as most of his work. In order to secure his release from prison in 1749, he had had to promise never to publish anything that might disturb or undermine the authorities ever again, and nor did he. The *Encyclopédie ou dictionnaire raisonné des sciences, des arts et des métiers*, on which he was already in 1749 hard at work (and which his imprisonment interrupted), which he co-edited with Jean le Rond d'Alembert until its publication was banned in 1759 and d'Alembert gave up on it, and which Diderot carried on preparing in secret, bringing out the remaining volumes of text in 1765 (there were 17 in all), and 11 volumes of plates in 1772, bringing the grand total to 28 volumes, was too massive an enterprise to endanger, and in itself exposed him to a good deal of risk anyway. Instead, from then on, he only published a couple of philosophical works (*Lettre sur les sourds et muets,* 1751; *Pensées sur l'interprétation de la nature,* 1753), a few plays (*Le Fils naturel,* 1757; *Le Père de famille,* 1758), and various other short texts, including the *Additions aux pensées philosophiques* (1770) and the *Regrets sur ma vieille robe de chambre* (1772).[27] And of this, only the *Lettre de M. Diderot à MM. Briasson et Le Breton*, Diderot's intervention in the case brought by Luneau de Boisjermain against the publishers of the *Encyclopédie*, actually carried his name in black and white.[28] Indeed, the plays caused a scandal anyway, as he was accused of plagiarism, while he himself was mercilessly satirised in Palissot's play *Les philosophes* of 1760 as part of a large-scale anti-*Encyclopédie* campaign; in sum, he was already a target, and already at risk. Thus, many of the works for which he is now most famous—his novels *Jacques le fataliste* or *La Religieuse*, or his dialogues, the scientifically exploratory *Rêve de d'Alembert* and the morally outrageous *Neveu de Rameau*, went

---

to 1821. See below for further information about the precise circumstances of their publication.

27  For the complete list, see Adams, 'Liste chronologique des éditions', in his *Bibliographie des œuvres de Diderot, 1739–1900* (Ferney-Voltaire: Centre international d'étude du XVIIIe siècle, 2000), vol. 1, pp. 53–76.

28  See Kate E. Tunstall, 'La fabrique du *Diderot-philosophe*, 1765–1782', *Les Dossiers du Grihl*, 2 (2017), https://doi.org/10.4000/dossiersgrihl.6793, especially paragraphs 25–26; J. Lough, 'Luneau de Boisjermain v. the Publishers of the *Encyclopédie*', *SVEC*, 23 (1963), 115–77; Adams, *Bibliographie des œuvres*, vol. 2, pp. 211–12.

unpublished during his lifetime. However, all of these works, with the exception of the then completely unknown *Neveu de Rameau* and also the *Éléments de physiologie*, had been circulated in a manuscript periodical, the *Correspondance littéraire*, sent only to a very restricted number of very elevated personnages, including Catherine II, across Europe and in Russia. Manuscripts were not subject to the same censorship laws, and in any case this manuscript magazine's royal readers extended their protection to it; Catherine indeed extended her protection directly to Diderot, buying his books and manuscripts and making him the salaried-librarian of his own books. Diderot died in 1784, and his books and a set of his manuscripts were sent off to Catherine; the books are now lost but the manuscripts are still in St Petersburg.

His novels and various short stories started leaking into print from copies of the *Correspondance littéraire* in the 1790s, and at this point, his literary executor, Naigeon, as we will hear, was galvanized into action, bringing out his edition of Diderot's *Œuvres* in fifteen volumes in 1798; he still omitted the *Rêve de d'Alembert*, the *Éléments de physiologie*, and the *Neveu de Rameau*, judging them too dangerous. In 1805, the *Neveu de Rameau* came out as *Rameaus Neffe*, in German, translated by none other than that titan of German letters, Goethe. So it was out of the bag. That left the *Rêve de d'Alembert* and the *Éléments de physiologie*, which Naigeon meshed into a new work, taking up one quarter of the *Mémoires historiques et philosophiques sur la vie et les ouvrages de Denis Diderot*, and which, as mentioned, would be published in 1823, thirteen years after Naigeon's death, and which therefore constitutes the first sort-of publication of both of those works. The *Rêve de d'Alembert* itself would be published entire in 1830, and from that moment it has had its own separate life. I say 'sort-of publication': we will see exactly what I mean in the chapter devoted to it, and in the connected digital edition of Naigeon's *Mémoires* that I offer as part of this study.[29] Suffice it to say that in the published version of the *Mémoires*, the discussion of these two texts take up 100 pages, and that of those 100 pages, 80 are woven from verbatim but unacknowledged and massively reorganised passages from these two works, with about 30 pages from the *Rêve* and about 50 from the *Éléments*. So this means that there are 80 pages of Diderot's writing in the *Mémoires*, and they are all about physiology.

---

29  See https://naigeons-diderot.mml.ox.ac.uk/index.htm.

So this is the extent to which we can and cannot say that the *Mémoires* constitute the first publication of both the *Rêve de d'Alembert* and the *Éléments de physiologie*. It is the first time that lines written by Diderot from both works appeared in print, but they did not appear as he wrote them, it wasn't clear that they were quotation—it looks like a paraphrase of what Diderot thought—and they are in a book whose author is not Diderot but Naigeon. The sheer extent of his reworking, as well, perhaps, as the relative unpopularity of the *Mémoires*—they have been plundered for anecdotes about Diderot but not taken seriously otherwise, and not been the object of any research in themselves—along with the availability from 1830 of the engaging and quirky *Rêve de d'Alembert*, has meant that it has never been contemplated that the *Mémoires* might constitute their first publication.[30] The *Éléments de physiologie*, unlike every other one of his works, did not come out separately and acquire its own identity in those crucial first fifty years after Diderot's death when his œuvre was being pieced together. It would not come out until 1875, in the critical edition in 20 volumes by scholars Jules Assézat and Maurice Tourneux. However, this was another bad moment for the *Éléments de physiologie*: Assézat and Tourneux published the early draft they had found in the St Petersburg archive of Diderot manuscripts. And so the reputation of the *Éléments de physiologie* was fixed: insofar as it existed at all, it was as an unfinished project. Not even the publication of the complete draft in 1964, subsequent to the emergence in 1948 of the complete set of Diderot's manuscripts which had gone to his daughter (a thrilling story),[31] has shifted that view. This book, however, attempts to overturn it.

The next chapter maps current scholarship on the *Éléments de physiologie*, and explores why it has stuck with the view of the *Éléments de physiologie* as an incomplete text; there is a perfect storm of reasons.

---

30 I should add though that Motoichi Terada's 2019 edition gives the relevant pages from Naigeon in an appendix, fully referenced to the *Rêve de d'Alembert* and to the *Éléments de physiologie* in its early draft form. This is a question we will return to in Chapter 12.

31 Herbert Dieckmann, 'L'épopée du Fonds Vandeul', *Revue d'histoire littéraire de la France*, 85.6 (1985), 963–77.

# 2. 'Toutes les imperfections de l'inachèvement'[1]
## The Mystification about the Manuscript Fragments

The general view about the *Éléments de physiologie*, as those who have an overview of Denis Diderot's production will know, is that they are a fragmentary series of reading notes and scattered thoughts scribbled by the ageing philosopher, and which have some form of undefined but underpinning relation to the *Rêve de d'Alembert*. This chapter will look closely at these views and try to understand where they come from, given that, as has been suggested and hopefully also demonstrated, at least to some extent, the *Éléments de physiologie* are not a fragmentary series of reading notes. However, many influential and important voices do maintain that this is the case.

Jean Mayer, authority on Diderot and science, and twice editor (1964, 1987) of the mature version of the *Éléments* brought to light in the Vandeul archive by Herbert Dieckmann in 1948, states in his book *Diderot, homme de science* (1959) that the *Éléments de physiologie* display 'toutes les imperfections de l'inachèvement' [all the flaws of incompletion].[2] His

---

1 Jean Mayer, *Diderot, homme de science* (Rennes: Imprimerie Bretonne, 1959), p. 273. Translation: 'All the flaws of incompletion'.
2 Mayer, *Diderot, homme de science*, p. 273. Later statements in the editions themselves show that Mayer would come to modify this early view, presumably after prolonged contact with the completed version of the *Éléments de physiologie* itself. In his DPV

1987 edition would implicitly disagree with that earlier statement, stating that 'Diderot avait poussé le travail jusqu'à l'achèvement' [Diderot's work on it had got to the point of completion], although he continued to maintain that the *Éléments* 'souffrent visiblement d'une documentation scientifique encombrante et mal dominée' [visibly suffer from a cumbersome and poorly mastered amount of scientific documentation][3] and that we should not be unduly concerned if Diderot contradicts himself as these are only his reading notes.[4] The preeminent historian of the eighteenth-century life sciences, Jacques Roger, did not consider this work a work at all, but rather, '[des] notes de travail rassemblées sous le titre d'*Éléments de physiologie*' [working notes brought together under the title of *Elements of physiology*].[5] Roger goes so far as to say that he prefers to use the earlier incomplete draft which we call the Saint-Petersburg version after the archive where it is held. The reason? Because the more mature version 'tend à masquer, sinon les grandes influences subies, du moins les chapitres où chacune d'entre elles s'est plus précisément exercée' [tends to mask, if not its major influences, at least the areas where they have been most specifically influential].[6] His judgement—that the *Éléments* is a bundle of working notes and not a finished work—becomes the reason that he cannot use the final version, precisely because it is not just a bundle of working notes. He thereby reveals—consciously or not—that what he really values is what makes his job as a source-tracing historian of science easier, that is, early drafts in their magpie state. The issue is not that he should prefer the early draft but that he should define the completed work in relation to that preference, and thereby considerably deform it. And it would not matter

---

    edition he writes that 'Diderot a poussé le travail jusqu'à l'achèvement [...]' [Diderot worked on it to the point of completion], *Éléments de physiologie*, ed. by Jean Mayer, *Œuvres complètes*, DPV (Paris: Hermann, 1987), vol. 17, pp. 261–574 (p. 273). In his 1964 edition he had already stated that the *Éléments de physiologie* was in many ways superior to other such physiological works of the time. *Éléments de physiologie*, ed. by Jean Mayer (Paris: Didier, 1964), p. lvi.

3    DPV 286.

4    'Mais ce sont là des notes de lecture: Diderot ne souscrit pas à toutes les opinions qu'il rapporte' [But there are just reading notes : Diderot doesn't subscribe to all the opinions he records]. DPV 349n.: note starts on p. 348.

5    Jacques Roger, *Les sciences de la vie dans la pensée Française du XVIIIe siècle: la génération des animaux de Descartes à l'Encyclopédie*, 2nd edn (Paris: A. Colin, 1971), p. 699.

6    Roger, *Les sciences de la vie*, p. 672.

that he was biased and wrong in his judgement if he and Mayer hadn't had considerable and persisting influence.

In the Pléiade volume of Diderot's *Œuvres philosophiques* (2010), the *Éléments de physiologie* do not appear in their own right but are subordinated as an appendix of thirty pages of cherry-picked extracts connected to the *Rêve de d'Alembert*. Eminent Diderot scholars Michel Delon and Barbara de Negroni justify this decision by calling the *Éléments de physiologie* a 'texte technique' [technical text], and by explaining that it provides information about what medical sources Diderot was using when composing the *Rêve de d'Alembert*.[7] And indeed, the thirty pages of extracts we find in the Pléiade volume of the *Œuvres philosophiques* hardly contribute to making the *Éléments* seem like a completed work in its own right; on the contrary, they sustain the myth of the *Éléments'* fragmentary character by producing a newly fragmented version. The editors are not without precedent in only publishing extracts: Laurent Versini did the same thing in his 1994 volume of Diderot's philosophical works. Versini's fragments are explicitly chosen according to criteria of omission: he omits what he considers to be tiresome descriptions and lists of anatomy and physiology, which are, he says, out of place in 'une collection d'œuvres philosophiques ou littéraires' [a collection of philosophical or literary works].[8] When Delon and Negroni call it a 'texte technique', therefore, they are simply confirming Versini's view that it just does not suit our taste (or come up to our standards) as scholars of literature and thought.

Between, on the one hand, the historians of science who declare that the *Éléments* are incomplete and/or nothing more than a bundle of working notes, dismissing the completed version because it gets in the way of source-hunting, and, on the other, literary scholars who accept and relay these opinions while also adding to the general rejection of this work with further damning judgements about its tiresome technical descriptions and implied lack of literary quality, the *Éléments*

---

7   Denis Diderot, *Œuvres philosophiques*, ed. by Michel Delon and Barbara de Negroni (Paris: Gallimard, 2010), p. 1253. Chronologically, this is a little misleading, given that Diderot wrote the *Éléments de physiologie* after the *Rêve*, see Chapter 1, but presumably what is meant is that the *Éléments de physiologie* tells us about Diderot's medical knowledge more generally, which is fair enough.

8   Laurent Versini, 'Introduction [to *Éléments de physiologie*]', in Denis Diderot, *Œuvres*, ed. by Laurent Versini (Paris: R. Laffont, 1994), vol. 1: *Philosophie*, p. 1259.

*de physiologie* has not recently stood much chance of establishing a reputation on its own terms. In the case of this text more than any of Diderot's others, the disciplinary specialisations and identities of the modern university system have meant that it falls between stools, failing to conform to our various expectations of style or content. The story about its fragmentary nature, however, has nothing to do with modern institutional specificities: it is a much older one.

The story about the fragments is generally traced to and substantiated by the account given by Diderot's literary executor, Jacques-André Naigeon. In his *Mémoires historiques et philosophiques sur la vie et les ouvrages de Denis Diderot*, published posthumously in 1823 (although dated to 1821, like the rest of the Brière edition, of which this was the last volume), Naigeon wrote that Diderot never completed his work on physiology and only left 'quelques matériaux épars et sans aucun ordre entre eux' [a few scattered materials with no internal order], further alleging that these scattered materials would only make sense 'aux yeux du philosophe assez instruit pour couver les idées neuves et fécondes dont Diderot a semé ses recherches' [to the philosopher who is sufficiently knowledgeable to appreciate the new and fertile ideas that Diderot planted in his work].[9] He also emphasised Diderot's debt to the great physiologist Albrecht von Haller, saying he had read Haller's work on *Physiologie* twice through 'la plume à la main' [pen in hand]: this has always been understood to tell us that Diderot's pen was ready to note down whatever he found useful in the 'source' text, and therefore that he is in someway *subservient* to it.[10] This is despite the fact that it could just as easily be read as meaning that he considerably corrected or responded to or amplified the source text, as he famously did in the case of the *Observations sur Hemsterhuis*, the *Réfutation d'Helvétius* or just generally.

The ninth volume of the great and first *Œuvres complètes* edition of the 1870s, undertaken by Jules Assézat and Maurice Tourneux and based on the archive of Diderot manuscripts which had been sent to

---

9  Jacques-André Naigeon, *Mémoires historiques et philosophiques sur la vie et les ouvrages de Denis Diderot* (Paris: J. L. L. Brière, '1821' [1823]; repr. Geneva: Slatkine Reprints, 1970), p. 291.

10 Naigeon writes that Diderot 'avait lu deux fois, et la plume à la main, sa grande *physiologie*' [read his great *physiology* twice, pen in hand] (*Mémoires historiques et philosophiques*, p. 222n).

Catherine the Great in St Petersburg after his death in 1784, contains the first print-published version of the *Éléments de physiologie* in its entirety, although as scholars would later discover, the so-called St Petersburg manuscript was a copy of a relatively early draft which Diderot would subsequently substantially reorganise and add to. In his introduction to the St Petersburg version, Jules Assézat closely paraphrases Naigeon's description of the *Éléments*, although he does not say so. Diderot, he wrote, 'lisait la plume à la main tous les livres qui lui parvenaient, et il en tirait ce qui pouvait l'éclairer dans ses recherches. Ce sont ces notes, intitulées Éléments de physiologie, qui forment un volume in-4° de la collection des manuscrits de la bibliothèque de l'Ermitage, que nous publions [...]' [read all the books that he could get hold of, pen in hand, and took from them anything that helped advance his work. It is these notes, entitled *Elements of physiology*, forming a quarto volume in the manuscript collection of the Hermitage library, which we are publishing here].[11] The fact that Assézat, without knowing it, only had access to an inferior version, adds a further complicating layer to the story, in that Naigeon's account would have seemed more accurately to describe the manuscript he worked from, although even that is hardly fragmentary, producing a substantial 190 printed pages. The most complete version we now know of, and the one which current editions use, was rediscovered by the great Diderot scholar Herbert Dieckmann in 1948 in the collection of manuscripts which passed to Diderot's daughter, Angélique Vandeul, at his death in 1784, and thereafter down through her family. Dieckmann himself had written an important article in 1938 examining Naigeon's treatment of the *Rêve de d'Alembert* and the *Physiologie* in his *Mémoires historiques et philosophiques*: he was the first scholar to bring to light that those *Mémoires* in fact quote verbatim from both these works.[12] His preference was clearly for the *Rêve*, which, given that he, like Assézat, was at that point working with the earlier version,

---

11   Denis Diderot, *Œuvres complètes*, ed. by Jules Assézat and Maurice Tourneux (Paris: Garnier Frères, 1875), vol. 9, p. 237. He elaborates further: 'ce caractère de notes, prises au jour le jour et rassemblées à la hâte, fait de cet ouvrage tout autre chose qu'un traité didactique' [this note-like character it has, of having been jotted down from one day to the next, makes this work completely different from a didactic treatise], p. 238.

12   Herbert Dieckmann, 'J.-A. Naigeon's Analysis of Diderot's *Rêve de d'Alembert*', *Modern Language Notes*, 53.7 (1938), 479–86, https://doi.org/10.2307/2912683.

is perhaps not surprising.¹³ Dieckmann's consistent assumption is that the *Éléments de Physiologie* was, or was planned to be, part of a longer version of the *Rêve*. Naigeon's story of, on the one hand, the disordered manuscript fragments, and, on the other, the reading notes, persist in assessments of the *Éléments* today, as we have seen in the influential accounts of Jean Mayer and Jacques Roger quoted at the beginning of this chapter. Naigeon's assertions about fragments and reading notes therefore come full circle, not only being repeated as authoritative evidence in every introductory presentation of the *Physiologie* that exists, and by every one of the critics mentioned thus far, but to some extent also used to define what the *Physiologie* is, and therefore what it is not, thereby dismissing the actual evidence of the text itself.

It's an odd situation, and one in which Naigeon's account has been decisive. Even Paolo Quintili's and Motoichi Terada's editions of the *Éléments de physiologie* (2004 and 2019 respectively), both of which forcefully argue for the importance of this late text, continue to plough the same furrow, quoting Naigeon, adding further information about Diderot's medical sources.¹⁴ There are very few scholarly pages which look at this text on its own terms, as opposed to as some sort of basket containing a mish-mash of Diderot's medical interests. This is because of what Naigeon said in his *Mémoires historiques et philosophiques* in 1823, and which every critic since has quoted as the gospel truth, compounded with this issue of the two very different stages of manuscript completion, their staggered publication dates, and the fact that Assézat's confirmation of Naigeon's story, although based on an incomplete draft, has nonetheless influenced later scholars from Dieckmann to the present, all of whom continue to relay this same account. The result is a sort of received wisdom about the *Physiologie* which means that when it is mentioned—if it is mentioned in non-Diderot-specific literature at all—it is as an incomplete text, a pipe dream of Diderot's. That's what

---

13  Dieckmann remarks with surprise that 'Sometimes Naigeon seems to prefer even the *Éléments*: once he chooses the formulation of the Éléments, though the same passage is found in the *Rêve* with only minor variants'. Dieckmann, 'J.-A. Naigeon's Analysis', 484. He is referring to *Mémoires historiques et philosophiques*, p. 260.

14  Motoichi Terada describes it as situated 'à mi-chemin entre un composé mosaïque de notes de lecture et un discours scientifique' [half-way between a mosaic made out of reading notes and a scientific discourse], *Éléments de physiologie*, ed. by Motoichi Terada (Paris: Éditions Matériologiques, 2019), p. 9 [hereafter MT].

Jean Starobinski called it in passing in his otherwise inspiring study of the intellectual history of the twinned concept of *Action et Réaction*.[15]

So if this story started with Naigeon, did he simply get it wrong? If he is the source for this story, and if the story appears to be starkly out of tune with the textual evidence, then we need to look again at his *Mémoires historiques et philosophiques* to see exactly what he says. He devotes 100 pages out of 416—that is, just about a quarter of the whole—to discussing Diderot's views on physiology. Of these 100 pages, 83—presented as a description or paraphrase—are almost entirely verbatim quotation from the *Rêve* and the *Physiologie*, extremely carefully assembled and sewn together. It's about a third *Rêve*, and two thirds *Physiologie*.[16] The more substantial borrowing is from the *Physiologie* not the *Rêve*, and there are fifty pages of quotation from it, which is obviously only a small part of the whole, but nonetheless, not merely a few scattered fragments. Just to be clear, in his *Mémoires historiques et philosophiques*, Naigeon describes Diderot's entire production, from the texts that were print-published and known during Diderot's lifetime such as the *Lettre sur les aveugles*, the *Encyclopédie* articles or the plays, to those with a limited manuscript circulation through the journal *Correspondance littéraire* such as the art criticism of the *Salons*, the fictional travelogue the *Supplément au voyage de Bougainville* or the novels *La Religieuse* and *Jacques le fataliste*, or only in

---

15  Jean Starobinski writes: 'Diderot rêva d'une anthropologie d'inspiration médicale quand il entreprit ses *Éléments de physiologie*, restés inachevés' [Diderot dreamed of writing a medically-inspired anthropological work when he undertook the *Éléments de physiologie*, which remained unfinished], in *Action et réaction: vie et aventures d'un couple* (Paris: Seuil, 1999), p. 146. See also the important intellectual historian Ann Thomson who mentions in passing Diderot's 'medical notes entitled *Éléments de physiologie*, the result of his medical reading [which] includ[e] vague formulations resembling La Mettrie's', in *Bodies of Thought: Science, Religion, and the Soul in the Early Enlightenment* (Oxford: Oxford University Press, 2008), p. 221. The 'vague formulations' to which she refers relate to the paragraph about the flesh pincers which we will quote in full in Chapter 4.

16  We shall be analysing this in Chapter 12; see also the connected digital edition of Naigeon's *Mémoires* at https://naigeons-diderot.mml.ox.ac.uk/index.htm. Motoichi Terada agrees with this analysis, referencing my article: Caroline Warman, 'Naigeon, éditeur de Diderot physiologiste', *Diderot Studies*, 34 (2014), 283–302, MT 56, 63. It was my great good luck that while finalising this digital edition of the *Mémoires*, Motoichi Terada brought out his edition of the *Éléments de physiologie*, which also reproduces Naigeon's *Mémoires*, see his 'Annexe: le précis du *Rêve* (Naigeon, *Mémoires*, pp. 207–91), avec des notes sur les emprunts au *Rêve* et aux *EP*', pp. 513–93. This enabled me to check my results against his; my work as a whole has much benefitted from his.

uncirculated manuscript, such as the searing social satire of the *Neveu de Rameau*. Yet there are only two texts from which he quotes substantially, the *Rêve* and the *Physiologie*, and of those two, the *Physiologie* takes up twice as much space as the *Rêve*. Of all Diderot's production, therefore, it is the one to which Naigeon gives most visibility, and which he must consider to be the most important. There is a stark difference therefore between the story he tells about the scattered fragments and reading notes and the way in which he prioritises this text for quotation above all others. It looks as if he's being deliberately misleading. Why?

We only begin to get an answer to this question when we look at some of the paratexts and also at the different versions of the *Physiologie*.

## From Elements to Fragments

Before returning to Paris from St Petersburg in 1774, Diderot had a new version of the *Rêve de d'Alembert* copied for Catherine II. It gave new names to the interlocutors—instead of Diderot, Jean le Rond d'Alembert, Julie de Lespinasse and Théophile de Bordeu, we have the playwright Nicolas Boindin, the grammarian César Chesneau Dumarsais, Mlle Boucher (daughter of painter François Boucher), and the *philosophe* Julien Offray de La Mettrie. The manuscript, entitled *Les deux Dialogues*, is fairly substantial (113 folios) and presents an intermediary version of the text we now know—more developed than the first drafts of the *Rêve de d'Alembert* but not yet in its final form.[17] It was preceded by an 'Avertissement' [Foreword] in the form of a letter directly addressing Her Imperial Majesty which explained that the original *Dialogues* had had to be destroyed because the original players insisted on having their fictional counterparts eradicated. This is the first instantiation of the myth of the destruction of the *Rêve* in response to d'Alembert and Lespinasse's supposed deep displeasure at featuring in the text.[18] The

---

[17] Georges Dulac describes this manuscript in detail in *Le Rêve de d'Alembert*, DPV, vol. 17, p. 76.

[18] Colas Duflo discusses the supposed destruction of the *Rêve de d'Alembert* on the orders of the supposedly embarrassed d'Alembert in the introduction to his edition: 'Il est difficile de croire que D, qui s'est souvent vanté d'être un champion de la mystification, n'ait pas encore une fois utilisé cet art utile. Jacques Roger maintient cependant qu'on "ne peut suspecter D de mauvaise foi en la circonstance" et que Grimm a dû garder une copie, sans en avertir D, qui serait "miraculeusement"

'avertissement' explains that the reassembled version 'n'est qu'une statue brisée, mais si brisée, qu'il fut presque impossible, même à l'artiste de la réparer' [nothing but a shattered statue, so very shattered that not even the artist could put it back together] and further that there remained 'un grand nombre de pièces dont il [l'artiste] ne put reconnaître la véritable place' [a large number of pieces whose proper place not even [the artist] could find again]. These pieces were all gathered at the end of the *Deux dialogues* and presented as ready for reintegration, despite not being from the original *Rêve* at all.[19] There are thirty pages of them, in the form of aphoristic remarks about physiology and sensation, gathered under thematic headings and entitled, in explicit echo of the 'avertissement', 'Fragments dont on ne put reconnaître la véritable place' [Fragments whose proper place could not be recognised].[20] This is a recognisable early draft of the *Éléments de physiologie*.[21]

So the first instance of the *Éléments de physiologie* being claimed to be fragmentary comes from Diderot himself, here, in 1774. Insofar as it introduces a masked version of the *Rêve*, masked not least because of the fears he expresses in the 'Avertissement' for his peace, fortune, life, honour, and reputation should it ever be leaked or published, we can see why Diderot might want to call them 'fragments': it's part of the disguise. Insofar also as these supposed *Fragments* are indeed a very early draft, we can see that it makes sense: they are incomplete, although the time sequence is back to front: they are not relics of what has been but seeds of what will be. But there is another game going on here

---

réapparue après la mort de Julie de Lespinasse (Intro de l'éd GF-Flam 1965, p. 21). Jean Varloot, pour sa part, pense que Diderot "simula un autodafé du manuscrit" (Introduction de l'édition DPV, p. 27). Il n'est peut-être ni possible ni très utile de trancher la question' [it is hard to believe that D, who had often boasted of being a champion of mystification, didn't once again deploy this useful skill here. Jacques Roger however maintains that "on this occasion we cannot suspect Diderot of being in bad faith" and that Grimm must have kept a copy without telling D, which "miraculously" reappeared after Julie de Lespinasse died. Jean Varloot thinks that Diderot "pretended to burn the manuscript". It is perhaps neither possible nor particularly useful to determine the truth of the matter]. Denis Diderot, *Le Rêve de d'Alembert*, ed. by Colas Duflo (Paris: GF Flammarion, 2002), p. 29, n. 3.

19 'Avertissement' DPV 17 221–23; *Éléments de physiologie*, ed. by Paolo Quintili (Paris: Champion, 2004), pp. 415–18 [hereafter PQ].
20 DPV 225–60 (title page: p. 225)/PQ 418–50 (title page: p. 418).
21 This early draft can be consulted in *Le manuscrit de Pétersbourg/1774/Avertissement des deux dialogues/Fragments dont on n'a pu trouver la véritable place*, ed. by George Dulac in DPV, vol. 17, pp. 213–60.

too, of which we begin to catch a glimpse when we discover that this specific 'Avertissement' exists in two further manuscript versions and is clearly therefore not an incidental but a crucial part of the text. The second version of the 'Avertissement', now in the Fonds Vandeul, again introduces the *Rêve de d'Alembert*, again alleging that 'Ce n'est qu'une statue brisée, mais si brisée qu'il fut presque impossible à l'artiste de la réparer. Il est resté autour de lui nombre de fragments dont il n'a pu retrouver la véritable place' [this is nothing but a shattered statue, so very shattered that not even the artist could put it back together. Around it there remain a number of fragments whose proper place not even (the artist) could find again].[22] A subsequent, and third, version was, like the first, sent to Catherine, this time after Diderot's death, along with a complete set of his manuscripts, but this one did not introduce the *Rêve*. Instead, it directly preceded the first complete draft of the *Éléments de physiologie*, now known as the St Petersburg version, and first printed in the Assézat-Tourneux edition of Diderot's complete works, as we have mentioned.[23] By this point, these supposed fragments were 190 pages long. So there is a conscious repeated connection on the part of Diderot between this introduction with its invocation of the shattered sculpture and the 'fragments dont [l'artiste] n'a pu reconnaître la véritable place'.[24] We see this conscious connection underlined even more explicitly when we set the 'Avertissement' alongside the opening pages of the *Éléments de physiologie* (in both the St Petersburg and Vandeul versions).[25]

> La chaîne des êtres n'est pas interrompue par la diversité des formes. La **forme** n'est souvent qu'un **masque** qui trompe, et **le chaînon qui**

---

22   Spelling *sic*. Bibliothèque nationale de France, NAF 13.731, ff3rv–4r: the quote is ff3rv. This is the manuscript known as V2, see DPV 17, pp. 213 and 83. Dulac says this 'Préface' is 'écrite d'une autre main' [written in a different hand] from the rest of the copy: in fact the handwriting is very recognisably that of *copiste* E (according to Paul Vernière's system, *Diderot, ses manuscrits et ses copistes* (Paris: Klincksieck, 1967), the same who was responsible for the ms. of the *Éléments de physiologie* in the Fonds Vandeul. The wording has changed slightly: 'fragments dont [l'auteur] n'a pu *reconnaître*' [1774 version, and heading of the 1774 fragments] or '*retrouver* la véritable place' [NAF 13.731 and AT IX 251]'.
23   AT IX 251.
24   See above, note 21, in Chapter 2.
25   In the St Petersburg version, it is in the second paragraph; in the Vandeul version, it is in the fifth.

**paraît manquer** réside peut-être dans un être connu, à qui les progrès de l'anatomie comparée n'ont encore pu **assigner sa véritable place**.[26]

The chain of being is not interrupted by the diversity of its forms. Form is often nothing other than a deceptive mask, and the link which seems to be missing may perhaps be found in a known being, which the advances in comparative anatomy have not yet managed to assign to its proper place.

The textual echo between the 'Avertissement''s 'fragments dont on n'a pu reconnaître la véritable place' and the 'chaînons' whose place in the 'chaîne des êtres' the progress of research in comparative anatomy 'n'[a] pas encore pu assigner sa véritable place' is glaring, the repetition drawing attention to the phrasing. What is Diderot's point?[27] Might he be suggesting an implicit parallel between text and content, and emphasising replicating structures of seeming fragmentation in a context of incomplete knowledge?

In the Vandeul manuscript, the 'Avertissement' we have been considering in its three iterations is removed and replaced with a new one which retains the claim about the fragments but sets it within a completely different framing narrative:

Éléments de Physiologie 1778

AVERTISSEMENT

En lisant les ouvrages du Baron de Haller M$^r$ *** conçut le projet de rédiger des Éléments de physiologie. Pendant plusieurs mois il recueillit ce qui lui parut propre ou essentiel à entrer dans ces Éléments. Les notes et extraits étaient sur des feuillets épars et isolés. La mort ayant empêché M$^r$ *** d'exécuter le projet, dont il n'avait fait que préparer les matériaux, on a cru devoir les réunir en une seule copie. Quelque incomplets qu'ils soient, et malgré le défaut d'ordre qu'on n'a pu y mettre, on pense que le public recevra avec plaisir ces fragments, et qu'un jour quelque personne

---

26   DPV 295–96/PQ 108/MT 118, my bolding. SP AT IX 253 is the second paragraph; the syntax is very slightly different from the quoted text above: 'Il ne faut pas croire que la chaîne des êtres...'—the rest is the same, apart from a slight difference in punctuation.

27   The model of the chain and its links is of course part of what Diderot is drawing attention to, and I address this topic below, see Chapter 3. See also: Yves Citton, *L'Envers de la liberté: l'invention d'un imaginaire Spinoziste dans la France des lumières* (Paris: Éditions Amsterdam, 2006), pp. 85–89; and Arthur O. Lovejoy's famous study, *The Great Chain of Being* (Cambridge, MA: Harvard University Press, 1936; repr. 2001), esp. pp. 227–41.

entreprendra d'après le plan et les idées de M^r *** l'ouvrage qu'il n'a fait qu'ébaucher.[28]

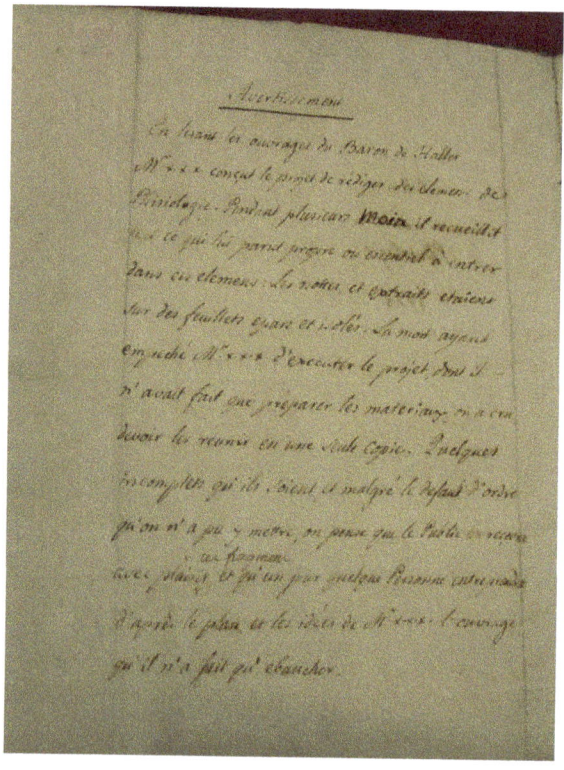

Fig. 2.1 The new 'Avertissement', BnF, Manuscrits, NAF 13762, f. 1v, Denis Diderot (copyist 'E'), c. 1780, Pen and paper, Denis Diderot *Éléments de physiologie*, Fonds Vandeul, Bibliothèque nationale de France, CC-BY

FOREWORD

It was on reading the works of Baron Haller that M^r *** came up with the project of writing a book on the Elements of physiology. He spent many months gathering whatever he thought was relevant or essential to

---

28 DPV 293/PQ 105/MT 115. See also Herbert Dieckmann, *Inventaire du fonds vandeul et inédits de Diderot* (Genève: TLF Droz, 1951), pp. 76–78. NAF 17.362, Copiste E. There are two emendations on the ms. copy, neither in E's hand: 'mois'[months] replaces the original 'années' [years], and the original 'le public les recevra' [the public will welcome them] has become the syntactically clearer 'le public recevra [...] ces fragments' [the public will welcome these fragments]: the correcting hand may be Vandeul's.

include in these Elements. His notes and extracts were on scattered and separate scraps of paper. Death having prevented M$^r$ *** from completing the project, for which he had only got as far as preparing the materials, it was felt they should be assembled into a single copy. However incomplete they may be, and despite the flaws in the order that has been chosen, it is hoped that the public will welcome these fragments with pleasure, and that one day somebody will undertake the work according to the plans and ideas that M$^r$ *** was merely able to sketch out.

This is a new version of the story about the fragments, at once more elaborate, more specific with respect to the details, and even more strikingly at odds with the text itself, in this its most complete version, filling 152 manuscript recto-verso pages of continuous text, and between 210 and 250 printed pages in Mayer's, Quintili's and Terada's annotated editions. Terada comments with surprise at the notion that this could be described as merely 'une ébauche d'ouvrage' [a sketch for a book] and adds that 'il y a certainement quelque mystification dans cette notice' [there is certainly some mystification going on in this preface].[29] Dieckmann and Quintili think it is so at odds with the text it purportedly introduces that it must in fact be part of the earlier St Petersburg version which, in their view, it more accurately describes.[30] There is no evidence that this is the case: the copyist is the same, it appears on the first page of the bound manuscript notebook and is not a later insertion, and the St Petersburg version had its own 'avertissement', as we have seen. On the contrary, Dieckmann and Quintili's bewilderment is further evidence of the extent to which this particular story about incompletion has been taken as the literal truth, without it ever occurring to anyone apart from Terada that the *Éléments*, in common with Diderot's other works, might contain playful and mystificatory features that themselves enclose a

---

29 MT 115n and MT 34 respectively.
30 Dieckmann observes 'on est surpris de trouver l'Avertissement en tête de ce volume; il appartient plutôt au manuscrit de Leningrad' [it is surprising to find the Notice at the beginning of this volume; it really belongs to the Leningrad manuscript], in his *Inventaire*, p. 77. Paolo Quintili takes this further, considering that this 'Avertissement' may well be posthumous precisely because it reflects the nature of the SP ms. rather than the Vandeul one (PQ 105, n. 2; see also DPV 293). Jean Mayer, in his 1987 DPV edition, appears to think that certain 'réviseurs' wrote this 'Avertissement' (DPV 17, p. 272); this seems unlikely for the reasons discussed above, and also because the same copyist, 'E' in Vernière's denomination, who copied out the entire manuscript, also did the 'Avertissement'; the hand is the same.

message in some way intimately connected with the questions the text was trying to raise.

This particular 'avertissement' asserts the incompleteness of the text it introduces even more insistently than the previous one, while doing so on the basis of an entirely different scenario. It retains the notion of the fragment, but integrates it into a story about long preparation interrupted by death, implicitly invoking loyal friends left behind to look after the 'feuillets épars et isolés' [scattered and separate scraps of paper], who have made a great effort to bring the 'fragments' together, who hope the public will take pleasure in them, and that one day some person will undertake to flesh out the plan and ideas M<sup>r</sup>*** has only sketched out. Incomplete, disordered, written on scraps of paper? The *Éléments de physiologie* is none of these things, and nor is the manuscript notebook which contains it.[31] Interrupted by death and advertising the date 1778, when Diderot did not die until 1784? Just a plan and some ideas, brought together in a single copy, while awaiting completion? None of this describes the *Éléments de physiologie* even remotely, but it does by contrast very precisely recall the fate and story of a landmark work, the posthumous so-called *Pensées* of the mathematician and Jansenist thinker Blaise Pascal.[32] Is this just a coincidence?

Pascal's project, one on which he was working during the last years of his life and despite his paralysing ill health, was to have been an apology of the Christian faith, an 'apologie' being in English an 'apology' or 'apologia' and meaning 'a written defence or justification' (OED); Pascal's particular aim seems to have been to convince atheists to believe in God, hence the famous 'pari de Pascal' [Pascal's wager], which argues that atheists might as well believe in God as they have nothing to lose.

It was famously not written out in continuous prose but made from many separate fragments written on scraps of paper. The Pascal family and their Jansenist circle at Port-Royal worked for years to produce what they saw as the best version, now known as the Port-Royal edition, and

---

[31] NAF 17.362; see also Jean Mayer's careful description of the 'tome cartonné' DPV 17, pp. 287–88.

[32] For a luminously clear introduction to Pascal and Pascal studies, see Richard Parish, 'Blaise Pascal', *French Studies*, 71.4 (2017), 539–50, https://doi.org/10.1093/fs/knx215.

in fact it was not what we would call a comprehensive or even a faithful edition, as it often ignored Pascal's own organisation (he had many of the separate fragments carefully ordered in specific thematic folders or 'liasses') and set aside a vast number of fragments which were not thought to be appropriate. Their title in the first editions of 1669, 1670, and 1688 was given as *Pensées de M. Pascal sur la religion et sur quelques autres sujets, qui ont esté trouvées après sa mort parmy ses papiers* [Thoughts of Mr Pascal on religion and on various other subjects which were found after his death amongst his papers]: the notion of these 'thoughts' having been found after his death amongst his papers is therefore a central part of the identity of the published work. The title page of the 1688 edition advertises itself as being 'augmentée de beaucoup de Pensées' [augmented with many Thoughts] so the difficulty and incompleteness of the editions was a feature of the *Pensées* from the very beginning. Jean Filleau de la Chaise had even written a book entitled *Discours sur les pensées de M. Pascal où l'on essaye de faire voire quel estoit son dessein* [Discourse on the thoughts of Mr. Pascal where an attempt is made to see what his design was]. It came out in 1672, two years after the original Port-Royal edition, and in it he expressed the fear that 'quantité de gens seront sans doute choqués d'y trouver si peu d'ordre' [many people will no doubt be shocked at the lack of order they find in it].[33]

Étienne Périer, Pascal's nephew, had alluded explicitly to this lack of organisation or connective logic in his introduction to the Port-Royal edition:

> on les trouva [les papiers] tous ensemble enfilés en diverses liasses, mais sans aucun ordre et sans aucune suite.[34]

> they [the papers] were found all kept together in different folders but they weren't in any order or sequence.

This description is very close to what Diderot would write in the revised 'Avertissement' at the beginning of his *Éléments*, down to his 'feuillets épars et isolés' and 'défaut d'ordre'. The version Naigeon gave in his

---

33  Jean Filleau de La Chaise, *Discours sur les pensées de M. Pascal où l'on essaye de faire voire quel estoit son dessein* (Paris: Guillaume Desprez, 1672), p. 3.
34  Blaise Pascal, *Les Provinciales, Pensées, et Opuscules divers*, ed. by Gérard Ferreyrolles and Philippe Sellier (Paris: Livre de Poche 'La Pochothèque', 2004), p. 831.

*Mémoires sur la vie et les ouvrages de Denis Diderot* closely echoes both Diderot's 'Avertissement' and Périer's own words:

> il n'a laissé de l'important ouvrage qu'il projetait [...] que **quelques matériaux épars et sans aucun ordre entre eux**.[35]
>
> of the substantial work he was planning he left nothing [...] apart from a few scattered materials that didn't follow any order

It is difficult to deny the similarities between Diderot's revised 'Avertissement' with its story about posthumous publication and disordered fragments and the story of Pascal's *Pensées*, even down to the actual wording. They are very similar. This suggests two initial conclusions: firstly, that Diderot was quite specifically evoking Pascal, and secondly, that it is not with Naigeon that this story about fragments and disorder commences, but with Diderot; Naigeon merely relayed it. It is clear enough that the notion of fragments had been a crucial part of his presentation of the *Éléments* from the very first drafts, but it is only with the final version that it develops into a story implicitly referencing Pascal.

Do we now have enough evidence to stop calling the *Éléments de physiologie* fragmentary, and to say instead that it seems as if this particular story about fragments is a disguise devised by the notoriously tricksy author? If so, the question then becomes why he did it, with a subsidiary enquiry into why no one has ever noticed. Perhaps the confusion over the two drafts, along with the view that Naigeon was faithfully transcribing what really happened as opposed to just as faithfully transcribing Diderot's mystification, explains why this has become the official account of the *Éléments*. In later chapters we will add more detail to the general picture of confusion surrounding this text when we look at the complex relationship between its publication history and Diderot's reputation during the French Revolution. In the rest of this chapter, however, we will attempt to address what this Pascal parallel that Diderot sets up at the very beginning of the *Éléments* is supposed to do.

---

35 Naigeon, *Mémoires historiques et philosophiques sur la vie et les ouvrages de Denis Diderot*, p. 291.

Significantly for the argument being made here, two new editions of Pascal's *Pensées*, the first to significantly reorder the Port-Royal version, came out while Diderot was composing his *Éléments de physiologie*, one in 1776 (with a revised version in 1778), and the other in 1779. The first was a polemical 'more methodical' reordering, by the *philosophe* and mathematician Condorcet, and the other was a serious contribution to Pascal scholarship, retrieving and making available material which had not until then been known.[36] This latter edition, by Charles Bossut, which came out in 1779, thereafter dominated until well into the nineteenth century.

Condorcet was a mathematician, thinker, and protégé of D'Alembert, Diderot's *Encyclopédie* co-editor, and he brought out his revised edition of the *Pensées*, advertising itself as being more methodical, in 1776. In 1778, this edition was republished, this time with annotations by Voltaire, who calls himself the 'second éditeur'. Voltaire's first annotation, relating to the title, is feistily judgmental and reductive in the normal Voltairean way, and immediately seizes on the issue of fragments, disorder, and the posthumous edition by a group of friends.

> (\*) Ce n'est point ainsi que Pascal avait arrangé ses pensées; car il ne les avait point arrangés du tout, il les jeta au hasard. Ses amis après sa mort les mirent dans un ordre; l'auteur de l'*Éloge* les a mises dans un autre, et ce nouvel ordre est plus méthodique. *Second éditeur.*[37]

> (\*) This is not at all how Pascal had arranged his thoughts, as he hadn't arranged them in the slightest, he just set them down at random. After his death, his friends put them in one order; the author of the *Éloge* [In Praise of Pascal] put them in another one, and this new order is more methodical. *Second editor.*

Voltaire had of course previously engaged with Pascal's *Pensées* in the last of his *Lettres philosophiques*, published in 1734, and the annotation above is a paraphrase from that earlier text, in whose opening paragraph he had written of the *Pensées* which Pascal 'avait jetées au hasard sur le papier' [had randomly set down on paper], talking of his respect for

---

36 *Éloge et Pensées de Pascal, édition établie par Condorcet et annotée par Voltaire*, ed. by Richard Parish, in *Œuvres complètes de Voltaire* (Oxford: Voltaire Foundation, 1968–), 80A (2008); *Œuvres*, ed. by Abbé Charles Bossut, 5 vols (The Hague [Paris]: Detune, 1779).

37 *Éloge et Pensées de Pascal* [Condorcet/Voltaire], p. 129.

'le génie et l'éloquence de Pascal' [the genius and eloquence of Pascal] declaring that 'c'est en admirant son génie que je combats quelques-unes de ses idées' [it is while admiring his genius that I contest some of his ideas].[38] Voltaire's Letter 25 does indeed go on to combat Pascal's ideas, quoting gobbets of the *Pensées* whose logic and view of Christianity and mankind he contests at every turn. For Voltaire, Pascal's genius and eloquence—and, we should add, his engagement with reason in discussing matters of faith—make him an important reference point, while his Jansenist world view makes him an important adversary for the optimistic pro-tolerance pro-mercantilist thinker that is the Voltaire of the 1730s. What he is in 1778 when the Condorcet edition with its Voltaire amendments came out is on his deathbed, at the end of about twenty years of ceaseless campaigning against religious intolerance.[39] The tone of his comments has therefore sharpened, as we will see.

Bossut's multi-volume edition of Pascal's complete works (including, of course, the *Pensées*) came out in 1779 and would have been known to Diderot, if for no other reason than that the careful description of Pascal's calculating machine that Diderot had written for the *Encyclopédie* article MACHINE ARITHMÉTIQUE was reprinted in its fourth volume: the Pascal scholar Arnoux Straudo believes that this article and its reappearance in Pascal's *Œuvres complètes* were responsible for the revival of Pascal's reputation as a scientist, forming the basis of subsequent descriptions.[40]

---

[38] Voltaire, *Lettres philosophiques*, ed. by Frédéric Deloffre (Paris: Gallimard Folio, 1986), p. 156.

[39] It was, apparently, the last work he published, and he was beadily following up on its progress only two weeks before he died: 'Je voudrais bien savoir si le *Pascal Condorcet* est fini. Je vous prie de vous en informer à Grasset de Genêve' [I would be very keen to know if the *Pascal Condorcet* is finished. Please be so kind as to check with Grasset in Geneva]. 'Voltaire [François Marie Arouet] to Jean Louis Wagnière: Thursday, 14 May 1778', in *Electronic Enlightenment Scholarly Edition of Correspondence*, ed. by Robert McNamee et al., 2018, https://doi.org/10.13051/ee:doc/voltfrVF1290322a1c. With thanks to Richard Parish for this information.

[40] Straudo writes that: 'Le travail de Diderot sera d'une grande utilité pour la fortune scientifique de Pascal: reproduit en effet dans l'édition des *oeuvres de Blaise Pascal* de Bossut [IV.34-50] et dans l'*Encyclopédie méthodique* [*Mathématiques*, t.1 (Paris 1784), p. 136-42], il servira de base à des descriptions ultérieures' [Diderot's work would be extremely useful for Pascal's academic fate : reproduced in Bossut's edition of the *Works of Blaise Pascal* and in the *Encyclopédie méthodique*, it would serve as a basis for later descriptions] (*La fortune de Pascal en France au XVIIIe siècle*, SVEC 351 (Oxford: Voltaire Foundation, 1997), p. 206).

Might it be the case therefore that these two new editions, with their prominent discussions of fragments and ordering and their claims to improve on previous editions, could have suggested to Diderot a new approach to his existing line about the *Éléments de physiologie*'s fragmentary nature?

One wonders therefore whether the date of 1778 on the title page of the Vandeul manuscript which we know to be erroneous and which the two editors Mayer and Quintili have found bizarre might be some form of signal to indicate proximity to the Condorcet/Voltaire edition of Pascal's *Pensées*, or even to Voltaire's death? Death, after all, features in the 'avertissement' as the obstacle to the completion of the project. In 1778, not only Voltaire but also Diderot's erstwhile friend Jean-Jacques Rousseau died, within six weeks of each other. 1778 is a death year for the *philosophes*, a moment with which Diderot may well have chosen to associate his not-yet-happened death. However, it is no more than speculation that Diderot chose this date as a significant one, and if so, that it might have been for these reasons.

Whether or not the date given on the first page of the manuscript is a later addition, there is a temporal proximity between the ongoing composition of Diderot's *Physiologie* and the publication of two new editions of Pascal's *Pensées*, both of which very publicly reopen the issue of their order and incompletion. It adds further circumstantial evidence about where this repeatedly relayed and manifestly false myth about the fragmentary nature of Diderot's last work came from. But we may not need this very localised literary history to make the case; it just helps us to see that the case is there. After all, the 'avertissement' letter which Diderot wrote to Catherine II in 1774, and which was re-sent to her as the introduction to the *Éléments de physiologie* in 1785, predates these Pascal editions, and draws attention repeatedly to the notion of fragments, dispersal, and rearrangement, as we have seen.

So the notion of fragmentation and the implicit reference to Pascal are planted at the opening of Diderot's *Physiologie*. Why is this? Why is it fundamental to the project of the *Éléments de physiologie* to first establish the Pascalian parallel? Pascal's *Pensées* were of course, and as already mentioned, the mosaic fragments of his long-mulled-over and never-completed apology of the Christian faith, in parts conceived of as a dialogue with an atheist whom Pascal is seeking to convert.

His 'written defence or justification' of the Christian faith had a huge impact from the moment of its publication. His arguments constituted a crucial reference for anyone interested in debating religion and its relation to knowledge in the century after his death, which was more or less everyone engaged in any aspect of knowledge at all, Voltaire being a case in point. But the *Pensées* and their arguments were nonetheless fragmentary and their relation to the never-achieved whole a matter for public discussion, dispute, and rearrangement. Might Diderot be using this opening allusion to the incompletion of Pascal's *Pensées* as a way of throwing down the gauntlet, the literal *notification* or 'avertissement' of a challenge to religious accounts of nature and man? The carefully crafted wholeness of the *Éléments*, starting with the big picture of nature and its infinitely varied beings, moving through the properties of matter and the different life forms, subsequently focusing in on human anatomy, and then presenting an extended assessment of sensation, the brain and human consciousness and self-consciousness, ending with a reverie about death, stands in interconnected and thorough contrast to the fractured *Pensées*. The *Éléments de physiologie* looks like the atheist's response to—and rebuttal of—the arguments of the Christian who had been trying to convert him to faith.

We know, after all, that Diderot likes to dialogue, rewrite, contest, refute: we have examples of this throughout his œuvre. We also, of course, know that he likes the aphoristic form of the 'pensée' which both recalls Pascal and is a sort of tribute to him: Diderot's *Pensées philosophiques* (1746) is one of the earliest publications of the emerging writer, and, as the prominent co-editor of the *Encyclopédie*, he returns publicly to the form with the *Pensées sur l'interprétation de la nature* (1753) continuing with it in the *Additions aux pensées philosophiques* (1763).[41] Indeed, he inserts a transformed version of at least one of his own *Pensées philosophiques* into the *Éléments*. In its first version it reads as follows:

---

41 The 'Additions' were written in 1762, manuscript-published in the Correspondance littéraire in 1763, print-published in 1770 in Naigeon's *Recueil philosophique*, and there (falsely) attributed to Vauvenargues. See David Adams, *Bibliographie des œuvres de Diderot, 1739–1900*, 2 vols (Ferney-Voltaire: Centre international d'étude du XVIIIe siècle, 2000). With thanks to Kate E. Tunstall for this detail.

> Le vrai martyr attend la mort; l'enthousiaste y court.⁴²
>
> The true martyr waits for death; the enthusiast runs towards it.

In the *Éléments*, it has become this:

> L'enfant court à la mort les yeux fermés : l'homme est stationnaire ; le vieillard y arrive le dos tourné.⁴³
>
> The child runs towards death with their eyes shut; the man is stationary; the old man approaches it with his back turned.

The shared scenario involves the more or less rapid movement of different sorts of people (different in terms of religious fervour or in age) towards death. Yet what was in the 1746 version an implicit criticism of the zealot who courts death has turned in the mature version into an aphorism about the growth and decline of the individual over time, and about their attitude to death according to their age. The idea and its expression are doubly materialist, being embodied (eyes closed, back turned), and also because the position of the body in space and time determines the experience and happiness of the individual. The criticism of religious enthusiasm in the first formulation gains a new edge in the context of the revision, in that being carried away by religious feelings is implicitly now presented as a youthful impulse which the older, wiser man moves beyond.

There are other such instances of Diderot incorporating his youthful *Pensées* into the older text: it is not my aim here, however, to focus on this particular aspect of Diderot's auto-intertextuality but rather to show that the 'pensée' is a form that Diderot continuously works with and indeed (as in this case) reworks. Pascal himself is explicitly named twice in the *Éléments*, once as an example of someone who was supposed never to have forgotten anything he had done, read, or thought 'depuis l'âge de raison' [since reaching the age of reason] and once, in the conclusion, where he is cited as having said about God that 'on ne sait ni ce qu'il est, ni s'il est' [we are incapable of knowing either what he is or whether he

---

42 Denis Diderot, *Pensées philosophiques, Additions aux pensées*, ed. by Jean-Claude Bourdin (Paris: GF Flammarion, 2007), p. 76 ('Pensée' 39).
43 DPV 313/PQ 129/MT 136.

is].⁴⁴ So, in sum, Pascal is both an implicit and an explicit reference point in the *Éléments de physiologie*, and the 'pensée' form so strongly associated with him is also present throughout Diderot's œuvre, including in this particular work. But this isn't all. There is reason to think that Diderot is engaging with specific arguments and *pensées*, and that the two writers surprisingly share common anchoring points or questions, even if their answers radically diverge. As Diderot observes, appositely enough in his own *Pensées philosophiques*, there are 'arsenaux communs' for the believer and the unbeliever alike:

> C'est en cherchant des preuves que j'ai trouvé des difficultés. Les livres qui contiennent les motifs de ma croyance m'offrent en même temps les raisons de l'incrédulité. Ce sont des arsenaux communs.⁴⁵
>
> It is when I was looking for proofs that I found difficulties. The books which contain the motives for my belief also and at the same time give me the reasons for unbelief. They contain ammunition for both sides.

We will therefore now turn to what I have suggested might be common points of reference, or even an arsenal of tools or weapons that Diderot could use, redeploy, or even turn against their creator. The three editions of Pascal's *Pensées* that Diderot would have had access to, that is, the Port-Royal, the Condorcet/Voltaire, and the Bossut, form the corpus of *pensées* which has been considered here. Suggestive parallels with *pensées* that were not yet available in print have been left aside, except in one case which we will come to in due course.

---

44 Pascal's prodigious memory: DPV 473/PQ 301/MT 289; Pascal on God: DPV 515/PQ 358/MT 327; Pascal in English *Pensées*, trans. by Roger Ariew (Indianapolis, IN: Hackett, 2005), p. 212. Pascal had written, 'Nous sommes donc incapables de connaître ni ce qu'il est ni s'il est.' In the Le Guern edition (used by DPV), this is part of composite fragment 397; in the widely-used Sellier, this is part of composite fragment 680 (p. 1210); the concordance tables in the Brunschvicg edition record this composite fragment in many different parts of the Port-Royal and Bossut editions. For Port-Royal edition, see VII 1 and 2, XXVIII.69; for Bossut, see II iii.1; II iii.4 and 5; II xvii.63. It appears in abridged form in Condorcet/Voltaire, ed. Parish, pp. 161-62, Article III §1 (with grateful thanks to Richard Parish for locating it).

45 Diderot, *Pensées philosophiques*, pp. 89–90 ('Pensée' 61).

## Pascal and Diderot: Common Reference Points

### Instinct

Both Pascal and Diderot consider instinct to be central to understanding the nature of man, both repeatedly ask about the relation of part to whole and the extent to which part is independent of or dependent on whole, and both consider that one's outlook on the world and experience of it are determined by varying levels and emphases of perception as well as by illness.

'Deux choses instruisent l'homme de toute sa nature: l'instinct et l'expérience' [Two things teach man about his whole nature: instinct and experience] writes Pascal, in a fragment which appears to have been first published in Bossut's edition and would not have been out of place in Diderot's work.[46] And where of course, for Pascal, nature is not an entity which excludes God, while for Diderot it is, instinct is of vital importance for both thinkers as they try to access what nature is, divested of custom. Thus, Diderot writes: 'L'instinct guide mieux l'animal que l'homme. Dans l'animal il est pur, dans l'homme il est égaré par sa raison et ses lumières' [Instinct guides animals better than humans. In animals it is unalloyed whereas in humans it is misled by their reason and knowledge].[47] When Pascal, echoing Montaigne, writes suspiciously of custom as 'une seconde nature, qui détruit la première' [a second nature that destroys the first], fearing that even nature may possibly be a form of custom, and therefore unnatural, he is also showing 'l'homme égaré'—man misled, unable to

---

[46] Op. cit., p.897, § 161 (Sellier, section VIII, 'Contrariétés'); Bossut I.iv.10 (Brunchsvicg §396); Blaise Pascal, *Pensées*, trans. by Roger Ariew (Indianapolis, IN: Hackett, 2005), p. 34. Ariew follows Sellier's ordering. I have used Sellier's concordance to produce the Brunschvicg numbering, and used the Brunchsvicg concordance to get to the Port-Royal and Bossut editions (it doesn't give the Condorcet/Voltaire edition).

[47] DPV 315/PQ 131/MT 138. In this section Diderot is also invisibly referencing La Mettrie's *Traité de l'âme*: 'L'instinct consiste dans des dispositions corporelles purement mécaniques, qui font agir les animaux *sans nulle délibération, indépendamment de toute expérience*' [instinct consists in purely mechanical bodily dispositions which make animals act *without any deliberation and independently of any experience*] (*Traité de l'âme*, in La Mettrie, *Œuvres philosophiques*, ed. by Francine Markovits, 2 vols (Paris: Fayard, 1987), vol. 1, p.185, added emphasis indicating the verbatim borrowing).

access 'real' nature.⁴⁸ In a fragment from the St Petersburg draft of the *Éléments de physiologie* which never made it into the Vandeul version, Diderot had written: 'Nous ne pouvons connaître l'instinct parce qu'il est détruit par notre éducation. Il est plus éveillé dans le sauvage' [We cannot understand instinct because it is destroyed by our education. It is keener in savages].⁴⁹ So while they are agreed on the importance of instinct as well as its compromised nature in man, Diderot will elevate the 'savage' man or animal over 'civilised' man as the former is closer to nature, less compromised in his reactions, as we see in this comic if compressed little scenario about a worm who unites instinct and experience: 'Expérience sur le ver: attendez qu'il sorte, piquez-le, il se détournera, il rentrera dans la terre, craindra de sortir etc' [Experiment on a worm: wait for it to come out, prick it, it will turn away, go back into the ground, fear to come out etc].⁵⁰ Out comes the worm, gets poked by the experimental human, dives back down into the earth and won't come out again. Its instinct makes it escape, and its experience of being poked gives it fear and thereby teaches it not to come out again. The worm has learnt the lesson which natural instinct has taught it, and it has turned, wisely.⁵¹

## Pleasure, Thought, and the Definition of the Human

Pascal sarcastically asks what it is within us that feels pleasure.⁵²

> Qu'est-ce qui sent du plaisir en nous ? Est-ce la main, est-ce le bras, est-ce la chair, est-ce le sang? On verra qu'il faut que ce soit quelque chose d'immatériel.⁵³

---

48  Op. cit., p.897, § 159 (Sellier, section VIII, 'Contrariétés'); Port-Royal: XXV.15; Bossut I.vi.19 (Brunchsvicg §93). *Pensées*, trans. by Ariew, p. 34. Sellier refers us to Montaigne, *Essais*, III, 10, p. 1010: 'L'accoutumance est une seconde nature, et non moins puissante' [custom is a second nature, and no less powerful].
49  PQ 140, 'FNR' (Fragment non repris). DPV 325 doesn't reference this FNR.
50  DPV 314/PQ 131/MT 138.
51  Sellier § 176 also considers the question of instinct. With thanks to Richard Parish for this addition.
52  In Sellier's edition, this 'pensée' precedes the fragment entitled 'Contre le pyrrhonisme' (§141). 'Pyrrhonism' is a synonym of scepticism, the position of rational doubt which Pascal works so hard to present as untenable and even incompletely rational in itself (see Pascal's wager, which as Parish points out is 'more correctly the fragment *Infini: Rien* [B 233; L 418; S 680]'. Parish, 'Blaise Pascal', p. 543.
53  Op. cit., p. 889, §140 (Sellier, section VII, Grandeur); Port-Royal XXXIII.8; Bossut I.iv.8 (Brunchsvicg §339bis). *Pensées*, trans. by Ariew, p. 30.

What feels pleasure in us? Is it our hand, our arm, flesh, blood? We will see that it must be something immaterial.

His triumphant 'we will see that it must be something immaterial' is blocked by Diderot, who takes this question extremely seriously and will musingly say that 'je pense que le plaisir n'est point dans l'oeil' [I think that the feeling of pleasure is by no means in the eye][54] without implying either that this is a statement of the obvious, absurd in any way, or that if pleasure isn't located in the eye, it cannot be material. Indeed, he will flatly contradict Pascal's position when he states that 'chaque organe a son plaisir et sa douleur particulière' [each organ has its own particular pleasure and pain].[55] When Pascal declares, this time in dialogue with René Descartes, that thought is what defines human difference from the rest of nature, Diderot again contradicts him. Pascal had written:

> Je puis bien concevoir un homme sans main, pieds, tête, car ce n'est que l'expérience qui nous apprend que la tête est plus nécessaire que les pieds. Mais je ne puis concevoir l'homme sans pensée. Ce serait une pierre ou une brute.[56]

> I can certainly conceive of a man without hands, feet, head, for it is only experience that teaches us the head is more necessary than the feet. But I cannot conceive of man without thought. He would be a stone or a beast.

Diderot writes in sharp contradistinction as follows:

> Dans l'état parfait de santé, où il n'y a aucune sensation prédominante qui fasse discerner une partie du corps, état que tout homme a quelque fois éprouvé, l'homme n'existe qu'en un point du cerveau: il est tout au lieu de la pensée; peut-être en examinant de fort près trouverait-on que

---

54 DPV 456/PQ 281/MT 272.
55 DPV 499/PQ 336/MT 313. See Chapter 4, particularly Bordeu-inspired vitalism.
56 Pascal, *Pensées*, p. 891, §143 (Sellier, section VII, Grandeur); Port-Royal XXIII.1; Bossut I.iv.2 (Brunchsvicg §339). *Pensées*, trans. by Ariew, p. 31. Sellier gives an intertext from Descartes: 'Nous connaissons manifestement que, pour être, nous n'avons pas besoin d'extension, de figure, d'être en aucun lieu, ni d'aucune autre telle chose qu'on peut attribuer au corps, et que nous sommes par cela seul que nous pensons' [We manifestly know that, in order to be, we have no need of extension, shape, location or of any other such thing that might be attributed to a body, and that we exist solely because we think] (Descartes, *Principes* I, 8, in *Œuvres*, ed. Charles Adam and Paul Tannery (Paris : Vrin, 1964), vol. 9 : II, *édition révisée*, p. 28).

> triste ou gai, dans la peine ou le plaisir, il est toujours tout au lieu de la sensation.[57]

> In a perfect state of health, when no single dominant sensation draws attention to any particular part of the body, a state which everyone has experienced sometimes, then a person exists only in one point in their brain and is completely absorbed in the thought; perhaps if we looked very closely we would discover that when someone is sad or happy, in pain, or feeling pleasure, they are always completely absorbed by their sensation.

Diderot's response to the definition of man as inevitably connected to thought is to reframe the question in bodily terms: what is the predominant sensation? If there is none, and if the person is in perfect health, then they will be entirely focused on their thought, or in Diderot's expression, entirely 'in the place of the thought'. He then transposes this idea onto the notion of feeling, pain and pleasure (notably absent in the previous hypothesis of the thought place), to suggest that the person when feeling would be entirely focused on the sensation, located inside it. This reframing completely displaces thought from its elevated position as ultimate, different, and essentially defining. Thought is only *part* of what is going on, only *part* of our consciousness, unless we enjoy such perfect health that we have no predominant sensation, in which case we can exist totally in our thought. He goes on to deny that humans are always thinking anyway:

> Est-ce qu'on pense quand on est vivement chatouillé? est-ce qu'on pense dans la jouissance des sexes? est-ce qu'on pense quand on est vivement affecté par la poésie, par la musique ou la peinture? Est-ce qu'on pense quand on voit son enfant en péril? Est-ce qu'on pense au milieu d'un combat?[58]

> Are we thinking when we are being intensely tickled? are we thinking when we are enjoying sexual ecstasy? are we thinking when we are intensely affected by poetry, music, or painting? Are we thinking we see our child in danger? Are we thinking in the midst of a fight?

What an array of differently intense situations! From close bodily contact whether pleasurable or painful (being tickled, having sex, fighting), to heightened emotion in response to the arts, or fear for

---

57  DPV 330/PQ 146/MT 151. Part 1, chapter 3 ('Homme'), §2 ('Pensée').
58  DPV 330/PQ 146-47/MT 151.

a child's safety, in none of these moments do we think, says Diderot. His definition of what is human includes these moments of strong, even violent sensation, and these moments preclude thought: logically therefore, Diderot's definition of what is human contests Pascal's (and Descartes's), reasserting the dominance of sensation over thought, and here in fact limiting the primacy of thought to neutral balance, which is tantamount to the total absence of sensation.

In terms of the *process* of thinking, however, Diderot seems to accept Pascal's view so totally as to quote him, albeit invisibly and possibly also unknowingly. This is Pascal's *pensée* about only being able to think about one thing at a time, and we also find it in La Mettrie's *Traité de l'âme* [Treatise on the soul].[59] It suggests that unpublished versions of Pascal's *Pensées* were circulating, in this case attaining print publication via the intermediary of La Mettrie. This is the sole example in this chapter where we use a passage from Pascal which was not, so far as I can tell, available in any of the published editions, and yet it is also the only occasion on which the phrasing is so close that it seems like direct quotation. This is what Pascal had written:

> Une seule pensée nous occupe. Nous ne pouvons penser à deux choses à la fois.[60]
>
> A single thought occupies us. We cannot think of two things at the same time.

In La Mettrie we read this:

> Nous ne pensons qu'à une seule chose à la fois.[61]
>
> We can only think of one thing at a time.

In Diderot's version, this becomes:

> Nous ne pouvons être qu'à une seule chose à la fois.[62]
>
> We can only be focused on one thing at a time.

---

59 We look at this trio of elsewhere, see Chapter 3.
60 Pascal, *Pensées*, p. 1081. S§453. *Pensées*, trans. by Ariew, p. 142.
61 La Mettrie, *Traité de l'âme*, pp. 212–13 and elsewhere: 'l'Ame ne peut avoir qu'une seule idée distincte à la fois' [the soul can only have one distinct idea at a time] (p. 186).
62 DPV 468/PQ 294/MT 283.

Diderot—we must assume—is using La Mettrie, without necessarily knowing that Pascal is the hidden source. It remains nonetheless within the realms of possibility that whatever La Mettrie had access to in terms of circulating Pascalian manuscripts, Diderot also had access to. The filiation in any case is clear, and Diderot's shift from a focus on *thought* to one which emphasises instead a more diffuse (and sensory) *being* is consistent with the displacement of thought from its central position that we have already been looking at.

## Limbs and Body: Subordination and Independence

Pascal uses the reference point or example of the body again and again to make his Christian arguments about the primacy of spirit or mind over its subordinate parts; this works just as well when he is talking about the church and its members as when he is talking about thought or pleasure and whether it's located in the body or not. In the *Pensées* (Liasse XXVII) entitled 'Morale chrétienne', he makes a point about how a Christian is part of a greater body, recalling the words and terms of St Paul, who had written 'Si l'un des membres souffre, tous les autres souffrent avec lui' [If one member suffers, all members suffer with it] (1 Corinthians 12: 26).[63] Pascal creates an extended analogy with body parts which quite quickly acquires a fictional life of its own that is not strictly plausible:

> Etre membre est n'avoir de vie, d'être et de mouvement que par l'esprit du corps et pour le corps. Le membre séparé ne voyant plus le corps auquel il appartient n'a plus qu'un être périssant et mourant. Cependant il croit être un tout et, ne se voyant point de corps dont il dépende, il croit ne dépendre que de soi et veut se faire centre et corps lui-même.[64]

> To be a member is to have life, existence, and motion only for the body and through the spirit of the body. The separated member, no longer seeing the body to which it belongs, has only a perishing and moribund existence. Yet it believes itself a whole, and, not seeing the body on which

---

63 The Bible is quoted in the Jansenist theologian Louis-Isaac Lemaistre de Sacy's French translation of 1667; the English is from Thomas Nelson's New King James Version of 1982.
64 1022 §404 (Sellier XXVII 'Morale chrétienne'); Port-Royal XXIX.3; Ult XXIX. 5 and 8; Bossut II.xvii.70 (Brunchsvicg §483). *Pensées*, trans. by Ariew, p. 105.

it depends, it believes it depends only on itself and wants to make itself its only center and body.

The separated limb has a being which is perishing and dying, as Pascal vividly puts it; thus far the analogy works in parallel. But this separated limb believes it has its own being, that it is complete in itself, that it relies on itself and is its own centre and body. This immediately departs from anatomical plausibility. Presumably the fact that this analogy develops in an absurd direction is part of Pascal's point, viz, that it is absurd to contemplate such a division. Diderot, however, will produce an interestingly equivalent yet literalised version of the relationship between body and selfish member. In his version, the body and its different parts are not an analogy for anything; they are a direct description of the physiological processes of ageing. Meet the selfish old tendon:

> Peu à peu le tendon s'affaisse, il se sèche, il se durcit, il cesse de vivre, du moins d'une vie commune à tout le système; peut-être ne fait-il que s'isoler, se séparer de la société dont il ne partage ni les peines, ni les plaisirs et à laquelle il ne rend plus rien.[65]
>
> Bit by bit the tendon declines, dries up, hardens, and stops living, at least stops living the life common to the whole system; perhaps all it's doing is isolating itself, separating itself from the society whose pains and pleasures it no longer shares, and to which it no longer contributes anything.

And although this depiction is not ironically absurd as Pascal's had been, it has a certain satirical humour or detachment, and in fact Diderot maintains the notion of the importance of contributing to something beyond one's own immediate identity. The society here is the body as a whole. Elsewhere, as we have already indicated above but will also develop further in Chapter 4, Diderot considers at length the extent to which a body part has its own identity within the larger body, and whether it can exist alone. He will say, about organs, that 'tous ont leur vie particulière' [they all have their own particular life], and that 'si l'organe vit, il a donc une vie propre et séparée du reste du système'

---

65  DPV 311/PQ 127/MT 135 (part 1, chapter 2 'Animal'; subsection 'Vie'). There's something about this selfish old tendon that is strongly reminiscent of the sorts of hyper-realised descriptions of wicked old people that we meet in Dickens.

[if the organ is living, it follows that it has its own life separate from the rest of the system].[66] An extended comparison of wooden versus flesh pincers (that is, fingers) is part of this same discussion:[67] it asks us to ask what the ability to feel pain means for flesh, however small or insignificant the piece of flesh, or sentient life, is. If it is sentient, it can feel pain; if it can feel pain, then probably, we assume, care should be taken not to inflict it, and probably also it should be respected as having its own identity. This question of whether the smaller parts have their own identity or not and whether they are subservient or not deeply divides Pascal and Diderot.[68] Pascal will consider the independence of body parts almost with derision in order to reassert their subordination, as here:

> Si les pieds et les mains avaient une volonté particulière, jamais ils ne seraient dans leur ordre qu'en soumettant cette volonté particulière à la volonté première qui gouverne le corps entier. Hors de là, ils sont dans le désordre et dans le malheur. Mais en ne voulant que le bien du corps ils font leur propre bien.[69]
>
> If the feet and hands had a will of their own, they would never be in their order except by submitting this particular will to the primary will governing the whole body. Outside of this, they are in disorder and misfortune. But in wanting only the good of the body, they accomplish their own good.

Against which Diderot will assert (and as we quoted a few pages ago): 'Chaque organe a son plaisir et sa douleur [...] sa volonté [...]' [Each organ has its pleasure, its pain [...], its will].[70] Although I have just extracted the key terms in order to make the parallel with Pascal clearer, the ellipses should not be taken as indicating that this is a passing remark. On the contrary, the whole paragraph runs as follows:

> Chaque organe a son plaisir et sa douleur particulière, sa position, sa construction, sa chaîne, sa fonction, ses maladies accidentelles, héréditaires, ses dégoûts, ses appétits, ses remèdes, ses sensations, sa

---

66   Both quotations from DPV 498–99/PQ 335/MT 312.
67   DPV 449/PQ 274/MT 265–66, quoted in full below.
68   We will examine how this aspect of Diderot's thought is influenced by Montpellier vitalism in Chapter 4, 'Major Debates in Physiology: Mechanism and Vitalism'.
69   1023–24 §406. *Pensées*, trans. by Ariew, p. 106.
70   DPV 499/PQ 336/MT 312, quoted above.

volonté, ses mouvements, sa nutrition, ses stimulants, son traitement approprié, sa naissance, son développement. Qu'a de plus un animal?[71]

Each organ has its particular pleasure and pain, its position, its construction, its chain, its function, its accidental or hereditary illnesses, its dislikes, its appetites, its remedies, its sensations, its will, its movements, its nutrition, its stimulants, its appropriate treatment, its birth, its growth. What more does an animal have?

For Diderot therefore, the idea of integrity of existence of the different body parts is an important one, and not an object of derision. The question both Pascal and Diderot pose, however, is the same: does the member, limb, organ or just simply part of a body have its own separate existence, or does it not?

## Illness

Where they both meet in an important way is on the distorting (Pascal) or determining (Diderot) effect of illness. Both return to it repeatedly. Pascal writes:

> Nous avons un autre principe d'erreur, les maladies. Elles nous gâtent le jugement et le sens. Et si les grandes l'altèrent sensiblement, je ne doute pas que les petites n'y fassent impression à leur proportion.[72]
>
> We have another principle of error, illnesses. They impair our judgement and our senses. And if major illnesses disturb them noticeably, I do not doubt that lesser ones make a proportionate impression.

Diderot puts it differently, removing the moralising notion of 'error', although retaining the idea that the way illness or a bodily disorder make us behave is literally a *dis*order, and therefore that bodily order is preferable and can be returned to:

> Effet réciproque de la sensation sur les objets et des objets sur la sensation. Je suis heureux, tout ce qui m'entoure s'embellit. Je souffre, tout ce qui m'entoure s'obscurcit. [...]

---

71  DPV 499/PQ 336/MT 313.
72  Pascal, *Pensées*, p. 860, §78 (following Sellier spelling and punctuation); PR XXV.11; Cond/Volt, p. 190, §XII (cf fn87); Bossut I.VI., §XIV. *Pensées*, trans. by Ariew, p. 15. Sellier points out that this is close to Montaigne *Essais* II.12, pp. 564–65: Montaigne is a common source and reference point for both Pascal and Diderot.

Un peu de bile dont la circulation dans le foie est embarrassée change toute la couleur des idées: elles deviennent noires, mélancoliques, on se déplaît partout où on est. [...]

Et c'est à de pareilles causes que tient notre raison, nos goûts, nos aversions, nos désirs, notre caractère, nos actions, notre morale, nos vices, nos vertus, notre bonheur et notre malheur, le bonheur et le malheur de ceux qui nous entourent![73]

Reciprocal effect of sensation on objects and of objects on sensation. I am happy, and everything around me becomes beautiful. I am in pain, and everything around me is plunged in gloom. [...]

A little bile not circulating properly in the liver changes the colour of our ideas completely: they become dark, melancholy, and we are displeased wherever we are. [...]

And it's causes like this that determine our reason, our tastes, our aversions, our desires, our character, our actions, our morals, our vices, our virtues, our happiness and our unhappiness, the happiness and unhappiness of those who are close to us!

This extended passage from Diderot provides an interesting commentary on Pascal's reflection about how nature makes us miserable in all states and that this misery is worsened by contrast with what our desires show us of a happier state; Pascal says that this contrast can never be resolved:

(§) La nature nous rendant toujours malheureux, en tous états, nos désirs nous figurent un état heureux, parce qu'ils joignent à l'état où nous sommes, les plaisirs de l'état où nous ne sommes pas; et quand nous arriverions à ces plaisirs nous ne serions pas heureux pour cela, parce que nous aurions d'autres désirs conformes à un nouvel état.[74]

(§) Since nature makes us constantly unhappy in every condition, our desires depict for us a happy condition, because they join to the condition in which we are, the pleasures of the condition in which we are not. And if we attained these pleasures, we would not be happy even then, because we would have other desires relating to this new condition.

The section sign (§) appears at the beginning of this paragraph in the Condorcet/Voltaire edition, and tells us that the 'second éditeur', that is,

---

73 DPV 461/PQ 287/MT 277. These are the closing paragraphs of Part 3, chapter 1, on 'Sensation'.
74 Cond/Volt ed. Parish, p. 230 §XXIII; Parish gives the PR reference to the 1728 edition, as being p. 13 (1728); S§529; PR XXIX.15; Bossut I.vii.5; Brunchsvicg §109. *Pensées*, trans. by Ariew, p. 165 (slightly modified).

Voltaire himself, has something to say. His interventions are normally acerbic or derisive in some way, and nor does he disappoint here:

> (§) La nature ne nous rend pas toujours malheureux. Pascal parle toujours en malade qui veut que le monde entier souffre. *Second éditeur.*[75]
>
> (§) Nature does not make us constantly unhappy. Pascal always speaks like a sick man who wants the whole world to suffer. *Second editor.*

What provokes Voltaire's ire and insult here is Pascal's *a priori* (and Christian Jansenist) position about nature always making us miserable. No, says Voltaire: Pascal was speaking as a sick man, and he wants everyone to suffer like him. Diderot's position—not directed specifically at Pascal—is not about jealousy or mean-spiritedness; it is about the effect of illness on one's outlook. As we quoted earlier, 'Je suis heureux, tout ce qui m'entoure s'embellit. Je souffre, tout ce qui m'entoure s'obscurcit' [I am happy, and everything around me grows beautiful. I am in pain, and everything around me is plunged in gloom]. This is something Pascal talks about, adding a subtle relativisation on thinking about being ill when well (he subsequently develops the theme of contrasting states, and wishing for something we do not have: in Sellier these two passages are brought together in §529, but in the Condorcet/Voltaire edition they're far apart): 'Quand on se porte bien, on ne comprend pas comment on pourrait faire si on était malade' [When we are well, we wonder how we could manage if we were ill].[76]

## Change, Variation, and Monstrosity

Yet where Pascal uses these points to lambast human fallibility and weakness (even man's grandeur lies in the recognition that he is wretched), and further, to draw attention to the instability of nature, Diderot, agreeing with the determining function of illness, fully embraces Pascal's depiction of natural change, clearly taking on and

---

75 Ibid.
76 S§529; Cond/Volt ed. Parish, p.289 §XIII; PRXXIX.23. *Pensées*, trans. by Ariew, p. 165.

arguing on behalf of the atheist. Pascal expresses the atheist point of view in order immediately afterwards to contest it. The first line is the atheist, the second the contestation:

> Toutes choses changent et se succèdent.
> Vous vous trompez, il y a... [77]
>
> All things change and succeed one another.
> You are wrong; there is...

All things change, pass, and are replaced, says Pascal's atheist: No, the man of faith replies, you are wrong, there is.... and the gap remains; there is no completed contestation. On the other hand, in the *Éléments de physiologie*, the statement about continous change is continuously repeated, sometimes unchanged, ironically enough:

> Nul état fixe dans le corps animal: il décroît quand il ne croît plus.[78]
>
> There is no fixed state in the animal body: it starts shrinking once it stops growing.
>
> L'ordre général change sans cesse: au milieu de cette vicissitude la durée de l'espèce peut-elle rester la même?[79]
>
> The general order is constantly changing: in the midst of this vicissitude how can the continuation of the species stay the same?
>
> Mais l'ordre général change sans cesse.[80]
>
> But the general order constantly changes.

Thus, for Diderot, the state of nature, whether on the level of the human or the species or at any other level, is indeed one of flux, and no one individual or species or the particular form it takes is therefore *un*natural or to be rejected. Nothing can be monstrous: the term itself is without meaning. This is in stark contrast with Pascal's dialectical moralising approach:

> S'il se vante, je l'abaisse

---

[77] Pascal, *Pensées*, p. 843, §38; PR VI.4; Bossut: II.vi.8. *Pensées*, trans. by Ariew, p. 7.
[78] DPV 312/PQ 127/MT 135.
[79] DPV 322/PQ 137/MT 144.
[80] DPV 444/PQ 265/MT 261.

> S'il s'abaisse, je le vante
> Et le contredis toujours
> Jusques à ce qu'il comprenne
> Qu'il est un monstre incompréhensible.[81]

> If he exalts himself, I humble him.
> If he humbles himself, I exalt him.
> And I continue to contradict him
> Until he comprehends
> That he is an incomprehensible monster.

This fragment provokes another explosion of wrath from Voltaire, as follows:

> Vrai discours de malade. *Second éditeur*.[82]

> Truly the speech of a sick man. *Second editor*.

Diderot addresses the question of monstrosity, without the vicious edge that characterises Voltaire's intervention, although also without naming or invoking Pascal. What Diderot is dealing with is the notion, not the person:

> Qu'est-ce qu'un monstre ? Un être, dont la durée est incompatible avec l'ordre subsistant.
> Mais l'ordre général change sans cesse. [....] S'amender, se détériorer sont des termes relatifs aux individus d'une espèce entre eux, et aux différentes espèces entre elles.[83]

> What is a monster? A being, whose continuing existence is incompatible with the existing order.
> But the general order changes constantly. [....] To grow better or deteriorate are terms relative to the individuals within any species, and also to the different species amongst themselves.

---

81  Pascal, *Pensées*, p. 898, §163; PR XXI.4; Bossut II.i.4; Cond/Volt, p. 219, §3. *Pensées*, trans. by Ariew, p. 34.
82  Cond/Volt, p. 219 §3.
83  DPV 444/PQ 265/MT 261.

For Diderot, monstrosity is simply relative difference, and relative difference is in fact the norm.[84] So the notion of rejection of one sort, type, or species, or of pronouncing one sort to be the proper version and others deformed ones, or even (or in particular) the idea that nature is monstrous at all, is directly addressed and dismissed. Monstrosity becomes instead a form of weak synonym for change, indicating the continuous variation between forms. In sum, Diderot directly and without shame employs and redirects the terms of Pascal's condemnation, whether they refer to nature or to the position of the atheist.

## Perfection/Perfectionnement

The important motif of perfection is a case in point. For Pascal, following the Biblical Book of Genesis and its account of the expulsion of Adam and Eve from the Garden of Eden, perfection is the thing we had but lost through giving in to an impulse of our own nature, specifically the desire for knowledge and the lure of power.

> Mais, malheureux que nous sommes, et plus que s'il n'y avait point de grandeur dans notre condition, nous avons une idée du bonheur et ne pouvons y arriver, nous sentons une image de la vérité et ne possédons que le mensonge, incapables d'ignorer absolument et de savoir certainement, tant il est manifeste que nous avons été dans un degré de perfection dont nous sommes malheureusement déchus.[85]

> But, wretched as we are—and more so than if there had been no greatness in our condition—we have an idea of happiness and cannot reach it. We perceive an image of truth and possess only a lie. Being incapable of absolute ignorance and certain knowledge, it is obvious that we once had a degree of perfection from which we have unhappily fallen.

---

[84] Work on Diderot's interest in the area of monstrosity includes Andrew Curran, *Sublime Disorder: Physical Monstrosity in Diderot's Universe* (Oxford: Voltaire Foundation, 2001); Emita Hill, *The Role of 'le monstre' in Diderot's Thought* (Banbury: Voltaire Foundation, 1972); Charles Wolfe, *Monsters and Philosophy* (London: College Publications, 2005). We return to this question in Chapter 3.

[85] Pascal, *Pensées*, pp. 901–02, §164; PR XXI.1, 4; III.5, 6, 8; XXVIII.30; Bossut II.i.1, 4; II.V.3, 4; II.xvii.23 (Brunscvicg §434). *Pensées*, trans. by Ariew, pp. 36–37. Sellier and Brunschvicg both have this as one *pensée*, Port-Royal and Bossut as many different fragments.

This passage is densely packed with overlaid binaries about greatness, abjection, misery, happiness, truth, lies, knowledge, ignorance, what is obvious or obscure, the manifest past and the unattainable future, what we feel and desire as opposed to what we actually possess and cannot avoid being aware of, what we did once have but have since lost. It is a desperate picture and a tragic situation: misery with the consciousness of its own condition and a sense not just of entrapment but that it could have been otherwise, that we could have retained perfection.

For Diderot, perfection is not a noun but a verb, a dynamic process.[86] In this first extract, he also presents it in tension with its polar opposite, vice, although increased perfection and increased vice are paradoxically and ironically coupled together:

> Je ne sais s'il n'en est pas de la morale ainsi que de la médecine qui n'a commencé à se perfectionner qu'à mesure que les vices de l'homme ont rendu les maladies plus communes, plus compliquées, et plus dangereuses.[87]
>
> I do not know that morals are any different from medicine which only started improving as human vices made disease more common, more complex, and more dangerous.

To paraphrase, morality and medicine, that is to say knowledge of morality and medicine, develop, advance, improve, become more *perfect*, as human vices produce an increase in the incidence and variety of diseases, which are now more common, complex, and dangerous than they once were. The parallel here with Pascal's story of our lost perfection is obvious, even if the origin is located elsewhere (not in the Garden of Eden but in Nature), and even if the term 'perfectionner' is now an ironic process (and a verb) rather than a lost state (and a noun).

Diderot is expressing a view we also find in Rousseau's *Discours sur l'origine de l'inégalité* (1754), written of course when he and Rousseau were still close, and where Rousseau states that:

---

[86] This point is influenced by Wilda Anderson's pithily expressed insight that 'philosophy in eighteenth-century France... was not a noun, but a verb'. 'Eighteenth-Century Philosophy', in *The Cambridge History of French Literature*, ed. by William Burgwinkle, Nicholas Hammond, and Emma Wilson (Cambridge: Cambridge University Press, 2011), pp. 404–11 (p. 404), https://doi.org/10.1017/chol9780521897860.047.

[87] DPV 512/PQ 354/MT 325.

la pluspart de nos maux sont notre propre ouvrage, et [...] nous les aurions presque tous évités, en conservant la maniére de vivre simple, uniforme, et solitaire qui nous étoit prescrite par la Nature. Si elle nous a destinés à être sains, j'ose presque assurer, que l'état de réflexion est un état contre Nature, et que l'homme qui médite est un animal dépravé.[88]

Most of our ills are of our own making, nearly all of which we might have avoided by preserving the simple, unchanging, and solitary way of life prescribed for us by nature. If nature has destined us to be healthy, I would almost venture to assert that the state of reflection is contrary to nature and that the man who meditates is a perverse animal.

The *Éléments* repeats this view: 'Rien n'est plus contraire à la nature que la méditation habituelle ou l'état du savant' [nothing is more contrary to nature than habitual medition or the profession of the scholar] which had also been forthrightly expressed by La Mettrie in *L'Homme-machine* [Man a machine] (1747) and constituted the subject of a book by the influential Swiss physician Samuel-Auguste Tissot, *De la santé des gens de lettres* [On the health of men of letters] (1775).[89] La Mettrie had written that 'La Nature nous a tous créés uniquement pour être heureux' [Nature created us all solely to be happy] and that it is 'par une espèce d'abus de nos facultés organiques que nous [...] sommes devenus [savants]' [we have perhaps become men of learning by a sort of misuse of our organic faculties].[90] We see Diderot, Rousseau, and La Mettrie reversing the causal links in Pascal's presentation of happiness, misery, nature and knowledge, while retaining a parallel account of the descent from a prior and better state. In a form of ironic twist, Rousseau's 'animal dépravé' [perverse animal] is the 'homme qui médite' [meditative man] which should be understood here not (just) as a form of savage self-satire but

---

88 Jean-Jacques Rousseau, *Œuvres complètes*, ed. by Bernard Gagnebin and Marcel Raymond (Paris: Gallimard Pléiade, 1964), vol. 3, p. 138. For further references, see also the related note, p. 1310; and Jean-Jacques Rousseau, *Discourse on Inequality*, trans. by Franklin Philip (Oxford: Oxford University Press, 1994), p. 30.
89 DPV 511/PQ 352/MT 324, and related note. La Mettrie, 'L'homme-Machine', in *Œuvres philosophiques*, vol. 1, p. 92. Anne C. Vila examines the pathology of the scholar in her illuminating study, *Suffering Scholars: Pathologies of the Intellectual in Enlightenment France* (Philadelphia, PA: University of Pennsylvania Press, 2018), https://doi.org/10.9783/9780812294804.
90 La Mettrie, 'L'homme-Machine', in *Œuvres philosophiques*, vol. 1, p. 92; trans. Ann Thomson in La Mettrie, *Machine Man and Other Writings*, ed. and trans. by Ann Thomson (Cambridge: Cambridge University Press, 1996), p. 22 (slightly amended for the context).

as the complete rejection of Pascal's position with respect to man and nature. It is in this context that Pascal, as a man of great learning who made discoveries about natural philosophy ('science'), who was the inventor of the first calculator, a profound reasoner, and ultimately a very influential Jansenist theologian, someone whose health, some thought, suffered as a result of his intense scholarly application and self-denial, becomes the target of *ad hominem* attack such as we found in Voltaire's repeated comments, quoted earlier, saying Pascal 'parle toujours en malade', that he has a 'vrai discours de malade'.[91] It is difficult not to see in Diderot's laconic remark 'Le génie suppose toujours quelque désordre dans la machine' [genius always carries with it the idea of some disorder in the machine] some form of (non-exclusive) allusion to Pascal, not least because of his association with the calculator or 'Machine arithmétique' about which Diderot had written an important article for the *Encyclopédie*.[92]

Diderot does not only use *perfectionner*, 'to perfect', in an ironic coupling with the notion of decline, he also uses it more positively, as an activity we can work at. Here he really recasts the term of 'perfection' with its religious association of loss and sin, propelling it instead into a process of education and improvement, particularly focusing on those erstwhile drivers of temptation and misapprehension, the senses:

> Nous exerçons nos sens comme la nature nous les a donnés et que les besoins et les circonstances l'exigent: mais nous ne les perfectionnons

---

91   See above.
92   DPV 508/PQ 348/MT 322. III.ix 'Maladies.' See also Straudo, *La fortune de Pascal*, as cited above, note 40, in Chapter 2. The question of the flaws of the genius was a subject which much preoccupied Diderot, as is well known. See *Le Neveu de Rameau*, ed. Marian Hobson (Cambridge: Open Book Publishers, 2016), pp. 103, 105, https://doi.org/10.11647/OBP.0098; *Le Rêve de d'Alembert*, ed. by Colas Duflo (Paris: GF Flammarion, 2002), p. 153. On Diderot and genius, see Herbert Dieckmann, 'Diderot's Conception of Genius', *Journal of the History of Ideas*, 2.2 (1941), 151–82, https://doi.org/10.2307/2707111; Otis E. Fellows, 'The Theme of Genius in Diderot's Neveu de Rameau', *Diderot Studies*, 2 (1952), 168–99; Angelika Schober, 'Aspects du génie chez Diderot et D'Alembert', *Diderot Studies*, 23 (1988), 143–49; Laurence Mall, 'L'Ego-philosophie à la manière de Diderot (*Réfutation d'Helvétius*)', *Littérature*, 165 (2012), 16–30, https://doi.org/10.3917/litt.165.0016; Jean-Alexandre Perras, *L'exception exemplaire: inventions et usages du génie (XVIe-XVIIIe siècle)* (Paris: Garnier, 2015); Konstanze Baron and Robert Fajen, eds, *Diderot, le génie des lumières: Nature, normes, transgressions* (Paris: Garnier, 2019).

> pas; nous ne nous apprenons pas à voir, à flairer, à sentir, à écouter, à moins que notre profession nous y force.⁹³
>
> We use our senses as nature gave them to us and as our needs and circumstances require: but we do not perfect them; we do not teach ourselves to see, to smell, to feel, to listen, unless our profession forces us to.

Diderot here expresses real faith in the senses, if that is not too confusing a way of putting it, given that the rejection of religious faith underpins everything the *Éléments de physiologie* is about. The point of using the expression is to indicate that the senses are not presented as false portals of knowledge, as misleading or deluding, but rather in their functional and practical capacity, as the gifts of nature, and as being subject to improvement. There is real hope here, in learning to use our senses better, in perfecting them, even if this is presented as something which we do *not* do unless our profession forces us to. Diderot's negative formulation (we do not improve our senses unless we have to) automatically suggests that we could and that we ought to. So the noun 'perfection', a place we have long left behind, is replaced with a process of learning to improve or perfect our natural senses. It's a big shift.⁹⁴

This is the shift which the *Éléments de physiologie* is trying to effect. It involves rejecting notions of the soul, explaining the phenomena of nature in terms of matter, seeing a human as an individual member of a species and as determined by its body, its needs, and its capacities, and using its brain to 'conceive clearly' the truth and produce 'clear ideas'.⁹⁵ This is the point Diderot returns to in the conclusion of the *Éléments de physiologie*, asking how it has come to be that there is no madness that has not been said by some *philosophe* or other, why all these 'auteurs, dont les ouvrages sont remplis de visions' [authors whose works are packed with visions] despise those whose 'accurate and firm minds only allow to be true that which can be clearly conceived'.⁹⁶ Pascal is explicitly brought into this discussion as the genius who 'dit expressément de Dieu: *on ne sait ni ce qu'il est, ni s'il est*' [specifically said about God that *we do not*

---

93 DPV 456–57/PQ 282/MT 272.
94 The topic of 'perfectionnement' will be important for Garat, Cabanis, and Destutt de Tracy, as will be discussed in some detail in Chapters 8 and 9.
95 DPV 514/PQ 356–57/MT 326.
96 DPV 514/PQ 356/MT 326.

*know what he is or whether he is*]: here Pascal is at once a representative of those who have visions and despise those who wish to be able to conceive of things clearly, and also a thinker who is way beyond them. This is the whole sentence:

> Ils assurent que l'existence de Dieu est évidente et Pascal dit expressément de Dieu : *on ne sait ni ce qu'il est, ni s'il est.*[97]
>
> They assert that the existence of God is obvious yet Pascal specifically says about God that *we do not know what he is or whether he is.*

'Ils', that is, these 'auteurs', are therefore lesser than Pascal: they assert that God's existence is obvious where Pascal had specifically argued that such assertion is not possible because we do not know what he is nor whether he is. The 'et Pascal' carries a sense of amazement and rhetorical flourish: it's a 'yet Pascal says the opposite'; it's an 'if Pascal says this they should pay attention', it's also an '*even* Pascal admits we know nothing about God', he being a visionary *and* a genius.[98] So Pascal represents for Diderot the man of genius who is beyond the common run of stupid complacent authors and also an example of those who get caught up in their own visions and can no longer see clearly. Pascal is his ultimate interlocutor, the man whose arguments he respects, and whom he therefore has to disprove. It is interesting therefore to consider that the snippet we have just shown Diderot quoting comes from the section now known as 'le pari de Pascal', Pascal's wager, in which he argues that the non-believer might as well believe in God as he has much to gain and nothing to lose. In this particular section, Pascal is looking at the idea of trying to understand God, equipped only by our 'lumières naturelles', that is to say, our natural intelligence, as opposed to faith. Needless to say, for Pascal, our natural illumination gets us precisely nowhere. This is the passage:

---

97 DPV 515/PQ 358/MT 327.
98 Diderot continues as follows: 'L'existence de Dieu évidente ! Et l'homme de génie est arrêté par la difficulté d'un enfant; et Leibniz est obligé, pour la résoudre, de produire avec des efforts de tête incroyables, un système qui ne résout pas la difficulté et qui en fait naître milles autres !' [The existence of God obvious ! And so the man of genius is blocked by a child's problem; and Leibniz is obliged, in order to solve it, and with unbelievable efforts of mind, to come up with a system that does not solve the problem and gives rise to a thousand others] (DPV 515/PQ 359/MT 327). When Diderot evokes the 'homme de génie', therefore, he is alluding to Pascal and also transitioning to Leibniz, so he's not *only* referring to Pascal.

> Parlons maintenant selon les lumières naturelles.
>
> S'il y a un Dieu, il est infiniment incompréhensible, puisque, n'ayant ni parties ni bornes, il n'a nul rapport à nous. Nous sommes donc incapables de connaître ni ce qu'il est, ni s'il est.[99]
>
> Let us now speak according to our natural lights.
>
> If there is a God, he is infinitely incomprehensible, since, having neither parts nor limits, he bears no relation to us. We are therefore incapable of knowing either what he is or whether he is.

So what Pascal really said was that if we try to understand God we will fail because we cannot apprehend him, and the argument he subsequently develops is that we must therefore go via faith. Although he *does* say that God cannot be understood by our natural intelligence, he is *not* saying that God might not therefore exist, and indeed the whole point of Pascal's wager is that it's a rational argument directed at those who insist on having things presented rationally, that *even if* we cannot understand what God is or prove his existence we might as well still believe in him, because the benefits would be worth it.

It is by no means obvious therefore that Diderot clearly scores a point over Pascal when he writes that (even) Pascal says about God that we do not know what he is nor if he is, given that Diderot selectively uses the snippet fragment he fragments from the bigger fragment. Whether he scores a point or not is irrelevant: the issue is that Pascal is a crucial interlocutor for Diderot, both explicitly and implicitly: if convincing the atheist or Pyrrhonian sceptic is Pascal's explicit and implicit aim, then convincing the Christian is Diderot's explicit and implicit aim. They each represent what the other is seeking to refute, and the *Éléments de physiologie* bears witness to the importance Diderot gave to this task. The *Éléments de physiologie* tries to describe nature from component parts to complete system, it tries to show how all the mechanisms fit together and relate to one another, whether in the first part which looks at nature's building blocks and processes, in the second with the fullness of its physiological description of the human body, in the final part which tackles the thorny questions of thought, emotion, behaviour, and illness, or in the general scrupulousness with which Diderot indicates what

---

[99] Pascal, *Pensées*, p. 1210, §680; PR VII.1, 2; XXVIII.69; Bossut II.iii.1; II iii.4 and 5; II.xvii.63 (Brunschvicg §233); *Pensées*, trans. by Ariew, p. 212.

is or isn't known. It is as complete and thorough an atheist materialist challenge to the Christian apologist as it was possible to write at that time.

## Fragmented Disorder

Whether this challenge was more or less ordered than what it was trying to refute was a crucial element of Diderot's reply, and not just because Pascal's *Pensées* were famously fragmented. Pascal himself had insulted his subject, 'man', in one fragment, asserting that he would not dignify it by presenting in an ordered fashion, as he wanted to show that human nature was incapable of being ordered in the first place. This is what he wrote:

> Pyrrhonisme.
> J'écrirai ici mes pensées sans ordre, et non pas peut-être dans une confusion sans dessein. C'est le véritable ordre, et qui marquera toujours mon objet par le désordre même.
> Je ferais trop d'honneur à mon sujet, si je le traitais avec ordre, puisque je veux montrer qu'il en est incapable.[100]

> Skepticism.
> I will write my thoughts here without order, but not perhaps in unplanned confusion. This is true order, and it will always indicate my aim by its very disorder.
> I would be honouring my subject too much if I treated it with order, since I want to show that it is incapable of it.

This fragment does not feature in the Port-Royal edition. It does appear in the Bossut and Condorcet/Voltaire editions, although in the latter shorn of its elucidating title, such that it seems as if 'mon sujet' might be his own attempt to talk about the Christian faith or, as some commentators have suggested, the human condition.[101] Nevertheless, his intention to demonstrate that *something* is incapable of order is clear, and in the Condorcet/Voltaire edition, the general title of this section, and of which this is the first fragment, is 'De l'incertitude de nos connaissances

---

100 Pascal, *Pensées*, p. 1084, §457. Not in Port-Royal edition; Bossut I.ix.55 (Brunschvicg §434); Cond/Volt, p. 185. *Pensées*, trans. by Ariew, p. 144.
101 See Richard Parish's elucidory note, Cond/Volt, p. 185.

naturelles'. Pascal himself is throwing down the gauntlet, and making the whole issue turn on whether something (man, natural knowledge) is capable of order. The insult is that he is not going to bother ordering his own thoughts: it will be a symbolic confusion.

It is a cruel twist of fate, therefore, that Pascal was unable to finish his manuscript, and left only disordered fragments, or in any case, fragments the order of which has been disputed for centuries and probably never will be finally resolved. It's a cruel twist of fate or an ironic moral for his tale, depending on your point of view, but it makes it even clearer why Diderot included an 'Avertissement' presenting his own *Éléments de physiologie* as a heap of fragments: Pascal hung his attempt to write an Apology for the Christian faith on his ability to prove that unbelief was a disorderly mess of degraded and deluded mind, yet he failed; his Apology was a shocking mess, shocking to some in any case.[102] Voltaire would go so far as to call the *Pensées* the product of an ill mind, but Diderot never did. Instead, he evoked the famous *Pensées* at the very beginning of his own Apology of Atheist materialism so as to resoundingly demonstrate and prove the deep coherence and order of nature, yet he also was hoist with his own petard, and everyone ever since has blithely talked about these fragments of the great philosopher's late, last, uncompleted magnum opus. How unfortunate! How funny!

---

102  As Jean Filleau de la Chaise said, quoted above in note 33. Jean Filleau de la Chaise, *Discours sur les pensées*, p. 3.

# 3. Material World and Embodied Mind

Denis Diderot's subjects of material world and embodied mind were not new when he came to write about them in the *Eléments de physiologie* in the 1770s, nor had they been new when he had written about them before, in his *Pensées philosophiques* (published 1746), *Lettre sur les aveugles* (published 1749), *Pensées sur l'interprétation de la nature* (published 1753), *Rêve de d'Alembert* (drafted 1769), *Principes philosophiques sur la matière et le mouvement* (written 1770), *Observations sur Hemsterhuis* and *Réfutation d'Helvétius* (both written 1773), or of course in the many articles he contributed to the *Encyclopédie* (published 1751–65). The sorts of concepts and frameworks he was using were already present in Aristotle's *Physics*, which discusses nature, change, time, continuity, and finalism, and also in the *Metaphysics*, which thinks about man, desire, knowledge, the senses (in particular, sight), animals, and memory, asserting that knowledge is based on perception, or, as Diderot put it in the *Réfutation d'Helvétius*, crediting Aristotle for being the first ever to say it: 'il n'y a [...] rien dans l'entendement qui n'[ait] été antérieurement dans la sensation' [there is nothing in our understanding which has not first passed through sensation], although Diderot's formulation is a direct French translation of the medieval theologian Thomas Aquinas's version, 'nihil est in intellectu quod non sit prius in sensu' [there is nothing in the mind which was not first in the senses].[1] As this double

---

1   Aquinas, Thomas, *Quaestiones disputatae de veritate*, 3 vols (Rome: Editori di San Tommaso, 1970–76) II, 3, 19, as Roland Desné and Gerhardt Stenger, point out, *Réfutation d'Helvétius*, ed. by Roland Desné, Didier Kahn, Annette Lorenceau and

quotation which is also a refutation amply demonstrates, Diderot is writing in a thriving and self-aware tradition, one which goes back to Ancient Greece, and in so doing, he is also taking sides in similarly long-lived arguments—about the operation of nature, about infinity, about the existence or otherwise of immaterial beings: his particular tradition is that of Epicureanism. Epicurus, forty years younger than Aristotle, taught that everything in nature is made from atoms and from the fortuitous ways in which they combine to create different beings: whether there is any role for divine powers in this is a moot point, but ethics are important (virtue and happiness being interchangeable). His writings are mostly lost but his teaching survives in the Roman poet Lucretius's masterpiece, *De rerum natura*, a poem which Diderot often quotes or alludes to, most prominently perhaps in his epigraph to the *Pensées sur l'interprétation de la nature*: 'Quae sunt in luce tuemur/ E tenebris' [From the darkness, we can see what is in the light].[2]

Diderot's moment in this tradition comes at a pivotal point after more than a hundred years of increasingly clamorous consensus that a true understanding of the world derives alone from the information or 'ideas' our senses give us.[3] Perhaps I will want to argue that the *Éléments de physiologie* is the culmination or final statement in the particular (materialist) offshoot of the empiricism debate (René Descartes asserted that we are born with innate ideas; John Locke denied it) that focuses on what sensation and sensibility are, and who or what has it, whether it is in fact innate or latent in all matter, and whether, if so, that means that matter can think. The stakes were high: theological accounts of the soul and of the order of the universe, of divine reasons and aims, accounts which underpinned social structures and laws, both for this life and the hereafter, were at risk of being dislodged from their position as truth. As indeed they were dislodged, to be replaced by accounts of nature and its laws and behaviour. A quick way of explaining this in English is to say

---

Gerhardt Stenger, in *Œuvres complètes*, DPV (Paris: Hermann, 2004), vol. 24, pp. 215-478: 515, n. 90.

2  Denis Diderot, *Pensées sur l'interprétation de la nature*, ed. by Jean Varloot and Herbert Dieckmann, in *Œuvres complètes*, DPV (Paris: Hermann), vol. 9, pp. 1-111 : p. 337.

3  On Diderot's closely-argued position in relation to empiricism, see Kate E. Tunstall, *Blindness and Enlightenment: An Essay* (London: Bloomsbury, 2011). On empiricism more generally, see Marion Chottin, *Le Partage de l'empirisme: une histoire du problème de Molyneux aux XVIIe et XVIIIe siècles* (Paris: Champion, 2014).

that increasingly from the end of the eighteenth century onwards, the word 'knowledge' is replaced by 'science', its Latinate synonym. And 'science', in English, means empirical descriptions of nature. (In French, this shift is not so niftily condensable: broadly, though, the branches of knowledge covered by eighteenth-century 'natural philosophy' become the modern-day sciences.) Of course, religion as practice and law did not disappear, and it remains an important presence in contemporary society. However, the ability of the church authorities to use the articles of belief to influence the way natural philosophy was conducted or to condemn its findings as being against religion or morality, was curtailed, not immediately, not irrevocably, but as it became more and more accepted that the accounts of the world and universe given by natural philosophy were, if incomplete, nonetheless verifiable, whereas religious accounts of nature and creation were not subject to verification.

What we are cosily calling 'Diderot's moment in the tradition' takes place, of course, within specific social technologies, networks and structures. These make his intervention possible and also determine its form and content.[4] One of those, already implicitly evoked, is the transmission of the written word, in letter, manuscript or print, to smaller or greater audiences, at a given moment or across the generations. Another, more immediate, is the discussion that took place in the female-led salons, which was no less impactful for lacking a written, posterity-providing form.[5] More official (and of course, exclusively male) are the learned societies which were being set up from the end of the seventeenth century to facilitate the exchange of research amongst their learned members, and whose meetings were carefully recorded in the archives that researchers now mine. The size of all these groups, even including print readers, was limited: connections, qualifications, language, and literacy were all needed for doors to be opened. And, of course, official censorship existed to make sure that those doors stayed shut when the authorities deemed that what might come in or go out of them posed a threat to ecclesiastical or monarchical orthodoxy. This was

---

4   On the connection between Diderot's materialism and his style of thinking in writing, see Caroline Jacot-Grapa, *Dans le vif du sujet: Diderot, corps et âme* (Paris: Classiques Garnier, 2009).

5   Dena Goodman, *The Republic of Letters: A Cultural History of the French Enlightenment* (Ithaca: Cornell University Press, 1994); Carla Hesse, *The Other Enlightenment: How French Women Became Modern* (Princeton, NJ: Princeton University Press, 2001).

the context of Diderot's entire working life, but the pressure building for change, or perhaps we should say the consensus that these 'new' forms of knowledge needed wider dissemination, grew throughout it. So when I talk about his 'intervention', perhaps I ought to say increasingly busy iterations of the same points. Diderot was busy repeating himself and kindred writers as often and as well as he could (although not as often as Voltaire). This chapter will look at what those iterations were, and at whom he was iterating.

It will be for later chapters to look at what happened next, a lurchingly complicated story that could not have been foreseen at the moment of Diderot's death in 1784. Within the broad-brush context of the rise of science, the stage was set for the (by then) widely supported establishment or expansion of institutions to disseminate the new perspectives of natural philosophy. This narrative is broadly familiar to us from Michel Foucault's influential account of the institutionalisation of the different academic disciplines around the turn of the nineteenth century, along with their ensuing professionalisation within the universities. Of course, in France, this process is part of the Revolution, whose new political structures undid and remade the previous institutions of learning more than once. The École normale, emerging briefly in 1795, aimed to make contemporaneous learning available to those who would go and teach it across the new Republic, while the research institution replacing the various academies of the ex-'kingdom', the Institut national des sciences et des arts, also set up in 1795 and also subject to regime upheavals, redefined the various branches of knowledge, and established specific groups to provide a platform for France's world-leading research. In both these institutions, those who had known Diderot and whose ideas were aligned with his had important roles, and I will turn to them in due course.

Many writers had been writing about nature, matter, man, and mind, in the previous 100 years, and they had been broadly in agreement in approach (empiricism) and in the way they presented man as completely determined by his material embodiment (as dependent on and moulded by his senses).[6] They had even often been in agreement

---

6   It is perhaps a bit tendentious to talk about general agreement in this context. Specialists tend to state instead that materialism 'ne constitue en rien une doctrine unifiée' [in no way constitutes a unified doctrine]: Adrien Paschoud and Barbara

about the ways in which they tried to prove their points, drawing on similar or even the same research, and on similar or even the same fictional hypotheses. Diderot is at the end of this tradition, to which he responds in detail, point by point, and which he closes off by presenting an unanswerable fusion of natural philosophy (drawing on physics, chemistry, what would come to be called 'biology', and medicine) and philosophy (theories of consciousness and identity related to memory), such that whether there is a soul can no longer be a serious question in the investigation of man's nature, and the medical sciences no longer have to deal with it.

So who and what was Diderot iterating, refining, or responding to in the *Éléments de physiologie*? In brief, Baruch Spinoza, Gottfried Wilhelm Leibniz, Jean Meslier, Bernard le Bovier de Fontenelle, Julien Offray de La Mettrie, Étienne Bonnot de Condillac, Georges-Louis Lerclerc de Buffon, Charles Bonnet, Jean-Jacques Rousseau, Claude Adrien Helvétius and François Hemsterhuis. Current editions of the *Éléments de physiologie* provide important scholarly apparatus about Diderot's medical sources, but give relatively little information about his philosophical ones, although Motoichi Terada has begun to add to our knowledge in this area.[7] This is no doubt because the *Eléménts de*

---

Selmeci Castioni, 'Le matérialisme au XVIIIe siècle en France: enjeux et perspectives', in *Matérialisme(s) en France au XVIIIe siècle. Entre littérature et philosophie*, ed. by Adrien Paschoud and Barbara Selmeci Castioni (Berlin: Frank and Timme, 2019), pp. 7–11 (p. 7). This is of course true, but whatever this non-unified non-doctrine is, it is nonetheless recognisable enough in its general positions for the same authors to say that 'it swarms through writings of remarkable diversity' (ibid., p. 8). My emphasis is on the common ground these swarming texts share rather than their differences. Yves Citton follows a somewhat similar approach in his *L'Envers de la liberté: l'invention d'un imaginaire Spinoziste dans la France des lumières* (Paris: Éditions Amsterdam, 2006), esp. pp. 28–33. See also Sophie Audidière, Jean-Claude Bourdin, and Francine Markovits, eds, *Matérialistes Français du XVIIIe siècle* (Paris: Presses Universitaires de France, 2006); Ann Thomson, *Bodies of Thought: Science, Religion, and the Soul in the Early Enlightenment* (Oxford: Oxford University Press, 2008); Franck Salaün, *L'Ordre des mœurs: essai sur la place du matérialisme dans la société française du XVIIIe siècle (1734-1784)* (Paris: Éditions Kimé, 1996), esp. pp. 41–78; and Colas Duflo, *Diderot philosophe* (Paris: Champion, 2003), pp. 65–267.

7   Terada's edition gives some source material and resonances from ancient authors Aristotle, Cicero, Epictetus, and Seneca, and early modern philosophers (and while the distinction between medical writers and philosophers is often a false one, La Mettrie being a case in point, this list follows the received view about who is a medical professional and who is a more generally philosophical writer): Francis Bacon, Pierre Bayle, Condillac, Marin Cureau de la Chambre, Daniel Heinsius, d'Holbach, La Mettrie, Leibniz, Montaigne, Pascal, and Spinoza. See also the

*physiologie* has not received much recognition as a serious philosophical text. This chapter cannot single-handedly change such a state of affairs, and indeed it has a relatively limited aim, which is simply to look at how the *Eléménts de physiologie* picks up and responds to philosophical arguments about material man, to see which voices are present in the *Éléments*, to see how many voices there are, and to see how this text brings them together and makes it seem as if they are a sort of call and echo chorus.

It is of course true that a good number or perhaps all of these (natural) philosophers and writers, taken separately, would, if charged, have strenuously rejected any association with materialism, and one of the necessary limitations of this chapter is that it never does take any of them separately. Their works are not looked at on their own terms, as a whole, or in the specific context of their production, and the way in which various sentences are lifted from them and woven together distorts their work, examining it from the retrospective point of view, or rather through the lens, of the *Éléments de physiologie*.[8]

Another layer of severe restriction is applied to the number of voices we argue Diderot is engaging with here. Although a list that includes Spinoza, Leibniz, Meslier, Fontenelle, La Mettrie, Condillac, Buffon, Bonnet, Rousseau, Helvétius and Hemsterhuis, not to mention Pascal, is hardly short or unambitious, other voices whom we might expect to see here are absent: no Descartes, no Pierre Gassendi, no Locke or Thomas Hobbes, no David Hume, and no ancient philosophers at all. Montaigne peeps in with Lucretius via Meslier, but that's all. If the space limitations already invoked also apply here—what can one really cover in a single chapter?—the question of the lens also does; these are the writers whose

---

relevant pages of his introduction: 'Les *Éléments de physiologie* dans la philosophie du dernier Diderot', in *Éléments de physiologie*, ed. by Motoichi Terada (Paris: Éditions Matériologiques, 2019), pp. 14–26 [hereafter MT].

[8] Readers wishing for a greater overview or more detail are encouraged to consult on materialism: as already cited in note 6 above, Audidière et al., *Matérialistes français*; Citton, *L'Envers de la liberté*; Salaün, *L'Ordre des mœurs*; Thomson, *Bodies of Thought*; and also Olivier Bloch, *Le Matérialisme* (Paris: Presses Universitaires de France, 1985); Jonathan Israel, *Radical Enlightenment: Philosophy and the Making of Modernity 1650-1750* (Oxford: Oxford University Press, 2001). For a specific focus on Diderot's place within all this, see: Duflo, *Diderot philosophe*; Jacot-Grapa, *Dans le vif du sujet*; Tunstall, *Blindness and Enlightenment*; and also Timo Kaitaro, *Diderot's Holism* (Frankfurt a.M.: Peter Lang, 1997).

presence I perceive most strongly in the *Éléments de physiologie*. That does not mean there are not other ones, while—very obviously—my own limitations are also operating to shape, frame, and constrain what and whom this chapter considers. It will be exciting when more work is done on philosophy in the *Éléments de physiologie*, more voices traced, its own contribution better understood.[9] My hope is that what I argue here about how particular philosophical positions relating to the material universe on the one hand and empiricism on the other appear to be being consistently enounced, asserted, and repeated over the course of a hundred years, and about how the *Éléments de physiologie*, bringing these numerous strands together in an unprecedentedly open way, helps us see that this is the case, will be accepted as offering a productive approach.

## How to Use This Chapter

The system of materialist and empiricist philosophy we are looking at here has been broken down into relatively small parts for ease of treatment, and is summarised in italics at the beginning of each section, followed by supporting passages presented chronologically in order to bring out the dialogic aspect of this repeating-relaying conversation. The headings below list the subsections in order, and together they provide a summary of the topics addressed by the *Éléments de physiologie*, in particular its first and third parts. Readers who would prefer a shorter version and who would rather be directed straight to the *Éléments* without preamble can simply hop from one subsection to the next, reading the italicised paragraph at the beginning, and seeing how the *Éléments de physiologie* intervenes at the end.

    a.  Nature, Order, and Natural Patterns
    b.  The Necessary Order of Nature
          The Order of Nature: Unchanging or in Flux
             i.  The Gouty Man and the Fire
            ii.  From Recycled Cases to the Specific

---

9    As Motoichi Terada does, for example, when he examines the connections between, on the one hand, sensibility and vanity, and on the other, Diderot's political philosophy, in his 'Les *Éléments de physiologie* dans la philosophie du dernier Diderot', *Éléments de physiologie*, ed. Motoichi Terada, pp. 19–26.

    c. Matter in Flux
    d. The Natural Processes of Material Transformation
        i. Reproduction
        ii. The Beginning and End of Death
        iii. The Beginning and End of Sensation
    e. Knowledge Derived from the Senses
        i. Knowledge from the Senses: Anti-Abstraction
        ii. Sensory-Deprivation Fictions
    f. Multi-Tasking and Levels of Awareness: Thinking and Walking
    g. Selfhood and Memory
    h. The Pursuit of Happiness

## a. Nature, Order, and Natural Patterns

*There is an order to nature and this order has no gaps, write Leibniz, Bonnet, and Diderot. This is expressed in Leibniz's formulation that there is no jump in nature (Leibniz, Bonnet). This natural order replicates itself in the body, and in mental processes of perception and idea, writes Spinoza (and Condillac and Diderot), and should be followed in productions of the mind such as books, writes Buffon.*

We start with Leibniz's concept of there being no gaps or *jumps* in nature:

> Rien ne se fait tout d'un coup, & c'est une de mes grandes maximes & des plus vérifiées, que la *nature ne fait jamais de sauts*. J'appellois cela *la loi de la continuité*, lorsque j'en parlois autre fois dans les nouvelles de la république des lettres; & l'usage de cette loi est très-considerable dans la Physique.[10]

> Nothing is done in a single leap, and it is one of my great maxims and is amongst the most verified, that *nature never makes a leap*. I called that *the law of continuity* when I was talking about it before in the *Nouvelles de la République des Lettres*; & and the use of this law is very widespread in Physics.

He advertises his ownership of what he calls his 'maxims', calls it the 'law of continuity', and explains its history in his own work. This particular extract is from the *Nouveaux essais sur l'entendement humain*

---

10  Gottfried Wilhelm Leibniz, *Nouveaux essais sur l'entendement humain (avant-propos et livre premier)*, ed. by Émile Boutroux (Paris: Librairie Delagrave, 1927), p. 11.

written in 1707 or 1711 in response to Locke's *Essay concerning Human Understanding*, but not print-published until 1764 or 1765, although it is thought that parts of it were probably circulating in manuscript form, and were more or less well-known to the philosophical community.[11] We meet the formulation in almost identical form in Bonnet's *Corps organisés* of 1762:

> La nature ne va point par sauts. Tout a sa raison suffisante, ou sa cause prochaine & immédiate. L'état actuel d'un Corps est la suite ou le produit de son état antécédent; ou pour parler plus juste, l'état actuel d'un Corps est détérminé par son état antécédent.[12]
>
> Nature does not proceed in leaps. Everything has its sufficient reason or its near and immediate cause. The current state of a body is the consequence or product of its previous state, or to put it more accurately, the current state of a body is determined by its previous state.

In Bonnet, as with Leibniz, the formula refers directly to the continuous linked chain of cause and effect ('raison suffisante' is of course also a Leibnizian formula, known in parodic form through the absurd sayings of Pangloss, the idiot tutor in Voltaire's *Candide*); this chain maps the patterns of logic onto the behaviour of nature, working on the assumption that logic itself is part of nature.

Diderot picks it up at least three times, once in the text that we know of as his *Observations sur Hemsterhuis* (1773), once in the *Réfutation d'Helvétius* (composed the same year) and once more in the *Éléments de physiologie*. Hemsterhuis is reflecting on the fact that he is not in control of his own thoughts, stating (rather obviously perhaps) that given that this is the case, there must be a cause prompting his (otherwise uncontrollable) thoughts. He writes:

> Puisque je ne suis pas maître de penser à ce que je veux, et qu'une longue expérience me l'a appris, il faut bien que j'y sois porté par une cause.[13]

---

11 Adrien Paschoud, 'Matérialisme, ordre naturel et imaginaire cosmologique dans *L'Homme-plante* (1748) de La Mettrie', in *Penser l'ordre naturel, 1680–1810*, ed. by Adrien Paschoud and Nathalie Vuillemin (Oxford: Voltaire Foundation, 2012), pp. 51-66 (p. 52n).

12 Charles Bonnet, *Considérations sur les corps organisés* [1762], in *Œuvres d'histoire naturelle et de philosophie*, 18 tomes in 10 vols (Neuchâtel: chez S. Fauche, 1779–83), vol. 3, t. 5, p. 87.

13 François Hemsterhuis in *Observations sur La 'Lettre sur l'homme et ses rapports' de Hemsterhuis*, ed. by Gerhardt Stenger, in *Œuvres complètes*, DPV (Paris: Hermann,

> Given that, as long experience has taught me, I am not in charge of what I think about, it must be that I am impelled to think about it by a cause.

Diderot writes in response to this passage that:

> Toute cause est un effet me paraît un axiome.
>
> Sans quoi la nature agirait à tout moment *per saltum*; ce qui n'est jamais vrai.[14]

> That every cause is an effect seems to me to be an axiom.
>
> Without it nature would be continuously acting *per saltum* [by leaps], which is never the case.

In this version the formula has taken on a Latin tinge: 'par saut' has moved into 'per saltum'. In the *Réfutation d'Helvétius*, written in the same year and manuscript-published in the *Correspondance littéraire* (1783–86),[15] we are back in French, also in the context of *natural cause and effect thought*:

> Rien ne se fait par saut dans la nature; et l'éclair subit et rapide qui passe dans l'esprit, tient à un phénomène antérieur avec lequel on en reconnaîtrait la liaison, si l'on n'était pas infiniment plus pressé de jouir de sa lueur que d'en rechercher la cause.[16]

> Nothing is done in a single leap in nature; and the sudden flash of lightning that passes through the mind derives from a previous phenomenon, and we would recognise the link if we were not in much more of a hurry to enjoy the illumination it brings than to seek its cause.

In the *Éléments de physiologie* we hear it again, but it is explicitly rather than just implicitly applied to the patterns and organisation of nature in general:

---

2004), vol. 24, pp. 479-767; 309.
14  Ibid.
15  *Réfutation d'Helvétius*, ed. by Roland Desné, Didier Kahn, Antoinette Lorenceau, and Gerhardt Stenger, in *Œuvres complètes*, DPV (Paris: Hermann, 2004), vol. 24, p. 440.
16  *Réfutation d'Helvétius*, p. 626. The editors note the recapitulation and the Leibnizian origin, but omit the later reference in *Éléments de physiologie* Denis Diderot, *Éléments de physiologie*, ed. by Jean Mayer, *Œuvres complètes*, DPV (Paris: Hermann, 1987), vol. 17, pp. 261–574 (p.483); Diderot, *Éléments de physiologie*, ed. by Paolo Quintili (Paris: Champion, 2004), p. 314; Diderot, *Éléments de physiologie*, ed. by Motoichi Terada (Paris: Éditions Matériologiques, 2019), p. 298 [hereafter notated as DPV 483/PQ 314/MT 298].

> Rien ne se fait par saut dans la nature; tout y est lié. L'animal, l'homme, tout être est soumis à cette loi générale.[17]
>
> Nothing is done in a single leap in nature, everything is connected up. Animals, humans, everything is subject to this general law.

'Tout y est lié' is the explanation and commentary for 'rien ne se fait par saut dans la nature': sequential links of cause and effect bind the whole; there are no gaps.

\*\*\*

For Spinoza, things, ideas, and body, are all connected in the same way, replicating and following the same natural patterns.[18]

> The order and connection of ideas is the same as the order and connection of things (by IIP7), and vice versa, the order and connection of things is the same as the order and connection of ideas (by IIP6C and P7). So just as the order and connection of ideas happens in the mind according to the order and connection of affections of the body (by IIP18), so vice versa (by IIIP2), the order and connection of affections of the body happens as thoughts and ideas of things are ordered and connected in the mind, q.e.d.[19]

If there is a natural order to things and ideas and affections in the body, sometimes that natural order is lost, and needs to be found again, as he argues in his *Traité de la réforme de l'entendement*:

> Le but est d'avoir des idées claires et distinctes, [...] Ensuite, pour ramener toutes ces idées à l'unité, nous nous efforcerons de les enchaîner et de les ordonner de telle façon que notre esprit, autant qu'il se peut faire, reproduise objectivement ce qui est formellement dans la nature, prise dans sa totalité aussi bien que dans ses parties.[20]
>
> The aim is to have clear and distinct ideas [...]. Thereafter, to unify all these ideas, we will attempt to link them up and order them in such a

---

17  DPV 483/PQ 314/MT 298.
18  This feature of 'concaténation' is neatly analysed by Citton in his *L'Envers de la liberté*, pp. 85–89. See also Arthur O. Lovejoy, *The Great Chain of Being* (Cambridge, MA: Harvard University Press, 1936; repr. 2001), esp. pp. 227–41.
19  Spinoza, *Ethics*, trans. by Edwin Curley with an introduction by Stuart Hampshire (London: Penguin, 1996), p. 163.
20  Spinoza, *Traité de la réforme de l'entendement et de la meilleure voie à suivre pour parvenir à la vraie connaissance des choses*, ed. and trans. by A. Koyré (Paris: Vrin, 1951), §91.

way that our mind, insofar as it is able to, reproduces objectively that which is formally in nature, nature being taken in its totality as well as in its parts.

Spinoza's aim is to have clear and distinct ideas which reproduce objectively what is in nature, that is to say, its forms, and also to show others how to do the same.

Condillac presents a similar notion that nature, ideas, and the exposition of truth are all, or should all, be linked in similar ways. His insistence on knowledge as purveyed by the senses has an obvious Lockean genealogy (but Spinoza said it first, as did many others, back to the acceptable Aristotle and the more worrying Epicurus).[21] In his *Essai sur l'origine des connaissances humaines* of 1746, Condillac mentions this perfect match between nature, our knowledge of it, and our presentation of it:

> La nature indique elle-même l'ordre qu'on doit tenir dans l'exposition de la vérité ; car si toutes nos connaissances viennent des sens, il est évident que c'est aux idées sensibles à préparer l'intelligence des notions abstraites.[22]
>
> Nature herself indicates the order we need to follow when setting out the truth, for if all our knowledge comes from the senses, it is obvious that it is the sensory ideas which pave the way for the understanding of abstract notions.

Buffon again references this idea of a perfect match between the works of nature and the works of the natural philosopher. The aim of the author, he explains in his *Discours sur le style*, given on his admission to the Académie française in 1753, is to imitate Nature as closely as he can: if he succeeds he will create 'immortal monuments':

> si [l'esprit humain] imite la Nature dans sa marche et dans son travail, s'il s'élève par la contemplation aux vérités les plus sublimes, s'il les réunit,

---

[21] Locke of course was less polemical to acknowledge as a source, see John Yolton, *Locke and French Materialism* (Oxford: Oxford University Press, 1991), https://doi.org/10.1093/acprof:oso/9780198242741.001.0001.

[22] Condillac, *Essai sur l'origine des connaissances humaines* [1746], ed. by Jean-Claude Pariente and Martine Pécharman (Paris: Vrin, 2014), p. 326 (II.II § 52).

s'il les enchaîne, s'il en forme un systeme par la réflexion, il établira sur des fondements inébranlables des monuments immortels.[23]

If [the human mind] imitates nature in its approach and in its work, if by dint of contemplation it is able to raise itself up to the most sublime truths, if it can bring them together and link them, if by dint of reflection it can shape it into one system, it will establish immortal monuments on unshakeable foundations.

The key idea is for the author to imitate Nature in his *approach*, literally his *walk* or in his *steps*, his *proceeding* would be the closest translation perhaps, and in his work: the book must replicate nature in order and organisation: what this means is that the author must raise himself to the contemplation of the most sublime truths, bring them together, link them up, and form a complete system. In fact Buffon uses the notion of authorship of books to establish nature as the best and most perfect author, or even, in the second extract below, not just the author but the book itself, a perpetually living book. Buffon is conceptualising this sort of difficult-to-imagine collapsing reversing relationship between the thing doing the doing and the thing which is made that we also see in Spinoza's double definition of Nature as *natura naturans* (the power nature has to determine its own laws) and *natura naturata* (the concept of nature as completely determined), and will meet again when looking at Diderot's model of memory as the self-reading, self-writing book. Here, however, is Buffon on the perfect form of natural creation; he is playing with the term 'ouvrage' [work] as book:

Pourquoi les ouvrages de la Nature sont-ils si parfaits? C'est que chaque ouvrage est un tout [...][24]

Why are the works of Nature always so perfect? Because every work is a whole.

la Nature est elle-même un ouvrage perpétuellement vivant.[25]

Nature itself is a work, a perpetually living one.

---

23 Buffon, 'Discours sur le style', in *Œuvres*, ed. by Stéphane Schmitt and Cédric Crémière (Paris: Gallimard Pléiade, 2007), p. 424, https://doi.org/10.5962/bhl.title.53421.
24 Buffon, 'Discours sur le style', pp. 423–24.
25 Buffon, *Histoire naturelle*, vol. XII [1764], in *Œuvres*, ed. by Stéphane Schmitt and Cédric Crémière (Paris: Gallimard Pléiade, 2007), pp. 424, 985.

For Buffon, nature and the book (should) match up perfectly in a mutually illuminating manner.

Diderot also sees nature and thought matching up: everything in nature is ordered and linked, and everything we write about nature necessarily follows the same pattern:

> Le type de nos raisonnements les plus étendus, leur liaison, leur conséquence est nécessaire dans notre entendement, comme l'enchaînement, la liaison des effets, des causes [,] des objets, des qualités des objets l'est dans la nature.[26]

> The pattern of our most extensive chains of reasoning, their connections and sequencing, is a necessary one within our understanding, as the connection, linking of effects, causes, objects, and the qualities of the objects within nature also is.

We see how faithfully these philosophers can choose to relay each other when they are not disputing other differences when we see how they quote each other, or pick up each other's specific phrasings, and therefore that it is reasonable to present them as more together than apart, more similar than different, more deeply united in their concerted efforts to understand nature and human understanding than divided on particular points—although of course some of the time we are looking at continuities, and other times at refinements and new versions.

As this last extract from the *Éléments* indicates, this natural order or pattern is 'necessary', determined by a fundamental model of cause and effect.

## b. The Necessary Order of Nature

*The order of nature is itself determined, writes Spinoza. Humans themselves are determined, and free will does not exist, writes Meslier. But there is reason, writes Condillac. Fontenelle wonders what the role of the instinct is. Diderot suggests that if there is any difference between the rest of living nature and the human, it is merely a question of extent.*

Spinoza had said this in his *Ethics*: 'the order of nature' is determined, and therefore 'things could have been produced in no other way and no

---

26  DPV 463/PQ 289/MT 279.

other order'.²⁷ Humans are also determined by the laws of nature, and therefore free will does not exist.

Despite being determined by these same laws of nature, humans do not recognise that this is the case, says Spinoza:

> It will be sufficient here if I take as a foundation what everyone must acknowledge: that all men are born ignorant of the causes of things, and that they all want to seek their own advantage, and are conscious of this appetite. From these (assumptions) it follows, *first*, that men think themselves free, because they are conscious of their volitions and their appetite, and do not think, even in their dreams, of the causes by which they are disposed to wanting and willing, because they are ignorant of (those causes).²⁸

Meslier, in his *Anti-Fénelon*, quotes and responds to Fénelon's trumpeted declaration *'Je suis libre\*, et je n'en puis douter [...]'* with the following abrupt refutation:

> \* Nous sommes libres dès que nous faisons ce que nous voulons sans contrainte; nous ne sommes point autrement libres.²⁹

> \* We are free from the moment we do what we want free of constraint, and we are not otherwise free in the slightest.

The stage is set here for a stand-off between reason and free will on the one hand (in this context, part of the demonstration of the existence of God), and Nature and instinct on the other, inevitably part of a demonstration that God is *not* part of the workings of Nature (unless God is defined *as* Nature).

It was generally agreed that instinct was common to all animals, but was not part of thought, a faculty which set humans apart from other animals, and was God-given. It was on this basis that Descartes could build his argument stating that animals had no soul. Fontenelle's fragment 'Sur l'instinct', published in 1757–58, thought to be a response to Nicolas Malebranche, asked whether instinct is voluntary

---

27  Spinoza, *Ethics*, p. 22 (§II.73).
28  Spinoza, *Ethics*, p. 26 (§II.78).
29  Jean Meslier, *Anti-Fenelon*, in *Œuvres complètes*, ed. by Roland Desné, Preface and Notes by Jean Deprun, Roland Desné et Albert Soboul, 3 vols (Paris: Éditions anthropos, 1970–72), vol. 3, pp. 262–63.

or involuntary.³⁰ Condillac, in his 1746 *Essai*, agrees with the view that instinct is beyond our control, and maintains the barriers between it and what he calls here the 'operations of the soul'.

> L'instinct n'est qu'une imagination dont l'exercice n'est point du tout à nos ordres, mais qui, par sa vivacité, concourt parfaitement à la conservation de notre être. Il exclut la mémoire, la réflexion et les autres opérations de l'âme. [...] Enfin la raison résulte de toutes les opérations de l'âme bien conduite.³¹
>
> Instinct is nothing other than a sort of imagination whose exercise can in no way be controlled by us, but which, with its lively responsiveness, perfectly contributes to the preservation of our being. It excludes memory, reflection, and the other operations of the soul. [...] In short, reason is the result of all operations of the well-regulated soul.

But if, in his *Essai*, Condillac will write that 'la raison' 'couronne l'entendement' [reason crowns the understanding], by the time he writes his *Traité sur la sensation*, he no longer separates instinct and reason quite so firmly.³²

Diderot, writing the *Éléments de physiologie*, will be prepared to tersely assert that 'Je veux, n'est qu'un mot' [I want, is nothing more than a phrase].³³ The will ('la volonté') is discussed purely as a function of nature's needs and appetites. Our nature determines us. And it determines what we think and what we do. As we saw with Hemsterhuis, one is not always the master of one's thoughts, and there is always a cause for this: Diderot agreed, and took the opportunity to reaffirm the law of sequential cause and effect. From Spinoza's point of view, there will be a reason for our 'volitions and appetites' but we

---

30   Bernard le Bovier de Fontenelle, *Fragments d'un traité de la raison humaine*, in *Œuvres complètes*, ed. by Alain Niderst, 10 vols (Paris: Fayard, 1996), vol. 7, p. 6.
31   Condillac, *Essai sur l'origine des connaissances humaines* [1746], ed. by Jean-Claude Pariente and Martine Pécharman (Paris: Vrin, 2014), p. 133 (I.II § 95).
32   Condillac, *Essai sur l'origine des connaissances humaines*, ed. by Pariente et Pécharman, p. 132 (I.II §92). In the *Traité des sensations*, 'raison' never features in a chapter title; the process of thought moves sequentially from sensation to impression, idea, memory thereof, comparison to another memory of a different sensation, which leads to abstraction, and so on. The whole process is one long chain. See for example Étienne Bonnot de Condillac, *Traité des sensations*, ed. by Christiane Frémont (Paris: Fayard, 1984), pp. 125–27 (part 1, ch. 8, § 'La statue devient capable de réflexion', etc.).
33   DPV 483/PQ 314/MT 298.

ourselves may not know what it is. Free will and reason occupy an ever smaller space in accounts of the mind. Instinct begins to take the place of reason. And indeed, in the third part of the *Éléments de physiologie*, with all its extended discussion of the brain and thought, there is no chapter on reason at all.[34] There is more to say on the topic of instinct and also modes of perception which are paradoxically not perceived by the perceiving subject, but its place is in a later section of this chapter, once nature and its laws have been discussed (and instinct has been discussed as part of human nature being determined just like the rest of nature), and we have moved on to look in more detail at the human understanding.

For the moment, we return to the discussion of the order of nature, and whether this order is eternal or subject to change.

## c. The Order of Nature: Unchanging or in Flux?

*That order, however, is not an unchanging one: the universe and species themselves are in flux, write Leibniz, Meslier and Bonnet. (Buffon disagrees: he thinks nature is fixed.) Human individuals are also more or less in flux, writes Meslier: they vary according to their constitution, age, and health, from one person to the next, and over the course of their own lifetime (Buffon agrees). Madmen and fools embody these differences, as do sudden bursts of strength overcoming debility in the face of fear or overwhelming need. The man immobilised by gout will suddenly run away from fire, Condillac and Buffon tell us, or lift burning wooden panels from a building (Diderot bizarrely claims that Buffon himself did this).*

As we have already quoted, Spinoza had stated that 'the order of nature' is determined, and therefore 'things could have been produced in no other way and no other order'.[35] Hemsterhuis echoes this view very closely:

---

34 Although in part one, 'Des êtres', in the third chapter, entitled 'Homme' the first sub-heading is 'Raison'. However, from the first sentence, it is displaced in favour of 'instinct': 'La raison ou l'instinct de l'homme est déterminé par son organisation [...]' [The reason or instinct of a man is determined by his organisation] (DPV 328/ PQ 144/MT 149).

35 Spinoza, *Ethics*, p. 33 (22 II/73).

> Ce qui existe par soi-même, et dont l'essence est d'exister, existe nécessairement, et nécessairement d'une façon déterminée. Existant nécessairement, il serait contradictoire qu'il n'existât pas, ou qu'il existât d'une façon autrement déterminée.[36]
>
> That which exists by itself, and whose essence is to exist, exists necessarily, and necessarily in a determined way. Existing necessarily, it would be contradictory for it not to exist, or for it to exist in a way that was determined differently.

Diderot agrees and then diverges. The divergence rides on the nature, or essence, of matter: is it *homogenous* or *heterogeneous*, that is, are the basic building blocks of matter all identical ('homogenous') or are they different ('heterogeneous')? The answer to this question, as we now know, is that they are different: this is what the periodic table tells us: the elements are essentially different, and from their combinations all things in nature are made. But natural philosophy was not ready to pronounce on the question at this stage. (Antoine Lavoisier's groundbreaking *Traité élémentaire de chimie*, with its first list of elements, would be published in 1789).[37] Diderot was already convinced that nature was heterogeneous, and as he explains, what is at stake is whether nature in its current form is unchanging or, to give it its divine resonance, 'eternal', or not: in his view its essential reactivity, or continuing change in reaction to everything around it, its 'vicissitude', means that while it is determined by natural laws (including the laws of cause and effect), and while it will eternally be so, it will also be subject to perpetual change. So, when Spinoza and Hemsterhuis state that nature's current forms are determined and will be unchanging, Diderot, responding directly to Hemsterhuis, disagrees:

> \* Je ne crois pas cela.
>
> Je crois que la forme actuelle sous laquelle la matière existe est nécessaire et déterminée; ainsi que toutes les formes diverses qu'elle prendra successivement à toute éternité.

---

[36] Hemsterhuis in Diderot, *Observations sur La 'Lettre sur l'homme et ses rapports' de Hemsterhuis*, ed. by Gerhardt Stenger, in *Œuvres complètes*, DPV (Paris: Hermann, 2004), vol. 24, p. 284.

[37] Even the term 'element' is not a given here: what Lavoisier meant by 'element' is not the same as an element in the periodic table as understood by Dmitri Mendeleev or as redefined in the twentieth century according to atomic number. With thanks to François Pépin for this point.

Mais cette vicissitude, ce développement qui est en flux perpétuel est nécessaire. C'est une suite de son essence et de son hétérogénéité.

Et je ne vois nulle contradiction à cette supposition.

Si elle est essentiellement hétérogène; elle est essentiellement en vicissitude.[38]

\* I do not believe that.

I believe that the current form in which matter exists is necessary and determined as are all the different forms it will take successively and for all eternity.

But this vicissitude, this development which is in perpetual flux is necessary. It is the consequence of its essence and its heterogeneity.

And I see no contradiction in this supposition.

If it is essentially heterogeneous then it is essentially subject to vicissitude.

Not all authors are willing to say this, and of course the extent to which Diderot writing these notes in Hemsterhuis's book and then handing them back to him with the strict injunction to keep them completely secret actually counts as saying it at all is debatable. But Diderot did plant his views in a number of different textual flowerbeds, including this one: in his 1753 print-published *Pensées sur l'interprétation de la nature* he suggested that Nature's productions are infinitely varied;[39] in the *Rêve de d'Alembert*, his character d'Alembert muses on the 'flux perpétuel', and this theme is further developed in the *Eléménts de physiologie*.[40]

Meslier had depicted a broad-brush canvas of perpetual motion and perpetual variation in his *Mémoire des pensées et sentiments* (written probably in the 1720s just prior to his death in 1729 and better known as his *Testament* after Voltaire's famous abridgement which appeared in 1761). In its structure and iterative style, Meslier's *Mémoire* is a written instantiation of infinite variation. One such evocation runs as follows:

> En un mot toute action suit naturellement et necessairement la nature du mouvement de l'être qui se meut. Tout cela est clair et certain, et comme d'ailleurs tous les divers mouvemens dont je viens de parler, se peuvent encore modifier en infinies sortes et manieres, et que tous les êtres qui sont en mouvement et qui sont les plus petites parties de la matière se

---

38 Diderot, *Observations sur La 'Lettre sur l'homme et ses rapports' de Hemsterhuis*, p. 284.
39 Diderot, *Pensées sur l'interprétation de la nature*, DPV, vol. 9, p. 291 ('pensée' 12).
40 Diderot, *Le Rêve de d'Alembert*, DPV, p. 138; *Eléments de physiologie*, DPV 312/PQ 127/MT 135; DPV 322/PQ 137/MT 144; DPV 444/PQ 265/MT 261, as quoted above.

peuvent mesler, se combiner, se joindre, se lier, s'accrocher, et s'unir ensemble, ou se heurter les unes contre les autres, se repousser les unes les autres, se separer, s'écarter, et se disperser les unes des autres, en infinies sortes et manieres.[41]

In a word all action naturally and necessarily follows the nature of the movement of the moving being. All this is clear and certain, and moreover all these diverse movements that I have just been speaking about can further modify themselves in infinite ways and manners, and all the beings which are moving and which are the smallest parts of matter can mix, combine, join, link, hold on, and unite together, or alternatively crash into one another, repel, separate, diverge and disperse in infinite ways and manners.

The naturalist Charles Bonnet bravely evokes species change in the natural world and in living beings in his *Palingénésie philosophique* (1769), published the same year that the *Rêve de d'Alembert* was first drafted. Bonnet had already invoked 'l'evolution, loi de la nature' in his *Corps organisés*.[42] In the *Palingénésie philosophique*, he evokes '[des] idées sur l'état passé & sur l'état futur des Etres vivans' [ideas on the past state and on the future state of living beings], and seeks to disarm disapproval, official or otherwise, by insisting (in Pluchian mode)[43] on the beauty of the spectacle, 'cette ravissante Scene de métamorphoses' [this ravishing scene of metamorphoses].[44] The result of all this change would be that 'Nous contemplerions un monde tout nouveau, un Ensemble de Choses dont nous ne saurions nous faire actuellement aucune idée' [we would

---

41 Meslier, *Mémoire des pensées et sentiments de Jean Meslier*, in *Œuvres complètes*, ed. by Roland Desné, préface et notes par Jean Deprun, Roland Desné et Albert Soboul, vol. 2, p. 443.
42 Charles Bonnet, *Considérations sur les corps organisés* [1762], in *Œuvres d'histoire naturelle et de philosophie*, vol. 3, t. 5, p. 303.
43 Noël-Antoine Pluche (1688–1761) was the author of the *Spectacle de la nature* (1732–42), famous for its argument that God's existence could be proved by reference to the beauty of nature, an argument which Diderot contested in Saunderson's (invented) death-bed speech (*Lettre sur les aveugles* [1749], in Denis Diderot, *Lettre sur les aveugles: à l'usage de ceux qui voient; Lettre sur les sourds et muets: à l'usage de ceux qui entendent et qui parlent*, ed. by Marian Hobson and Simon Harvey (Paris: GF Flammarion, 2000)).
44 In the *Palingénésie philosophique* [1769], Bonnet evokes (in the title) 'idées sur l'état passé & sur l'état futur des Etres vivans' (Bonnet, *Œuvres d'histoire naturelle et de philosophie*, vol. 7, t. 15, p. 171).

be contemplating a completely new world, an ensemble of things about which we currently have absolutely no idea at all].[45]

There are, as already suggested, material variations which are more familiar and less obviously paradigmatically challenging. There are malformed bodies: in eighteenth-century terms, 'monsters'. Emita Hill, Andrew Curran and Charles Wolfe have all written fine and complementary studies of the monster as concept, as thought experiment and as fiction in Diderot.[46] As we know, Diderot was interested in understanding the range and also random nature of 'monstrous' forms, and in using them to show the material variability of nature and its laws.[47] Bonnet had said in his *Corps organisés* (1762) that

> On nomme Monstre toute production organisée, dans laquelle la conformation, l'arrangement, ou le nombre de quelques-unes des parties ne suivent pas les règles ordinaires.[48]

> We term a Monster any organised production in which the structure, arrangement or number of any of its parts do not conform to ordinary rules.

Buffon discusses natural monstrosity, but is not ready to suggest species modification and transformation over time, instead piously confirming that the 'ordonnance [de la nature] est fixe pour le nombre, le maintien et l'équilibre des espèces' [order of nature is fixed in relation to the amount, the preservation, and the balance of species].[49] He states, as is generally accepted in all of these works of natural philosophy, that individuals themselves vary one from the next, and over the course of their own lives: change is a modus vivendi and the 'habitude [de la nature] vari[e] autant qu'il est possible dans toutes les formes individuelles' [nature

---

45   Bonnet, *Palingénésie philosophique*, in *Œuvres d'histoire naturelle et de philosophie*, vol. 7, t. 15, p. 392.
46   See Emita Hill, Andrew Curran, and Charles Wolfe on monsters in Diderot's thought; see also Wes Williams for earlier deployments of the concept. Andrew Curran, *Sublime Disorder: Physical Monstrosity in Diderot's Universe* (Oxford: Voltaire Foundation, 2001); Emita Hill, *The Role of 'le monstre' in Diderot's Thought* (Banbury: Voltaire Foundation, 1972); Charles Wolfe, *Monsters and Philosophy* (London: College Publications, 2005); Wes Williams, *Monsters and Their Meanings in Early Modern Culture* (Oxford: Oxford University Press, 2011), https://doi.org/10.1093/acprof:oso/9780199577026.001.0001.
47   We touched on the question of monsters and monstrosity in the previous chapter.
48   Bonnet, *Corps organisés*, p. 102.
49   Buffon, *De la nature. Seconde vue* in *Histoire naturelle*, vol. 13 [1765], *Œuvres*, p. 999.

habitually varies as much as possible across all individual forms].⁵⁰ Bodies are in flux, had said Leibniz in his *Monadologie*, comparing bodies to rivers:

> Car tous les corps sont dans un flux perpétuel comme des rivières ; et des parties y entrent et en sortent continuellement.⁵¹

> For all bodies are in perpetual flux like rivers, and parts are continually coming in and going out of them.

While the allusion to rivers in flux nods to Heraclitus's alleged remark about never stepping into the same river twice, it was not a truism, philosophical, medical or otherwise, to state that bodies were also in flux. Meslier also said that bodies are in flux, quoting Montaigne's *Apologie de Raimond Sebond* to do so, and thereby inserting Montaigne's Lucretian commentary that our thoughts, judgements, and soul suffer and are affected by these continual alterations. Montaigne's own relation to Epicureanism is an interesting one that is not part of the story we are telling here, but it is perhaps useful to note that he deeply admired Lucretius's poem, and cited it very frequently.⁵² Montaigne's role in the transmission of *De rerum natura* is important, as these particular pages from Meslier's *Testament* demonstrate: there is extensive quotation from Lucretius, and it is all lifted from Montaigne's *Apologie de Raymond Sebond*.⁵³

---

50  Ibid.
51  Gottfried Wilhelm Leibniz, 'Monadologie', in *Principes de la nature et de la grace fondés en raison et principes de la philosophie ou monadologie*, ed. by André Robinet (Paris: Presses Universitaires de France, 1954), p. 113 (§71); *Monadology: An Edition for Students*, ed. and trans. by Nicholas Rescher (London: Routledge, 2002), p. 234 (translation lightly amended).
52  See Michael Screech, *Montaigne's Annotated Copy of Lucretius: A Transcription and Study of the Manuscript, Notes and Pen-Marks* (Geneva: Droz, 1998) and Wes Williams, '"Well Said/Well Thought": How Montaigne Read His Lucretius', in *Lucretius and the Early Modern*, ed. by David Norbrook, Stephen Harrison, and Philip Hardie (Oxford: Oxford University Press, 2015), pp. 136–61, https://doi.org/10.1093/acprof:oso/9780198713845.003.0007.
53  Meslier, *Mémoire des pensées et sentiments de Jean Meslier*, in *Œuvres complètes*, ed. by Desné, vol. 3, p. 48 n. 2.

> *Il est certain,* dit le judicieux Montaigne, *que nos pensées, que nos jugemens, et que les facultés de notre âme souffrent selon les mouvemens, et les alterations du corps; lesquelles alterations sont continuëlles.*⁵⁴

> It is certain, says the judicious Montaigne, *that our thoughts, our judgements, and the faculties of our soul suffer according to the movements and alterations of the body, these alterations being unceasing.*

There are two strands to draw out of this particular tradition of conceptualising individual bodies in flux: firstly, the expanding-diminishing model of a body that will grow, flourish, and then decline and die, and secondly, the idea that illness and other changes can affect and alter its abilities and character at any given moment. I will take these strands one after the other. The first is a typically lofty example of the ineluctable forces of nature from the pen of Buffon:

> Tout change dans la Nature, tout s'altère, tout périt ; le corps de l'homme n'est pas plûtôt arrivé à son point de perfection, qu'il commence à déchoir.⁵⁵

> Everything changes in Nature, everything alters, everything perishes; no sooner has the body of man reached its peak of perfection than it starts to decline.

In 1753, Diderot will pick up this notion of the flourishing and death of an individual to push back to the bigger question: might not a species follow the same pattern?

> [...] dans les règnes animal et végétal, un individu commence, pour ainsi dire, s'accroît, dure, dépérit et passe; n'en serait-il pas de même des espèces entières?⁵⁶

> In the animal and vegetable realms, an individual starts, so to say, grows, lasts, declines and passes; might it not also be the same for whole species?

Although as we have already seen, Buffon will refuse to countenance such a notion.⁵⁷

---

54 Meslier, *Mémoire des pensées et sentiments de Jean Meslier*, in *Œuvres complètes*, ed. by Desné, vol. 3, p. 53 (from Montaigne's *Apologie de Raimond Sebond*).
55 Buffon, *De l'homme* in *Histoire naturelle*, vol. 2 [1749], *Œuvres*, p. 262.
56 Diderot, *Pensées sur l'interprétation de la nature*, DPV, vol. 9, p. 331.
57 Barbara de Negroni comments on Buffon's opposition to 'les thèses transformistes', in Diderot, *Pensées sur l'interprétation de la nature*, in *Œuvres*, p. 1206, n. 143.

The principal of continual change in bodies is asserted again in the section on 'Mort' [Death] in the *Éléments de physiologie*: 'Nul état fixe dans le corps animal: il décroît quand il ne croît plus' [There is no fixed state in the animal body: it starts shrinking once it stops growing].[58]

The second strand is the notion of illness, which we have already seen in Montaigne via Meslier, and also in the previous chapter, in relation to Pascal.[59] Bonnet will restate it in eighteenth-century physiological vocabulary:

> Une maladie peut déranger toute l'Economie du Cerveau & anéantir l'Imagination, la Mémoire, le Raisonnement; elle n'annéantit pas l'Ame, & néanmoins elle est réduite à l'état de l'Ame de la Brute.[60]

> An illness can upset the whole economy of the brain and annihilate imagination, memory, and reason; it does not annihilate the soul, which is nonetheless reduced to the state of the soul of a beast.

In the *Éléments de physiologie*, this view is the underlying assumption for the whole work and references to it are ubiquitous. Here is one, from part 1, 'Des Etres', chapter III, 'Homme', sub-section 'Raison':

> Les facultés de l'homme se perdent sans retour, comme elles se perdent momentanément, c'est la même cause, dont l'effet dure ou cesse. Exemples pris de la lassitude, de la maladie, de la convalescence, de la passion, de l'ivresse, du sommeil, c'est ainsi que l'homme est successivement ingénieux ou stupide, patient ou colère, jamais le même; le plus constant est celui qui change le moins.[61]

> Human faculties can be irrevocably lost just as they can be momentarily lost, the cause is the same, whether the effect endures or not. Examples can be found in tiredness, illness, convalescence, passion, drunkenness, sleep, and thus is man successively ingenious or stupid, patient or angry, never the same; the most constant is he who changes the least.

---

58 DPV 312/PQ 127/MT 135.
59 See above.
60 Bonnet, *Analyse abrégée de l'Essai analytique sur les Facultés de l'Ame* [?1764], in *Œuvres d'histoire naturelle et de philosophie*, vol. 8, t. 15, p. 38.
61 DPV 329/PQ 145/MT 150.

## i. The Gouty Man and the Fire

Thus far, these relaying maxims and patterns remain rather generalised. There are also specific examples which get picked up and reused. One such is the inverse example of the gouty man, enfeebled by his illness yet given remarkable strength by experiencing extreme emotion.

Here is Condillac's version:

> Un homme, tourmenté par la goutte et qui ne peut se soutenir, revoit au moment qu'il s'y attendait le moins, un fils qu'il croyait perdu : plus de douleur. Un instant après le feu se met à sa maison : plus de faiblesse. Il est déjà hors du danger quand on songe à le secourir. Son imagination subitement et vivement frappée, réagit sur toutes les parties de son corps, et y produit la révolution qui le sauve.[62]

> A man, tormented by gout and unable to support his own weight, sees at the moment he least expected it a son whom he'd thought lost: no more pain. An instant later his house catches fire: no more weakness. By the time anyone thinks of giving him any assistance, he has already got out of danger. The effect of imagination having been suddenly and deeply struck reaches every part of his body and produces the revolution which saves him.

This sentimental fiction of Condillac's staggers under the weight of its implausibly compacted drama of the gouty father, the return of a son believed dead, and a sudden dangerous blaze, and fails to make any convincing physiological point. The version we meet in the *Eléménts de physiologie* is this (the gouty man has disappeared to be replaced by three separate characters):

> \* Mr de Buffon voit la flamme s'échapper avec de la fumée à travers les fentes d'un lambris; il arrache le lambris; il prend entre ses bras les planches à demi brûlées et les porte dans sa cour et il se trouve qu'un cheval n'ébranlerait pas le fardeau qu'il a porté. Une femme délicate est attaquée de vapeurs hystériques, de fureur utérine et trois hommes ne peuvent contenir celle qu'un seul d'entre eux aurait renversée, liée dans son état de santé. Le feu prend à la maison d'un avare, il prend son

---

62 Condillac, *Essai sur l'origine des connaissances humaines*, ed. by Pariente and Pécharman, p. 129 (I.II, §88).

coffre-fort et le porte dans son jardin, d'où il ne l'aurait pas remué pour dix fois la somme qu'il contenait.[63]

\* Mr de Buffon sees flames and smoke escaping through the slits of a piece of wooden pannelling; he tears it off; he carries the half-burnt planks in his arms out into the courtyard and it emerges that a horse would not have been able to shift the load he carried. A delicate woman is attacked by hysterical vapours and uterine fury and three men are unable to restrain a person whom one of them could have knocked over and tied up unaided had she been in a state of health. The house of a miser catches light, he picks up his strong box and carries it into his garden, and then wouldn't have been able to move it for ten times the sum it contained.

Diderot's three cases have fewer elements within them, taken separately, and although each one presents an extreme instance that certainly does contain melodramatic qualities, the physiological point about the body being capable of surprising strength in certain crisis circumstances (here, anxiety about treasured possessions—or just treasure—and hysteria)[64] is clear. It is curious nonetheless that Buffon is referenced (we have not been able to find the source for this anecdote),[65] and even more curious that Buffon features not as a natural philosopher organising and presenting anecdotal evidence, but as a player himself. Is there something at stake here, even if it's just a joke about the ponderous Buffon skipping about with huge weights? An implicit parallel with the miser, mocking Buffon for his pride in his wood panelling? Condillac is not named or alluded to, but his version tells us that these sorts of

---

63 DPV 327/PQ 143n/MT 149.
64 See Sabine Arnaud, *On Hysteria: The Invention of a Medical Category between 1670 & 1820* (Chicago: Chicago University Press, 2015), https://doi.org/10.7208/chicago/9780226275680.001.0001.
65 DPV and Terada have no references for this anecdote; PQ references the source in Buffon, *Histoire naturelle*, t.II, p. 429, 'Histoire naturelle de l'homme. De la nature de l'homme', but it does not seem to be there. Substantial hunting in Pietro Corsi et al.'s online edition of Buffon's work also failed to turn up the anecdote (http://www.cn2sv.cnrs.fr/article142.html). Buffon scholar Stéphane Schmitt supplies two references in Buffon to extraordinary strength in extraordinary straits, both in the *Supplément*, vol. 4, p. 372 ('Addition à l'article de l'accouchement' on labour pains) and p. 387 ('Addition à l'article de la puberté' on a young man in an 'état de délire convulsif' [a state of convulsive delirium]), but neither of these refer to Buffon himself. With thanks to Pietro Corsi and Stéphane Schmitt for helping to look.

examples, particularly involving fire, pre-existed Buffon's alleged experience, and were popping up in separate but overlapping texts.

## ii. From Recycled Cases to the Specific

Memory is a recurring topic of interest to all these authors thinking about how the brain works (as we have already seen and will see again): stupidity, genius, and madness are used throughout these texts as conditions that illuminate the phenomena of memory, and vice versa. La Mettrie's *Traité de l'âme* (1745) states that 'les sots raisonnent mal, ils ont si peu de mémoire' [idiots reason poorly, they have so little memory], and makes a link with the mad, whose ideas (he says) are disconnected, and in this sense 'idiots' are mad too, their ideas also being disconnected.[66] Condillac's *Essai sur l'origine des connaissances humaines* (1746) makes the same analogy: the man without memory (and therefore also without imagination), being completely unable to link his ideas, would be incapable of thought at all, and would be an imbecile; the man who had too much memory and too much imagination would similarly be unable to think, also failing to have properly linked consecutive thoughts, and would be mad.[67] Diderot's version is less boxily categorising, and also less assertive: inexperience as well as failure or loss of memory will all have an effect on a man's ability to link his ideas, and all lead to the same phenomenon, that is, that the man will *seem* mad.

> Si faute d'expérience les phénomènes ne s'enchaînent pas, si faute de mémoire ils ne peuvent s'enchaîner, si par la perte de la mémoire ils se décousent, l'homme paraît fou.[68]
>
> If for lack of experience phenomena don't link up, if for lack of memory they cannot be linked, if for loss of memory they become disconnected, a man will seem mad.

In all these circumstances, memory, sanity, and health exist in a sensitive and easily-disturbed relationship to each other, and Diderot

---

66  Julien Offray de La Mettrie, *Traité de l'âme*, in *Œuvres philosophiques*, ed. by Francine Markovits, 2 vols (Paris: Fayard, 1987), vol. 1, p. 216.
67  Condillac, *Essai sur l'origine des connaissances humaines*, ed. by Pariente and Pécharman, pp. 98–99 (I.II, §34).
68  DPV 464/PQ 289/MT 279. See also 'Il y a des phénomènes de mémoire qui ont conduit à la stupidité, à la folie' (DPV 473/PQ 301/MT 289).

gives a number of examples involving that relationship being lost,[69] or even never established, as in the case of the boy who lived with bears until the age of ten, who had no language other than bear grunts when brought into 'civilization', and who, once he had learnt language, could not remember his pre-language years with the bears. Diderot does not give all these details, tersely stating that 'Les signes servent beaucoup à la mémoire. Un enfant de dix ans, élevé par les ours, resta sans mémoire' [signs assist memory a great deal. A child of ten, brought up by bears, remained without memory].[70] The background can be found in the anecdote's previous appearances: in La Mettrie's *Traité de l'âme*, in La Mettrie's possible source, Jean-Pierre Crousaz's *Logique* (1720), although here the boy is a man, and in Condillac's *Essai* and again in his *Traité*: it comes (and Condillac gives the note accurately in his *Essai*) from Bernard Connor's *Evangelium medicum, seu medicina mystica*, published in London in 1697, and emerges again in Rousseau's *Discours sur l'origine de l'inégalité*, note III.[71]

The point here is that these writers all use this same example. There are other such cases, the blind boy operated on by Cheselden or the deaf man from Chartres being two more.[72] Diderot does not use these

---

69   DPV 469–70/PQ 297–98/MT 285–86; DPV 472–73/PQ 300–01/MT 288–89. He also talks about the volatility of the mind during fever or delirium, when the clever man and the fool can swap places owing to bodily illness. He considers that this is as important a deciding aspect of a person's intelligence as the perfection or otherwise of their senses (Helvétius's general view), see *Réfutation d'Helvétius*, DPV, vol. 24, p. 515.
70   DPV 470/PQ 298/MT 286.
71   La Mettrie, *Traité de l'âme*, p.236; Jean-Pierre Crousaz', *La Logique, ou Système de réflexions qui peuvent contribuer à la netteté et l'étendue de nos connaissances*, 2nd edn (Amsterdam: L'Honoré et Châtelain, 1720), vol. 1, p. 32; Condillac's *Essai*, §23, and *Traité*, p. 254–55; Bernard Connor, *Evangelium medicum, seu medicina mystica*, London in 1697, pp. 133–34; Rousseau's *Discours sur l'origine de l'inégalité*, note III in the *Œuvres complètes*, ed. by Bernard Gagnebin and Marcel Raymond (Paris: Gallimard Pléiade, 1964), vol. 3, p. 196, and p. 1361, n. 5.
72   'Aveugle-né' [man born blind]: Voltaire's account seems to kick-start this particular series: Voltaire, *Éléments de la philosophie de Newton*, ed. by Robert L. Walters and W.H. Barber, *Œuvres complètes de Voltaire* (Oxford: Voltaire Foundation, 1992), vol. 15, ch. 7. See Crousaz, *Logique*, vol. 1, pp. 33–34; La Mettrie, *Traité de l'âme*, pp. 227–28; Condillac, *Essai sur l'origine des connaissances humaines*, p. 186 (I.VI §15); Diderot's *Lettre sur les aveugles* (1749); Buffon, *Histoire naturelle*, vol. 3 (1749), p. 314; Condillac, *Traité des sensations* (1753), III.V, p. 195. See Tunstall, *Blindness and Enlightenment*, pp. 133–36. 'Sourd de Chartres' [the man from Chartres born deaf]: Crousaz, *Logique*, vol. 1, p. 34; La Mettrie, *Traité de l'âme*, pp. 225–26; Condillac, *Essai*, pp. 156–57 (I.II.IV, §13), pp. 156–57; Buffon, *Histoire naturelle* (1749), p. 348.

particular examples in the *Éléments de physiologie*, although they had appeared elsewhere in his œuvre. But they feature consistently across this corpus of texts that we are looking at, all of which provide material for the *Éléments de physiologie*. In the *Lettre sur les sourds et muets*, Diderot alludes to 'nos muets de convention' [our typical dumb people] and to the 'questions dont on leur demanderait la réponse' [the questions we would ask them to answer] as if those questions were always the same, and the deaf and dumb cases also the same.[73] This common corpus tells us that, as Diderot hints, the same examples and questions bear down on all these thinkers. One of the features that typifies the *Éléments de physiologie* is that while he often does work with familiar positions or examples, he does so in concentrated form, often adding newer, more personal, or stranger examples.

We can observe this shift from the general position (that humans differ from each other and over the course of any one life time according to physiology and state of health) to the striking and specific exemplification, in the change from the exasperated *Réfutation d'Helvétius* to the *Éléments de physiologie*. In the former, Diderot lambasts Helvétius for stating that humans are essentially the same everywhere, without regard for the sort of society they live in, and equally without regard to their physiological condition generally or at any given moment. He orders his reader to open the books of anatomists, doctors and physiologists, and to think about how a slight fever can make us quicker or slower. He asks us whether we have ever had a headache, implicitly challenging us to consider the effect it has on our thought processes. And meanwhile the 'vous', the collective you he is addressing, shades into a direct challenge to Helvétius himself (by then dead), chastising him for not having said a word about 'les fous' [mad people].[74]

In the *Éléments de physiologie*, this fieriness has cooled into detached description: the mental drama he records is all the more vivid for it. The notion that our state of mind at any given moment depends on our precise physiological condition gains a curious scenario: Diderot turns himself into a narrative of the husband and father whose familial anxiety is caused by a slightly fast pulse:

---

73  Diderot, *Lettre sur les sourds et muets*, ed. by Hobson and Harvey, pp. 95, 96.
74  Diderot, *Réfutation d'Helvétius*, DPV, vol. 24, p. 620.

L'action des nerfs porte au cerveau des désirs singuliers, les fantaisies les plus bizarres, des affections, des frayeurs: Il me semble que j'entends crier ma femme: on attaque ma fille, elle m'appelle à son secours; je vois les murs s'ébranler autour de moi: le plafond est prêt à tomber sur ma tête; je me sens pusillanime, je me tâte le pouls, j'y découvre un petit mouvement fébrile: la cause de ma frayeur connue, elle cesse.[75]

The action of the nerves transmits strange desires to the brain, the most bizarre fantasies, affections, and fears: I seem to hear my wife crying out: my daughter is being attacked, she is calling me for help; I see the walls shake around me: the ceiling is about to fall on my head; I feel fearful, I check my pulse, I find it is beating slightly feverishly: as soon as I know what the cause for my fright is, it ceases.

So, nature is in flux, and man is in flux.

## d. Matter in Flux

*Matter can move from one form to another, not in the sense that stones and other materials might suddenly get up and start arranging themselves into a building (a lumbering joke Meslier makes) but in the course of natural material processes, write Meslier, Buffon and Bonnet. These processes include absorption by nutrition, says Bonnet, while any given being at any given moment is a composite of different substances or bodies, write Spinoza and Buffon. This can be exemplified by the differences between different sorts of matter such as stone and flesh, and transformations between them. Rousseau challenges any philosopher to come and tell him how a lump of rock can become a living creature. And what is the likelihood that nature in all its extraordinary functions and variety could have come about without a guiding hand, just by chance? Diderot's answer can be found in the first part of the 'Rêve de d'Alembert'.*

Meslier is quick to reject cartoonish versions of materialist thinking which simplify to the point of nonsense the notion of the circulation of matter. It is not, he says, that the materials of a house jump up and start building themselves:

> Pareillement il seroit ridicule de dire ou de penser que les pierres et les bois qui composent une maison se seroient façonnés, assemblés, rangés,

---
[75] DPV 359/PQ 179/MT 179.

et attachés d'eux mêmes ensemble pour bastir une maison, puisque tous ces materiaux là n'ont en eux mêmes aucun mouvement.[76]

Similarly it would be absurd to say or to think that the stones and pieces of wood that make up a house could have carved themselves, got assembled, arranged and bound all by themselves to build a house, because none of those materials in themselves have any movement.

He explains how matter moves from one form to another in humans or animals through the simple processes of drinking and eating, and he also strikes a blow against abstraction (which these writers repeatedly do) by pointing out that it is not some general sort of unspecified matter which thinks, it's matter in human or animal form (provocatively presenting them as interchangeable, and without comment here on the anti-Cartesian notion of the thinking animal):

> Ce n'est pas précisément la matière qui pense, mais c'est l'homme ou l'animal composé de matière, qui pense, qui boit, qui mange, qui marche, qui dort; et comme les parties d'une pierre ou d'un morceau de fer ou de quelque autre chose que ce soit peuvent par leurs différentes modifications devenir chair et os et composer un corps organique et vivant, elles peuvent par conséquent faire un homme ou quelque autre animal capable de sentiment et de connaissance, et pour cela il ne faut point d'autre arrangement ni d'autres mouvements que ceux qui se trouvent ordinairement dans les hommes ou dans les autres animaux.[77]

It's not exactly matter which thinks, but the human or the animal made of matter which thinks, drinks, eats, walks, and sleeps; and just as the parts of a stone or a piece of iron or whatever else it might be can, by going through different modifications, become flesh and bone and compose an organic living body, they can also therefore make a human or some other animal capable of feeling and knowledge, and for that nothing is needed apart from the arrangement or movements that are ordinarily found in humans or other animals.

---

76 Meslier, *Mémoire des pensées et sentiments de Jean Meslier*, in *Œuvres complètes*, ed. by Desné, vol. 2, p. 460.
77 Meslier, *Anti-Fénelon*, ed. by Jean Deprun, in Meslier, *Œuvres complètes*, ed. by Desné, vol. 3, p. 244, n. 22. Deprun quotes Vernière as saying (in his *Spinoza et la pensée française avant la Révolution*, 1954, t. 2, p. 368, n. 3) that Meslier 'décrit, cinquante ans avant Diderot, le processus d'"animalisation" du *Rêve de d'Alembert*' [describes, fifty years before Diderot, the process of "animalisation" from the *D'Alembert's Dream*].

This view of the individual (whether animal or human) as composite and as depending on its particular organisation for any specific character or capacities was also shared by Spinoza and Buffon. Spinoza simply states:

> The human body is composed of a great many individuals of different natures, each of which is highly composite.[78]

Buffon's amplifying style presents the same point differently and more repetitively, but is substantively identical:

> [...] un individu n'est qu'un tout uniformément organisé dans toutes ses parties intérieures, un composé d'une infinité de figures semblables et de parties similaires, un assemblage de germes ou de petits individus de la même espèce, lesquels peuvent tous se développer de la même façon, suivant les circonstances, et former de nouveaux tous composés comme le premier.[79]

> An individual is nothing more than a whole uniformly organised in all its internal parts, a compound of infinite shapes and similar parts, an assemblage of seeds or of mini individuals of the same species which are all capable of developing in the same way, circumstances permitting, and forming new ones all put together just like the first.

Buffon always takes great care to avoid provocation and also to avoid seeming materialist (the two being synonymous), so he will not touch directly on anything which casts doubt on the divine, and rather than talking about how inert matter might acquire or already possess in latent form the ability to think, he looks at it the other way round, describing how living matter becomes dead matter. This is a clever move, as it implicitly retains the notion of the movement between different forms of matter:

> [...] il me paroît que la division générale qu'on devroit faire de la matière, est *matière vivante* et *matière morte*, au lieu de dire matière organisée et matière brute ; le brut n'est que le mort, je pourrois le prouver par cette quantité énorme de coquilles et d'autres dépouilles des animaux vivans qui font la principale substance des pierres, des marbres, des craies et des marnes, des terres, des tourbes, et de plusieurs autres matières que

---

78  Spinoza, *Ethics*, p. 44: II/102, postulate 1. See above, on Bordeu and the composite animals.
79  Buffon, *Histoire des animaux* in *Histoire naturelle*, vol. 2 [1749], *Œuvres*, p. 144.

nous appellons brutes, et qui ne sont que les débris et les parties mortes d'animaux ou de végétaux [...].[80]

It seems to me that the general division that one should make in matter is that of *living matter* and *dead matter*, instead of talking about organised matter and base matter; base matter is nothing other than dead matter, and I would be able to prove it with the vast quantity of shells and other animal remains which make up the principle substance of all sorts of stone, marble, chalk, clay, earth, peat, and many other sorts of matter which we call base, and which are nothing other than the debris and dead parts of animals or plants.

Bonnet, who is also averse to making any pronouncements that may seem to undermine religion, and who in fact goes to great lengths to demonstrate his piety with fervent prayers and thanks to God,[81] avoids generalising statement insofar as he can, instead talking in detail about the different forms of embodied matter and about the similarities and divergences between plant and animal life:

Comme la Plante, [l'Animal] végete: comme elle, il reçoit du dehors l'aliment qui le fait croître: comme elle, il multiplie. Mais à ces différentes actions, se joint chez lui le sentiment ou la perception de ce qui se passe dans son intérieur.[82]

Like the plant, the animal vegetates: like it, the animal receives nourishment from outside that makes it grow: like it, the animal multiplies. But to these different actions can also be added feeling or the perception of what takes place inside it.

Bonnet as we see is looking hard at the processes—here nutrition and reproduction—that are shared by both kinds of life form, and what differentiates the animal from the vegetable is qualitative in the sense that it is completely different but also quantitative in that it is an addition to a shared common root. He also looks a great deal at nutrition and at changing shape and size over time, as influenced by nutrition;[83] we see Diderot picking this point up in the *Observations sur Hemsterhuis*, where he reflects with interest that thanks to the food he has ingested,

---

80   Buffon, *Histoire des animaux* in *Histoire naturelle*, vol. 2 [1749], *Œuvres*, p. 157.
81   See for example Bonnet, *Contemplation de la nature* [1764] in *Œuvres d'histoire naturelle et de philosophie*, vol. 4, t. 7, pp. 185, 187.
82   Bonnet, *Contemplation de la nature* [1764], pp. 177–78.
83   Bonnet, *Corps organisés*, p. 100.

and having as a baby 'experienced sensation over the length of a foot and a half', he now 'experiences sensation along the length of five feet and a bit'.[84] Diderot finds these transformative processes fascinating and also moving: he becomes exasperated with Hemsterhuis's plodding exposition of this materialist doxa:

> Et ce passage d'un règne à un autre, et ces êtres intermédiaires qui semblent appartenir à la plante et à l'animal, ne vous touchent-ils point?[85]
>
> And this journey from one kingdom to another, and these intermediary beings which seem to belong to both plant and animal life, do they not move you?

Diderot's point is that it is touching and awe-inspiring to contemplate, and indeed it is a particular feature of his materialism that he finds it so exciting and dynamic, where others simply see the petrifying gaping absence of the divine. Perhaps this is part of what Élisabeth de Fontenay is alluding to in the captivating title of her study on Diderot, *Le Matérialisme enchanté*.[86]

One of Diderot's principal and gloomiest interlocutors, Jean-Jacques Rousseau, who makes sure that his later works reject materialism, morosely engages with the question of the transformability of matter in an important footnote to the 'Profession de foi du vicaire savoyard' in *Émile* (1762). As we see, rocks are still playing a key role in the debate, and Meslier had failed to do away with them:

> Il me semble que loin de dire que les rochers pensent, la philosophie moderne a découvert au contraire que les hommes ne pensent point [...] Mais s'il est vrai que toute matière sente, où concevrai-je l'unité sensitive ou le moi individuel ? sera-ce dans chaque molécule de matière ou dans des corps agrégatifs ? Placerai-je également cette unité dans les fluides et dans les solides, dans les mixtes et dans les éléments ? il n'y a, dit-on, que

---

84 And he continues: 'Comment suis-je parvenu avec l'âge à sentir sur une longueur de cinq pieds et quelques pouces. J'ai mangé. J'ai digéré. J'ai animalisé' [How, with age, did I manage to feel along the length of five feet and a few inches. I ate. I digested. I animalised]. Diderot, *Observations sur La 'Lettre sur l'homme et ses rapports' de Hemsterhuis*, DPV, vol. 24, p. 304 (§136). The editors comment that he probably found the word 'animaliser' in Bonnet who uses it a lot or alternatively in Buffon.
85 Diderot, *Observations sur La 'Lettre sur l'homme et ses rapports' de Hemsterhuis*, DPV, vol. 24, p. 291.
86 Elisabeth Fontenay, *Le Matérialisme enchanté* (Paris: B. Grasset, 1981).

des individus dans la nature! Mais quels sont ces individus ? Cette pierre est-elle un individu ou une agrégation d'individus ?[87]

It seems to me that far from saying that rocks think, modern philosophy has discovered, on the contrary, that men do not think. [...] But if it is true that all matter can feel, then where shall I conceive the sensitive unity or the individual *I* to be? Will it be in each molecule of matter or in the aggregate bodies? Shall I put this unity equally in fluids and solids, in compounds and elements? There are, it is said, only individuals in nature. But what are these individuals? Is this stone an individual or an aggregate of individuals?

There is no room to unpack Rousseau's multiple referents, which surely include Diderot, here.[88] What is important for our purposes is to see that Rousseau cogently presents some of the problems with this aspect of materialist theory: they are problems which Diderot will pay close attention to, and reply to, in both the *Rêve de d'Alembert* and the *Éléments de physiologie*.[89]

## e. The Natural Processes of Material Transformation

*These natural processes of the material transformation of any living body include not only nutrition but reproduction and also death and decomposition. Reproduction involves the metamorphoses of forms and moreover their identical reproduction from one generation to another, writes Buffon with amazement. However, the moment when an actual living being can be said to have died is very difficult to determine: for example, at what point is a drowned man really dead, asks Leibniz? It is also difficult to identify the beginning and the end of*

---

87  Rousseau, *Émile*, in *Œuvres complètes*, vol. 4, p. 584 (authorial footnote); Jean-Jacques Rousseau, *Emile*, trans. by Allan Bloom (London: Penguin, 1979), p. 279 (slightly amended).
88  See the editorial footnote, Rousseau, *Œuvres complètes*, vol. 4, pp. 1540–41 for an overview of the philosophical interlocutors. François Pépin also reads the 'Profession de foi du vicaire savoyard' as containing anti-Diderot anti-materialist polemic, in his *La Philosophie expérimentale de Diderot et la chimie: philosophie, sciences et arts* (Paris: Classiques Garnier, 2012), pp. 480–83.
89  See the first part of the *Rêve de d'Alembert*, the 'Suite d'un entretien entre M. d'Alembert et M. Diderot' which is all about this question; see also d'Alembert's dream-speech ('Laissez là vos individus' etc, *Le Rêve de d'Alembert*, DPV, vol. 17, p. 138 (and in *Le Rêve de d'Alembert*, ed. by Duflo, p. 104) and in the *Éléments de physiologie*, see 'L'homme peut donc être regardé comme un assemblage d'animaux', DPV 501/PQ 338/MT 314 (and quoted above).

sensation, write Buffon and Bonnet. La Mettrie and Condillac take this to an extreme, and wonder whether an atom can think: they are genuinely asking the sort of question that we just saw Rousseau deriding.

## i. Reproduction

Diderot is moved when he contemplates the steps between one life form and another: Buffon asks us to feel admiration and wonder as we look at how a species renews itself and at how long that species can last (by extension therefore, he suggests that it does not necessarily last forever—this is something Diderot thinks about quite explicitly, both in the *Rêve de d'Alembert* and the *Éléments de physiologie*):

> Cependant, quelqu'admirable que cet ouvrage [le corps d'un animal] nous paroisse, ce n'est pas dans l'individu qu'est la plus grande merveille, c'est dans la succession, dans le renouvellement et dans la durée des espèces que la Nature paroît tout-à-fait inconcevable.[90]

> Yet, however admirable this work [the body of an animal] may appear to us, it is not even a single individual which is the greatest marvel, it's in the succession, the renewal and the continuation of species that nature appears utterly inconceivable.

There are long chapters in the *Éléménts de physiologie* about human reproduction, its mechanisms, its organs, its mysteries and its mistakes: this is matter visibly moving through transformative processes, and Diderot's curiosity about how it works and how it affects human experience—the two parts going hand in hand—is inexhaustible.

## ii. The Beginning and End of Death

Buffon's reclassification of matter into *matière vivante* and *matière morte* does not of course preclude its movement from one state to the other, and indeed his definition assumes transformation over time, in that what is dead must have once lived, because otherwise it cannot have died. This seems unproblematic. However, the difficulty is in assessing when death has occurred. What we now call a coma is the test case which is often referred to; in Diderot this discussion will be refracted through

---

[90] Buffon, *Histoire des animaux* in *Histoire naturelle*, vol. 2 [1749], Œuvres, pp. 134–35.

the tale of a man thought to be drowned who then comes back to life.[91] Leibniz was debating the issue in his *Monadology*, written in French in 1714, the year after Diderot's birth (perhaps, by 1714, he had reached a foot and a half in length).[92] As usual, Leibniz was in the middle of a polemic with the Cartesians:

> Ils ont confondu avec le vulgaire un long étourdissement avec une mort à la rigueur.[93]

> They, like the uneducated, mistook an extended lack of consciousness for actual death.

Buffon casts this sort of question in more diplomatic terms, preferring instead to talk about 'l'incertitude des signes de la mort', writing that:

> [...] entre la mort et la vie il n'y a souvent qu'une nuance si foible, qu'on ne peut l'apercevoir même avec toutes les lumières de l'art de la Médecine et de l'observation la plus attentive [...][94]

> the difference between death and life is often so faint that it is imperceptible even to those equipped with all the knowledge of the art of Medicine and with the keenest powers of observation.

The issue turns on sensation and perception: if the person does not respond to stimulus and appears to feel nothing, and if the observing doctor cannot perceive any movement, pulse or breathing, then the person may still not be dead, but they cannot be reached by the normal processes of empirical investigation, that is by sensation or perception. So there is a methodological problem. In the *Éléments de physiologie*, in a sub-section on the soul, or rather, the meaninglessness of the notion, Diderot asks about life and sensibility in the seeming absence

---

91 *Éléments de physiologie*, DPV 333/PQ 151/MT 154 and also in Cabanis, see below.
92 In fact, Diderot was the first translator into French of the Latin version of the *Monadology*, in his *Encyclopédie* article 'Leibnitzianisme' in *Encyclopédie ou dictionnaire raisonné des sciences, des arts et des métiers, par une société de gens de lettres*, ed. by Denis Diderot and Jean le Rond d'Alembert, 28 vols (Paris: Briasson, David, Le Breton, Durand, 1751-72), vol. 9 (1765), pp. 369b-379b. With thanks to François Pépin for this information.
93 Leibniz, *Monadologie*, p. 14.
94 Buffon, *Histoire naturelle de l'homme* in *Histoire naturelle*, vol. 2 [1749], in *Œuvres*, p. 279.

of both.[95] He specifically considers melancholic lethargy, catalepsy and drowning:

> Où est-elle [l'âme] dans le noyé, qu'on rappelle à la vie de l'état de mort, ou d'un état qui lui ressemble tellement, que si le noyé n'avait point été secouru, il aurait persévéré dans cet état sans éprouver d'autre changement qu'une torpeur plus profonde.[96]

> Where is it [the soul] in the drowned man, who can be recalled to life from the state of death, or from a state which resembles it so closely, that if the drowned man had not been treated, he would have continued in that same state without experiencing any change other than a deeper torpor.

The question turns on when sensation begins or ends in a living person, whether animals or even plants have feeling, and what sensation with limited brain power might mean in terms of experience. Buffon states quite clearly that the 'espèce de sentiment' [sort of feeling] that is mechanical sensation is very widely shared, and that it is by no means easy to differentiate the animal from the plant kingdoms according to that criterion: 'Cette différence entre les animaux et les végétaux non seulement n'est pas générale, mais même n'est pas bien décidée' [this difference between animals and plants is not only not a general one, it is not even clear or agreed upon].[97]

### iii. The Beginning and End of Sensation

Bonnet asks at which level of organised bodies feeling is first manifested, and he does not appear to have an answer:

> Mais quel est précisément l'échellon où le sentiment commence à se manifester?
>
> Du Polype ou de la Moule à une Plante, la distance paroït bien petite.[98]

> But what exactly is the stage at which feeling starts to be manifested?

---

95 DPV 333–34/PQ 150–51/MT 154.
96 DPV 333/PQ 151/MT 154.
97 Buffon, *Histoire des animaux* in *Histoire naturelle*, vol. 2 [1749], in *Œuvres*, p. 137.
98 Bonnet, *Contemplation de la nature*, in *Œuvres d'histoire naturelle et de philosophie*, vol. 4, t. 7, p. 179.

> From the polyp or from the mussel to a plant, the difference seems extremely slight.

La Mettrie inverts the model, not asking how low down the ladder feeling begins, instead showing us a human, from the top of the ladder, pushed right down to the bottom and reduced to the state of a thinking atom:

> un homme qui perdroit toute mémoire, seroit un atome pensant.[99]
>
> someone who lost all their memory would be a thinking atom.

Of course, the idea of a thinking atom is a contradiction in terms for those who plot nature along a line from simple to complex, and in any case what La Mettrie probably means is a *feeling* atom rather than a *thinking* one, thought requiring memory. Rousseau's critique of this sort of thinking is more coherent than La Mettrie's, but it still collapses over its own logic:

> J'ai fait tous mes efforts pour concevoir une molécule vivante, sans pouvoir en venir à bout. L'idée de la matière sentant sans avoir des sens me paraît inintelligible et contradictoire. Pour adopter ou rejeter cette idée, il faudrait commencer par la comprendre, et j'avoue que je n'ai pas ce bonheur-là.[100]
>
> I have made every effort to conceive of a living molecule but I have not succeeded. The idea of matter sensing without having senses appears unintelligible and contradictory to me. To accept or to reject this idea, one would have to begin by understanding it, and I admit that I have not been so fortunate.

Rousseau strips the model back one stage further, to the idea of a *living molecule*. In his view, living is synonymous with *feeling*, and so he assumes the model is one with a molecule that feels, although as he then adds, it does not have any senses, so it cannot. Diderot's version is most consistent, and although it does claim that the molecule can feel, it does not confuse the issue by also giving it sensory organs:

---

99 La Mettrie, *Traité de l'âme*, p. 172.
100 Rousseau, *Émile*, in *Œuvres complètes*, vol. 4, p. 575 (authorial footnote); *Emile*, trans. by Allan Bloom, p. 273 (slightly amended).

> L'homme, réduit à un sens, serait fou: il ne reste que la sensibilité, qualité aveugle, à la molécule vivante; rien de si folle qu'elle [...][101]
>
> A human being reduced to one sense would be mad: the only thing left in the living molecule would be sensibility, a blind quality; there's nothing so mad as that [...]

Here we see him thinking in his habitually condensed way about the different levels of sensation as well as the different levels of complexity in organised bodies; we see him comparing the most developed (man) with the least developed (the living molecule), and we see it assessed in relation to medical and/or moral criteria: the man with only one sense would be mad; sensation is all that the living molecule has, and there is nothing madder than it. Here what neither the one-sensed man nor the simply sensory molecule possess is control or self-awareness: they, unlike the writer Diderot in this passage, cannot conduct any comparisons.

## f. Knowledge Derived from the Senses

*The only possible way to know anything is through the senses, write Spinoza and Condillac. La Mettrie, Buffon, Condillac, and Bonnet all set up and follow through the fiction of an initially sensorily-deprived person to work through the implications of this model. Abstract points or examples that are not based in nature, must be avoided, write Spinoza, Fontenelle, Buffon, Bonnet. Condillac's examples tend to be hypothetical fictions, and impossible in nature. Geometers (or mathematicians, as we might call them) can become figures of fun, as we will see, and geometry is often presented as the opposite of knowledge (by Meslier, La Mettrie, and Buffon: even Spinoza calls his own geometrical method 'cumbersome'—twice). Precise research must be drawn on, and in fact there is a corpus of recycled examples. (Condillac, La Mettrie, and Buffon had all written about the man born deaf, from Chartres, and the child brought up by bears in Russia).*[102]

---

101 DPV 486/PQ 318/MT 301.
102 As mentioned before.

## i. Knowledge from the Senses: Anti-Abstraction

The only possible way to know anything is through the senses, write Spinoza, Meslier, and Condillac. Spinoza's *Traité de la réforme de l'entendement*, written in 1661, affirms the importance of empirical method and does so well before Locke's *Essay concerning Human Understanding* (1689): to point out this chronology is not to dislodge Locke from his eminent perch or give Spinoza more prominence but simply to indicate that Locke was not the first to make these arguments, as we said earlier in the chapter. The really important point is that this position with respect to knowledge, that is to say, that it is derived from the external world via the senses, was reiterated in very similar terms over and over again throughout this period and that the reiterations seem to have been part of this century-long effort to get this view accepted, not just by some, and not as a particular philosophical stance, but as the truth. This is what defines this particular group of writers—that they keep repeating themselves and each other—and also what defines Diderot's contribution, which is that after the magisterial synthesis which the *Eléments de physiologie* constitutes, it was no longer necessary to repeat the same things, and natural philosophy could move on; we will see whether the second part of this book bears out such a view.

The reason these writers or philosophers of the mid-seventeenth to the late-eighteenth centuries endlessly repeat the same things, without necessarily or even very often mentioning their other interlocutors or predecessors, is because the validity of their views about nature and the human mind were indeed questioned. In this context therefore it is not right to veer between judgements about originality and plagiarism, or even to cast aspersions about their relative boldness or by contrast the veiled diplomacy of their writings: in a hostile atmosphere of active censorship and the aggressive protection of orthodoxy, it is not really possible for non-orthodox writers and thinkers to exist in a relationship of progress and development from one to the next. Their relationship to one another may well have been fraught with polemic, rivalry, and disagreement, and demonstrably often was, but their relationship to the philosophical positions they were trying to get accepted meant that they simply needed to keep repeating them in various iterations until after more than a hundred years they were accepted.

This, therefore, is what Spinoza writes:

> [...] avant tout il nous est nécessaire de tirer toujours toutes nos idées de choses physiques.[103]

> before anything else we need always to draw all our ideas from physical things.

> [il faut] savoir nous servir de nos sens et faire, d'après des règles et dans un ordre arrêté, des expériences suffisantes pour déterminer la chose que l'on étudie.[104]

> [it is necessary] to know how to use our senses and conduct, according to rules and in an established order, experiments which are sufficient to define the thing being studied.

Spinoza frames his statements as injunctions: we *must* draw our ideas from physical things; we *must* learn how to use our senses and work out how to conduct reasoned and ordered experiments so that we can understand the thing we are studying. Meslier does not express this as an injunction which exhorts us to work and effort, instead presenting our sensory understanding of the world as an innate and effortless ability which he admires:

> J'admire à la vérité cette faculté, et cette puissance que nous avons naturellement de penser, de voir, de sentir, ou de connoitre tout ce que nous faisons, tout ce qui se présente à nous, à nos sens, et à notre entendement.[105]

> I truly admire that faculty and power which we naturally have to think, to see, to feel, or to know everything we are doing, everything that appears to us, to our senses, and to our understanding.

Condillac in the following passage from the *Traité des sensations* of 1754 does not exhort or admire, he states. He sees all our mental operations and emotions as deriving at root from the same thing—sensation. Here the reader may notice a certain analogy with the way in which matter was described in the earlier part of this chapter: the model of the base

---

103 Spinoza, *Traité de la réforme de l'entendement*, §99.
104 Spinoza, *Traité de la réforme de l'entendement*, §103.
105 Meslier, *Mémoire des pensées et sentiments de Jean Meslier*, in *Œuvres complètes*, ed. by Desné, vol. 2, p. 399.

material from which everything is made but which undergoes infinite transformations is the same:

> Le jugement, la réflexion, les desirs, les passions, etc., ne sont que la sensation même qui se transforme différemment.[106]
>
> Judgement, reflection, desires, passions, etc., are nothing other than sensation itself, differently transformed.

Diderot's own *Pensées sur l'interprétation de la nature*, published the same year as Condillac's *Traité*, and in which he draws on the Pascalian tradition of the 'pensée' to produce neatly-shaped maxims, pronounces on this subject as follows:

> Nous avons trois moyens principaux; l'observation de la Nature, la réflexion et l'expérience. L'observation recueille les faits, la réflexion les combine, l'expérience vérifie le résultat de la combinaison.[107]
>
> We have three principal means; the observation of nature, reflection and experience. Observation gathers facts, reflection combines them, experience verifies the result of their combination.

Logically, therefore, these empiricist thinkers—including here Spinoza, Fontenelle, Buffon and Bonnet—wish to avoid any abstract points or examples that are not based in nature. Spinoza sees abstraction as being liable to induce error:

> Il faut ajouter que cette sorte d'erreur provient de ce que l'on conçoit les choses d'une façon trop abstraite.[108]
>
> We should add that this sort of mistake arises from conceptualising things in too abstract a manner.

Fontenelle explains why mathematical thinking does not work when thinking about nature. He does not criticise mathematical thinking in itself; it is simply a mismatch, in that the information available about the physical world is incomplete and therefore liable to error. He writes in his 'Loi de la pensée' [Law of thought]:

---

106 Condillac, *Traité des sensations*, p. 11.
107 Diderot, *Pensées sur l'interprétation de la nature*, DPV, vol. 9, p. 293 ('Pensée' 15).
108 Spinoza, *Traité de la réforme de l'entendement*, §75.

> Comme je vois l'être mathématique entier, nulle idée ne lui peut être contraire; car je le vois par-tout de la même manière, toujours par une idée simple.
>
> Mais comme je ne ne vois pas entier l'être physique de l'homme, je puis appliquer à la partie inconnue de cet être physique une idée prise ailleurs, et qui lui sera contraire. [...]
>
> Ainsi je ne puis concevoir les choses autrement qu'elles ne sont, que lorsqu'une partie de leur être m'est inconnue. Si je connoissois le tout, j'y verrais nécessité absolue d'être ainsi.........[109]

> A complete mathematical being, as I see it, can have no idea contrary to it, for I see it in the same way from all points, always via a simple idea.
>
> But as I cannot see the physical being of a human in their entirety, I might apply to the unknown part of this physical being an idea taken from elsewhere, and which will be contrary to it. [...]
>
> Thus I am only able to conceive of things as other than they are when a part of their being is unknown to me. If I knew them in their entirety, I would see the absolute necessity of their being as they are.

Meslier wages war on abstraction, and makes a conceptually important point when he rejects the idea of talking about matter in an unembodied form:

> De même manière que quoique la santé, et la maladie ne soient que des modifications de la matière, ce ne seroit cependant point proprement la matiere qui se porteroit bien, ni qui seroit malade.[110]

> Similarly, although health and illness are nothing other than modifications of matter, it would still not be at all right to say that it was the matter that was well or ill.

It is not matter that is healthy or ill; it is an animal or a human that is.[111]

Nor is Meslier's attack on abstraction itself abstract; it is specifically targeted at Cartesians and/or geometers. To what extent these two terms are interchangeable is not clear, but usage suggests that the earlier

---

109 Fontenelle, 'Loi de la pensée', in 'Fragments d'un traité de la raison humaine', in *Œuvres complètes*, ed. by Alain Niderst (Paris: Fayard, 1996), vol. 7, pp. 475–98, p. 494.
110 Meslier, *Mémoire des pensées et sentiments de Jean Meslier*, in *Œuvres complètes*, ed. by Desné, vol. 3, p. 90.
111 This is a similar sort of idea to what we saw Meslier expressing in the *Anti-Fénelon* about it not being *matter* that thinks, but a person, etc. (see above).

texts tend to talk about Cartesians when making this anti-abstraction argument, whereas the later ones attack geometers instead. Meslier is in the earlier camp, and his philippic is typically vitriolic. The difficulty is in deciding which particular iteration of his abuse is most pertinent, and in working out where to cut it:

> Donc il est ridicule à nos cartésiens de pretendre que nos pensées, que nos raisonnemens, que nos connoissances, que nos desirs, que nos volontés, et que les sentimens que nous avons de plaisir, ou de douleur, d'amour ou de haine, de joye et de tristesse... etc., ne soient pas des modifications de la matiere sous pretexte que ces sortes de modifications de notre âme ne sont point étendües en longueur, en largeur, et en profondeur, et sous prétexte qu'elles ne sont ni rondes, ni carrées, et qu'elles ne peuvent (être) divisées ou coupées en pieces et en morceaux.[112]

> It is therefore ridiculous of our Cartesians to claim that our thoughts, arguments, knowledge, desires, will, or the feelings that we have of pleasure, pain, love or hatred, of joy or sadness... etc., cannot be modifications of matter, on the pretext that these sorts of modifications of our soul do not stretch out lengthways, widthways, or have any depth, and on the pretext that they are not round or square and that they cannot be cut up into little bits and pieces.

His particular angle (although perhaps that geometrical metaphor is not one he would have chosen himself) is that Cartesians only conceive of material embodiment in bluntly physical, measurable terms, and that their view that our soul—which Meslier here equates with our thoughts, our reasoning, our knowledge, our desire, our impulses, and feelings of pleasure, pain, love, hatred, joy and sadness—cannot be material because none of these thoughts or feelings is physically locatable, is ridiculously reductive of what matter is. (Interestingly, as a critique of those who are supposed to wish to account for emotion and experience in measurable and even algebraic terms, it is almost identical to what Henri Bergson will later argue in his *Données immédiates de la conscience* of 1889.)

La Mettrie is a spiritual son of Meslier, in his energetic tirades at least: in his *Traité de l'âme* (1745) he lambasts geometers and their inability

---

[112] Meslier, *Mémoire des pensées et sentiments de Jean Meslier*, in *Œuvres complètes*, ed. by Desné, vol. 3, p. 33. Spinoza refers to fictions such as having an 'âme carrée' [a square soul] (*Traité sur la réforme de l'entendement*, p. 58).

to work outside their 'petite sphère', giving a fairly comprehensive list of the things he considers them incapable of: physics, astronomy, metaphysics, ethics, physiology, and literature.[113]

Buffon, whose style is normally so different from both Meslier and La Mettrie, is as opposed to the notion of geometry and abstraction in the study of nature as they are, and nearly as hyperbolic:

> Toutes ces abstractions sont des échafaudages pour soûtenir notre jugement, et combien n'avons-nous pas brodé sur ce petit nombre de définitions qu'emploie la Géométrie ! nous avons appelé simple tout ce qui se réduit à ces définitions, et nous appellons composé tout ce qui ne peut s'y réduire aisément, [...] toutes ces figures géométriques n'existent que dans notre imagination, [...] Dans la Nature au contraire, l'abstrait n'existe point, rien n'est simple et tout est composé [...][114]

> All these abstractions are scaffolding we use to support our judgement. How many times have we embroidered on the very few definitions that Geometry uses! We called simple everything that could be reduced to these definitions, and composed everything which cannot easily be reduced to them, [...] all those geometric figures exist only in our imagination, [...] In nature on the contrary, there is no abstract, nothing is simple and everything is composed.

Buffon's critique posits that the conceptual model geometry gives us of 'simple' and 'complex', that is a few 'simple' definitions built up into complex structures ('échafaudages') is purely abstract, and a sort of fiction that exists in our imagination, while in nature, there is no abstract, and there is no simple: everything is complex.

Diderot has his own pithy ways of expressing his opposition to abstraction. We meet them throughout his œuvre. In the early *Pensées philosophiques* (1746) we find:

> Toutes les billevesées de la métaphysique ne valent pas un argument *ad hominem*.[115]

---

113 La Mettrie, *Traité de l'âme*, p. 199.
114 Buffon, *Histoire des animaux* in *Histoire naturelle*, vol. 2 [1749], in *Œuvres*, p. 145.
115 Diderot, *Pensées philosophiques*, ed. by Michel Delon, in *Œuvres philosophiques*, ed. by Michel Delon and Barbara de Negroni (Paris: Gallimard, 2010), p. 8 ('Pensée' 17), and also Denis Diderot, *Pensées philosophiques, Additions aux pensées*, ed. by Jean-Claude Bourdin (Paris: GF Flammarion, 2007), p. 8 ('Pensée' 17).

All the nonsense of metaphysics is not worth a single *ad hominem* argument.

We meet it again in less condensed form in the *Pensées sur l'interprétation de la nature* (1753):

> On en a conclu que c'était à la philosophie expérimentale à rectifier les calculs de la géométrie, et cette conséquence a été avouée même par les géomètres. Mais à quoi bon corriger le calcul géométrique par l'expérience? N'est-il pas plus court de s'en tenir au résultat de celle-ci?[116]

> It was concluded that it was the job of experimental philosophy to correct the calculations of geometry, and this consequence has been accepted by the geometers themselves. But what is the point of correcting geometric calculation by experience and experiment? Isn't it quicker just to use the results of the latter?

He rejects any equation (le mot juste) of geometry and 'experimental philosophy', that is, the study of nature, asserting that there is no need to correct mathematical calculation with an experiment: he recommends instead simply leaving the calculations aside, and sticking with the results of the experiment. This would constitute knowledge and information about the works of nature, that is to say, the truth, where a calculation cannot, because it's an abstraction.

In the *Principes philosophiques sur la matière et du mouvement* of 1770 he returns to the same theme, interestingly (for the editor of the *Encyclopédie*) rejecting the sort of thinking which seems to want to be rigorous by relying on uniform definitions. Diderot rejects the uniformity:

> Il ne faut jamais dire, quand on est physicien, *le corps comme corps*; car ce n'est plus faire de la physique, c'est faire des abstractions qui ne mènent à rien.[117]

> As a natural philosopher, one should never say *the body as body*, because that means stopping doing natural philosophy, and instead creating abstractions which lead nowhere.

---

116 Diderot, *Pensées sur l'interprétation de la nature*, DPV, vol. 9, p. 286 ('Pensée' 2).
117 Diderot, *Principes philosophiques sur la matière et le mouvement*, ed. by Barbara de Negroni in *Œuvres philosophiques*, ed. by Michel Delon and Barbara de Negroni (Paris: Gallimard, 2010), p. 449.

As we have seen, all these writers have reservations about the usefulness of geometrical abstraction, and some of them reject it outright. They want empirical evidence and specific case studies, and interestingly, there is a corpus of examples which they recycle. Condillac and La Mettrie write about the English boy born blind, whose cataracts were removed by William Cheselden, the man born deaf from Chartres, and the child brought up by bears in Lithuania; Buffon also writes about the bear child. Diderot of course also engages with this material particularly fully in his *Lettre sur les aveugles* (1749) and *Lettre sur les sourds et muets* (1751), while the anecdote about the child growing up with bears features in the *Éléments de physiologie*.[118]

## ii. Sensory-Deprivation Fictions

Surprisingly perhaps, given that empiricism has an avowed status approaching a dogma amongst these writers, they often resort to fictions, specifically imaginary stories of sensory deprivation. Perhaps, however, we ought not to be surprised: insofar as there is a rather limited number of known cases, all of which are multiply recycled, it is likely that these Lockean writers will wish to find other ways of testing or investigating or simply communicating their hypotheses. A 'fiction' was indeed often the only way to test out the sort of hypothesis we would now blithely call 'scientific' in an era when other forms of testing were simply not possible for lack of technical capability, if for no other reason. By 'fiction', therefore, we mean following through a given idea in the imagination rather than in reality.[119] La Mettrie, freely adapting the early Christian apologist Arnobius's 'belle conjecture' [beautiful conjecture]—one of the 'plus beaux morceaux de l'Antiquité' [the most exquisite pieces of Antiquity], he says—imagines a baby kept underground in complete sensory deprivation and without human contact until adulthood in the

---

118 See above, for the references to these recycled cases. See also Caroline Warman, 'Comment écrire le vécu? Diderot et le problème matérialiste de l'abstraction', in *Matérialisme(s) en France au XVIIIe siècle. Entre littérature et philosophie*, ed. by Adrien Paschoud and Barbara Selmeci Castioni (Berlin: Frank and Timme, 2019), pp. 103–13.

119 See Richard Scholar and Alexis Tadié, eds, *Fiction and the Frontiers of Knowledge in Europe, 1500–1800* (Farnham: Ashgate, 2010), https://doi.org/10.4324/9781315582276.

*Traité de l'âme* (La Mettrie's fictions and examples are often cruel).[120] Buffon imagines a fully-grown man emerging into consciousness, asking

> Si cet homme vouloit nous faire l'histoire de ses premières pensées, qu'auroit-il à nous dire ? quelle seroit cette histoire ? Je ne puis me dispenser de le faire parler lui-même, afin d'en rendre les faits plus sensibles : ce récit philosophique qui sera court, ne sera pas une digression inutile.[121]
>
> If this man were to want to tell us the story of his first thoughts, what would he say? What would this story be? I cannot allow myself not to make him speak for himself, so that the facts make a greater impression: this philosophical tale will not take long, and will not be a pointless digression.

What follows is Buffon's fictional first-person narrative of this suddenly-awoken man's experience: 'je ne savais ce que j'étais, où j'étais, d'où je venais' [I did not know what I was, where I was, or where I came from], he says (might the famous opening of Diderot's *Jacques le fataliste* be echoing these words?).[122] Buffon's man gushes his amazement over several pages ('je tombais de surprise en surprise' [I tumbled from one surprise to the next])[123] as he coherently and implausibly recounts his sensations and experiences in sequence. Condillac's *Traité des sensations* (1753) famously follows through the fiction of a marble statue first being endowed with sight, then all the other senses in turn (interestingly, he was accused of plagiarising Buffon, while Condillac

---

120 La Mettrie, *Traité de l'âme*, pp. 241–42; See *L'Homme-machine*, in *Œuvres philosophiques*, vol. 1, pp. 99–100 where La Mettrie lists examples of organs continuing to work after death, mixing instructions about how to conduct the experiments with anecdotes about a drunken soldier beheading a rooster and suggestions about dissecting executed criminals, or p. 113, where he describes the flexible state of an amniotic sac immediately before birth, adding that this was a phenomenon 'que j'ai eu le plaisir d'observer dans une femme, morte un moment avant l'Accouchement' [that I had the pleasure of observing in a woman who had died a moment before giving birth], or in the *Traité de l'âme*, p. 240, where La Mettrie boastfully recalls the honour the Maréchal de Saxe did him in providing details about a girl who ate her sister.
121 Buffon, 'Des sens en général', in *Histoire naturelle*, vol. 3 [1749], in *Œuvres*, pp. 302–06 (p. 302).
122 Buffon, 'Des sens en général', p. 302.
123 Buffon, 'Des sens en général', p. 304.

himself rebuts accusations of having plagiarised Diderot's *Lettre sur les sourds et muets*).[124]

In his *Essai analytique sur les facultés de l'âme*, which he did not publish until 1760, Bonnet claims to have been working on a very similar fiction when Condillac's *Traité* was published, and hence felt unable to publish his own version, despite his reservations at Condillac's approach. As we see, his starting point is relatively close both to Buffon (the adult using his senses for the first time) and to Condillac (because he is also using a statue that comes to life):

> Recourons donc à une fiction: elle ne sera pas la Nature; mais elle aura son fondement dans la Nature. [...] Imaginons un Homme dont tous les Sens sont en bon état, mais qui n'a point encore commencé à en faire usage.[125]
>
> Let's have recourse to a fiction: it won't be nature, but it will have its basis in nature. [...] Let's imagine a man whose senses are all in good shape, but who has never yet started to use them.

Let's imagine a man whose senses are all in good working order, but who hasn't yet started to use them. Let's! These fictions are all variously implausible, and also surprisingly unempirical and unphysiological, given that the various case studies of the lifting of sensory deprivation which these writers all allude to show that people have to *learn* to use their senses.[126]

The contrast between the recommended empirical approach and actual practice seems to be most extreme in the case of Condillac and his

---

[124] Buffon, *Œuvres*, p. 1465, n. 15; Condillac, 'Réponse à un reproche qui m'a été fait sur le projet exécuté dans le Traité des sensations', *Traité des sensations*, pp. 277–81.

[125] Condillac, 'Avis important au lecteur', *Traité des sensations*, p. 9.

[126] Rousseau rather entertainingly parodies this particular trope when he has the Savoyard vicar turn the argument back against materialist thinkers: 'Supposons un sourd qui nie l'existence des sons, parce qu'ils n'ont jamais frappé son oreille. [...] Plus je réfléchis sur la pensée et sur la nature de l'esprit humain, plus je trouve que le raisonnement des matérialistes ressemble à celui de ce sourd' [Let us suppose a deaf man who denies the existence of sounds because they have never struck his ear. [...] The more I reflect on thought and on the nature of the human mind, the more I find that the reasoning of materialists resembles that of this deaf man] (*Émile*, in *Œuvres complètes*, vol. 4, p. 585; *Emile*, trans. by Bloom, p. 279-80). Although Rousseau's analogy wittily turns materialists into deaf people, it perhaps gives the materialist standpoint more room for manoeuvre than may first appear, in that the cognitive model of sensory perception is still the referent: faith is like an extra sense, it's not extra-sensory.

statue. His discussion of the human mind is not rooted in any remotely physiologically plausible terms:

> J'avertis donc qu'il est très-important de se mettre exactement à la place de la statue que nous allons observer. Il faut commencer d'exister avec elle, n'avoir qu'un seul sens, quand elle n'en a qu'un [...]: en un mot, il faut n'être que ce qu'elle est.[127]

> I point out therefore that it is very important to put yourself in the exact position of the statue that we are going to be observing. We must start existing with her, have only one sense when she only has one [...]: in a word, we must be nothing other than what she is.

He orders us as readers to put ourselves exactly in the position of the thing we are observing, and to experience its staged and incremental perception with it, while remaining ourselves; we have finally to be *nothing but* it, while simultaneously being the aware readers he wants to persuade. Then there is the fact that this newly-sensorily aware being is made of marble ('l'extérieur tout de marbre' [exterior all of marble]):[128] which not even the most diehard materialist (which Condillac himself is very far from being) would ever attempt to argue possessed the ability to feel.

Diderot will unpick these sorts of inconsistencies in various ways. The first part of *Le Rêve de d'Alembert* (written 1769), stages a discussion between two philosophers: Diderot himself, and his *Encyclopédie* co-editor, the mathematician d'Alembert. Diderot talks d'Alembert through the steps by which a marble statue can become human and acquire sensation: first it must be ground into powder, then added to earth in which food is grown, then become absorbed into the growing plant, and then eaten by the man, finally being absorbed into his flesh and acquiring the ability to feel. This is a hypothesis which is plausible within nature, unlike Condillac's version. In his *Réfutation suivie de l'ouvrage d'Helvétius intitulé 'De L'homme'*, written in 1773–74, that is after the *Rêve de d'Alembert*, and, along with the *Observations sur Hemsterhuis*, an important staging post between the *Rêve* and the *Éléments de physiologie*, we see Diderot being sharper with the woolly thinking that underpins this frequently-recycled trope. The

---

127 Condillac, *Traité des sensations*, p. 9.
128 Condillac, *Traité des sensations*, p. 11.

supposition Diderot is responding to sets forth a statue-man. This is what Helvétius had written:

> Supposons un homme absolument insensible. Mais il serait, dira-t-on, sans idées, par conséquence une pure statue. Soit. Admettons cependant qu'il pût exister et même penser [...]. [129]
>
> Let us suppose a completely unfeeling man. But he would be, it is said, without ideas, and by consequence a pure statue. Fine. But let us accept nonetheless that he could exist and even think.

Diderot reacts as follows, and we see him reply not only to Helvétius but also to Condillac, although his name is not mentioned.

> 'Vous supposez un *homme impassible.*' Mais un homme impassible à votre manière est un bloc de marbre... Vous demandez que ce bloc de marbre pense et ne sente pas ; ce sont deux absurdités : un bloc de marbre ne saurait penser, et il ne saurait non plus penser sans sentir, que sentir sans penser.[130]
>
> 'You suppose a *man without sensation.*' But your sort of man without sensation is a block of marble... You want the block of marble to think and not feel; that is absurd twice over: a block of marble is unable to think, and it would be as unable to think without feeling as it would be to feel without thinking.

For Diderot, this sort of fiction is an absurdity. Of course, as we know, in his own overtly fictional work, that is to say in novels like *La Religieuse* or *Jacques le fataliste*, he always draws attention to the ways in which fiction tests or stretches the truth. In the *Éléments de physiologie*, he never deploys a fictional hypothesis of the statue sort, always using instead a case study or anecdote rooted (or supposedly rooted) in nature and/or lived experience to make or interrogate a particular point. The eagle-eyed reader will have noted the qualification here: his cases are rooted or at least *supposedly* rooted in nature or experience.

Part of what makes Diderot into such an extraordinary writer is that he can always work on (at least) two levels: firstly, working through the implications and ramifications of a given case or model with forensic consistency, while also dialoguing with or even parodying all

---

129 Helvétius, in Diderot, *Réfutation d'Helvétius*, DPV, vol. 24, p. 533.
130 Diderot, *Réfutation d'Helvétius*, DPV, vol. 24, p. 533.

those who have written on similar areas or cases before.[131] We will see an interesting example of this in the next section. In this part we have been looking initially at how the philosophers of this extended period repeatedly claimed that knowledge derives exclusively from sensory perception, then at the case studies they used and recycled, and at the philosophical fictions they also used and recycled, while continuing to seek acceptance for their views. We have also seen how Diderot pointed out and rejected the artificiality of these fictions, insisting on using empirical information, however initially inexplicable.

In the next section, we will move on to look at how these writers understood what happened next in the cognitive sequence: we have five senses, give or take one or two, and they give us ideas. How does that work? Can we *think* of more than one thing at a time? Can we *do* more than one thing at a time?

## g. Multi-Tasking and Levels of Awareness: Thinking and Walking

*It is possible to focus on only one idea at any given time, wrote Pascal and La Mettrie. Ideas flow one from another in a natural sequence: they are born from one another, write Crousaz and La Mettrie. However, our brains may operate on two levels at once, a conscious and an unconscious one, writes Fontenelle. The particular fiction deployed here is of a person walking without realising what he is doing (this person is never a woman). In Spinoza's version and in Fontenelle's, he is sleepwalking; in Leibniz's, he is not paying attention; in Condillac's, he walks right across Paris. In Diderot, he gains a philosophical identity, walks, thinks, forgets, and never trips over.*

Pascal formulates the notion that we can only think about one thing at a time with typical forthright certainty and brevity (and we looked at this in the previous chapter):

---

131  For a brilliant investigation of this doubleness, see Tunstall's study of the *Lettre sur les aveugles*, in *Blindness and Enlightenment*.

> Une seule pensée nous occupe. Nous ne pouvons penser à deux choses à la fois.[132]

> A single thought occupies us. We cannot think of two things at the same time.

La Mettrie says the same thing in his *Traité de l'âme*, and his use of the word 'âme', looking slightly dissonant in this context, shows us that he (provocatively) means it to be understood as *mind*.

> l'Ame ne peut avoir qu'une seule idée distincte à la fois.[133]

> The soul can only have one distinct idea at once.

We encounter this view again—closest to its Pascalian formulation—in the *Éléments*:

> Nous ne pouvons être qu'à une seule chose à la fois.[134]

> We can only be focused on one thing at a time.

But if we can only think of one thing at a time, one thought gives rise to another, in a sort of naturally logical sequence: as La Mettrie puts it, quoting Crousaz almost verbatim:

> *Toutes les pensées,* comme l'observe judicieusement Crousaz, *naissent les unes des autres; la pensée,* (ou plutôt l'Âme dont la pensée n'est qu'un accident,) *se varie et passe par différens états; et suivant la variété de ses états et de ses manières d'être, ou de penser, elle parvient à la connoissance, tantôt d'une chose, tantôt d'une autre. Elle se sent elle-même, elle est à elle-même son objet immédiat; et en se sentant ainsi, elle se représente des choses différentes de soi.*[135]

> *All thoughts,* as Crousaz judiciously observes, *are born from one another; thought* (or rather the soul, of which thought is a mere accident) *varies and passes through different states; and according to the variety of its states and ways of being or thinking, it arrives at knowledge, sometimes of one thing and sometimes of another. It can feel itself, it is its own immediate object; and being*

---

132 Blaise Pascal, *Les Provinciales, Pensées, et Opuscules divers*, ed. by Gérard Ferreyrolles and Philippe Sellier (Paris: Livre de Poche 'La Pochothèque', 2004), p. 1081 (S§453). Blaise Pascal, *Pensées*, trans. by Roger Ariew (Indianapolis, IN: Hackett, 2005), p. 142. Quoted above.
133 La Mettrie, *Traité de l'âme*, p. 186.
134 DPV 468/PQ 294/MT 283.
135 La Mettrie, *Traité de l'âme*, p. 217; Crousaz, *La Logique* (1718), vol. 2, p. 416.

> able to feel itself in this way, it is able to represent things to itself that are not the same as itself.

Crousaz's formulation seems to have been a successful one: Diderot not only uses it in the *Éléments*, but also approves it explicitly:

> Toutes les pensées naissent les unes des autres; cela me semble évident.[136]
>
> All thoughts are born from one other; this seems obvious to me.

However, if one thought is considered as following on from the previous one in a temporal sequence, there can be multiple levels of simultaneous perception, not all of which are actually clearly perceived by us. These perceptions can be followed by decision and action which again are not always conscious. These thinkers are trying to work out how instinct relates to reason and to come up with models that account for different levels of consciousness. Spinoza sets out the problems: they relate in part to our faulty knowledge of bodily functions, in part to questions of divergent behaviour when conscious or unconscious and to related issues of transgression, and in part to the abilities and independence of the body as separate from the mind. Here he evokes the issue of the sleepwalker:

> For no one has yet come to know the structure of the body so accurately that he could explain all its functions—not to mention that many things are observed in the lower animals which far surpass human ingenuity, and that sleepwalkers do a great many things in their sleep which they would not dare to do awake. This shows well enough that the body itself, simply from the laws of its own nature, can do many things which its mind wonders at.[137]

Leibniz is fully engaged with these questions. In his *Nouveaux essais sur l'entendement humain* he describes the 'infinity of perceptions within us' that we do not notice but which all together have an effect, and of which we are aware, at least in a nebulous way:

---

136 DPV 335/PQ 153/MT 156. François Pépin analyses the Leibnizian context to this sentence in his article: 'Diderot et Leibniz Face à la chimie du vivant', in *Leibniz et Diderot: rencontres et transformations*, ed. by Christian Leduc, François Pépin, Anne-Lise Rey, and Mitia Rioux-Beaulne (Paris: Vrin, 2015), pp. 211–35 (p. 222), https://doi.org/10.4000/books.pum.2153.

137 Spinoza, *Ethics*, p. 72.

> [...] il y a mille marques, qui font juger qu'il y a à tout moment une infinité de perceptions en nous, mais sans Apperception et sans Reflexion, c'est à dire des changements dans l'Ame même, dont nous ne nous appercevons pas, parce que ces impressions sont où trop petites & en trop grand nombre, ou trop unies, en sorte qu'elles n'ont rien d'assez distinguant à part, mais jointes à d'autres, elles ne laissent pas de faire leur effet, & de se faire sentir dans l'assemblage, au moins confusément.[138]

> There are a thousand signs that lead us to judge that at any moment there are an infinity of perceptions within us taking place without apperception or reflection, that is to say changes in the soul itself which we do not perceive because these impressions are either too tiny or too numerous or too clumped together, such that there is nothing to distinguish them separately. However, once joined up to others, they do not fail to have their effect and make themselves felt in the assemblage, at least in some confused way.

These *petites perceptions* are what create our tastes and understanding of the world, link us to the world around us.

> Ces petites perceptions sont donc de plus grande efficace qu'on ne pense. Ce sont elles, qui forment ce je ne say quoy, ces gouts, ces images des qualités des sens, claires dans l'assemblage, mais confuses dans les parties; ces impressions que les corps, qui nous environnent, font sur nous & qui enveloppent l'infini; cette liaison que chaque être a avec tout le reste de l'univers.[139]

> These tiny perceptions are much more effective that one might think. It is they who form that je-ne-sais-quoi, those tastes, and those images produced by the qualities of the senses, which are clear when they are put together but confused in their constituent parts; those impressions which the bodies which surround us make on us and which envelop the infinite; that link which every being has with all the rest of the universe.

---

138 Leibniz, *Essais sur l'entendement humain*, pp. 8–9.
139 Leibniz, *Essais sur l'entendement humain*, p. 10. See Richard Scholar, *The Je-Ne-Sais-Quoi in Early Modern Europe: Encounters with a Certain Something* (Oxford: Oxford University Press, 2005), https://doi.org/10.1093/acprof:oso/9780199274406.001.0001 for a helpful discussion of this particular passage, pp. 169–71. With thanks to Richard Scholar for supplying this reference when Covid-19 restrictions prevented me from consulting his book myself. I have also (mostly) used his translation of this passage, which I am happy to record was better than my own!

And they are at work all the time, affecting us in determining our seemingly random decisions in the most concrete form. For Leibniz, they are not random in the slightest:

> (...) ce sont ces petites perceptions qui nous déterminent en bien de rencontres sans qu'on y pense, & qui trompent le vulgaire par l'apparence d'une *indifference d'equilibre*, comme si nous étions indifférens de tourner par exemple à droite ou à gauche.[140]

> It is these tiny perceptions which determine our actions in many encounters without us thinking about it, and which deceive the uneducated by making it seem as if we were paying no attention or were *indifferent* to our balance, as if, for example, we were indifferent as to whether we turned right or left.

Along with the reference to the sleepwalker which Spinoza uses, Leibniz's particular scenario of someone walking along without seeming to use his rational mind to direct him will appear repeatedly in interesting variations: Diderot uses it at least three times, as we will see. Fontenelle's 'Fragment on the instinct', possibly circulating before its first publication in 1757–58, has moved the scenario away from pure sleepwalking: in his version, a man is walking along in a reverie:

> Je suppose un homme qui rêve en marchant, et rencontre en son chemin un pieu dont l'image se peint dans son oeil, mais dont il ne se détourne point, parce qu'il n'y fait point attention.[141]

> Suppose a man who is day-dreaming as he walks along and who encounters a post on his path, the image of which is depicted in his eye, but which does not cause him to swerve because he's not paying it any attention.

Fontenelle discusses at length whether the man does or does not see the post, and whether his ability to see it or not is dependent on whether he is thinking about the post or not. Fontenelle does not resolve his story, and we never find out whether the man did or did not step round the post, although it is established that he could have done. Fontenelle concludes that 'Le cerveau de cet homme supposé est en même temps

---

140 Leibniz, *Essais sur l'entendement humain*, pp. 10–11.
141 Fontenelle, 'Sur l'instinct', in 'Fragments d'un traité de la raison humaine', in *Œuvres complètes*, ed. by Alain Niderst (Paris: Fayard, 1996), vol. 7, pp. 475–98 (p. 470).

dans deux états' [the brain of the man we are imagining is in two states at once].[142] Condillac uses the same example in much extended form in the *Essai*, and he is clearly working with Leibniz's model of the unperceived perceptions, and for him, there is no debate about whether the walking man will avoid the post—now he is in a named place, Paris: not only will the post not trip him up, but he will seamlessly avoid all obstacles:

> L'imagination produit même souvent en nous des effets qui paraîtraient devoir appartenir à la réflexion la plus présente. Quoique fort occupés d'une idée, les objets qui nous environnent continuent d'agir sur nos sens : les perceptions qu'ils occasionnent en réveillent d'autres auxquelles elles sont liées, et celles-ci déterminent certains mouvements dans notre corps. Si toutes ces choses nous affectent moins vivement que l'idée qui nous occupe, elles ne peuvent nous en distraire, et par là il arrive que, sans réfléchir sur ce que nous faisons, nous agissons de la même manière que si notre conduite était raisonnée : il n'y a personne qui ne l'ait éprouvé. Un homme traverse Paris et évite tous les embarras avec les mêmes précautions que s'il ne pensait qu'à ce qu'il fait : cependant il est assuré qu'il était occupé de toute autre chose. Bien plus, il arrive même souvent que, quoique notre esprit ne soit point à ce qu'on nous demande, nous y répondons exactement; c'est que les mots qui expriment la question sont liés à ceux qui forment la réponse, et que les derniers déterminent les mouvements propres à les articuler. La liaison des idées est le principe de tous ces phénomènes.[143]

> Imagination surprisingly often produces effects in us which would seem to necessarily result from the most immediate reflection. Even when we are completely occupied with an idea we're having, the objects which surround us continue to act on our senses: the perceptions which they occasion trigger other connected ones, which in turn determine certain movements in our body. If all these things affect us less vigorously than the idea occupying us, they do not distract us from it, and so it can happen that, without thinking about what we're doing, we continue doing it as if our conduct were rationally decided upon: there's no one who hasn't experienced this. A man walks across Paris and avoids every obstacle with as much care as if he were thinking about it, and yet it is certain that he was thinking about something completely different. Moreover, it surprisingly often happens that, although our mind is not focused on

---

142 Fontenelle, 'Sur l'instinct', p. 472.
143 Condillac, *Essai sur l'origine des connaissances humaines*, ed. by Pariente and Pécharman, p. 103 (I.II. §. 42). He goes on to account for this phenomenon with instinct, which he discredits elsewhere, as we know.

what we are being asked, we answer correctly; the reason being that the words used to formulate the question are connected to those that provide the reply, and that the latter trigger the right movements to articulate it. The way ideas are linked up is the principle underpinning all these phenomena.

This clearly-explained extract is worth giving in full for the link it provides between Leibniz's discussion of unperceived but determining perceptions, Fontenelle's example of the man who successfully walks along while thinking about something else, and Diderot's subsequent elaborations of these themes. Links themselves also become the focus in Condillac's conclusion when he declares that the 'liaison' or linking of ideas is behind all these phenomena. Here the notion of the natural logical sequencing of ideas that we were looking at earlier reappears. For Condillac, however, the phenomena he is describing here are part of instinct, and instinct is still subordinate to reason. Diderot will be continuously interested in instinct throughout his works for the direct access it gives to the laws of nature. In this 'pensée' he explicitly subverts the hierarchy of reason over nature:

> L'instinct va sans cesse regardant, goûtant, touchant, écoutant; et il y aurait peut-être plus de physique expérimentale à apprendre en étudiant les animaux qu'en suivant les cours d'un professeur.[144]
>
> Instinct moves along constantly watching, tasting, feeling, listening, and there may be more experimental natural philosophy to be learnt from studying animals than from attending the lessons of a professor.

In fact, Diderot rarely uses the term 'reason' (there is no chapter on reason in the *Éléments*, as we mentioned earlier): he prefers to talk about the will ('la volonté') whose conscious exercise he also considers to be much exaggerated. In the *Rêve*, Diderot re-uses the scenario of the man acting without consciously willing his actions to turn it into a full portrait of d'Alembert himself, as drawn rather aggressively by his interlocutor, the fictionalised Montpellier vitalist Bordeu, who rounds on d'Alembert when he asks whether Bordeu really does believe that free will is nothing more than the life-long cumulative result of continual small movements of desire and aversion:

---

144 Diderot, *Pensées sur l'interprétation de la nature*, DPV, vol. 9, p. 290 ('Pensée' 10).

> Et c'est vous qui me faites cette question! Vous qui livré à des spéculations profondes, avez passé les deux tiers de votre vie à rêver les yeux ouverts et à agir sans vouloir [...].[145]

> Fancy that question coming from you! You who, buried in your abstruse speculations, have spent two-thirds of your life dreaming with your eyes open and acting quite without volition [...]

We meet this scenario again in the *Observations sur Hemsterhuis* of 1774. This time the role of the philosopher (and therefore supreme rationalist) is played by Hemsterhuis, and the narrative is a little more elaborate:

> Il ne me serait pas difficile de démontrer que Mr Hemsterhuis a passé les trois quarts de sa vie sans vouloir.
>
> Il sort de chez lui la tête occupée d'optique ou de métaphysique; sans vouloir sortir, il est poussé hors de sa porte par un souvenir; chemin faisant, il évite des obstacles, sans y penser; il se rappelle un oubli qui le ramène chez lui, il y revient; et il exécute la chose qu'il avait oublié de faire, toujours à sa pensée. C'est alors qu'il est bien évidemment un automate chassé, détourné, ramené par des causes qui disposent de lui aussi impérieusement, qu'un choc dispose d'un corps choqué.
>
> Sa rêverie philosophique cesse, et il ne sait rien ni de ce qu'il a dit, ni de ce qu'il a fait.[146]

> It would not be difficult for me to show that Mr Hemsterhuis has spent three quarters of his life without exercising his will.
>
> He goes out of his house with his head full of optics or metaphysics; without choosing to go out, he is impelled out of his door by a memory; as he walks along, he avoids any obstacles without thinking about them; he remembers something he had forgotten and so goes back home, where he carries out the thing he'd forgotten to do, still preoccupied with his thoughts. And in this case he is absolutely obviously an automaton, driven out of doors, guided around obstacles, and brought back by causes that propel him as imperiously as a collision propels a body that has been collided into.
>
> Once his philosophical reverie ceases, he has absolutely no idea of what he has been saying or doing.

---

[145] Diderot, *Le Rêve de d'Alembert*, DPV, vol. 17, p. 185; Denis Diderot, *Rameau's Nephew and D'Alembert's Dream*, trans. by Leonard Tancock (London: Penguin, 1966), pp. 216–17.

[146] Diderot, *Observations sur La 'Lettre sur l'homme et ses rapports' de Hemsterhuis*, DPV, vol. 24, p. 308.

We have the single Fontenellian post multiplied into the Condillacian multiple obstacles as Hemsterhuis walks out of his house and unconsciously makes his way somewhere. The narrative has two novel elements—firstly, there is a rather complicated to and fro between remembering and forgetting: Hemsterhuis leaves home because he has remembered something, and then he comes back again because he has forgotten something else. He is doing his remembering and forgetting without conscious awareness, 'toujours à sa pensée'—still immersed in his thought about optics or metaphysics: in Diderot's words, he is an automaton, a body simply moving as pushed. Secondly—and still on the theme of memory—once he emerges from his 'rêverie philosophique' he has no memory of what he has said or done. This, for Diderot, appears to be tantamount to not having been consciously aware of making any decisions: what will be remembered, is what was being consciously thought because that is where the attention and the will were.

This scenario appears again in the *Éléments*, not once but twice, in the chapters on the will (III.vi, 'Volonté') and on the organs (III.viii, 'Des organes'). Diderot separates out the two strands of conscious decision-making and instinct, and develops both into fuller narrative elaborations.

> Histoire expérimentale de [l'homme réel, agissant, occupé et mû]. Je le suis et l'examine; c'était un géomètre. [...] La rue, où demeure cet ami, est embarrassée de pierres, notre géomètre serpente entre ces pierres, il s'arrête tout court. Il se rappelle que ses lettres sont restées sur sa table, ouvertes, non cachetées [...] il revient sur ses pas, il allume sa bougie, il cachette ses lettres, il les porte lui-même à la poste; de la poste il regagne la maison où il se propose de dîner; il y entre, il s'y trouve au milieu d'une société de philosophes ses amis. On parle de la liberté et il soutient à cor et à cri que l'homme est libre: je le laisse dire, mais à la chute du jour, je le tire en un coin et je lui demande compte de ses actions. Il ne sait rien, mais rien de tout ce qu'il a fait; et je vois que machine pure, simple, et passive de différents motifs qui l'ont mû, loin d'avoir été libre, il n'a pas même produit un seul acte exprès de sa volonté [...].[147]

> Experimental story [of a man who is real, acting, occupied, and propelled]. I follow him and watch him closely: this man is a mathematician. [...] The road where this friend lives is cluttered with stones, our mathematician

---

147 DPV 485/PQ 315–16/MT 300.

weaves between them and then stops short. He remembers that his letters are still on his table, open, and unsealed [...] he goes back home, lights his candle, seals his letters, takes them to the post-office himself, and from there goes to the house where he means to dine; in he goes and finds himself in the midst of a group of philosophers who are his friends. Freedom is the topic of discussion, and he makes a great fuss about maintaining that man is free. I let him get on with it, but in the evening, I pull him aside and ask him to give me an account of what he's been doing. He has absolutely no idea of his actions, and I see that he is a pure and simple machine, the passive recipient of the different motives which have driven him, and that far from being free, he has not produced one single action specifically of his own volition [...].

The narrative illustrates the underlying philosophical question much more clearly than the others while still retaining certain familiar features—the road with the stones, the deep reverie, the forgetting, and then—new features, these—the philosophical discussion about free will amongst like-minded friends, and the presence of the watching friend throughout, who calls him to account. This narrative has been taken to be a return to Bordeu's portrait of d'Alembert, with Diderot as the wise observer, and the baron d'Holbach as the friend at whose house he was debating philosophy and eating dinner. It is highly plausible that Diderot was indeed thinking directly about these particular friends, not least because in the Saint-Petersburg manuscript of the *Éléments de physiologie* he specifies the actual road on which d'Holbach lived, rue Royale-Saint-Roch.[148] However, this is not the only reading: as we have seen, one philosopher can be replaced by another, and the narrative has a very real existence in prior tellings that do not describe an outing by d'Alembert one fine day. And of course, Diderot uses it again—this time without d'Alembert—just a few pages later:

> Comment se fait-il que nous traversions Paris, à travers toutes sortes d'obstacles, profondément occupés d'une idée, par conséquent parfaitement distraits sur tout ce qui se rencontre, se passe, nous touche, s'oppose à nous, nous environne, sans accidents, sans nous tuer, sans blesser les autres? Comment se fait-il que dans les choses de pure habitude et de pure sensation nous les fassions d'autant mieux que nous y pensons moins? Nous montons parfaitement bien notre escalier,

---

148 DPV p. 485, n. 369.

pendant la nuit, si nous n'y pensons pas. Nous commençons à tatonner quand nous y pensons. Le jour, l'esprit occupé, nous le montons, nous le descendons comme s'il faisait nuit. Il y a plus: il fait nuit en plein midi, dans les rues, pour celui qui pense prondément et nuit profonde. L'œil nous mène; nous sommes l'aveugle. L'œil est le chien qui nous conduit [...].[149]

How does it happen that we can walk right across Paris and around all sorts of obstacles when we're profoundly preoccupied by an idea, and hence perfectly unaware of everything on our route, everything taking place, affecting us, blocking us, surrounding us, and do all this without mishap, without getting killed or hurting anyone? How does it happen that in the case of things related to pure habit or pure sensation, the less we think about them, the better we do them? We can get up our stairs perfectly at night-time, as long as we aren't thinking about what we're doing. The instant we start thinking about it, we start groping our way. By day, when our mind is preoccupied, we go up and down them as if it were night-time. There's more: at mid-day it's night-time and darkest night too for someone in the streets who's deep in thought. Our eyes lead us; we are blind. Our eyes are the dog which guides us [...].

This is the same scenario, but 'we' (the author and his readers, in companionable complicity) are now the actors, walking across Paris oblivious to everything while never falling over and never knocking anyone else over either. For all our conscious awareness of our surroundings, it might as well be pitch black. And indeed, we are blind: our eye (just the one) leads us; it is a guide dog for the blind. Diderot continues to develop this idea: our organs (our senses, our inner organs, and even our limbs all count as organs for Diderot) have their own animal life and independence (and we will look further at this idea in the next chapter). Thus: 'l'œil est un animal dans un animal, exerçant très bien ses fonctions tout seul' [the eye is an animal within an animal, carrying out its functions very well all by itself]:[150] over the course of the rest of the chapter, Diderot calmly works through the idea of the independence of organs, how they have their own tastes and dislikes, illnesses and varying states of health. The logical conclusion is inevitably that:

---

149 DPV 499–500/PQ 336–37/MT 313. Terada signals a further passage which also addresses the question of involuntary movement, from Marat's *De l'homme*, see *Éléments*, ed. by Terada, p. 496, Source X.
150 DPV 500/PQ 337/MT 314.

> L'homme peut donc être regardé comme un assemblage d'animaux [...].[151]
>
> Man can therefore be regarded as an assemblage of animals [...].

This provides the new starting point for Diderot's consideration of bodily and emotional states, along with logical consequences for differing ethical positions. It is very thorough-going determinism, and it leaves selfhood and identity in a somewhat precarious position.

## h. Selfhood and Memory

*If we are only ephemeral body, and not eternal soul or reason, then what are we? The body has a self, and that self is coterminous with memory, write Condillac and Bonnet. What then is memory? Memory must be some kind of imprint, agree Spinoza, Leibniz, La Mettrie, Condillac, Bonnet, and Diderot: or is it? asks Bonnet; there are interesting phenomena related to the memory of different languages, and to memorising verse, explain Spinoza, La Mettrie and Diderot. Diderot considers brain and memory as a self-reading self-writing book.*

When Condillac considers the question of the statue's self, this is what he decides:

> Son *moi* n'est que la collection des sensations qu'elle [la statue] éprouve, et de celles que la mémoire lui rappelle.[152]
>
> Her *self* is nothing other than the collection of sensations which she [the statue] feels, and which come to her memory.

Condillac leaves no room for manoeuvre: the self is *nothing but* the combined feelings of the statue, along with those sensations retained by the memory. It is a hardline reductive definition, particularly for those of us whose memory is faulty. Not all philosophers are willing to be so brutal. Bonnet for example cannot quite bring himself to say it, when writing about *his* statue's 'personality':

---

151 DPV 501/PQ 338/MT 314.
152 Condillac, *Traité des sensations*, p. 56 (I.vi): there's an obvious translation problem here in gendering or not gendering the statue. Condillac uses the feminine form automatically, because statue is a feminine noun, and the female characterisation he develops is also supported by the fact that the statue is also of a woman. We therefore also follow the feminine.

> Sa personnalité est devenue plus composée; parce que le Moi s'est approprié par la Réminiscence un plus grand nombre de sensations. Son Essence personnelle a reçu successivement de nouvelles déterminations. Je sens que cette proposition exige que je la développe un peu plus.¹⁵³

> Her personality became more complex because the self acquired a greater number of sensations through its memory. Her personal essence was successively determined in new ways by this means. I feel that this proposition requires further development.

Bonnet does say that 'personality' becomes more complex the more sensations its memory has banked up; he also says that someone's 'personal essence' acquires new aspects over time with sensations; finally he admits that he needs to go into it a bit further. These various statements transmit a certain sense of unease, and the following paragraphs, in which he supposedly 'develops this proposition a bit more' (as he puts it), do not so much add anything, as say it again a few times while using the word 'âme' [soul]. Rousseau's *Émile* says the same thing more directly, and, in being more personal, avoids the dogmatic reductiveness that characterises Condillac:

> Je sens mon âme; je la connois par le sentiment et par la pensée [....] Ce que je sais bien c'est que l'identité du *moi* ne se prolonge que par la mémoire, et que pour être le même en effet, il faut que je me souvienne d'avoir été.¹⁵⁴

> I sense my soul. I know it through feeling and thought. [...] What I know for sure is that the identity of the *self* is prolonged only by memory, and that in order to be actually the same I must remember having been.

Rousseau not only brings in the term of identity, he notices the thorny issue of continuity, and imposes continuous memory on himself: in order to be the same person he *must* remember what he was before. Diderot will consistently identify the self with memory, while also probing the various implications of continuity and interruption. In the *Rêve de d'Alembert*, d'Alembert asks Bordeu how he has managed to stay himself despite continuous change:

---

153 Bonnet, *Essai analytique sur les facultés de l'âme* [1760], in *Œuvres d'histoire naturelle et de philosophie*, vol. 8, t. 14, p. 212 (§702).
154 Rousseau, *Émile*, in *Œuvres complètes*, vol. 4, p. 590; *Emile*, trans. by Bloom, p. 283 (slightly amended).

> D'ALEMBERT: A travers toutes les vicissitudes [...] comment suis-je resté moi pour les autres et pour moi?[155]
>
> Taking into account all the changes [...], how have I kept my own personality for myself as well as for others?

Bordeu replies, with reference to an animal's sense of self (the conversation has been moving surreally):

> BORDEU: Que c'était par la mémoire qu'il était lui pour les autres et pour lui: et j'ajouterais par la lenteur des vicissitudes.[156]
>
> That it remained itself both for others and for itself thanks to memory. And I would add because of the gradualness of the change.

That because of the slow rate of change he has remained recognisable to himself and to others is perhaps not a particularly reassuring doctrine. In the *Observations sur Hemsterhuis*, Diderot testily scratches out Hemsterhuis's association of self with soul:

> \* Le *moi* est le résultat de la mémoire qui attache à un individu, la suite de [ses] sensations. Si je suis un individu, c'est *moi*. Si c'est un autre individu, c'est *lui*. Le *lui* et le *moi* naissent du même principe.[157]
>
> \* The *self* is the result of memory attaching a sequence of sensations to an individual. If I am an individual, that's *me*. If it's another individual, then it's *him*. The *him* and the *me* are born from the same principle.

So selfhood is the *result* of memory attached to an individual. And the difference between *me* and *him* is nothing more mysterious than that *I* have one set of sensations strung together into memories, and *he* has a different set. The *Éléments de physiologie* contains a very rich and fascinating chapter on memory, full of curious anecdotes, set piece recollections, and bizarre imagery, all of which test and stretch our notions of what memory might be and how it works. But it does

---

155 Denis Diderot, *Rêve de d'Alembert*, DPV, vol. 17, p. 164; *Rameau's Nephew and D'Alembert's Dream*, trans. by Leonard Tancock (London: Penguin, 1966), p. 201.
156 Diderot, *Rêve de d'Alembert*, DPV, vol. 17, p. 164; *Rameau's Nephew and D'Alembert's Dream*, trans. by Tancock, p. 201.
157 Diderot, *Observations sur La 'Lettre sur l'homme et ses rapports' de Hemsterhuis*, ed. by Stenger, in *Œuvres complètes*, DPV, vol. 24, p. 329 (Diderot's note number 191, responding to Hemsterhuis's 'notre âme, notre *moi*').

not move from its fundamental position that, as it tersely puts it: 'La mémoire constitue le soi' [memory constitutes the self].[158]

What then is memory? Is it an imprint? The notion that memory is an imprint in the waxy substance of the brain is age-old. It goes back to Pindar, Plato and Aristotle. Bacon, Descartes and Leibniz use it. Locke in fact uses the idea of white paper with writing, but Swift, paraphrasing him, reintroduces the wax motif with his *tabula rasa*.[159] It seems to be the only model for memory ever used. Spinoza wrote in the *Traité de la réforme de l'entendement*:

> Que sera donc la mémoire ? Rien d'autre que la sensation des empreintes qui sont dans le cerveau, jointe à une pensée relative à une durée déterminée de cette sensation, comme le montre la réminiscence.[160]

> What will memory be then? Nothing other than the sensation of the imprints which are in the brain, in connection with a thought relating to the specific duration of this sensation, as we see in the case of reminiscence.

La Mettrie has a general notion of all forms being created from matter *as wax takes the shape of a seal*:

> Ces modifications [de forme] reçoivent leur être, ou leur existence, de la matière même, comme l'empreinte d'un cachet la reçoit de la cire qu'elle modifie.[161]

> These modifications [in form] receive their being, or their existence, from matter itself, just as the imprint of a seal receives its shape from the wax which it modifies.

Memory is simply an extension of this metaphor:

---

158 DPV 471/PQ 298/MT 286.
159 See Brad Pasanek's wonderful resource, hosted by the University of Virginia 'The Mind as a Metaphor' (http://metaphors.lib.virginia.edu/about). The works referred to are, respectively, Pindar, *Olympian 10*; Plato, *Theaetetus*; Aristotle, *De memoria* (On Memory); Bacon, *Temporis Partus Masculus* (The Masculine Birth of Time); Descartes, *Rules for the direction of the mind*; Leibniz, *New Essays on Human Understanding*; Locke, *An Essay concerning Human Understanding*; Swift, *Critical Essay upon the Faculties of the Mind*.
160 Spinoza, *Traité de la réforme de l'entendement*, §83.
161 La Mettrie, *Traité de l'âme*, p. 131.

> La cause de la mémoire est tout-à-fait mécanique, comme elle-même; elle paroît dépendre de ce que les impressions corporelles du cerveau, qui sont les traces d'idées qui se suivent, sont voisines [...][162]

> The cause of memory, like memory itself, is entirely mechanical; it seems to depend on the proximity to each other of the corporeal impressions in the brain, which are the traces of the sequences of ideas [...]

Memories are sensations which have been impressed on the mind, leaving traces of ideas. Condillac also applies the analogy very literally when considering what will remain in the memory and what will not:

> Si la succession en renferme un grand nombre, l'impression des dernières, comme la plus nouvelle, sera la plus forte; celle des premières s'affoiblira par des degrés insensibles, s'éteindra tout-à-fait, et elles seront comme non avenues.[163]

> If the sequence contains a great number, the impression made by the most recent ones, like the newest, will be the strongest; the impression made by the first ones will become fainter by imperceptible degrees, disappear completely, and it will be as if they had never happened.

This explains how a sensation can become a memory, that is, by leaving a lasting impression (we see how ubiquitous this model also is in English when we use a metaphorically identical but very common phrase like 'leaving a lasting impression'). But it does not explain how a memory is later recalled. The impression model really struggles to deal with this aspect. Here is Condillac's attempt:

> Quand une idée se retrace à la statue, ce n'est donc pas qu'elle se soit conservée dans le corps ou dans l'âme: c'est que le mouvement, qui en est la cause physique et occasionnelle, se reproduit dans le cerveau.*[164]

> When an idea is retraced in the statue, it's not as if it had been kept in the body or soul, it's that the movement (which is the physical and occasional cause of the idea) is reproduced in the brain.

So, in sum, it is not that the memory is an object which is kept in a store until needed; it's that the same movement re-occurs in the brain... Condillac's assertive style does not hide the fact that this particular

---

162 La Mettrie, *Traité de l'âme*, p. 172.
163 Condillac, *Traité des sensations*, p. 23 (I.ii).
164 Condillac, *Traité des sensations*, pp. 33–34 (I.ii).

explanation departs from his earlier model, and in so doing, stops making sense. In fact, as is obvious, his account has gone beyond what the wax imprint model can explain, and, having no precise knowledge of how a returning memory works, he is obliged to resort to a different mechanical model to do with movement.

Bonnet is simply more open about his lack of knowledge and his perplexity in this area. He turns Condillac's model into a question, asking whether memories endure because of the mechanical energy with which they are first felt. But then he answers it sceptically, and with reference to the physiological composition of the brain:

> Mais, ces mouvements que l'objet imprime à l'Organe ne se conserveroient-ils point dans le Cerveau par l'énergie de sa méchanique? [...]
>
> [...] on a de la peine à concevoir la conservation du mouvement dans une Partie aussi molle que paroît l'être le Cerveau.[165]
>
> But are these movements which the object impresses on the organ not preserved in the brain according to the energy of its mechanical operation?
>
> It is tricky to conceive of movement being preserved in a part as soft as the brain appears to be.

Elsewhere he goes even further, chastising himself for his earlier feebleness in simply re-using this old wax-imprint model. In fact his model was one of fibres (related to the idea of nerve fibres)[166] but we see in the following passage how the vocabulary of *traces*, *pressure*, and *movement* remain.

> Je n'ai rien dit de ces traces, de ces ébauches qu'on suppose si gratuitement dans le cerveau, toutes les fois qu'on parle de l'Imagination & de la Mémoire: j'avoue, que n'ayant pu m'en former aucune idée, j'ai jugé plus philosophique d'admettre que les mêmes organes qui, ébranlés par les Objets, nous donnent tant de perceptions diverses, sont faits de manière que leurs parties constituantes reçoivent de l'action des objets certaines déterminations d'où résulte une tendance à se mouvoir dans un sens plutôt que dans un autre.[167]

---

165 Bonnet, *Essai analytique sur les facultés de l'âme* [1760], pp. 40, 42 (§55).
166 See Tobias Cheung's article on fibres: 'Omnis Fibra Ex Fibra: Fibre OEconomies in Bonnet's and Diderot's Models of Organic Order', *Early Science and Medicine*, vol. 15, no. 1–2, 2010, pp. 66–104.
167 Bonnet, *Analyse abrégée de l'Essai analytique sur les Facultés de l'âme*, pp. 27–28.

I have said nothing of these traces, these sketches in the brain which we so freely mention every time we talk of imagination and memory: I admit that, having been unable to form any idea of them myself, I judged that it would be more philosophical to suppose that these same organs which, shaken by objects, give us so many different perceptions, are made such that their constituent parts receive from the action of these objects certain determinations from which arises a tendency to move in one way or another.

Diderot takes all of these aspects and sends them into a spin.

Pour expliquer le mécanisme de la mémoire il faut regarder la substance molle du cerveau comme une masse d'une cire sensible et vivante, mais susceptible de toutes sortes de formes, n'en perdant aucune de celles qu'elle a reçues et en recevant, sans cesse, de nouvelles qu'elle garde. Voilà le livre. Mais où est le lecteur? Le lecteur c'est le livre même. Car ce livre est sentant, vivant, parlant ou communiquant par des sons, par des traits,[168] l'ordre de ses sensations; et comment se lit-il lui-même? En sentant ce qu'il est et en le manifestant par des sons.

Ou la chose se trouve écrite, ou elle ne se trouve pas écrite. Si elle ne se trouve point écrite, on l'ignore. Au moment où elle s'écrit, on l'apprend.

Selon la manière dont elle était écrite, on la savait nouvellement ou depuis longtemps.

Si l'écriture s'affaiblit, on l'oublie, si l'écriture s'efface, elle est oubliée, si l'écriture se revivifie, on se la rappelle.[169]

To explain the mechanism of the memory it is necessary to view the soft parts of the brain as a mass of sensitive and living wax, but one which can take on all sorts of forms, losing none of those it has had, and ceaselessly taking on new ones which it will always retain. That is the book. But where is the reader? The reader is the book itself. For this book feels, lives, speaks or communicates its sensations in order, with sounds, with lines; and how does it read itself? By feeling what it is and by manifesting that through sounds.

Either the thing happens to be written, or it doesn't. If it doesn't happen to be written, we don't know it. The instant it is written, we learn it.

Depending on the manner in which it was written, we learnt it anew or had known it for a long time.

---

168 *Trait* is hard to translate in that it means *lines* or *strokes* (of hand-writing), but also *features* (as in expressions). Diderot probably means all these things.
169 DPV 470/PQ 297/MT 285–86.

If the writing weakens, we forget it, if the writing is rubbed out, it is forgotten, if the writing comes back to life, we remember it.

Diderot takes the image of the malleable wax and makes the brain into a living, moving, reacting, self-sculpting mass that permanently contains its own past forms. This, he says, without signalling the change of image, is the book. What book? Diderot is picking up the other strand of this model: having investigated the notion of waxy forms, he returns to the notion that it is a *book* written on wax tablets (as Pindar, Plato, etc, had said). But if it is a book, it needs a reader, or so we are given to understand by virtue of his question asking where the reader is. Because of course the brain is not passive (unlike the wax in this age-old topos), and if we are going to remember something, we have to actively do something. So the brain reads itself, not by mechanical movement, as Condillac had stated and Bonnet had wondered, but in feeling its own existence. Thus far we have three self-performing actions, or rather, operations which are both active and passive at once:[170] sculpting, reading, and feeling. 'La chose'—the thing (not yet a *memory*)—is the sensation which is either written or not written—or rather *happens or not* to be written (there is no agency behind it being written or not) in the waxy book, and if it does *not* happen to be written, we are unaware of it, and at the moment of it being written—or writing itself—we learn it. Still this is not memory, it is sensation that we feel and therefore learn, or do not feel and therefore do not know. *La manière* of its writing—the manner or perhaps we could go so far as to say the *style* of the writing is what determines whether this thing is something we are learning anew or which we had known for a long while. And this thing, in the sentence we have just been looking at, is presumably a sensation which is familiar, and therefore one which we have had before and *remember*, or it is a new one, for which there is no existing trace. In the last sentence, forgetting explicitly ties us to questions of writing, given that this model tells us that if the writing fades we forget the thing, and once the writing has gone, it is completely forgotten, unless the writing comes back to life, in which case the thing will then be remembered.

---

170  Citton analyses the same passage and the binary relationship between active and passive in his *L'Envers de la liberté*, pp. 479–80.

The density of this image, its helter-skelter shifts, and its sheer implausibility make the passage very striking. Its bizarreness obliges us to linger on it, and it is perhaps therefore an illustration of what is written here about the *manner* of how something is presented making all the difference between it being entirely familiar and altogether fresh and novel (or memorable, of course). Thinking about his extended metaphor in the context of the earlier commentators, we can see that Diderot tests out and strains the various features of this well-known, even well-worn image. He pushes it as far as it will go, and farther. In so doing, he shows us where the weaknesses lie, and how a metaphor can carry meaning and implications that have their own shaping force. Its very peculiarity draws attention to the conceptual and imaginative oddities and the implausibility of what it is that this model of the mind and memory is expected to do, and what features it appears to be required to accommodate and perform. And of course, memory does actually perform all the functions Diderot describes the self-reading, self-writing, self-performing book as doing. The philosopher of mind and specialist on memory, Krista Lawlor, writing more than two centuries later, identifies the features characterising memory as being autobiography, self-consciousness, memory traces, connectionism, trace and cue, re-presentation, reflexive thinking, and metarepresentational thought. She concludes that what is comprehensively lacking is 'a specific model of how working memory might function to preserve content, while acknowledging that memory involves reconstruction'.[171] Diderot's straining multi-model simultaneously provides a commentary on the inadequacies of the ubiquitous imagery, a precise description of what the brain and memory actually does, and also performs memorable writing that does indeed do that thing of leaving a lasting impression.

If all the self consists of is cumulative sensation over time, with memory also being a sensation felt in the present, then we depend entirely on our sensations for the quality of our selfhood. As Diderot put it to Hemsterhuis, just after having stated that 'Le *moi* est le résultat

---

171 Krista Lawlor, 'Memory', in *The Oxford Handbook of Philosophy of Mind*, ed. by Ansgar Beckermann, Brian P. McLaughlin, and Sven Walter (Oxford: Clarendon Press, 2009), p. 674, https://doi.org/10.1093/oxfordhb/9780199262618.003.0039.

de la mémoire [...]' [the *self* is the result of the memory], 'Ce *moi* veut être heureux' [this *self* wants to be happy].[172]

## i. The Pursuit of Happiness

*It is a virtue and therefore a duty to seek our self-preservation, nourishment, and happiness, write Spinoza, La Mettrie and Diderot.*

Spinoza argues that if the multiple nourishment needs of the multiple body are met, then both it and the mind will be able to function well. He puts it more poetically than that:

> [...] the human body is composed of a great many parts of different natures, which require continuous and varied food so that the whole body may be equally capable of doing everything which can follow from its nature, and consequently, so that the mind may also be equally capable of conceiving many things.[173]

He goes on to argue that anything that boosts human happiness is good, specifically because it will boost the power of the human body and mind:

> Since those things are good which assist the parts of the body to perform their function, and joy consists in the fact that man's power, insofar as he consists of mind and body, is aided or increased, all things which bring joy are good.[174]

To boost one's ability to function properly in terms of body and mind is, concludes Spinoza, virtuous, and indeed 'the foundation of virtue':

> [...] the foundation of virtue is this very striving to preserve one's own being, and [...] happiness consists in a man's being able to preserve his being [175]

As La Mettrie less carefully puts it in *L'Homme-machine*:

---

172 Diderot, *Observations sur La 'Lettre sur l'homme et ses rapports' de Hemsterhuis*, DPV, vol. 24, p. 330 (Diderot's note 192).
173 Spinoza, *Ethics*, p. 159 (§ XXVII).
174 Spinoza, *Ethics*, p. 159 (§ XXX).
175 Spinoza, *Ethics*, p. 125 (II/222 (i)). Terada also suggests Spinozan sources for Diderot's thinking in this area, see e.g. Spinoza, *Ethics*, proposition XIX, quoted MT 480.

> La Nature nous a tous créés uniquement pour être heureux; ouï tous, depuis le ver qui rampe, jusqu'à l'Aigle qui se perd dans la Nuë.[176]
>
> Nature created us all solely to be happy—yes, all, from the worm crawling along to the eagle soaring on high.[177]

The *Éléments* agrees, and summarises this joint physiological and ethical position at the beginning of the chapter entitled 'Passions':

> Il n'y a qu'une seule passion, celle d'être heureux.[178]
>
> There is only one passion, and that is to be happy.

The chapter goes on to demonstrate how the fulfillment of bodily needs and happiness go hand in hand, as do sickness, frustration and misery. The final sentence of the *Éléments* recapitulates this in firm form:

> Il n'y a qu'une vertu, la justice; qu'un devoir, de se rendre heureux; qu'un corollaire, de ne pas se surfaire la vie et de ne pas craindre la mort.[179]
>
> There is only one virtue: justice; only one duty: to make oneself happy; and only one corollary, not to overvalue one's life and not to fear death.

One's duty is to oneself, and it is to promote one's own happiness, while not clinging onto life and not fearing death. On this virtuous, upright, deeply Epicurean sentiment, the *Éléments de physiologie* ends.

\*

In this chapter I have tried to present the key structuring aspects of these theories of nature and the human understanding, or mind, or brain, and I have tried to show how Diderot fits them together into one seamless materialist system. I have also tried to bring out how these key structuring aspects appear again and again, and how their motifs often follow similar patterns and models, despite normal variation from one author to another. It is often not clear who was reading whom and therefore being influenced by whom; the reading routes are carefully hidden in the case of this often highly censored material. However, if it

---

176 La Mettrie, *L'Homme-machine*, p. 92.
177 La Mettrie, *Machine Man* in *Machine Man and Other Writings*, trans. and ed. by Ann Thomson (Cambridge: Cambridge University Press, 1996), p. 22.
178 DPV 486/PQ 317/MT 301.
179 DPV 514/PQ 362/MT 328. Terada usefully points us in the direction of Spinoza, *Ethics*, proposition XX, and to Boulainvillier's *Réfutation de Spinoza* for other close source material.

seems clear enough that Diderot knew all these writers well (sometimes personally), the aim of this chapter has not primarily been to trace their influence or impact on the *Éléments de physiologie*. What instead I hope to have shown is that he is picking up these multifarious elements, responding to them, and creating a synthesis which no other author had previously brought together, in a style which was more explicit and forthright about its materialist determinism than any other, and therefore able to look at and probe its consequences and implications more clearly. This text is obviously not the first in which Diderot sought to express materialist positions: it is the last, and it contains aspects and developments of all those which lead to it, from the *Pensées philosophiques* of 1746 onwards. In the *Observations sur Hemsterhuis* and the *Réfutation d'Helvétius*, he repeatedly refers to his 'philosophie', a philosophy which, we infer, is more complex, thorough, instantiated, and rigorous than what these two interlocutors had proposed.[180] He can only be referring to the *Éléments*, already underway at that time.[181]

---

180 Diderot speaks of 'ma philosophie' [my philosophy], 'mon mot' [what I have to say], and 'ma philosophie' [my philosophy] in *Observations sur La 'Lettre sur l'homme et ses rapports' de Hemsterhuis*, DPV, vol. 24, p. 261, 262, and 340 respectively, and again of 'ma philosophie' in *Réfutation d'Helvétius*, DPV, vol. 24, p. 588.
181 See above, note 13, in Chapter 1.

# 4. Diderot the Physiologist

In 1764, Toussaint Bordenave, a surgeon respected both for his practical experience and his mastery of Latin, which made him doubly useful to his many students, brought out for their use an *Essai sur la physiologie*. His aim was to give a comprehensive but concise overview of the workings of the human body, and he drew closely on the work of the preeminent Swiss physiologist Albrecht von Haller, whose works were all written in Latin, and whose own condensed handbook on the subject, the *Primae lineae physiologiae*, Bordenave would later translate into French under the title *Éléments de physiologie*, no doubt driven by his continuing pedagogical impulse. His 1764 *Essai* is printed in a handy duodecimo size, and has 253 pages: he packs a lot of definition and description into his pages, and here, to give a flavour of it, is how he defines giving birth, from a physiological point of view:

> L'Accouchement est une fonction naturelle, par laquelle le foetus parvenu a un certain terme est expulsé au-dehors.[1]
>
> Delivery is a natural function by which the foetus having reached a certain term is expelled outside.

There is nothing wrong with this definition from a mid-to-late eighteenth-century point of view; it is clear and concise, while its emphasis on delivery as a natural function shows that Bordenave is within the mainstream of Haller-influenced physiological thinking in seeing physiology as not just anatomy but as the ensemble of (partly mechanical) processes within a living body. However, it is not exactly whizzy. It uses impersonal almost

---

1   Toussaint Bordenave, *Essai sur la physiologie* (Paris: P. Al. Le Prieur, 1764), p. 203.

© Caroline Warman, CC BY 4.0   https://doi.org/10.11647/OBP.0199.04

abstract substantives ('l'accouchement''; 'le foetus'; 'une fonction'; 'un terme') that completely detach the process from any specific living (and presumably gendered) body. It is also simultaneously tautologous (the foetus is not just 'expelled', but 'expelled outside') and incomplete: there is no mention of what this foetus is expelled out of—we assume *a/the* body. Bordenave's definition is generalised and at once over-emphatic and underspecified. Compare it with what Denis Diderot says in the *Éléments de physiologie*:

> 'L'accouchement est une espèce de vomissement [...].'[2]
>
> Delivery is a sort of vomiting [...].

In essence, he is saying the same thing as Bordenave, but he is more severely concise and direct. He avoids the formalising and repetitive language so common to definitions ('it is a natural function by which', etc), and he also sidesteps the depersonalised mechanical model implicit in the notion of automatic expulsion. In comparing delivery to vomiting, he communicates the idea of the foetus being 'expelled outside' with piercing clarity, presenting it as an experience all humans (male as well as female) can relate to and have a bodily memory of, one that carries physical sensation and its associated emotional response in the shape of extreme discomfort.[3] His definition is sparer, less formalised, much more violent, and much more effective. Its brevity and impact are typical of Diderot's *Éléments de physiologie* more widely. He systematically avoids generalisation and abstraction and tends to communicate his point by connecting it to relatable experience, whether by example or—as here—by analogy. This chapter will look at Diderot's *Physiology* next to other introductory overviews to the subject from the period, and will aim to show where it is similar to them and of course also where it diverges. It is not attempting to take into account the variety and specificity of Diderot's medical reading

---

2   Denis Diderot, *Éléments de physiologie*, ed. by Jean Mayer, *Œuvres complètes*, DPV (Paris: Hermann, 1987), vol. 17, pp. 261–574 (p.440); Diderot, *Éléments de physiologie*, ed. by Paolo Quintili (Paris: Champion, 2004), p. 261; Diderot, *Éléments de physiologie*, ed. by Motoichi Terada (Paris: Éditions Matériologiques, 2019), p. 257 [hereafter notated as DPV 440/PQ 261/MT 257].

3   This is not the first time we have mentioned vomiting. See also the mouthless oyster in Chapter 1.

and influences: fine work has already been done in this area by Jean Mayer, Paolo Quintili, and Motoichi Terada.[4] One of the things we will be arguing is, as has already been sketched out, that Diderot's *Physiology* is better written and therefore that, quite concretely, it is a better introduction to physiology than many others were, or it would have been, had it been published. The vexed question of its publication history however is for later chapters.

***

But what is physiology? This is not a question which we have even touched on yet. The definition which Paris-trained medic Pierre Tarin (1725–61) gives in his *Encyclopédie* article is this:

> PHYSIOLOGIE, s. f. de Φύσις, *nature*, & λόγος, *discours*, partie de la Médecine, qui considere ce en quoi consiste la vie, ce que c'est que la santé, & quels en sont les effets. *Voyez* Vie & Santé. On l'appelle aussi économie animale, traité de l'usage des *parties;* & ses objets se nomment communément *choses naturelles* ou *conformes aux lois de la nature. Voyez* Naturel & Nature.[5]

> PHYSIOLOGY, feminine noun from Φύσις, *nature*, & λόγος, *discourse*, part of Medicine, which looks at what life consists of, what health is, and what their effects are. *See* Life & Health. It is also called *animal economy, treatise of the use of parts*; and its objects are commonly called *things which are natural* or *which conform to the laws of nature*. *See* Natural & Nature.

So, it is part of medicine, it specifically asks what life is, what health is, and what the effects of life and health are. It can also be called *animal economy* and *treatise of the use of parts*, and what it (all this) looks at,

---

4   See their editions, and also Jean Mayer, *Diderot, homme de science* (Rennes: Imprimerie Bretonne, 1959). See also Gilles Barroux's study of the importance of medical knowledge for Diderot's materialism: *Le Cabinet médical de Diderot: la part de la médecine dans l'élaboration d'une philosophie matérialiste* (Paris: Éditions Matériologiques, 2018), although Barroux does not specifically focus on the *Éléments de physiologie*.

5   Pierre Tarin, 'Physiologie,' *Encyclopédie ou dictionnaire raisonné des sciences, des arts et des métiers, par une société de gens de lettres*, ed. Diderot and D'Alembert (Paris: Briasson, David, Le Breton, Durand, 1751-1772), vol. 12 (1765), p. 537, http://artflsrv02.uchicago.edu/cgi-bin/philologic/getobject.pl?c.11:1364.encyclopedie0416. See also the critical online edition *Édition numérique collaborative et critique de l'Encyclopédie* ed. by Alexandre Guilbaud, Alain Cernuschi, Marie Léca-Tsiomis and Irène Passeron, http://enccre.academie-sciences.fr/encyclopedie/. Also quoted in PQ, p. 11.

that is, the objects of its attention, are commonly known as *things which are natural or conform to the laws of nature*. One of the characteristic features of the *Encyclopédie* is the way in which it integrates cross-references to connected articles: the immediate ring of closest related articles to 'physiologie' are Life, Health, Natural, and Nature. We notice, therefore, that the terms *human* and *body* do not feature in this first most concentrated nugget of the definition, although they appear in the first line of the next paragraph, which commences a more detailed exposition and description (the whole article is just over a thousand words). So physiology, despite belonging to medicine and therefore being inevitably and implicitly connected to human beings and illness, is in fact explicitly concerned with general questions about life and health. Beyond that, it is also to do with the animal economy, how the different parts of the body work together, and about how things are natural, how they do or do not conform to the laws of nature. Physiology could not therefore be called a limited field of enquiry, and it is not even principally to do with the human body.

In his article, Tarin mentions three authorities: firstly, Montaigne, a remark of whose he uses to cast ridicule on daft concretisations of the soul, and the other two—Herman Boerhaave and Albrecht von Haller—to indicate the two greatest authorities in the field. Tarin had in fact executed a first translation of Haller's *Primae lineae physiologiae* ('First Lines', 1747): it was published under the title *Éléments de physiologie* in 1752, and was the only translation available in French until Bordenave's tighter version of 1769 (this will be the version Diderot uses for his *Éléments de physiologie* as we can tell from the echoes in the phrasing; we will come to this aspect in due course). So Tarin very thoroughly associates his work with Haller, as indeed all the writers about physiology mentioned in this chapter do. Where there is polemic, it is not about whether Haller was or was not an authority on the workings of the human body. Haller himself would later write the revised and extended version of Tarin's definition for Jean-Baptiste Robinet's edition of the *Supplément* to the *Encyclopédie* (1776, 4 vols); Haller expanded it to nearly 25,000 words, relating in chronological order who made what discoveries in physiology from Pythagoras onwards: he jettisons Tarin's article apart from that first nugget definition which he retains as the introductory paragraph.[6]

Diderot's 'Système figuré des connoissances humaines', that provocatively rearranged fold-out map of human knowledge which features at the beginning of the *Encyclopédie*, in fact places physiology as a subset of zoology, on a par with anatomy, medecine, and then a group of associated veterinary areas ('la vétérinaire', horse-riding, hunting, fishing, and falconry).[7] Medicine has its own subsets, not including physiology. These are: hygiene (the art of preventing disease), pathology and 'seméiotique' (respectively the knowledge of disease and of its signs and symptoms), and therapeutics (the art of healing). By contrast, in the *text* accompanying the diagram of the 'système figuré', Diderot presents things slightly differently: medicine *either* focuses on the 'economy of the human body' and theorises ('raisonne') its anatomy, this area becoming physiology, *or* deals with illness and health, and how to avoid, recognise, and cure the former, and reinforce the latter.[8] So there is clearly some variation in the understanding of where physiology sits as a branch of knowledge (whether or not it is a subset of medicine; its relation to anatomy), and within that, what it covers. We can tell that this is not just a question of uncertainty but of debate, even polemic, when we read that the influential Parisian medic and writer, Félix Vicq d'Azyr (1748–94) made a point of combining

---

6   Albrecht von Haller (and Pierre Tarin), 'Physiologie', in *Supplément à l'Encyclopédie ou Dictionnaire raisonné des Sciences, des Arts & des Métiers par une Société de Gens de lettres*, ed. by Jean-Baptiste Robinet, 4 vols (Amsterdam: M.M. Rey, 1776–77), vol. 4 (1777), p. 344, http://artflsrv02.uchicago.edu/cgi-bin/philologic/getobject. pl?c.3:496.supplement2.

7   Religion, for example, appears as a sub-section of, in the first instance, 'Reason', secondly 'Philosophie', thirdly 'Science de Dieu', and fourthly 'Théologie naturelle, Théologie révelée'. Only then comes 'Religion', immediately qualified by 'd'où par abus, superstitions' [whence, by abuse, superstitions]. The 'Système figuré des connoissances humaines' was first published as part of the prospectus of the *Encyclopédie* in 1750, and, as already indicated, features at the head of the first volume of the *Encyclopédie* proper (volume 1 was published in 1751), https://encyclopedie. uchicago.edu/content/système-figuré-des-connaissances-humaines-0. See also the critical online edition *Édition numérique collaborative et critique de l'Encyclopédie* ed. by Alexandre Guilbaud, Alain Cernuschi, Marie Léca-Tsiomis and Irène Passeron, http://enccre.academie-sciences.fr/encyclopedie/.

8   Denis Diderot, 'Prospectus' (1750), p. 8, see http://artflsrv02.uchicago.edu/cgi-bin/extras/diderotimg.pl?0035_pg8_section3.jpg (the link for the prospectus as a whole is https://encyclopedie.uchicago.edu/node/174).

physiology and anatomy in his teaching: Laurence Brockliss and Colin Jones tell us that he 'founded each part of his physiology course on an anatomical description of a vital organ'.[9] Diderot also lobbies, in the final chapter of his *Éléments de physiologie*, for post-mortem dissection to be much more widespread; his argument is that only through anatomy can the science of medicine progress.[10]

Why should this be an issue? Indeed, what is the issue? It is not easy for the modern reader to comprehend the arguments of past centuries: for us, it is perfectly obvious that the detailed knowledge of the human body is in fact synonymous with advanced anatomical knowledge and furthermore, that anatomy and physiology occupy overlapping areas of biology. What this means, however, is that thinkers like Vicq and, before him, Diderot, won the argument, and that—to put it one way—our understanding of the sciences comes down to us from such as them— and to put it another—that they influenced the shape of things to come. This is not to exaggerate the importance of any particular moment or group of thinkers—every link or generation in a genealogy is a crucial one, without which the cumulative inheritance would be different. The more general point is to recognise and understand that the field of knowledge broadly conceived is the result of a complex and multi-generational intellectual genealogy, and within the context of this study, the aim is to look at one of those generations and, insofar as possible, at the precise historical conditions of its production. For instance, when we blithely throw the term 'biology' into the discussion as if it were a given, we ought perhaps to consider that neither term nor concept existed when Diderot was writing. It seems to have emerged in response to the debates pervading the wider fields of natural philosophy, physiology, and zoology, and its adoption was propelled into general usage by the French naturalist Jean-Baptiste Lamarck (1744–1829).[11] The fact that the

---

9 Laurence Brockliss and Colin Jones, *The Medical World of Early Modern France* (Oxford: Clarendon Press, 1997), p. 426. They refer to Félix Vicq d'Azyr, 'Discours sur l'anatomie: premier discours, Plan d'un cours d'anatomie', in *Œuvres de Vicq d'Azyr*, ed. by J.-L. Moreau de la Sarthe (Paris: Duprat-Duverger, 1805), vol. 1, pp. 35–124, https://doi.org/10.5962/bhl.title.48727.
10 DPV 513–14/ PQ 354–55/ MT 325–26.
11 Shirley A. Roe tells us that 'around 1800, the word "biology" began to be used independently by Lamarck and Bichat in France, and Karl Friedrich Burdach and Gottfried Reinhold Treviranus in Germany' (Roe, 'The Life Sciences', in *The Cambridge History of Science: Volume 4, Eighteenth-Century Science*, ed. by Roy Porter

now familiar field of biology did not exist in the period we are looking at, but very soon would, is itself an indicator of the considerable change and reorganisation of the map of knowledge that was occurring at the time. François Duchesneau, eminent historian of eighteenth-century French physiology, puts it this way: 'Le XVIIIe siècle, suggérions-nous, voit la transition des théories de l'être vivant à la théorie physiologique' [The Eighteenth Century, we would suggest, sees a transition, from theories of the living being to physiological theory].[12] This is a pithy encapsulation of an immense epistemological shift. Yet its retrospective assessment consigns the variation around the definition that we have been briefly sketching to a hazy past, as Duchesneau goes on to make clear:

> La physiologie, division de la philosophie naturelle sans spécificité de méthodes ou de concepts thématiques dans la période précédente, acquiert l'autonomie d'un savoir empirique strictement délimité avec les *Elementa physiologiae corporis humani* (1757–1766) de Haller.[13]
>
> Physiology, a part of natural philosophy without, in the preceding period, any specific methods or thematic concepts, gains autonomy as an empirical and strictly defined body of knowledge with the publication of Haller's *Elementa physiologiae corporis humani* (1757–1766).

For Duchesneau therefore, the watershed is Haller, who establishes physiology as a defined empirical science. Haller's impact was immense and Duchesneau's clear statement gives him due prominence. It is however interesting to note that pre-Hallerian physiology is simply brushed aside as having been 'sans spécificité'; such an attitude derives from a notion of history as progress, one which is particularly hard to avoid when looking at the history of science, where we have manifest and endless evidence that things can be done 'now' which weren't possible or even conceivable 'before'. So, to be clear: we are not suggesting that there is anything wrong, as in factually incorrect or

---

(Cambridge: Cambridge University Press, 2003), pp. 397–416 (p. 416), https://doi.org/10.1017/chol9780521572439.018). Charles Wolfe analyses the knotty context and specifically the contribution of vitalism to the emergence of 'biology' in his study *La Philosophie de la biologie avant la biologie: une histoire du vitalisme* (Paris: Classiques Garnier, 2019).

12  François Duchesneau, *La Physiologie des lumières: empirisme, modèles et théories*, Histoire et philosophie des sciences (Paris: Classiques Garnier, 2012), p. 685.

13  Ibid.

intellectually faulty, with that sort of march-of-science history or with that view of the truth. It is just not what we are looking at: our focus is on the constituent elements and strands within physiology in the latter half of the eighteenth century in France so that we can understand what physiology was understood to be, what its debates were, what Diderot's position in all this was, and finally, what his contribution was or might have been.

## Major Debates in Physiology: Mechanism and Vitalism

The major debates around physiology, its definition and its mapping within medical knowledge more broadly turned on the approaches generally known as mechanism and vitalism. Mechanism was, as its name suggests, the theory that the body was best understood as a mechanism or machine, an infinitely complex assemblage of working parts, with pumps (such as the heart) and levers (such as the muscles), and so forth. René Descartes' understanding of the body is exactly this. As the mention of Descartes serves to remind us, mechanism usefully hives off discussion of the soul, while continuing to press for empirical investigation of the body. Its primary tools of research are anatomy and dissection: if the body is a mechanism, then what better way to understand it than to take it apart? The pre-eminent mechanist was Dutch anatomist and chemist Herman Boerhaave (1668–1738) who taught generations of students at Leiden, amongst whom were the aforementioned Haller, the medically-trained philosopher La Mettrie (1709–51), author of *L'Homme-machine* (1747), and Louis de Jaucourt (1704–79), contributor of no fewer than seventeen thousand articles to the *Encyclopédie* including some on physiology and chemistry.[14] An important sub-section of mechanism is iatromechanism ('iatro' is a prefix from the Greek word for 'physician'); the crucial contribution its adherents made was to bring chemistry into the mechanist fold, viewing chemical processes in mechanical terms; iatrochemistry applies this approach to the body, seeing it as a *chemical* machine, with functions

---

14  The leading contributors in these areas however were Venel (chemistry) and, in the area of physiology and medecine, Tarin and Ménuret de Chambaud. On chemistry in the *Encyclopédie*, see Christine Lehman and François Pépin, 'La Chimie et l'Encyclopédie', *Corpus, revue de philosophie*, 56 (2009).

such as digestion or secretion being understood as primarily chemical processes.[15]

Vitalism, with *vita*—'life'—at its core, picks up something we have already touched on, that is to say, the enquiry into what life actually is. Vitalist medicine, particularly associated with the medical school of Montpellier, sees the body as the ensemble of its living functions; it is particularly interested in the life of the organs which it conceptualises according to a model of interdependent independence.[16] For vitalists, to dissect a cadaver is a subordinate if not pointless activity, as the key object of enquiry—life—is no longer present. Hence the wide-spread practice of (animal) vivisection in the eighteenth century, amongst both mechanists and vitalists, given that the former understood the importance of looking at the living machine, and that the latter realised the need for detailed knowledge of physiology, that is, of the body's constituent parts and how they work together in the 'animal economy'.[17] The cleft stick that this put actual physiologists in is well if disturbingly expressed by Vicq d'Azyr in his heartfelt account of, on the one hand, dissecting a body whose muscles and nerves no longer respond to 'the instrument' and whose dead silence is a great enigma, and on the other, the awfulness of attempting to see or understand any phenomenon at all while inflicting extreme pain and fear on a live animal, in the midst of its convulsions, screams, and pouring blood. The first passage records post-mortem dissection; the second describes vivisection.

> [...] tout est insensible, tout est muet; le muscle ne se roidit plus sous l'instrument qui le blesse; le nerf est déchiré sans exciter ni trouble ni douleur; toute connexion, toute sympathie sont détruites, et les corps

---

15 Laurence Brockliss and Colin Jones provide a helpful survey of iatromechanism and its main proponents, see in *The Medical World of Early Modern France* (Oxford: Clarendon Press, 1997), pp. 419–33. See also Kurt Ballstadt's deft mapping of Diderot's attitude to iatromechanism in his *Diderot: Natural Philosopher*, SVEC 2008:09 (Oxford: Voltaire Foundation, 2008), pp. 204–05.
16 See Roselyne Rey, *Naissance et développement du vitalisme en France de la deuxième moitié du 18e siècle à la fin du premier empire*, SVEC 381 (Oxford: Voltaire Foundation, 2000); Elizabeth Williams, *A Cultural History of Medical Vitalism in Enlightenment Montpellier* (Ashgate: Aldershot, 2003); and Pascal Nouvel, *Repenser le vitalisme* (Paris: Presses Universitaires de France, 2011). For a more condensed introduction, see Timo Kaitaro, *Diderot's Holism* (Frankfurt a.M.: Peter Lang, 1997), pp. 117–23.
17 Rey, *Naissance et développement*, p. 139 (on animal economy); p. 405 (on vivisection).

des animaux dans cet état sont une grande énigme pour celui qui les dissèque.[18]

Everything is unresponsive, everything is mute; the muscle no longer stiffens at the touch of the instrument which injures it; the nerve can be severed without provoking disturbance or pain; every connection, every sympathy is destroyed, and the bodies of animals in this state are a great enigma for he who dissects them.

Vicq contrasts the process of the post-mortem we have just read with the distress and uproar of vivisection:

[...] pour un animal retenu par des liens, le plus léger mouvement est le signal de la douleur et redouble ses craintes; tout son corps se contracte, chacune de ses parties se soulève contre l'ennemi qui la menace ou qui la tourmente. Parmi des flots de sang et des convulsions, au milieu des cris aigus et des angoisses, comment ne pas se tromper sur le siège du sentiment? Qui pourroit se flatter, dans un bouleversement aussi général, de retrouver les traces des mouvements naturels? et quelles précautions, quelle sagacité ne faut-il pas pour en tirer quelques résultats utiles?[19]

For an animal who is tied down, the slightest movement is the signal of pain and intensifies its fear; its whole body contracts, each part of it rises up against the enemy which threatens or torments it. Amidst the pouring blood, the convulsions, the piercing screams and the anguish, how can we hope to find the root of the feeling? Who could suppose, within such general paroxyms, that it was ever possible to discern the trace of any natural movement? And what infinite amounts of care and sagacity are required to be able to draw any useful results from it!

Vicq is an expressive, self-questioning, and impassioned writer as well as an important physiologist, and he draws attention here to one of eighteenth-century culture's defining characteristics, its interest in the question of *sensibility*, that is to say, the ability to feel sensation. Manifestly, life and sensibility are almost synonymous here.[20] Haller's extensive research into the property of sensation in bodies, and his careful differentiation of it into *irritation* and *sensation*, constitute his most important actual discovery, as distinct from his wider importance

---

18 Félix Vicq d'Azyr, *Traité d'anatomie et de physiologie* (Paris: Didot l'Aîné, 1786), vol. 1, p. 2.
19 Vicq, *Traité d'anatomie*, p. 3.
20 This is an aspect we shall return to in Chapter 9, '1796-97: Cabanis and Destutt de Tracy at the Institut national'.

as the author of a comprehensive and empirically-based account of human physiology.²¹

Irritation is a reactive convulsive property of human tissue; it is not necessarily consciously felt, unlike sensation, which operates through the nerves, and therefore by definition is felt. An easy way to grasp the distinction is to think of irritation in relation to the muscles: muscular action happens without our being particularly conscious of it (think of heart beats, for instance), whereas pain causes sensation, of which we are aware and to which we respond. Haller's work on irritability was of great importance in helping physiologists to think about the specific properties of muscle fibre (or more widely what will come to be known as human tissue), and indeed Diderot was extremely interested in this aspect. In part, what the physiological concept of irritation did was provide fodder for materialist thinkers. If materialism posited that nothing exists in the universe other than matter in different combinations, and therefore that everything is made of matter, then one of its main questions was how matter could feel, and subsequently, if it could think; its many detractors derisively called on materialists to explain this, satirically asking if they thought rocks could think. Jean-Jacques Rousseau was one such, as we saw in the previous chapter.²² Haller himself was a devout Calvinist, and within physiology, firmly situated in the mechanist camp, and he rejected appropriations or extensions of his work which denied or questioned the existence of the soul.²³ However, the concept of irritability did make it possible to see that matter could

---

21 Andrew Clark gives an approachable and concise account of sensibility and irritability in his *Diderot's Part* (Ashgate: Aldershot, 2008), pp. 49–53, https://doi.org/10.4324/9781315257853; see also Hubert Steinke, 'Haller's Concept of Irritability and Sensibility and its Reception in France', *Mécanisme et vitalisme*, ed. by Mariana Saad, special issue of *La Lettre de la maison Française d'Oxford*, 14 (2001), 37–70; and Duchesneau's authoritative *La Physiologie des lumières*, pp. 217–58.

22 'Il me semble que loin de dire que les rochers pensent la philosophie moderne a découvert au contraire que les hommes ne pensent point' [It seems to me that far from saying that rocks think, modern philosophy has discovered, on the contrary, that men do not think], Jean-Jacques Rousseau, 'Profession de foi du vicaire savoyard', in *Émile* (1762), *Œuvres complètes*, ed. by Bernard Gagnebin and Marcel Raymond (Paris: Gallimard Pléiade, 1964), vol. 4, p. 584n; *Emile*, trans. by Allan Bloom (London: Penguin, 1979), p. 279 (slightly amended), as discussed above in Chapter 3.

23 For an immensely careful and illuminating account of this quarrel, see Marian Hobson, 'Sensibility and Spectacle: the Medical Context for the "Paradox"', in *Diderot and Rousseau: Networks of Enlightenment*, ed. by Kate E. Tunstall and Caroline

be reactive or responsive *without* consciousness, with a form of life and independence distinct from thought, whether or not thought was considered to be immaterial. Furthermore, a model according to which some sorts of organised matter have irritability and others sensibility makes it possible to conceptualise sensibility as a further development of irritability, and therefore to see it, and consciousness more widely, as a property of matter rather than of the soul.

Leading vitalists such as Théophile de Bordeu (familiar to readers of Diderot in the shape of the doctor in *Le Rêve de d'Alembert*) were directly challenged by Haller for using a notion of sensibility which was too broad-brush, giving too much self-organising autonomy and movement to the parts of the body.[24] Yet Bordeu, in his work on the glands (1751), on the pulse (1756), and later on chronic diseases (1775), again and again returns to the question of the relation of part to whole, to the extent to which we can say that organs do or do not have their own particular life, using as his investigative principle this notion of the sensibility of flesh. The great anatomist Xavier Bichat (1771–1802), whose ground-breaking microscopy work on human tissue would found the medical sub-discipline of histology, claims Bordeu along with Haller as two of his three medical masters, so if one single thing is clear it is that this quarrel around sensibility and irritability was a productive one.[25] What may not yet be particularly clear is how working on the organs, on the relationship of part to whole, and on their interdependence or independence is at all the same thing as looking at the properties of sensibility or irritability in human fibre, or what we now call tissue. This is because the definition of what an organ is has changed, and this is in part due to Bordeu and others like him. In the first edition of the *Dictionnaire de l'Académie française* (1694), the organ is the 'instrument de quelque faculté dans l'animal' [the instrument of some faculty in

---

Warman (Oxford: Voltaire Foundation, 2011), pp. 65–90 (esp. pp. 75–83, 'The Sensibility/Irritability Quarrel').

24 Marian Hobson, 'Sensibility and Spectacle', p. 76.
25 Rey, *Naissance et développement*, p. 371. Bichat's third master was Lazzaro Spallanzani (1729–99), and he shouldn't really be relegated to a footnote. He is celebrated for his work refuting the theory of the spontaneous generation of matter, for establishing once and for all that human reproduction requires both ovum and sperm, and for showing that digestion is not a muscular process whereby the stomach physically grinds the food but a chemical one in which the food is turned into a solution by the action of acid.

the animal]; in the second edition (1762), it has become a 'partie du corps servant aux sensations et aux opérations de l'animal' [part of the body of use to the sensations and operations of the animal]; it changes in the sixth edition (1835) to become 'partie du corps organisé, laquelle remplit quelque fonction nécessaire ou utile de la vie' [part of the organised body, filling some necessary or useful function of life].[26] This final definition is more or less the one we now work with, focusing on our vital functions, but it is clear that there is considerable change over the century, from 'instrument of some faculty' to 'part of the body of use to the sensations and operations of the animal' which is at once very important and very general. It might as well just mean 'body part', and the definition indicates a sort of problem with working out which bits exactly are of use, and in what way. This is where Bordeu's insistence on the relation of part to whole was so important; it allowed physiologists to distinguish what exactly was a part that had autonomy, what wasn't, and how those parts communicated. In his *Recherches sur les glandes*, Bordeu uses the metaphor of the swarm of bees to explore this idea. I would probably want to argue that Diderot's famous development in the *Rêve de d'Alembert* of this exact same metaphor fed back into Bordeu's thinking as we see it in the *Recherches sur les maladies chroniques*, where his model of the organisation of organs has moved on from the mechanical bee cog idea to take into account a more organic vitalist concept of reciprocity within the organism.[27] As the previous sentence makes manifest, 'organ' and its multiple cognates are all coming under some pressure during this period: the term 'organism' is invented at the beginning of the century; 'organisation' has its own quite specific physiological meaning which also mutates throughout the century.[28]

---

26 ARTFL's database of French dictionaries, Dictionnaires d'autrefois (https://artfl-project.uchicago.edu/content/dictionnaires-dautrefois), is a vital tool for tracking definition shifts across time, see https://artflsrv03.uchicago.edu/philologic4/publicdicos/query?report=bibliography&head=organe.

27 See Warman, 'L'âme et la vie de l'organe dans la pensée vitaliste de Bordeu, Diderot et Bichat', in *Repenser le vitalisme*, ed. by Pascal Nouvel (Paris: Presses universitaires de France, 2011), pp. 157–65; esp. p.162.

28 'Organism' was coined in Latin in 1706 by George Ernst Stahl (1660–1734). See Georges Canguilhem, 'Du singulier et de la singularité en épistémologie biologique', in *Études d'histoire et de philosophie des sciences*, 2nd edn (Paris: Vrin, 1970), pp. 223–34, as cited by Duchesneau, *La Physiologie des lumières*, p. 26. For a neat encapsulation of what the word 'organisation' itself means and comes to mean during this period, see Rey, *Naissance et développement*, p. 177, as quoted

This general account of the definitions and theories influencing physiology in the eighteenth century, specifically in France, and specifically with a view to enabling the reader to judge where Diderot locates himself, is inevitably cursory and reductive, forefronting certain aspects and omitting others. There is a longer heritage to the way in which physiological thought underpins vitalism than has so far been suggested; the chemist and physiologist Georg Ernst von Stahl (1660–1734) who has just been invisibly referenced (as the coiner of the term 'organism') conceptualised the soul in terms of energy which moved the inert matter of the body: his theory is known as animism.[29] Stahl's animism was a crucial trigger for the development of vitalism in Montpellier through François Boissier de Sauvages (1706–67) who taught physiology and pathology there from 1734, and through him on Montpellier students such as Bordeu who qualified as a physician in 1744,[30] and Paul-Joseph Barthez (1734–1806) who qualified ten years later in 1754, becoming known for his crusading theory of the 'principe vital'. Laurence Brockliss and Colin Jones explain this theory

---

by Alexandre Wenger, *Le Médecin et le philosophe: Théophile de Bordeu selon Diderot* (Paris: Hermann, 2012), pp. 84–85.

29  Paolo Quintili, 'Introduction', in Diderot, *Éléments de physiologie*, ed. by Paolo Quintili (Paris: Champion, 2004), pp. 34–35; Brockliss and Jones, *The Medical World*, pp. 427–29; and in greater detail Duchesneau, *La Physiologie des lumières*, pp. 25–67.

30  On Bordeu: Pierre Roussel, *Éloge historique de M. Théophile de Bordeu* (Paris: Ruault et Mequignon, 1788), p. 7. Pierre Roussel was himself a Montpellier doctor trained in vitalism; his *Système physique et moral de la femme* (Paris: Vincent, 1775) was well-received, and features on the reading list Diderot drew up for himself (see 'Notes de la main de mon père sur la physiologie', Diderot, *Éléments de physiologie*, ed. by P. Quintili, p. 389, and for the editor's commentary, pp. 33–34). François Pépin convincingly argues that Stahl's influence on Enlightenment vitalism is not in the mode of direct adoption, extension, or application, but is about countering his dualism: 'il n'y a aucun lien possible entre l'animisme de Stahl et le vitalisme des Lumières. Il faut au contraire considérer que ce vitalisme se construit en large part contre Stahl, l'enjeu étant, non seulement d'étudier le vivant à partir du vivant en soulignant sa spécificité, mais d'inscrire les processus et les fonctions organiques dans le corps organique lui-même' [there is no possible link between Stahl's animism and Enlightenment vitalism. On the contrary, one should think of this sort of vitalism as constructed largely against Stahl, the issue being not only to study what life is in the living and thereby underline its specificity, but also to think of organic processes and functions in the context of the organic body itself]. François Pépin, 'Diderot et Leibniz face à la chimie du vivant' in *Leibniz et Diderot: rencontres et transformations*, ed. by Christian Leduc, François Pépin, Anne-Lise Rey, and Mitia Rioux-Beaulne (Paris: Vrin, 2015), pp. 211–35 (p. 235), https://doi.org/10.4000/books.pum.2153.

in their usual succinct and helpful way: the vital principal 'was both a sensible and motor force, varied in its power from organ to organ, and operated sympathetically so that its activation in one spot could lead to its activation in another'.[31] Barthez's *Nouveaux éléments de la science de l'homme* (1778) is rather unlike the other works of physiology looked at in this chapter, in that it focuses uniquely on the presentation of its own theory, and is therefore neither introductory nor comprehensive.[32] It is nonetheless worth mentioning because of Barthez's prominence as a vitalist looking at organs and their interconnectedness in ways not dissimilar to Bordeu's thinking on the matter, and because his title, *Nouveaux éléments de la science de l'homme*, seems to promise something both introductory ('elements') and revisionary ('new'), setting itself apart from other texts by choosing to describe its object as 'the knowledge of man' rather than 'physiology'. Diderot includes Barthez's book in the reading list he drew up for himself when working on his own *Éléments de physiologie*, but in fact only mentions the 'principe vital' once in the finished work.[33]

There is a further crucial ingredient that needs adding into the mix of concepts and models which Diderot had available to him, and it has already been mentioned both in relation to mechanism and vitalism: chemistry. Seminal mechanist and animist-vitalist physiologists Boerhaave and Stahl were both also chemists; their understanding of chemistry unsurprisingly splits along mechanical and vitalist lines. It was however the later research of Diderot's chemistry tutor Guillaume-François Rouelle (1703–70) and *Encyclopédie* contributor Gabriel François Venel (1723–75) that most influenced to Diderot's thinking, and which leads François Pépin in his monumental study of the importance of chemistry for Diderot to conclude that chemistry provides him more than anything else with a 'modèle de penser' [model with which to

---

31  Brockliss and Jones, *The Medical World*, p. 429.
32  Paul-Joseph Barthez, *Nouveaux éléments de la science de l'homme* [1778], 2 vols, 2nd edn (Paris: Goujon et Brunot, 1806).
33  'Notes de la main de mon père sur la physiologie', Diderot, *Éléments de physiologie*, ed. by Quintili, p. 389 (and for the editor's discussion of Barthez, pp. 43–44); the 'principe vital' is mentioned within the text on p. 126, almost in passing as a synonym for 'life', and therefore without any particular emphasis or attention being drawn to it. Terada adds depth to our knowledge of the extent to which Barthez contributes to Diderot's thinking in the *Éléments de physiologie*, see esp. MT 161n, 168n, 174n.

think] and 'une source de modèles et d'orientations pour penser la nature et des processus' [a source of models and perspectives to use for conceptualising nature and natural processes].[34] Fermentation will be one such specifically chemical notion which, in Diderot's hands, becomes a tool for thinking about change in matter, in bodies, and in species.[35]

In sum, eighteenth-century physiology can be understood as covering a spectrum of enquiry from the workings of bodies to life itself. Bodies themselves were understood to be a mixture of solids and fluids and needed to be investigated as such. There was great emphasis on the properties of flesh, specifically sensation and irritation, on the organs, their functions, and how they communicated or contributed to the body as a whole. These bodily functions generally include the following list: circulation, secretion, nutrition, digestion, respiration, sensation, and reproduction. The brain was mostly a mystery, although its physical appearance and constituent parts were recorded in ever greater detail.[36] Diderot's *Éléments de physiologie*, like other general works of physiology, contains all these aspects, and takes up its own particular positions on them.

It might be helpful to indicate where critical literature has generally situated Diderot with respect to his physiological sources. The first point to make therefore, specifically in relation to this question, is that a clear differentiation has tended to be made between him and physiological writers who underwent professional medical training; he is understood to be at one remove from physiological research. Thus, he is seen to draw rather selectively on the careful physiological or anatomical descriptions of others, without also importing their conceptual frameworks.[37] This

---

34 François Pépin, *La Philosophie expérimentale de Diderot et la chimie: philosophie, sciences et arts* (Paris: Classiques Garnier, 2012), p. 696.
35 Pépin, *La Philosophie expérimentale*, pp. 718–19.
36 Vicq's *Traité d'anatomie et de physiologie*, coming out in 1786, two years after Diderot's death, presents itself as ground-breaking in its investigations of the brain. It advertises itself as being the first of many volumes but in fact there was only one (was it too expensive a publication project?), and that one only covers dissections of the brain. The plates, of which there are seventy, are exquisite (*Traité d'anatomie et de physiologie: avec des planches coloriées représentant au naturel les divers organes de l'homme et des animaux* (Paris: de l'Imprimerie de Franç. Amb. Didot l'Aîné, 1786).
37 This is the case with respect to Jean-Paul Marat, Adriaan van der Spiegel (also known as Adrianus Spiegelius), Lorenz Heister, Marin Cureau de la Chambre, and

also applies to what is termed his appropriation and repurposing of the arguments or ideas of others, such that, as Andrew Clark puts it, their 'meaning must be renegotiated'.[38] Jean Mayer hones in on how he rewrites his 'informants': 'il ne prendra chez ses informateurs que l'essentiel, simplifiant leur prose, comme Pascal lorsqu'il s'inspire de Montaigne ou de Charron' [he will take from his informants only the essential, simplifying their prose, like Pascal does when taking inspiration from Montaigne or Charron].[39] One might say that the definition of giving birth that opens the chapter is a good example of this stylistic paring down, but it is an interesting question as to whether what Diderot does is simpler, precisely. Paolo Quintili has a nicely paradoxical way of expressing the balance between source text and its new home: he talks of the 'originalité de la synthèse diderotienne' [the originality of the diderotian synthesis].[40] Motoichi Terada follows the same line when he talks about 'l'éclectisme diderotien, qui tisse un texte original à partir d'emprunts variés' [diderotian eclecticism, weaving an original text from various borrowings].[41] Alexandre Wenger and others characterise the recycling of pre-existing elements by reference to that mutating, splitting and reforming basic organism of nature, the polyp: they call it Diderot's 'style-polype'.[42] Clark will see this in transformational terms, talking about 'a poetics of physiology', and in part what he is doing is extending the implicit analogy between physiological theory and its stylistic expression that Wenger is also using; Clark pushes it further, establishing a parallel between the physiological focus on the relationship between part and whole which has already been alluded to in relation to Bordeu, and Diderot's new 'assemblages'.[43] François Pépin will emphasise instead (and in less exalted terms) just how hard it is to

---

others (Quintili, 'Introduction', p. 36), and also with respect to Roussel and A. L. Thomas on the female variety of the human (Quintili, p. 40).
38 Quintili, 'Introduction', p. 76 (specifically with respect to Haller); Kaitaro, *Diderot's Holism*, p. 14; Andrew Clark, *Diderot's Part* (Ashgate: Aldershot, 2008), p. 75, https://doi.org/10.4324/9781315257853.
39 Mayer, *Diderot, homme de science*, p. 317.
40 Quintili, 'Introduction', p. 99.
41 MT 54.
42 Wenger, *Le Médecin et le philosophe*, p. 90; he references essays by Jacques Proust, 'Diderot et la philosophie du polype', *Revues des sciences humaines*, 182 (1981), 21–30, and May Spangler, 'Sciences, philosophie et littérature: le polype de Diderot', *RDE*, 23 (1997), 89–107, https://doi.org/10.3406/rde.1997.1391.
43 Clark, *Diderot's Part*, pp. 84, 81 respectively.

'séparer ce qui appartiendrait à un savoir constitué en dehors de l'œuvre de Diderot et ce que celui-ci en fait' [separate what belongs to specialist knowledge from outside Diderot's œuvre and what he does with it].[44] It seems helpful here to heed Wenger's remark about the relationship between Diderot's text and the field of physiology, despite the fact that he is referring to the *Rêve de d'Alembert* rather than the *Éléments de physiologie*: 'ce texte, partie d'un tout dont l'achèvement se situe toujours dans le futur, est appelé à être révisé sans cesse' [this text, part of a whole whose completion is always located somewhere in the future, requires constant revision].[45] Hopefully, this reminds us why Diderot needs to draw on quite so many sources: it is not that he lacks originality or is a plagiarist, but rather that the area covered by physiology is vast and that he is integrating new developments; as a field of knowledge (what we now call a *science*) it was changing all the time, ceaselessly revised, modified, added to, whether in terms of specific details that came to be better understood, or in terms of the over-arching theories that make sense of the cumulative mass of local description and information. To have a single text which contained all this, was both introductory (in the sense that 'éléments' provide the basics), complete, up-to-date and accurate (in that it covered all constituent parts and how they operate together), and clear (in that the details did not overwhelm a sense of the whole) was (and remains) extremely challenging.

## 'Il faudroit enfin un Descartes ou un Leibniz'[46]

Physiologists of the period were aware of the difficulties of the genre, and repeatedly mention it as a challenge or a problem. Vitalist contributer to the *Encyclopédie* Ménuret de Chambaud gives a long list of what is required 'pour faire une bonne physiologie' [to do a good physiology] in his article OBSERVATION.[47] Bordeu lambasts the 'faiseurs de physiologie ordinaire' ['the makers [writers/compilers]

---

44  Pépin, *La Philosophie expérimentale*, p. 696.
45  Wenger, *Le Médecin et le philosophe*, p. 99.
46  ['ultimately what is needed is a Descartes or a Leibniz'].
47  Ménuret de Chambaud, 'Observation', *Encyclopédie*, vol. 11, pp. 313–21 (p. 319), http://artflsrv02.uchicago.edu/cgi-bin/philologic/getobject.pl?c.10:1051:2.encyclopedie0416.3346788.3346794. See also the critical online edition *Édition numérique collaborative et critique de l'Encyclopédie* ed. by Alexandre Guilbaud,

of ordinary physiology'] and Bordenave, lobbying for the qualities of his own *Essai sur la physiologie*, writes that 'Je sçais qu'on ne manque point de Livres sur la Physiologie, mais ils sont ou trop abrégés, ou trop étendus, ou au-dessus de la portée des Etudians' ['I know that there is no lack of books on physiology, but they're either too short, too long, or beyond the reach of students.'].[48] Perhaps here he is allowing himself to criticise Haller, whose summum, the *Elementa physiologiae corporis humani*, ran to eight relatively indigestible (and Latin) volumes (1757–66); perhaps however Bordenave's subsequent translation of Haller's *Primae lineae* (1769) is an implicit avowal that his own *Essai* had not turned out to be quite so authoritative or popular as he had hoped. Vicq d'Azyr will be very critical of the sloppy and discursive writing styles of his brother physiologists (sadly, no sisters): 'Ce qui a le plus contribué à rendre les descriptions informes et prolixes, c'est l'usage où la plupart des auteurs sont de s'interrompre pour disserter sur ce qu'ils exposent' [What has contributed the most to the shapelessness and verbosity of [physiological] description is the habit that most authors have of interrupting themselves to comment on what they are describing].[49] But then Vicq only completed the first volume of his ambitious and no doubt extremely expensive entreprise, the *Traité d'anatomie et de physiologie*, while Bordeu never did get round to writing a 'physiologie'. He did however call for a philosophical genius to do so: 'Il faudroit enfin un Descartes ou un Leibniz, pour débrouiller ce qui concerne les causes, l'ordre, le rapport, les variations, l'harmonie, et les lois des fonctions de l'économie animale' [ultimately what is needed is a Descartes or a Leibniz to disentangle everything relating to the causes, order, connections, variations, harmony, and laws of the functions of the animal economy].[50] An interesting and surely significant appeal, this, in a book we know Diderot read, written by a friend of his whom he will later transform into a major voicepiece for materialist and medical theory in *Le Rêve de d'Alembert* (1769). Certainly, Diderot's own

---

Alain Cernuschi, Marie Léca-Tsiomis and Irène Passeron, http://enccre.academie-sciences.fr/encyclopedie/. Cited in Quintili, 'Introduction', p. 21.
48 Bordenave, *Essai sur la physiologie*, p. iii.
49 Vicq, *Traité d'anatomie*, pp. 49–50.
50 Théophile de Bordeu, *Œuvres complètes de Bordeu: précédées d'une notice sur sa vie et sur ses ouvrages*, ed. by Anthelme Richerand (Paris: Caille et Ravier, 1818), vol. 1, p. 208.

*Physiologie* does attempt to cover all these aspects, although he leaves speculation about impenetrable causes aside, exorting us instead to start with the facts.[51] So, if on the one hand there was a sense of the need for a 'bonne physiologie' to rise above the 'faiseurs de physiologie ordinaire', to avoid tedious commentary, to be neither too short, too long or too hard for the student to understand, and if, on the other hand, at least one of these physiologists considered that the only person able to balance all the different aspects would be a philosopher of the stature of a Descartes or a Leibniz, then it does look as if there was room and even appetite for such as Diderot to have a go.

Indeed, in his 1964 edition of Diderot's *Éléments de physiologie*, Jean Mayer 'noted that it is superior, in many respects, to most other such tracts that were available at the time'.[52] Kurt Ballstadt is more effusive than the cautious Mayer: he calls it 'Diderot's second encyclopedia' and his *'pièce de résistance'*.[53] Even Jean Rostand, who only knew the *Éléments* in the early incomplete draft (published by Assézat and Tourneux from the manuscript in the St Petersburg archive) writes the following words in praise of the *Éléments*: 'Enfin, indépendamment de leur contenu scientifique, que de formules vives et plaisantes, dans les *Éléments de physiologie,* nous font souvenir du grand écrivain qu'était Diderot' [Also, scientific content apart, how truly the vigorous and striking expressions we find in the *Éléments de physiologie* remind us of what a great writer Diderot was].[54]

Of course, we already know that there is another side to this story of praise: viz, that critics often refer to it as incomplete.[55] We looked at how the mystification about fragments came to have purchase in Chapter 2. We will not open that question again here, returning instead

---

51  DPV 336/PQ 154/MT 156.
52  See Jean Mayer's first edition of the text (as opposed to his subsequent DPV edition), *Éléments de physiologie* (Paris: Didier, 1964), p. lvi, cited by Ballstadt, *Diderot: Natural Philosopher*, p. 209.
53  Ballstadt, *Diderot: Natural Philosopher*, pp. 209, 214, respectively.
54  Jean Rostand, 'Diderot et la biologie', *Revue d'histoire des sciences et de leurs applications*, 5.1 (1952), 5–17 (p. 15), https://doi.org/10.3406/rhs.1952.2892. Quoted in Wenger, *Le Médecin et le philosophe*, p. 114. This is in the context of Wenger strongly criticising Rostand for the way in which he fails to take into consideration the performative and dialogic aspects of the *Rêve de d'Alembert*: Wenger considers that this remark about the *Éléments* is Rostand's way of compensating for having 'consciously amputated' the *Rêve* of its crucial stylistic dimension.
55  See above.

to the comparative analysis of different introductory works to the field of physiology in France in the second half of the eighteenth century. A simple way to grasp the continuities or differences in emphasis and approach is to compare their structure and contents, and to do so in chronological order of their publication (or, in the case of Diderot, composition). This handful of works, starting with Haller, have been chosen to span the period just before and after Diderot was writing so as to get some sense of what the field was like, and also in reference to their title: they need to be attempting some form of introduction or overview of physiology. Specialist works, even if they are known to have influenced Diderot's thinking on physiology, will not therefore be taken into consideration.[56]

## Introductory Physiologies: Structures and Contents

The master Haller's one-volume *Primae lineae physiologiae* (1747) and his eight-volume master work the *Elementa physiologiae* (1757–66) move through the same sequence of body parts and functions. As he is the reference point for every subsequent physiologist we will be looking at, the sequence is worth describing. The *Primae lineae*, or *Éléments de physiologie* as both Tarin and Bordenave's translations call it, plunges straight into a description of the fibre after only the briefest introduction. The *Elementa physiologiae* itself does not have a great deal of introductory matter, and after only a few pages establishing the recent history of new discoveries in physiology and anatomy and one introductory page on the wider subject of physiology and proper methods of observation, also gets straight into detailed description of the fibre.[57] The *Primae lineae* has thirty-five chapters (there is no superstructure grouping these chapters into various parts), and their headings contain about an equal number of named body parts or elements of the body (such as cellular tissue and fat, or the heart, the brain, the intestines, etc) and functions (such as circulation, secretion, nutrition, muscular movement, etc). As we already said, Haller's *Elementa* moves through the same sequence

---

56   The interested reader may wish instead to consult Motoichi Terada's edition, with its panoply of helpfully-reproduced sources.
57   The volumes of Haller's *Elementa physiologiae corporis humani* are online at https://catalog.hathitrust.org/Record/008593541.

as the *Primae lineae*, although grouped into separate volumes. The first volume looks at the fibre, blood vessels, circulation of the blood and at the heart. Volume 2 looks in greater detail at the character of blood and then at secretions. Volume 3 looks at respiration and the voice; volume 4 at the brain, nerves, and muscles. Volume 5 treats the internal and external senses. Volume 6 looks at deglutition, the stomach, the stomach lining, the spleen, pancreas and liver. Volume 7 turns to the intestine, the digestive fluid chyle, urine, semen and 'women's matters'. The final volume deals with the life of the foetus. Interestingly, there is no main heading dealing with the skeleton or with bones more generally.

Bordenave's *Essai sur la physiologie* (1764) is close to Haller in terms of content and order with one principal difference: he also has a substantial first part entitled 'Des Élémens ou principes en général' which looks at the properties of matter and their different elements, including a section on sources of heat (air, water, oil, salt and earth). His 'Parties qui constituent le corps de l'homme' [constituent parts of the human body] then broadly follows Haller's sequence, with an increased focus on bodily functions as opposed to body parts in the chapter titles. Bordenave also inserts a chapter on sensibility and irritability in a prominently early position (after chapters on Fibre and then Cellular Tissue and Fat), which also draws closely on Haller.

Diderot's *Éléments de physiologie*, which in terms of the dates of its composition (c.1773–c.84) falls between Bordenave and Vicq d'Azyr (1786), also has a first part. He names it 'Des Etres', and it starts, like Bordenave, with elements, matter, and molecules, moving on to consider life in its 'végéto-animal', 'animal', and human forms. He makes some strongly vitalist statements: 'Sans la vie rien ne s'explique' [without life nothing can be explained] and 'Sans la vie, nulle distinction entre l'homme et son cadavre' [without life, there is no distinction between a man and his corpse].[58] He considers both sensibility and irritability as general properties of living things, looking in turn at life, death, movement, reproduction, species, size, the morality (or behaviour) of animals, their grace and beauty. In the chapter on Man he looks at reason, thought, and soul. His second part, the 'Éléments et parties du corps humain' [Elements and parts of the human body] is famously the

---

58  *Éléments de physiologie*, PQ 126.

part which is closest to Haller, with a first chapter on the fibre, and a first line of that first chapter which reproduces a sentence of Haller's almost word for word.[59] However, this chapter on 'Fibre' is preceded by a very unHallerian introduction, opening with the following sentence:

> L'homme a toutes les sortes d'existence: l'inertie, la sensibilité, la vie végétale, la vie polypeuse, la vie animale, la vie humaine.[60]
>
> Man has every kind of existence: inertia, feeling, vegetable life, polypous life, human life.

Diderot's framing gives a decidedly materialist orientation to this second part on the 'Elements and parts of the human body', emphasising its relationship to the contextualising first part on 'Beings' more widely. It contains twenty-five chapters, and all, apart from one ('Génération'), have an element or part of the human body as their title, and are not therefore organised according to abstracted bodily functions. In general, it contains a good deal of Hallerian physiology, but the order is different, starting with no fewer than four chapters on the basic constituent parts of flesh (fibre, cellular tissue, membranes, fat), then moving to the brain and nerves, thereafter muscles generally, then heart, blood, arteries and the lymphatic system, glands and other secretions, and bit by bit down the torso from chest to stomach and organs of digestion and excretion, and finally the reproductive organs, ending with the foetus.[61] It packs a great deal of very succinct description into about a third of the length of Haller's *Primae lineae*.

---

59  'En physiologie la fibre est ce que la ligne est en mathématiques' [in physiology the fibre is what the line is in mathematics], (PQ 156): Editors Jean Mayer and Paolo Quintili remind us of Haller's Latin: 'Fibra enim physiologo id est, quod linea geometrae' (*Elementa physiologiae*, vol. 1, p. 2, quoted DPV 338n and *Éléments de physiologie* PQ 156n). Clark draws attention to Diderot's meaningful substitution of *mathematics* for *geometry*, and points out that Diderot may have got the phrasing from Haller, but that it wasn't original to Haller either. Haller got it from Francis Glisson (1597–1677), Professor of Physic at Cambridge from 1636. Clark, *Diderot's Part*, p. 75.

60  DPV 337/PQ 155/MT 157.

61  Mayer points out that this second part is influenced in its broad conception by Bordeu's emphasis on the triumvirate of brain, heart, and stomach, as well as being packed with physiological information from Haller's *Primae lineae* and *Elementa physiologiae*. Mayer, *Diderot, homme de science*, pp. 279–80. Terada shows that while the earlier draft of the *Éléments de physiologie*, which we call SP, follows Haller's conceptual ordering of subjects, the mature one, known as V, departs from it (MT 53).

The third part contains the 'Phénomènes du cerveau' [phenomena of the brain], and most of it does not have an equivalent in Haller.[62] In its opening chapter, Diderot describes sensation and the sensory organs, to which the *Primae lineae* had given six separate chapters, book-ended by the topics of muscular movement and sleep; 'Sleep' in Haller's treatment is then followed by twelve chapters on hunger and aspects of digestion. Diderot, as we see, organises things very differently: from sensation he moves to 'the understanding', memory, imagination, sleep, the will, passions, organs (which looks, Bordeu-fashion, at the extent of their independence and dependence), diseases, and finally the conclusion. Memory in fact is briefly treated in Haller as part of a chapter on 'internal senses', while sleep, as we have seen, has its own chapter. They do not have the rest of the chapter headings in common. So Diderot's *Physiology* has its own quite distinct character, commencing with matter and living beings, then describing the human body, and finally moving to the mind and looking at our experience of the outside world and of ourselves, as rooted in our physiology and its particularities or (more often than not) pecularities.

Vicq's *Traité d'anatomie et de physiologie* (1786) has a fifty-page opening discourse in which he discusses the difficulty of the subject, opines that physiologists should not attempt to track down causes but base their analyses on effects, as has only just begun to be attempted by '[les] écrivains les plus modernes' [the most modern writers] and that enough is now known, however imperfect, to supply 'des résultats utiles à la Médecine et à la Philosophie' [useful results for both medicine and philosophy].[63] The structure that he announces gives headings only to nine identified bodily functions, in the following order: digestion, nutrition, circulation, respiration, secretion, ossification, reproduction, irritability, sensibility.[64] It is interesting to see ossification appear here, as bones do not feature as a chapter heading in the previous works we have been considering. Exactly how Vicq would have managed the structure cannot be predicted, given that all we have is this first volume. Apart

---

62  Terada discusses, with respect to the ordering of *Éléments de physiologie*, part 3, what he calls 'la singularité du châpitrage' [the peculiarity of the chapter divisions] (MT 97).
63  Vicq, *Traité d'anatomie*, pp. 6–7.
64  Vicq, *Traité d'anatomie*, p. 15.

from its introductory discourse, it contains a seventy-page physiological vocabulary list with definitions, and then moves on to the plates describing the brain.

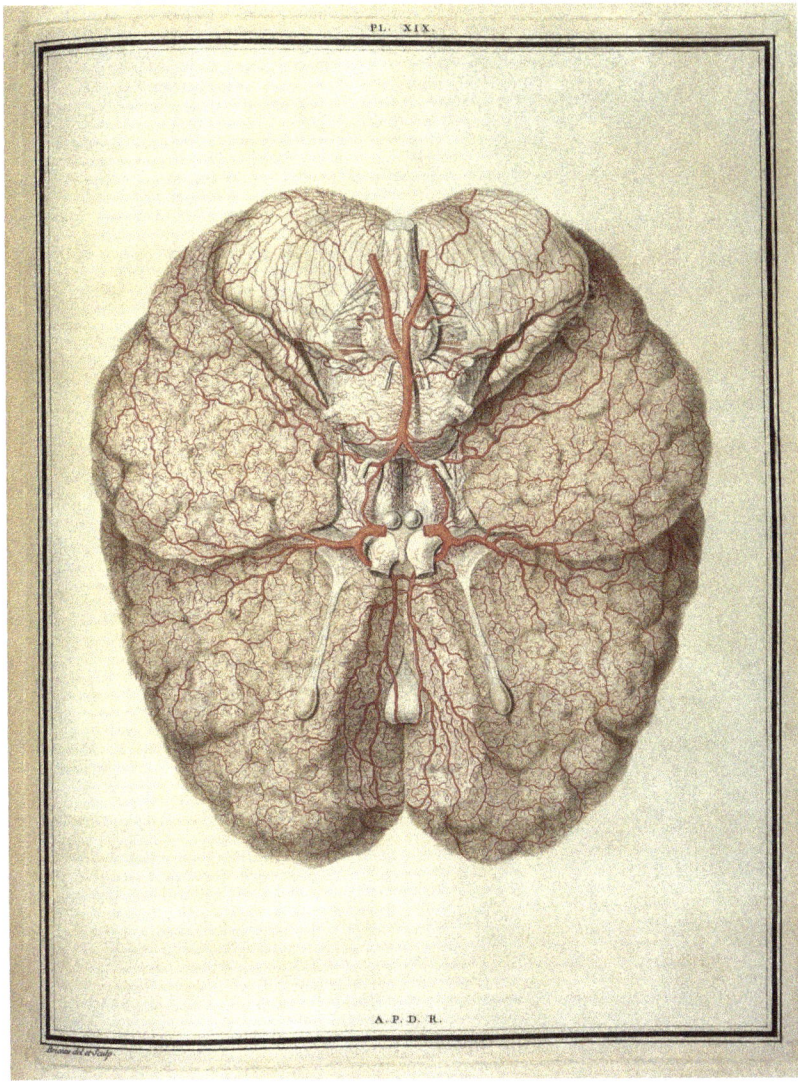

Fig. 4.1 Felix Vicq D'Azyr, *Traité d'anatomie et de physiologie*, EPB F694. Plate 19, engraving showing dissection of the brain, Wellcome Collection, https://wellcomecollection.org/works/yprjdx8t, CC BY 4.0

The final work we will be looking at, the *Nouveaux élémens de physiologie*, signals its revisionary and introductory aim very clearly. Its author, Anthelme Richerand, would go on to edit Bordeu's complete works.⁶⁵ Dedicated to the influential ideologue Pierre-Jean-Georges Cabanis (whom we will be discussing in '9. 1796–97: Cabanis and Destutt de Tracy at the Institut national'), it appeared in 1801 and by 1811 was being reprinted in its fifth revised edition.⁶⁶ His *Nouveaux élémens* spans two volumes and has two parts: the shorter introductory first part discusses natural beings, differences between organic and inorganic bodies, animal and vegetable properties, life, sensibility, a series of Barthez-influenced chapters on sympathies between different parts of the body and on habit and the 'principe vital'. Part two looks at the vital functions (digestion, absorption, circulation, respiration, secretion, nutrition, sensation, reproduction) and also contains separate chapters on movement, voice and speech, ending with a survey of ageing and variety in temperament, death and decay. The chapter on sensation (which falls at the beginning of volume 2) has subsections on the understanding, on passions, sleep and sleepwalking. The opening topics in part one are, of course, strikingly close to Diderot's own opening section.⁶⁷

Of all these figures, Haller is the only one not to include introductory matter setting human physiology in a vaster context, whatever that might be. It is interesting to consider the extent to which his omission of these sorts of questions might well be one of the factors enabling historians of science such as François Duchesneau to identify him as a founder of modern physiology, introducing a sort of medical modernity which is in fact synonymous with the abandonment of philosophical enquiry. Haller himself would have been anxiously determined to adhere to a religious and Calvinistic understanding of creation, and therefore left these questions aside precisely because they were important and polemical. The modern science of physiology with its delimited definition does not include such contextualising questions in its introductory

---

65  Bordeu, *Œuvres complètes*, ed. by Richerand.
66  Anthelme Richerand, *Nouveaux élémens de physiologie*, 5th edn (Paris: Caille et Ravier, 1811).
67  We do not have the space here to develop this particular parallel, but Richerand appears again later in the book in '9. 1796–97: Cabanis and Destutt de Tracy at the Institut national'.

overview textbooks.⁶⁸ However, most of the physiologists mentioned in this chapter—Bordeu, Tarin, Bordenave, Barthez, Diderot, Vicq, and Richerand—all of whom were aware of and variously influenced by Haller's work, did emphasise such questions, and perhaps this is because of the increasingly dominant vitalism in French physiology of the period. As François Victor Mérat de Vaumartoise, co-editor of the *Dictionnaire des sciences médicales* (1812–22) remarked in his definition of 'Vitalistes', 'il n'est guère permis à l'époque actuelle de n'être pas vitaliste; les progrès des sciences médicales nous ont ramené de toutes parts à cette croyance en nous montrant le vide des autres opinions, et la puissance des forces de la vie' [it is hardly acceptable in current times not to be vitalist; the progress of the medical sciences has in every instance reinforced the validity of this view while demonstating the nullity of any other opinion, as well as the power of the forces of life].⁶⁹ If Vaumartoise's strident assertion in fact indicates the continuing presence of debate rather than the contrary, there is no real doubt that physiology of the period did see itself as linked to understanding what life was.

Diderot will answer this question from an unhesitatingly materialist point of view, and this, therefore, is what makes his *Physiologie* distinctive. The actual number of pages taken up by the description of

---

68 Walter F. Boron and Emile L. Boulpaep open their Physiological textbook with the title question 'What is physiology?'. This is their definition: 'Physiology is the dynamic study of life. Physiology describes the 'vital' functions of living organisms and their organs, cells, and molecules. For centuries, the discipline of physiology has been closely intertwined with medicine. Although physiology is not primarily concerned with structure – as is the case for anatomy, histology, and structural biology – structure and function are inextricably linked beause the living structures perform the functions.' Walter F. Boron and Emile L. Boulpaep, *Medical Physiology*, 3rd edn (Philadephia, PA: Elsevier, 2017), p. 2. It is interesting to note, given the earlier discussion of the aims and conversely pitfalls of physiology manuals, that Boron and Boulpaep also have a sense of the difficulty of the entreprise: 'We were intrigued by an idea suggested to us by W.B. Saunders: write a modern textbook of physiology that combines the expertise of a multi-author book with the consistency of a single pen' (Preface to the First Edition, p. ix).

69 François Victor Mérat de Vaumartoise, 'Vitalistes', in *Dictionnaire des sciences médicales*, ed. by François Pierre de Chaumeton and F.V.M. de Vaumartoise (Paris: Panckoucke and Plomteux, 1812–22), vol. 58, p. 281. See also my 'Charts and Signposts: Following Vitalism and Mechanism through the *Encyclopédie*, the *Encyclopédie méthodique* and the *Dictionnaire des sciences médicales*', *Mécanisme et vitalisme*, ed. by Mariana Saad, special issue of *La Lettre de la maison Française d'Oxford*, 14 (2001), 85–104 (p. 96).

human physiology is proportionally smaller than these other writers, while the opening and final sections on, firstly, the elements of life and death, and secondly, sensation, the mind, and experience, are proportionally greater. His *Physiologie* is characterised by descriptions which are more severely concise and selective than those of his peers, and also by a consistently anti-abstract approach. He gives many more case studies, examples, and anecdotes than these other writers who consistently describe a universalised body. For him, instead, it is always about a particular body in time and space, whether his own or someone else's.[70] If nature is matter and life is sensibility, and physiology is nature, matter, life and sensibility all in one conjoined mass, then what does that feel like? The point being, presumably, that that conjoined mass is what we are, no more or less and for no longer than it continues to function. This approach is what characterises Diderot's particular brand of materialist vitalism. We will now turn to look at these two aspects of concise description and anti-abstraction in more detail.

\*\*\*

Here is how Haller describes what the chest is, what it's made of and what its three-dimensional form is:

> Nous appellons POITRINE ou THORAX une espece de cage composée d'os & de cartilages, dont les intervalles sont remplis par des muscles; elle a la figure d'un cône obtus, plus étroit à la partie supérieure et presque ellyptique; cependant applati en devant et divisé à sa partie postérieure par une éminence.[71]

> We will call CHEST or THORAX a sort of cage made of bone and cartilage with muscles filling the spaces in between; its shape is of an obtuse cone, narrower at the top and almost elliptical, flattened on the front and divided at the back by an eminence or raised part.

---

70　See Diderot, *Éléments de physiologie*, 'j'avais 66 ans quand je me disais ces vérités' [I was 66 years old when I told myself these truths] (DPV 313/PQ 129/MT 136); 'Il me semble que j'entends crier ma femme' [I seem to hear my wife cry out] (DPV 359/PQ 179/MT 179).

71　Haller, *Éléments de physiologie*, trans. by Toussaint Bordenave (Paris: chez Guillyn, 1769) vol. 1, p. 158 (ch. X: De la respiration, §CCLXXVIII), https://doi.org/10.5962/bhl.title.43392. Spelling and accents: sic.

A sort of cage made of bone and cartilage with muscles filling the spaces in between is relatively straightforward to visualise, although rather grotesque if taken literally. The second part with its sequential geometrical description is less easy to absorb or translate into an image. An obtuse cone, narrower at the top, almost elliptical, that is flatter on the front and divided at the back by an eminence, or raised part? If I did not know already what a chest looked like, I would have no idea how to translate this description into a meaningful shape. Elsewhere, it is described not as an obtuse cone but as a truncated one (a 'cône tronqué').[72] Bordenave followed this definition very closely in his own attempt at a concise physiological manual. He writes:

> La Poitrine ou Thorax est une espece de cage composé d'os, de cartilages et de muscles. Sa figure dans l'homme pourroit être comparé à un cône tronqué, applati sur le devant, dont la base est inférieure. Son plus grand diamètre est d'un coté à l'autre, et le plus petit de la partie antérieure à la postérieure.[73]

> The Chest or Thorax is a sort of cage made of bone, cartilage, and muscle. Its shape in humans is comparable to a truncated cone, flattened on the front, and whose base is at the bottom. Its widest diameter is from one side to the other, and the narrowest from the front to the back.

As we see, the 'sort of cage' image is reproduced identically, although Bordenave adds a quick gloss to clarify that the geometrical description which follows relates to its shape as found in a human being. Thereafter he slightly rephrases Haller: using the notion of 'truncated cone', he retains the description of the flattened front, but instead of saying that it is narrower at the top, he says that the base—i.e. the wider part—is at the bottom; he then starts talking about diameter, anterior and posterior.

In terms of ekphrasis, his description is not very helpful. His and Haller's descriptive method would work to a certain extent if the text were accompanied by a diagram, although arguably the diagram would render the description redundant. As a stand-alone description, it is simply confusing. Compare with Diderot's description:

---

72 Haller, *Éléments de physiologie*, trans. by Bordenave, vol. 1, p. 36 (ch. V: Du coeur, §LXXV).
73 Bordenave, *Essai sur la physiologie*, p. 102.

*Poitrine*, grande cavité formée par les côtes, le cou et le diaphragme.⁷⁴

*Chest*, large cavity formed by the ribs, the neck, and the diaphragm.

His brevity is so startling as to be almost comical when compared to the efforts of Haller and Bordenave. He does not overlay his description with metaphorical cages, or geometrical abstractions and measurements. He simply calls the chest a large cavity formed by the ribs, the neck, and the diaphragm, producing an image in words which is immediately comprehensible and visualisable, keeping a consistent and unencumbered focus on what he is talking about—the body itself.

This approach to physiological description which I have called more severely concise and selective than that of his peers derives from unparalleled experience of describing things in words—the decades of work on the *Encyclopédie* articles and plates, and the experimental ekphrasis of painting and sculpture we find in the *Salons*. The concision is not an end in itself; it is about the clarity and efficacy of the textual description of a physical object, such that description becomes evocation in the most direct way possible. Freed from the labyrinth of detail that ensnares other physiologists (however much they attempt to clarify, explain, and make accessible in their various manuals, essays, and translations), Diderot starts but does not end with description. He defines, evokes, gives odd variants that may illuminate or may challenge existing knowledge, explains how the part or function of the body he is describing works with the whole, and he moralises, by which I mean, he comments on connected behaviour. This is the pattern that dominates in his *Éléments de physiologie*, and any one page would give examples of it. We will simply look here at the brief ninety-word sub-section describing the organ of taste, without however contrasting it with Haller's more exhaustive physiological description; hopefully the way in which Diderot selectively uses and departs from Haller is now clear.⁷⁵ The passage is relatively terse and not particularly striking.

---

74   DPV 392/PQ 210/ MT 211.
75   Haller, *Éléments de physiologie*, ch. XV: 'Du Goût', §CDXLVIII-CDLVIII; tr. Tarin, pp. 103–06; tr. Bordenave, t. 2, pp. 18–26. Terada shows that in this section Diderot also draws on Antoine Le Camus's *Médecine de l'esprit*, see MT 454, source notes xv–xviii.

*Goût*

Si l'impression se fait sur les papilles de la langue, la sensation est du goût.

Si le siège du goût est dans la langue, il s'affaiblit en approchant de l'épiglotte. Une fille, qui pour toute langue n'avait qu'un tubercule, goûtait. La langue a des papilles de deux espèces, des tronquées et des frangiformes.

Le palais, le tour de la bouche, le gosier sont encore des organes servant au goût.

Le goût est le dernier des organes qui s'éteigne : il n'est donc pas étonnant que les vieillards aiment la table.[76]

*Taste*

If an impression is made on the papillae of the tongue, the sensation is one of taste.

Taste is based in the tongue and is weaker closer to the epiglottis. A girl, who had nothing but a tubercle for a tongue, could still taste. The tongue has two sorts of papilla, truncated and fungiform.

The palate, the whole mouth, and the gullet are also organs which contribute to taste.

Taste is the last organ to go, which explains why old people like eating so much.

Diderot defines and distinguishes taste in the wider context of sensation in general, locating it principally in the tongue but also looking at a counter-example which shows that even with only a sort of protuberance for a tongue, the organ of taste can still function. However, this counter-example is not generalised, unlike my gloss of it; Diderot turns the counter-example into a living case by attaching it—albeit cursorily—to the experience of one particular girl. He moves without explanation or any transitionary gestures to the different sorts of papillae (containing the taste buds), then surveying the subsidiary taste organs, to return at the end to taste as a sensory organ amongst others, to its life (its growth and decline) within the life of the body as a whole. The final clause moves further outwards, connecting physiology and its cycles to a sort of common knowledge or received wisdom

---

76  DPV 449–50/PQ 274–75/MT 266.

about old people, their behaviour and preferences. The passage as a whole is very economical (more than this commentary on it is able to be!), and gives only key points: what is taste; where is it located; what are its physiological mechanisms; what are its limits; what is its life cycle; what are the implications of this for human experience.

These will be Diderot's questions for every part of the body; if the patterns and processes of physiology determine, frame, and initiate every interrogation, it is never confined to them, and will always move on to consider the related aspect of human experience, bringing in observations of more or less moralising character and connecting them to shared knowledge about human life, its phases and types. Thus he consistently avoids abstraction by always asking the same question: what does it feel like? And by consistently asking this question, Diderot also avoids the sort of dehumanised approach which underpins Haller's work, and is objectionable to read when it breaks surface, such as in the following instance, where Haller talks in comparative terms about the properties of skin:

> La surface interne de l'épiderme est plus *pulpeuse*, demi-fluide & comme composée de *mucus*; celle des Européens se sépare difficilement, celle des Nègres d'Afrique plus aisément [...].⁷⁷
>
> The internal surface of the epidermis is more *pulpy*, semi-fluid and as if made of *mucus*; in Europeans, it can only be separated with difficulty, whereas in African Negroes it is much easier.

Of course, Haller is not trying to section the epidermis of living Europeans and Africans but is alluding to his difficulties in dissecting corpses; his vivisectional experiments related to animals, and this is a subject we touched on earlier in the chapter. Nonetheless, the generalisation about white and black skins has a nasty resonance, not least because Haller does not talk about white skin and black skin, he talks about Europeans and Negroes from Africa, which in the context of the eighteenth century means colonisers and colonised, masters and slaves. Furthermore, there is an implicit notion of hierarchy in the idea of the tougher European skin, as Haller's following remarks, likening

---

77　Haller, *Éléments de physiologie*, trans. by Bordenave, vol. 2, pp. 4–5 (§CDXXIX). Haller's italics.

black skin to animal skin, make all too clear.[78] And although Diderot copies almost word-for-word some parts of this chapter on the sense of touch, including Haller's definition of skin, he places this particular comparison of Haller's elsewhere, in his chapter on Membranes, and he removes the connected remark about the similarity with animal skin.[79] What we do find in Diderot is an extended meditation on the difference between flesh, which is endowed with sensation, and wood, which is not. Again, Diderot is asking the question: what does it feel like? And it may well be that this passage is at least in part a subterranean reaction to Haller, and an implicit correction. It's a bravura piece, and here it is:

> Pourquoi tant de différence dans le pincer d'une tenaille de bois ou de fer et d'une tenaille de chair, ou de deux doigts ?
>
> La tenaille de bois ne sent pas, celle de chair sent ; la tenaille de bois ne souffre pas, celle de chair souffre, la tenaille de bois n'est pas chatouillée, la tenaille de chair l'est. La tenaille de bois ne se refuse pas à sa rupture, la tenaille de chair s'y refuse. La tenaille de bois ne sent ni sa force, ni sa faiblesse, la tenaille de chair la sent : la tenaille de bois, après sa rupture, ne se meut pas, la tenaille de chair se meut [ ...] la tenaille de chair était en conspiration, et reste en sympathie avec d'autres organes. La tenaille de bois ne s'accroissait, ni ne vivait, la tenaille de chair avait un

---

78   'Chez ces derniers [les Nègres d'Afrique] elle est vraiment membraneuse, solide et séparable, ainsi que dans le palais des animaux' [In the latter (African negroes) it is truly membranous, solid and separatable, similar to the palates of animals] (Haller, *Éléments de physiologie*, trans. by Bordenave, vol. 2, p. 4). Diderot uses this passage in his chapter on Membranes, but without the comparison to animal skin, see DPV 344/PQ 162/MT 163.

79   'Ce qu'on appelle PEAU, est un tissu dense, composé d'une grande quantité de cellules extrémement rapprochées, dont les fibres sont entrelacées et embarrassées les unes dans les autres; elle est conséquemment *extensible, contractile & poreuse*' [What is called SKIN is a dense tissue composed of a great number of cells which are extremely close together and whose fibres are interlaced and entangled; it is consequently *extensible, contractile & porous*] (Haller, *Éléments de physiologie*, trans. by Bordenave, vol. 2, p. 2 [§ CDXXVI]; Haller's capitals and italics). And here is Diderot: 'La peau est un tissu dense, composé d'un grand nombre de cellules rapprochées, dont les fibres sont entrelacées et embarrassées les unes dans les autres. Elle est extensible, contractile & poreuse' [The skin is a dense tissue composed of a great number of cells which are close together and whose fibres are interlaced and entangled ; it is consequently extensible, contractile & porous] (DPV 447/PQ 272/MT 163). He has simply removed the adverbs and the typographical emphasis. See the previous footnote for the reference to the Membrane chapter.

accroissement, et sa vie. En général dans l'animal et dans chacune de ses parties, vie, sensibilité, irritation. Rien de pareil dans la matière brute.[80]

> Why is there such a difference between the pinch of wooden or iron pincers and of flesh pincers, or of two fingers?
>
> The wooden pincers don't feel anything, the flesh ones do; the wooden pincers have no pain, the flesh pincers do, the wooden pincers don't feel any tickling, the flesh pincers do. The wooden pincers do not put up any resistance to being ripped apart, the flesh pincers do. The wooden pincers have no sensation of their strength or weakness, the flesh pincers do: the wooden pincers, once torn apart, don't twitch, the flesh pincers do (...) the flesh pincers conspired with other organs, and remain in sympathy with them. The wooden pincers didn't grow or live, the flesh pincers had growth, and their own life. In general in the animal and in each of its parts, there is life, sensibility, irritability. There's nothing of the sort in raw matter.

This peculiar comparison of flesh pincers and wooden ones is peculiar precisely because it is depersonalised. If at the beginning we are reminded that the analogy is with fingers, thereafter Diderot prefers to use the defamiliarised image of the flesh pincers, thereby emphasising the parallel with the tool made from inanimate matter so as to pursue the imaginative investigation of what sensation is and how it works. It also inverts the expected perspective, in the same way that the comparison between love and a piece of fruit that this study opens with also did. There, we were asked to think about the question of desire from the point of view of the piece of fruit; here, instead of exploring the question of painful sensation being inflicted *by* pincers, we are thinking of painful sensation inflicted *on* pincers. And although this analogy is depersonalised, it is not abstract, because it is relatable; it asks its reader to relate to the questions, to follow the thought experiment, and to use that imaginative experience to consider life as characterised by sensation, or in this instance, pain. The narrative moves from the pleasurable notion of a tickling sensation to the violent one of severing, the flesh twitching in reaction to being severed, still 'in sympathy' with the other organs it is no longer attached to. And further, it uses this two-part notion of severing and connection to ponder the relation of part

---

80  DPV 449/PQ 274/MT 265–66.

to whole, a question which was much debated at the time, as we have already mentioned.

Diderot's 'what does it feel like' means, as we have said, that we hear about many people, including himself, in the course of these pages. Perhaps the most remarkable and certainly the longest examples recount, in a footnote which swells to take up the whole page, the stories of two couples who fall pregnant when it should have been anatomically impossible for them to do so.[81]

Fig. 4.2 The swollen footnote, BnF, Manuscrits, NAF 13762, f. 96v.-97r., Denis Diderot (copyist 'E'), c. 1780, Pen and Paper, Denis Diderot, *Éléments de physiologie*, Fonds Vandeul, Bibliothèque nationale de France, CC-BY

---

81 I further analyse these cases in my chapter '"Autre fait arrivé au château de Nicklspurg, en Moravie": Diderot and the Horrid Case Study', in *The Dark Thread: From Tragical Histories to Gothic Tales*, ed. by John D. Lyons (Newark: University of Delaware Press, 2019), pp. 149–59. I thank John D. Lyons and the University of Delaware Press for allowing me to re-use some of that analysis here, and I would also like to record my gratitude to Professor Lyons and the University of Virginia for the generous funding which made it possible for me to attend the 'Dark Thread' conference (from which the edited book emerged) in Charleston, March 2016.

172                    *The Atheist's Bible*

The footnote is in Part II of the *Éléments de physiologie*, in the long chapter on reproduction and how it occurs.[82] (Diderot presents five different theories.) This footnote gives two examples from two different sources of the statement in the main body of the text about it being possible to get pregnant even when—as he carefully puts it—the woman is infibulated, that is, without any apparent vagina. The first case relates how the lover of a young woman with this particular problem is not put off, but simply requires her to indulge him in a different way, as the text coyly says, going on to report that she happily obliged.

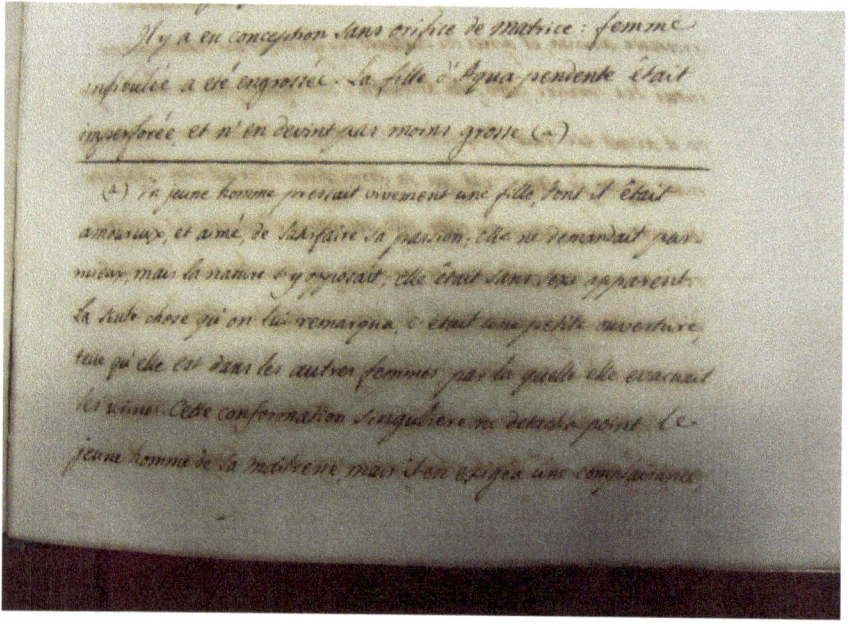

Fig. 4.3 The resourceful lovers, BnF, Manuscrits, NAF 13762, f. 96r., Denis Diderot (copyist 'E'), c. 1780, Pen and paper, Denis Diderot, *Éléments de physiologie*, Fonds Vandeul, Bibliothèque nationale de France, CC-BY

Her stomach starts to swell and she calls a doctor, who pronounces her pregnant. She has no difficulty proving to him that this is impossible, and yet her stomach and bosom continue to swell, and she calls him a second time. He swears she is pregnant, but the young

---
82  DPV 429–31/PQ 249–51/MT 247–48.

woman and her lover pay no attention. After nine months she has terrible pains, and after horrendous tearing a baby is born 'by the same route he was conceived'. Diderot finishes by saying he does not know whether the mother and child died or not, but that her particular 'formation' is in no way uncommon. He then supplies his scholarly source.[83]

The second instance, repeated verbatim from an account by 'Mr Nuch' in the *Journal historique et politique*, is alluringly introduced as 'another true story that took place in the castle of Nicklsburg in Moravia'—a good gothic setting for a lurid story. It involves a twenty-two-year-old soldier whose stomach started swelling and who complained of nausea. He was treated for dropsy, although to no effect. His stomach kept growing, but he felt fine, and it had no impact on his ability to carry out his duties which he kept on with very cheerfully.

Then, on 3 February 1774 he suddenly had acute pains in his lumbar region. First he was treated with sedatives, which did not work, then they gave him a lumbar puncture which also did not work. They tried bleeding him. Nothing worked, and the pains just grew worse and worse. He started going into convulsions. After ninety-seven hours of suffering, he died. This was all so surprising and baffling that an autopsy was performed, and imagine everyone's surprise—interjects Nuch—when they discovered a sort of cyst or sac in the soldier's abdomen in which they found a perfectly formed—although dead—baby boy. This sack was of course a uterus which communicated with the rectum by means

---

83   He writes, 'je tiens ce fait de Monsr Louis, secrétaire de l'académie de chirurgie' [I got this fact from Mr Louis, secretary of the academy of surgery]: Antoine Louis (1723–92), whom Diderot infers had related it directly to him, was a friend of his and contributor to the *Encyclopédie*. Louis had published on this topic *An imperforata mulier possit concipere?* (1755) (DPV 429, n. 269/PQ 250, n. 86/MT 247, n. 182). Mayer, Quintili, and Terada give a rejected fragment from the St Petersburg draft which explains that Louis left this anecdote out of the '*Mémoires* de notre Académie de Chirurgie' (which Louis had founded) because decency would not allow otherwise (DPV 429/PQ 249/MT 247). Mayer also adds (n. 269) that this case is mentioned by Haller (*Elementa*, t.VIII, I$^{re}$ partie, p. 22). In fact this is not accurate; in Haller, anything specific about the case is removed, which is alluded to very briefly and in generalised terms: 'Etiam per anum, in quem vagina patebat, maritus feminam impraegnavit: alii uxoris urethrae ad venerem abusi sunt' [Furthermore, a husband impregnated a woman through the anus, which connected with her vagina; others misused the wife's urethra for intercourse]. With thanks to Ilya Afanasyev and Gustav Zamore for the translation.

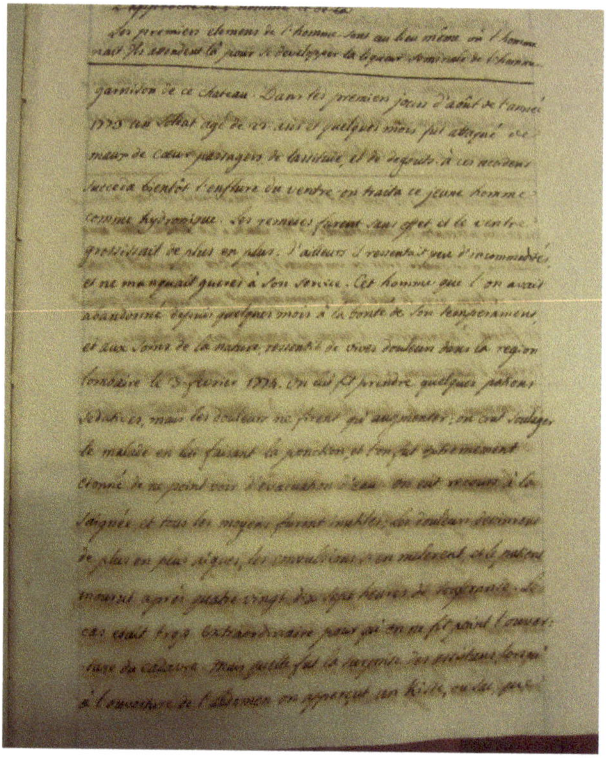

Fig. 4.4 The pregnant soldier carries on his duties blissfully unaware, BnF, Manuscrits, NAF 13762, f. 96r., Denis Diderot (copyist 'E'), c. 1780, Pen and paper, Denis Diderot, *Éléments de physiologie*, Fonds Vandeul, Bibliothèque nationale de France, CC-BY

of a very narrow tube that was even smaller, we read, than the ink feeder in a fountain pen. Otherwise, the soldier was 'perfectly' male both internally and externally. The unnamed and unpersonalised observers then remember that the soldier had complained he felt something moving inside him about thirty hours before he died. The story ends balefully: 'they' are in no doubt about how this all happened, but just for the avoidance of doubt, they seize the soldier's bedfellow, clap him in irons and repeatedly 'threaten him' until he finally admits what 'they' had 'violently suspected'. And there, with a cursory reference to the source, the footnote ends.[84]

---

84 *Gazette des Deux-Ponts* (1775), number 22. At the beginning of the anecdote, he had also referenced 'Mr Nuch, chirurgien-major des troupes de la garnison de ce

Of course the history of medicine and of law is full of bizarre 'cases' that sometimes leap off the page in a way that brings their subjects to life—as many have noticed, not least Natalie Zemon Davis in her work on Martin Guerre and on the pardon cases in *Fiction in the Archives*.[85] Such cases offer a very rich and deep meeting of high and low cultures, where the educated writer—a literate observer, whether lawyer or doctor— commits to writing the events and words of those being observed, generally according to certain forms of professional code. These sorts of 'cases' are obviously both problematic and revealing in equal measure, but when a writer such as Diderot extracts them from their original context and re-uses them, they begin to resonate in an entirely new way; as Clark put it, and as we quoted a few pages earlier, their 'meaning must be renegotiated'.[86] Diderot's adoption and framing of these two tales and the way in which he brings them together gives them great prominence, even just in terms of space on the page. Lightly sketched as they are, both stories are full of human detail and character—the lovers in the first story who eagerly find a way round the woman's irregular physical formation, and who repeatedly reject the doctor's prognosis; in the second, the cheerful character of the soldier who willingly gets on with his duties, and the intimacy of the hidden relationship. The economy of the telling and the narrative trajectory increase—I would argue—the impact of the shadows around the story—that which is not known, or not said. The brutal statement about not knowing whether the mother and child died in the first case prods the reader to notice the callousness of the reporting observer, while also returning attention to the human outcome—certainly shocking and probably tragic for those involved. The shape of the Moravian story is not dissimilar, in that the relation of the everyday duties and interactions also end in baffled suffering and tragedy. In this case however, it seems more intensely tragic: the soldier suffers for ninety-seven hours, he does die, and so does the child, while his 'bedfellow' or rather his *lover* not only loses him, but is imprisoned because of their relationship, the violence of the suspicion being a transposition, we assume, of the way in which

---

château' as having certified it. See DPV 430, n. 270/PQ 250, n. 87/MT 247 (the entire source is given MT 433–35, *Journal historique et politique*, Genève, 1775, pp. 296–98).

85   Natalie Zemon Davis, *Fiction in the Archives: Pardon Tales and Their Tellers in Sixteenth-Century France* (Cambridge: Polity Press, 1987).

86   See above.

he is treated. These cases sharply juxtapose the precise and sceptical empiricism of the doctor anatomist with a complex human situation in time—the emphasis is not only on the person with the malformed body but on the human relationships he or she has, and on the consequences of the bodily malformation on those relationships. The distance of the recording eye in combination with the intensity, strangeness, and tragedy of the human events make for a powerful mix.

The effect that the presence of these and other such narratives have on the *Éléments de physiologie* as a whole is to make sure we do not get lost in abstractions about physiology, matter and its movement. They tell us what it feels like to be a piece of matter, or a piece of malformed matter, experiencing love and tragedy. These people or characters are not special, not heroic, yet their experience is still intense, still worthy of attention and compassion. They are part of Diderot's answer to the philosophical question about what happens to identity, individuality, and the all-round unique specialness and perfection of the human being when viewed as nothing more or less than the temporary happenstance of material organisation and physiology. These notions of uniqueness with their theological and hierarchical dimensions may all fall away when humans are viewed as a certain species of animal, and what is left may well be both fragile and impermanent, but perception and experience—what it feels like to be alive—are no less complex or intense. Or, in these cases, tragic.

To briefly sum up: what distinguishes Diderot's *Éléments de physiologie* from similar introductory surveys of the period is in part the way in which it is framed with materialist questions (about matter, life, experience, illness, and death). It is also characterised by its much sharper style, and by a resolutely anti-abstract approach; again we can link this to Diderot's materialism and his interrogation of it, refusing to universalise. The basics of physiology involve, for Diderot, understanding our experience of being alive, of being ill, of feeling desire, of being driven by it.

# PART TWO

# THE *ÉLÉMENTS DE PHYSIOLOGIE*, 1790–1823

# 5. 1790: Naigeon and the *Adresse à l'Assemblée nationale*

In 1784 Diderot died. The following year, the set of manuscripts which Diderot had prepared for Catherine II were sent off to her along with all his books.¹ No catalogue of his library survives, and the books themselves have been dispersed or lost.² The manuscripts, however, would go on to form the basis of the edition of his complete works that Jules Assézat and Maurice Tourneux prepared, and which came out in twenty volumes between 1875 and 1877. The *Éléments de physiologie* is to be found in volume nine, but this version, as indicated in Chapter 2, was an early draft of the text. Diderot had had another complete set of his manuscripts made, and these passed to his daughter, Angélique de Vandeul. Jacques-André Naigeon (1738–1810), a member of d'Holbach's circle younger than Diderot by a generation, and, like him, a co-writer of the baron's most famous work, the *Système de la nature* (1770), was named in Diderot's will as his literary executor.³ It is to him that we now turn.

Jacques-André Naigeon's contribution to the Diderot story—as editor and guardian of Diderot's works and reputation—was decisive,

---

1   Gerhardt Stenger, *Diderot, le combattant de la liberté* (Paris: Perrin, 2013), pp. 703–04.
2   Sergeï V. Korolev has attempted to reconstitute it, see his study, *La Bibliothèque de Diderot. Vers une reconstitution* (Ferney-Voltaire: Centre international d'Études du dix-huitième siècle, 2014).
3   Denis Diderot, 7 June 1773, quoted in Maurice Tourneux, Review of Ernest Dupuy's edition of the *Paradoxe sur le comédien*, *Revue d'histoire littéraire de la France*, 9.3 (1902), 500–18 (p. 506); also Denis Diderot, *Correspondance*, ed. by Georges Roth and Jean Varloot, 15 vols (Paris: Minuit, 1955–70), vol. 12, p. 231 (3 June 1773). Naigeon would also quote it, and we give the text in its entirety in Chapter 10.

and did not perhaps always work to Diderot's advantage or to his own. This however is more owing to the unpredictable unfolding of what we now know as the French Revolution as if it was one event with one identity, and which Naigeon misread more than once, than to any innate inadequacy on his part. The remainder of this study is therefore as much about the Revolution and its cultural politics and polemics as it is about Naigeon or Diderot or any of the other figures we will be looking at. Its twists and turns cannot be relegated to some sort of decorative backdrop; it is the 'context' here which directly influences the form any 'text' can take, with some truly odd, even distorting, results in the case of the hardline atheist materialist *Éléments de physiologie*. I will argue that for Naigeon, it was Diderot's most important text bar none, and that pages 207–90 of his *Mémoires historiques et philosophiques sur la vie et les ouvrages de Denis Diderot* constitute its first, disguised, publication. This, however, did not occur until 1823, thirteen years after Naigeon's death. This is despite Naigeon's advertising the *Mémoires* as early as 1792 in the article on 'Diderot' he wrote for the philosophy volumes of the *Encyclopédie méthodique* and again in his preface to Diderot's *Œuvres* which came out in 1798. Yet, even in 1823, it was immediately banned and the publisher fined.[4] As we can see from even this short overview, the story is convoluted in chronological terms and stretches beyond Naigeon's named publication of Diderot's *Œuvres* in 1798 across different texts with different genres, from the dictionary entry to the intellectual biography, and from the early years of the Revolution to the reign of the ultra conservative Charles X. Given this complexity, it seems clearest therefore simply to follow the years through in chronological order. This will involve moving between Naigeon and other players, specifically the politician-philosopher-lecturer Dominique-Joseph Garat and the philosophers Pierre-Jean-Georges Cabanis and Antoine Louis Claude Destutt de Tracy, later known as Ideologues after Destutt's neologism of 'Idéologie', important figures who were not necessarily in sympathy with Naigeon and whom we will introduce in greater detail in due course.

The story starts though with the first of Naigeon's publications to touch on any of Diderot's works since the latter's death, and the first

---

4   David Adams, *Bibliographie des œuvres de Diderot, 1739–1900*, 2 vols (Ferney-Voltaire: Centre international d'étude du XVIIIe siècle, 2000), vol. 2, p. 141.

(and last)[5] to engage directly with Revolutionary politics, seeking to influence decisions in the making.[6] This is his *Adresse à l'Assemblée nationale sur la liberté des opinions, sur celle de la presse*, published in Paris in February 1790.[7]

Detailed work by Pascale Pellerin, Raymond Trousson, and René Tarin has explored and explained why the consecrating glory bestowed on Voltaire and Rousseau is emphatically denied to Diderot throughout the Revolutionary years. They show how, for different reasons and at different moments, Diderot is persistently perceived as, in Pellerin's words, 'violent, extrémiste, ennemi implacable des rois et des prêtres' [violent, extremist, and an implacable enemy of kings and priests].[8] As Pellerin argues, this perception seems to be set on its juggernaut course by Naigeon's vitriolically anti-clerical *Adresse à l'Assemblée nationale*, which tarnished Diderot by association. Naigeon's description of priests as 'des espèces de bêtes féroces qu'il faut enchaîner et emmuseler, lorsqu'on ne veut pas être dévoré' [species of wild beasts that must be chained and muzzled if one wishes to avoid being devoured] was quoted and requoted in a relay race of righteous indignation, and rapidly associated with Diderot.[9] This impression, that 'derrière chaque phrase de Naigeon, le public observe l'ombre de Diderot' [behind each sentence Naigeon wrote, the public saw the shadow of Diderot],[10] and that that shade was a vengeful and violent one, was confirmed by Louis-Sébastien Mercier's damaging anecdote, published in 1791, that Diderot used to say that 'le genre humain [...] ne sera heureux que quand on aura étranglé le dernier

---

5  Apart from the censored preface to his edition of Montaigne, although that never made it to publication (see discussion below).

6  I regret that Mario Cosenza's study of Naigeon, *All'ombra dei Lumi: Jacques-André Naigeon philosophe* (Naples: FedOAPress, 2020) came out too late for my research to benefit from it. It is free to read here: http://www.fedoabooks.unina.it/index.php/fedoapress/catalog/book/190.

7  Jacques-André Naigeon specifies the month in which the *Adresse* was published in the 'Discours préliminaire' to his 3-volume dictionary: *Encyclopédie méthodique: Philosophie ancienne et moderne*, 3 vols (Paris: Panckoucke, 1791–94), vol. 1, pp. i–xxvi (p. xxii: the printed number on this page is 'xii' but this is an error): 'cet écrit a été publié dans le mois de février 1790' [this text was published in the month of February 1790].

8  Pascale Pellerin, 'Naigeon: une certaine image de Diderot sous la Révolution', *Recherches sur Diderot et sur l'Encyclopédie*, 29.2 (2000), 25–44 (p. 26), https://doi.org/10.4000/rde.104.

9  Pellerin, 'Naigeon: une certaine image de Diderot sous la Révolution', 37.

10  Pellerin, 'Naigeon: une certaine image de Diderot sous la Révolution', 35.

roi avec les boyaux du dernier prêtre'[11] [the human species [...] will not be happy until the last king has been strangled with the guts of the last priest], and for all that Naigeon carefully and accurately restores this expression back to its rightful source, the parish priest Jean Meslier, in the article on him which appeared in the third volume of the *Philosophie ancienne et moderne* in 1794, it remained indelibly associated with Diderot, not least because of his poem, *Les Eleuthéromanes*, later published in 1796, contains a rephrasing of exactly this.[12] So we see what the issue is, and it does not really matter a great deal that the exact phrase did not originate with him and in fact reached its pithy apogee in a reworking of Meslier authored by Voltaire in 1762, and thus that Diderot is the third not the first to come out with this threat to the twin authorities of church and monarchy; his being associated with it is not incorrect. And of course it gives superb ammunition to the anti-revolutionaries: Jean-François de La Harpe (1739–1803), literary critic and erstwhile *philosophe* in the ambit of Voltaire, whose imprisonment in 1794 is credited with transforming his views into reactionary conservatism, influenced generations to come when he wrote in his *Cours de littérature* of 1797 that Diderot was 'un auteur immoral et subversif mais aussi sanguinaire' [not only an immoral and subversive author but also a blood-thirsty one].[13]

And yet this is not the whole story. The Diderot (or the La Harpe) of 1797 was not the Diderot (or the La Harpe) of 1790. And Naigeon's *Adresse* was not universally negatively received; on the contrary, great swathes of it—twelve pages, no less—were quoted verbatim and approvingly in the *Mercure de France* in its issue of 5 March 1791, the journalist explaining that he preferred to provide the original given that his own views were identical: 'nous nous sommes étendus sur ces idées et au lieu d'y mêler les nôtres qui sont absolument conformes à celles de l'Auteur, nous avons cité, en le resserrant, tout son système' [we examined these ideas and instead of mixing ours in with them decided, given that they

---

11 L. S. Mercier, *De J. J. Rousseau considéré comme l'un des premiers auteurs de la Révolution* (Paris: Buisson, 1791), vol. 2, p. 137; quoted in Raymond Trousson, *Images de Diderot en France, 1784–1913* (Paris: Champion, 1997), pp. 29–30.
12 Diderot, *Les Éleuthéromanes*, ed. by Jean Varloot, in *Œuvres complètes*, ed. by H. Dieckmann, Jacques Proust, Jean Varloot (Paris: Hermann, 1975) [hereafter DPV], vol. 20, pp. 549–55.
13 René Tarin, *Diderot et la Révolution française: controverses et polémique autour d'un philosophe* (Paris: Champion, 2001), p. 143.

follow the Author's exactly, to quote, in condensed version, his whole system].[14] And when we read the *Adresse*, we discover that the 'public' was not wrong to observe Diderot's shade hovering behind Naigeon, as Pellerin put it: Naigeon in fact directly quotes, without acknowledging it, from a number of Diderot's works. We find lengthy paragraphs from his *Plan d'une université pour le gouvernement de Russie*, and also sentences or recognisable expressions from the *Éléments de physiologie*, his letters, *Jacques le fataliste*, and the 'Prière du sceptique'.[15] Naigeon also invisibly quotes from D'Holbach's *Système de la nature*, and (extensively) from his own articles on Cardan and Mirabeau, due to appear in 1792 and 'An II' (1793–94) in volumes 2 and 3 of the *Philosophie ancienne et moderne* (there may well be more extensive quotation even than this, but I have not been able to source any more).

From the point of view of this study, then, it looks as if Naigeon was using his *Adresse* to prepare the way for his multi-staged Diderot publication project, and also as an advert or appetiser for his forthcoming *Philosophie ancienne et moderne*, with its important 'Diderot' article. If so, as we have already intimated, it did not work very well. It was his first misstep. But we can see from the text itself that he thought the time was ripe: 'quand on a quelque chose de bon à dire, il faut se presser' [when you have something good to say, you must hurry up and say it].[16] In the pages that follow we will look at what 'the good thing' he had to say was, and why it was urgent.

The goal of Naigeon's one-hundred-page argument with its two lengthy notes, bringing the page count to 140, is in his sub-title: 'Examen philosophique de ces questions; 1°. Doit-on parler de Dieu, & en général de religion, dans une déclaration des droits de l'homme? 2°. La liberté des opinions, quelqu'en soit l'objet; celle du culte & la liberté de la Presse peuvent-elles être légitimement circonscrites & gênées de quelque manière que ce soit, par le Législateur?' [Philosophical

---

14 *Mercure de France* 1791: 5 mars 1791; 'Nouvelles littéraires', pp. 128–41 (p. 141).
15 It is not clear whether the 'Prière du sceptique' really was authored by Diderot. Adams does not include it in his *Bibliographie des œuvres*, but Christian Albertan and Anne-Marie Chouillet conclude that it was his, see Christian Albertan and Anne-Marie Chouillet, 'Autographes et documents', *Recherches sur Diderot et sur l'Encyclopédie*, 36 (2004), paragraphs 14–15, https://doi.org/10.4000/rde.618.
16 Jacques-André Naigeon, *Adresse à l'Assemblée nationale sur la liberté des opinions, sur celle de la presse, etc.* (Paris: Volland, 1790), p. 9.

examination of the following questions; 1. Should God and religion in general be mentioned in a declaration of the rights of man? 2. Can the freedom to have any opinion about any object, the freedom of worship and of the press ever be legitimately circumscribed and blocked in any way whatsoever by the Legislator?]. The answer Naigeon gives to both questions is an emphatic no. To the first one: 'Les seules matières où il soit permis de parler de Dieu, sont celles de Théologie [...]. Il faut le bannir de toutes les autres, sans exception [...]' [the only subject in which God may be discussed is Theology [...] It must be banished from absolutely every other one without exception].[17] And to the second:

> Le commerce des pensées ne doit être, sous quelque prétexte que ce soit, ni plus gêné, ni plus restreint que celui des denrées et des marchandises; c'est le même principe général d'utilité et de justice appliqué à des objets divers. S'il est des circonstances difficiles et momentanées, où la liberté absolue du commerce puisse être modifiée, suspendue même pour un temps, dans quelques-unes de ses parties; ce qu'il n'est pas de mon sujet d'examiner, il n'est aucun cas, sans exception où celle de penser et d'imprimer, puisse être légitimement limitée.[18]

> The trade in thoughts must not, on any pretext whatsoever, be blocked or hindered any more than the trade in foodstuffs and goods; this is the same general principle of utility and justice applied to different objects. If there are any difficult and momentary circumstances in which the absolute freedom of trade can be amended or even suspended for a short time in any particular aspect is not something I can examine here. However, there is no case or exception when the freedom to think and to publish can be legitimately limited.

Naigeon's argument is an interesting one: the free circulation of thought is as important as the free circulation of goods, and can never be legitimately restricted. His view, expounded at length, is that personal satires, calumny or libel, can have no negative impact if they are false, and that they will mostly cancel each other out (p. 72) or be boringly written (the only unexpiable crime, he writes, p. 74, sounding very like Voltaire), that 'un bon Gouvernement' would never tolerate unjust defamation, and further, that, while 'un libelle diffamatoire' [a defamatory libel] only imperils individuals, the freedom of the press is

---

17 Naigeon, *Adresse*, p. 21.
18 Naigeon, *Adresse*, p. 76.

a 'bien général' [general good] (p. 77). It is this entire section which the *Mercure de France* approvingly quotes at length, with some gaps.[19]

These two views, broadly, on the one hand, that church and state should be separate and discussion of God limited to theological debate, and on the other, that freedom of the press should be absolute, are not particularly radical in Revolutionary France. Naigeon's anti-clerical pro-tolerance pro-free speech stance is not even particularly far from the Voltaire of the *Lettres philosophiques* (1734). So it is interesting that this particular publication is associated in scholarly literature with an expression of anti-clericalism deemed excessive, and indeed typical of Naigeon.[20] This view seems to replicate and pursue the anti-Revolutionary rhetoric so effectively harnessed by La Harpe. Naigeon certainly does express unbridled animosity towards priests with their institutional power but that is not the only feature of his text, and as we have already seen, other aspects were also given the limelight, and viewed as well-expressed and important.[21]

Let us turn to the aspect which is of most importance to this study, that is, Naigeon's quotation from or stewardship of Diderot's writings and thought, not omitting the *Éléments de physiologie*. As Naigeon's quotation of Diderot's texts in the *Adresse* seems not to be fully recognised, I will give it in full.[22] Apart from the fact that this will hopefully be of interest to scholars of Diderot and Naigeon anyway, the relevance for this specific argument is to begin to chart and track the patterns of Naigeon's quotation of and references to Diderot, which we will follow through his other publications all the way to the *Mémoires* of 1823.

---

19  Direct quotation (as opposed to paraphrase which begins and ends the Mercure review) is to be found in *Mercure de France* 1791: 5 mars 1791; pp. 133–39, relating to Naigeon's *Adresse*, pp. 60–79.
20  See for example Pellerin, 'Naigeon', 33, 36.
21  See for example *Mercure de France* 1791, p. 140, as quoted above.
22  Roland Mortier gives an 'analyse détaillée de son contenu' [detailed analysis of its content], remarking how Naigeon 'se place [...] sous l'égide de Diderot, dont l'autorité sera évoquée discrètement à d'autres occasions' [places himself (...) under the auspices of Diderot, whose authority will be discreetly evoked on other occasions], one of these occasions being part of the section about the 'Sorbonnistes' which we quote below, but Mortier doesn't name the source text or give precise references, so it's not entirely clear whether he saw Naigeon's 'discreet evocation' of Diderot as being in the order of quotation or just allusion. Roland Mortier, 'Naigeon critique de la déclaration des droits', *RDE*, 20 (1996), 103–13 (pp. 105, 107, 108, 111), https://doi.org/10.3406/rde.1996.1325.

## Quotation and Allusion

The two most extensive verbatim quotations from Diderot are from his (then) unpublished *Plan d'une université pour le gouvernement de Russie*, and here both the title and the author are kept strictly quiet, although each passage is given in quotation marks and attributed to 'un philosophe' (in the first instance) and 'un philosophe moderne' (in the second). This text, sent by Diderot to Catherine II in 1775 (and not implemented by her), was a continuation of what are now known as his *Mélanges pour Catherine II* and in which he planned the earlier stages of education.[23] The two passages Naigeon quotes are anti-clerical. The first proposes that churches be turned into lunatic asylums, with the priests kept on to look after the inmates, and the second claims that priests trained at the Sorbonne are all either deist or atheist, and all the more intolerant and disputatious for it; he shudders at the idea that such men should be allowed to propound their fanatical theories to the population as a whole. Here are the passages.

Naigeon is talking about how the population as a whole is ignorant and superstitious and ripe for fanaticism. This reminds him of:

> ce que disoit un philosophe avec cette éloquence et cette énergie que donnent la hardiesse et la profondeur des pensées. 'Le gros d'une nation restera toujours ignorant, peureux et par conséquent superstitieux. L'athéisme peut être la doctrine d'une petite école, mais jamais celle d'un grand nombre de citoyens, encore moins celle d'une nation un peu civilisée. La croyance de l'existence de Dieu, ou la vieille souche restera donc toujours: or qui sait ce que cette souche abandonnée à sa libre végétation, peut produire de monstrueux? Je ne conserverois donc pas les prêtres comme des dépositaires de vérités, mais comme des obstacles à des erreurs possibles et plus monstrueuses encore; non comme les précepteurs des gens sensés, mais comme les gardiens des fous; et leurs églises je les laisserois subsister comme l'azile ou les petites maisons d'une certaine espece d'imbécilles qui pourroient devenir furieux, si on les négligeoit entiérement'.[24]

---

[23] See Laurent Versini, 'Introduction [to *Plan d'une université*]', in Denis Diderot, *Œuvres*, ed. by Laurent Versini (Paris: R. Laffont, 1995), vol. 3: *Politique*, p. 411.

[24] Naigeon, *Adresse*, pp. 33–34. The section in quotation marks ('le gros d'une nation' to 'entièrement') is from the *Plan d'une université pour le gouvernement de Russie*, in Diderot, *Œuvres complètes*, ed. by Jules Assézat and Maurice Tourneux, 20 vols (Paris: Garnier Frères, 1875–77), vol. 3, p. 518, https://fr.wikisource.org/wiki/Plan_d'une_Université_pour_le_gouvernement_de_Russie.

what a philosopher said with that eloquence and energy that bold and deep thoughts bestow on the speaker. 'Most of a nation will always stay ignorant, fearful and, in conquence, superstitious. Atheism may be the doctrine of a small school, but never of a large number of citizens and even less of a nation that is somewhat civilized. Belief in the existence of God or the old stock will therefore always remain: yet who knows what monstrosity this old root, left to grow freely, might produce? I would never therefore allow the priests to stay on as the depositories of truth but I would keep them to block other possible errors, possibly even more monstrous; not as tutors for sensible people, but as wardens of asylums for the insane. As for their churches, I would allow them to continue to exist as the asylums or special refuges for the sort of imbecile that might become violent if they were completely neglected.

We notice how he characterises this 'philosophe' as possessing the eloquence and energy that audacious and profound thought bestows; this is a not atypical description of Diderot.

In the second passage, Naigeon has been relaying a remark about how those who teach theology do not believe in a word they say yet spend more time than anyone else engaged in disputation and lecturing; as before, this leads him into his quotation:

> sa remarque se trouve confirmée par celle d'un Philosophe moderne qui avoit fait autrefois sa Licence à Paris, & qui regardoit la Faculté de Théologie, comme une excellente école d'incrédulité. 'Il n'y a guère de Sorbonnistes, dit-il, qui ne recelent sous leur fourure ou le déisme ou l'athéisme; ils n'en sont que plus intolérans & plus brouillons; ils le sont ou par caractere, ou par intérêt, ou par hypocrisie. Ce sont les sujets de l'Etat les plus inutiles, les plus intraitables & les plus dangereux. Eux & leurs adhérens, Prêtres ou Moines, ont souvent abusé du droit de haranguer le peuple assemblé. Si j'étois Souverain, & que je pensasse que tous les jours de Fêtes et de Dimanches, entre onze heures et midi, cent cinquante mille de mes Sujets disent à tous les autres, & leur font croire, au nom de Dieu, tout ce qui convient au démon du fanatisme & de l'orgueil qui les possède, j'en frémirois de terreur.'[25]

[this] remark is confirmed by what was said by a modern philosopher who had previously studied for his degree in Paris, and who regarded

---

25  Naigeon, *Adresse*, pp. 46n–47n. The section in quotation marks ('Sorbonistes' to 'terreur') is from the *Plan d'une université pour le gouvernement de Russie*, in Diderot, *Œuvres complètes de Diderot*, ed. by Assézat and Tourneux, vol. 3, p. 438, https://fr.wikisource.org/wiki/Plan_d'une_Université_pour_le_gouvernement_de_Russie.

the Faculty of Theology as an excellent school for incredulity. 'There is not a single Sorbonne-trained priest', said he, 'who does not hide either deism or atheism beneath the fur-lined gown of their office; they're all the more intolerant and argumentative because of it, whether by character, interest, or simple hypocrisy. They and their supporters, priests or monks, have often abused their right to harangue their congregations. If I were the sovereign, and I thought that every Sunday and feast day, between eleven o'clock and mid-day, one hundred and fifty thousand of my subjects were saying to all the rest of them whatever the demon of fanaticism and pride possessing them inspired them to say, and making them believe it in the name of God, I would be shuddering with fear.'

Both these passages are striking, and strikingly disrespectful. It is perhaps not surprising, given the outraged reaction that Naigeon's *Adresse* provoked at least in some quarters, and moreover the way in which its more extreme expressions of anti-clericism were attributed to and blamed on Diderot (not incorrectly, as we are beginning to see), that Naigeon did not return to the *Plan d'une université* in either his 'Diderot' article or in his fifteen-volume *Œuvres de Diderot* of 1798. It does, however, occupy twenty pages of his *Mémoires sur Diderot* (pp. 352–73), where we meet these exact same passages again, along with many others.[26]

These two passages are, to my knowledge, the most extensive quotations from Diderot in the *Adresse*, and, as we have seen, they are prominently presented as quotations from the conversation of 'un philosophe'. Yet there are other sorts of quotation which are not demarcated from the text in any way. In the paragraph following the first passage (about priests guarding imbeciles kept in churches), Naigeon immediately follows on with a further substantial sentence, this one extracted from a letter Diderot wrote about meeting the unorthodox priest Dom Deschamps.[27] It is thought to have been addressed to Mme de Maux, and it only survives because Naigeon copied it into a notebook of extracts from Diderot's works and letters which is now part of the

---

26 The first passage is replicated in Naigeon's *Mémoires historiques et philosophiques sur la vie et les ouvrages de Diderot* (Paris: J. L. L. Brière, 1821 [1823]; repr. Geneva: Slatkine Reprints, 1970), pp. 360–61, and the second on p. 358. (And it reappears in the original manuscript of Naigeon's *Mémoires*, F. 216.).
27 Léger Marie Deschamps (1716–74), known as 'Dom Deschamps', Benedictine monk and radical atheist thinker.

Fonds Vandeul in the Bibliothèque nationale.[28] And the *Adresse* is where Naigeon subsequently placed this passage. In the letter, Diderot explains he is paraphrasing Deschamps's views on the destructive consequences of social inequality. In the quotation, Naigeon simply quotes the idea without the framing introduction. It is:

> [...] l'idée d'un état social où l'on arriveroit en partant de l'état sauvage, en passant par l'état policé au sortir duquel on a l'expérience de la vanité des choses les plus importantes, et où l'on conçoit enfin que l'espèce humaine sera malheureuse, tant qu'il y aura des Rois, des Prêtres, des Magistrats, des Loix, un tien, un mien, les mots de vice et de vertu, etc.[29]
>
> the idea of a social state that could ultimately be arrived at, having started from a primitive state and moving through a civilized state on the way, at the end of which people would have experienced the emptiness of all the most important things, and would finally understand that the human species will be miserable for as long as there are kings, priests, magistrates, laws, a yours, a mine, the words of vice and virtue, etc.

Here, the 'etc.' signals the end of this particular passage, and in fact it is how Naigeon tends to indicate a cut, as we will see more clearly when we look at the *Mémoires sur Diderot*. However, that cut is invisible to the reader unaware of Naigeon's codes, and he then proceeds to argue that any reference to God, while useful in a legal code or charter, is completely unnecessary in a Declaration of Rights. It is not perfectly clear why one passage would be set apart from the rest of the text as an official quotation from 'un philosophe' and the other invisibly embedded, other, perhaps, than if it is owing to the desire to give those particular extracts of the *Plan d'une université* a bit more visibility, possibly with a view to later publication, which, if so, was dropped. It is not the passage's status as an informal letter per se, as Naigeon does not always invisibly embed

---

28 See Diderot's letter to Mme de Maux, 31 August 1769, in Diderot, *Œuvres complètes*, ed. by Roger Lewinter, 15 vols (Paris: Club Français du Livre, 1969–73), vol. 8, p. 895; Bibliothèque nationale de France, NAF 13783 134v.

29 Ibid. Pellerin states that this precise text 'faisait référence à deux passages du *Supplément [au voyage de Bougainville]*' [refers to two passages from the *Supplément au voyage de Bougainville*], citing the 'adieux du vieillard' and the dialogue between Orou and l'aumônier (Pellerin, 'Naigeon', 30), and of course she's not wrong that these passages resonate, but it's rather that the letter will (as often happened) have provided the source that Diderot later worked up into a finished text (the *Supplément* appeared in Grimm's *Correspondance littéraire* in the course of 1773–74).

extracts from Diderot's letters. The *Adresse* proper opens with an extract from a letter which offers a sort of moral fable:

> Un philosophe faisoit un jour cette question à un homme du monde: si le bal de l'opéra duroit toute l'année, que pensez-vous qu'il en arrivât? – Ce qui en arriveroit! C'est que tous les masques se reconnoitroient. – Eh bien, reprit le philosophe, ces masques-là sont les symboles de nos erreurs: souhaitez que le bal dure & ils finiront tous par être reconnus.[30]

> One day, a philosopher put this question to a man of the world: 'If the masked balls at the opera were on all year round, what do you think would happen?' 'What would happen? People would end up recognising all the different masks.' 'Well,' replied the philosopher, 'those masks symbolise our errors: you should hope that the balls carry on because then every single one will end up being seen through.'

As we have already begun to see, the relation of what 'un philosophe' said or did is a sure sign of the beginning of a quotation, and often (but not always)[31] directly refers to Diderot. This extract, too, comes from a letter to Mme de Maux. The dialogical dialectical style is very familiar from our reading of Diderot, particularly from texts such as the *Rêve de d'Alembert* or the *Neveu de Rameau*, and indeed summer 1769, when this letter was written, is when he composed the *Rêve*, even if the moralising talk of masks and error feels closer to the *Neveu*. So, in sum, Naigeon does quote from the letters more than once, and he varies the way in which he presents or embeds his extracts.

At points, he even paraphrases them. One such, from what will become perhaps the most requoted part of the *Adresse*, certainly in anti-Revolutionary texts, is where, in a development of the theme about

---

30 Naigeon, *Adresse*, p. 11, quoting Diderot, letter to Mme de Maux, mai 1769?; in Diderot, *Correspondance*, *Œuvres*, ed. by Versini (Paris: Laffont, 1997), vol. 5, p. 947; *Œuvres complètes*, ed. by Lewinter, vol. 8, pp. 852–53 (source copy Naigeon NAF 13783 132v). Identical except for N's 'souhaitez'; Diderot wrote more piously: 'priez Dieu' [pray to God]. This same opening passage will be regarded as striking and quoted by Jean-Philibert Damiron in his study on Naigeon (and others), *Mémoire sur Naigeon et accessoirement sur Sylvain Maréchal et Delalande* (Paris: Durand, 1857), reprinted in *Mémoires sur les Encyclopédistes* (Genève: Slatkine reprints, 1968), p. 411. Damiron does not know that this is a quotation from an unpublished letter.

31 Other allusions to the views of perspectives of 'un philosophe' are to be found in Naigeon, *Adresse*, pp. 33, 46n, 55, 90, 91, 98; the references on pp. 11, 33, and 46n are to Diderot as we have seen; 55 is to Cardan; and the others are non-specific.

which sections of the law or constitution God, religion, and priests may (or may not) appear in, Naigeon describes priests as:

> des espèces de bêtes féroces qu'il faut enchaîner et emmuseler, lorsqu'on ne veut pas en être dévoré.[32]
>
> species of wild beasts that must be chained and muzzled if one wishes to avoid being devoured

We mentioned this extract in our introduction to Naigeon's *Adresse*, and only return to it here to replace it in the context of an argument whose features we are beginning to be acquainted with. On the following page of the *Adresse*, Naigeon quotes—still invisibly—from the *Système de la nature*[33] (1.29-30):

> [...] l'histoire de Dieu est écrite en caractères de sang dans les annales de tous les peuples du monde [...] [34]
>
> the history of God is written in characters of blood in the annals of all the peoples of the world

Naigeon was, as we know, one of d'Holbach's assistants in the writing of the *Système de la nature*, along with Diderot. The extent of their contribution is not known; it is perfectly possible that Naigeon wrote this particular bit, or even Diderot himself. This hazy multiple authorship raises interesting questions about whether it is important (let alone possible) to identify any one voice over any other one.[35] For the time

---

32  Naigeon, *Adresse*, p. 37. Quoted by Pellerin, 'Naigeon', 35, 43: '... Moi, Naigeon, Encyclopédiste gagé, je ne puis croire que ce soit troubler l'ordre établi par la loi, que de mettre au grand jour mes principes Didérotiques, et de soutenir avec ce grand Maître de politique et de morale, qu'il n'y aura de bonheur sur la Terre, que le jour, où le dernier des Rois sera étranglé avec les boyaux du dernier des Prêtres' [I, Naigeon, a sworn Encyclopedist, cannot believe that it would disturb the order established by law to expose my Diderotian principles to the light of day and claim with this great Master of politics and morals that there will be no happiness on Earth until the day that the last King is strangled with the guts of the last Priest]. Naigeon also quotes this image in his 'Discours préliminaire', p. xxii. The footnote is about Meslier but refers also the Naigeon's *Adresse*.

33  D'Holbach, *Système de la nature*, ed. Josiane Boulad-Ayoub, 2 vols (Paris : Fayard, 1990), vol. 1, p. 30.

34  Naigeon, *Adresse*, p. 38.

35  See also Caroline Warman, 'Garden Centres Must Become the Jacobin Clubs of the New Revolution', *Voltaire Foundation*, 20 November 2018, https://voltairefoundation.wordpress.com/2018/11/20/garden-centres-must-become-the-jacobin-clubs-of-the-new-revolution/.

being, let us leave it that Naigeon does lift and re-use recognizable chunks of Diderot's words, and that, given that this study is attempting to establish whether a particular work of Diderot's was circulating and if so, where and how, it is a necessary part of our process and method to trace and place quotation of this sort.

It is perhaps appropriate therefore that I now turn to the three very glancing quotations from the *Éléments de physiologie* that I have found in the *Adresse*. These passages are devoid of the vitriolic anti-clericism we have seen thus far, but they also question God, while the materialist theory underpinning the rejection of religion comes more clearly into view. The first is at the very end of a footnote, mainly quoting Thomas Hobbes, which itself expands on a point being made in the main body of the text about banning discussion and even the name of God from all areas of study apart from theology. Naigeon adds this:

> Pascal dit expressément de Dieu, qu'on ne sait ni ce qu'il est, ni si il est.[36]
>
> Pascal specifically says about God that we do not know what he is or whether he is.

In the conclusion to the *Éléments de physiologie*, we read this:

> Pascal dit expressément de Dieu, qu'on ne sait ni ce qu'il est, ni s'il est.[37]
>
> Pascal specifically says about God that we do not know what he is or whether he is.

The reference is slight, and its positioning at the end of a long footnote could hardly be less eye-catching. One might also feel sceptical about this being attributable to Diderot given that it is a reference to Blaise Pascal, and yet to the sceptic I would make two points; firstly, that this formula gives a rather specific twist to what Pascal had written in what is now known as his 'wager' or 'le pari de Pascal' (and which we discussed in Chapter 2), and secondly that 'expressément' does

---

[36] Naigeon, *Adresse*, p. 21n; see discussion of this particular passage in Chapter 2. Reference to Denis Diderot, *Éléments de physiologie*, ed. by Jean Mayer, *Œuvres complètes*, DPV (Paris: Hermann, 1987), vol. 17, pp. 261–574 (p.515); Diderot, *Éléments de physiologie*, ed. by Paolo Quintili (Paris: Champion, 2004), p. 358; Diderot, *Éléments de physiologie*, ed. by Motoichi Terada (Paris: Éditions Matériologiques, 2019), p. 327 [hereafter notated as DPV 515/PQ 358/MT 327].

[37] DPV 515/PQ 358/MT 327.

not feature in the Pascal text; this sentence with its emphatic adverb does not sound like a cliché or a received idea; it sounds very written. Furthermore, it is not possible that Naigeon was still unaware of the *Éléments de physiologie* in 1790: he had had continuous access to the manuscripts at least from Diderot's death on, and probably earlier, and as has been mentioned, integrated many pages from the *Éléments* into the *Mémoires* which he had been writing from 1784 onwards.[38] It seems safe therefore to conclude that Naigeon is indeed quoting from it here, and that it has a marginal but perceptible presence in the *Adresse*. And indeed it is already there, twice, in the opening pages, where Naigeon declares that what the Assemblée nationale needs is 'un esprit vaste et sage qui arrête et dessine le plan dans lequel ils doivent entrer' [a mind of great depth and wisdom to decide on and sketch out the plan that the members of the Assemblée nationale need to adopt]; he says moreover that 'les matériaux existent, il est vrai, mais épars et sans liaison, sans rapports entre eux' [the materials exist, it is true, but they are scattered, disconnected, without relationships between them].[39] He goes on to say that for the Assemblée nationale's work, 'il importe, sur-tout, que les fondemens en soient solides, & le choix n'en est pas indifférent, car ici, comme dans beaucoup d'autres cas, il n'y a qu'une seule manière d'être bien, & mille manieres d'être mal' [the most important thing is that the foundations be solid, and the choices it makes do matter, for here, as in many other cases, there is only one way to be well, and thousands of ways of being bad].[40]

These 'matériaux' which are 'épars et sans liaison' [scattered and disconnected] recall the 'Avertissement' of the *Éléments de physiologie*, a passage we have already analysed in some detail, also in connection with Pascal, and which evokes the incomplete 'matériaux' written on its 'feuillets épars et isolés' [on scattered and separate scraps of paper] in contrapuntal echo to the introduction to Pascal's *Pensées* by his nephew, Étienne Périer, in which he describes his uncle's fragments as being 'quelques matériaux épars et sans aucun ordre entre eux' [a

---

38 Jacques-André Naigeon, 'Diderot', in *Encyclopédie méthodique: Philosophie ancienne et moderne*, vol. 2, pp. 153–228 (p. 153); 'Avertissement des Éditeurs', in Naigeon, *Mémoires sur la vie et les ouvrages de Diderot*, p. v.
39 Naigeon, *Adresse*, p. 12.
40 Naigeon, *Adresse*, pp. 12–13.

few scattered materials with no internal order]. We see these allusions re-echoing here in the opening pages of Naigeon's *Adresse*, and they will return in his *Mémoires*.[41]

He follows on, as we saw, with this allusion to the single way of being good or well as opposed to the thousand ways of being bad or unwell, which he introduces as being applicable in many other cases. Here is the one he was probably thinking of:

> Il n'est qu'une manière de se porter bien; il y en a une infinité de se porter mal.[42]

> There is only one way of being well, but there are thousands of ways of being ill.

This is the opening sentence to the chapter on 'Maladies' in the third and final part of the *Éléments*. 'Se porter' in Diderot's words has become 'être' in Naigeon's, to pull it away from its relevance to health, and yet, 'être bien/être mal' is rather clunky, particularly if what Naigeon is referring to here is the Assemblée nationale's decision-making processes. It seems as if he did not wish to alter the original sentence beyond recognisability, instead affirming its sententious or axiomatic nature, rather than making it fit better in the context.

So, what have we got here with respect to the *Éléments de physiologie*? Not much in terms of quantity, but some discernable references, one from its opening pages and another from its close, along with this third one about health and the variety of 'ill' ways of doing things, or simply of 'being' in the awkward rephrasing we find here, itself embedded in Naigeon's own opening paragraphs, which, as we have already seen, are rich in precise quotation from Diderot. In sum, a marginal presence, yet in the sense that margins can also be the frame, or perhaps, to bring in Naigeon's own metaphor of '[des] fondemens [...] solides', that on which the rest is built or which provides the 'matériaux' out of which it is built, *bref*, the assumptions that underpin Naigeon's argument. Of such a sort is the definition of man from 'un point de vue plus philosophique' [a more philosophical view-point]—more philosophical, that is, than the religious view of man—as a 'portion nécessairement organisée d'une

---

41  Naigeon, *Mémoires sur la vie et les ouvrages de Diderot*, p. 291; discussed in Chapter 2.
42  DPV 508/PQ 347/MT 321.

matière éternelle, nécessaire' [a necessarily organised portion of eternal and necessary matter]: this definition of man is lifted from Diderot's 'Prière du sceptique' [The Sceptic's prayer].[43] The *necessity* of human material organisation, that is, its determined character, resurfaces again in the remark in passing about 'ces hommes malheureusement nés' [these humans born in an unfortunate form] who cannot be influenced or contained by law; this is specifically in the context of the importance of everyone having 'le droit de tout dire et de tout imprimer' [the right to say and publish anything] (p. 86); those who are 'malheureusement nés' [born in unfortunate form] must simply be destroyed, given that they cannot be punished. This particular formula appears to be related to the French version of Hobbes, but is most recognisable as the view of Jacques's captain: 'il prétendait qu'on était heureusement ou malheureusement né' [his claim was that one was born in a fortunate or unfortunate form].[44]

## Naigeon's Strategy

To summarise and characterise Naigeon's referencing of Diderot in the *Adresse*, then, we can say firstly, that Diderot is clearly present in this text in the form of exact quotation from a range of works, none of which were published in 1790 (although *Jacques le fataliste* had been circulated in the manuscript periodical, the *Correspondance littéraire*); secondly, that Diderot's name is never given; thirdly, that Naigeon sometimes signals that he is quoting, by the simple deployment of quotation marks, and that these quotations are attributed to 'un philosophe'; and finally, that a rough characterisation of the Diderot texts deployed here would suggest that they are primarily anti-clerical, secondarily anti-authoritarian and anti-hierarchical, and lastly, materialist. The verb 'deployed' suggests a

---

43 Despite some question about the authorship of this piece, as referenced above, recent scholarship considers that this 'Prière du sceptique' was by Diderot: see Albertan and Chouillet, 'Autographes et documents', paragraphs 14–15.

44 Naigeon, *Adresse*, p. 87. 'Hommes malheureusement nés' may be a Hobbesian formula in French clothes; also in *Jacques le fataliste*: '[Jacques] prétendait qu'on était heureusement ou malheureusement nés', see DPV, vol. 23, p. 189; also 'dans une lettre à SV, Diderot écrit que la plupart des hommes "naissent moitié sots et moitié fous "' [in a letter to Sophie Volland, Diderot writes that most men 'are born half stupid and half mad'], Diderot, *Correspondance*, ed. by Roth and Varloot, vol. 3, p. 98.

strategy on Naigeon's part. Are we right to use such a verb? Is there a strategy at work in his supposed 'deployment' of Diderot in this text, and if so, what is it? Of course, in asking this question, we set aside Naigeon's explicit aim of convincing the *Assemblée nationale* to omit any mention of God and also to enshrine freedom of speech in the *Déclaration des droits de l'homme et du citoyen* as this is not the concern of our study. The question is thus not how Naigeon uses Diderot to boost his arguments, but more specifically, whether Naigeon uses this text as an occasion to publicise or publish Diderot, and if so, how.

Without being able to produce a conclusive answer, we can nonetheless look at what Naigeon does say generally about readers, publication, timeliness, and quotation. In an early footnote, for example, he apologises for not having had enough time to integrate the footnotes with the main body of the text, but states that the 'Lecteur attentif & intelligent' [attentive and intelligent reader] will have no trouble linking the ideas and seeing the 'rapport très-immédiat' [very direct relationship] between the different text levels.[45] This tells us immediately that Naigeon has an ideal reader in mind, and that this reader will understand his text in a way that others, undescribed but existing in implicit contrast to this 'attentive and intelligent reader', will not. So there are different levels of readers and different levels of understanding, and some will see what the text really means, whereas others will not. This is a hierarchisation of the elite reader that we will meet again in the *Mémoires*, when, specifically in the context of the 'quelques matériaux épars et sans aucun ordre entre eux' which we mentioned only a few paragraphs back in connection with the 'Avertissement' to the *Éléments de physiologie* and its allusion to Pascal's *Pensées*, Naigeon says that these ideas, however scattered, will nonetheless have meaning 'aux yeux du philosophe assez instruit pour couver les idées neuves et fécondes dont Diderot a semé ses recherches' [in the eyes of the philosopher who is

---

45 Naigeon, *Adresse*, p. 2. Naigeon makes a further appeal in the *Adresse* to a more advanced sort of reader when he talks about the 'lecteur accoutumé à se rendre compte de toutes ses pensées' [reader accustomed to justify his thoughts to himself] (*Adresse*, p. 62). This phrasing recalls one of Diderot's letters to Sophie Volland, where he talks about the pleasure of 'se rendre compte à soi-même de ses opinions' [justifying one's opinions to oneself] (Letter to SV, 14.7.62, quoted in Roland Mortier, 'Diderot et le problème de l'expressivité: de la pensée au dialogue heuristique', *Cahiers de l'AIEF*, 13.1 (1961), 283–97, https://doi.org/10.3406/caief.1961.2204).

sufficiently knowledgeable to appreciate the new and fertile ideas that Diderot planted in his work].[46] So, looking at this notion of the ideal reader from the perspective of the *Mémoires*, we see that s/he (probably 'he' for Naigeon) is ideal specifically in the way in which he will be learned enough to appreciate the new and productive ideas that Diderot seeded across his research. The ideal reader is one who is capable of appreciating Diderot.

The ideal writer, on the other hand, says what he means and publishes at the right time. Claude Adrien Helvétius's *De l'homme* had met neither of these criteria, Naigeon tells us:

> comme il avoit résolu de le faire imprimer, malgré les conseils de ses amis qui prévoyoient les suites funestes de son imprudence, il craint de laisser pénétrer ses vrais sentimens; mais on les apperçoit au travers du voile dont il cherche en vain à se couvrir.[47]

> as he was determined to publish it, despite the advice of his friends, who foresaw the disastrous consequences of his imprudence, he was fearful of allowing his real views to be detected. Yet they are still perceptible through the veil with which he seeks in vain to cover them.

Helvétius wished to publish but also wished to get round censorship by disguising his real meaning; the result is a disaster, in that he fails to avoid censorship, and his attempt to disguise his real meaning leads, claims Naigeon, to pages and pages of tedious and confusing argumentation—'des longueurs accablantes'.[48] This sort of writing which attempted to disguise its real meaning had a name: 'la double doctrine'.[49] According to Naigeon, this is what Helvétius was using, and not only was it a failure, it was unworthy of a 'philosophe'. Thus we read that:

> L'usage de la double doctrine convient mieux à un Hiérophante dont l'intérêt est d'obscurcir les notions les plus claires, & qui ne vit que de l'ignorance & de la crédulité des Peuples, qu'à un Philosophe [...][50]

---

46 Naigeon, *Mémoires sur la vie et les ouvrages de Denis Diderot*, p. 291.
47 Naigeon, *Adresse*, p. 28n.
48 Naigeon, *Adresse*, p. 29n (this is a continuation of the note on p. 28).
49 For a thorough analysis of libertine rhetoric, see Isabelle Moreau, *'Guérir du sot': Les Stratégies d'écriture des libertins à l'âge classique* (Paris: Champion, 2007).
50 Naigeon, *Adresse*, p. 28n.

The deployment of the double doctrine better befits a hierophant in whose interest it is to make the clearest notions as obscure as possible, and whose survival depends upon the ignorance and credulity of the people, than it does a philosopher.

The brave, wise, and virtuous *philosophe* does not publish primarily for glory ('Helvétius aimoit la gloire' [Helvétius loved glory]), against the advice of his friends, resorting to 'vains subterfuges' in order to protect himself and thereby making his book incomprehensible. The *philosophe* tells the truth, whatever it costs, even if that means foregoing publication. Naigeon goes on to reprove Newton for having chosen to appease the theologians by giving some weak proofs of the existence of God (pp. 30–32), only subsequently quoting from a *philosophe* who wrote 'avec cette éloquence et cette énergie que donnent la hardiesse et la profondeur des pensées' [that eloquence and energy that bold and deep thoughts bestow on the speaker] and about most people being ignorant, afraid, and superstitious. This is the passage we have already quoted, starting 'Le gros d'une nation' [most of a nation] and that quotation is from Diderot. In this long castigation of writers who failed in their duty or judgement in one way or another, therefore, it is Diderot who is presented as the shining counter-example, even though his name is hidden.

This all seems quite clear, even stridently so. Naigeon is in charge, and although Helvétius did not understand when the right time to publish was, Naigeon does, and that time is now, as he had said in his introduction:

> [...] quand on a quelque chose de bon à dire, il faut se presser; car on est presque sûr que la vérité qu'on découvre aujourd'hui, & qu'on n'annonce pas, sera trouvée & publiée demain par un autre. Il est très-indifférent, sans doute, que l'Auteur d'une grande découverte s'appelle *Newton* ou *Leibniz*; ce [qui] importe beaucoup, c'est que cette découverte se fasse; mais il n'en est pas moins vrai que le soin de sa propre gloire n'est pas à dédaigner, & qu'il ne faut pas paroître suivre ceux qu'on peut précéder, ou à côté desquels on a droit de se placer.[51]

when you have something good to say, you must hurry up and say it; because you can be almost sure that the truth you discover today and

---

51 Naigeon, *Adresse*, pp. 9–10.

don't publicise will be found and publicised by someone else tomorrow. It is completely irrelevant, no doubt, whether the name of the author of a great discovery is *Newton* or *Leibniz*; what is really important, is that this discovery should be made. And yet it is no less true that one's own glory should not be neglected, and that one should not allow it to seem that one has followed in the footsteps of those one has preceded, or in whose company one has the right to stand.

Or is he quite so clear? This particular argument seems to be coming from a different angle. The right moment to publish in this presentation is based not on issues of censorship and prudence but on getting a move on and making sure someone else does not grab one's rightful glory. Is he contradicting himself? Perhaps there is no need to set Naigeon's two positions against one another, as if he were in bad faith for lambasting Helvétius's interest in glory; perhaps it is enough simply to say that what Naigeon says in his introduction and what he says twenty pages later are two separate things, that so far as Naigeon is concerned, times have changed, and the interests of the nation require him to say 'quelque chose de bon' [something good] straightaway, and not neglect his own reputation—or that of the author whose manuscripts it is his job to look after and disseminate as he sees fit—in the meantime. But in any case, as we know, Naigeon's confidence, both in the timing of his (and Diderot's) anti-clerical message and in the readiness of his readers to hear it, was—ironically—completely misplaced.

Thus far, in our attempt to understand whether Naigeon has a strategy, we have looked at what he says about readers, publication, and timeliness. He presents a strident display of confidence and knowledge combined, a sense of knowing better, that is not so much persuasive as dogmatic and dominant, and yet as we have also seen, there is a perceptible thread of self-contradiction that undermines some of what he says. We have not yet analysed an important aspect for this study, that is, his strategies or practices of quotation more generally.

Describing these practices of quotation reveals an economy that is so mixed that it is hard to discern any strategy. This is not to suggest that the result is a textual (or authorial) mess but rather that it is extremely complex. As we have already seen, he quotes Diderot on multiple occasions and from multiple texts, and also in multiple ways, while never actually naming him.[52] Some of the quotation is made textually prominent and visible as quotation by the straightforward use of quotation marks; some of it is introduced by 'un philosophe disoit' [a philosopher said] or 'un philosophe faisoit un jour cette question' [a philosopher one day asked this question]—and we note the emphasis here on orality and conversation rather than on written texts—and some of it is not given textual prominance of any sort but is invisibly embedded in a sentence—this may be simply an expression we can trace to a Diderot text or which echoes a Diderot text quite closely but does not replicate it exactly. But Diderot is not the only author he quotes. We also meet La Rochefoucauld half way through a sentence, his 'il n'y a rien d'absolument bon et d'absolument mauvais' [there is nothing absolutely good or absolutely bad] recycled into a statement presenting itself not as quotation but as a declaration of the truth.[53] It would be tempting to extrapolate from this that for Naigeon, writing and philosophising is not about a display of authorial attribution and sources, but about a depersonalised or rather a de-authorialised establishment of the truth, if we did not have the counter-evidence of the paragraph on publishing in order to stamp one's name on a discovery and maintain one's rightful glory. Furthermore, in fact, we also find a great deal of attributed citation, predominantly from Latin authors. Tacitus and Horace appear frequently to lend their classical authority and clinch a point.[54] Pierre Bayle is named and precisely referenced.[55] Yet Lucretius is also quoted in Latin, without being named

---

52   Elsewhere we have studied some of the striking behaviour around naming sources (or more often, not naming them) in the 1790s, and it seems that Naigeon's practice of calling Diderot 'un philosophe' fits quite neatly into that analysis whereby certain unproblematic authorities are named, while others (generally Diderot) are anonymised. See Caroline Warman, 'Caught between Neologism and the Unmentionable: The Politics of Naming and Non-naming in 1790s France', *Romance Studies*, 31 (2013), 264–76, https://doi.org/10.1179/0263990413Z.00000000051.
53   Naigeon, *Adresse*, p. 81; from François de La Rochefoucauld, *Réflexions ou sentences et maximes morales* (1665).
54   See for example Naigeon, *Adresse*, p. 5n (Horace); p. 41n (Tacitus). References to Tacitus in this period carry a particular polemical and political charge, see Catherine Volpilhac-Auger, *Tacite en France de Montesquieu à Chateaubriand* (Oxford: Voltaire Foundation, 1993).
55   Naigeon, *Adresse*, p. 84n (quotation from Pierre Bayle's *Dictionnaire historique et critique* (Paris: Éditions Sociales, 1974), vol. 2, p. 2494, article PORTIUS).

or referenced.⁵⁶ Naigeon quotes a line of *De rerum natura* advising the writer to 'bathe his work in the charm of the muses' ('musaeo contingens cuncta lepore'), and he places it at the end of a paragraph discussing how best to write about 'des matières philosophiques' [philosophical matters]. This is suggestive; Lucretius's Epicurean poem about a world of atoms is an important text and model for the thinkers (and covert materialists) of the Early Modern period.⁵⁷ The fact that Naigeon is at pains to advertise the references of all Latin sources *apart from* Lucretius means he is treated in the same way as Naigeon's principle unnamed source, Diderot, and they are thereby associated.⁵⁸ One wonders what the non-naming here is supposed to do. Presumably a learned reader, 'un lecteur attentif & intelligent' [an attentive and intelligent reader], will not have very much trouble recognising Lucretius, and we know that contemporaneous readers did espy Diderot's presence within Naigeon's pages, even if, we assume, they were not acquainted with the specific texts being used.

So Naigeon is hiding quotation in full view, at least to some extent. Is this a form of provocation directed either at the authorities or to the reader? Or is it a game of associations and connections? Or both? Or a series of implicit directions to the informed reader, so that they knew they were dealing with a text with a materialist undertow? Could it be all of these things? It is not very clear precisely how this functions or how we are supposed to read its allusions and intertextual flags, but it is clear, paradoxically, that the text is not quite so clear or so open as Naigeon's loud rejection of the 'double doctrine'—saying one thing while meaning another—would have us believe. In the *Adresse*, he also quotes—unacknowledged—whole pages of his own articles on 'Cardan' and 'Mirabeau' from his forthcoming three-volume philosophical dictionary, *La Philosophie ancienne et moderne*.⁵⁹ These three volumes

---

56 Naigeon, *Adresse*, p. 4: 'musaeo contingens cuncta lepore', from *De rerum natura*, book 1, line 934, meaning 'bathing all with the charm of the muses'.
57 See for example David Norbrook, Stephen Harrison, and Philip Hardie, eds, *Lucretius and the Early Modern* (Oxford: Oxford University Press, 2015), https://doi.org/10.1093/acprof:oso/9780198713845.001.0001.
58 See also Naigeon's quotation of Lucretius in support of an allusion to Diderot and an injunction to crush fanaticism in his 'Discours préliminaire', *Encyclopédie méthodique: Philosophie ancienne et moderne*, vol. 1, p. xxiii.
59 Naigeon, *Adresse*, pp. 53–55 ('Cardan') and pp. 101–9 ('Mirabeau'). The *Philosophie ancienne et moderne* was part of Panckoucke's immense *Encyclopédie méthodique*

were published in 1791, 1792, and in the Revolutionary 'An II', that is, 22 September 1793–21 September 1794. 'Cardan' fills or rather constitutes the Supplement at the end of vol. 2 (alphabetically it should have appeared in vol. 1, which runs 'Académiciens' to 'Collins'), and 'Mirabeau' appeared in vol. 3, in its expected alphabetical position, although it is not about Mirabeau at all but is instead a summary of the *Système de la nature* which had been (falsely) published under Mirabeau's name by its real author, the baron d'Holbach, and his co-authors Diderot and Naigeon.[60] And in a neat piece of reciprocal cross-text symmetry, where 'Cardan' provides the entirety of the supplement to vol. 2, the extract from 'Mirabeau' provides almost the entirety of the nine-page first note of the 'Additions' to the *Adresse*. Naigeon is right to appeal to the 'lecteur attentif'; he needs an attentive reader, as the rest of us get hopelessly confused!

Confusion aside, there may be a few observations we could fairly make. Firstly, that these pieces of writing are not 'neat', to pick up on that adjective used a few lines back. The *Adresse* is not really a speech, and its different parts do need a 'lecteur attentif' to make sense of them all; the philosophical dictionary is not really a dictionary in any alphabetical sense—the entries are not published in clearly-planned alphabetical order, and 'Mirabeau' does not refer to 'Mirabeau', as the first line declares. And we clearly cannot argue that Naigeon thought of 'Cardan' late in the publishing process, and therefore put it as a sort of rushed afterthought at the end of vol. 2, firstly because an article sixty-seven pages long is not a rushed afterthought, and secondly, because he was already citing extensive passages from it in 1790. It may of course be the other way round, and that he developed passages from the *Adresse* in these later articles. It is not very easy to tell, and now is not the place to attempt any sort of conclusive analysis. What we can say is that there is some sort of overlap between the two works, that the *Adresse* and the three volumes of the dictionary are published in quite close proximity,

---

project, aiming to update Diderot and d'Alembert's *Encyclopédie*, although dividing it into separate thematised volumes, hence the subsection under Naigeon's editorship on 'La Philosophie ancienne et moderne'.

60  Naigeon, 'Cardan', *Philosophie ancienne et moderne*, vol. 2 (1792), pp. 873–940; the section quoted or pre-quoted by Naigeon in the *Adresse* appears on p. 989; 'Mirabeau', vol. 3 (an II), pp. 239–326; the section quoted in the *Adresse* appears on pp. 241–42.

that even if Naigeon is not citing paragraphs from articles he has already prepared, he will already have been working on the dictionary, and yet he does not use the opportunity provided by the *Adresse* to explicitly advertise that other work. So the citation, if citation it is, is not about advertisement.

Is he simply self-plagiarising? Is all this citation simply about Naigeon plundering the texts to which he had access, including his own? On the question of plagiarism, Naigeon himself has something to say, in the very 'Cardan' article we have been discussing. He has been talking about Cardan's 'larcins' [thefts] from Aristotle, Theophrastus, Hippocrates, Galen, Celsus, and Dioscorides, and in particular from Pliny.[61] He has this to say:

> [Pliny] n'oublie point de nommer les sçavans qui lui en ont fourni les matériaux ; tandisque *Cardan*, bien loin de suivre cet exemple que l'équité, la reconnoissance, & l'intérêt même de sa gloire lui prescrivoient également, a voulu faire croire qu'en écrivant sur tant de sujets divers, il n'y employoit, pour me servir de l'expression de Montaigne, que *ses propres & naturels moyens*. C'est cette affectation à cacher les sources où il avoit puisé une partie de son savoir, qui l'a fait accuser de plagiat; & il faut avouer que ce n'est pas sans fondement. Scaliger assure même que le livre de *Cardan* sur l'immortalité de l'ame, n'est qu'un assemblage de plusieurs lambeaux pris ça et là, & que pour couvrir son vol, il mêla des déclamations ridicules aux doctrines qu'il avoit tirées des écrits de Pomponace & d'Augustin Niphus.[62]

> [Pliny] never forgets to name the scholars whose works he has borrowed from, while *Cardan*, far from following this example which fairness, gratitude and even the interests of his glory equally prescribed, wanted everyone to think that in writing on all these diverse subjects, he employed nothing, to use Montaigne's expression, other than his *own natural means*. It's this affectation of hiding the sources from which he drew part of his knowledge that caused him to be accused of plagiarism, and we have to admit that this charge is not a baseless one. Scaliger goes so far as to assert that Cardan's book on the immortality of the soul is nothing other than an assemblage of numerous bits and pieces gathered from here and there, and that to cover up his theft, he mixed various ridiculous declamations in with the doctrines that he had taken from Pomponazzi & Agostino Nifo.

---

61   Naigeon, 'Cardan', p. 931.
62   Naigeon, 'Cardan', p. 932.

And, on this page alone, backing up not only his punctilious references to Montaigne and Scaliger but providing other learned allusions, we find no fewer than seven notes giving Latin original and detailed source information. So, Naigeon knows that making a text from 'un assemblage de plusieurs lambeaux pris ça et là' [assemblage of numerous bits and pieces gathered from here and there] can be seen as theft. Here he calls the practice of hiding a source an 'affectation'. He acknowledges that accusations of plagiarism are not unfounded. He further says that fairness, gratitude, and even Cardan's reputation or glory required him to acknowledge his borrowings, but that Cardan pretended they were all his anyway. How curious this is! The impression of virtuous and scholarly authorship is further reinforced by the closing signature: 'cet article est du citoyen Naigeon' [this article is by Citizen Naigeon].[63] The 'lecteur instruit' [knowledgeable reader], Naigeon further adds, will be able to make their own mind up about Cardan's work, and about what is true and useful, and what its faults are.[64] That appeal to the superior sort of reader again! We really do need him (and he is definitely male)! Of course, here the dates may well be significant, and Naigeon's reproof of the naughty Cardan who is otherwise, as a 'médecin philosophe' [medical philosopher] much praised, may be a form of response to Naigeon's own critics who had derided the Naigeon of the *Adresse* as Diderot's lapdog or monkey.[65] Yet Naigeon was not accused of plagiarism, so far as I know.

If this display of righteous reproof and virtuous referencing is a response to Naigeon's critics, then it takes the form of a simple denial, and of course it is a straightforward lie insofar as it applies to Naigeon's own work. But one wonders whether there is something more complex going on than either denial or local inconsistency. Perhaps what we find here is the 'double doctrine' Naigeon had lambasted Helvétius for. Perhaps that very reproof was itself an example of the 'double doctrine' in action, whereby Naigeon was really disseminating the work he claimed to criticise, an ironic denunciation that not only gave further page space to

---

63   Naigeon, 'Cardan', p. 940.
64   Naigeon, 'Cardan', p. 938.
65   Naigeon, 'Cardan', p. 938; La Harpe famously called Naigeon 'le singe de Diderot' [Diderot's monkey], see Jean-François La Harpe, *Œuvres*, 16 vols (Paris: Verdière, 1820), vol. 11, p. 41.

Helvétius but also advertised to the 'attentive' or 'informed' reader that censorship-bypassing codes of clandestine rhetoric were in operation in the *Adresse*? That he considered that some prudence was required is evident from the fact that while he did reference and name some sources, he never named Diderot, and that he was right to be cautious is only too clear from the outraged responses of some—but not all—reviewers. In any case, so far as the reputations of both Naigeon and Diderot were concerned, the damage was done anyway. Whatever the reasons informing Naigeon's explicit condemnation of plagiarism in the case of Cardan, however, we can see that it would have been impossible for Naigeon as a writer who did also embed unacknowledged quotation in his work not to notice the irony. Whether his readers—or perhaps just the really attentive and informed one—noticed, and were even meant to do so, is not a question we can resolve here. We can, however, say that Naigeon is a more complicated and tricksy writer than has been considered to be the case, and we can also say that in the *Adresse*, he did disseminate some of Diderot's hitherto unpublished manuscripts, drawing on some of the most intensely anti-authoritarian passages to do so, moreover. The extent to which this was an organised strategy of publication, of which the 'Diderot' article he wrote for the *Encyclopédie méthodique* was another part, with his edition of Diderot's *Œuvres* of 1798 and the *Mémoires historiques et philosophiques* of 1823 completing the quartet, is not something we can yet determine, although we will continue to track which Diderot texts Naigeon named or published or described, and where, and how. We now turn to the article on 'Diderot'.

# 6. 1792: Naigeon's Article on 'Diderot' in the *Encyclopédie méthodique Philosophie ancienne et moderne*

The article 'Diderot' which we find in the second volume of Jacques-André Naigeon's philosophical dictionary does not, of course, hide either Denis Diderot's name or the extracts from his work.[1] Published in 1792, it was written, Naigeon tells us, in November 1789, very close to (and quite possibly overlapping with) the writing and publication of the *Adresse à l'Assemblée nationale* in February 1790 (another date which Naigeon himself supplies).[2] At seventy-five double-columned pages, it is a substantial article, and indeed it is here that Diderot's significant if brief *Principes philosophiques sur la matière et le mouvement*, written in 1770, are first published, as Naigeon is pleased to announce, all three pages of them.[3] So this article holds an important place in the story of the publication of Diderot's works, in part for the *Principes philosophiques* and in part for the details Naigeon supplies about his 'intime ami'

---

1   Jacques-André Naigeon, 'Diderot', in *Encyclopédie méthodique: Philosophie ancienne et moderne* (Paris: Panckoucke, 1792), vol. 2, pp. 153–228.

2   Naigeon, 'Diderot', *Philosophie ancienne et moderne*, vol. 2 (1792), p. 153, n. 3: 'on écrit ceci au mois de novembre'. For the dating of the *Adresse*, see above.

3   Naigeon, 'Diderot', pp. 192–95. See also Michel Delon's edition, in Denis Diderot, *Œuvres complètes*, ed. by H. Dieckmann, Jacques Proust, Jean Varloot (Paris: Hermann, 1975), [hereafter DPV], vol. 17 (1987), p. 10.

© Caroline Warman, CC BY 4.0              https://doi.org/10.11647/OBP.0199.06

[intimate friend].[4] And yet it is not quite what one might expect. It does not give a comprehensive list let alone survey of Diderot's works, which, for example, Naigeon does do in the case of Condillac, the article about whom fills the first 135 pages of this same volume, even though he complains bitterly about the 'extrême secheresse' [extreme dryness] of Condillac's writing and the courage and patience needed to wade through it all, and even though the first extracts he quotes in it are in fact from Diderot, as part of his demonstration that the 'idée mère' [mother idea] for Condillac's famous statue was Diderot's.[5] So there is an odd disproportion here; odd in that Condillac gets almost twice as many pages despite the philosophical priority being given very clearly to Diderot, and despite the fact that Naigeon claims to find Condillac hard going. Why is this?

There seem to be two connected reasons; firstly and most explicitly, because Naigeon states on the first page of the article that he has reserved the longer discussion of Diderot's Œuvres for his Mémoires, but possibly also out of caution. It is an article that does not foray far into the Diderot œuvre; apart from the brief Principes philosophiques mentioned above, Naigeon limits discussion to Diderot's published works and to various extracts and reviews. Thus we also hear about the Pensées philosophiques (pub. 1746), the Additions aux pensées philosophiques (pub. 1770), the Lettre sur les aveugles (pub. 1749)—presented in gobbet form as twenty-nine numbered 'pensées' along with an exposition of its treatment of the Molyneux problem—the Lettre sur les sourds et muets (pub. 1751), the Pensées sur l'interprétation de la nature (pub. 1753), along with some extracts on education, some sixty 'Reflexions philosophiques sur divers sujets', and various reviews emphasising the importance of style. This is a presentation of Diderot's writings that has four distinguishing features; firstly, their status as (mostly) published; secondly, their speculative philosophical nature; thirdly, the emphasis on the importance of style in philosophical writing; and fourthly, their arrangement in 'pensée' or

---

4   Naigeon, 'Diderot', p. 153.
5   Naigeon, 'Condillac', Philosophie ancienne et moderne, vol. 2 (1792), pp. 1–135 ('extrême secheresse', p. 105; pp. 5–7 for the discussion of how Condillac's Traité des sensations was inspired by Diderot's Lettre sur les sourds et muets; the quotation fills more than two columns, pp. 6–7).

gobbet form.⁶ This version of Diderot is an authoritative, predominantly published, often gnomic thinker, who pronounces on important matters connected to the philosophical or educational matters of the day. If Naigeon is stoutly defending and often re-stating Diderot's importance here, then, he is nonetheless not adding very much to what is already published and known, apart from the three pages of the *Principes philosophiques*. So there are some reasons to think that this version of Diderot is indeed a cautious one.

However, as mentioned, this article comes complete with opening and closing references to the *Mémoires historiques et philosophiques*, references which make clear its subservience to this grander, deeper, longer work which readers are explicitly advised to consult despite the fact that it hasn't yet been published. Furthermore, of the three paragraphs on the first page of this article, two of them discuss not Diderot and his writing but Naigeon's internal debates about when to publish these *Mémoires*. The dominant position this discussion is given, at the very head of the article, communicate how difficult it was for Naigeon to work out how to publish what and when, and how continuously the political situation affected his choices. So if there was a strategy on Naigeon's part to publish Diderot's work in phases, we can see how it was repeatedly changed and updated. Thus he talks of 'ces *mémoires* que je n'aurois pu faire imprimer, il y a six mois' [these memoirs which I would not have been able to publish six months ago] without inviting the persecution of ministers and judges—and it is here that he inserts the footnote dating the writing of the article to November 1789—and of 'ces *mémoires* pensés & écrits par-tout avec cette liberté si nécessaire dans les matières philosophiques' [these memoirs were thoroughly conceptualised and written with that freedom which is so crucial in philosophical matters] and which *now*, thanks to the 'heureuse révolution qui s'est opérée dans l'ordre des choses' [happy revolution which has occurred in the order of things] 'pourroient être insérés tout entiers dans cet article' [could be inserted entire into this article].⁷ 'Liberté' here is in no way an empty rhetorical flourish, nor even an uncomplicated echo of one of the Revolution's slogans; it has a specific meaning in this context, of course,

---

6    For Naigeon's remarks on Diderot's style, see 'Diderot', pp. 154, 164, 217; for Diderot's stinging review of the translation of Beccaria's *Recherches sur le style*, see p. 223.
7    All quotations from Naigeon, 'Diderot', p. 153.

related to free-thinking and the 'libertins' or free-thinkers, who are to be understood in seventeenth-century terms as those who do not conform to the orthodoxy of the church, and in eighteenth-century terms more insultingly as those who are immoral or amoral, and is therefore a term directly associated with atheism and materialism. This is Naigeon's 'liberté' [freedom], and it is an attitude and a style, as he tells us, that one writes and thinks with: 'pensés & écrits par-tout avec cette liberté'. So the printed matter discussed in the article comes attached to a silent and extensive supplement in the form of these free-thinking *Mémoires*: 'quoiqu'ils ne soient point encore imprimés, j'y renvoye néanmoins le lecteur' [although they have not yet been published, I nonetheless refer the reader to them].[8]

So why, if the 'heureuse révolution' [happy revolution] is now propitious to free expression, does he choose *not* to publish them within the article? He gives four reasons in his first explanation, and two in his second. Firstly, then, they would take up too much space; secondly, they have a different 'objet' or aim, thirdly, they could not be written in the same style and with the same details, and fourthly, he would not be able to have the same 'excursions' or digressions. His subsequent explanation makes a pact with the reader to fulfil a duty towards his late friend and write these *Mémoires* which his predilection for peace and quiet ('l'amour du repos'), along with some other, more urgent, more imperious considerations ('des considérations peut-être encore plus fortes, plus impérieuses'), have prevented him from doing. 'Mais un jour plus pur nous luit': a brighter day beckons. Six reasons for not publishing or not having written them yet, including this ominous last one, with its allusion to important considerations! No one has ever accused Naigeon of being a minimalist, but this is a clear case not purely of maximalism but of making sure that the reader's attention is repeatedly fixed on these *Mémoires*. Six reasons, a cross-reference to the unpublished memoirs, and substantial discussion on this opening page, along with a further cross-reference within the body of the article, and a final one on the closing page serve to emphasise and re-emphasise how incomplete the article is without the *Mémoires*, and how important

---

8   All quotations from ibid.

this latter work is for the understanding of Diderot.[9] And we know that what specifically characterises the *Mémoires* is 'cette liberté si nécessaire dans les matières philosophiques' [that freedom which is so crucial in philosophical matters]. In fact, the cross-reference on the closing page is even more specific. Here it is:

> Ce seroit ici le lieu de parler de plusieurs ouvrages purement philosophiques qui se trouvent parmi les manuscrits de Diderot ; mais j'ai donné, dans les mémoires sur sa vie, une analyse raisonnée de celui de ces ouvrages qui m'a paru le plus profond : j'entre même à ce sujet dans des détails qui ne seront pas sans quelque utilité pour les lecteurs qui s'occupent de ces matières difficiles, et qui, déjà éclairés par leurs propres méditations, seront capables de suivre et de cultiver les idées de ce philosophe.[10]

> This would be the place to speak about the many purely philosophical works amongst Diderot's manuscripts. However, I have given, in the memoirs about his life, an analytical account of the particular work of his that I thought most profound: I even go, on this subject, into details which will not be without some use for those readers who make it their business to consider these difficult matters, and who, already enlightened by their own meditations, will be capable of following and developing the ideas of this philosopher.

Here we meet again that invitation which we saw in the *Adresse* to those special readers who engage with difficult matters and are capable of following and developing Diderot's ideas. And in fact it is not all Diderot's writings or a group of them that Naigeon wishes to draw attention to here, it is a single one: 'celui de ces ouvrages qui m'a paru le plus profond'—the particular one he considers to be the most profound. Examination of the *Mémoires*—which, despite these repeated references to its existence and imminent publication will remain unpublished until 1823—will show that he was talking about the *Éléments de physiologie*, which, with a tally of fifty pages of re-woven quotation, the *Rêve* coming

---

9   Naigeon writes, regarding Diderot's imprisonment at the château de Vincennes in 1749: 'De plus longs détails sur cette affaire seroient déplacés dans cet article; on les trouvera dans les *mémoires* dont j'ai parlé ci-dessus, & j'y renvoye le lecteur' [it would be misplaced to give more detail on this affair in this article ; more information can be found in the *memoirs* I mentioned above, and I refer the reader to them] ('Diderot', p. 166).
10  Naigeon, 'Diderot', p. 228.

in second at about thirty, and no other work anywhere near, is the single text to which he gives most prominence. As we will see, he is still advertising it as well as advertising that he is still working on it in the preface to the Œuvres de Diderot which he published in 1798. We will come to that preface, as well as to the *Mémoires* themselves in due course, according to the chronological approach which we adopt here and which aims on the one hand to provide some order and sense of an unfurling narrative, whereby what follows is aware of and informed by what has preceded, and on the other to give a sense of the complexity and unpredictability of the context. In the meantime, we will leave Naigeon, so active and vocal in these early 1790s, with his repeated allusions to Diderot and to the *Mémoires*, and his intimations of a work characterised by particular freedom, one that was more profound than any other. Naigeon was not a marginal figure, as the many reactions to his *Adresse*, and the centrality of his position as editor of the *Philosophie ancienne et moderne* volumes, go to show. His readers, and perhaps not just those especially alert and erudite ones he kept winking at, will have been aware that there was more Diderot in the offing, that there was a particularly important free-thinking text which they had not yet seen. The *Éléments de physiologie*, unnamed at this point though it was, but quoted in the *Adresse* and alluded to in 'Diderot', thus already has a shadowy presence in print, repeatedly signalled both as imminent and as hugely important. And for any readers who knew how, or who simply knew where Naigeon lived, the *Mémoires* were accessible in draft manuscript form, perhaps even the *Éléments de physiologie* themselves. In any case, someone apart from Naigeon had a copy, as we will now go on to discuss.

# 7. 1794: 'Le citoyen Garron', the Comité d'instruction publique, and the Lost Manuscript of the *Éléments de physiologie*

This person appears to have been called 'le citoyen Garron'. We know of his existence from the 1837 catalogue of Parisian bookseller Pierre Leblanc. In a letter dated 'Germinal quartidi 4, l'an II de la République', that is, 24 March 1794, he presented a manuscript of the *Éléments de physiologie* to the Comité d'instruction publique [Committee for Public Eduction] of the Convention nationale. Leblanc was selling both the presentation letter and the manuscript itself. Marvellous detective work by Maurice Tourneux established that the manuscript was still on Leblanc's lists until 9 March 1846, when it disappeared; in 1954, Jean Pommier discovered that the manuscript had been sold only three days later, on Thursday 12 March 1846, for the quite high sum of 220 francs, to a certain 'pottier'. Editor of the *Éléments,* Jean Mayer, who records these transactions in such beautifully precise detail, was not able to trace the manuscript any further, and nor was Paolo Quintili in his edition of 2004.[1] It remains unlocated, yet it seems unlikely that

---

1 See Denis Diderot, *Éléments de physiologie*, ed. by Jean Mayer, *Œuvres complètes*, DPV (Paris: Hermann, 1987), vol. 17, pp. 261–574 (p. 270, n. 28), [hereafter DPV]; Diderot, *Éléments de physiologie*, ed. by Paolo Quintili (Paris: Champion, 2004), p. 32 [hereafter PQ]. Mayer harvests these details from two sources by Maurice Tourneux (both now freely consultable on Gallica), *Les Manuscrits de Diderot conservés en Russie*

it has been destroyed, given its identity as an expensively-acquired manuscript with documented provenance and a supremely famous author, and also given well-worn traditions within families of wealth stewardship and transmission. Let us hope that it emerges from a strong box some day.

This manuscript was described in some detail by Hippolyte Walferdin (1795–1880), a native of Langres like Denis Diderot, a politician, sometime inventor, and one of the editors of the Brière edition of Diderot's works in twenty-two volumes (1821–23), of which Jacques-André Naigeon's *Mémoires historiques et philosophiques sur la vie et les ouvrages de Denis Diderot* was the last volume, and also, separately, of the *Salons*.[2] Walferdin describes a manuscript entitled 'Physiologie' that falls into three parts, of which the first two 'se composent de descriptions d'un organe etc...' [are made up of descriptions of organs and so on]—a description which is accurate insofar as it goes but does not express (or invite) much interest; he states that it is not until towards the end of the second part and in the third part that Diderot starts drawing any conclusions. He goes on to say that he only spent an hour examining it but that he recognises from those last two parts a number of passages, specifically the ones about the miser and the woman written about by the scientist Girolamo Fabrici d'Acquapendente, and says they come either from the *Rêve de d'Alembert* or the *Mémoires*. In fact, they are not from the *Rêve* but from the *Mémoires*, Naigeon having lifted them verbatim from the *Éléments de physiologie*, although it is not hard to see why Walferdin isn't quite sure, given the way Naigeon knits them

---

(Paris: Imprimerie nationale, 1885), pp. 27–28; and Tourneux's angry review of Ernest Dupuy's edition of the *Paradoxe sur le comédien* which appeared in the *Revue d'histoire littéraire de la France*, 9.3 (1902), 500–18 (pp. 506–07); Tourneux confirms that historian of the Revolutionary papers, James Guillaume, has checked there is no trace in the papers of this committee (p. 506n). See also Jean Pommier, 'Lueurs nouvelles sur les manuscrits de Diderot', *Bulletin du bibliophile*, 5 (1954), 201–17. It is worth drawing attention here to the fact that in 1885 Tourneux dated the letter 'an IV', whereas in 1902 he dated it as 'an II'. Pommier addresses this discrepancy and clarifies that the correct date (as transcribed in the auction catalogue) is 'l'an $2^e$' (Pommier, 'Lueurs nouvelles', p. 207); he further explains that the day of the month is the first 'quartidi' of Germinal, that is to say '4 Germinal', which translates in the Gregorian calendar as 24 March 1794 (Pommier, 'Lueurs nouvelles', pp. 209–10, n. 3).

2   See Denis Diderot, *Œuvres complètes*, ed. by Jules Assézat and Maurice Tourneux, 20 vols (Paris: Garnier Frères, 1875–77), vol. 10, p. 88, https://fr.wikisource.org/wiki/Page:Diderot_-_Œuvres_complètes,_éd._Assézat,_X.djvu/98.

together in the *Mémoires*. How he does that will be the subject of Chapter 12. Walferdin clearly knows the *Mémoires* and Diderot's writings well, and he is trying to work out where this unpublished manuscript fits; he records Naigeon's note about Diderot having copied out extracts from Haller's *Physiologie* which he burnt once he had finished writing on the subject, and he mentions a manuscript 'des éléments de physiologie et mélanges [...] sur les passions' [including elements of physiology and varia [...] on the passions] which Jean-Baptiste-Alexandre Paulin had not published;[3] Walferdin notices that there is 'quelque chose sur les passions' in the Leblanc manuscript too.

What is interesting here is the palimpsest of different manuscripts and topics, and the confusion created by the slippage between them. What was in Naigeon's *Mémoires* described merely as extensive extracts from Haller which Diderot used and then burnt once he had completed 'les deux dialogues' [the two dialogues], is almost imperceptibly upgraded in Walferdin's description to 'les mémoires sur la physiologie' [notes on physiology] which Diderot had burnt once he finished writing *Le Rêve de d'Alembert*. He considers that this manuscript was the point of departure for the *Rêve*. He further records that the manuscript contains a crossed-out paragraph contradicting Jean-Paul Marat's theory of the soul, noting that Marat's work came out in 1775, and that Diderot died in 1784 (thereby unwittingly providing the evidence that the *Éléments* was written after the *Rêve*, composed in 1769), that Naigeon claims Diderot had planned to write a physiological thesis in the form of a series of letters to Naigeon himself, and that this particular manuscript bears no resemblance to a series of letters. He ends with a laconic remark that the manuscript seems to come from a certain 'Mr Moette de Versailles' who he believes was the translator of *Lucina sine concubitu*.[4]

There is enough information here to draw a few clear conclusions. Firstly, that this was a separate manuscript copy of the *Éléments*; the

---

3   Jacques-André Naigeon, *Mémoires historiques et philosophiques sur la vie et les ouvrages de Denis Diderot* (Paris: J. L. L. Brière, 1821 [1823]; repr. Geneva: Slatkine Reprints, 1970), p. 222n. Jean-Baptiste-Alexandre Paulin (1800–59) brought out the important *Mémoires, correspondance et ouvrages inédits de Diderot, publiés d'après les manuscrits confiés en mourant par l'auteur à Grimm* in four volumes in 1830: this is where the *Rêve de d'Alembert*, amongst other texts, was first published in full.

4   Note transcribed in full, Mayer DPV 270–71. Walferdin's note is in the Bibliothèque de la ville de Reims (ms 2127), with the manuscript of Naigeon's *Mémoires sur Diderot*.

two we still have did not, so far as we know, ever leave their archive repositories, and nor is the passage lambasting Marat crossed out in either version.[5] Secondly, it must be a mature iteration of the work and therefore similar (if not identical) to the Vandeul full-length copy in that it is organised in three parts. Thirdly, it had readers beyond the restricted circle of those whom we know for sure had access to the manuscript in one version or another, that is, Naigeon, Diderot's daughter and her husband, and Catherine II of Russia. These readers were the Citoyen Garron (the person who sent the manuscript), the members and/or clerks of the Comité d'instruction publique (to whom it was sent), and 'Mr Moette de Versailles' (in whose hands it ended up).

This 'Mr Moette de Versailles' and translator from English of *Lucina sine concubitu* is Jean-Pierre Moët (1721–1806). The *Lucina* was the work of Sir John Hill, a lurid mixture of medicine and prurience, as well as a satire against the Royal Society, published under the name Abraham Johnson. It examines various cases of women becoming pregnant without intercourse.[6] This is a topic which Diderot examines in connection with abnormal genital configurations and pregnancies in both sexes,[7] and about which Acquapendente (whose presence in this manuscript is one of the few details Walferdin noticed, as we saw) also wrote.[8] What we also know about Moët is that he was a freemason of importance, having held prominent positions in the Grand Orient in the 1750s and 1760s, that he was also involved in the theatre, being co-director (with Charles Simon Favart and others) of the Opéra Comique (1757–63), that he translated Emanuel Swedenborg from Latin (his translations were published posthumously), that he was the son of a well-regarded bookseller, and that, according to the entry in Jean Sgard's *Dictionnaire des journalistes*, 'il se piquait d'être encyclopédiste' [he liked to make out he was a contributor to the *Encyclopédie*].[9]

---

5   SP AT p. 378; DPV 334/PQ 153; Naigeon, *Mémoires historiques et philosophiques*, p. 221 (Marat is not named).
6   Sir John Hill, *Lucina sine concubitu* (London: M. Cooper, 1750).
7   See *Éléments de physiologie*, Part 2, Chapter 24 on 'Génération' [Reproduction], esp. DPV 428–33/PQ 248–53/ *Éléments de physiologie*, ed. by Motoichi Terada (Paris: Éditions Matériologiques, 2019), pp. 242–50 [hereafter MT], and above.
8   Girolamo Fabrici d'Acquapendente (1537–1619), author of *De formatione ovi et pulli tractatus accuratissimus* (Patavii [Padova]: A. Bencii, 1621). DPV 429/PQ 249/MT 246.
9   See Marie-Rose de Labriolle, 'Moët', in *Dictionnaire des journalistes, 1600–1789*, ed. by Jean Sgard (Oxford: Voltaire Foundation, 1999), http://dictionnaire-journalistes.

Moët was therefore a man with connections in multiple arenas of Enlightenment sociability. We do not appear to know what he was doing in the 1790s or early 1800s, but given that he was the person in whose hands the copy of the *Éléments de physiologie* sent to the Comité d'instruction publique ended up, he must be a player of some sort, while conversely, his various affiliations tell us something about the groups that might have been interested in Diderot's work on physiology—perhaps those special readers to whom Naigeon repeatedly alluded. In this light, Moët's connections to medical texts and to the religiously unorthodox freemasons seem particularly resonant. Furthermore, if we consider his profile, and his repeatedly collaborative roles, whether as translator or journalist or within the theatre or as a freemason, it seems unlikely that he kept himself out of circulation, detached, private. The opposite seems more likely to be the case, that is, that he came across the manuscript because of his connections, and that he would have continued to share it with kindred spirits. Speculation aside, we can add him to the list of known readers of this text. But what of the 'citoyen Garron' and the members of the Comité d'instruction publique? How, if it was presented to the Convention as a form of national treasure via this important Committee, did it find its way to Moët, and why?

Any answer to these questions cannot be more than hesitant, as we only have circumstantial evidence, and there is no record or trace of it in the archives of the Comité d'instruction publique, published by the remarkable scholar James Guillaume at the end of the nineteenth century.[10] Guillaume himself confirmed this lacuna to Maurice

---

gazettes18e.fr/journaliste/581-jean-pierre-moet. See also Alain Bernheim, 'The *Mémoire justificatif* of La Chaussée and Freemasonry in Paris until 1773', originally published in *Ars Quatuor Coronatorum*, 104 (1992): 'On 'the 19th day of the 6th moon of the year 2299 of the rebuilding of the second Temple of the Great Architect of the Universe (vulgar era, 25 September 1763)... Jean-Pierre Moët... General Secretary and Grand Orator of the Most Worshipful Grand Lodge of France' was elected Sovereign of the *Conseil d'Orient*, and a certificate to that effect was delivered to him.' (Source given as *Bibliothèque nationale*, FM$^5$ 37). http://www.freemasons-freemasonry.com/bernheim25.html.

10 *Procès-verbaux du comité d'instruction publique de la convention nationale publiés et annotés*, ed. by James Guillaume, 7 vols (Paris: Imprimerie nationale, 1891–1957) : vol. 4 (1891) is the specific volume, covering 21 March 1794 – 28 August 1794, it would have been mentioned in.

Tourneux.[11] What we do know, however, is that the Comité d'instruction publique was extremely concerned about the fate of manuscripts and books, and that it published numerous decrees and instructions relating to their preservation and forbidding destruction. On 25 Ventôse an II (15 March 1794), it adopted the proposal made by its feeder committee, the Commission temporaire des arts, on 'la manière d'inventorier et de conserver tous les objets qui peuvent servir aux arts, aux sciences et à l'enseignement' [the methods for making an inventory and looking after all the objects that may be of use to the arts, sciences, and for teaching purposes];[12] it is interesting therefore, that the manuscript of the *Éléments de physiologie* was sent when it was, just nine days later, on 4 Germinal an II (24 March 1794). It is just possible—but of course completely unprovable—that it was offered to the Comité in direct response to that instruction. So why is it not mentioned in their records? Would they really have been so uninterested in a work on this topic, written by a figure of the stature of Diderot, that they would not have bothered even to mention it in passing?

In fact, on the contrary: there was a flurry of reports on saving and stocking books and manuscripts for the nation at exactly this moment. Prominent member of the Comité d'instruction publique, Henri Grégoire (better known as Abbé Grégoire) published his *Rapport sur la bibliographie* only a few weeks later on 22 Germinal an II (11 April 1794), its aim being to prevent the dispersal and loss of the books and precious objects of the nation; he describes the state of human knowledge and the steps that still need to be made, and he does so by invoking the progress already made by the 'rédacteurs de *l'Encyclopédie*' [editors of the *Encyclopédie*].[13] He talks of bringing together all these materials and

---

11   Maurice Tourneux's review of Ernest Dupuy's edition of the *Paradoxe sur le comédien* which appeared in the *Revue d'histoire littéraire de la France*, 9.3 (1902), 500–18 (p. 506n).

12   See the French senate webpage recording how preserving heritage became part of governmental responsibilities : 'Au service d'une politique nationale du patrimoine : le rôle incontournable du Centre des monuments nationaux', https://www.senat.fr/rap/r09-599/r09-59933.html. The remit of the Commission temporaire des arts is explained here: https://data.bnf.fr/fr/13533855/france_convention_nationale__commission_des_arts/. It existed between 18 December 1793 and 19 December 1795, that is, a relatively short time, hence the 'temporaire' in its name.

13   Henri Grégoire, 'Rapport sur la bibliographie', in *Procès-verbaux du comité d'instruction publique de la convention nationale publiés et annotés*, ed. by James Guillaume, vol. 4, pp. 120–29.

of transmitting them to the generations of the future. His instructions were immediately sent off around France, to be adopted with immediate effect.[14] This is not the report of a man to disregard an unpublished work by Diderot, one of those 'rédacteurs de *l'Encyclopédie*' he had explicitly mentioned. Grégoire's report of 22 Germinal came hot on the heels of another report dated 15 Germinal (itself only nine days after the letter and manuscript were sent), specifically on how to set up a depository for manuscripts: this report was written by Félix Vicq d'Azyr, not only a key member of the Commission temporaire des arts, but one of the most prominent anatomists of the time;[15] his recommendations were adopted.[16] On other occasions, Vicq d'Azyr and 'le citoyen Poirier', that is, ex-Benedictine monk Dom Germain Poirier (1724–1803),[17] are charged with examining and requisitioning manuscripts for the state, including those of the 'ci-devant Académie des sciences' [what was hitherto known as the Académie des sciences]; Vicq is recorded as announcing that 'parmi ces manuscrits des pièces infiniment précieuses pour les sciences et les arts, notamment des lettres écrites de la main même de Descartes' [amongst these manuscripts there are pieces which are infinitely precious for the arts and sciences, in particular letters handwritten by Descartes himself].[18] It seems vanishingly unlikely that a manuscript of Diderot's on the subject of physiology would have gone unnoticed by someone like Vicq d'Azyr.

Furthermore, the Comité d'instruction publique itself was highly organised and interested in its own records: it appointed a 'chef des archives de la Commission' ('committee' and 'commission' seem to be used interchangeably) on the 29 Germinal an II (18 April 1794);[19] it had a

---

14 Grégoire, 'Rapport sur la bibliographie', p. 129.
15 Félix Vicq d'Azyr featured in Chapter 4 for his work on the brain.
16 *Procès-verbaux de la commission temporaire des arts*, ed. by Louis Tuetey (Paris: Imprimerie nationale, 1912), p. 125.
17 H. Dufresne, 'Une vocation historique: Dom Germain Poirier 1724-1803', *Bulletin des bibliothèques de France*, 11 (1956), 755–66, http://bbf.enssib.fr/consulter/bbf-1956-11-0755-001. See Tourneux Review of Dupuy's *Paradoxe* (1902), p. 507, about Poirier being tasked by Diderot's family to hunt through Grimm papers for anything of Diderot's.
18 *Procès-verbaux de la commission*, ed. by Tuetey, p. 175 (20 Floréal an II/9 May 1794); for another example, see 5 Floréal an II/24 April 1794, pp. 148–49.
19 This is Dagobert Eustase Broquet, aged thirty-one, with extensive experience as a private tutor in languages and literature and 18 months study of 'l'art de guérir': *Procès-verbaux du comité*, ed. by Guillaume, vol. 4, p. 229 (29 Germinal an II).

sub-section (distinct from the Commission des arts) with no fewer than ten clerks specifically tasked with bibliography and cataloguing, and whose bureau chief, le citoyen Bardel, receives particular congratulation for his tireless efforts.[20] Meanwhile, le citoyen Mathieu reports on the correct internal procedures for recording items received, which, as Guillaume notes, was probably in response to an instruction to assess the secretariat's functioning, its lapses and possible losses.[21] So even if, as we see, there is a suggestion that things may have gone missing, this committee is far from indifferent to that happening, and is actively attempting to address the issue.

I mentioned only having circumstantial evidence to offer about what might have happened to this particular manuscript of the *Éléments de physiologie*. We have simply no idea why, assuming it did actually reach the Comité d'instruction publique, it was not recorded and kept, or why, if it was disappeared on purpose, that is, either hidden or stolen, the letter of gift would have been preserved with it, given that that would be evidence of irregularity, at the very least. But what we can see from this rapid survey of the archiving and cataloguing operations of the Comité d'instruction publique and of its public statements and instructions about the preservation of manuscripts and books during precisely this period is that it is unlikely that the absence of Diderot's manuscript was a simple oversight.

The more we pore over such documentation as there is, the less likely the oversight option seems. Naigeon worked for the Commission temporaire des arts, for example. He appears not to have been a fully-fledged member like his brother Jean-Claude (1753–1832), a painter known as Naigeon l'aîné, that is Naigeon senior, despite the fact that he was younger than Jacques-André (1735–1810). Yet, despite not being a fully-fledged member of the Commission temporaire des arts, our

---

20 *Procès-verbaux du comité*, ed. by Guillaume, vol. 4, p. 775 (23 Messidor an II).
21 Mathieu's report on procedures to follow within the secretariat with respect to recording and processing items received can be found in the *Procès-verbaux du comité*, ed. by Guillaume, vol. 4, pp. 775–77, and Guillaume's note, p. 776n. It is interesting therefore to note that despite all this bibliographical activity, there is no catalogue extant of the 12,000 books that the Comité d'instruction publique held, and which were transferred en masse to the library of the Assemblée nationale in 1796, after the termination of the Comité d'instruction publique's activities in October 1795.

Naigeon's signature appears in the register of the final session.[22] Was he working there in March 1794? An official member whose presence is not in doubt was the naturalist Jean-Baptiste Lamarck, whose *Recherches sur l'organisation des corps vivants* (1802) shared a number of the preoccupations we find in the *Éléments de physiologie*, particularly the first part, 'Des Êtres', and whose wary attitude to the generality of his readers as well as evocation of some superior individuals is strongly reminiscent of the attitude we have already seen Naigeon taking.[23] So, it seems likely the *Éléments* would have found an eager reader in Lamarck, were he ever to have come across them.[24] The secretary of the Comité d'instruction publique itself was a medical man, René-François Plaichard de la Choltière, and the records repeatedly mention medical works or questions being referred to him for review and report.[25] Moreover, one of the tasks of the Comité d'instruction publique at this time was the setting up of medical schools.[26] Again, it seems implausible that someone like him, with the role he had, would have been uninterested in Diderot's *Éléments de physiologie*.

It is of course not impossible that Diderot's manuscript was unrecorded or missed out of incompetence, but that it wasn't simply thrown away we know from the fact that it ended up with Moët. What seems perhaps more likely is that it was intercepted, hidden, secreted or stolen, in full knowledge of its interest. By whom and at what level

---

22 *Procès-verbaux de la commission*, ed. by Tuetey, p. ix, n. 5 (5 Nivôse an IV/26 December 1795). Guillaume lists the published members of the Commission temporaire des arts: *Procès-verbaux du comité*, ed. by Guillaume, vol. 3, pp. 502–03.

23 J.-B. Lamarck, *Recherches sur l'organisation des corps vivans*, ed. by J. M. Drouin (Paris: Fayard, 1986), pp. 55–56 (p. 59).

24 For reasons of space, and also because I'd already bitten off far more than I could chew, I regretfully set aside pursuing potential links with Lamarck. I go a little bit further in my article: Caroline Warman, 'Caught between Neologism and the Unmentionable: The Politics of Naming and Non-naming in 1790s France', *Romance Studies*, 31 (2013), 264–76, https://doi.org/10.1179/0263990413Z.00000000051.

25 For example, medical works are sent to Plaichard on 11 Germinal (p. 59), 29 Prairial (p. 652), 1er Thermidor (p. 835), 27 Thermidor (p. 941). This is a representative not an exhaustive list. Guillaume records the members of the Comité d'instruction publique in his 'Introduction': *Procès-verbaux du comité*, ed. by Guillaume, vol. 4, pp. ii–x.

26 Laurence Brockliss and Colin Jones, *The Medical World of Early Modern France* (Oxford: Clarendon Press, 1997), pp. 804–11; and Eugène Despois, *Le Vandalisme revolutionnaire: fondations litteraires, scientifiques et artistiques de la convention* (Paris: Germer Baillière, 1868), p. 116.

of seniority, again, we cannot know. Raymond Trousson, although he does not mention the *Éléments de physiologie*, wonders how various unpublished manuscripts of Diderot's somehow made their way into the pages of the pro-*philosophe* journal, the *Décade philosophique*. He speculates that the most likely route for these leaks is via its own editor, Pierre Ginguené (1748–1816), who, as deputy to the 'Commissaire' of the Comité d'instruction publique, Dominique-Joseph Garat (1749–1833) from January 1795, and then Commissaire himself from August 1795, and finally (briefly) its Director General, before its closure, would have had access to the depository where the confiscated papers of the ex-editor of the *Correspondance littéraire*, Friedrich Melchior, Baron von Grimm, were held.[27] Something of this order seems likely to be the case, although it could not have been Ginguené or Garat at this point (that is, March 1794), as they seem not yet to have been involved in the Comité d'instruction publique. Indeed, they were both about to be arrested, and Garat would be sentenced to death, surviving only thanks to the fall of Maximilien Robespierre.[28]

This is perhaps the point at which we should remind ourselves what was happening in Revolutionary Paris at this moment, beyond the Comité d'instruction publique and its bibliographical instructions and concerns. On the day the letter presenting the *Éléments de physiologie* to the Comité was dated, 4 Germinal (24 March), the Hébertistes were all executed. Georges Danton, Camille Desmoulins and others were executed on the 16 Germinal (5 April). This is the height of the Terror, and Diderot himself was not exempt from Robespierre's condemnatory attentions at this point: on 18 Floréal (7 May), four days after Ginguené had been arrested, Robespierre made a speech condemning the Encyclopedists, calling them charlatans, and accusing them of having persecuted 'la vertu et le génie de la liberté en la personne de ce Jean-Jacques' [the virtue and genius of freedom as embodied in the person of

---

27 Raymond Trousson, *Images de Diderot en France, 1784–1913* (Paris: Champion, 1997), p. 42. See also William Murray's *Dictionnaire des journalistes* entry on 'Garat' and Jean Roussel's on 'Ginguené' for the exact dates of these various offices: William Murray, 'Garat', in *Dictionnaire des journalistes, 1600-1789*, ed. by Jean Sgard (Oxford: Voltaire Foundation, 1999), http://dictionnaire-journalistes.gazettes18e.fr/journaliste/329-dominique-garat; and Jean Roussel, 'Ginguené', in *Dictionnaire*, http://dictionnaire-journalistes.gazettes18e.fr/journaliste/343-pierre-ginguene.

28 See Murray, 'Garat' and Roussel, 'Ginguené', in *Dictionnaire des journalistes*, ed. by Sgard.

Jean-Jacques Rousseau].[29] This was not the moment for one of the most prominent committees of the Revolutionary government to be recording as a national treasure a manuscript of this condemned charlatan.[30] Much better to keep it quiet.[31]

Why did 'le citoyen Garron' send it at this point, then? Was he a blinkered idiot? Paolo Quintili suggests that it was probably because of the plans for the Écoles normales that were at that point being considered.[32] It is true that the École des armes et des poudres (Weaponry and Gunpowder School), set up to disseminate knowledge about arms production across the embattled Republic, and thereby massively and rapidly increase it, was being presented as a new model for hyper-efficient education during precisely this period, and that the Comité d'instruction publique would pick up the baton in an announcement of 29 Floréal an II (20 May 1794) about its intention 'à propager l'instruction publique sur le territoire entier de la République par des moyens révolutionnaires semblables à ceux qui ont été déjà employés pour les armes, la poudre et le salpêtre' [to propagate public education across the entire territory of the Republic by the revolutionary means already employed for weaponry, gunpowder and saltpetre].[33] So it is possible

---

29  René Tarin, *Diderot et la Révolution française: controverses et polémique autour d'un philosophe* (Paris: Champion, 2001), p. 60.
30  Receiving manuscripts of Rousseau's, however, was a cause for celebration and public announcements: see 7 Fructidor, '293e séance: 'offre de manuscrits de Rousseau (par Jussieu et Girod)', along with Gregoire's response, *Procès-verbaux du comité*, ed. by Guillaume, vol. 4, p. 977.
31  Paolo Quintili writes that 'Garron non poteva scegliere periodo peggiore' [Garron could not choose a worse time], concluding that 'La Convenzione non solo non s'interessò agli Éléments ma ne respinse il manoscritto senza che se ne trovi più alcuna traccia fra i *procès-verbaux* delle sue commissioni' [the Convention did not only take no interest in the *Elements* but also rejected the manscript without there being any trace left in the *procès-verbeaux* of its committees]. There is no specific evidence to support the hypothesis that the Convention *rejected* the manuscript, other than the absence of any trace in the *Procès-verbaux*. Paolo Quintili, 'Diderot e la Rivoluzione francese: miti, modelli, riferimenti nel secolo XXI', *Quaderni materialisti*, 2 (2003), 81–106 (p. 105).
32  Quintili, 'Diderot e la Rivoluzione', p. 105.
33  *Procès-verbaux du comité*, ed. by Guillaume, vol. 4, p. 451. Quoted in Dominique Julia, 'La Fondation de l'école normale de l'an III', in *L'École normale de l'an III: une institution révolutionnaire et ses élèves, Introduction historique à l'édition des Leçons*, ed. by Dominique Julia (Paris: Éditions Rue d'Ulm, 2016), pp. 83–104 (p. 86). I discuss the rise and fall of the École normale further here: Caroline Warman, '"The Revolution Is to the Human Mind What the African Sun is to Vegetation": Revolution, Heat, and the Normal School Project', *The Critical Genealogy of Normality*,

that plans to set up new schools for the education of the new Republic are what triggered the gift, and it is also possible that the manuscript was sent in response to the Comité's adoption on 25 Ventôse (15 March) of the Commission temporaire des arts' recommendation regarding 'la manière d'inventorier et de conserver tous les objets qui peuvent servir aux arts, aux sciences et à l'enseignement' [the methods for making an inventory and looking after all the objects that may be of use to the arts, sciences, and for teaching purposes], as already mentioned; a combination of the two is also possible. We cannot determine with any certainty why it was sent when it was, and one of the reasons for this is that we do not actually know who 'le citoyen Garron' is.

The sales catalogue describes the content of his letter:

> En tête du volume se trouve une Lettre datée de Germinal quartidi 4, l'an IV de la République, par laquelle le citoyen Garron présente au comité d'Instruction Publique cet Ouvrage, qu'il reçut du citoyen Diderot quelque temps avant sa mort, comme un témoignage de sa confiance et de son amitié.[34]

> At the front of the volume there is a letter dated Germinal quartidi 4, year 4 of the Republic, in which Citizen Garron presents to the Committee of Public Education this work which he was given by Citizen Diderot some time before his death as a mark of his trust and friendship.

This description sounds very much like a close paraphrase or perhaps even a quotation. We will not be far from the truth if we suppose that 'le citoyen Garron' said something like 'je présente au comité d'Instruction Publique cet Ouvrage, que je reçus du citoyen Diderot quelque temps avant sa mort, comme un témoignage de sa confiance et de son amitié' [I present to the Committee of Public Education this work which I was given by Citizen Diderot some time before his death as a mark of his trust and friendship].

It tells us two things about 'le citoyen Garron' therefore: firstly, he is filled with revolutionary and republican fervour, given that he is so ceremoniously making a presentation of the manuscript to the new government, and also given that Diderot has become 'le citoyen Diderot'.

---

ed. by Peter Cryle, special issue, *History of Human Sciences* (2020), 1-18, https://doi.org/10.1177/0952695120946992.

34 Tourneux, *Les Manuscrits de Diderot conservés en Russie*, p. 28; Pommier, 'Lueurs nouvelles', p. 202.

Secondly, we learn that he is a friend of Diderot's, someone in whom Diderot has confidence, and to whom he wishes to leave something supremely precious. We do not know of anyone by this name this close to Diderot. We are stumped. If it is a pseudonym, we do not have any answers either. However, in the section that follows, we will look at some of the possibilities for who 'Garron' might be.

Tourneux tersely brushes aside the name 'Garron', saying it is 'vraisemblablement' [probably] Pierre-Henri Marron (1754–1832), a French Huguenot pastor who arrived in Paris in 1782. In support of this identification, Tourneux cites the opinion of bookseller and historian Étienne Charavay (1848–99), according to whom the 'M' of Marron's signature was very similar to a 'G'.[35] But is there any evidence Diderot and Marron ever met?

Emboldened by the notion that the name may have been mistranscribed, and by similar evidence of mistranscription in the archives of the Comité d'Instruction Publique itself,[36] some interesting possibilities, all of which may be completely erroneous, suggest themselves. They can be divided into two camps: firstly, those whom we know knew Diderot; secondly, those who were active in the Republican government in some way.

So, Jean-Baptiste Garant or Garand (c.1730–80) has nearly the right name, and knew Diderot a bit and executed the only portrait of Diderot that Diderot himself really liked.[37]

---

35  Tourneux, *Les Manuscrits de Diderot conservés en Russie*, p. 28.
36  See the confusion around the collection left by the émigré of a certain 'Jeannin Flammant'; Guillaume comments that 'il faut probablement identifier ce 'Jeannin Flammant' avec le 'Jeannin Chamblanc' ou 'Jallin-Chamblant' à l'occasion duquel avait été rendu le decret du 10 octobre 1792' [this 'Jeannin Flammant' should probably identified as 'Jeannin Chamblanc' or 'Jallin-Chamblant']. *Procès-verbaux du comité*, ed. by Guillaume, vol. 4, p. 945n.
37  In his *Salon de 1767*, he wrote that 'Je n'ai jamais été bien fait que par un pauvre diable appelé Garant' [my likeness has never been done well apart from by a poor devil called Garant]: Denis Diderot, *Salon de 1767*, ed. by Else Marie Bukdahl, Michel Delon, and Annette Lorenceau (Paris: Hermann, 1995), p. 83. The portrait no longer exists, but the engraving commissioned by Grimm does: Denis Diderot (c. 1760), by Jean-Baptiste Garand, https://commons.wikimedia.org/wiki/File:Denis_Diderot_by_Jean-Baptiste_Garand.jpg.

Fig. 7.1 Portrait of Diderot by Jean-Baptiste Garand, as engraved by Pierre Chenu, Jean-Baptiste Garand; engraver Pierre Chenu, 1760, Photo by Spiessens (2013), Wikimedia, https://upload.wikimedia.org/wikipedia/commons/8/88/Denis_Diderot_by_Jean-Baptiste_Garand.jpg, Public Domain

Against Garand's case are the fact that they did not know each other at all well, and that he had died in 1780, and could not therefore have been the author of a letter written in 1794. So it seems unlikely that it was him.

Next, we can offer Gaschon (first name and dates unknown), who seems to have been a banker of some sort, and who was a close and trusted friend of the Volland family. Roger Lewinter tells us that 'Mme Volland et Sophie plaçaient de fortes sommes par son entremise : 8,000 livres le 31 décembre 1771, et 20,000 en 1781' [Mme Volland and Sophie invested large sums with his help: 8,000 livres on 31 December 1771, and 20,000 in 1781].[38] Diderot mentions him quite regularly and affectionately in his letters to the Vollands during the period 1759 to 1774. But could 'sch' really be mistaken for 'rr'? Perhaps.

Third in this series is Dominique-Joseph Garat (1749–1833), a figure who bridges these two camps as both an acquaintance of Diderot and as someone active in the Republican government. Indeed, he has already appeared in this chapter as a Revolutionary politician on the verge of arrest and as someone who would later be involved with the very

---

38  Denis Diderot, *Œuvres complètes*, ed. by Roger Lewinter, 15 vols (Paris: Club Français du Livre, 1969–73), vol. 3, p. 754, n. 6 (relating to a letter from Diderot to Sophie dated Langres, 31 juillet 1759).

committee to which the manuscript and dedicatory letter was sent. He was Minister of Justice after Danton, and at the latter's recommendation, from 9 October 1792; from 14 March 1793 until his resignation on 20 August 1793 he was Minister of the Interior; arrested in September 1793, then released under house arrest, he was rearrested in 1794 and condemned to death on 2 Thermidor 1794, and not immediately released after the fall of Robespierre.[39] He only emerged from prison at the demand of various members of the new Convention, who wanted him to be appointed Commissaire of the Comité d'instruction publique, which he duly was, as we have seen. He would go on to be a key mover in the establishment of the École normale, also lecturing there himself.

As a young journalist for the Mercure de France in 1779, he had penned a remarkable—and now famous—portrait of Diderot in a state of almost crazed exaltation, as someone who could not stop talking, who whacked Garat's thigh for emphasis as if it were his own, and who, continually inspired, ranged from theatre to legislation to antiquity and history, whose imagination transported him to any place, subject, and time.[40] Diderot himself, having read this portrait, declared that he was 'point éloigné d'aimer' [not far from loving] Garat.[41] Garat seems like an option; an 'r' more or less seems insignificant, while a hasty 't' can look like a messy 'n' without too much of a stretch, and indeed does.

Fig. 7.2 Garat's signature from the registers of the Académie française, Dominique-Joseph Garat, ?1803, Pen and Paper, Académie française, http://www.academie-francaise.fr/les-immortels/dominique-joseph-garat, CC-BY

---

39   Murray, 'Garat', in *Dictionnaire des journalistes*, ed. by Jean Sgard (Oxford: Voltaire Foundation, 1999).
40   Garat dans le *Mercure de France*, 15 February 1779. Reprinted in Denis Diderot, *Correspondance*, ed. by Georges Roth and Jean Varloot (Paris: Minuit, 1955–70), vol. 15, pp. 130–31.
41   Diderot, *Correspondance*, vol. 15, p. 131, n. 14.

Against Garat being the signatory is his own celebrity or notoriety as a politician of the Revolution; would his signature not have been quite well known, and his name not recognised? Whether or not Garat owned and sent the manuscript, the lectures on the 'analyse de l'entendement' [analysis of the human understanding] that he went on to give at the École normale overlap strikingly at points with the third part of the *Éléments de physiologie*, and Garat therefore has to be part of our story. We will examine those lectures in a later section.

The first candidate clearly in our second camp, that is, those active in the Republican government, rather than straddling both like Garat, is the Assemblée nationale deputy, anti-slavery campaigner and lawyer, Jean-Philippe Garran de Coulon (1748–1816), known during the Revolutionary years as 'Jean-Philippe Garran'. He would have been an admirer of Guillaume-Thomas Raynal's *Histoire des deux Indes* (to which Diderot contributed so substantially), he had contributed to the 'Jurisprudence' volumes of the *Encyclopédie méthodique*[42] and, as a deputy, he published on a wide number of subjects, including disasters in the colonies, the sentencing of Louis XVI, and the government of Poland.[43] In favour of Garran is his name, his networks and interests. He would probably have considered that any substantial manuscript by Diderot would be important, without himself being particularly invested in the subject of physiology. This may be a reason supporting the idea that he would have gifted any such manuscript to the Republic. However, against him is any evidence that he knew Diderot in the slightest.

Finally, we have a homonymic 'Caron' who petitioned to be taken on as a clerk for the Comité d'instruction publique on 15 Messidor (3 July

---

42 The *Encyclopédie méthodique* was divided into different subject areas (including three on philosophy, edited by Naigeon, as discussed in Chapter 6) and ran to more than 200 volumes in all.

43 See *Encyclopédie méthodique. Jurisprudence*, ed. by M. Lerasle and 'un ensemble de juristes' of whom Garran de Coulon is one (A Paris, chez Panckoucke), 1782–89, 10 vols (see BnF catalogue entry: https://catalogue.bnf.fr/ark:/12148/cb307966921); Garran as unique author, *Opinion de J.-Ph. Garran,... sur les causes et les remèdes des désastres des colonies, lue à la séance du 29 février 1792...* (Paris: Impr. nationale, [n.p.]); *Sur le jugement de Louis XVI* (Paris: chez les directeurs de l'imprimerie du Cercle social, 1793); *Recherches politiques sur l'état ancien et moderne de la Pologne, appliquées à sa dernière révolution* (Paris: impr. de J.-J. Smits, an III [1794]). There is an engraving of him here: https://gallica.bnf.fr/ark:/12148/btv1b6943332w.

1794) and was duly given a job on 19 Thermidor (6 August 1794).[44] His petition has not survived, and we have no information about him, other than that he was taken on. Was he Pierre-Siméon Caron (1757–1806), a theatrical impresario and book collector who had some success with a puppet show in 1784, and who might possibly have known the Jean-Pierre Moët in whose hands the manuscript ended up. This Caron published a curious collection of 11 volumes of rare and licentious works, and he sounds more like the eponymous anti-hero of the *Neveu de Rameau* than a conscientious clerk.[45] The clerk and the puppeteer/book collector/writer are quite likely to be two separate people, neither of whom had anything to do with the manuscript. And while we are on the name 'Caron', a more famous (and probably equally unlikely candidate) is Pierre-Augustin Caron de Beaumarchais (1732–99), that is, the famous playwright, who was well-known to Diderot, but never close; there is only one (rather formal) letter from Diderot to Beaumarchais.[46]

To summarise: there is no obvious Garron. Tourneux, on weak evidence, suggests the Protestant pastor Pierre-Henri Marron. We, in turn, and on the basis of no evidence at all, but simply working around possible mistranscriptions and homonyms of the name itself amongst those who knew Diderot, and who therefore had some claim to friendship, propose the painter Jean-Baptiste Garand (who had been dead since 1780), the Volland intimate and banker Gaschon, the journalist and Revolutionary politician Dominique-Joseph Garat or even Beaumarchais, who would have styled himself 'le citoyen Caron' during the Revolution. More weakly even, because we lack evidence of acquaintance of any sort, we offer Assemblée nationale deputy Garran de Coulon, who, as 'le citoyen Garran', at least has the merit of having almost the right name, and, finally, the unknown clerk of the Comité d'instruction publique, taken on five months after the manuscript was sent. What this tells us more than anything is that it is almost pointless to try to identify a candidate because we simply do not have enough information; we are not even in a position to suggest that it might be a

---

44 *Procès verbaux du comité d'instruction publique*, ed. by Guillaume, vol. 4, pp. 741 and 907 respectively.
45 Pierre Siméon Caron, *Collection d'anciennes facéties*, 6 vols (Paris: [n.p.], 1798–1806).
46 Diderot to Beaumarchais, in *Œuvres complètes*, ed. by Lewinter, vol. 12, pp. 789–91 (letter of 5 August 1777).

pseudonym. And how quickly our efforts descend into the farcical, with late eighteenth-century Paris turning into a caricature of itself! What? A puppeteer and publisher of lewd old books? Beaumarchais the sometime gunrunner and spy? We might as well set to writing storylines for the computer game *Assassin's Creed*, where bibliographer, ex-Benedictine monk, and Vicq d'Azyr's co-worker Germain Poirier does indeed feature in some exciting manner.[47] Will some other researcher have better luck? I hope so.

Meanwhile, the name that stands out as most plausible, because the name could have been misread, because he did know Diderot, because he was clearly an admirer, and because he did go on to address very similar topics, is Garat. Whether or not the manuscript came from him, it is to him that we now turn, in order to explore the echoes between his lectures and Diderot's text. His future position as Commissaire of the Comité d'instruction publique means, after all, that if anyone could have had access to this manuscript, it would have been him.

---

47  For example: https://assassinscreed.fandom.com/wiki/Dom_Poirier.

# 8. 1794–95: Garat and the École normale

We already know a bit about Dominique-Joseph Garat from the previous section. We know that he had been a journalist, had met Denis Diderot and immortalised him in the pages of the *Mercure de France*; we know that he was a politician of some visibility during the Revolution. We also know that he was appointed Commissaire of the Comité d'instruction publique after his release from prison and the lifting of his death sentence, that he wrote the report on whose basis the École normale was set up, and was heavily responsible for its conceptualisation, organised as it was around his own lectures on the *Analyse de l'entendement*.[1]

A few more details seem necessary to understand Garat's background and perhaps also to make better sense of some of the hypotheses this chapter will advance.[2] His admiring portrait of Diderot was in fact something of a professional speciality: he was a celebrated and prize-winning author of eulogies of French statesmen and advisors to kings

---

1  Pierre-Louis Roederer (1754–1835) wrote that: 'le cours de Garat devait être le cours préliminaire de tous les autres' [Garat's lectures were to be the foundation of all the rest], *Journal de Paris*, 7 March 1795. Quoted in Jean Dhombres, 'Lettres et sciences: la cohabitation de 1795 à l'école normale', in *L'École normale de l'an III*, ed. by Jean Dhombres (Paris: Éditions ENS, 2008), vol. 4, p. 17, https://doi.org/10.4000/books.editionsulm.1445.

2  Sources for the information that follows (and more) are: William Murray, 'Garat', in *Dictionnaire des journalistes, 1600-1789*, ed. by Jean Sgard (Oxford: Voltaire Foundation, 1999), http://dictionnaire-journalistes.gazettes18e.fr/journaliste/329-dominique-garat and Gérard Gengembre, 'Introduction', in *Leçons d'analyse et d'entendement de Garat*, ed. by G. Gengembre et al., in *L'École Normale de l'an III*, ed. by Jean Dhombres, vol. 4, pp. 45–50, https://doi.org/10.4000/books.editionsulm.1458.

through the ages, and also of Enlightenment scientist Bernard le Bovier de Fontenelle.[3] (In 1820, he would return to the subject of Fontenelle in his *Mémoires sur la vie de M. Suard, sur ses écrits et sur le dix-huitième siècle* [Memoirs on the life of Mr Suard, his writings, and on the eighteenth century], a curious work that we shall have occasion to discuss in Chapter 11.)[4] He attended Mme Helvétius's influential salon in Auteuil, as Diderot also had (although they probably did not overlap), and he was also a member from 1779 of the connected masonic lodge which astronomer Jérôme Lalande had set up in 1776 with Mme Helvétius's support, the *Loge des Neuf Sœurs*.[5] Two further members of both Salon and Lodge are the doctor philosopher Pierre-Jean-Georges Cabanis (1757–1808) and his friend the philosopher Antoine Louis Claude Destutt de Tracy (1754–1836); all three, roughly of the same generation (Garat was born in 1749), would write on sensations, ideas, and human understanding, although at this point (1794–95) none of them had yet published anything on this particular area; Garat's published *École normale* lectures would be their first text of this sort, to be rapidly followed by Cabanis and Destutt de Tracy, as we shall see in the next section/chapter. But we are getting ahead of ourselves.

It seems as if initially Garat had no plan to deliver lectures on this topic himself; the Swiss philosophe and naturalist Charles Bonnet was named instead.[6] Bonnet's *Essai analytique sur les facultés de l'âme* (1760) would be much praised by Garat (a house speciality, as we have seen) in his first lecture; he declares that 'nul n'a connu mieux que lui le mécanisme de la pensée' [no one knew the workings of thought better than he].[7] This is not the first time Bonnet has featured in this study; we looked at Bonnet's contribution in Chapter 3. But Bonnet was unable

---

3 Michel de l'Hospital (1778), Abbé Suger (1779), Charles de Sainte-Maure (1781) and Fontenelle (1784). The Académie Française awarded the last three prizes. Murray, 'Garat', in *Dictionnaire des journalistes*.
4 Dominique-Joseph Garat, *Mémoires historiques sur la vie de M. Suard, sur ses écrits, et sur le XVIIIe siècle; par Dominique-Joseph Garat*, 2 vols (Paris: A. Belin, 1820).
5 See Louis Amiable, *Une loge maçonnique d'avant 1789: La Loge des Neuf Sœurs*, ed. by Charles Porset (Paris: Éditions maçonniques de France, 2014), pp. 35, 245–46. See also Dominique Julia, 'La Mise en œuvre du décret du 9 brumaire: les mesures préparatoires', in *L'École normale de l'an III: une institution révolutionnaire et ses Élèves*, ed. by Dominique Julia (Paris: Éditions Rue d'Ulm, 2016), pp. 115–69 (p. 130).
6 Julia, 'La Mise en œuvre du décret du 9 brumaire: les mesures préparatoires', p. 119.
7 Dominique-Joseph Garat, *Leçons d'analyse et d'entendement* [1796], ed. by G. Gengembre et al., *L'École normale de l'an III*, ed. by Jean Dhombres, vol. 4, p. 74.

to take up the position, as he had unfortunately died eighteen months before, in May 1793. As Dominique Julia wryly observes, it makes one wonder what effect the Revolutionary upheavals were having on communication networks within the republic of letters.[8] It is indeed curious that the death of such an important scholar would not have been known in Paris.[9] Might Garat have put forward the celebrated Bonnet as a blind, in full knowledge that he had died the year before, in order to offer himself up as a replacement in seeming humility and selflessness?

Partly what we are evoking here—in the hypothetical republic of letters, or more specifically in the Cercle d'Auteuil or the Loge des Neuf Sœurs—are a series of unofficial networks whose workings, efficacy and reach are not perfectly visible or readable to us, although we can trace membership and speculate on connections. The case of the Comité d'instruction publique and its École normale are different. These are prominent, official, even show-case parts of the government of the new Republic. So they have a different relationship to records, accountability, and reputation. We have already discussed the records of the Comité d'instruction publique, so we already know that while its official workings and records may tell a story of transparent officialdom, there are also many gaps and unknowables. Yet it does matter that they are official organs of the government and also that they are self-consciously new creations of it, reflecting its republican values, because this means that when they speak, they speak for the government. They are public not private; institutional not individual. And we cannot therefore separate content from form. Perhaps we never can, but if we are even considering suggesting that anything from the *Éléments de physiologie* might have made its way into Garat's *Cours*, from, that is, a clandestine and unavowable materialist manuscript written by one of Maximilien Robespierre's *personae non gratae,* and which the Comité d'instruction publique avoided recording when given it, and onto one of the most visible stages of the virtuous new Republic, then it seems obvious that

---

8    Julia, 'La Mise en œuvre du décret du 9 brumaire: les mesures préparatoires', p. 119.
9    Richard Whatmore considers it unlikely that news of Bonnet's death would not have got through to Paris, as communication between Geneva and Paris was good, email 22.2.2019; see also Richard Whatmore, 'Revolution and Empire', in *Against War and Empire: Geneva, Britain and France in the Eighteenth Century* (New Haven: Yale University Press, 2012), pp. 228–70 (ch. 7), for ample evidence of letters getting through between the two cities.

anything revealing any aspect of its origins will have had to be well hidden. Its form would have to be completely different. It would have to fit and reflect the École normale. And thus the first question to address is what was the École normale? What was its form, its function, its mode? Were these disputed? Was it successful?

## The École normale of 1795, its rise and demise

So, although the idea and indeed the name of the Normal School as a training academy for teachers was imported from Germany, its conceptualisation as a rapid revolutioniser of teaching across the new Republic was directly borrowed from a highly successful *military* model.[10] This was the project to bring citizen students from across the country to the École des armes et des poudres (Weaponry and Gunpowder School) to learn to make canons and the saltpetre and gunpowder to go with them, the idea being that not only would the students learn to make them but that they would return to their districts and then run foundries, and that the military production line would be vastly increased: this was an urgent national need in 1794, when France was engaged in fighting Spain, Portugal, Austria, Prussia, Hanover, and Britain. It worked, and it also functioned as a way of spreading Revolutionary fervour, as the students returned to their districts with offical governmental bulletins in hand.[11] The decree setting it up and requiring each district to send two citizens aged between twenty-five and thirty within five days, was announced on 14 Pluviôse an II (2 Feb 1794), and the lessons, lasting three 'decades' i.e. thirty days (a 'decade' referring to ten *days* rather than years), were due to start on the 1er Ventôse; this duly happened,

---

10 See Étienne François, 'L'École normale: une création allemande?', in *L'École normale de l'an III*, pp. 31–49. Some of the following analysis can also be found (more fully developed and more fully focused on the École normale itself) in Caroline Warman, "The Revolution Is to the Human Mind What the African Sun is to Vegetation": Revolution, Heat, and the Normal School Project', *The Critical Genealogy of Normality*, ed. by Peter Cryle, special issue, *History of Human Sciences* (2020), 1-18, https://doi.org/10.1177/0952695120946992. I would like to express my thanks to Peter Cryle and to the *History of Human Sciences* for allowing me to draw on my article here, and also acknowledge my gratitude to Peter Cryle (again) and Elizabeth Stephens for inviting me to their ARC-funded conference workshop on the Critical Genealogy of Normality in Italy, June 2018, where this work was first presented.

11 Quoted by Dominique Julia, 'La Fondation de l'école normale de l'an III', in *L'École normale de l'an III*, pp. 83–104 (p. 86).

and the first graduates of this school were returning to set up or revolutionise their local foundries by 2 Germinal (22 March 1794), just after a grand 'fête civique' to mark the end of the lessons, in which the pupils ceremonially presented the saltpetre, gunpowder and one bronze canon that they had made to the Convention nationale.[12] Jacobin politician Bertrand Barère (1755–1841), member of the Comité de salut public (Committee of public safety) under Robespierre and one of the few who survived his fall to continue as a member of the government, is loud in his acclamation:

> L'ancien régime aurait demandé trois ans pour ouvrir des écoles, pour former des élèves, pour faire des cours de chimie ou d'armurerie. Le nouveau régime a tout accéléré. [...] C'est ainsi que l'influence de la liberté rend tous les fruits précoces et les institutions faciles.[13]

> The old régime would have asked for three years to open schools, train students, and complete lessons in chemistry or armoury. The new régime has accelerated everything. [...] This is the influence of freedom, it makes all fruit ripen early, it makes institutions easy.

This is a curious passage. It naturalises the industrial production of weaponry as a harvest as it also naturalises acceleration in terms of an *early* harvest, and of course it also naturalises the new régime and the process of freedom as a sort of sun. But it took a while (even in these accelerated times) for it to get off the ground. It was Robert Lindet's report on the state of the nation, delivered on behalf of the Comité de salut public to the Convention nationale on the 4e jour des sans-culottides an II (20 September 1794) that reactivated the project. Lindet's aim was to make ignorance and darkness—les ténèbres—disappear, and to spread light and knowledge. He wanted the Convention nationale to 'éclairer le peuple, de l'attacher à la Révolution' [enlighten the people and make them love the Revolution, bind them to it]: he thinks all French citizens should be educated to be like those from the canton du Valais in Switzerland:

> Dans le Valais, tout habitant sait cultiver son champ, les arts et les sciences ; toute maison renferme une collection des meilleurs livres, des

---

12   Quoted by Julia, 'La Fondation de l'école', p. 85.
13   Archives parlementaires, 1ere série, t. 85, Paris, Éditions du CNRS, 1964, p. 208–09, quoted in Julia, 'La Fondation de l'école', p. 85.

outils les plus ingénieux des différents arts et métiers et des instruments d'agriculture, dont le possesseur sait faire usage.[14]

In the Valais, every inhabitant knows how to cultivate his field, the arts and crafts, and knowledge more generally; every house contains a collection of the best books and also of the best tools for arts and crafts, as well as for agriculture, and their owner knows how to use them all, moreover.

The response of the Convention nationale to Robert Lindet's call for action was to instruct the Comité d'instruction publique to produce a report within 2 'décades' (that is, twenty days), and its official document used the same terminology of acceleration we saw in Bertrand Barère's speech:

La Convention nationale, voulant accélérer l'époque où elle pourra faire répandre dans toute la République l'instruction d'une manière uniforme, charge son Comité d'instruction publique de lui présenter, dans deux décades, un projet d'écoles normales [...][15]

The National Convention, wishing to accelerate that time when it will be able to spread education uniformly across the Republic, charges its Committee of Public Education to present to it, in 20 days, a project for normal schools [...]

This is where Garat comes in. He duly wrote the report—although it came in 10 days late—and it was delivered by government minister Joseph Lakanal.[16]

On 9 Brumaire (30 October 1794), Garat's report was adopted and decreed. One citizen for every 20,000 population was to be sent by each district to Paris by the end of 'Frimaire' (December). Each future 'élève' or pupil of the École normale would be reimbursed for their travel expenses and paid an allowance. 1500–1600 new pupils duly arrived in Paris.

---

[14] Robert Lindet, 'Rapport sur l'état de la France', in *L'École normale de l'an III: une institution révolutionnaire et ses élèves (2). Textes fondateurs, pétitions, correspondances et autres documents (janvier-mai 1795)*, ed. by Dominique Julia (Paris: Éditions rue d'Ulm, 2016), p. 42.
[15] Quoted in Julia, 'La Fondation de l'école', p. 94.
[16] 'Rapport sur l'établissement des écoles normales', in *L'École normale de l'an III: une institution révolutionnaire et ses élèves (2). Textes fondateurs, pétitions, correspondances et autres documents (janvier-mai 1795)*, ed. by Dominique Julia (Paris: Éditions rue d'Ulm, 2016), pp. 43–49.

The official opening session was on 1er Pluviôse an III, where high levels of enthusiasm and repeated applause were reported.[17] The subjects taught were to be Maths, Geometry, Chemistry, Physics, Natural History, Agriculture, Literature, The Analysis of the [human] Understanding, Morals, The Art of Speaking, Geography, and Political Economics. The idea was that each lesson would be followed at a distance of a few days by a debate; in the lesson the professor alone would speak, but in the debate, the pupils would be allowed to intervene. The lecturers were not allowed to read out their work but had to speak it, supposedly improvising. Stenographers would take down what was said, and present proofs of the lessons to the lecturers three days later, which the lecturers would have three hours to correct, and which would then be printed and distributed to the students, who would be able to use them to prepare for the debates. The debates were also taken down by the stenographers, and given to the lecturers to correct—this time they had three weeks to do it. The student speakers however were not given proofs, and were unable to participate in the corrections, as at least one of them bitterly complained.[18] In fact the debates stopped occurring relatively quickly—around the end of the month of Ventôse (that is, 20 March 1795).[19] After increasing discussion about the École normale and its functioning, some of which was also to do with the practical living conditions of the students and the sheer expense of it all, the École normale was closed down on 30 Floréal an IV (19 May 1795), with most of the lessons still incomplete.[20] The stenographed corrected versions of lessons and debates would be publicly published, as it were, only a few months later, in the autumn of 1795 (l'an IV de la République), and dispatched to all the students in their home districts.[21]

---

17  Dominique Julia, 'Le Déroulement des leçons dans l'amphithéâtre du muséum', in *L'École normale de l'an III*, pp. 333–70 (p. 344).

18  This is Louis de St Martin, quoted by Stéphane Baciocchi and Julia in 'Un hiver à Paris', in *L'École normale de l'an III*, pp. 307–70 (p. 317).

19  Dominique Julia, 'Les "Conférences" de l'école normale: typologie des débats', in *L'École normale de l'an III*, pp. 371–421 (p. 388).

20  Stéphane Baciocchi and Dominique Julia, 'La Dissolution de l'école', in *L'École normale de l'an III*, pp. 425–62 (p. 440).

21  They were republished in an extended edition in 1800–01 and then again in 1808, and are now the subject of a critical edition (1992–2008). See Dominique Julia, 'Sources et bibliographie', *L'École normale de l'an III*, pp. 616–17, and also ch. 14 'Le Destin ultérieur des Leçons: les éditions des *Séances des écoles normales*', pp. 463–81.

The school had been a mixed success. it was supposed to have been only four months long, as indeed it was, but it had started late and none of the lessons were completed. Whether it would repeat on a yearly basis had not been addressed.[22] But, in any case, it was supposed to operate rapidly and efficiently, and it was relatively obvious that this had not happened.

The material organisation had been patchy, and the concrete conditions appalling, for both organisational and natural reasons. Students had arrived by the end of Frimaire (20 December) as they had been ordered to, but lessons did not start until a month later, whereas the modest allowances and travel expenses promised to the students by the Convention were not forthcoming until the lessons actually started. No accommodation had been provided for the students, of whom there were between 1500–1600, and the venue for lessons, the amphitheatre or lecture hall of the Muséum d'histoire naturelle, could only accommodate about half of them. It was also one of the coldest winters of the century and the Seine froze over so no supplies of wood or food could get into the city, which made conditions even worse. There were therefore 1,500 disgruntled students knocking about Paris, and there was some anxiety about the possibility of unrest. Once the lessons actually started, they still did not follow the advertised rota: some of the professors did not finish their lessons (Garat was one), some did not come at all (André Thouin, supposed to teach Agriculture, stayed in Belgium with the French army; Bernardin de Saint-Pierre, due to teach 'Morale', came late), and some were simply inaudible.[23] Despite the main mission of the École normale being to train teachers so as to facilitate the rapid onward transmission of all this knowledge, few of the lessons addressed the actual mechanics of teaching. One of the principal pillars of this particular lecture format was that they would be taken down by stenographers who would then write them up, and they had to be printed and distributed to the students in time for them to prepare for the planned follow-up debates.

---

22  The whole project was disbanded and not repeated again, as it had initially been supposed to, see the *Projet du comité d'instruction publique*, 1er Prarial an II, 20 May 1794, article 13, in *L'École normale de l'an III: une institution révolutionnaire et ses élèves (2). Textes fondateurs, pétitions, correspondances et autres documents (janvier-mai 1795)*, ed. by Julia, p. 41.

23  Julia, 'La Mise en œuvre du décret du 9 brumaire: les mesures préparatoires', p. 121; and Julia, 'Le Déroulement des leçons', p. 334.

Yet the stenographers never managed to turn the lectures round in time and, subject to the same appalling conditions as everyone else, became ill and went off sick. Some of the debates became heated and politically contentious—Garat for instance was accused of preaching materialism and atheism, as we will see, and he was not the only one.[24] Some students started making representations to the Convention to be allowed home—many had families needing support.

Meanwhile, the École normale—which was originally a Jacobin initiative from before Robespierre's fall—came under the suspicion because of it. The Assemblée des quatre sections réunies d'Auxerre officially wrote to the Convention on 30 Ventôse (20 March 1795) to ask for an 'épuration générale de l'École normale' [general purification of the École normale] whose élèves, they say, were chosen under Robespierre.[25]

None of this made the operation of the École normale easy, and indeed it never ran smoothly. It did not behave as it was conceived of behaving, that is, rapidly, efficiently, without loss of substance or speed in the transmission.

Interestingly, it was the speed and extent of the ambition that one deputy honed in on in the debate of 27 April 1795 about whether to

---

24 Stéphane Baciocchi and Dominique Julia give details of these accusations in their article 'La Dissolution de l'école': Antoine-Alexandre Barbier 'est formellement accusé par le Conseil général de la commune d'avoir "comme Chaumette prêché l'athéisme et d'en avoir fait une profession de foi publique"' [is formally accused by the General Council of the commmune of having 'like Chaumette preached atheism and of having made a public avowal of his faith in it']; Pierre Fontanier was denounced on 2 Germinal (22 March 1795) for atheism along with 'les commissaires qui, pour convertir le peuple à la raison, lui prêchaient l'athéisme en style révolutionnaire' [the commissioners who, in order to convert the people to reason, preached atheism in the revolutionary style]; Joseph Fourier (one of the élèves who in fact teaches maths to the other élèves) wrote to his friend Bonnard on 28 Ventôse an III (18 March 1795): 'J'entends toutes sortes de contes à ce sujet. Je n'ajouterai jamais foi à de pareilles sottises, et ce qui rend tout ceci incroyable encore, c'est qu'on me présente, dit-on, comme un dilapidateur et un ivrogne' [I am hearing all sorts of stories on this topic. I will never believe in such nonsense, and what makes it even more unbelievable is that apparently I am being presented as a spendthrift and drunkard] ('La Dissolution de l'école', pp. 431, 431, 433 respectively). On Fontanier, see also http://lakanal-1795.huma-num.fr/wiki/Fontanier_Pierre from the *Prosopographie des élèves nommés à l'école normale de l'an III*, ed. by Stéphane Baciocchi and Dominique Julia, http://lakanal-1795.huma-num.fr/wiki/Présentation.

25 Baciocchi and Julia, 'La Dissolution de l'école', pp. 437–38.

close down the École normale or not. This is what Pierre-Marie-Augustin Guyomar, député (elected representative) des Côtes-du-Nord and cloth merchant from Guingamp, said:

> Lorsque l'École normale fut établie, la manie des anciens gouvernants régnait encore ; on croyait alors qu'on pouvait faire des savants en quatre mois ; on voulait *révolutionner* jusqu'à la science [...]. J'observerai que vouloir des cultivateurs faire des savants, c'est une brillante chimère ; pourvu qu'ils sachent lire, écrire et compter, c'est tout ce qui leur est nécessaire.[26]

> When the École normale was set up, the mania of the old rulers still held sway; it was then thought that it was possible to make scholars in four months; they wanted to *revolutionise* everything, even knowledge [...] In my view, to want to make scholars out of farmers is a brilliant chimera; as long as they can read, write, and count, that's all they need.

In 'manie des anciens gouvernants' we recognise of course a criticism of the Jacobins, now presented as obsessives and subject to mania. The speed is presented as ridiculous, as is the aim we heard positively presented by Lindet in his report to the convention on 20 Sept 1794, only seven months earlier (and subsequent to the fall of the Jacobin régime), that is, to imitate the inhabitants of the Swiss canton of Valais, who read and are interested in their fields and in arts and sciences. Lindet's aim had been to create an equality that was also an aspiration. Guyomar's restatement of the needs of farmers is a back-to-basics sort of notion, and makes something as complex and ambitious as the École normale in its 1795 incarnation appear broadly redundant, even a sort of perversion, a monster of mixed parts, like the mythical chimera.

## Garat's Lectures on the Analysis of Human Understanding

Garat is right in the middle of all this. His role in orientating the ambition of the school was decisive: he wanted the school no longer

---

26 Guyomar, as relayed by the *Journal de France* no. 942, 8 Floréal an III (27 April 1795), in *Une institution et ses élèves (2): Textes fondateurs*, ed. by Julia, Appendix 3 (Les débats à la Convention), p. 67; also quoted in Baciocchi and Julia, 'La Dissolution de l'école', p. 445.

simply to train teachers but to be 'la première École du monde' [the first School in the world].[27] He chose the subjects and put forward lecturers with whom he had long-standing intellectual affinities, as Julia puts it.[28] He also tried to get Cabanis to join them (he declined on health grounds).[29] And as mentioned, once Bonnet's hoped-for contribution was no longer an option, and Garat had begun to occupy the conceptual space initially (or supposedly) intended for the Genevan naturalist, he gave his own lectures on the Analysis of the Understanding centre stage, presenting their analysis of analysis as the starting point and touchstone of everything else, as we will see.

Why would the Analysis of the Understanding come before all other subjects and be presented as the foundation of all? In common-sense terms, because once one learns to think and learns to learn, then one can learn anything. Thus, Garat envisages his pupils going out to teach learning in general, forming efficient clear minds. This aim is, in his words, perfectly specific: 'il n'y a qu'une seule manière de bien penser' [there is only one way of thinking properly], and is the foundation 'de tout ce qu'il y a de plus grand et de plus réel dans les espérances conçues pour le perfectionnement de l'esprit humain et pour l'amélioration universelle des destinées humaines' [of everything that is grandest and most real in the hopes conceived for the perfecting of the human mind and the universal improvement of human destinies].[30] We see the aims, values, and claims of the Republican government in this sentence. In any case, to discover this single manner of thinking well or, in alternative terms, of directing the mind ('l'esprit'), there is 'un seul moyen' [a single means] which is 'de le bien connaître, de le suivre pas à pas dans tout ce qui lui arrive et dans tout ce qu'il fait, depuis les sensations qui lui sont communes avec les animaux, jusqu'aux conceptions les plus compliquées de la plus vaste intelligence' [to know it well, to follow it step by step in everything that happens to it and everything it does, from

---

27 Garat, letter to Lakanal, 15 Nivôse an III (4 January 1795), quoted in Julia, 'La Mise en œuvre du décret du 9 brumaire: les mesures préparatoires', p. 120. See also Gérard Gengembre, 'Introduction', *Leçons d'analyse et d'entendement de Garat*, p. 48.
28 Julia, 'La Mise en œuvre du décret du 9 brumaire: les mesures préparatoires', p. 132.
29 Julia, 'La Mise en œuvre du décret du 9 brumaire: les mesures préparatoires', p. 152, n. 40 (from the same letter of 15 Nivôse to Lakanal, see note 27).
30 Garat, *Leçons d'analyse et d'entendement*, ed. by G. Gengembre et al., in *L'École Normale de l'an III*, ed. by Jean Dhombres (Paris: Éditions ENS), pp. 43–160 (p. 85).

the sensations it shares with animals all the way to the most complicated conceptions of the greatest intelligence].[31]

As this term 'sensations' immediately tells us, Garat's programme is to teach the theory of sense-based knowledge with which we engaged briefly in Chapter 3; whether in doing this he also addresses how to teach learning is a moot point. However, he describes the processes by which a sensation becomes an idea and can then be compared to another sensation-based idea; from comparison we come to judgement, and connectedly to memory and imagination. He also talks about how language is a part of this process. In doing so, Garat 'adopte un sensualisme dans la continuité de Diderot' [adopts a sort of sensationalism following on from Diderot], as Béatrice Didier summarily puts it in her introduction to Garat's lectures.[32] But Didier might easily also have said Buffon or Condillac or Bonnet or any number of other adherents of sensationist empiricism. Condillac and Bonnet indeed are often mentioned by Garat; Diderot never. The aim of these lectures is, declares Garat, no less than to establish 'une science toute nouvelle, qui ne remonte pas plus haut que Bacon' [a completely new science, which goes no further back than Bacon], and the first thing he addresses therefore is the history of this new science.[33] Eulogy-like, his 'Première leçon' runs through Francis Bacon, John Locke, Thomas Sydenham (1624–89, English physician), Bonnet and Condillac, with glancing references to César Chesneau Dumarsais, Isaac Newton, Galileo, and Johannes Kepler.[34] We note in passing the preponderance on this list of

---

31   Garat, *Leçons d'analyse et d'entendement*, p. 67 (Programme).
32   Béatrice Didier, 'Les cours littéraires de l'an III: tradition et innovation', in *L'École normale de l'an III*, ed. by Jean Dhombres, vol. 4, p. 30. Michèle Crampe-Casnabet argues that Garat presents a 'reduced' (rather than reductive) version of sensualism; see her 'Garat à l'École normale: une entreprise de réduction du sensualisme', in *Langages de la Révolution, 1770-1815). Actes du 4ᵉ colloque international de lexicologie politique* (Paris: Klincksieck, 1995), pp. 177–84.
33   Garat, *Leçons d'analyse et d'entendement*, p. 69 (Programme).
34   Garat, *Leçons d'analyse et d'entendement*, pp. 71–73 (Bacon); pp. 73–74 (Locke); p. 74 (Sydenham, Bonnet); pp. 74–75 (Condillac); p. 75 (Dumarsais); pp. 72–73 (Newton), p. 75 (Galileo, Kepler). His 'Seconde leçon' will range beyond these references, bringing in classical authorities Plato, Virgil and Horace, and from 'recent' European thought, Michel de Montaigne, Nicolas Malebranche, Gottfried Wilhelm Leibniz, Montesquieu, Jean-Jacques Rousseau, and altogether in a clump, 'les Lavoisier, les Berthollet et les Laplace' (p. 83): of all these, only Rousseau is more than a passing reference (p. 86). Garat will deploy his pluralising trope—'les Lavoisier' etc, i.e. people like Lavoisier— again, see below. Jean-Luc Chappey looks

seventeenth-century rather than recent luminaries, and the presence of only two Frenchmen, Condillac and Dumarsais.

His conviction that human understanding or reason is sense-based leads logically to a second conviction, which is that in order to understand thought, we need to understand sensation. The connections between thought and sensation, and beyond them, the capacities of a given human being, are emphasised from the very beginning of his lectures.

> Tout ce que fait l'homme, tout ce qu'il veut, et même, à beaucoup d'égards, tout ce qu'il peut, dépend, en dernière analyse, de la manière dont il sent les choses, dont il les voit, dont il en raisonne, dont il les *entend*, en quelque sorte.[35]
>
> Everything man does, everything he wants, and often, in many respects, everything he is capable of, depends, in the final analysis, on how he feels things, how he sees them, what he thinks about them, how he *makes sense* of them, in some way.

Thus, it is not surprising to discover in his second lecture a particular push to improve, or in his term 'perfectionner' [to perfect], the functioning of our senses. He does not, however, draw attention to this in the plan (also in the second lecture) he outlines, whereby what he identifies as 'sections' (rather than separate lectures) will address firstly, the senses, sensations, and the origin of understanding (p. 77); secondly, the *faculties* of the human understanding (his italics, p. 80); thirdly, the theory of ideas of all sorts (p. 83); fourthly, the immediate and intimate way in which the theory of language or languages is connected to the theory of ideas (p. 86); and fifthly, method, and how 'bien *sentir*, bien se servir de ses facultés, bien former ses idées, bien parler [...] ne sont qu'une seule et même chose' [to *sense* well, to be able to use one's faculties well, to form one's ideas well, to speak well [...] are one and the same thing] (his italics, p. 89). We have already seen his rhetorical tendency to focus

---

at the importance of lists and the way in which they construct 'l'unité d'un groupe d'individus' [the unity of a group of individuals] during the Revolution, and although his remarks refer to a slightly earlier period and are specifically interested in biographical dictionaries, they are also illuminating here, see Jean-Luc Chappey, *Ordres et désordres biographiques: dictionnaires, listes de noms, réputation des Lumières à Wikipédia* (Seyssel: Champ Vallon, 2013), p. 176.

35  Garat, *Leçons d'analyse et d'entendement*, p. 65 (Programme).

on a *single* way of thinking properly and a *single* way of directing the mind, and here we see him present the proper ways to feel, use one's faculties, form ideas, and speak, as being one *single* thing. So, he has a plan, and it seems coherent, emphatically so. This, however, is all we have, apart from the two debates, in which he mainly repeats what he had already said in the lectures, and also defends himself against various accusations levelled at him, one by an anonymous letter, and the other by one of his students, the theosophist Louis-Claude de Saint-Martin (1743–1803), of connections to either atheism or materialism.[36] (We will turn to these accusations in due course.) This is all we have because the lecture transcriptions that we do have are incomplete, and there are no transcriptions at all for lessons we know from other sources that he did give.[37] Furthermore, he did not complete his lecture course.[38]

However, the material we do have is cause for interest in itself. As will already be evident, Condillac's influence is overt, and it was noticed by the students.[39] In this context, the word 'analyse' is almost

---

36   The 'Programme' and 'Première leçon' were given on 11 Pluviôse an III (30 January 1795). The 'Seconde leçon' was given on 23 Pluviôse (11 February). The 'premier débat' and 'second débat' took place on 29 Pluviôse (17 February) and 9 Ventôse (27 February) respectively. For an outline of the content of Garat's lectures and debates, see 'Chronologie et résumés des leçons et des débats', *Leçons d'analyse de l'entendement*, in *L'École normale de l'an III*, vol. 4, pp. 63–64.

37   The final part of the second lecture is missing (p. 63). A lecture from 19 Pluviôse an III (7 February 1795) is missing from the record: in the second debate (9 Ventôse/27 February) Garat reads out a letter from Saint-Martin referring to 'la conférence du 19 pluviôse' (p. 100), and another student, Duhamel, also mentions it in his remarks in the same debate (p. 113). There are eyebrow-raised reviews in the press of a lecture he supposedly gave on 4 Ventôse (22 February) which appears to have discussed a theory of a sixth sense connected to love (the press accounts focus with fascinated sarcasm on a detail about a heightened sense of smell connected to sex): see le *Courrier universel du citoyen Husson* (9 Ventôse/27 February), p. 2, and also the *Courrier universel ou l'Écho de Paris, des départements et de l'étranger* (30 Floréal an III/19 May 1795), quoted by Julia, 'Le Déroulement des leçons', p. 356. Julia also refers to a memoir by Charles-Marie de Salaberry which mentions this lecture, *Mon voyage au Mont d'Or* (1802). Finally, Paul Dupuy gives two further dates for missing transcriptions of lectures from the 18 and 24 Ventôse (8 and 14 March respectively); they are mentioned in the *Feuille de la République* (Paul Dupuy, 'L'École normale de l'an III', in *Le Centenaire de l'École normale*, édition *du Bicentenaire* [1895] (Paris: Presses de l'École normale supérieure, 1994), pp. 1–200 (p. 170), https://doi.org/10.4000/books.editionsulm.1538.

38   We don't know why this is, but there are at least two plausible explanations, which we discuss below.

39   L'élève Fournier wrote a letter describing Garat, specifically mentioning his enthusiastic admiration for Condillac (and Bacon and Locke), see Jean-Robert

automatically associated with Condillac; 'Condillacian analysis' is a well-known and influential mode of analysis with a wide range of applications in 'Enlightenment' thought.[40] His posthumously published work, *La Logique* (1780) seems particularly pertinent in connection to Garat's lectures—its full title is *La Logique ou les premiers développemens de l'art de penser*, and the relevance to Garat is not hard to see.[41] Divided into two parts, it first focuses on 'Comment la nature même nous enseigne l'analyse' [How nature itself teaches us analysis], containing chapters such as 'Que l'analyse est l'unique méthode pour acquérir des connoissances' [How analysis is the only method to acquire any knowledge] (Chapter 2), 'Que l'analyse fait les esprits justes' [How analysis produces accurate minds] (Chapter 3), 'Analyse des facultés de l'âme' [Analysis of the faculties of the soul] (Chapter 7).[42] The second part is entitled 'L'analyse considérée dans ses moyens et dans ses effets, ou l'art de raisonner réduit à une langue bien faite' [Analysis considered in its means and effects, or the art of reasoning reduced to well-made language].[43] Garat is not only influenced by Condillac, he is clearly modelling his lectures on *La Logique*, already a well-known

---

Armogathe, 'Garat et l'école normale de l'an III', *Corpus, revue de philosophie*, 14–15 (1990), 143–54 (p. 149).

40  As Arnaud Orain puts it, 'Condillac would raise algebraic analysis to the status of method [for] all science. The famous philosopher labeled analysis as a means for the "invention" of ideas: by comparing two ideas which are "known" the thinker is going to engender a third, which then leads to an "unknown"—a new—idea. Now Condillacian "analysis" was to become *the* great scientific method of the age of Enlightenment and was to be defended, in particular, by D'Alembert in the *Encyclopédie* for all fields of knowledge as the "method of invention"'. See Arnaud Orain, 'Physiocratic Arithmetic versus *Ratios*: The Analytical Economics of Jean-Joseph-Louis Graslin', in *The Economic Turn: Recasting Political Economy in Enlightenment Europe*, ed. by Steven L. Kaplan and Sophus A. Reinert (London: Anthem Press, 2019), pp. 193–220 (p. 208), https://doi.org/10.2307/j.ctvb1htk7.12. Orain refers to Condillac's 1749 *Traité des systèmes* (*Œuvres philosophiques*, ed. by Georges le Roy (Paris: Presses Universitaires de France, 1948), vol. 1, pp. 119–217, 213n); and d'Alembert's entry on 'Éléments d'une science', in *Encyclopédie ou dictionnaire raisonné des sciences, des arts et des métiers, par une société de gens de lettres*, ed. by Denis Diderot and Jean le Rond d'Alembert, 28 vols (Paris: Briasson, David, Le Breton, Durand, 1751–72), University of Chicago: ARTFL Encyclopédie Project (Autumn 2017 Edition), ed. by Robert Morrissey and Glenn Roe, http://encyclopedie.uchicago.edu/, vol. 5 (1755), p. 495a.

41  Condillac, 'La logique', in *Œuvres philosophiques*, vol. 2, pp. 369–416.

42  Condillac, 'La logique', pp. 374, 376, and 384, respectively.

43  Condillac, 'La logique', p. 393. There are many passages on reforming and perfecting language; see for example 'La logique', II.iii–iv, pp. 399–400.

text and claimed repeatedly by Antoine Lavoisier as his inspiration in reforming chemical nomenclature and language in the 'Discours préliminaire' of his seminal *Traité élémentaire de chimie* (1789).[44] The famous Condillac is Garat's pre-eminent authority, referred to in the course of the lectures alone eight times, ahead of Locke with seven mentions and Bacon with six. Yet the direction Garat takes his lectures in, insofar as we have them, is not quite the same. Instead of this specific Condillacian focus on perfecting language, Garat looks at perfecting the senses, and claims total novelty in even asking whether it can be done.[45] In the conclusion to this second lecture, he makes sure to anchor this question in Condillacian technique, emphasising that all this will be done 'analytiquement'.[46] And yet the claim for a completely new area, however Condillacian, has been made.

Nor are all of the references to Condillac entirely eulogizing. Garat wonders whether 'la sécheresse de ses narrations dépouillées de toute imagination et de toute beauté de style' [the dryness of his accounts devoid of any imagination or stylistic beauty] can be forgiven.[47] On the faculty of imagination, he chastises his eminent forebears—whom he lumps together—for insufficiently separating out the operations of memory, judgement and reason from imagination:

> les Locke même, et les Condillac, n'ont pu éviter le vague de certaines idées ; c'est pour avoir négligé de faire ces distinctions qu'on a eu, sur l'imagination, des opinions si opposées ; qu'on a regardé cette faculté

---

[44] Antoine Lavoisier, *Traité élémentaire de chimie, présenté dans un ordre nouveau et d'après les découvertes modernes* (Paris: Cuchet, 1789), pp. v, xx, xxxi–xxxii, https://doi.org/10.5962/bhl.title.67783.

[45] 'Il n'y a pas lieu de s'étonner que de pareilles questions n'aient pas été faites dans les siècles où l'on était persuadé que nos connaissances n'étaient point originaires de nos sensations; mais il y a lieu à s'étonner que depuis un siècle que cette vérité a été mise dans un si grand jour, on n'ait pas même songé à les faire' (*Leçons d'analyse et d'entendement*, Seconde leçon, p. 79, analysed and translated below).

[46] 'Nous serons assurés à l'avance qu'il n'existe et ne peut exister d'autre moyen de bien voir et de bien observer, de bien penser et de bien s'énoncer, que de s'énoncer, de penser, d'observer et de voir analytiquement [...]' [We can be sure in advance that there neither exists or could exist any other way of seeing well and observing well, of thinking well and speaking well, than of speaking, thinking, observing, and seeing with the analytic method] (*Leçons d'analyse et d'entendement*, Seconde leçon, p. 89).

[47] Garat, *Leçons d'analyse et d'entendement*, p. 75 (Première leçon).

brillante de l'entendement, tantôt comme la *folle* de la maison, tantôt comme la *divinité* [...].⁴⁸

Even the Lockes and the Condillacs were unable to avoid vagueness in certain ideas; it's because these careful distinctions were not made that there have been such opposing views about the imagination, and that this brilliant faculty of the understanding has sometimes been regarded as the resident *madwoman* of the house, and sometimes as a *goddess* [...]

Interestingly, in the *Mémoires historiques et philosophiques*, Jacques-André Naigeon would also accuse Locke and Condillac of vagueness on the 'operations de l'entendement humain', and he attributes the accusation to Diderot.⁴⁹ On the question of 'moral ideas', Garat again marks a separation between Condillac and his own, more embodied and experience-based, view.

Condillac a pensé que nous formons les idées physiques sur des modèles que nous présente la nature, et les idées morales sans modèles. Je ne crois pas cette opinion de Condillac très exacte ; je la soumettrai à votre examen : vous jugerez si nos idées morales, mémoire les notions sur les vices et les vertus, n'ont pas leur *modèle* dans nos diverses actions et dans leurs effets, comme les idées physiques ont leur modèle dans les objets extérieurs qui frappent nos sens.⁵⁰

Condillac thought that we form our physical ideas according to the models which nature gives us, and our moral ideas without models. I do not believe that this opinion of Condillac's is quite right; I will set it out for your consideration, and you will judge whether our moral ideas, that is to say, our notions of the vices and virtues, do not have their own *model* in our different actions and their effects, as the physical ideas have their model in the external objects which strike our senses.

So Condillac is an important presence, but Garat does not treat his work as if he were a strict disciple. He credits it, gestures to it, and diverges from it. There is no reason to be automatically suspicious of this sort of academic strategy; do we not all use and acknowledge the work of those who have come before us, while seeking to carve out a small niche for our own contribution? And yet there is some reason to be

---

48   Garat, *Leçons d'analyse et d'entendement*, p. 81 (Seconde leçon, original italics).
49   Naigeon, *Mémoires historiques et philosophiques sur la vie et les ouvrages de Denis Diderot* (Paris: J. L. L. Brière, 1821 [1823]; repr. Geneva: Slatkine Reprints, 1970), p. 207.
50   Garat, *Leçons d'analyse et d'entendement*, p. 84 (Seconde leçon, original italics).

suspicious in this particular case, because the specific aspects on which Garat diverges from Condillac are ones which are already present in Diderot's *Éléments de physiologie*. Diderot recommends improving the senses, and wonders why we do not,[51] he considers imagination to be a crucial tool of the mind,[52] while his chapter on the passions looks consistently and uniquely at passion and action as determined by nature.[53] These are striking parallels: could they be coincidental? Or— one step up—do they demonstrate a general awareness of Diderot's thought in this area, as imbibed through discussion at Mme Helvétius's salon d'Auteuil? Or, a further step up, do Garat's lectures suggest that he must have been aware of the *Éléments de physiologie* specifically? A direct comparison of the texts will quickly reveal whether there is anything in the suggestion that Garat may have been aware of or even using the *Éléments de physiologie*.

The following passages, all drawn from the second lecture of 23 Pluviôse (11 February), fill out the areas of possible proximity mentioned above, that is, broadly, sensation and the senses, their variation and improvability ('perfectionnement'); the imagination and its role in the mind; and finally, passions and natural determinism. The order is not quite the same as Garat presents them in, as I have chosen to follow the normal logical sequencing from simple to complex that all these works on the human understanding follow; that Garat does not quite do the same thing here is partly because he is announcing what he will do, not systematically doing it (which as we know he never does get round to doing, for reasons we will address in due course). However, they all come from the same dense few pages (pp. 79–82). Garat's statement comes first, and, for ease of comparison, is followed immediately by the closest equivalent from the *Éléments de physiologie*. My own commentary will be limited to drawing out their similarity or divergence.

---

51   Denis Diderot, *Éléments de physiologie*, ed. by Jean Mayer, *Œuvres complètes*, DPV (Paris: Hermann, 1987), vol. 17, pp. 261–574 (pp. 455–57) [hereafter DPV]/ Diderot, *Éléments de physiologie*, ed. by Paolo Quintili (Paris: Champion, 2004), p. 282 [hereafter PQ]/Diderot, *Éléments de physiologie*, ed. by Motoichi Terada (Paris: Éditions Matériologiques, 2019), p. 272 [hereafter MT].
52   DPV 475/PQ 303/MT 290.
53   DPV 486–98/PQ 317–34/MT 301–11.

## a. The Variation of Sensations

[Garat] La sensibilité elle-même [...] parait différer d'un homme à un homme, et dans le même homme, d'un instant à un autre instant.[54]

Sensibility itself [...] appears to differ from one man to the next, and within the same man, from one moment to the next.

[Diderot] La variété des sensations s'explique, ce me semble, assez bien par la variété des manières dont un même organe peut être affecté [...].[55]
De là ce qui est peine dans un instant, devient plaisir dans un autre ; de là ce qui est plaisir pour moi, est peine pour vous [...].[56]

The variety of sensations can be quite well explained, it seems to me, by the variety of ways in which a single organ can be affected [...].
Hence what is pain one moment becomes pleasure the next; hence what is pleasure for me is pain for you [...].

For Garat, sensibility differs from one man to the next, and within one man from one instant to the next. For Diderot, the variety of sensations can be explained, he thinks, by considering the many ways in which the same organ can be affected, and thus what is pain one moment is pleasure the next, and what is pleasure for me is pain for you. Garat expresses the same opinion as Diderot, although Diderot has a more thinking-aloud quality. He is also more physiological, mentioning organs,[57] and he specifies pain and pleasure and who is feeling them (you and me), where Garat is more abstract and detached.

## b. Misleading Senses; Senses Which Correct Each Other

[Garat] Lorsqu'un de nos sens est prêt à nous tromper, tous les autres sont prêts à nous avertir de sa supercherie.[58]

When one of our senses is poised to deceive us, all the others are poised to warn us of its deception.

---

54  Garat, *Leçons d'analyse et d'entendement*, p. 80 (Seconde leçon).
55  DPV 459/PQ 285/MT 275.
56  DPV 460/PQ 285/MT 275.
57  An organ, as we may remember from Chapter 4, is a general physiological term for any body part, including the sensory organs.
58  Garat, *Leçons d'analyse et d'entendement*, p. 78 (Seconde leçon).

> [Diderot] Combien l'organe de l'œil serait trompeur, si son jugement n'était pas sans cesse rectifié par le toucher.[59]
>
> What a deceiver the organ of the eye would be if its judgement were not constantly rectified by the touch.

Garat explains that when one sense is about to mislead us, the others all jump in to alert us to its trickery. Diderot remarks on how misleading the eye would be if its views were not ceaselessly corrected by the sense of touch. Where Garat gives one (unnamed) sense being corrected by all the others, Diderot avoids the abstracts, not even generalising the sense of sight but specifically focusing on the 'organ of the eye' being corrected by touch. They both use the word 'tromper' in different forms. In the following example, which considers blindness in connection to the other senses, Garat also brings together sight and touch:

> [Garat] Vous savez, et vous y pensez peut-être avant que je vous en parle, vous savez quelle étendue, quelle finesse, quelle sagacité presque miraculeuse, l'organe du tact acquiert dans les infortunés que la nature ou des accidens ont privés de l'organe de la vue.[60]
>
> You know, and perhaps you are thinking about it before I mention it to you, you know what range, what subtlety, what almost miraculous discernment, the organ of touch acquires in those unfortunate people whom nature or accident have deprived of the organ of sight.
>
> [Diderot] Il est vrai que quelquefois le vice naturel d'un organe se répare par l'exercice plus fréquent d'un autre. Si l'aveugle a perdu la sensation des formes et de tous les sentiments qui en émanent, il est bien plus sensible aux cris [...].[61]
>
> It is true that sometimes the natural defect of an organ can be compensated by the more frequent exercise of another. If the blind man has lost the sensation of shapes and all the feelings that arise from them, he will nonetheless be much more sensitive to different calls.

Garat evokes the extraordinary levels of subtle information the sense of touch can provide a blind person with; he suggests his audience is already thinking of the example before he even mentions it. This tells

---

59 DPV 457/PQ 282/MT 273.
60 Garat, *Leçons d'analyse et d'entendement*, p. 79 (Seconde leçon).
61 DPV 508/PQ 347/MT 321.

us how widespread familiarity with this sort of sensationist thinking was during this period, after a century of print discussion about it.[62] Diderot's well-known *Lettre sur les aveugles* (1749), is presumably an automatic reference point for any such discussions, and it is interesting to see how Garat refers to unspoken associations that his audience already have with what he is saying, ones that must here include the otherwise unmentioned Diderot.[63] Is it an overly suspicious reading to suggest that Garat's reference to the listeners' thoughts is a way of *avoiding* mentioning Diderot's name? Whether or not it is a conscious strategy of simultaneous avoidance and evocation, he certainly does not mention Diderot. The text from the *Éléments de physiologie* is similar if not identical to Garat's. Diderot states—in general mode—that it is true that a fault in one organ is often compensated for by using another one more frequently. He turns to the experience of a blind person who loses the sensation of shapes and connected feelings, but who becomes much more sensitive to calls or shouts.

### c. Perfecting the Senses, in Particular, the Sense of Touch

[Garat] Nos sens qui sont aussi des organes de notre corps, et les plus délicats de tous, ne pourroient-ils pas de même par des exercices bien appropriés à ce but, acquérir plus de finesse, plus d'énergie, plus d'étendue?[64]

Could our senses, also organs of our body and the most delicate of all, not also by means of carefully tailored exercises gain greater precision, more energy and range?

[Diderot] Nous exerçons nos sens comme la nature nous les a donnés et que les besoins et les circonstanc s l'exigent : mais nous ne les perfectionnons pas : nous ne nous apprenons pas à voir, à flairer, à sentir, à ecouter, à moins que notre profession ne nous y force.[65]

---

62  See above, Chapter 3, section 'Knowledge Derived from the Senses'.
63  Garat does mention Diderot's name once, in the first debate, as one of those, along with Rousseau and Claude Adrien Helvétius (Diderot comes last), in whose works 'la métaphysique' has been identified and criticised. This in itself is an odd claim. (Garat, *Leçons d'analyse et d'entendement*, p. 95 (Premier débat)).
64  Garat, *Leçons d'analyse et d'entendement*, p. 79 (Seconde leçon).
65  DPV 456–57/PQ 282/MT 272.

We exercise our senses as nature gave them to us and as need and circumstance dictate, but we do not perfect them; we do not teach ourselves to see, to smell, to feel, to hear, unless our profession forces us to.

Garat considers that sensory organs are parts of our body, and can therefore, like other parts of the body, be improved by means of carefully-crafted exercises. They would thereby acquire more precision, force, and reach. Diderot takes it from the other end; he states that we use our senses as nature has given them to us and as need and circumstance require but we do not work on them to make them better; we do not teach ourselves to see, scent, feel, or listen unless our profession forces us to. This explicit criticism constitutes an implicit recommendation, suggesting that we should do. In the next extracts, Garat asks whether it would be possible to create an art of seeing or an art of touching; Diderot imagines what a perfected art of touching would be able to do.

[Garat] Est-il possible de créer un art de *voir*, qui apprendrait à voir plus rapidement et à de plus grandes distances, un plus grand nombre d'objets à-la-fois sous toutes leurs formes et avec les nuances les plus légères de leurs couleurs ? Est-il possible de créer *un art de toucher* qui apprendrait à distinguer et à démêler rapidement sur la surface des corps, des formes, des contours, des polis et des asperités que nous ne pouvons pas même soupçonner, parce que nous ne nous sommes pas exercés à les démêler par nos sensations, et à les distinguer par des noms ?[66]

Is it possible to create an art of *seeing*, which would teach us to see a greater number of objects faster and at greater distances, and also in all the detail of their shapes and the slightest tones of their coloring? Is it possible to create *an art of touch* which would teach us to distinguish and rapidly tell apart the shapes, contours, the smoothness and roughness of the surfaces of bodies to an extent that we cannot even suspect at the moment because we are not practiced in using our sensations to tell them apart, and we have no names for these qualities?

[Diderot] Je conçois un toucher si exquis qu'il suppléerait aux quatre autres sens. Il serait diversement affecté selon les odeurs, les saveurs, les formes et les couleurs.[67]

I conceive of a touch so exquisite that it would replace the four other senses. It would be differently affected by different smells, tastes, shapes and colours.

---

66 Garat, *Leçons d'analyse et d'entendement*, p. 79 (Seconde leçon).
67 DPV 448/PQ 273/MT 265.

Garat asks whether it is possible to create an art of seeing which would teach us to see a greater number of objects in greater precision both of colour and shape, and to do this quicker and at greater distances. He wonders whether it is possible to create an art of touch which would make it possible for someone to perceive and distinguish subtleties of shape, outline, and surface that are currently unimaginable, because we have no practice in differentiating these sorts of sensation, and we do not have any words to describe them. Diderot is briefer and less exhortatory. He simply, ecstatically, and slightly surreally imagines a sense of touch that would be so exquisite it would replace the other four senses, and would be differently affected by smell, flavour, shape, and colour.

Interestingly, Garat follows this passage with an exclamation of amazement that no one before has thought to consider how to improve or extend sensory perception:

> Il n'y a pas lieu de s'étonner que de pareilles questions n'aient pas été faites dans les siècles où l'on était persuadé que nos connaissances n'étaient point originaires de no s sensations; mais il y a lieu à s'étonner que depuis un siècle que cette vérité a été mise dans un si grand jour, on n'ait pas même songé à les faire.[68]

> There's no reason to be surprised that such questions were not raised in those centuries when people were persuaded that our knowledge did not originate with our sensations; but there is reason to be surprised that in the century since this truth has been made so illuminatingly clear, no one has even thought to ask them.

Given that the *Éléments de physiologie* does draw attention to exactly this area, one is almost inclined to think this is a pointed remark.

### d. Perfecting the Senses: The Eyesight of the Savage Who Sees a Ship Far Out at Sea

> [Garat] Des voyageurs assurent que des hottentots, du haut des rochers du cap de Bonne-Espérance, découvrent à l'œil nud, dans l'immensité de l'océan, des vaisseaux que les européens peuvent à peine percevoir avec le telescope.[69]

---

68  Garat, *Leçons d'analyse et d'entendement*, p. 79 (Seconde leçon).
69  Ibid.

> Travellers tell us that from the top of the rocks of the Cape of Good Hope, Hottentots can see ships out in the vastness of the sea with their bare eyes, ships which Europeans are scarcely able to see with a telescope.

> [Diderot] Un mot sur les formes vagues et indécises pour l'œil. Par exemple, je ne vois en mer qu'un point nébuleux qui ne me dit rien, mais ce point nebuleux est un vaisseau pour celui qui l'a souvent observé et peut-être un vaisseau tres distinct. Comment cela s est-il fait ? D'abord, ce n'était pour le sauvage, comme pour moi, qu'un point nébuleux.[70]

> A word on shapes which are vague and unclear to the eye. For example, I can't see out at sea anything but a nebulous and meaningless blob, but that nebulous blob is a ship for someone who's often seen it, and perhaps even a very distinct ship. How has that happened? Initially it was nothing for the savage but a nebulous blob, just as it is for me.

Garat's comparison of the 'primitive' man who can see better than a European is presented via the medium of travellers' anecdotes. He tells of the 'Hottentot', who, looking out at sea from the cliffs of the Cape of Good Hope, see ships that Europeans can barely see even with the aid of a telescope. Diderot's is more personal. He compares his own vision, which tells him there is a blob out at sea, to that of someone who is used to looking far out at sea, a person who is subsequently described as a savage; this person sees not a blob but a precisely-delineated ship. An earlier passage in the *Éléments de physiologie*, in the section on sight, had already clarified the comparison envisaged, i.e. that practice makes perfect, and that the 'savage' provides the exemplary model.

> [Diderot] Tel qui ne voit pas comme le sauvage, verrait comme lui, si son œil était exercé.[71]

> Someone who can't see as well as a savage would be able to if he practiced looking more.

Garat takes the idea of practising and perfecting the range of one's senses in some rather concrete directions. He suggests that the way in

---

70 DPV 476/PQ 304–05/MT 291. Terada supplies Diderot's probable source in Jean-Paul Marat's *De l'homme*, MT 475, n. iii. It is of course possible that Garat also draws on Marat irrespective of whether or not he also draws on Diderot. My argument that he is using the *Éléments de physiologie* has to be based on the sheer accumulation of similarities rather than on any single passage.
71 DPV 457/PQ 282/MT 273.

which Galileo's telescope successfully extended the normal boundaries of human vision should be a model for what can be achieved *without* any enabling instrument, and simply by dint of greater skill:

> [Garat] Galilée a prodigieusement étendu, par le secours d'un instrument [le téléscope], la portée de l'organe de la vue; mais ne peut-il pas exister pour tous les organes de tous nos sens des moyens d'étendre leur sphère sans le secours d'aucun instrument, et seulement par une manière plus heureuse ou plus habile de s'en servir?[72]
>
> Galileo hugely extended the reach of the organ of sight with the help of an instrument [the telescope], but are there no means by which we might extend the sphere of all our sensory organs without recourse to an instrument, and simply by learning a better or more skilful way of using them?

There is no follow-up here to *how* this might be achieved, just this comparison with an instrument, and then a suggestion that *somehow* such extensions should be possible; perhaps 'extension' is the wrong term, simply a transposed metaphor deriving from the image of the telescope, and that what we should really call it is 'internalisation'?[73] There is something curious here about how an external and mechanical tool, normally used to supplement natural sensory capacities, is here given as a model for what the senses could do by themselves if only they tried. Garat is suggesting that humans could internalise the functions of external tools. It is a rather bizarre application of the idea that the senses might be improvable, perfectible, and it does not seem clearly realisable in any way at all. A humbler way of increasing productivity is also offered; the cup of coffee:

---

72  Garat, *Leçons d'analyse et d'entendement*, p. 79 (Seconde leçon).
73  Diderot's witness on matters of blindness, the 'aveugle-né du Puiseaux' [man born-blind of Puiseaux], makes some striking remarks about telescopes, and Garat may have them in mind here. However, the 'aveugle-né du Puiseaux' does not want to have a telescope or sight at all; he'd rather have long arms. See Diderot, *Lettre sur les aveugles: à l'usage de ceux qui voient; Lettre sur les sourds et muets: à l'usage de ceux qui entendent et qui parlent*, ed. by Marian Hobson and Simon Harvey (Paris: GF Flammarion, 2000), pp. 33, 35 ; Tunstall, Kate E., *Blindness and Enlightenment: An Essay, with a new translation of Diderot's Letter on the Blind (1749) and a translation of La Mothe Le Vayer's 'Of a Man-Born-Blind' (1653)* (London: Bloomsbury, 2011), pp. 173, 176. With thanks to François Pépin for this reminder.

> [Garat] Une tasse de café ne donne pas du génie ; mais elle donne au génie le mouvement avec lequel il va produire et créer.[74]
>
> A cup of coffee does not bestow genius, but it does bestow on the genius the impetus he needs to produce and create.

It does not bestow genius, but it propels a genius into movement so that he can start producing and creating; it gets a genius going. We find no such passages in the *Éléments de physiologie* about internalising or transposing a telescope-like capacity to other senses, or about drinking coffee.

### e. Memory and Imagination

Memory, however, is something both Garat and Diderot consider to have been wrongly overlooked:

> [Garat] La mémoire n'a pas toujours obtenu et n'obtient pas encore une grande considération parmi les philosophes.[75]
>
> Memory has not always attracted much interest amongst philosophers, and it still doesn't.

> [Diderot] L'empire de la mémoire sur la raison n'a jamais été assez examiné.[76]
>
> The power memory has over reason has never been sufficiently examined.

We have already quoted the passage in which Garat chastises writers such as 'the Lockes and the Condillacs' for being a bit vague about the imagination, 'cette faculté brillante de l'entendement' (p. 81). For Diderot, imagination is more important than memory; the first has the power to move and inspire, while the latter is simply a faithful copyist.

> L'imagination est un coloriste, la mémoire est un copiste fidèle. L'imagination agite plus et l'orateur et l'auditeur que la mémoire.[77]
>
> Imagination is a colourist, memory is a faithful copyist. The imagination stirs up both orator and listener more than memory does.

---

74 Garat, *Leçons d'analyse et d'entendement*, p. 80 (Seconde leçon).
75 Garat, *Leçons d'analyse et d'entendement*, p. 81 (Seconde leçon).
76 DPV 474/PQ 302/MT 289.
77 DPV 480/PQ 309/MT 295.

So there is a similar estimation of the importance of imagination for both. How do they define it?

> [Garat] Qu'est-ce, en effet, Que l'imagination? c'est la faculté de se peindre les objets absents, comme s'ils étaient présents encore, avec tous leurs traits, toutes leurs formes, toutes leurs couleurs, avec toutes les circonstances de tems et de lieu qui les précèdent, les accompagnent et les suivent.[78]

> What, in fact, is imagination? It's the capacity to paint absent objects to oneself as if they were still present, with all their features, all their forms, all their colours, all the circumstances of the time and place which came before them, went alongside them, and which followed them.

> [Diderot] Faculté de se peindre les objets absents, comme s'ils étaient presents, d'emprunter des objets sensibles des images qui servent de comparaison, d'attacher à un mot abstrait un corps, voilà l'idée que j'ai de l'imagination.[79]

> The capacity to paint absent objects to oneself as if they were present, to borrow from perceptible objects images that serve for comparison, to attach a body to an abstract word, that is the idea I have of imagination.

Here, for the first time, we have a word-for-word echo. The definition that Diderot claims as his personal view ('l'idée que j'ai de l'imagination') is identically replicated in Garat: imagination is the 'faculté de se peindre les objets absents, comme s'ils étaient présents' [capacity to paint absent objects to oneself as if they were present]. Garat fills in his initial proposition by detailing the sorts of ways in which absent objects might be depicted as if they were present. Diderot sketches his in more gnomically: he talks about taking images from sensory objects so as to enable comparison, and of putting an abstract term together with a body (presumably so as to give it life? He does not say so). So the first part of the definition is identical, although the second diverges.

Is this evidence that Garat was using the *Éléments de physiologie*? One might counter the idea that here Garat really must be copying Diderot by saying that this definition sounds so simple it cannot be unique just to them; it must be a very common formulation. But where else do we find this potentially very common formulation? A wide search has not

---

78   Garat, *Leçons d'analyse et d'entendement*, p. 81 (Seconde leçon).
79   DPV 475/PQ 302/MT 290.

turned it up yet.[80] Importantly, Condillac does not define imagination in this way, and although he does indeed use the counter-balancing notion of the absent or present object, he uses it to discuss how comparison works.[81] Condillac's definition of imagination is this: 'les idées qu'on se fait sont des images qui n'ont de réalité que dans l'esprit ; et la réflexion qui fait ces images, prend le nom *d'imagination*' [the ideas that one has are images with no reality other than in the mind; the reflection that these images produce takes the name of *imagination*].[82] What Diderot and Garat do, whether separately or together, briskly rewrites Condillac.

Immediately following Garat's description of imagination, as quoted above, he is moved to exclaim:

> [Garat] Qui ne voit qu'une pareille faculté, qui tient plus longtemps les objets sous vos yeux, vous donne le temps et les moyens de les contempler plus à loisir, de les considérer sous toutes leurs faces, pour en saisir tous les rapports ; de rapprocher les objets absents des objets présents et de les comparer, comme si tous étaient présents encore ?[83]

> Who doesn't see that such a capacity, which keeps objects before your eyes for longer, gives you the time and the means to contemplate them at greater leisure, to consider them from all different sides and capture all the relationships between them, to bring absent objects close to the objects which are present and to compare them as if they were all still there?

> [Diderot] L'homme à imagination se promène, dans sa tête, comme un curieux dans un palais.[84]

---

80  Nor has Motoichi Terada found anything. He comments, about this chapter as a whole, that 'Diderot rédige ce chapitre avec peu de sources explicites' [Diderot writes this chapter with few explicit sources] (MT 290, n. 233).

81  In his paragraphs on comparison, Condillac writes this: 'Un objet est présent ou absent. S'il est présent, l'attention est la sensation qu'il fait actuellement sur nous; s'il est absent, l'attention est le souvenir de la sensation qu'il a faite. C'est à ce souvenir que nous devons le pouvoir d'exercer la faculté de comparer des objets absens comme des objets présens. Nous traiterons bientôt de la mémoire' [An object is present or absent. If it is present, the attention is the sensation that it makes on us at that moment; if it is absent, the attention is the memory of the sensation that it did make. It is to this memory that we owe the power of exercising the faculty of comparing objects that are absent in the same way as we compare objects that are present] (Condillac, 'La logique', I.vii, p. 385, just a few paragraphs above his definition of the imagination, see the following note).

82  Condillac, 'La logique', I.vii, p. 385.

83  Garat, *Leçons d'analyse et d'entendement*, pp. 81–82 (Seconde leçon).

84  DPV 475/PQ 303/MT 290.

The imaginative man walks about, in his head, like a curious person in a palace.

Garat's rhetorical question addresses a 'you' who gets to contemplate objects at leisure; he ends with a repetition of the definition he had already given. Diderot's imaginative man strolls around his head like a curious visitor in a palace. Their central image of the man who is either leisurely (Garat) or strolling (Diderot) contemplating the objects of his curiosity has a certain parallelism.

At this point, Garat begins to describe people ('des hommes') with intense levels of imagination. Imagination, sensibility, calculation, vision, and discovery go hand-in-hand. He draws a rousing picture of the genius, whose imagination is like an army scout and a military commander, or like the rays that precede sunrise, whose intuitions lead to the greatest discoveries. And this, he concludes, is what constitutes the great philosopher: someone whose reason is practically nothing but one huge imagination working according to strict rules.

> L'imagination est l'attribut des hommes de la sensibilité la plus forte et la plus exquise : elle est cette sensibilité meme ; et plus on sent, plus on a de moyens de voir, d'apprendre et de créer. L'observation et le calcul vérifient ; mais c'est l'imagination qui marche en avant pour découvrir ce qu'il faut soumettre au calcul et à l'observation. Elle est entre les facultés de l'entendement, ce que sont dans les armées, ces avant-gardes qui vont aux *reconnaissances,* qui devinent et voient en même-tems dans quelle forêt l'ennemi peut être caché, et les sommités dont il faut s'emparer pour tout voir et pour tout dominer. C'est à l'imagination qu'appartiennent ces pressentimens, qui sont comme ces jets de lumière qui précèdent le soleil, avant que son globe apparu sur l'horizon, ait dissipé les ténèbres. L'histoire des sciences en fait foi ; les découvertes les plus sublimes et les plus utiles au genre humain ont commencé par n'etre que les soupçons de quelqes hommes de génie ; et la raison des grands philosophes n'a été presque jamais qu'une imagination vaste, soumise à des règles exactes. En un mot quand on n'a que de l'imagination, et qu'on en a beaucoup, on est à-peu-pres un fou ; quand on n'a que de la raison, on peut n'être qu'un homme assez commun ; quand on a une raison sévère et une imagination brillante, on est un homme de génie.[85]

> Imagination is the attribute of men with the most powerful and exquisite sensibility: it is sensibility itself; and the more we feel, the more ways

---
85  Garat, *Leçons d'analyse et d'entendement*, p. 82 (Seconde leçon).

of seeing, learning, and creating we have. Observation and calculation verify, but it is the imagination which walks ahead to discover what needs to be calculated and observed. The relationship of the imagination to the faculties of the understanding is the same as that of the reconnoitring scouts to the army, simultaneously intuiting and seeing which forest the army might be hiding in, which vantage points need to be seized in order to gain total overview and total sway. It's to the imagination that these presentiments belong: they are like those rays of light that pierce through before the sun rises above the horizon and dispels the shadows. The history of knowledge shows this to be the case; those discoveries which are most sublime and useful to the human race started by being no more than the guesses of a few men of genius, and the reason of the great philosophers has almost never been other than a vast imagination subjected to exact rules. In a word, when one only has imagination, and a lot of it, one is almost mad; when one only has reason, one might only be a rather mediocre person, but when one possesses severe reason and a brilliant imagination, one is a man of genius.

On reading this, one is unavoidably reminded of the portrait Garat drew of Diderot in 1779, someone he described then lle grand homme dont j'avais tant de fois admiré le génie' [the great man whose genius I had so often admired].[86] Garat makes it really hard for us here to continue to maintain a sceptical attitude towards the notion that he may have been drawing on Diderot's work. In the space of two paragraphs, he distances himself from those who are otherwise loudly trumpeted as the masters in this area, he gives a definition of the imagination which is word-for-word identical to Diderot's which he then illustrates with the image of a person engaged in unhurried contemplation, an image we also find in Diderot, and finally, he launches into rapturous description of the genius's imagination, their imagination being tantamount to an extremely fine sensibility, and whose intuitions are the discoveries of the future, which itself is strongly reminiscent of the intensely admiring portrait of Diderot he had published sixteen years earlier.

\*\*\*

---

[86] Garat in the *Mercure de France*, 15 February 1779. Reprinted in Denis Diderot, *Correspondance*, ed. by Georges Roth and Jean Varloot (Paris: Minuit, 1955–70), vol. 15, pp. 130–31. See above.

Summarising the results of this comparison, we see that there are repeated points of similarity: Diderot talks about the variation of sensory perception within one person over time and from one person to the next; so does Garat. Diderot explains that a sense operating alone would make mistakes, but that the senses work together to correct each other's misperception; so does Garat. Diderot talks about perfecting or improving the senses, and how professional expertise leads to much greater skill in the use of one sense or another; Garat talks about developing skills in each separate sense, and remarks on how extraordinary it is that no one has thought about this before. Diderot discusses this point with the aid of a comparison between the practised 'savage' and the unpractised and practically blind 'European'; so does Garat. Diderot states that the question of memory has never been sufficiently considered; so does Garat. Diderot defines the imagination as the faculty of creating images of absent objects as if they were present; so does Garat. Some differences: Garat extends his thinking about how to improve sensory perception firstly by asking whether we cannot all internalise telescopes; Diderot does not (although they do feature in his *Lettre sur les aveugles*): Garat talks about the effect of coffee on speeding up the cogs of a genius (although coffee cannot actually create genius in the first place); Diderot does not. Garat includes a rhapsodic passage that culminates with a description of the 'grand philosophe' and the 'homme de génie' and the importance of their imaginative insights that is rather similar to what he had written about Diderot before. In none of this is there a single mention of Diderot's name. Does this mean he is absent? On the contrary, I think he is present.

There seem to be simply too many parallels for this to be just a coincidence, or the coincidental use of the same sources by both Diderot and Garat. One or two, maybe. But not at this density and level of similarity. I conclude therefore that Garat is demonstrating not only a general awareness of Diderot's thought but a detailed awareness of the relevant sections of part III of the *Éléments de physiologie*. Whether it was him who also wrote the letter gifting the manuscript to the Comité d'instruction publique, as surmised in the previous section, or whether, as Commissioner of this same Comité d'instruction publique, he might have taken the manuscript under his protection (or nicked it), and then planned to use it for his own lectures on human understanding (which, as we may remember, he was not initially planning to do, hoping to bring Bonnet in; he himself would probably have lectured on ancient history as he did elsewhere),[87] we simply cannot know. We do not have enough evidence. But we probably do have enough evidence to say, now, that Garat did have access to the third part of the *Éléments*, and that we can see that he did from close comparison of the texts. What he would have gone on to do in his lectures, had he completed them, or had the transcriptions of those he did give themselves been completed and published, again, we cannot know. What we do have are the two debates that followed these lectures, including Garat's rebuttal of a letter accusing him of atheism and also the attack on him made by one of the students, Louis-Claude de Saint-Martin, who accused him of materialism. In the context, this is highly salient material, and we turn to it now.

## Saint-Martin's attack on Garat

The idea of the debates was to allow some discussion of the lecture material to take place. As we mentioned earlier, the lectures themselves were supposed to have been transcribed in good time before the debate for the students to mull them over, but they never were. In the case of the two debates relating to Garat's lectures that we have, it looks less like discussion than like fire-fighting. Letters and questions have been sent in to Garat, and he is trying to reply to them; students also ask questions directly. There is a certain formality and politeness (and much use of the appellation 'Citoyen'), but at points it becomes heated. The first one took place on 29 Pluviôse (17 February) and the second on 9 Ventôse (27 February).[88] Garat opens the first one with a detailed rebuttal of an anonymous letter he has received, in which his morality and belief in the immortality of the soul are challenged.[89] Garat swipes away the challenge without too much trouble, but related challenges

---

87 Garat lectures on history at the lycée called the *Athénée* from 1786 onwards and continues to do so during the Revolution (Gengembre, 'Introduction', pp. 46, 49).
88 See notes above for the details of the dates on which other lessons or debates by Garat may have taken place.
89 Jean-Robert Armogathe argues that this letter was written by La Harpe, and was part of an ongoing spat between the two. Jean-Robert Armogathe, 'Garat et l'école normale de l'an III', p. 152.

return in the second debate, which in its printed version is fifty pages long (as opposed to ten pages for the first debate, and six and twelve for the first and second lectures respectively). In fact, part of the reason for this is that Saint-Martin subsequently expanded his objections into a letter, which was published separately in 1795 and included in the 1802 edition of the *Débats*.[90] That the exchange of views started taking on a momentum of its own is relatively clear from this length and from the publication record.[91]

The first stage of Saint-Martin's attack ends with this demand:

> Citoyen professeur, nous pouvons donc sortir de ce doute déséperant, auquel vous nous aviez réduits ; nous pouvons, dis-je, devant tous les hommes qui voudront réfléchir aux observations que je vous représente, prononcer hautement que la matière ne pense pas : et c'est là le troisième amendement que je sollicite.[92]

> Citizen Professor, we can thus get out of the despairing doubt to which you have reduced us; we can, I repeat, in front of all those who will wish to think about the observations which I present to you, loudly proclaim that matter does not think: and that is the third amendment which I seek.

Garat has a long response, which boils down to this: I never said that in the first place. Here it is:

> J'ai été plus circonspect encore que Locke; je n'ai ni énoncé, ni annoncé aucune opinion sur les rapports de la matière et de la pensée: cependant on a dit, on a imprimé plusieurs fois dans les journaux et dans les pamphlets que je faisais de la matière une sustance éternelle, et de la pensée un de ses attributs. Vous-même, citoyen, vous dont je suis loin d'accuser les intentions, vous paraissez croire que ces deux assertions ont été avancées par moi dans cette École.
>
> J'ai regret d'entrer dans ces explications; mais on les a rendues trop nécessaires. Jamais je n'ai dit que la matière est éternelle: jamais je n'ai dit que la matière pense; jamais je ne le dirai.[93]

---

90   See Garat, *Leçons d'analyse et d'entendement*, pp. 117–52 (Second débat). Saint-Martin had published it under the title *Lettre à un ami ou Considérations politiques, philosophiques et religieuses sur la Révolution française, suivi du Précis d'une conférence publique entre un élève des Écoles normales et le professeur Garat* (Paris, 1795).
91   See also Julia's analysis of 'Saint-Martin contre Garat' in 'Les "Conférences" de l'école normale: typologie des débats', *L'École normale de l'an III*, pp. 403–06.
92   Garat, *Leçons d'analyse et d'entendement*, p. 103 (Second débat).
93   Garat, *Leçons d'analyse et d'entendement*, p. 112 (Second débat).

> I have been even more circumspect than Locke; I have neither expressed nor declared any opinion on the connections between matter and thought, but nonetheless people have said and often written in newspapers and pamphlets that I was defining matter as an eternal substance and stating that thought was one of its attributes. You yourself, Citizen, whose intentions I am far from calling into question, you seem to believe that these two assertions have been advanced by me in this School.
>
> I regret having to go into these explanations, but it has become all too necessary to do so. Never have I said that matter was eternal: never have I said that matter could think; and never will I do so.

He goes further; he separates the question of matter completely from sensation, so that he does not have to address the former. This is his explicit policy, in which, as he says, he follows Condillac:

> L'abbé de Condillac, qui parle peu de religion, écarte presque toujours ces faits matériels associés aux causes et aux actes de l'intelligence: en cela j'ai imité et j'imiterai toujours Condillac; non de peur de paraître matérialiste; si je l'étais, je craindrais peu de le paraître: non de peur de le devenir dans ces recherches physiologiques; si le matérialisme était une vérité, je le croirais utile comme toutes les vérités; mais parce que tout ce mécanisme de nos nerfs, de leur système et de leurs rapports avec le cerveau et les sensations, est beaucoup trop mal connu encore.[94]
>
> Reverend Condillac, who speaks little about religion, almost always avoids the material facts associated with the causes and actions of intelligence: in that I have always imitated Condillac and always will; not for fear of seeming like a materialist; if I were one, I wouldn't worry much about seeming to be; not for fear of becoming one by undertaking research in physiology; if materialism was true, I would find it useful like all truths are; but because this mechanism of the nerves, of their network and of the links between the brain and sensations, is still much too poorly understood.

This is an illuminating passage, not least for the way in which it bestows a religious identity on Condillac, who was indeed a tonsured priest. However, in all the many previous mentions of his name, he had not once been given that clerical title. So, Garat is clearly using it here for protection, as a shield specifically to fend off these accusations of materialism (which is, as we have already seen, understood to be

---

94  Garat, *Leçons d'analyse et d'entendement*, p. 113 (Second débat).

a synonym for irreligion). And secondly, it brings to the fore Garat's general understanding of what Condillac can do for him (and what Garat thinks Condillac does for himself as well), which is avoid any connection to materialism by dint of never mentioning anything to do with it, 'it' being interpreted directly by Garat here as any aspect of physiology.[95] It is very helpful to see Garat make this pair of associations so overtly—materialism and irreligion; materialism and physiology— and show us how he considers he can best protect himself from any such attack. He subsequently and almost immediately makes a further raid on religious language in an attempt to close down the issue, when he declares that sensations are 'les premiers phénomènes dont se saisit la bonne métaphysique';[96] what good metaphysics starts with (note also his use of the theological term 'metaphysics'):

> Voilà ma profession de foi, puisqu'il a fallu en faire une. Il est bien clair que ceux qui ont supposé que je faisais ici une espèce de cours de matérialisme m'ont accusé, et ne m'ont pas compris.[97]

> And there's my profession of faith, seeing as I had to make one. It is very clear that those who supposed that I was giving some sort of course in materialism have accused me without understanding me.

His profession of faith, there it is. An affirmation of belief rather than 'a sort of course in materialism'; an either/or situation in which it was absolutely necessary to deny and quash the latter proposition. Unfortunately for him, it did not work. As mentioned, Saint-Martin amplified the dispute further by pursuing it via publication with his *Lettre à un ami ou Considérations politiques, philosophiques et religieuses sur la Révolution française*, suivi du *Précis d'une conférence publique entre un élève*

---

95 Naigeon and Cabanis explicitly criticise Condillac's silence with respect to physiology and consider it a serious weakness, as we will see. Their view that he *should* be mentioning physiology suggests that they favour Diderot's physiologically-based account of the mind. In the case of Naigeon, we know this to be true, because his *Mémoires* publish the first version of the *Éléments*; in Cabanis's, the argument has to be made with greater circumspection; for Cabanis, see below, for Naigeon, see his comment 'Condillac n'en avait pas même une teinture superficielle [de la médecine] : ignorance qui influe sur toute sa philosophie, et qui réduit à un petit nombre de pages ce qu'elle a d'utile' [Condillac had not the slightest knowledge of medicine, and his ignorance of it has an impact on his entire philosophy, reducing its usefulness to a very few pages], *Mémoires historiques et philosophiques*, p. 216.
96 Garat, *Leçons d'analyse et d'entendement*, p. 113 (Second débat).
97 Ibid.

*des Écoles normales et le professeur Garat* (Paris, 1795), which the editors of the 1802 edition included in the debates, possibly in order to prevent it flairing up yet again, although in fact any further developments were stopped short with Saint-Martin's death in 1803. In that *Lettre à un ami*, Saint-Martin directly and sarcastically addressed Garat's Condillac strategy:

> J'admire toutefois comment vous vous êtes garanti du matérialisme en vous rangeant, comme vous le faites, sous les enseignes de Condillac.[98]
>
> Nonetheless I admire how you have protected yourself from materialism by standing, as you do, under the banner of Condillac.

In a way, all he is doing here is echoing what Garat himself had already said, that is, that he is a follower of Condillac and therefore cannot be reproached with materialism, but it is helpful to have Saint-Martin confirm that he also considers that that is what Garat is doing. He then proceeds to deride Garat for thinking that Condillac might be able to shield him, as within the pages of that philosopher's work there are practically 'pas de passages qui ne me repoussent' [no pages which do not repel me].[99] Saint-Martin does not even like Bacon very much.

Saint-Martin was a spiritualist, and his first work, *Des erreurs et de la vérité*, was published in 1775. Born in 1743, he was more than fifty when he was a student at the École normale, and he was therefore older than Garat himself (the decree requiring districts to send students to the new *École normale* specified that they should be between twenty-five and thirty years old, as we saw).[100] So he is not a typical student in any way; he may well have been looking for a dispute of this sort in order to publicise his own work and position. If so, he certainly found it. In his autobiography, unpublished until 1961, he declared with great self-satisfaction that his friends thought he personally had brought down the École normale, and thus thwarted its aim, clear to him from

---

98  Garat, *Leçons d'analyse et d'entendement*, p. 134 (Second débat).
99  Ibid.
100 On Saint-Martin, see Gérard Gengembre, 'Introduction aux cours sur l'analyse de l'entendement', pp. 56–61, 'Appendice n°12 – L'élève Louis-Claude de Saint-Martin' in *Une institution révolutionnaire et ses élèves (2): Textes fondateurs*, ed. by Julia, pp. 287–307, and also Nicole Jacques-Lefèvre, *Louis-Claude de Saint-Martin, le philosophe inconnu (1743-1803): un illuministe au siècle des lumières* (Paris: Dervy, 2003), esp. pp. 183–204.

the beginning, of establishing 'atheism and the doctrine of matter throughout the Republic':

> Ce but m'avait paru assez clair dès le commencement. C'était d'établir l'athéisme et la doctrine de la matière dans toute la République, et plusieurs de mes camarades ont pensé que ma séance avec Garat avait été le coup de grâce de l'École.[101]
>
> This aim seemed clear enough to me from the very start. It was to establish atheism and the doctrine of matter throughout the Republic, and many of my friends thought that my session with Garat was the killer blow for the School.

Dominique Julia dismisses these claims as 'guère plausibles' [scarcely plausible].[102] Earlier in this chapter, we briefly sketched in the multiple reasons the École normale folded: there was an increasing volume of denunciations and even demands for an 'épuration générale' of any lurking Jacobins, there were attacks in the press, the élèves petitioned to go home. Some of the criticisms were about how the content of the lectures was too advanced and that the specific aspect of *how to teach* had been neglected. Stéphane Baciocchi and Dominique Julia lay this all out in their remarkable chapter on 'La Dissolution de l'école'.[103] It is clear from their analysis that there were multiple factors leading to it being closed down. Saint-Martin's accusation of materialism is yet another attack, and therefore joins a host of problems that the École was experiencing.

With respect to Garat himself and his decision not to complete his lectures or to publish the ones he had completed, the landscape is a little different. On 19 Ventôse an III (9 March 1795), that is to say, ten days after the bruising second debate took place on 9 Ventôse (27 February), Garat was attacked from a different direction, denounced to the Convention by Louis-Philippe Dumont (deputy of Calvados) as the defender of the September Massacres of 1792 and an actor in the insurrection of 31 May 1793: the Convention decrees that 'la conduite des chefs et auteurs

---

101 Saint-Martin, *Mon portrait historique et philosophique (1789–1803)*, § 537; in 'Appendice n°12 – L'élève Louis-Claude de Saint-Martin', Appendix 12, in *Une institution révolutionnaire et ses élèves (2): Textes fondateurs*, p. 293. For details on the autobiography and its publication by Robert Amadou, see ibid., p. 285.
102 Julia, 'Les "Conférences" de l'école normale: typologie des débats', p. 406.
103 Baciocchi and Julia, 'La Dissolution de l'école', pp. 425–62.

de l'insurrection du 31 mai (vieux style) sera examinée par le Comité de sûreté générale' [the conduct of the leaders and instigators of the insurrection of 31 May (old style) will be examined by the Committee of General Safety].[104] Dominique Julia states that Garat abandoned his functions at the École normale from this moment, specifically in order to defend himself, publishing his defence in May of that year.[105] This was his *Mémoires sur la Révolution ou exposé de ma conduite dans les affaires et les fonctions publiques*, completed two days before the closure of the school on 30 Floréal an IV (19 May 1795).[106] And yet, if the *Feuille de la République* is to be believed, Garat did give one further lecture, on 24 Ventôse (14 March).[107] However, the urgency of Garat's need to deal with this denunciation and the ensuing action by the Comité de sûreté générale is unarguable.

But is it for this reason alone that Garat failed to complete his lectures, announced with such fanfare as something he had been thinking about for twenty years and which caused him bitter regret not to have completed when he was 'au pied de l'échafaud', [at the foot of the scaffold] as he had rousingly announced in the closing words of his first lecture?[108] He could have completed them later, once he had been cleared of the suspicions against him, which he duly was.[109] The 1800–01 edition of the Cercle social was still plaintively requesting that he do so, printing on the very first page of their volumes 7 and 8 that 'le citoyen Garat n'a plus qu'à réviser également ses premières Leçons sur l'analyse de l'entendement humain; et les Élèves des Écoles normales

---

104 Quoted in Julia, 'La Mise en œuvre du décret du 9 brumaire: les mesures préparatoires', p. 129.
105 Armogathe says Garat finished writing his *Mémoires sur la Révolution* on 17 May 1795/28 Floréal de l'an III, see Armogathe, 'Garat et l'école normale', p. 152.
106 Dominique-Joseph Garat, *Mémoires sur la Révolution ou exposé de ma conduite dans les affaires et les fonctions publiques* (Paris: J. J. Smits, l'an III de la République [necessarily 1795 and not 1794, as the BnF catalogue has it]). Gengembre says that this was much more than a simple self-defence, reminding us that this 'brochure obtient un réel succès' [this brochure had real success] (Gengembre, 'Introduction aux leçons d'analyse de l'entendement de Garat', p. 48).
107 See above, note 37 in this chapter, as mentioned in Dupuy, 'L'École normale de l'an III', in *Le Centenaire de l'École normale*, p. 170.
108 Garat, *Leçons d'analyse et d'entendement*, p. 76 (Première leçon). This statement does somewhat go against the fact that we know he hadn't initially planned to give them, intending this topic for Bonnet, as mentioned. It may have had a merely rhetorical function, to create a sense of excitement and urgency.
109 Julia, 'La Mise en œuvre du décret du 9 brumaire: les mesures préparatoires', p. 129.

ne tarderont pas à en jouir' [Citizen Garat has only to revise his first Lectures on the analysis of the human understanding, and the Pupils of the Écoles normales will immediately be able to enjoy them].[110] But he never did release either the unpublished transcriptions or the ungiven lectures. He could have completed this long-contemplated work, and there was clearly an appetite for him to do so; the publishers certainly thought so. I tend to agree, therefore, with nineteenth-century historian Paul Dupuy, who said that he believed that 'la raison pour laquelle la plus grande partie de son enseignement fait défaut dans le journal sténographique des séances, c'est qu'il a craint de donner prise à ses ennemis qui l'accusaient d'athéisme' [the reason for which most of his lectures are missing from the Stenographic Journal of the sessions is that he feared to give ammunition to his enemies who were accusing him of atheism] and that 'au milieu du déchaînement de rancunes qui le menaçait et finit par l'atteindre le 19 Ventôse, il jugea sans doute plus prudent de ne plus laisser imprimer ses leçons' [in the midst of the torrent of resentment that threatened and finally overwhelmed him on 19 Ventôse, he no doubt judged it wiser not to allow his lectures to be published].[111] He stopped, fearing further controversy, perhaps not only for himself, but also for the theories of the understanding he had only begun to reveal, and which had become inextricably linked with accusations of atheism and materialism, theories which we have argued were influenced by Diderot's *Éléments de physiologie*. In stopping his own publication, he prevented the association from continuing, and he did not return to the theme in print until his curious *Mémoires sur Suard et sur le dix-huitième siècle* (1820), which we will be examining in a later chapter. His particular analysis of human understanding, however, passed over to Cabanis and Destutt de Tracy, proponents of 'Idéologie', as the latter would come to name it in 1796; they claimed his *Cours* as their source text.[112] In November 1795, Cabanis and Destutt were invited,

---

110 *Séances des écoles normales, recueillies par des sténographes, et revues par les professeurs*. Nouvelle édition: débats, vols 7–8 (Paris: Cercle-social, 1800–01), pages unnumbered (opening page).
111 Dupuy, 'L'École normale de l'an III' in *Le Centenaire de l'École normale*, [1895] p. 171. This hypothesis is alluded to, without commentary, by Julia, 'Le Déroulement des leçons', p. 361, n. 24.
112 See Pierre-Jean-Georges Cabanis, *Rapports du physique et du moral de l'homme: introduction de Serge Nicolas suivie des commentaires de François Thurot et A.L.C. Destutt de Tracy*, 2 vols (Paris: L'Harmattan, 2005 [Facsimile of the 1802 1st edition]), vol. 1,

along with Garat, to become members of the Institut national, decreed on 3 Brumaire an IV (25 October 1795), five months almost to the day that the École normale had closed. The Institut national replaced the erstwhile Académies royales as a stage for French research, and it was devoid of troublesome students. Garat, Cabanis, and Destutt were made members of the Section Analyse des idées [Analysis of Ideas Section], and it is to that institution and the lectures Cabanis and Destutt de Tracy gave there that we now turn.

---

p. xiv (Preface) [for the avoidance of doubt, this is the edition hereafter referenced when quoting from this work]. See also Marc Regaldo, *Un milieu intellectuel: la Décade philosophique (1794-1807)*, 5 vols (Thesis--Université de Paris IV: Paris-Sorbonne, 1976), vol. 5, p. 725. We find a short but precise overview of the connections between Garat, Cabanis, and Destutt de Tracy in Mariana Saad, *Cabanis, comprendre l'homme pour changer le monde* (Paris: Classiques Garnier, 2016), pp. 28–35.

# 9. 1796–97: Cabanis and Destutt de Tracy at the Institut national

Pierre Daunou (1761–1840) rose to prominence as the author of the Constitution de l'an III (1795) which ushered in the Directorate, and also as the mover behind the law of 3 Brumaire an IV (25 October 1795) reforming public education and known as the Loi Daunou.[1] This law set down rules for primary, secondary, and 'specialised' education, and it also created the Institut national des sciences et des arts, of which he then became president. Before the Revolution, like Dominique-Joseph Garat, Daunou had been a minor author and a winner of academy prizes—with a study of Boileau's literary influence (Académie de Nîmes, 1787) and an investigation into the origins, extent, and limits of paternal authority (Académie de Berlin, 1788).[2] He had also been, like Garat, a regular member of Mme Helvétius' salon in Auteuil, and continued to be.[3] Daunou's Institut national des sciences et des arts was set up with the following aims:

---

1 Loi Daunou, adopted on 5 Fructidor an III (22 August 1795). Wikipedia Contributors, 'Lou Daunou', *Wikipedia*, 20 February 2020, https://fr.wikipedia.org/wiki/Loi_Daunou.

2 See *De l'influence littéraire de Boileau* in Nîmes (1787), and a *Mémoire sur l'origine, l'étendue et les limites de l'autorité paternelle* in Berlin (1788). For an insightful exploration of this particular characteristic of eighteenth-century France, see Jeremy L. Caradonna, *The Enlightenment in Practice: Academic Prize Contests and Intellectual Culture in France, 1670–1794* (Ithaca: Cornell University Press, 2012).

3 There are many descriptions of this salon and their role in it. The major study is (still) Antoine Guillois, *Le Salon de Madame Helvétius: Cabanis et les idéologues* (Paris: Calmann Levy, 1894). Mariana Saad neatly sums up what is known in her *Cabanis, comprendre l'homme pour changer le monde* (Paris: Classiques Garnier, 2016), pp. 20–21.

© Caroline Warman, CC BY 4.0   https://doi.org/10.11647/OBP.0199.09

1.° à perfectionner les sciences et les arts par des recherches non interrompues, par la publication des découvertes, par la correspondance avec les sociétés savantes et étrangères ; 2.° à suivre, conformément aux lois et aux arrêtés du directoire exécutif, les travaux scientifiques et littéraires qui auront pour objet l'utilité générale et la gloire de la république.[4]

1. To perfect the sciences and arts by means of uninterrupted research, by means of the publication of discoveries, by means of correspondence with learned societies in France and abroad; 2. To undertake, in accordance with the laws and decrees of the executive directory, scientific and literary work whose purpose is the general utility of all and the glory of the republic.

There had been no single research institution of this sort before. The various (previously royal) Académies had been dissolved in 1793. As we saw, the École normale awkwardly straddled the gap between research and teacher-training institutions. The Institut national des sciences et des arts emphatically reintroduced the research focus, specified in this passage as being *uninterrupted*. Uninterrupted by students and their awkward questions, certainly, because there were none.

It had three departments or 'classes': the 'sciences physiques et mathématiques', the 'sciences morales et politiques', and 'littérature et beaux-arts', and the three 'classes' were divided into a number of 'sections'. First in the list of 'sections' for the 'sciences morales et politiques' was the '*Analyse des sensations et des idées*'. Each section had six Parisian members and six associate members from around France: in the case of the 'Section Analyse des sensations et des idées', Garat and Pierre-Jean-Georges Cabanis were Parisian members, and Antoine Louis Claude Destutt de Tracy, resident in Auteuil, an associate member.[5] The Institut national held its meeting at the Louvre, renamed

---

4    '1795. Texte de la loi créant l'Institut national des sciences et des arts', *Textes Rares*, http://pages.textesrares.com/index.php/Rubriques/1795.-Texte-de-la-loi-creant-lInstitut-national-des-sciences-et-des-arts.html and https://books.google.co.uk/books?id=dy5bAAAAQAAJ&printsec=frontcover&dq=Institut+national+de+la+République+française&hl=en&sa=X&ved=0ahUKEwjxp7_IorvgAhWTUhUIHe3vA2wQ6AEINTAB#v=onepage&q=Institut%20national%20de%20la%20République%20française&f=false.

5    The members are all given at the beginning of volume 3: *Mémoires de l'Institut national des sciences et des arts: sciences morales et politiques* (Paris: Baudouin, 1798 /99), vol. 3, pp. iv–viii.

the Palais national des sciences et des arts. Their lectures were published in the *Mémoires de l'Institut national des sciences et des arts*: in the case of the 'classe' of Sciences morales et politiques, only five volumes were published, as Napoleon Bonaparte closed it down in 1803.[6] No lecture by Garat is recorded, which, in the context of the furore around his lectures at the École normale, is unsurprising and yet stark; it is not as if he did not have anything to say on the subject, as we know, and what he had said was left incomplete.[7] Cabanis and Destutt de Tracy, however, did give numerous lectures, all of which were published, initially in installments in the *Mémoires de l'Institut*, and then separately. Cabanis's became the *Rapports du physique et du moral*, first published in 1802, and then in a revised edition in 1805, with further posthumous editions in 1815 and 1824. Destutt de Tracy's were published as the *Mémoire sur la faculté de penser* in the *Mémoires de l'Institut*, to which he added the *Dissertation sur quelques questions d'idéologie*, a new extended version in the *Projet d'éléménts d'idéologie à l'usage des écoles centrales de la République française* (1801), then the *Idéologie proprement dite* of 1804, which was the first volume of the *Éléments d'idéologie*. This grew into four volumes, was completed in 1815, and republished in 1824.

As we see therefore, unlike Garat's, the lectures of Cabanis and Destutt de Tracy not only made it into publication in the *Mémoires* but also flourished as separate works through various editions. And as we also see when we look at the publication dates, these works are published not so much separately as in tandem. This impression is further reinforced when we see that it was Destutt who wrote the eighty-page summary or 'Table analytique' for the second edition of Cabanis's *Rapports sur le physique et le moral* (1805).[8] Their focus on the 'analyse des sensations et des idées' is a shared one, and when we read their works, it is clear that the project is a shared one whose ideas benefit from the amplification they receive from being said twice, or rather, not just twice but many many times over by two different voices occupying slightly different positions on the same terrain, one more physiologically-informed

---

6   The volumes came out between An IV (1795/96) and An XII (1803/04).
7   Garat was sent as French Ambassador to Naples in 1798, but his tenure was brief.
8   Pierre-Jean-Georges Cabanis, *Rapports du physique et du moral de l'homme* (Paris: Crapart, Caille et Ravier, 1805), vol. 2, pp. 559–640. Pierre Sue provided an index for this same edition, pp. 651–720.

(Cabanis), the other self-consciously occupying the same space as Condillac, with his work not just on sensations but on grammar and logic (Destutt). The style of both is strikingly ceremonious and oral, emphasising the origin of these texts as lectures delivered at the Institut national. As we will see, both writers retain these markers of oral delivery generally, alongside references to the Institut specifically, and thereby stake a firm claim to virtuous republican authority and identity. As Jean Starobinski remarks with customary incisiveness in his analysis of 'la chaire, la tribune, le barreau', that is, of sermons, political speeches, and legal utterances, 'le lieu d'où l'on parle', that is, where one speaks from, is crucially important in determining or even authorising its meaning, and neither Cabanis nor Destutt de Tracy intend to let us forget it.[9] We will return to these markers of style in due course, but first we need to see what they actually said, in order to establish whether or not their lectures are relevant to the argument we are attempting to make here, that is, that Diderot's *Éléments de physiologie* was known by these writers, and that its influence can be perceived at various moments in their writings. Thus far, all that has been established is that they were in the same section of the same class as Garat at the Institut national, and that they would have known him anyway as a fellow-member of the Cercle d'Auteuil, Mme Helvétius's salon, and that the same goes for Daunou (although he was in a different section of the same 'Classe des Sciences morales et politiques': his section was 'Sciences sociales, et Législation').[10] Jacques-André Naigeon, too, was made a member of the Institut national, Classe des Sciences morales et politiques, but the section he was invited to be part of, interestingly, was 'Morale'.[11] One sees why he would not have been invited to join the section 'Analyse des sens et des idées'—his reputation as a diehard atheist and his public association with Diderot would hardly have helped keep the field of their enquiries controversy-free where, as we will see, there is some real proximity to Diderot and to materialism in their work.

---

9    Jean Starobinski, 'La Chaire, la tribune, le barreau', in *Les Lieux de mémoire. II. La Nation*, ed. by Pierre Nora (Paris: Gallimard, 1986), vol. 3, pp. 425–86 (p. 481).
10   See *Institut national de la République française* (Paris: Baudouin, Brumaire An VI [Oct–Nov 1797]), Lois et réglement, liste des membres.
11   Naigeon doesn't appear to have given any lectures.

Both Cabanis and Destutt de Tracy make the 'analyse des sens' into the analysis of life itself. In so doing, they are more ambitious than Garat. He starts with sensation, the senses, their flaws, correctibility, and perfectibility. And indeed he does not get a lot further than that. But Cabanis and Destutt cover more ground, and use more words. Once comfortably commenced, and with thousands of words to cushion him, Cabanis plants this aphoristic statement in the middle of a long and multi-claused sentence:

[...] vivre, c'est sentir [...].[12]

To live is to feel.

Destutt restates this foundational principle as a question, with the help of a judiciously-deployed synonym and syntactical reformulation:

Qu'est-ce qu'exister, si ce n'est le sentir?[13]

What is it to exist if it isn't to feel?

It is interesting to see how cautiously these formulas are planted and stated. By the time he gets to the *Idéologie proprement dite* of 1801, Destutt is able to state with more confidence and more prominence that:

---

12  Cabanis, *Rapports du physique et du moral de l'homme: introduction de Serge Nicolas suivie des commentaires de François Thurot et A.L.C. Destutt de Tracy*, 2 vols (Paris: L'Harmattan, 2005 [Facsimile of the 1802 1st edition]), vol. 1, p. 91 (lecture 2) [N.B. For the avoidance of doubt, where the edition is not specified in footnotes, this is the one used.].

13  Antoine Louis Claude Destutt de Tracy, *Mémoire sur la faculté de penser, De la métaphysique de Kant, et autres textes*, ed. by Anne Deneys and Henry Deneys (Paris: Fayard, 1992), p. 69; lecture 2. Destutt de Tracy gave his *Mémoire sur la faculté de penser* initially as four *Mémoires* in five installments; he then revised it and re-read it at the Institut; the *Mémoires de l'institut national*, vol. 1, give the text of the second reading, while recording the date of the very first lecture. The approved text has three parts, which are each sub-divided into chapters: part 1 has twenty-seven pages in the 1992 edition, and two chapters; part 2 has sixty-seven pages and six chapters; part 3 has forty-four pages and two chapters. We assume that part 1 constituted the first lecture, and that part 2 includes lectures 2 and 3, and maybe part of 4; part 3 therefore may include some of part 4, and certainly part 5. The dating between parts 1 and 2 in any case is clear: Destutt differentiates them temporally by talking about what he did 'dans la première partie' [in the first part] and what he is going to do 'Aujourd'hui' [today] (*Mémoire sur la faculté de penser*, p. 65 [Préface to part 2]).

Penser, sentir et exister ne sont pour nous qu'une seule chose.¹⁴

To think, to feel, and to exist are in our eyes nothing other than the same thing.

These statements are very close to one another, and very close also to the starker aphorism we find in Diderot's *Éléments de physiologie*, that:

Sentir, c'est vivre.¹⁵

To feel is to live.

Cabanis's 'vivre, c'est sentir' chiastically mirrors Diderot's 'sentir, c'est vivre', while Destutt's 'Qu'est-ce qu'exister, si ce n'est le sentir?' affirms the same parallelism between existing/being alive and feeling via a rhetorical question. The similarity of these statements by Diderot, Cabanis, and Destutt is striking, and yet it is hardly conclusive with respect to any putative influence by or presence of the *Éléments de physiologie* specifically. Perhaps all it does is show that Diderot, Cabanis and Destutt are in alignment with respect to a basic notion of sensationism. Interestingly, however, Destutt immediately follows his statement that 'Penser, sentir et exister ne sont pour nous qu'une seule chose' [To think, to feel, and to exist are in our eyes nothing other than the same thing] with the following curious remark: 'J'ai cru fermement ne l'avoir pas appris de Condillac' [I firmly believed I did not learn this from Condillac].¹⁶

For the suspicious reader, this is a gift. Is Destutt drawing attention to the fact that he did not learn it from Condillac in order to plant the idea of having learnt it from someone else, that is, Diderot? He could be. One might want to argue, on the basis of Condillac's *Traité des sensations* of 1754 or his less well-known but arguably more relevant *La Logique*, published posthumously in 1780, that sensation and life are obviously presented as equivalent in some sort of way, and this is certainly true.

---

14 Antoine Louis Claude Destutt de Tracy, *Idéologie proprement dite*, in *Œuvres complètes*, ed. by Claude Jolly (Paris: Vrin, 2012), vol. 3, p. 191.
15 Denis Diderot, *Éléments de physiologie*, ed. by Jean Mayer, *Œuvres complètes*, DPV (Paris: Hermann, 1987), vol. 17, pp. 261–574 (p. 447) [hereafter DPV] /Diderot, *Éléments de physiologie*, ed. by Paolo Quintili (Paris: Champion, 2004), p. 271 [hereafter PQ] /Diderot, *Éléments de physiologie*, ed. by Motoichi Terada (Paris: Éditions Matériologiques, 2019), p. 263 [hereafter MT].
16 Destutt de Tracy, *Idéologie proprement dite*, p. 191.

But we would have to point out nonetheless that Condillac never says so in so many words, and that his style is circumlocutory rather than pithy or aphoristic. That the little aphorisms in Cabanis and Destutt linking life, existence and sensation are very close to an almost identical aphorism we find in the *Éléments de physiologie* cannot be denied, but nor does it prove knowledge or influence. It is nonetheless suggestive, as is Destutt's curious statement about not having learnt it from Condillac. In any case, we cannot at this point *exclude* the notion that there *may have been* knowledge on their part of Diderot's *Éléments*, and that it might have influenced them. It is a possibility.

\*\*\*

Yet while we can see that it is a possibility, we also see how cautious Cabanis and Destutt are, how carefully they present this definition of life as sensation. Whether Diderot's influence is present or not is only part of a problem which requires them to avoid the sort of charge of materialism which Garat had been subjected to, and which had so quickly got out of hand. When Cabanis and Destutt pick up the baton, they do so protected by the newly founded Institut national, according to its codes, and therefore with new forms of virtuous distance between themselves, their work, and anything that could be called materialist. Part of this is the distance they keep from Naigeon, nicely muzzled in the 'Morale' section. Fortunately, moreover, one of the key terms of the Institut is the notion of improvement or 'perfecting': the Constitution de l'an III, article 298, states that 'Il y a, pour toute la République, un Institut National, chargé de recueillir les découvertes, de perfectionner les arts et les sciences' [There is, for the entire Republic, a National Insitute, charged with recording discoveries and with perfecting the arts and sciences].[17] The Loi du 3 Brumaire an IV, titre IV, article premier, states that the Institut National 'est destiné à perfectionner les sciences et les arts par des recherches non interrompues, par la publication des découvertes, par la correspondance avec les sociétés savantes et étrangères' [To perfect the sciences and arts by means of uninterrupted research, by means of the publication of discoveries, by means of correspondence

---

17 *Institut national de la République française* (Paris: Baudouin, Brumaire An VI (Oct–Nov 1797), p. 1.

with learned societies in France and abroad]:[18] we quoted this earlier. So, 'perfectionner', to perfect the sciences and arts, or more accurately translated, the different branches of knowledge and the different skills and crafts, is the fundamental aim of the Institut National. Cabanis and Destutt de Tracy have nothing to worry about therefore when they talk about *perfecting* the senses: they are speaking the language of the Institute itself, even if perfecting the senses is not the same operation as perfecting branches of knowledge or crafts, and is manifestly closer to materialist positions about the processes of embodied thought. Yet the term 'perfectionner' legitimises this area of their thinking, such that there is no evidence whatsoever of the sort of syntactical caution and embedding that we saw when, in passing, or as a rhetorical question, they defined life as sensation. We remember of course that Garat had also enthusiastically proposed learning to perfect the senses, and this shared feature of their thought provides a key link between his *Cours* and their *Mémoires*, and a perceptible moment of transmission from him to them. Whether Diderot is also behind this notion remains a moot point.

On reading Cabanis, we see how grand, how educational, this notion of perfecting the senses has become:[19]

> Si notre première étude est celle des instrumens que nous avons reçus immédiatement de la nature ; la seconde est celle des moyens qui peuvent modifier, corriger, perfectionner ces instrumens. Il ne suffit pas qu'un ouvrier connoisse les premiers outils de son art ; il faut qu'il connoisse également les outils nouveaux qui peuvent en agrandir, en perfectionner l'usage, et les méthodes par lesquelles on peut les employer avec plus de fruit.
>
> La nature produit l'homme avec des organes et des facultés déterminées : mais l'art peut accroître ses facultés, changer ou diriger leur emploi, créer en quelque sorte de nouveaux *organes*. C'est-là l'ouvrage de l'éducation, qui n'est, à proprement parler, que l'art des impressions et des habitudes.[20]
>
> If our first objects of study are the instruments which we have received directly from nature, the second are the means by which we may modify,

---

[18] *Institut national de la République française* (Paris: Baudouin, Brumaire An VI (Oct–Nov 1797), p. 3.
[19] Mariana Saad examines the importance of 'perfectibility' for Cabanis's thought more widely in her study: *Cabanis, comprendre l'homme*, pp. 239–68.
[20] Cabanis, *Rapports du physique et du moral de l'homme*, vol. 1, pp. 75–76 (lecture 1).

> correct, and perfect these instruments. It is not enough for a workman to know the basic tools of his craft; he must also know all the new tools which can expand and perfect it and the methods by which they can most fruitfully be used.
>
> Nature produces man with organs and faculties already directed to a certain purpose, but skill can extend his faculties, change or direct their use, and in a certain way create new *organs*. This is the job of education, which is nothing other, properly speaking, than the art of impressions and habits.

Cabanis's rather ceremonious and amplificatory style makes it hard to quote him briefly (unless snatching a tiny clause out of a big sentence, as I did earlier), but his meaning is clear: 'we' must study, firstly, the 'instruments' we receive from nature, and secondly, how to use them, and how to use them better; this, he declares, is the job of education. That what he means by 'instruments' and 'organes' denotes the senses and the physiology of their functioning is indicated by the fact that the 'Histoire physiologique des sensations' will provide the basis for his entire 'Programme'.[21] So, Cabanis is returning to that notion of working on the senses and improving them that Garat had proposed, but, although he does use the term 'instrument', he is not suggesting the actual internalisation of a tool as Garat had in the case of the telescope, nor does he mention coffee as a way of boosting the faculties.[22] His notion is about learning to use the 'organs' skilfully, of extending their range, and changing or directing their use. As such, it is closer to Diderot's remarks quoted earlier about practice and skill.[23]

The passage from Destutt—from his *Mémoire sur la faculté de penser*, first published in the *Mémoires de l'Institut* in 1798—is more ambitious again. He argues that if we come to understand the multiple, rapid, and often imperceptible sensations that give rise to our thoughts, we can begin to reform our sensations and our judgements, and thus, ultimately, begin to improve or *perfect* ourselves, and, subsequently, in

---

21 Cabanis, *Rapports du physique et du moral de l'homme*, vol. 1, p. 80 (lecture 1).
22 For extra verification, see Pierre Sue's remarkable index of 'Table des matières', published, along with Destutt de Tracy's highly helpful Table analytique, at the end of the second volume of the 1805 Second edition (pp. 651–720). There is no mention of 'téléscope' at all, and just two passing mentions of 'café'.
23 See above.

due Condillacian form, perfect signs and language. These are worthy objectives of the virtuous Republic.

> [...] il faut commencer par jeter un coup d'œil sur les effets du perfectionnement graduel des individus, du perfectionnement successif de l'espèce, de l'usage des signes, et de la rédaction perpétuelle de chacun de ces trois phénomènes sur les deux autres.[24]
>
> We must start by looking at the effects of the gradual perfecting of individuals, the successive perfecting of the species, the perfecting and the use of signs, and of the way each of these three phenomena perpetually rewrite the other two.

So, for Destutt de Tracy too, the perfecting of sensory skills is the first step in this far-reaching project of human improvement, at once individual and social.

This emphasis we see in Cabanis and Destutt de Tracy on the improvement of the senses looks outwards to the actual operation of our five senses, but also inwards to our understanding and ability to perceive internal sensation. This focus on internal sensation was not present in Garat's published *Cours*. It is present, however, in Diderot's *Éléments de physiologie*. In proper 'éléments d'une science' style, as Jean le Rond d'Alembert had defined the matter in the *Encyclopédie*, the *Éléments de physiologie* indicate 'la voie des découvertes à faire' [the path towards new discoveries].[25] Here is what Diderot had written:

---

24 Destutt de Tracy, *Mémoire sur la faculté de penser*, ed. by Anne and Henry Deneys, p. 136 (beginning part 3).
25 D'Alembert had explained 'Élémens des sciences' as follows: 'Des *élémens* bien faits, suivant le plan que nous avons exposé, & par des écrivains capables d'exécuter ce plan, auroient une double utilité: ils mettroient les bons esprits sur la voie des découvertes à faire, en leur présentant les découvertes déjà faites; de plus ils mettroient chacun plus à portée de distinguer les vraies découvertes d'avec les fausses; car tout ce qui ne pourroit point être ajoûté aux *élémens* d'une Science comme par forme de supplément, ne seroit point digne du nom de *découverte*. Voyez *ce mot. (O)*' [*Well-constructed basic elements*, according to the plan that we have presented, when they are prepared by authors capable of carrying out such a project, would be useful in two ways. In the first place they would be setting good minds on the road to future discoveries by presenting prior discoveries to them. And secondly, they would be putting everyone in a better position to distinguish true discoveries from false ones. For anything that could not be added as a supplement to the *basic elements* of a Science would not be worthy of being called a *discovery . See* Discovery.] *Encyclopédie ou dictionnaire raisonné des sciences, des arts et des métiers, par une société de gens de lettres*, ed. by Denis Diderot and Jean le Rond d'Alembert, 28 vols (Paris: Briasson, David, Le Breton, Durand, 1751–72), vol. 5, pp.

> Ce que nous connaissons le moins, ce sont les sens intimes, c'est nous, l'objet, l'impression, la représentation, l'attention.[26]

> What we know least are the intimate senses, that is, ourselves, the object, the impression, the representation, attention.

What is original about this is not the description of the route from external object to internal impression and representation, but the way in which this process connects to or in some way produces 'nous', that is 'ourselves', and the very notion of 'les sens intimes' [intimate senses] that enable our internal awareness and 'attention'. Cabanis does not use this term of 'les sens intimes' but he does assert that 'les impressions internes' [internal impressions] need looking at, and that this is a 'question nouvelle' [new question]. He asks why 'analyst philosophers' have not considered this before:

> Les philosophes analystes n'ont guère considéré jusqu'ici que les impressions qui viennent des objets extérieurs, et que l'organe de la pensée distingue, se représente, et combine : ce sont elles seulement qu'ils ont désignées sous le nom de *sensations* ; les autres restent pour eux dans le vague.[27]

> Analyst philosophers have barely considered until now anything but those impressions which come from external objects and which the organ of thought distinguishes, represents to itself, and combines: it is only to them that these philosophers have attributed the name of *sensations*: the rest remain in a sort of vague area for them.

Cabanis goes on to present two options: either to follow Condillac 'et quelques autres' [and various others] in assuming that all our ideas come via our senses from the outside world, or, alternatively, to ask whether 'les impressions internes' might be part of this process:

---

491–97 (p. 497), https://artflsrv03.uchicago.edu/philologic4/encyclopedie1117/navigate/5/1752/; «Elements of the sciences», translated by Lauren Yoder, *The Encyclopedia of Diderot & d'Alembert Collaborative Translation Project*. Ann Arbor: Michigan Publishing, University of Michigan Library, 2011, http://hdl.handle.net/2027/spo.did2222.0001.133. See also the critical online edition *Édition numérique collaborative et critique de l'Encyclopédie* ed. by Alexandre Guilbaud, Alain Cernuschi, Marie Léca-Tsiomis and Irène Passeron, http://enccre.academie-sciences.fr/encyclopedie/.

26  DPV 468/PQ 294/MT 283.
27  Cabanis, *Rapports du physique et du moral de l'homme*, vol. 1, p. 103 (lecture 2).

La question nouvelle qui se présente, est de savoir s'il est vrai, comme l'ont établi Condillac et quelques autres, que les idées et les déterminations morales se forment toutes et dépendent uniquement de ce qu'ils appellent *sensations*; si par conséquent, suivant la phrase reçue, toutes nos idées nous viennent des *sens*, et par les objets extérieurs: ou si les impressions internes contribuent également à la production des déterminations morales, et des idées, suivant certaines lois dont l'étude de l'homme sain et malade peut nous faire remarquer la constance [...].[28]

The new question that arises is to find out whether it is true, as Condillac and various others have established, that ideas and moral decisions are all formed from and depend solely on what they call *sensations*, and hence whether, to use the common phrase, all our ideas come from the senses and from external objects, or whether internal impressions contribute equally to the production of moral decisions and ideas, in accordance with certain laws which the study of humans in health and illness show to be equally constant [...].

As for Destutt de Tracy, he talks in his *Mémoire sur la faculté de penser* about the 'sentiment intime' using the same adjective that Diderot had, and in the *Idéologie proprement dite* about the 'sensations internes'.[29] Interestingly, in the recent critical edition of this latter text, editor Claude Jolly draws attention specifically to the idea of internal sensations, saying that neither Condillac nor Bonnet had gone beyond the five external senses and that this idea of a sixth internal sense is original to Cabanis, by whom Destutt de Tracy is directly influenced on this point.[30] And yet, as we know, Diderot had conceptualised this notion of 'les sens intimes', and not only that, he had also indicated that more work needed to be done to develop knowledge in this area. At the very least, it is of

---

28  Cabanis, *Rapports du physique et du moral de l'homme*, vol. 1, pp. 104–05 (lecture 2). He also talks about those signs which remain 'cachés dans l'intérieur; ils sont pour l'individu lui seul' [hidden within; they are for the individual alone] (vol. 1, p. 73); he references 'le *sens interne*' [the *internal sense*] (vol. 1, p. 231 ital. in orig.).

29  Destutt de Tracy, *Mémoire sur la faculté de penser*, p. 74 (Part II, §1); *Idéologie proprement dite*, p. 100.

30  Jolly comments as follows: 'Tant Condillac que Charles Bonnet réduisaient la sensibilité aux cinq sens. C'est Cabanis qui, dès les premiers mémoires lus dès l'an 4 (1796) devant la seconde classe de l'Institut national, a élargi son champ aux sensations internes. Destutt de Tracy lui est sur ce point directement redevable' [Condillac like Charles Bonnet reduced sensibility to the five senses. It is Cabanis who, from the very first memoirs read out in Year 4 (1796) to the second class at the Institut National, extended the field to internal sensations. Destutt de Tracy is directly indebted to him on this point.] (*Idéologie proprement dite*, p. 100n.).

interest to note that while neither Condillac or Bonnet had mentioned 'les sensations internes', Diderot had done, and therefore that Cabanis was not original in doing so. The coincidence of these points in the work of Cabanis and Destutt de Tracy, on the one hand, and in Diderot's, on the other, is striking.

There is also an interesting replication and development of an approach we already saw in Garat: there is total radio silence with respect to Diderot, even when talking about the cases of people born blind, which in this context is an almost automatic recall of the well-known *Lettre sur les aveugles*, and at the same time, while there are frequent mentions of the avowed master Condillac, very many of these are critical.[31] I hope I may be forgiven for showing this aspect via a mash-up of passages, the point that I am trying to make here being the multiplicity of anti-Condillacian statements, rather than the specific nature of the objections. Thus Cabanis, talking about 'les assertions de Condillac' [Condillac's assertions] criticises their 'extrême généralité' [extreme generality] which is 'absolument contraires aux faits' [completely in opposition to the facts]; he praises Claude Adrien Helvétius and Condillac only to regret that 'ils ont manqué l'un et l'autre de connoissances physiologiques, dont leurs ouvrages auroient pu profiter utilement' [they both lacked any physiological knowledge, and their works would have much benefited from it]; he asserts his own accuracy under a mask of worry about diverging from his views: 'Quand nous croyons nous écarter des vues de ce grand maître, il est bien nécessaire d'étudier soigneusement et d'assurer nos pas' [when we consider we may be diverging from the opinions of this great teacher, we must be extremely careful to watch where we step]; talks about 'une suite d'actions qui sont bien plus inexplicables encore, suivant la théorie de Condillac' [a series of actions that are even more inexplicable if we follow Condillac's theory]; and praises 'les belles analyses de Buffon, de Bonnet et de Condillac' [fine analyses of Buffon, Bonnet, and Condillac]

---

31  The 'aveugle-né' is mentioned in Cabanis, *Rapports du physique et du moral de l'homme*, vol. 2, p. 435; Destutt de Tracy, *Idéologie proprement dite*, p. 259. Critical mentions of Condillac follow in the main text. Respected Cabanis scholar Mariana Saad generally views him as being a faithful adherent of Condillacian theory, but does nonetheless point out how he contests 'un des points essentiels de la théorie de la connaissance de Condillac', which is the existence of an immaterial soul (Saad, *Cabanis, comprendre l'homme*, p. 30).

only then to point out 'une certaine fausse direction qu'elles pourraient faire prendre à l'idéologie et (le dirai-je sans détour?) sur les obstacles qu'elles sont peut-être capables d'opposer à ses progrès' [a sort of wrong direction that they might make ideology go in and (shall I say it without roundaboutation?) the obstacles that they might be capable of setting in its way] and, having indeed decided to say it straight, states that 'Rien sans doute ne ressemble moins à l'homme, tel qu'il est en effet, que ces statues [...]' [There is no question that there is nothing which resembles man as he really is less than these statues].[32] We see that where Cabanis does also contest the theories of thinkers apart from Condillac (Buffon and Bonnet, for instance), it is he who is the red thread throughout.[33]

Destutt de Tracy's criticisms of Condillac are more frequent and sharper in tone. In the *Mémoire sur la faculté de penser*, we find the following remarks: 'Est-il bien vrai, comme Condillac le dit, que [....]. Je ne le pense pas' [Is it really true, as Condillac says, that [...]. I don't think so]; 'Ici Condillac me paroît commencer à s'écarter de son exactitude ordinaire' [Here Condillac seems to me to depart from his usual precision]; 'Ici, quelque respect que j'aie pour Condillac, je dirai nettement que ce n'est pas le sentiment de la statue qui est *vague*, que c'est l'idée de l'auteur qui est louche et mal déterminée' [Here, whatever respect I have for Condillac, I have to say that it's not the statue's feeling which is *vague*, it's the author's concept which is askew and ill-defined]; 'Condillac, qu'il faut toujours citer, lors même qu'il ne satisfait pas entièrement [...]' [Condillac, whom one is always obliged to cite, even when he is not entirely satisfactory]; 'Je n'ai pas besoin de dire pourquoi je n'ai pas, comme Condillac, fait du raisonnement une partie particulière de la faculté de penser' [I have no need to say why I have not, unlike Condillac, made reason into a particular part of the faculty of thought]; 'Il n'est donc pas très-exact de dire avec Condillac

---

32 Cabanis (page references in order of appearance): *Rapports du physique et du moral de l'homme* vol. 1: Préface, p. xvi [the preface was first published in the 1802 edition]; lecture 1: p. 37; lecture 2: p. 113; p. 130; Part 10 (parts 7–12 of the 1802 *RPM* had not been given as lectures at the Institut national, and were new to the 1802 version), vol. 2, p. 442.

33 Other modern authorities Cabanis mentions (without necessarily contesting them) are Francis Bacon, René Descartes, Thomas Hobbes (p. 29); 36: John Locke (p. 36); 37: Bonnet, Helvétius, Condillac (p. 37). Authorities from Antiquity: Pythagoras, Democritus, Epicurus (p. 18); Hippocrates (p. 24-7); Aristotle (p. 29). All from *Rapports du physique et du moral de l'homme*, Lecture 1.

[...]' [It is therefore not very accurate to say, as Condillac does]: we see how these criticisms when stitched together begin to look like repeated resistance.³⁴ His *Dissertation sur quelques questions d'idéologie*, given as a lecture to the Institut national on 7 Prairial an VIII (27 May 1800) and published the following year, and ostensibly an occasion to praise Condillac on the occasion of the publication of his *Œuvres* in 1798 (a complete set of which Garat presented to the Convention), is a thorough-going critique of his work, as he himself notes: 'j'eus beaucoup moins l'air de commenter Condillac que de le combattre' [it looked much more as if I was disagreeing with Condillac than explaining his work]; drawing attention to contradiction even as he asserts the opposite: 'En disant cela je crois fermement ne faire que continuer Condillac, et non le contredire' [When I say this, I firmly believe that I am doing nothing other than continuing his work and not contradicting him]; is pleased to find some key shared ground (the implication being that this is rather rare): 'j'ai le bonheur de me rencontrer avec Condillac dans ces trois articles fondamentaux' [I am lucky enough to find myself in agreement with Condillac on these three fundamental articles] only to discover a further disagreement: 'je diffère essentiellement de Condillac' [I profoundly differ from Condillac], concluding that, if he is right, 'on doit m'accorder que [...] la première partie de son *Traité des sensations* tombe toute entière' [one must agree with me that (...) the first part of his *Treatise on sensations* falls away completely].³⁵ The *Idéologie proprement dite* continues in the same vein: Locke and Condillac are not 'exempts d'erreurs' [free of errors]; what is useful when tracking such errors in Condillac, 'c'est de voir ce qui a pu égarer cet homme habile' [is to see what misled this clever man]; later, we find this quite thorough-going statement: 'Je persiste donc à penser que la manière dont Condillac a composé notre intelligence est vicieuse; et que plus on y reflechira, plus on se convaincra que la pensée de l'homme ne consiste jamais qu'à sentir des sensations, des souvenirs, des jugements et des désirs' [I persist in thinking that the way in which Condillac constructed our intelligence is

---

34 Destutt de Tracy in order of appearance: *Mémoire sur la faculté de penser*: part 1 (lecture 1), pp. 43, 44, 45; part 2 (lectures 2 and 3), pp. 96, 124; part 3 (lecture 5), p. 169.
35 Destutt de Tracy, *Dissertation sur quelques questions d'idéologie* in *Mémoire sur la faculté de penser, De la métaphysique de Kant, et autres textes*, ed. by Anne Deneys and Henry Deneys (Paris: Fayard, 1992), pp. 181–201 (187, 189, 192, 193, 199).

defective, and that the more one thinks about it, the more one realizes that human thought never consists of anything other than feeling sensations, memories, judgements, and desires], and finally, as quoted before, 'Penser, sentir et exister ne sont pour nous qu'une seule et même chose. J'ai cru fermement ne l'avoir pas appris de Condillac' [To think, to feel, and to exist are in our eyes nothing other than the same thing. I firmly believe that I did not learn this from Condillac].[36] These are far from the only moments in the text when Destutt de Tracy criticises one aspect or another of Condillac's theory. It happens so frequently that it draws commentary from Tracy scholar and editor Claude Jolly: 'Par cette note, Tracy s'oppose une fois de plus à Condillac' [with this note, Tracy opposes Condillac yet again].[37]

Should we really understand this resolute and continuous countering of Condillac uniquely as the further substantiation of his theories through the critical attention brought to them by his philosophical offspring, whose contestation is actually evidence of their respect, and of their working within his frameworks to further develop them? It seems a bit of a weak justification for such extensive disagreement. And then of course we do have the Diderotian shadow hovering quite close by, however absent the name Diderot is. 1798 was not only the year in which Condillac's *Œuvres* were published and so ostentaciously presented to the Convention, but also the year Naigeon finally brought out his edition of Diderot's *Œuvres*. What was in them and how Naigeon framed them will be discussed in the next section, but in any case no one offered them to the Convention with a special speech. We have already noted how in one instance, when Destutt de Tracy says he is *not* following Condillac, there may be reason to believe that he is evoking Diderot in silent contrast. Just a few pages earlier than that passage, in a note he adds to the 1817 edition of the *Idéologie proprement dite*, Destutt de Tracy (again) both praises and criticises Condillac: he praises him for inventing the field, and he criticises him for not bringing his insights together into 'un traité unique qui contînt son système tout entier' [a single treatise which brought together his whole system].[38] On another page, he also wrote about how 'ce célèbre métaphysicien a

---

36 Destutt de Tracy, *Idéologie proprement dite*, pp. 76, 157n, 190, 191.
37 Destutt de Tracy, *Idéologie proprement dite*, p. 181n.
38 Destutt de Tracy, *Idéologie proprement dite*, p. 187n.

eu si peu d'émules dans la carrière qu'il a parcourue, que l'histoire de ses pensées est pour ainsi dire l'histoire de la science pendant ce long intervalle de temps' [this famous metaphysician had so few emulating him in the career he followed that the history of his thoughts is, so to say, the history of knowledge during this long period].[39] When we know that Diderot *had* brought all his insights in this area into 'un traité unique' and that he had *also* been writing and thinking about the same questions as Condillac over the same time span, from the *Lettre sur les aveugles* to the *Éléments de physiologie*, that he is a better candidate, as editor of the *Encyclopédie*, for the person whose thoughts are the history of knowledge at that time, and when we have some grounds already to think that Tracy did know that work, are we wrong to wonder whether that criticism of Condillac might be a shield here for discussion of that same work, or even a signal that it is being alluded to? These are the questions that we must now investigate further, through more detailed comparative inspection of the works of Diderot, Cabanis, and Destutt de Tracy.

In what follows, I will consider passages from Cabanis, first, and Destutt de Tracy, second, that seem to bear some striking resemblance to a similar passage in the *Éléments de physiologie* (although on one occasion I also refer to the *Rêve de d'Alembert*, also unpublished other than in the élite manuscript journal the *Correspondance littéraire*, where it had appeared in installments between August and November 1782). My underpinning enquiry is to establish whether the textual evidence allows us to assert that Cabanis and Destutt de Tracy knew the *Éléments de physiologie*. My aim is not necessarily to assert that they are parroting it or that they see their work as disseminating its theories, although they might be. It is also not to consider their theories as a whole, nor the extent to which these theories may or may not have been influenced by Diderot. These are all interesting and important questions, but they go beyond the purview of this study. Furthermore, because I have chosen not to discuss general parallels but only to put forward the most visible textual similarities, those which seem to be referring to specific passages in the *Éléments*, I am also not presenting the work of either Cabanis or Destutt de Tracy in a particularly coherent way—I am obliged to dart

---

39  Destutt de Tracy, *Dissertation sur quelques questions d'idéologie*, p. 184.

about from one passage to another without there necessarily being any connection between them, nor do I have space to supply much theoretical contextualisation. This is regrettable but I think unavoidable, given that this section is subservient to our larger investigation into whether the *Éléments de physiologie* was being read and drawn on in the 1790s.

## Cabanis and the *Éléments de physiologie*

There seem to be perceptible similarities between passages in the *Rapports sur le physique et le moral* and the *Éléments de physiologie* particularly in Cabanis's discussion of attention, of dream-thinking (although here we refer to *D'Alembert's Dream*), of the notion of the brain as a thought-secreting organ, in his presentation of the senses as having their separate memories, in his examples of exceptional strength, and in his consideration of drowned people. We will take them in that order, with Cabanis first, and Diderot after for ease of comparison, as we did in the section on Garat.

We start with the idea that attention and absorption come hand in hand with obliviousness to other things:

> [Cabanis] [...] l'être sensitif n'étant capable que d'une certaine somme d'attention, qui cesse de se diriger d'un côté, quand elle est absorbée de l'autre.[40]

> Given that the sensitive being is incapable of more than a certain amount of attention, it stops being directed on one side when it is absorbed on the other.

> [Diderot] Toutes sortes d'impressions se font, mais nous ne sommes jamais qu'à une. L'âme est au milieu de ses sensations comme un convive, à une table tumultueuse, qui cause avec son voisin, il n'entend pas les autres.[41]

---

40 Cabanis, *Rapports du physique et du moral de l'homme*, vol. 1, p. 134 (lecture 2).
41 DPV 467/PQ 294/MT 283. See also: 'Dans l'état parfait de santé, où il n'y a aucune sensation prédominante qui fasse discerner une partie du corps, état que tout homme a quelquefois éprouvé, l'homme n'existe qu'en un point du cerveau: il est tout au lieu de la pensée' [In a perfect state of health, when no single dominant sensation draws attention to any particular part of the body, a state which everyone has experienced sometimes, then a person exists only in one point in their brain and is completely absorbed in the thought] (DPV 330/PQ 146/MT 151) and here in Cabanis: 'Quand tous ses organes jouissent d'une activité moyenne, et en quelque

All sorts of impressions are being made, but we only ever focus on one. The soul in the midst of its sensations is like a guest at a boisterous dinner table. He's conversing with his neighbour, and he can't hear anyone else.

Cabanis asserts that 'the sensitive being' is only capable of a certain amount of attention, and that if it is all absorbed on one side, it will not notice what is happening on the other. This idea, in Diderot's version, had been illustrated with reference to a person at a noisy dinner table, literally absorbed on one side in a conversation and oblivious to everything else. If the idea is similar and the motif of being absorbed on one side and oblivious to the other relatively similar, how striking the difference in style is! Poor Cabanis. His statement looks almost lifeless next to the busy word picture in Diderot's illustration of the mind having a great chat at a dinner party. Interestingly, Cabanis comments directly on his flat style, also in connection with the question of attention:

> Notre intention n'est point de retracer des tableaux faits pour plaire à l'imagination; rien assurément ne seroit ici plus facile. Dans les sujets de cette nature, le physiologiste est sans cesse entouré d'images qui peuvent le captiver et le fasciner lui-même [...]. Nous voulons éloigner, au contraire, tout ce qui pourroit s'écarter de la plus froide observation: nous sommes, en effet, des observateurs, non des poètes; et dans la crainte de détourner l'attention que cet examen demande, par des impressions entièrement étrangères à notre but, nous aimons mieux n'offrir que le plus simple énoncé des opérations de la nature, et nous renfermer dans les bornes de la plus aride et de la plus froide exposition.[42]

> Our intention is not to paint pictures that the imagination will find attractive; certainly nothing would be easier here. In connection with subjects of this sort, the physiologist himself is constantly surrounded by images which are likely to captivate and fascinate him [...]. We wish, on the contrary, to set aside anything which might depart from the coldest observation: we are, in fact, observers and not poets; and for fear of distracting the attention that this enquiry requires with impressions which are entirely alien to our aim, we prefer to make nothing but

---

sorte proportionnelle, aucun ordre d'impressions ne domine; toutes se compensent et se confondent' [when all a person's organs are enjoying a moderate level of activity, no particular order of impressions dominates ; they all balance out and merge with one another] (*Rapports du physique et du moral de l'homme*, vol. 1, p. 134: lecture 2).

42  Cabanis, *Rapports du physique et du moral de l'homme*, vol. 1, pp. 312–13 (lecture 5).

the simplest assertions about the operations of nature, and to confine ourselves to the driest and coldest exposition.

He sets the imagination aside, he asserts his identity as an observer and not a poet, he embraces the statement and the cold aridity of exposition.[43] He is also, we note, rather verbose; because of this aspect of his style (which we will return to), we are often obliged to cut his sentences out of sheer practicality. The particular passage we have just looked at is only slightly cut, and it is interesting to contrast it with the following rather famous (and pithier) statement by Diderot, already quoted in connection to Garat:

> L'homme à imagination se promène, dans sa tête, comme un curieux dans un palais, où ses pas sont à chaque instant détournés par des objets intéressants.[44]
>
> The imaginative man walks about in his head like a curious person in a palace, his steps constantly drawn by interesting objects.

How curious to see not so much the similarity between these two passages—they are rather different—but the common reference point, that of the person with an imagination being attracted to first one thing and then another. When Cabanis says he will set aside imaginative tableaux—which he informs us all physiologists are ceaselessly surrounded with—he first evokes it and then rejects it; he evokes writing like a poet and then rejects that approach; he evokes the attention being distracted (détournée), only to reject distraction. He is doing a lot of rejecting, but he is also doing a lot of evoking, so much so, that one wonders whether he is in fact alluding to Diderot in this insistence on/rejection of imaginative style, an evocation which is also a resolve not to get distracted 'par des impressions entièrement étrangères à notre but' [with impressions which are entirely alien to our aim]: is this also a warning that he will not be diverted from his aim to establish the connections between 'le physique' and 'le moral', whatever sensitivity there is around the subject or around others who happen also to have treated it, possibly those who have treated it more poetically? If this is

---

43 Cabanis had in fact started his writing life under the aegis of the poet Antoine Roucher as a translator of the *Iliad* and poet himself.
44 DPV 475/PQ 303/MT 290.

so, then the allusion cannot be to any writer other than Diderot, and certainly not to Condillac, whose 'sécheresse' Garat had criticised, as we quoted above?[45] This may be a reach too far. Yet, we note his assertion that he will not be a poet, and in the first textual comparison we offered, looking at the workings and blind spots of attention, we can see that the contrast between Cabanis's and Diderot's versions is that of the bald statement to the poetical one.[46]

In this context therefore it seems relevant to ask whether the following passage, presenting the notion that the mind, with the aid of the imagination, can process ideas overnight, is a non-poetical treatment or re-writing of the same subject as addressed in the intensely poetical *Rêve de d'Alembert*:

> En effet, l'esprit peut continuer ses recherches* dans les songes; il peut être conduit par une certaine suite de raisonnemens, à des idées qu'il n'avoit pas [...]. Enfin, certaines séries d'impressions internes, qui se coordonnent avec des idées antérieures, peuvent mettre en jeu toutes les puissances de l'imagination, et même présenter à l'individu une suite d'événemens, dont il croira quelquefois, entendre dans une conversation régulière, le récit et les détails.[47]

> In fact, the mind can continue its research in dreams; it may be led by a certain series of reasons to ideas which it did not have before [...]. In short, a given series of internal impressions, in coordination with existing ideas, can get all the powers of the imagination going, and even present to an individual a series of events in which he will sometimes believe he is hearing a regular conversation with narration and details.

---

45 See above: 'la sécheresse de ses narrations dépouillées de toute imagination et de toute beauté de style' [the dryness of his accounts devoid of any imagination or stylistic beauty] (Première leçon, p. 75).

46 See also: 'une attention forte, une méditation profonde, peut suspendre l'action des organes sentans externes' [concentrated attention or deep meditation can suspend the action of the external sensory organs] (Cabanis, *Rapports du physique et du moral de l'homme*, vol. 1, p. 166); Diderot had discussed attention and distraction in *Éléments de physiologie* DPV 485/PQ 315–16/MT 300 and DPV 499–500/PQ 336–67/MT 313–14. Destutt de Tracy also engages with the question: 'Mais, dit-on, quand je fais *attention* à une sensation, j'en ai la conscience, et toutes les autres disparaissent. Hé bien! Les autres sont nulles; et vous avez une sensation: voilà tout' [But, it is said, when I pay *attention* to a sensation, I am conscious of it, and all the others disappear. Well then! The others are nothing, and you are having a sensation: that's all], *Idéologie proprement dite*, p. 189 (original italics).

47 Cabanis, *Rapports du physique et du moral de l'homme*, vol. 2, pp. 547–48 (Part 10 of the 1802 edition).

This description of the dreaming working mind, with all the powers of the imagination at play, including a regular conversation, a sustained narrative and local details, is not a bad description of the *Rêve de d'Alembert*. It is therefore almost funny to see that the asterisk following 'recherches' leads us to a footnote discussing guess who? It's Condillac:

> * Condillac m'a dit, qu'en travaillant à son cours d'études, il étoit souvent forcé de quitter, pour dormir, un travail déjà tout préparé, mais incomplet, et qu'à son réveil il l'avoit trouvé plus d'une fois terminé dans sa tête.

> * Condillac once told me that when working on his course of study [a sort of educational manual], he was often forced to interrupt, at bed time, some work that he had got completely ready but hadn't completed, and that when he woke up he more than once found it finished off in his head.

There is no reason this anecdote should not be perfectly true. It is just interesting to find it right here, appended to what sounds very much like a description of the *Rêve de d'Alembert*, sitting in a footnote that blocks that association by presenting an alternative and much more respectable source.

We see how speculative and associative this process of textual comparison and allusion is obliged to be. In the following passage, however, it is more straightforward. Cabanis presents the brain as an organ which produces or even secretes thought. We find this exact idea in the *Éléments de physiologie*. Here is Cabanis first, and Diderot second, as usual:

> [Cabanis] Pour se faire une idée juste des opérations de la pensée, il faut considérer le cerveau comme un organe particulier, destiné spécialement à la produire [...].[48]

> In order to gain an accurate idea of the operations of thought, it is necessary to consider the brain as a particular organ, specifically destined to produce it.

> [Cabanis] [...] le cerveau digère en quelque sorte les impressions; [...] il fait organiquement la sécrétion de la pensée.[49]

---

48   Cabanis, *Rapports du physique et du moral de l'homme*, vol. 1, p. 151 (lecture 2).
49   Cabanis, *Rapports du physique et du moral de l'homme*, vol. 1, p. 152 (lecture 2).

The brain digests impressions in a sort of way [...] it organically produces the secretion that is thought.

[Diderot] Le cerveau n'est qu'un organe secrétoire.[50]

The brain is nothing other than a secretory organ.

Serge Nicolas, editor of the facsimile 1802 edition *Rapports du physique et du moral de l'homme* (2005), draws particular attention to this notion of Cabanis's that the brain secretes thought, presenting it as a perfect case of Cabanis's anti-Cartesianism and prominent role as 'le plus illustre apologiste' [the most illustrious apologist] of materialism, the writer who will provide nineteenth-century materialists with 'leurs meilleurs arguments' [their best arguments].[51] He cites other 'esprits illustres' [illustrious minds] of the materialist camp—d'Holbach, La Mettrie and Helvétius. No Diderot mentioned. And in fact, no Buffon either; the idea was not original to Diderot, as Paolo Quintili points out when commenting on this statement in his edition of the *Éléments de physiologie*; it was Buffon's. Motoichi Terada adds a further three sources in Daniel de Laroche, Antoine Le Camus, and Jean-Paul Marat. Let's start with what Buffon had written:

> Le cerveau, au lieu d'être le siège des sensations, le principe du sentiment, ne sera donc qu'un organe de sécrétion et de nutrition.[52]

> The brain, instead of being the seat of sensation, the source of sensation, is therefore nothing other than an organ of secretion and nourishment.

It is interesting to see that when it comes to presenting an uncompromisingly materialist statement such as this idea of thought as a bodily secretion, both Buffon and Cabanis choose to wrap it up nicely in introductory clauses and qualifications; Diderot, however, strips this all away to its baldest version. No poetry here. Returning to the question of the genealogical transmission of this idea, however, we can see that

---

50   DPV 353/PQ 172/MT 172.
51   Serge Nicolas, 'Introduction', in Cabanis, *Rapports du physique et du moral de l'homme*, vol. 1, p. xi, n. 13. In his study on Cabanis, Yves Pouliquen also draws attention to the importance and originality of this feature of Cabanis's thought: *Cabanis, un idéologue: de Mirabeau à Bonaparte* (Paris: Odile Jacob, 2013), p. 175. Saad also underscores this point, in her *Cabanis, comprendre l'homme*, pp. 30, 149–50.
52   Buffon, *Histoire naturelle*, vol. 7 (1758), p. 122 ('Les animaux carnassiers'); reference given by Quintili in *Éléments de physiologie*, ed. by Quintili, p. 172, n. 20.

Diderot receives the idea either from Buffon or Marat (or both). Marat had written this:

> Le cerveau n'est qu'un organe secrétoire, & n'a aucun rapport à l'Ame, qu'en tant qu'il filtre plus ou moins de fluide & que ce fluide est plus ou moins élaboré: c'est à cet égard aussi qu'il influe sur l'intelligence.[53]

> The brain is nothing other than a secretory organ, and has no connection to the soul other than insofar as it filters more or less fluid, and that this fluid is more or less developed: it is in this respect also that it influences the intelligence.

Diderot's 'ne... que' is a direct repetition of Buffon's, and Marat seems also to repeat Buffon. Cabanis may have in mind Buffon, Diderot, Le Camus, Laroche, or Marat, singly or plurally: as Terada points out, 'c'est une opinion très répandue à l'époque' [this opinion was widely shared at the time].[54] Notice, however, that Diderot drops the nutritional aspect that Buffon includes as an equal part of his formula: for Buffon, the brain is nothing but an organ of secretion *and nutrition*. Diderot drops the Buffonian nutrition as he also drops Marat's inclusion of filters and fluid. In Cabanis, the notions of nutrition and filtered fluids are also absent, and although he does mention the associated process of digestion, it is in the form of an analogy to communicate the idea of thought as a secreted product of the brain, and not as a direct function of the brain itself. The more likely hypothesis therefore is that Cabanis is following Diderot and not Buffon or Marat, even if his style is somewhat more cautious.

***

We also find similarity in their views about sensory memory. Cabanis writes that:

> [...] je ne serois pas éloigné de penser que les sens, pris chacun à part, ont leur mémoire propre.[55]

---

53  Marat, *De l'homme*, 1775, vol. 2, p. 337, source given and partially cited by Terada, MT 360–61 n. xxi.
54  *Éléments de physiologie*, ed. by Terada, p. 172, n. 78.
55  Cabanis, *Rapports du physique et du moral de l'homme*, vol. 1, p. 229 (lecture 3).

> I am not far from thinking that the senses, taken separately, have their own memory.

He goes on to illustrate this idea by talking about standing in front of a sun-lit window, closing his eyes, and continuing to see the image of the window frame and glass panes.

In the *Éléments de physiologie*, we read this:

> Mémoire de la vue, mémoire de l'oreille, mémoire du goût, habitudes qui lient une longue suite de sensations et de mots, et de mouvements successifs et enchaînés d'organes.[56]

> Memory of sight, memory of the ear, memory of taste, habits which link a long series of sensations and words and also link successive and connected movements within the [sensory] organs.

He goes on to evoke visual memory when the eyes are shut (although he gives no example): 'les yeux fermés nous réveillent une longue succession de couleurs' [the eyes when closed waken a long string of colours], concluding that 'la mémoire peut donc être regardée comme un enchaînement fidèle de sensations, qui se réveillent successivement comme elles ont été reçues' [the memory can therefore be regarded as a faithful chain of sensations, which are successively aroused in the order in which they were received].[57] We can see that both Diderot and Cabanis are thinking explicitly about sensory memory, although Cabanis's admission that he is not far from thinking that each sense has its own memory is less affirmative than Diderot's formulation, while his rather concrete and undeveloped example of seeing an image remaining imprinted on his eyelids on closing his eyes is more tentative than Diderot's confident 'longue succession de couleurs'. Cabanis goes on to allude to auditory memory, to interruptions, and to sensory memories featuring in dreams or in the 'silence et l'obscurité de la nuit' [silence and darkness of the night], all topics which Diderot also discusses.[58] So these passages do bear out the notion that Cabanis is following the earlier text, grappling with its assertions, trying to think them through,

---

56 DPV 472/PQ 299/MT 287.
57 DPV 472/PQ 299/MT 287.
58 Cabanis, *Rapports du physique et du moral de l'homme*, vol. 1, p. 230 (lecture 3).

and that his *Rapports du physique et du moral de l'homme* bears the traces of this process.

We will just look at two more of these potential traces before turning to Destutt de Tracy. In the first, we see Cabanis arguing that 'the energetic passions' are capable of calling up unsuspected amounts of strength:

> [...] dans toutes les passions énergiques, chaque homme trouve en lui-même une vigueur qu'il ne soupçonnoit pas, et devient capable d'exécuter des mouvements dont l'idée seule l'eût effrayé dans des temps plus calmes.[59]

> In all the energetic passions, each person finds within themselves a vigour that they had not suspected, and becomes capable of executing movements the very idea of which would have frightened them in calmer times.

In the *Éléments de physiologie*, we find this:

> L'homme sain ne connaît pas toute sa force; j'en dis autant de l'homme tranquille.*
>
> > * Mr de Buffon voit la flamme s'échapper avec de la fumée à travers les fentes d'un lambris; il arrache le lambris; il prend entre ses bras les planches à demi brûlées et les porte dans sa cour et il se trouve qu'un cheval n'ébranlerait pas le fardeau qu'il a porté. Une femme délicate est attaquée de vapeurs hystériques, de fureur utérine et trois hommes ne peuvent contenir celle qu'un seul d'entre eux aurait renversée, liée dans son état de santé. Le feu prend à la maison d'un avare, il prend son coffre-fort et le porte dans son jardin, d'où il ne l'aurait pas remué pour dix fois la somme qu'il contenait.[60]

> The healthy man does not know the extent of his strength; I say the same applies to a tranquil man.*
>
> > *Mr de Buffon sees flames and smoke escaping through the slits of a piece of wooden pannelling; he tears it off; he carries the half-burnt planks in his arms out into the courtyard and it emerges that a horse would not have been able to move the load he carried. A delicate woman is attacked by hysterical vapours and uterine fury and three men are unable to restrain someone whom one of them could have knocked over and tied up unaided had she been in a state of health. The house of a miser catches light, he picks up his strong box and

---

59 Cabanis, *Rapports du physique et du moral de l'homme*, vol. 1, p. 200 (lecture 3).
60 DPV 327/PQ 143/MT 149.

carries it into his garden, and then wouldn't have been able to move it for ten times the sum it contained.

This is a passage we have looked at before.[61] There, we noted how it picks up a theme also treated by Condillac. Who's to say which one (or who else) Cabanis is engaging with? We cannot be sure. And yet, Condillac's version is neither particularly plausible nor physiologically-based, despite the mention of gout. Diderot focuses very specifically on extreme circumstances either of threat (to self or to something held precious) or illness, specifically hysteria. This is also what Cabanis looks at: a hysterical woman being stronger than a group of men trying to restrain her; sufferers from 'maladies maniaques' [manic illnesses] being able to break chains asunder, and finally, how the 'forces vivantes' [living forces] can suddenly, in 'toutes les passions énergiques', as quoted, bestow on every man ('homme') 'une vigueur qu'il ne soupçonnait pas'.[62] There is a clear parallel between the passages, supported by the appearance of the exceptionally strong hysterical woman in both, even though in Cabanis we find no specific anecdotes, and therefore no mention of Buffon saving his precious wood panels or the miser his strong box from fire.[63]

The last passage I wish to look at in this section is about the persistence of life, or specifically, sensibility, in the absence of any perceptible signs of it, specifically in the case of drowned persons.

Here is what Cabanis writes. He has been dealing with the sensibility irritability polemic, and in the following extract evokes 'others' who hold a particular position on the matter:

> Les autres, et l'on peut compter parmi eux plusieurs hommes de génie, objectent que la sensibilité subsiste dans les asphyxies, les léthargies, les apoplexies, en un mot dans les syncopes de tout genre, quoiqu'elle ne se manifeste alors par aucun acte précis qui la constate, quoiqu'elle ne laisse après elle aucune trace, aucun souvenir qui la confirme. Ils ajoutent qu'entre l'état d'un noyé qui revient à la vie, et l'état de celui dont la mort est irrévocable, la différence sera difficile à bien établir.[64]

---

61 See Chapter 3 in the section titled 'The Gouty Man and the Fire'.
62 Cabanis, *Rapports du physique et du moral de l'homme*, vol. 1, pp. 199–200 (lecture 3).
63 For the history of hysteria, see Sabine Arnaud, *On Hysteria: The Invention of a Medical Category between 1670 & 1820* (Chicago: Chicago University Press, 2015), https://doi.org/10.7208/chicago/9780226275680.001.0001.
64 Cabanis, *Rapports du physique et du moral de l'homme*, vol. 1, pp. 86–87 (lecture 2).

Others, and amongst them can be counted many men of genius, object that sensibility persists in different sorts of asphyxia, lethargy, and apoplexy, in a word in swoons of all sorts, although it is not evident in any precise action which might prove it, although it leaves no trace behind it, no memory to confirm it. They add that between the state of a drowned person who returns to life and the state of someone whose death is irrevocable, the difference is difficult to establish properly.

In the *Éléments de physiologie*, Diderot specifically looks at these questions, and we have quoted the following passage before.[65] He has evoked melancholic lethargy and catalepsy, and here he thinking about a drowned person:

> Où est-elle [l'âme] dans le noyé, qu'on rappelle à la vie de l'état de mort, ou d'un état qui lui ressemble tellement, que si le noyé n'avait point été secouru, il aurait persévéré dans cet état sans éprouver d'autre changement qu'une torpeur plus profonde.[66]

> Where is it [the soul] in the drowned man, who can be recalled to life from the state of death, or from a state which resembles it so closely, that if the drowned man had not been treated, he would have continued in that same state without experiencing any change other than a deeper torpor.

It is difficult to read Cabanis's allusion to 'plusieurs hommes de génie' [many men of genius] arguing about the persistence of sensibility, and see him record that 'they add' this further point about establishing life or death after drowning, without thinking about these precise pages from the *Éléments de physiologie*, where these specific subjects are treated in exactly this order. Furthermore, how interesting to see Cabanis anonymise this group of thinkers at the same time as asserting their status as men of genius. In the course of his presentation of the different arguments and views about sensibility and irritability, he has named Locke, Bonnet, Condillac, Helvétius, and Xavier Bichat, as well as Albrecht von Haller, the Stahlians, and the medical schools of Edinburgh and Montpellier.[67] So it is not as if he is averse to naming in general,

---

65 DPV 333–34/PQ 150–51/MT 154, discussed in Chapter 3, in the section titled 'The Natural Processes of Material Transformation'.
66 DPV 333/PQ 151/MT 154.
67 Cabanis, *Rapports du physique et du moral de l'homme*, vol. 1, pp. 84–88 (lecture 2). As mentioned earlier, Jean-Luc Chappey analyses the phenomenon and politics of the

although, as mentioned earlier, Diderot is not once named. In this context, therefore, it is striking to see Cabanis not only alluding to and semi-identifying (as geniuses) this new group, but also conveying to his reader that he aligns his own view with theirs.[68] We have to suppose—given the similarity of the texts—that he is referring ever so carefully to Diderot, and that he must be using the *Éléments de physiologie*.[69] Is there any other conclusion we can draw?

## Destutt de Tracy and the *Éléments de physiologie*

Destutt de Tracy's connection to Diderot and the *Éléments de physiologie* is not quite so clear. This is because he remains strictly within the 'rational' part of what, from his second lecture onwards, he calls 'l'idéologie rationelle';[70] we will turn to his coining of this influential neologism in a few pages. He distinguishes 'l'idéologie rationelle' from 'l'idéologie physiologique', stating that 'Idéologie' has two parts, the physiological and the rational, and that 'En parlant de la sensibilité et des facultés qui en dérivent, je n'ai point osé rechercher leurs causes physiologiques' [when talking about sensibility and the faculties which derive from it, I have not dared to research their physiological causes].[71] He is too modest to talk about what he does not master, so he does not talk physiology. This obviously makes it harder work to find any traces

---

list in his *Ordres et désordres biographiques: dictionnaires, listes de noms, réputation des Lumières à Wikipédia* (Seyssel: Champ Vallon, 2013), p. 176, quoted above.

68   This is not the only time Cabanis does this. He also talks about 'les écrivains qui se sont occupés avec quelque profondeur, de l'analyse des idées, de celle du langage [...] et des principes de la morale privée ou publique' physique' [the writers who have thought deeply about the analysis of ideas and of language (...) and about the principles of private and public morality], further specifying that these writers had all 'senti cette nécessité de se diriger, dans leurs recherches, d'après la connoissance de la nature humaine' [felt the need to orientate their research according to what we know about human nature] Cabanis, *Rapports du physique et du moral de l'homme*, vol. 1, p. vii (Préface)—this last qualification tells us that we are not talking about Condillac; Diderot seems alluded to, again.

69   I explore the question of non-naming as an allusive way of naming in my article: Caroline Warman, 'Caught between Neologism and the Unmentionable: The Politics of Naming and Non-naming in 1790s France', *Romance Studies*, 31 (2013), 264–76 (esp. pp. 266–67), https://doi.org/10.1179/0263990413Z.00000000051.

70   Destutt de Tracy, *Mémoire sur la faculté de penser*, p. 89 (Part II, §iv, probably lecture 3).

71   Ibid.

of Diderot's *Éléments de physiologie*, even supposing there were any in the first place. However, if he focuses on presenting a model of the mind and its functions in philosophically logical (and thus Condillacian) terms, he consistently refers to its physiological bases and relation to the body in general (he also continuously criticises Condillac, as we saw). His view of the mind and thought as fundamentally physiological is made even more explicit when he states, in the preface to the first stand-alone edition of the *Idéologie proprement dite* (a lightly reworked version of the *Mémoire sur la faculté de penser*) that ideology is a subsection of zoology: 'L'idéologie est une partie de la zoologie' [ideology is part of zoology].[72] Statements of thorough-going physiological determinism are ubiquitous. For example, having disputed the accuracy of the definition of need/s which Condillac gives in the *Traité des sensations*, he states that:

> je pense que nos premiers besoins [...] résultent directement de notre organisation [et qu'ils] sont des perceptions simples, de purs sentimens [...].[73]

> I think that our primary needs [...] are the direct result of our organization [and that they] are simple perceptions, pure feelings [...]

A few pages later (but within the same lecture chapter), he further states that:

> tout plaisir ou peine est un besoin, et toute sensation perçue est en elle-même un besoin.[74]

> every pain and pleasure is a need, and every perceived sensation is in itself a need.

In the third lecture chapter, he returns to the same theme, even more explicitly:

> [...] tout ce que nous pensons, tout ce que nous sommes, dérive de nos besoins physiques dans toute leur simplicité, de notre seule organisation.[75]

> everything that we think, everything that we are, derives from our physical needs in all their simplicity, from our organization alone.

---

72 Destutt de Tracy, *Idéologie proprement dite*, p. 75.
73 Destutt de Tracy, *Mémoire sur la faculté de penser*, p. 97 (Part II, §v, lecture 3 or 4).
74 Destutt de Tracy, *Mémoire sur la faculté de penser*, p. 99 (Part II, §v, lecture 3 or 4).
75 Destutt de Tracy, *Mémoire sur la faculté de penser*, p. 140 (Part III, §iv, lecture 4 or 5).

This view manifestly goes much further than anything Condillac said, while being very close to the sort of materialist physiological determinism which saturates the *Éléments de physiologie* from one end to the other. 'Organization' is a rather specific term, relating to particular eighteenth-century theories of the body, and should be understood as a sort of synonym for it, for the sort of body a person has, how it works, what its particular characteristics are. (We touched on 'organisation' in Chapter 4.) It is a crucial conceptual term for Diderot. Thus, in the chapter on *la volonté*, the will, we read this:

> Le désir est fils de l'organisation, le bonheur et le malheur, fils du bien-être ou du mal-être.[76]

> Desire is the child of the body's organization, while happiness and unhappiness are the children of well-being or the lack thereof.

One's whole being—one's health and happiness—derives from one's 'organisation'. Meanwhile, in the chapter on muscles we read this about pleasure and pain and their influence on all animal parts and functions:

> Le plaisir et la douleur ont été les premiers maîtres de l'animal: ce sont eux qui ont appris peut-être à toutes les parties leurs fonctions et les ont rendues habituelles et héréditaires.[77]

> Pleasure and pain were the animal's first teachers: it may be they who taught all its parts their functions and made them habitual and hereditary.

Sensibility—fundamentally either pleasurable or painful—is made responsible in this statement for developing not just muscle function, but all parts of the body and all its functions.

These assembled passages combine to make a different sort of argument from the earlier one about the proximity between Cabanis and Diderot; there it seems that there is a case for claiming specific connections or influence. Here, it is rather more diffuse. Nonetheless, the philosophical position Destutt de Tracy takes with respect to the body and mind, and the physiological bases of thought, feeling, and being, is measurably close to Diderot's. However, there are moments when the texts themselves seem very close, despite Destutt de Tracy's

---

76  DPV 486/PQ 317/MT 301.
77  DPV 366/PQ 186/MT 186–87.

general avoidance of physiological description and discussion. Here, for example, returning to the question of the will, the chapter dedicated to which we alluded to very briefly a few paragraphs ago, we read this. Here Diderot comes first:

> Je veux, n'est qu'un mot, examinez-le bien et vous ne trouverez jamais qu'impulsion, conscience et acquiescement: impulsion volontaire, conscience ou aséité, acquiescement ou attrait senti.[78]

> *I want* is nothing more than a phrase, examine it carefully and you will never find anything other than impulsion, consciousness and acquiescence: voluntary impulsion, consciousness or aseity, acquiescence or felt attraction.

Diderot reduces the expression of the will, *I want*, to desire, impulse or need, whether conscious or not: he says that *I want* is nothing more than a word. Destutt de Tracy has something similar to say about the word *freedom*:

> Plus j'y ai réfléchi, plus je me suis persuadé qu'être libre consiste à pouvoir agir en conséquence de sa volonté, et que le mot *liberté*, de quelque manière qu'on l'emploie, ne signifie rien, ou signifie la puissance de satisfaire ses désirs.[79]

> The more I thought about it, the more I became convinced that *being free* consists in being able to act in accordance with one's will, and that the word *freedom*, however it is used, signifies nothing, or signifies the power to satisfy one's desires.

He says that the word *freedom* is meaningless, or simply designates the power or ability to satisfy one's desires. There is a palpable parallelism between the texts here beyond the similarity of their positions on free will (i.e., that there is none); they both assert the emptiness of the words themselves, with, on the other hand, the identification of the will with the drive to fulfill desires.

On a separate note, it seems worth remarking Tracy's insistence on the word 'liberté' here. In the context of the French Revolution and its clarion call motif of 'liberté égalité fraternité' it is startling to see one of

---

78  DPV 484/PQ 314/MT 298.
79  Destutt de Tracy, *Mémoire sur la faculté de penser*, p. 104 (Part II, §v, lecture 3 or 4; original italics).

the Revolutionary government's official philosophers brush the notion of liberty aside in such a cursory fashion.[80] He immediately softens his sharpness by following up with an argument about how 'les vérités politiques' require 'us' to try to ensure that each other's desires harm others as little as possible and are directed to the fulfilment of the desires of all. Despite this political caveat, it remains a rather striking statement. Thus, as well as expressing philosophical and physiological views which, as we have shown, are tightly allied to similar views expressed by Diderot, Destutt de Tracy may well also be signalling a shift in the political weather of the Directorate, away from unconditional espousal of the notion of liberty, towards something more qualified.[81] Garat would soon publish his article in favour of coups d'état in *Le conservateur*.[82]

\*\*\*

When we review the very real proximity between the *Éléments de physiologie* and these lectures given in 1796–98 by Cabanis and Destutt de Tracy at the Institut national, and subsequently published, not only in the *Mémoires de l'Institut* (1798–1801) but then in their own separate editions (and re-editions), we cannot but be struck by their success. The institution protected, framed, and authorised their efforts, in a way that the fraught structures of the École normale had completely failed to do in the case of Garat. Their lectures were given the status of '[des] travaux scientifiques et littéraires qui auront pour objet l'utilité générale et la gloire de la république' [scientific and literary work whose purpose is the general utility of all and the glory of the republic] as quoted above, and decreed in the Loi Daunou of 3 Brumaire an IV (25 October 1795), Section Four, Article One.[83] Cabanis influenced the thinking of medical

---

80 See also Mona Ozouf's entry: 'Liberté', in *Dictionnaire critique de la Révolution française : Idées*, ed. by François Furet, Mona Ozouf, Bronislaw Baczko (Paris: Flammarion, 1992), pp. 253-73. (*Idées* was volume 4 of the initial *Dictionnaire critique de la Révolution française*, here published separately).
81 Destutt de Tracy, *Mémoire sur la faculté de penser*, pp. 104–05 (Part II, §v, lecture 3 or 4).
82 Garat, 'Considérations sur la dictature et les dictateurs' in *Le conservateur*, Nivôse/ Pluviôse an VI (January 1798). Garat set up and edited this journal with Daunou and Marie-Joseph Chénier (*Le Conservateur* 'journal politique, philosophique et littéraire', an V-VI, Garat, Daunou et (Marie-Joseph) Chénier, http://dictionnaire-journalistes.gazettes18e.fr/journaliste/329-dominique-garat.
83 See above.

luminaries such as Bichat (1771–1802), the ground-breaking anatomist and founder of histology (the study of human tissue).[84] Cabanis was also thought to be an authority by the physician Anthelme Richerand, who helped him turn the lectures into a book, and who dedicated the fifth edition of his own extremely successful *Nouveaux élémens de physiologie*, first published in 1801, to the memory of Cabanis.[85] (Richerand has already had a walk-on part in the chapter on physiology, and would later edit the medical writings of Diderot's friend, the Montpellier vitalist Théophile de Bordeu.)[86] And, as Jean Starobinski points out, Cabanis will remain a reference point up to and including Sigmund Freud, who refers to him in connection with dreams and mental illness in the *Interpretation of Dreams*.[87] The point, however, is not to discuss the reception of Cabanis and Destutt de Tracy (who also had great impact) in any depth, but simply to indicate that their work, whether considered separately or under their joint banner of 'Idéologie', had official status, was recognised as important, and did feed without delay into contemporaneous discussions of the brain-mind as an organ of the body. As Cabanis put it, or rather, as Destutt de Tracy made explicit, 'le moment est favorable'.[88] And in this case, unlike Naigeon, who, as we saw, also thought times were propitious, they were both right.[89] And

---

84   Xavier Bichat is discussed in Chapter 4; he seems to be alluding to Cabanis in his *Traité d'anatomie descriptive*, 5 vols (Paris: Brosson, Babon, 1801–03), vol. 1, p. xxiv); Cabanis complains about those who use his work without acknowledging him, and refers to Bichat, *Rapports du physique et du moral de l'homme*, vol. 1, pp. xxii–xxiii (Preface; the reference tying these remarks to Bichat is in the footnote [p. xxiii] recording his death). Martin Staum considers that Bichat distanced himself from Cabanis to some extent (*Cabanis: Enlightenment and Medical Philosophy in the French Revolution* (Princeton, NJ: Princeton University Press, 1980), p. 256).

85   Anthelme Richerand, *Nouveaux élémens de physiologie*, 5th edn (Paris: Caille et Ravier, 1811), opening page. (He also dedicates this edition to the memory of Fourcroy, who has also died since the fourth edition of 1807; Cabanis in 1808 and Fourcroy in 1810. The fourth edition had been dedicated just to Fourcroy.) Cabanis had acknowledged their relationship, thanking Richerand for his precious help, *Rapports du physique et du moral de l'homme*, vol. 1, p. xxxix (Preface).

86   See Chapter 4.

87   Jean Starobinski, *Action et réaction: vie et aventures d'un couple* (Paris: Seuil, 1999), p. 151.

88   Destutt de Tracy, 'Table analytique', in Cabanis, *Rapports du physique et du moral de l'homme*, vol. 1, pp. xxxii–liv (p. xxxii).

89   As discussed in Chapter 5 (Naigeon chastises Helvétius for choosing the wrong moment, and praises himself for knowing that the right time has come, wrongly as it emerges).

yet, as we see from the time lag between Cabanis's first printed preface in 1802 and its second outing in 1805, by which time it has acquired Destutt de Tracy's concise summary along with its terse expression that 'le moment est favorable', they proceed with caution. In 1796, when giving the first in the series of lectures which will find their way into print in the *Mémoires de l'Institut*, there is no preface, and no statement, however verbose, convoluted or in need of translation by his friend, that 'le moment est favorable'. At that point neither he nor Destutt de Tracy were quite sure whether the time was right or not, and there are many indications of nervy caution, of which the slow emergence into publication is only one.

They are very both careful to situate their lectures within the space from which they speak—'le lieu d'où l'on parle', as Starobinski put it—and those references to the space and to the original orality of their texts are retained through the various iterations.[90] Thus, Cabanis evokes the saying 'know thyself', quoting it in the original Greek and thereby establishing his own credentials as a learned person, stating that it 'est très-digne de servir d'inscription à cette salle, aussi bien qu'au temple de Delphes' [entirely worthy to serve as an inscription for this room, as well as for the temple in Delphi].[91] This is a neat piece of echo-chamber flattery, whereby Cabanis flatters his own venue while also making Antiquity relevant and current, and annexing the authority of both for himself. Furthermore, his insistence on where exactly he is speaking from is made explicit in his own footnote, asterisked to 'cette salle': 'Celle de l'institut national' [Institut national's meeting room].[92] Destutt de Tracy, for his part, alludes to critics, 'hors de cette enceinte' [beyond the enclosure of these walls] and how to prevent them blocking his progress, thereby turning the Institut national into a sort of protected circle.[93] He further evokes place and audience when, one page later, he approvingly quotes 'un membre de cette assemblée' [a member of this

---

90 Jean Starobinski, 'La Chaire, la tribune, le barreau', p. 481, quoted above.
91 Cabanis, *Rapports du physique et du moral de l'homme*, vol. 1, p. 159 (lecture 2).
92 Cabanis, *Rapports du physique et du moral de l'homme*, vol. 1, p. 159n (lecture 2: lower-case original).
93 Destutt de Tracy, *Mémoire sur la faculté de penser*, p. 65 (Introduction to part 2, i.e. lecture 2).

assembly].⁹⁴ Both ceremoniously address the 'citoyens' who listen to them in an allusion to and invocation of the desired listener, one who follows the etiquette of courteous Republican reciprocity and attention.⁹⁵ Destutt de Tracy explicitly tells his listeners/readers that he is doing what they asked him to do, binding both sides in a contract which he claims his lecture fulfills.⁹⁶ This of course is a way of diverting criticism, and perhaps we would not draw attention to this feature, brushing it aside as a piece of rhetoric, both habitual and innocuous, were it not for a context which we already know to be hostile to materialist thinking, and for other markers of anxiety within these texts. Both allude to the danger or difficulty specifically of navigating around these fraught subjects. Cabanis evokes his efforts to bring together anatomy and physiology on the one hand, and 'l'analyse philosophique' on the other, appealing to his audience in exactly the way alluded to above, while advertising his severe self-imposed discipline:

> [...] je vais surtout m'efforcer de remplir les lacunes qui séparent encore les observations de l'anatomie ou de la physiologie, et les résultats incontestables de l'analyse philosophique. Vous sentez, citoyens, que dans des matières si nouvelles, où le plus léger faux-pas peut conduire aux conséquences les plus erronées, il faut s'imposer une grande précision, une grande sévérité de language [...]⁹⁷

> I will make a particular effort to fill in the gaps that separate the observations of anatomy or physiology from the incontestable results of philosophical analysis. You will realise, citizens, that in the case of subjects which are so new, the slightest mis-step may lead to the most

---

94  Destutt de Tracy, *Mémoire sur la faculté de penser*, p. 66 (Introduction to part 2, i.e. lecture 2).
95  Destutt de Tracy, *Mémoire sur la faculté de penser*, pp. 37, 49, 133; *Dissertation sur quelques questions d'idéologie*, p. 183; Cabanis, *Rapports du physique et du moral de l'homme*, vol. 1, pp. 6, 22, 82, 113, 121, 159, etc. In the *Idéologie proprement dite*, on the other hand, Destutt addresses readers rather than listeners, and they are conceptualised as 'jeunes gens' [young people] or 'mes jeunes amis' [my young friends], see pp. 77, 83, 176, 185, 193, 249.
96  He writes: 'Mais une preuve que vous voulez examiner ces mêmes facultés [de l'entendement de l'homme] sous tous les aspects, c'est que vous avez composé votre première section d'analystes et de physiologistes' [but one proof that you do want to examine these same faculties (of human understanding) in all their aspects is that you have filled your first section with analysts and physiologists] (Destutt de Tracy, *Mémoire sur la faculté de penser*, pp. 72–73, part 2, i.e. lecture 2).
97  Cabanis, *Rapports du physique et du moral de l'homme*, vol. 1, pp. 83–84 (lecture 2).

erroneous consequences, and that we must impose the greatest precision on ourselves and be as severe as possible in our use of language.

These allusions, on the one hand to the efforts he will be making to connect physiology and philosophical analysis, and on the other to the 'totally erroneous consequences' that might ensue from making 'the slightest mis-step', with the appeal he makes to his audience of 'citizens' who feel, he claims, the importance of getting it right, given this very new subject, display the writer's anxiety and caution very clearly. He will make the same sort of moves when evoking how 'l'analyse philosophique' had previously separated off 'les observations embarrassantes qui regardent l'instinct' [troublesome observations about instinct], given that instinct has not been viewed as arising directly from sensation as such, and how these observations had been therefore regarded as 'comme erronées ou dangereuses dans leurs conséquences' [as erroneous or dangerous in their consequences].[98] Troublesome, erroneous, and dangerous are strong words. He does not explain why these observations were held to be all these things, and perhaps he does not need to, or rather, perhaps he needs not to. Cabanis carefully goes so far as to say that 'it is something perhaps' to have been able to show that the instinct is properly part of the 'l'analyse philosophique'. Destutt de Tracy says it is no wonder that knowledge of and opinions about human understanding vary so much, as 'il y a eu jusqu'à présent si peu de discussions libres sur ces sujets' [there have been so few free discussions on these subjects until now].[99] This is an interesting admission, given the ubiquitous allusions to the influence of the eminent and mostly unproblematic Condillac. Tracy's remark suggests that, counter to the much-repeated view that Condillac provides the modern impetus to advances in knowledge of the processes of human understanding, in fact, there have been very few free discussions about it; Condillac is what is left after the censorship. In the *Idéologie proprement dite*, where, as we have suggested, Destutt de Tracy is a little less tentative, he begins to discuss the 'natural state of matter' which, he says, is 'movement', and he goes on to elaborate:

---

98 Cabanis, *Rapports du physique et du moral de l'homme*, vol. 1, pp. 137–38 (lecture 2).
99 Destutt de Tracy, *Mémoire sur la faculté de penser*, p. 131 (II.6, i.e. lecture 4 or 5).

> [...] si je n'avais craint de trop choquer les idées reçues, j'aurais mis l'activité à la tête des propriétés des corps.[100]
>
> if I were not afraid to offend received ideas, I would have put activity at the head of the properties of bodies.

Of course, in stating his fears, he is also stating what he states he is afraid to say, that is, that activity is the most fundamental property of particles of matter ('corps' should be understood in this way, rather than as specifying human bodies). So, while he is not too afraid to make such a claim about the properties of matter, he still frames it tentatively, conditionally, and in connection to fear. And we know enough now to see that the seemingly simply polite formula of fearing to offend received opinion is not just a form of words: as Cabanis had put it, these 'observations embarrassantes' might be 'erronées ou dangereuses dans leurs conséquences'; they could 'tout brouiller de nouveau' [mess everything up again].[101] For all their care, their ceremonious verbiage, and the protection of their elevated and official position, it would not take much to bring them down.

\*\*\*

In these years of 1796, 1797, and 1798, when Cabanis and Destutt de Tracy were giving the first versions or first parts of what would later be published in separate editions, neither materialism nor Diderot's name were becoming any less polemical.[102] This is owing at least in part to the publications of the highly visible Jacobin Gracchus Babeuf, arrested for supposedly plotting to overthrow the state in May 1796, and whose

---

100 Destutt de Tracy, *Idéologie proprement dite*, p. 167.
101 Quoted above, Cabanis, *Rapports du physique et du moral de l'homme*, vol. 1, p. 138 (lecture 2).
102 Diderot's poem 'Les Eleuthéromanes', with its incendiary reference to strangling kings with the guts of priests, was first published and then rapidly re-published in September and November 1796; as we discussed before, this image is lifted from Meslier in Voltaire's version and was not original to Diderot. This did not stop it causing damage, and it was already associated with him thanks to Mercier, see above, and Naigeon had quoted snippets from it in his *Adresse à l'Assemblée nationale* of 1790. It was published in the *Décade philosophique* on 30 Fructidor an IV (16 September 1796) and in Roederer's *Journal d'économie politique* on 20 Brumaire an V (10 November 1796). Why these two journals, both friendly to Diderot and the cause of the 'philosophes', chose to publish it at this time, given its political sensitivity, and the fact that the Babeuf affair was already underway, is not clear.

trial, lasting from February to May 1797, would, as René Tarin puts it, place 'Diderot sous les feux de l'actualité' [in the firing line of current events].[103] As such, it affects our story directly. We now turn to Babeuf in order to understand what was at stake, what happened, and how Diderot was involved, not least because there are some grounds for thinking that this renewed negative publicity may have triggered Destutt's decision to create a new name for their school of thought.

Babeuf was not cautious, and he antagonised the government directly by using his journal the *Tribun du peuple* to campaign for the enactment of the never-enacted constitution of 1793.[104] This constitution, ratified but suspended for the duration of the Terror and now replaced by Daunou's new drafting of 1795 establishing the Directorate, had legislated for greater equality and redistribution of wealth. Babeuf was particularly virulent about the great evil of property, and he systematically, approvingly and lengthily quotes a work called the *Code de la nature* written by the now little-known philosopher Étienne-Gabriel Morelly (1717–78) which had initially been published in 1755 and which proposes that human laws should be modelled on nature. Here's the rub: Babeuf did not know that it was written by Morelly; he thought it had been written by Diderot, and he thought this because it had appeared in an unauthorised edition of Diderot's works in 1772.[105] In fact, Diderot had nothing to do with it. Unaware, Babeuf firmly annexes Diderot to his cause, exhorting his readers to 'écoute[r] Diderot, il ne vous laissera pas plus d'équivoque sur le secret du véritable et seul système de sociabilité conforme à la justice' [listen to Diderot, he will leave you in no doubt as to the

---

103 René Tarin, *Diderot et la Révolution française: controverses et polémique autour d'un philosophe* (Paris: Champion, 2001), p. 107.
104 Laura Mason considers Babeuf's inability to follow a cautious line in her brilliant analysis of the trial, see *The Last Revolutionaries: The Trial of Gracchus Babeuf and the Equals*, ch. 9, pp. 191–93 (of Mason's typescript: submitted for publication; details forthcoming). With grateful thanks to Laura Mason for so generously sharing her work.
105 Diderot, *Œuvres philosophiques de Mr D\*\*\**, 6 vols (Amsterdam: Marc-Michel Rey, 1772). The *Code de la nature* appears in volume 1. See Adams, *Bibliographie des œuvres de Diderot, 1739–1900*, 2 vols (Ferney-Voltaire: Centre international d'étude du XVIIIe siècle, 2000), vol. 1, p. 85. Adams explains that the claim that the famous publisher Marc-Michel Rey had anything to do with it was also false, p. 90.

secret of the true and only just system for society].[106] In March–April 1796, Babeuf stepped up the pressure on the government, writing a summary of his doctrine in fifteen principles and flyposting it around Paris. Here, he invoked nature (articles 1–3), stated that the Revolution was unfinished (article 11), and that the constitution of 1793 was the true law of the French (article 12), and that 'every citizen is expected to re-establish and defend in the Constitution of 1793 the wishes and the happiness of the people' (article 13). This went down badly with the authorities, and the Directoire responded with the laws of 27–28 Germinal an IV (16–17 April 1796) which decreed the death penalty for attempting by word or in writing to overthrow the established authority or re-establish the constitution of 1793.[107] Babeuf riposted on 5 Floréal (just three days after Tracy had given his first lecture on the 'faculté de penser'), stating that 'il n'est plus permis de se parler; il n'est plus permis de lire; il n'est plus permis de penser' [we are no longer permitted to speak to each other; we are no longer permitted to read; we are no longer permitted to think].[108] Just over a fortnight later, on 21 Floréal an IV (10 May), Babeuf and 'les Egaux' (the Equals), as they were known, were pre-emptively arrested on the basis of preventing an alleged coup d'état; renewed anti-Jacobin repression followed.

Now, Destutt de Tracy announced his new name for 'la science de la pensée' not in the first installment of his lectures on *la faculté de penser* but in the second. One might have expected a new investigation into the faculty of thought that was going to introduce a new name for itself to do so at the beginning. Tracy did not even allude to this issue in his first 'Mémoire' which took place on the 2 Floréal an IV (21 April 1796), the second being given on 2 Messidor an IV (20 June 1796). In between

---

106 Gracchus Babeuf, *Le Tribun du Peuple, ou le défenseur des droits de l'homme. An III–An IV* (Paris: Éditions d'Histoire Sociale, 1966), p. 93 (numéro 35, 9 Frimaire an IV/19 November 1795). Didier analyses Babeuf's debt to Diderot/Morelly in her essay 'Statut de l'Utopie chez Gracchus Babeuf', in *Présence de Babeuf: Lumières, Révolution, Communisme*, ed. by A. Maillard, Cl. Mazauric, and E. Walter (Paris: Publications de la Sorbonne, 1994), pp. 29–48 (p. 31), and Ian Birchall gives a good overview of his intellectual debts (Birchall, *The Spectre of Babeuf* (Basingstoke: Macmillan, 1997), p. 50).
107 John Anthony Scott, ed. and trans., *The Defense of Gracchus Babeuf before the High Court of Vendôme with an Essay by Herbert Marcuse and Illustrations by Thomas Cornell* (Amherst: University of Massachusetts Press, 1967), p. 11.
108 Babeuf, *Le Tribun du peuple*, pp. 297–98 (numéro 43).

those two sessions, Babeuf and associates were arrested. As we have seen, Babeuf's support for Diderot was very public, irrespective of the fact that he was really talking about Morelly. Destutt de Tracy would have known that this was a false attribution (Naigeon dealt with it with his usual outraged ferocity in the introduction to his *Œuvres de Diderot* of 1798), but it was very damaging nonetheless, and we can see why it might have been crucial for the continuation of the project on the *analysis of sensations and ideas*—an area which was strongly associated with Diderot however little his name ever appeared in connection to it— to maintain and indeed increase distance from the newly disreputable thinker, now tightly associated with someone designated as a traitor. This gives a new context to how Destutt de Tracy introduces his neologism, *ideology*. Here is the passage in full:

> Reste donc que la science de la pensée n'a point encore de nom. On pourroit lui donner celui de *psychologie*. Condillac y paroissoit disposé. Mais ce mot, qui veut dire *science de l'âme*, paroît suposer une connoissance de cet être que sûrement vous ne vous flattez pas de posséder; et il auroit encore l'inconvénient de faire croire que vous vous occupez de la recherche vague des causes premières, tandis que le but de tous vos travaux est la connoissance des effets et de leurs conséquences pratiques.
>
> Je préférerois donc de beaucoup que l'on adoptât le nom *d'idéologie*, ou science des idées.
>
> Il est très-sage, car il ne suppose rien de ce qui est douteux ou inconnu; il ne rappelle à l'esprit aucune idée de cause.
>
> Son sens est très-clair pour tout le monde, si l'on ne considère que celui du mot français *idée*; car chacun sait ce qu'il entend par une idée, quoique peu de gens sachent bien ce que c'est.
>
> Il est rigoureusement exact dans cette hypothèse; car *idéologie* est la traduction littérale de *science des idées*.[109]

It remains the case that the science of thought does not yet have a name. We could perhaps call it *psychology*. Condillac seemed willing to do that. But this word, which means *science of the soul*, seems to require knowledge of this being which you surely do not claim to possess; and it would also have the disadvantage of making it seem that you are occupied with vague research on primary causes, when the aim of your work is the knowledge of effects and their practical consequences.

---

109 Destutt de Tracy, *Mémoire sur la faculté de penser*, p. 71 (Part II, ch. 1, i.e. lecture 2, author's own italics).

> I would much prefer therefore that we adopted the term *ideology*, or science of ideas.
>
> It is very judicious, as it does not imply anything doubtful or unknown; it does not carry any reminder of any idea to do with causes.
>
> Its sense is very clear for everyone, if one just thinks about the French word *idea*, as everyone knows what they mean by an idea, although few people really know what it is.
>
> Everyone would be absolutely accurate in their hypothesis, for *ideology* is the literal translation *science of ideas*.

Très-sage: very wise or very sensible? Both! Tracy's explicit aim is to distance himself from discussions of the soul, but we can see that he also wants to avoid any association with doubt or with the past: he wants this science to look forward, to come from nowhere, to have 'aucune idée de cause', and not to incite doubt. Attempting to avoid association either with discourses of the soul or with philosophical doubt, Tracy has a tricky path to tread. 'Douteux': we have already seen the baggage that *doubt* carries: it is the term Louis-Claude de Saint-Martin used to attack Garat with. 'Aucune idée de cause' is also interesting: it avoids the issue of creation and God of course, and it also avoids nearer causes or influences. It cuts ties with Diderot very efficiently. And, as we know, Destutt de Tracy's *Mémoire sur la faculté de penser* would later be republished with the grander title, *Idéologie proprement dite*. To found a branch of knowledge is indeed to erase the idea that this knowledge pre-existed its foundation. What a brilliant strategy! And thus work that we know Diderot had been engaged in and which we have some compelling evidence for saying was directly influential for these philosophers henceforth known as 'idéologues' or 'idéologistes' after their newly-identified field, is taken further, and in fact the virtuous halls of learning of the new Republic gain credit for encouraging this *new science or branch of learning*, while the danger or repression that lies behind is completely hidden as is any affiliation with Diderot. *Très-sage* indeed.

Just how wise a move it was, whether strategic or strangely fortuitous, to create this distance between the 'idéologues' and Diderot, becomes even clearer when we consider Babeuf's trial. It lasted from February to May 1797, was a cause célèbre, much reported, and indeed the state itself anxiously published stenographed proceedings which were immediately disputed and rival proceedings published.[110] Babeuf's defence speech was very lengthy and detailed, and it started with a thorough consideration of his intellectual debts. The longest, most detailed, and most enthusiastic tribute is to 'Diderot' (that is, Morelly). There are seven pages of 'Diderot' tribute of which this is a typical sample:

> Il me reste à citer une grande autorité en garantie contre l'accusation de provocation [...]. Cette garantie imposante, c'est Diderot. C'est bien le plus déterminé, le plus intrépide, j'ai presque dit le plus fougueux athléte [sic] du système.[111]

> It still remains for me to cite a great authority as protection against the charge of provocation [...]. This imposing protector is Diderot. He is the most determined, the most intrepid, I am tempted to say the most passionate athlete of this system.

So, Diderot's reputation as a ferocious extremist will not be in any way toned down by being called 'a determined intrepid fiery athlete of anti-propertarianism' and by being called that approvingly by someone on trial for plotting to overthrow the state. Babeuf even claims that his plans are softened versions of Diderot's more hardcore texts, and seems to think that if he shows the court that who they are really accusing is Diderot, then they will yield to Diderot's intellectual authority, and also see that Babeuf is not really at fault himself.[112] He was wrong on both counts. Babeuf was sentenced to death on 26 May 1797 and guillotined the following day. Diderot was not in favour. As Tarin describes, 'La réaction s'acharne alors sur ce philosophe. Jugé responsable de tous les excès de

---

110 The official record: *Débats du procès, instruit par la Haute-Cour de Justice, contre Drouet, Babeuf et autres*, 6 vols (Paris: Baudouin, 1797). The rival record: *Journal de la Haute-Cour de Justice, ou L'écho des hommes libres, vrais et sensibles* (facsimile reprint: Paris: Edhis, 1966), edited by Pierre-Nicolas Hésine and his wife, Marie-Agathe Hénault. Laura Mason discusses the official versus rival set-up in her fascinating article, 'The "Bosom of Proof": Criminal Justice and the Renewal of Oral Culture during the French Revolution', *The Journal of Modern History*, 76.1 (March 2004), 29–61 (p. 50), https://doi.org/10.1086/421184.

111 Victor Advielle, *Histoire de Gracchus Babeuf et du babouvisme d'après de nombreux documents inédits*, 2 vols (Paris: chez l'auteur, 1884), vol. 2, pp. 52–59 (p. 52).

112 In the course of his defence, Babeuf says: 'Aux yeux des mêmes accusateurs, Diderot doit paraître le chef suprême de tous les conjurés' [In the eyes of these same accusers, Diderot must seem like the leader in chief of all the plotters] (Advielle, *Histoire de Gracchus Babeuf et du babouvisme*, vol. 2, p. 59).

la Révolution, le "héros des athées" sera présenté comme l'apôtre de la subversion' [reactionary factions then set upon the philosopher. Judged responsible for all the excesses of the Revolution, the 'atheists' hero' was represented as the apostle of subversion].[113] Jean-François de La Harpe (lecturer at the Institut like the *Idéologues* and l'Abbé Augustin Barruel are just two of those whose fanatical excoriation of Diderot Tarin cites.[114]

And who else was lending themselves to the cause of materialism in these years? Shall we mention Donatien Alphonse François, Marquis de Sade? I think we should. Sade's was a powerful voice, and it did not go unheard. His *Justine, ou les malheurs de la vertu* (published anonymously in 1791) was well-known, and (unsurprisingly) caused apoplexy. The seemingly pious *Aline et Valcour* and the utterly brazen *Philosophie dans le boudoir* both come out in 1795 (the former under Sade's name; the latter, anonymously). And then out come *La Nouvelle Justine* (1799) and *L'Histoire de Juliette* (1801).[115] They each contained long disquisitions on materialism.[116] These works were extremely popular and sold out rapidly. A luxury illustrated edition in preparation when Sade was arrested on 6 March 1801 was impounded and destroyed. Sade's extremely transgressive writings certainly contributed to the sensitivity around materialism and its alleged indecency, even if he probably also wrote them in reaction to that same sensitivity and with a view to provoking it. In 1805, famed astronomer (and founder of the Loge des Neuf Sœurs), Jérôme Lalande, publishing his supplement to Sylvain Maréchal's *Dictionnaire des athées anciens et modernes* (1800), will wistfully say: 'Je voudrais bien pouvoir citer M. de Sade; il a bien assez d'esprit, de raisonnement, d'érudition; mais ses infâmes romans de Justine et de Juliette, le font rejeter d'une secte où l'on ne parle que de vertu' [I

---

113 Tarin, *Diderot et la Révolution française*, p. 107; his footnote tells us that 'le héros des athées' [the atheists' hero] was one of the sarcastic terms used by l'abbé Augustin Barruel to lambast Diderot in his *Mémoires pour servir à l'histoire du Jacobinisme* (Hamburg: Fauche, 1798–99), t. 1, ch. 16, p. 335.

114 Tarin, *Diderot et la Révolution française*, pp. 107, 143 (La Harpe also lambasts Babeuf, p. 115).

115 The dating is complex because of false dates being published on the title pages. *L'Histoire de Juliette* was falsely dated to 1797, but in fact came out in 1801. See Michel Delon, 'Note sur le texte [de la *Nouvelle Justine*]', in Donatien Alphonse François, Marquis de Sade, *Œuvres*, ed. by Michel Delon (Paris: Gallimard Pléiade, 1995), vol. 2, p. 1271.

116 See Caroline Warman, *Sade: From Materialism to Pornography* (Oxford: Voltaire Foundation, 2002).

would very much like to include M. de Sade; he has more than enough intelligence, reason and erudition; but his disgraceful novels, Justine and Juliette, mean he must be excluded from a sect in which virtue is the only topic of discussion].[117] So Sade's simultaneous membership (how qualified he is! and Lalande says so from the vantage point of being one of the pre-eminent scientists in the land) and exclusion (how infamous his novels are!) give a sense of what an embarrassing case he was. Even more embarrassing, it seems as if Sade may have been affiliated in some way to the Loge des Neuf Sœurs that Lalande himself had founded, and of which Garat, Cabanis, and Destutt de Tracy were all members.[118] So there is some quite dangerous proximity here.[119] Thus, Sade was no help at all to anyone wishing to pursue materialist research from within the authorised spaces of the government. He only further confirmed the view that materialist tracts were immoral, obscene, and deranged.[120] With Babeuf on one side, trumpeting the wonders of 'Diderot's' ideas on social revolution, and Sade on the other, giving extended monologues on materialist theory to his most vicious characters, it is really no surprise that Destutt de Tracy evokes the safe space of the Institut national, 'cette enceinte' outside which critical voices persist and must be ignored. His coining of the neologism 'idéologie' establishes, in my view, a further layer of protection.

We have said that Cabanis and Destutt de Tracy were successful in their distancing and publication strategies (which include the reinforcing effect of their duet), and also in seeing their view of the inter-relation of

---

117 Sylvain Maréchal, *Dictionnaire des athées anciens et modernes, deuxième édition, augmentée des supplémens de J. Lalande, de plusieurs articles inédits, et d'une notice nouvelle sur Maréchal et ses ouvrages, par J.-B.-L. Germond* (Bruxelles: chez l'éditeur, 1833), p. 84, https://doi.org/10.1522/25051474.

118 Daniel Kerjan, in his entry on this Loge, states that 'Il est désormais établi que Mirabeau et Sade y furent affiliés' [it is henceforth accepted that Mirabeau and Sade were affiliated to it]: *Dictionnaire du grand orient de France au XVIIIe siècle: les cadres et les loges*, ed. by Daniel Kerjan, Alain le Bihan, and Pierre Mollier (Rennes: Presses Universitaires de Rennes, 2012), [p. x]. I have not been able to establish what the evidence for this claim is.

119 I explore what seem to be allusions to Sade in Garat's *Mémoires sur Suard* in my article: Caroline Warman, '"A Little Short Fat Man, Thirty-five Years of Age, Inconceivably Vigorous, and Hairy as a Bear": The Figure of the Philosopher in Sade', in *Sade's Sensibilities*, ed. by Kate Parker and Norbert Sclippa (Lewisburg: Bucknell University Press, 2015), pp. 103–17 (pp. 112–14).

120 Sade, imprisoned (again) in 1801, was interned in Charenton mental asylum in 1803 and died there in 1814.

body and mind influence the thinking of others. But they were not so successful as to avoid their section of the Institut national being closed down on the orders of Napoleon on 23 Jan 1803/3 pluviôse an XI, on the basis of his dislike for their criticism of his régime.[121] In fact, they had been key supporters of his in the Coup du 18 Brumaire (9 November 1799) which raised Napoleon to Consul; Cabanis had presented *Projet d'adresse au peuple français* to the Conseil des cinq-cents, printed at Saint-Cloud on 19 Brumaire (10 November), and on 25 frimaire an VIII (15 December 1799), he published his pro-Napoleonic *Quelques considérations sur l'organisation sociale et particulièrement sur la nouvelle constitution*.[122] He, Garat, and Destutt de Tracy were all made senators, which gave them an annual income of 25,000 Francs, and therefore brought financial security and ease.[123] However, the 'dictature sans dictateur' [dictatorship without a dictator][124] that Cabanis had praised and argued for in his *Quelques considérations* did not, of course, prove to be quite so dictator-free as he had supposed, and they fell under the displeasure of the Premier Consul, who, with his dynastic then religious and imperial ambitions was inevitably moving away from those who might have reminded him of how he came to power, and furthermore, might have held him to account. His irritation with them even when they were trying to please him is evident in his alleged remark after a three-hour speech Garat had given in praise of his victory at Marengo: 'conçois-tu un animal comme Garat? Quelle enfilade de mots! J'ai été obligé de l'écouter pendant trois heures' [have you ever seen an animal like Garat? What a string of words! I was forced to listen to him for three hours straight].[125] Whether Napoleon did say this or not, it is attested (by the Oxford English Dictionary, no less) that it was he who started the re-definition of 'idéologie', which the OED describes as 'abstract speculation; impractical or visionary theorizing'. As we saw, Tracy himself had gone to some pains to establish that his neologism was not abstract or impractical. Politically therefore, from 1803 if not earlier,

---

[121] Emmet Kennedy, '"Ideology" from Destutt de Tracy to Marx', *Journal of the History of Ideas*, 40.3 (1979), 353–68 (pp. 354–55), https://doi.org/10.2307/2709242.
[122] Yves Pouliquen discusses the role of the Ideologues in the Coup du 18 Brumaire in some detail. Pouliquen, *Cabanis, un idéologue*, pp. 152–56.
[123] Pouliquen, *Cabanis, un idéologue*, p. 163.
[124] Quoted in Pouliquen, *Cabanis, un idéologue*, p. 152.
[125] Pouliquen, *Cabanis, un idéologue*, p. 202 (14 juillet 1800/25 Messidor an VIII).

their influence was much reduced. However, maybe even in Napoleon's derisive redefinition of 'idéologie' as abstract theorising, we can see a mark of their success. If it is abstract theorising, then there is nothing for the censors to worry about, and indeed there is no sense that Cabanis's or Destutt de Tracy's publication plans met with any obstacles, unlike Sade (the luxury illustrated edition of whose *Nouvelle Justine* and *Histoire de Juliette* being destroyed down to the very last copy) or indeed Naigeon, whose introduction to his edition of the Bordeaux copy of Montaigne's *Essais* would be suppressed (by its own publisher, Pierre Didot) because of the direct appeal it contained to Napoleon to continue to control priests, this introduction being dated 15 Germinal, an X (5 April 1802), and thus due to appear three days before the ratification of the Concordat between Napoleon and the Pope on Easter Sunday 1802 (8 April 1802).[126] So we can see that there was active censorship and real political sensitivities to negotiate, and therefore measure the extent of Cabanis and Destutt de Tracy's success. The one possibly problematic text that Cabanis wrote, his *Lettre à Fauriel*, would not be published until 1824, sixteen years after his death, despite it having supposedly circulated in manuscript very freely.[127] It contains a more concise and more forthright statement of his materialist thinking than the *Rapports*, but is otherwise rather similar to it.[128] And nonetheless it attracted accusations of militant atheism, so much so that Cabanis's widow protested that the edition was inaccurate

---

126 As we discuss below. Philippe Desan, '"Cette espèce de manuscrit des *Essais*": l'édition Naigeon de 1802 et son "Avertissement" censuré', *Montaigne Studies*, 10 (Oct 1998), 7–34 (pp. 19, 33n). See also H. Mazel, 'La Fameuse Préface de Naigeon', *Bulletin de la société des amis de Montaigne*, 2.4 (1938), 28–29. Mazel states that, 'il ne reste de cette édition 1802 avec préface que huit exemplaires, ayant appartenu au Premier Consul, à ses hauts fonctionnaires, et à Didot' [of this 1802 edition with preface there are only eight copies left, having belonged to the First Consul, his high-ranking functionaries, and to the publisher, Didot], p. 29.

127 Pierre-Jean-Georges Cabanis, 'Lettre à M.F. sur les causes premières', in *Œuvres philosophiques*, ed. by Claude Lehec and Jean Cazeneuve (Paris: Presses Universitaires de France, 1956), vol. 2, pp. 255–98 (p. 256, n. 1). The 'Lettre' was written in 1806–07, and published in 1824 by J. F. Bérard, with notes. Bérard writes: 'Une foule de copies manuscrites de cette lettre sont répandues dans le public depuis la mort de Cabanis [en 1808]' [many manuscript copies of this letter spread amongst the public after Cabanis's death in 1808] (Cabanis, *Lettre, posthume et inédite de Cabanis à M. F\*\*\* sur les causes premières, avec des notes par F. Bérard* (Paris: Gabon, 1824).

128 See for example his discussion of the: 'Connaissance approfondie de l'organisation humaine', '[ses] besoins' (p. 260); 'l'être sensible doué d'imagination' (p. 265); 'la sensibilité' (p. 266); 'l'ouvrage du jeu des organes' (p. 267); 'les organes de l'homme' (p. 272); memory (p. 272); 'la percussion' or 'collision mutuelle des corps' (pp.

and that it traduced the image of her virtuous husband.[129] It was not inaccurate, it was just that atheism and materialism were still tightly associated, still publicly unavowable, and still subject to censorship. We alluded to Naigeon coming a-cropper in 1802; earlier we mentioned his outraged denial of Diderot's authorship of Morelly's *Code de la nature* in the introduction to his edition of Diderot's *Œuvres* of 1798. It is time to return to Naigeon and to these two introductions, each embattled for different reasons, before we reach the final installment of this story with Garat's *Mémoires sur le XVIIIe siècle et sur M. Suard* (1820) and Naigeon's *Mémoires sur la vie et les ouvrages de M. Diderot*, whose publication date is advertised on the title page as 1821, but which in fact came out in 1823 (and was banned in December of that year).[130]

Let us however close this chapter by returning to Cabanis and Destutt de Tracy to state that, without there being a signed and sworn affidavit as to their knowledge of Diderot's *Éléments de physiologie*, there is nonetheless considerable cumulative textual evidence that they did indeed know it, and furthermore, that they were influenced by its hypotheses and are attempting to pursue the lines of research it lays out. The strength of the argument is perhaps best shown when we turn it round: is it plausible, given their general position with respect to physiological determinism, and the multiple moments of textual synchronicity, that they had never read it and were not using it?

---

274, 280); 'le perfectionnement' (p. 295); materialist tableau (pp. 276–77); advice to avoid words 'athéisme' and 'matérialisme' (pp. 268, 271).
129 Cabanis, 'Lettre à M.F. sur les causes premières', p. 256, n. 1.
130 Adams, *Bibliographie des œuvres de Diderot, 1739–1900*, vol. 2, p. 141.

# 10. 1798, 1802: Naigeon, the *Œuvres de Diderot*, and the Censored Preface to Montaigne

We return now to Jacques-André Naigeon, member, like Dominique-Joseph Garat, Pierre-Jean-Georges Cabanis, and Antoine Louis Claude Destutt de Tracy, of the Institut national's Sciences morales et politiques class, although his section was 'Morale', as we may remember. No lecture of his finds its way into the *Mémoires de l'Institut national*, although he is recorded as having sat on a committee charged with determining the appropriate way of acknowledging the death of one of its members.[1] In 1798, however, he brought out Diderot's *Œuvres* in fifteen volumes, with an angry preface, explaining that he had had to defer his *Mémoires historiques et philosophiques sur la vie et les ouvrages de Denis Diderot* yet again because of the outrageous claims made about Diderot's authorship of the *Code de la nature*, and because other publishers were planning to bring out Diderot's works, replete with texts wrongly attributed to him, based on truncated versions of the texts; he is eloquent and multi-clausal in his ire.[2] And so out the *Œuvres* reluctantly come, with yet another headline allusion to the *Mémoires* whose composition he has

---

1 *Mémoires de l'Institut national des sciences et des arts: sciences morales et politiques* (Paris: Baudouin, Imprimeur de l'Institut national, an VII (Fructidor an VII/Aug-Sept 1799)), vol. 2, pp. 681–94.
2 Jacques-André Naigeon, 'Préface de l'éditeur', in Denis Diderot, *Œuvres* (Paris: Desray et Déterville, 1798), vol. 1, pp. v–xxxiii. 'Babœuf' is lambasted on pp. v–vi; other editions of Diderot's supposed *Œuvres* are lambasted on p. viii; Bouillon's faulty edition of his philosophy articles from the *Encyclopédie* are lambasted

unfortunately had to interrupt, on the first page of the 'Préface de l'éditeur' in the first volume, complete with supporting footnote; both allusion and supporting footnote are repeated only a few pages later.[3] This culminates in the following virtuous declaration (which follows on from further rebuttal of Diderot's authorship of the *Code de la nature* and its false principles):

> [...] je ne crus pas devoir balancer un moment à différer encore de quelques mois l'impression d'un ouvrage souvent annoncé, trop attendu peut-être, mais qui du moins ne sera pas sans quelque intérêt pour la famille et les amis de Diderot. Rassuré par cette idée consolante, je m'occupais aussi-tôt à mettre en ordre les matériaux que j'avois déjà recueillis pour l'édition que je projetois.[4]

> I thought it right not to hesitate about deferring for a further few months the publication of a work which had often been announced, and for which people had been waiting too long perhaps, but which at least will not be without some interest for the family and friends of Diderot. Reassured by this consoling idea, I turned straightaway to the materials that I had already gathered for the edition that I was planning and started putting them in order.

The order in which Naigeon presents his 'ouvrage' and the 'matériaux' is very telling, as are the words he chooses respectively for, on the one hand, the 'work' and on the other, the 'materials'. Even the syntax is a bit odd: his preceding criticism of the threat posed by these other projected *Œuvres de Diderot* with their erroneous and dangerous inclusion of the *Code de la nature*, leads one to suppose that he is saying he should not hesitate for a second to get on with his own planned (and authorised) *Œuvres de Diderot*, but no: it is that he should not hesitate for one second to put the *Mémoires* on the back-burner, despite the fact that it has frequently been announced and has perhaps been too long awaited. He does not turn to the edition of which this is supposed to be the preface until the following sentence. Everything he is saying tells us how important the *Mémoires* is, more important in his eyes than the *Œuvres* themselves. As we have already seen in relation to the article on

---

   on pp. xxiv–xxvi. He also attacks Grimm as an editor of Diderot's work in the *Correspondance littéraire* in vol. 13, pp. vi–viii.
3  Naigeon, 'Préface de l'éditeur', in Diderot, *Œuvres* (1798), vol. 1, pp. v, vii.
4  Naigeon, 'Préface de l'éditeur', in Diderot, *Œuvres* (1798), vol. 1, p. ix.

Diderot he wrote for the *Encyclopédie méthodique*, he repeatedly, urgently, draws our attention to them.[5] In an 'avertissement de l'éditeur' which we find in volume 12 of these *Œuvres*, sandwiched between the main text of *La Religieuse* and what we now know as the *Préface-annexe*, but which Naigeon entitles *Extrait de la Correspondance littéraire de M\*\*\*, année 1770*, he mentions them again, again with a supporting footnote, declaring that this volume 'sera très-incessamment sous presse' [will be published imminently].[6] He is also telling us when he was composing the *Mémoires*, or at least when he claimed to be writing them. His written statements, from the 'Diderot' article of 1792 to the preface to Diderot's *Œuvres*, tell us that he started work on it in the six months after Diderot's death, was busily engaged with it when writing the dictionary article, and was again busy with it in 1798, having not quite finished it (he had had to set it aside to bring out the edition, as he says in the preface), but very nearly (as he says in vol. 12). What is actually in it, of course he does not say, other than that it will deal with 'celui de ces ouvrages qui m'a paru le plus profond' [the particular work of his that I thought most profound].[7] No doubt this is why he attaches so much importance to it, and spends so much time over it. Why he did not publish it soon after the edition came out as he seems to have expected does not perhaps need much commentary, given what has already been said about the unabated (or perhaps renewed) hostility of the authorities towards materialism and Diderot during these years. Yet there is something more to be said about the way Naigeon presents Diderot's works and how he perceives his connection to them, and his role as editor and even censor.

As is already abundantly clear, Naigeon's commitment to Diderot is total, and yet it has a certain profile: it is morally pure, frequently evocative of the tight-knit circle of family and friends, and it likes a certain sort of seriousness. Thus, Naigeon evokes (in relation to writing the *Mémoires*) 'ce plaisir si doux, et si pur qu'on éprouve à faire une bonne action' [this very sweet and pure pleasure that we feel when we

---

5   See also Naigeon, 'Préface de l'éditeur', in Diderot, *Œuvres* (1798), vol. 1, p. xxiii.
6   Denis Diderot, *Œuvres* (Paris: Desray et Déterville, 1798), vol. 12, p. 261n.
7   Naigeon, 'Diderot', in *Encyclopédie méthodique: Philosophie ancienne et moderne*, 3 vols (Paris: Panckoucke, 1791–94), vol. 2 (1792), p. 228, quoted above in Chapter 2.

do something good],⁸ about how (again in relation to the *Mémoires*) it would not be 'sans quelque intérêt pour la famille et les amis de Diderot' [without some interest for the family and friends of Diderot],⁹ while also declaring that he is 'pour plusieurs ouvrages de Diderot, un censeur plus rigoureux que le public' [in the case of many of Diderot's works, a harsher censor than the public],¹⁰ which is, in fact, the rather odd and not merely defensive statement with which he closes his preface. This is a curiously intense combination of attitudes, the key to which is perhaps given on the penultimate page of the preface; this is the letter containing Diderot's instructions regarding his manuscripts, written in 1773 as Diderot prepared to depart for St Petersburg, and which Naigeon describes as follows: it is 'un écrit qui ne s'est jamais offert à mes yeux, sans me causer la plus tendre emotion' [a piece of writing that I was never able to look at without feeling the most tender emotion].¹¹ The mention of his eyes evokes first intellect and then tears. Giving this 'écrit' in full in a footnote, he states that he cannot deny himself the pleasure of copying out the note, the precious original of which he keeps safe, and which will transmit his name to posterity, to the 'vrais amis des lettres, et aux jeunes gens qui s'appliquent à l'étude de la philosophie rationnelle' [the true friends of letters and to those young people who apply themselves to the study of rational philosophy].¹² When we weigh up the respective gravitas of the true friends of letters and the young people who apply themselves to rational philosophy, it is clear that the prize goes to the youthful hard workers. Yet his own friendship for Diderot does not, he says, imply a lack of judgement: 'l'amitié ne m'a point fait illusion: peut-être même trouvera-t-on qu'elle m'a rendu quelquefois trop sévère' [friendship has not blinded me: perhaps people will even think that it has made me too harsh at times]; this is the statement that leads to his saying he has been a harsher censor even than the public. Clearly, then, he sees his role as one involving the exercise of judgement, understood as involving disapproval and censorship where

---

8    Naigeon, 'Préface de l'éditeur', in Diderot, *Œuvres* (1798), vol. 1, pp. vii–viii.
9    Naigeon, 'Préface de l'éditeur', in Diderot, *Œuvres* (1798), vol. 1, p. ix.
10   Naigeon, 'Préface de l'éditeur', in Diderot, *Œuvres* (1798), vol. 1, p. xxxiii.
11   Naigeon, 'Préface de l'éditeur', in Diderot, *Œuvres* (1798), vol. 1, p. xxxii.
12   Naigeon, 'Préface de l'éditeur', in Diderot, *Œuvres* (1798), vol. 1, p. xxxiin.

necessary. This interpretation does indeed seem to be supported by Diderot's instructions:

> Comme je fais un long voyage, et que j'ignore ce que le sort me prépare, s'il arrivoit qu'il disposât de ma vie, je recommande à ma femme et à mes enfants de remettre tous mes manuscrits à monsieur Naigeon, qui aura pour un homme qu'il a tendrement aimé, et qui l'a bien payé de retour, le soin d'arranger, de revoir et de publier tout ce qui lui paroîtra ne devoir nuire ni à ma mémoire, ni à la tranquillité de personne. C'est ma volonté, et j'espère qu'elle ne trouvera aucune contradiction. A Paris, ce juin 1773. Diderot.[13]

> As I am going on a long journey and do not know what fate may have in store for me, were it to happen that it took my life, I request my wife and children to hand over all my manuscripts to Mr Naigeon, who will have for a man whom he has tenderly loved, and who has amply repaid him, the task of organising, reviewing, and publishing anything which he considers will not do any damage to my memory or to anyone's security. This is my will, and I hope no one will contradict it. Paris, June 1773, Diderot

We see that the bond of love precedes (and sanctions) the bond of duty, and that Diderot does not prescribe complete publication, but only 'tout ce qui lui paroîtra ne devoir nuire ni à ma mémoire, ni à la tranquillité de personne' [anything which he considers will not do any damage to my memory or to anyone's security]. That the 'tranquillity' of Diderot's family or even Naigeon himself was in question, at whatever level of intensity, is indisputable; Diderot's reputation was already damaged, as we have seen. This edition is therefore an interpretation of Diderot's wishes that is also, one assumes, an attempt to repair that damage, restore his reputation, and ensure the tranquillity of all concerned. Certainly, Naigeon's predilection was for philosophy, as the works which he edited or co-wrote for the baron d'Holbach and during Diderot's lifetime attest. But that aspect is in any case the one he chooses to emphasise, given Diderot's instructions. And thus the fifteen-volume *Œuvres* present three volumes of philosophy, followed by one of (and on) drama, three volumes of philosophical articles

---

13   Naigeon, 'Préface de l'éditeur', in Diderot, *Œuvres* (1798), vol. 1, p. xxxiin; Denis Diderot, *Correspondance*, ed. by Georges Roth and Jean Varloot (Paris: Minuit, 1965), vol. 12, p. 231 (3 June 1773).

from the *Encyclopédie*, two about Antiquity (the work on Seneca and the reigns of Claudius and Nero), three of fiction, the final three with the art criticism of the *Salons* of 1765 and 1767. The three volumes of fiction, we note, are sandwiched in towards the end. Naigeon's Diderot is the mighty philosopher, the tireless servant of the *Encyclopédie*, the dramatist, the critic. And also, as it happens, the writer of some rather tasteless fiction, which Naigeon, as his true friend and *censor*, would have been very happy to have repressed, as he indicates on the final page and in the final note of the 'Préface': the word 'censeur' is followed by a footnote call, referring readers to the twelfth volume:

> *Voyez*, entre autres, tome XII de cette édition, l'Avertissement de l'Editeur, imprimé à la suite de *la Religieuse*, et les notes que j'ai jointes à l'écrit qui a pour titre: *Principes de politique des souverains*.

> See, amongst others, the Editor's Announcement, in volume 12 of this edition, published at the end of *The Nun*, and the notes that I have attached to the piece of writing entitled *Political Principles for Sovereigns*.

When we follow up this emphatically visible cross-reference, we find eleven pages of emphatic excoriation of the entirety of this *Extrait de la Correspondance littéraire de M\*\*\**, année 1770 (or 'Préface-annexe'), the letters of which, he declares, he would have 'certainement retranchées, si j'avois été le premier éditeur de ce roman' [have certainly cut, had I been the first editor of this novel],[14] because they are in bad taste and weaken the effect. Fortified by a witticism of Voltaire's, comparing publishers to sacristans who collect old rags and then get people to worship them, Naigeon sets out his own more discerning stall:

> 'Tous, dit [Voltaire], rassemblent des guenilles qu'ils veulent faire révérer. Mais on ne doit imprimer d'un auteur que ce qu'il a écrit de digne d'être lu. Avec cette règle honnête, il y auroit moins de livres et plus de goût dans le public.' Convaincu depuis long-tems de la vérité de cette observation, je n'ai pu voir sans peine qu'on imprimât *la Religieuse* et *Jacques le fataliste* avec tous les défauts qui les déparent plus ou moins aux yeux des lecteurs d'un goût sévère et délicat. Un éditeur qui [...] n'auroit eu pour chérir, pour respecter sa mémoire, d'autres motifs que les progrès qu'il a fait faire à la raison, à l'esprit philosophique, et la forte

---

[14] Naigeon, in Diderot, *Œuvres* (1798), vol. 12, p. 255.

impulsion qu'il a donnée à son siècle [...] auroit réduit *Jacques le Fataliste* à cent pages, ou peut-être même il ne l'eût jamais publié.¹⁵

As Voltaire puts it, 'They just assemble any old bits and pieces they want people to revere. But of any given author, only what is worthy of being read should be published. If this honest rule were followed, there would be fewer books and the public would have more taste.' Long convinced of the truth of this observation, I was pained to see that *The Nun and Jacques the Fatalist* were being published with all the defects which tarnish them more or less in the eyes of those readers with a severe and delicate taste. An editor whose [....] only reason to hold an author dear and to respect his memory was because of the advances he made in thought and philosophical thinking and the way he pushed the whole century forward [...] would have reduced *Jacques the Fatalist* to a hundred pages, or he might not have published it at all.

However, as he grumpily points out, 'ces retranchements, que *Jacques le Fataliste* et *la Religieuse* semblent exiger' [these cuts, which *Jacques the Fatalist* and *The Nun* seem to require] are now pointless: 'la première impression, toujours si difficile à effacer, est faite' [the first impression, always so difficult to eradicate, is made].¹⁶ Interesting, here, to see the two meanings of 'impression', that is, *printing* and *impression*, both being evoked and presented in complete alignment. One may wish to suggest that Naigeon's statements about the bad taste of Diderot's fiction and the desirability of cutting the bad parts are straightforwardly strategic on Naigeon's part, made with a view to preempting any attack on Diderot's virtue, and therefore that we should not take them at face value. After all, he does actually publish *Jacques le fataliste* and *La Religieuse* in the *Œuvres*, and he publishes the more straightforwardly obscene *Bijoux indiscrets* too. This 'Avertissement' and the remarks he makes in the 'Préface', from this point of view, would simply be false protestations of virtuous restraint, which actually make it possible for him to go ahead and publish the offending works in full, works which he himself does not approve of and would never have published, works which Diderot (he says) entirely recognised were unacceptable, but works which happen already to have been published, so he might as well go ahead and give them in corrected editions anyway. It would certainly be true to say that

---

15  Naigeon, in Diderot, *Œuvres* (1798), vol. 12, p. 260.
16  Naigeon, in Diderot, *Œuvres* (1798), vol. 12, p. 264.

it is strategic of Naigeon to present the novels in this way, but his being strategic does not necessarily preclude his agreeing with the position he articulates, that is, that both novels are weakened by the obscenity (he objects to the mother superior's orgasm) and the lack of nobility (he disapproves of Jacques's low station and low way of speaking). Of course, we cannot know what Naigeon *really* thought, but we can read what he says and look at what he does. And in this context, some of the things he says, in particular about *Jacques le fataliste*, seem to indicate a certain view about what would have been a more effective way for Diderot to write, one which may prove helpful when considering the *Mémoires*, and we meet again the reference to the 'lecteurs d'un goût sévère et délicat' [readers with a severe and delicate taste]. He writes that it is not that we do not find here and there 'des réflexions très-fines, souvent profondes, telles enfin qu'on les peut attendre d'un esprit ferme, étendu, hardi, et qui sait généraliser ses idées' [very subtle and often profound thoughts, such as we might expect to find in a firm, expansive, and bold mind, one which knows how to generalize its ideas] and he goes on to say:

> Mais ces réflexions si philosophiques, placées dans la bouche d'un valet, tel qu'il n'en exista jamais; amenées d'ailleurs peu naturellement, et n'étant point liées à un sujet grave, dont toutes les parties fortement enchaînées entre elles s'éclaircissent, se fortifient réciproquement, et forment un tout, un système UN, n'ont fait aucune sensation. Ce sont quelques paillettes d'or éparses, enfouies dans un fumier où personne assurément ne sera tenté de les chercher; et, par cela même, des idées isolées, stériles et perdues.[17]

> But these very philosophical thoughts, being placed in the mouth of a servant such as never did exist, introduced moreover in a highly unnatural way, entirely unconnected to any serious subject in which all the parts are strongly linked together and thereby illuminate and strengthen each other to construct a whole, one system AS ONE, made no sensation of any sort. They are merely a few scattered flecks of gold buried in a midden where for sure no one will feel any temptation to go and find them, and for this reason, they are ideas which are isolated, sterile, and lost.

---

17  Naigeon, in Diderot, *Œuvres* (1798), vol. 12, pp. 261–62.

What he criticises is the way in which the 'very subtle and often profound thoughts' are scattered about, *not* brought together or interlinked, and therefore *fail* to mutually illuminate and strengthen each other or to form a whole, and so go unnoticed. These thoughts are flecks of gold buried in a midden, no one will *want* to go and look for them, and thus the ideas remain isolated, sterile and lost. This view, in conjunction with his explicit statement about getting rid of three quarters of *Jacques le fataliste*, suggest that Naigeon has a particular technique in mind; the identification and collecting of these flecks of gold or ideas, freeing them from the muck, joining them together into a clearly connected, consistently serious whole so that they stop languishing in isolation and start being productive. The mind that can do this work, the firm, far-reaching, and audacious mind, is specifically one which knows how to generalise its ideas. If generalisation and seriousness is what Naigeon prizes, no wonder he does not like the all-too-specific, class-located, and generally ungeneralisable Jacques!

The rather striking repetition and typography in the phrase 'un système UN', which I have translated as *one system AS ONE*, is instructive in this respect: Naigeon wants something emphatically unified and generally applicable, probably something abstract. Interestingly, this phrase is also an allusion to and an echo of a formula we find in *Jacques le fataliste*. Diderot's phrase is in fact 'une cause une' (he does not appear to capitalise the second indefinite article). This same phrase also appears in the *Rêve de d'Alembert*, in the *Observations sur Hemsterhuis*, and in the *Réfutation d'Helvétius*.[18] We find something similar in the *Éléments de physiologie*: 'Sans la sensibilité et la loi de continuité dans la contexture animale, sans ces deux qualités l'animal ne peut être *un*' [Without sensibility and the law of continuity in the intermixture of animal parts, without these two qualities the animal cannot be *one*].[19] Here, as we see, the connected wholeness, the oneness, of the animal is emphasised typographically, via italicisation. Clearly, in any case, the notion of the

---

18   With thanks to Ruggero Sciuto for sending me these details, private correspondence, 23 August 2017.
19   Denis Diderot, *Éléments de physiologie*, ed. by Jean Mayer, *Œuvres complètes*, DPV (Paris: Hermann, 1987), vol. 17, pp. 261–574 (p. 307) [hereafter DPV]/Diderot, *Éléments de physiologie*, ed. by Paolo Quintili (Paris: Champion, 2004), p. 122 [hereafter PQ]/Diderot, *Éléments de physiologie*, ed. by Motoichi Terada (Paris: Éditions Matériologiques, 2019), p. 131 [hereafter MT].

connected whole is a recurrent one, and almost certainly a very subtle and profound thought of the variety Naigeon approves of, a 'paillette d'or' or fleck of gold. He uses the same syntactical emphasis when he talks elsewhere about Michel de Montaigne being 'un homme UN' [a man AS ONE].[20]

This 'elsewhere' in which he mentions Montaigne in fact comes from the editing project he was undertaking in parallel with the *Œuvres de Diderot*, the first appearance in print of the *Essais* in what is known as the 'Exemplaire de Bordeaux', in which Montaigne added copious annotations to the 1588 edition of his *Essais*, thereby extending the text by about a third.[21] Philippe Desan tells the story of how François de Neufchâteau (1750–1828), man of letters and politician, found out about this annotated copy in the 1770s and never forgot about it; as Minister of the Interior in 1798–99, he commanded that it be sent to Paris from the Bibliothèque publique de Bordeaux in preparation for a new edition, and it was Naigeon to whom he gave the task.[22] Naigeon, like him, was also a member of the Institut national, although Neufchâteau was in the 'classe des Lettres'; unlike Naigeon, but like Garat, Cabanis, and Destutt de Tracy, Neufchâteau was also a member of the Loge des Neuf Sœurs, and had been, from its creation. So, as we keep on finding, there are a good number of connections and overlapping relationships. Naigeon's edition was ready to come out in 1802, with an extensive preface including the usual anti-clerical rants and dated 'Paris, 15 Germinal, an X' (5 April 1802), just three days before the ratification, on Easter Day (18 Germinal/8 April) of the Concordat between Napoleon Bonaparte and the Pope in which Roman Catholicism was re-established as the principal religion of France. Naigeon's preface was not merely anti-clerical, it directly exhorted Napoleon to keep the priesthood under control.[23] And

---

20 Jacques-André Naigeon, 'Avertissement de l'éditeur', ed. by Philippe Desan, *Montaigne Studies*, 10 (Oct 1998), 35–78 (p. 36).

21 https://montaignestudies.uchicago.edu/h/bordeaux_copy/ (information in English); Nicolas Barbey, 'Comment Montaigne écrivait ses Essais : l'Exemplaire de Bordeaux', *Le Blog Gallica*, 6 July 2016, https://gallica.bnf.fr/blog/06072016/comment-montaigne-ecrivait-ses-essais-lexemplaire-de-bordeaux (information in French, and the digitised version).

22 Philippe Desan, 'Naigeon et l'"avertissement" censuré de l'édition des *Essais* de 1802', *Montaigne Studies*, 10 (1998), 7–33 (pp. 7–13).

23 Naigeon, 'Avertissement de l'éditeur', ed. by Desan, 72. (via Voltaire: 'Qui conduit des soldats, peut gouverner des prêtres' [who leads soldiers can govern priests]);

thus the preface was suppressed, by the publisher Didot himself; of the initial preface only a few pages were kept, and of the original print-run only eight copies survived, owned by Didot, Napoleon, and some of his top officials.[24] Meanwhile, the new edition of Montaigne duly came out, with its much briefer and politer preface. When we consult the original, however, which we now can, thanks to Desan's critical edition, we find an absolute gold mine (rather than just a few gold flecks interspersed in a giant midden) of curious and impassioned statements about what it means to be an editor, which help prepare us for the much longer curiosity that is the *Mémoires*.

Firstly, then, Naigeon claims that his edition is 'une copie rigoureusement exacte [...] Je ne crois pas avoir oublié un mot, une syllabe, une lettre' [a strictly accurate copy [...] I do not think I missed a word, a syllable or a letter].[25] This is a firm statement of total adherence to the autograph, and it is absolutely false: all the way through, Naigeon altered the spelling to make it more archaic. Thus 'aucteur' for 'auteur', 'doulce' for 'douce' and so on. Philippe Desan analyses the process of archaization in some detail, speculating with Pierre Bonnet that Naigeon did this in order to intensify 'l'apparence de sincérité' [appearance of sincerity].[26] From our point of view, in any case, the important thing is that Naigeon utterly denies having changed even a letter, while having in fact altered the spelling in a very thorough-going way. In fact, he has quite a curious idea of what it is to be a scholar and an editor: in his view, it is not an occupation or a service so much as a life or death passion, as we see in the following portrait, which first outlines the limitations of the scholar, and then, unexpectedly, starts to describe something *more imperious*:

---

further anti-clerical rants: p. 44 (this is also a rant against women), 65, 71 (on p. 73 he turns against the newspapers).

24 Desan details what happened, Desan, 'Naigeon et l'"avertissement" censuré de l'édition des *Essais* de 1802', 31–33, quoting in particular Gabriel Peignot (Gabriel Peignot, *Répertoire des bibliographies spéciales, curieuses et instructives*, 1810, Paris Renouard p. 92) and H. Mazel (H. Mazel, 'La Fameuse Préface de Naigeon', *Bulletin de la société des amis de Montaigne*, 2.4 (1938), 28–29).

25 Naigeon, 'Avertissement de l'éditeur', ed. by Desan, 44.

26 Desan, 'Naigeon et l'"avertissement" censuré de l'édition des *Essais* de 1802', 27. He is quoting Pierre Bonnet, 'Évolution et structure du texte des *Essais*', in *Pour une édition critique des Essais*, ed. by Marcel Françon (Cambridge: Schoenhof's Foreign Books, 1965), p. 16.

> L'érudit a dans la tête plus de mots que d'idées; il est sur-tout incapable de cette attention forte et continue, qui ne suffit pas sans doute pour reculer la limite d'une science ou d'un art, mais sans laquelle on ne fait guere de découvertes ni dans l'une ni dans l'autre. Il est même assez difficile que la culture des sciences exactes et expérimentales, ou celle de la philosophie rationnelle ait pour lui un grand attrait: une passion plus impérieuse le domine et l'entraîne; il faut qu'il y cède; sa raison, sa vie même en dépend; il faut qu'il corrige, qu'il restitue des textes, qu'il collationne des manuscrits, qu'il recueille des variantes, qu'il compile, ou qu'il meure.[27]

> The man of learning has more words than ideas in his head; above all, he is incapable of that intense and continued attention which is probably not enough in itself to push at the boundaries of the sciences or arts, but without which no discovery of any sort can be made in either. Even cultivating the exact and experimental sciences is quite difficult for him, and nor does rational philosophy have any great attraction: a more imperious passion dominates and drives him; he has to yield to it; his reason, even his life depends upon it; he has to correct and restore texts, compare manuscripts, gather variants, compile, or die.

This description of the desultory scholar with more words than ideas and not a lot of concentration or even that much interest transmutes in the most surprising way into the portrait of a person who is driven and obsessed by his editorial work, utterly unable to withstand the compulsion to correct and restore texts, collate manuscripts, list variants, and just simply compile—in the case of this last verb, there is not even an object; the activity itself is the driver. And without it, he will die. Why is Naigeon saying this? Has editorial work ever been described, before or since, with such fervour? In its intensity and strangeness, this passage sticks out of its context—a discussion of Pierre Coste's edition of the *Essais*—and it cannot be simply a description (either appreciative or mocking) of Coste as an editor, as Naigeon immediately follows on with a description of his own editorial conscientiousness.[28] Nor does he appear to be satirising himself, although a certain ironic self-consciousness is clearly on display. It sounds like nothing so much as a

---

27 Naigeon, 'Avertissement de l'éditeur', ed. by Desan, 49–50.
28 'J'ai vérifié sur le texte des meilleures éditions des auteurs classiques tous les passages cités par Montaigne' [I cross-checked in the best editions all the passages Montaigne quotes from classic authors] (Naigeon, 'Avertissement de l'éditeur', ed. by Desan, 50).

personal avowal—a confession, perhaps—of an overmastering passion, which in revealing itself also describes itself and details its activities. First in the list of activities are correcting and restoring texts, and as we see from what he did with the hitherto unpublished *Exemplaire de Bordeaux* of Montaigne's *Essais*, correcting and restoring do not necessarily involve following the autograph exactly; they might involve restoring the text to an invented idealised archaic version. When we consider this in parallel with Naigeon's remarks about an improved version of *Jacques le fataliste*, that is, one reduced by 75%, shorn of characterisation, and retaining only the golden flecks of the 'réflexions très-fines, souvent profondes', we begin to see that he had a very specific idea of editing, one that is indeed subservient to the text in production, but whereby that text is an ideal or idealised one, not necessarily the one that the author had produced. If Naigeon decides not to amend ('restore') texts which have already been published, it is because there is no point, as 'la première impression, toujours si difficile à effacer, est faite' [the first impression, always so difficult to eradicate, is made], but in the case of texts which have never been published, as with the *Exemplaire de Bordeaux*, there is more room for manoeuvre. In fact, with Montaigne's *Essais*, he contented himself with the archaising of the spelling and some reworking of the punctuation.[29] But from what we have seen before, and from what he says in the following passage, we can see that he envisages more far-reaching 'corrections', ones which, he alleges, *secretly delight the author of real taste*:

> Ces petites nettetés du style qui consistent, tantôt dans un simple choix d'expressions plus sonores, plus musicales, plus douces à l'oreille, ce juge si dédaigneux et superbe; tantôt dans la suppression de quelques ornements ambitieux; ici dans le soin d'eviter certaines formules dont le retour trop fréquent *manière* le style; là dans l'art d'éteindre à propos des lumieres trop brillantes qui nuisent à l'harmonie, à l'effet de l'ensemble, en multipliant les effets particuliers et secondaires: toutes ces diverses corrections, plus ou moins importantes, échappent sans doute aux gens du monde, la plupart peu instruits [...]: mais un écrivain de grand goût, un auteur qui se contente, comme Horace, d'un petit nombre de lecteurs, [...] s'applaudit en secret de ces corrections très légeres, minutieuses même en apparence, mais qui ajoutent d'autant plus de prix à un

---

29  On the question of punctuation, see Desan, 'Naigeon et l'"avertissement" censuré de l'édition des *Essais* de 1802', 26.

ouvrage, que les défauts qu'elles font disparoître étoient peu sensibles, et exigeoient, par cela même, pour être apperçus, un tact plus fin, plus sûr, et un sentiment plus exquis du beau et des convenances.[30]

Those little stylistic touches which consist sometimes in simply choosing expressions which are more sonorous, more musical, sweeter to the ear – that proud judge who is so hard to please – sometimes in suppressing a few ambitious ornaments, here in taking care to avoid certain expressions whose over-frequent appearance *manners* the style, there in the art of purposely dimming some of the illuminations which shine too bright and disrupt the harmony and effect of the whole, by multiplying some of the specific and secondary effects: all these diverse and more or less significant corrections no doubt escape the notice of people of the world, most of whom have very little education [...]: but a writer of great taste, an author who, like Horace, is happy with just a few readers,[...] secretly applauds these very slight corrections, minuscule in appearance, but which add all the more value to a work, the defects they remove having been barely perceptible in the first place and for that very reason having required a finer and more skilful touch and a more exquisite sentiment of beauty and of what is proper.

This lyrical flight in praise of the correction of texts is just one sentence, lightly abridged for the sake of length. Yet how full it still is! How much Naigeon has to say about the aesthetically enhancing capacities of correction! What a pile-up of carefully balanced clauses! This is a paean to the corrector, not to the writer, and also, not to the re-writer; this is not a description of Montaigne re-writing his own work, and in any case, as we know, Montaigne did not rewrite existing sentences so much as add to them. So this is not about Montaigne's amplificatory work on the *Essais* or about Naigeon's editing of them, given that his alterations were limited to the archaization of the spelling and the changing of the punctuation. This is very specifically about the corrector who does not himself (definitely a *him*; Naigeon sees the world he values as masculine)[31] generate a text but who comes along subsequently, and improves it in many ways, the corrections being 'plus ou moins importantes' [more or less significant] while remaining invisible to the

---

30 Naigeon, 'Avertissement de l'éditeur', ed. by Desan, 70–71.
31 We referenced his outbursts against women as well as priests above (Naigeon, 'Avertissement de l'éditeur', ed. by Desan, 44); he has some trouble managing what he thinks about Marie de Gournay, see Desan, 'Naigeon et l'"avertissement" censuré de l'édition des *Essais* de 1802', 28–29.

largely uneducated 'gens du monde' [people of the world]; they are also 'très légères' [very slight] and yet add great value to a work. There is a sort of see-saw of opposing negating statements in operation here: corrections might be quite extensive but they are invisible; they are very light yet they add a great deal. The corrector matches the writer in terms of taste: the writer 'of great taste' is highly appreciative of the work the corrector does; the corrector himself needs the most perfect and sure touch, the most exquisite feeling for beauty and propriety to be able to do the work he does. The writer writes; the corrector perfects, and brings the text to the highest pitch of beauty, a beauty which is defined, at least in part, by its propriety. The work of the corrector seems to take place at a higher level than the work of the writer; it takes priority.

So, we know what Naigeon thinks about editing and we know how he thinks Diderot should be edited. The preface he wrote to the *Œuvres de Diderot*, in combination with the self-exculpatory 'Avertissement de l'Editeur, imprimé à la suite de *la Religieuse*' and the original 'Avertissement de l'Editeur' for Montaigne's *Essais*, all of which are dated within four years of each other (1798–1802), provide us with statements which become increasingly revealing and idiosyncratic, whether that be in relation to the judgements that they make of what a writer gets wrong (in the first two texts, the writer is explicitly Diderot) and should change (or allow to be changed), or about the overwhelming passion that is editing for Naigeon, about how far-reaching he conceives the editing role as being in the case of hitherto unpublished texts, and finally, of the great status he attributes to the editor, greater it seems even than the writer, at least in terms of taste. This truly is an odd series of statements, and the closer we look at them, the odder they seem. They will be very helpful, though, when we come to look at the *Mémoires sur la vie et les ouvrages de Denis Diderot*, so often mentioned as imminent by Naigeon, and yet unpublished until 1823. This we soon will; it is the final text to consider, and the second of our final pair. Firstly, though, to Garat, whom we last heard of keeping his counsel at the Institut national.

# 11. 1820: Garat's *Mémoires historiques sur la vie de M. Suard, sur ses écrits, et sur le XVIIIe siècle*

We now jump forward in time, to two memoir pieces, Dominique-Joseph Garat's composed just prior to publication, and Jacques-André Naigeon's published posthumously. They are, to give them their full titles, Garat's *Mémoires historiques sur la vie de M. Suard, sur ses écrits, et sur le XVIIIe siècle* of 1820, and Naigeon's *Mémoires historiques et philosophiques sur la vie et les ouvrages de Denis Diderot*, with its advertised publication date of 1821, and its actual date of 1823. We take them in chronological order of publication according to our usual pattern, and it seems satisfying to do so in this particular case, given that Garat seems to nod to the imminent appearance of Naigeon's *Mémoires*, and that the *Mémoires* themselves are a fitting end to the book, offering what I will argue is the first publication of Denis Diderot's *Éléments de physiologie*, presented in a rearranged and abridged mesh with the *Rêve de d'Alembert* as it is.

Garat's *Mémoires historiques sur la vie de M. Suard, sur ses écrits, et sur le XVIIIe siècle*, or *Mémoires sur Suard* for short, is a curious work, alternately hyperbolic and guarded. The object of this biographical memoir, Jean-Baptiste-Antoine Suard (1732–1817), was a minor man of letters, editor and journalist; he was part of the world of the 'philosophes' and knew many of them, yet sometimes he represented the authorities (as 'Censeur des théâtres', he was responsible for banning Beaumarchais's *Mariage de Figaro*). Garat's *Mémoires sur Suard* are 900 pages long, split into two volumes, the first of which relates the history of French culture

© Caroline Warman, CC BY 4.0        https://doi.org/10.11647/OBP.0199.11

through the lens of conversation, the second offering a panorama of European literature, language by language.¹ This is all framed by and interspersed with information, anecdotes, and comments about Suard's life which are remarkable for their lack of enthusiasm. He is variously described as being lazy (1.221, 2.215), somnolent (2.213-214), writing less than his contemporaries and being less passionate (1.220), being timid (1.232), not being a very impressive speaker because of his weak voice and nervous tone (1.332), having a poor memory (2.129) and as having not written as much as he should have done (1.328). One of the most complimentary passages describes him as being capable of writing the history of France via conversation, but as not having done it (Garat is doing it instead, 1.171). Another goes so far as to say that if the hundred pieces he wrote, each separately excellent, were brought together, they would make a 'volume digne d'une haute considération et de toutes les places académiques' [a volume worthy of high consideration and of any academic post] (1.331). There are many other such weak compliments and barbed comments. It is understandable therefore that Suard's widow (Amélie Panckoucke) wrote her own briefer, more focused, and more amorously subservient version to counter Garat's, and brought it out in virtuous outrage the same year.² In sum, Suard seems to provide

---

1    Dominique-Joseph Garat, *Mémoires historiques sur la vie de M. Suard, sur ses écrits, et sur le XVIIIe siècle; par Dominique-Joseph Garat*, 2 vols (Paris: A. Belin, 1820). See the 'Table analytique', vol. 1, pp. i–xliv (p. vii): 'Nécessité de connaître l'histoire des conversations en France depuis le dixième siècle qu'elles ont commencé pour bien apprécier celles du dix-huitième' [Necessity of knowing the history of conversations in France from their commencement in the tenth century and onwards, in order properly to appreciate the conversations of the eighteenth]. See also 1.176 onwards.

2    'Une plume beaucoup plus habile avoit désiré se charger de ce soin; la connoissance parfaite que cet écrivain avoit du caractère et des vertus de M. Suard, les larmes abondantes qu'il répandoit sur sa tombe, m'ont fait céder à ses voeux. Mais ni mes intentions, ni celles que je lisois dans les dernières volontés de M. Suard n'ayant été remplies par cet écrit, dont à peine quelques fragments m'ont été communiqués, des considérations tres puissantes à mes yeux et dont je ne dois compte à personne, me décident à le désavouer auprès de mes amis' [a more skilful pen than mine had requested this task for himself ; the perfect knowledge that this writer had of Mr Suard's character and virtues, the abundant tears he shed over his tomb, made me grant his request. But neither my intentions nor those I read in the last wishes of Mr Suard having been fulfilled by this piece of writing, of which barely a few fragments have been shown to me, and owing to considerations which are very important to me, and which I need justify to no one, I have decided to tell my friends that I disavow his memoir]. Amélie Suard, *Essais de mémoires sur M. Suard* (Paris: Didot, 1820), pp. 2–3.

a rather desultory excuse for Garat to give an account of something, 900 pages-worth of it, that he finds more important, this something being to do, no doubt, with the other part of the title, 'le XVIIIe siècle' [the eighteenth century].

By the time Garat wrote the *Mémoires sur Suard*, he was no longer in the epicentre of power. The restoration of the Bourbon monarchy triggered his expulsion from the post-Revolutionary reinstated Académie française, and he returned to his native Basque country where he died in 1833, having refused an official invitation to rejoin the Académie française in 1829, although agreeing, when the Académie des sciences morales et politiques was set up in 1832 (or rather set back up, its ancestor, the 'Classe des sciences morales et politiques', having been closed down by Napoleon Bonaparte, as we saw in a previous chapter), to his election as member of the section 'Morale' (Destutt de Tracy was part of the section 'Philosophie').[3] Garat never took up this seat. Suard, in fact, had been one of the key movers in determining who should be expelled from the Académie française, its own entry on Suard stating that he 'prit une part regrettable à la réorganisation de 1816' [he played a regrettable role in the 1816 reorganisation].[4] Here, then, would be one reason for Garat's inability to praise Suard wholeheartedly: personal resentment towards the instigator of his expulsion. This, however, he denies, both at the opening of the two volumes and at their close.[5] Indeed, he may be hoping that these magnanimous *Mémoires* will contribute to his reinstatement; his statements about how much he misses his erstwhile colleagues and his declaration that his only remaining wish is to converse with them once more would seem to tend in that direction.[6] Also, as suggested above, he may wish his *Mémoires sur Suard* to be associated with other forthcoming *Mémoires*, possibly even Naigeon's on Diderot. As he says, 'beaucoup de mémoires restent encore à paraître' [many memoirs are yet to be published]. The passage that this snippet comes from is worth quoting in its entirety for the hints

---

3   Who held what seat ('fauteuil') and when is carefully recorded on the website of the Académie, see https://academiesciencesmoralesetpolitiques.fr/les-academiciens-de-1832-a-nos-jours/.
4   See http://www.academie-francaise.fr/les-immortels/jean-baptiste-antoine-suard.
5   Dominique-Joseph Garat, *Mémoires sur Suard*, vol. 1 ('Avertissement'), p. 5 (unnumbered); vol. 2, p. 444.
6   Garat, *Mémoires sur Suard*, vol. 1, pp. 5–6 (unnumbered).

that it gives of a hinterland of as-yet unknown truth. It describes Suard's conversation, Suard who chatted much more than he wrote ('M. Suard a beaucoup plus causé qu'il n'a écrit' [Mr Suard conversed very much more than he wrote], 1.173):

> Mais c'est dans les cercles, dans les cabinets, dans les entretiens, qu'il [Suard] les [des choses précieuses] a comme jetées; pour en apprécier le mérite et l'influence, il faudrait connaître parfaitement ce dix-huitième siècle sur lequel beaucoup de mémoires restent encore à paraître; il faudrait en comparer les conversations aux conversations des siècles qui l'ont précédé. On peut et on doit indiquer ici ces parallèles nécessaires et piquans; on ne peut les instituer; ils seraient trop longs et ne seraient pas complets; les matériaux ne manquent pas seulement; ceux que nous avons sont rarement assez sûrs.[7]

> But it's in small groups, in private studies, in conversations, that Suard scattered, as it were, these precious things; to appreciate their merit and influence, one would need to perfectly understand the eighteenth century, about which many memoirs are yet to be published; one would need to compare the conversations to the conversations of preceding centuries. One can and one must signal these necessary and illuminating parallels; one cannot undertake them oneself; they would be too long and would not be complete; it's not only the materials that are missing; those we do have are rarely trustworthy enough.

How curious, this imperative to indicate parallels with other conversationalists, to compare across the eighteenth century (which one would need to know *perfectly*), and with previous centuries.[8] How curious that these parallels are described as both *necessary* and 'piquant'—a difficult term to translate—Chambaud's French-English Dictionary in its 1815 edition suggests variously *pungent, keen, sharp, biting*. In modern parlance, one might perhaps say about a parallel that it was suggestive, meaningful, or revelatory. In any case, Garat declares that these parallels *must* be signalled but *must not* be spelled out. For

---

7 Garat, *Mémoires sur Suard*, vol. 1, pp. 173–74.
8 Benedetta Craveri has answered Garat's call, see *The Age of Conversation*, trans. by Teresa Waugh (New York: New York Review of Books, 2005). Craveri does not in fact mention Garat, but she does discuss Diderot, a famed talker, quoting Marmontel's engaging account (*The Age of Conversation*, pp. 360–62). Jon Mee explores this topic in the British context and specifically from the point of view of dissent and disagreement in his *Conversable Worlds: Literature, Contention, & Community 1762–1830* (Oxford: Oxford University Press, 2011).

this, he gives various weak excuses, saying it would take too long and there is not enough material, and it is not reliable enough anyway. Or perhaps he really means that it is not *safe* enough. There seems to be a certain measure of wary caution in evidence here, and as we know anyway, Garat was out of favour, and probably seeking to return to it. But, as we also see, Garat is not *only* being prudent, he is *also* planting some signs here. There are quite a lot of these throughout the book.

He talks about '[l'art de] cacher une partie de son idée' [the art of hiding part of one's idea] (I.212), taught primarily by Fontenelle, about how to 'exciter de ces surprises que la logique même est sûre de produire' [provoke some of those surprises that logic itself is sure to produce] (I.212), about how ellipses (or gaps for that which is not made explicit) are 'pour ainsi dire, l'algèbre moral des langues' [the moral algebra of languages, so to say] (II.184), about how a pamphlet written by Jean-François Marmontel against Jean-Jacques Rousseau evoked him without naming him once ('moins il le nommait, plus il le rappelait' [the less he named him, the more he brought him to mind] (II.239)), and of the 'travail lent et secret du dictionnaire' [slow secret work of the dictionary], which, by 'détermin[ant] les acceptions des mots' [determining the meanings of words] would later come to influence 'le cours de morale et de politique' [the course of moral and political life] (II.421). Elsewhere, when relaying discussions that Suard had with Laurence Sterne, author of *Tristam Shandy*, Sterne purportedly gives 'l'étude de Locke' [the study of Locke] as one of his three main influences (along with his 'sensibility' and also a daily portion of the Bible). John Locke is the trigger for an outburst of praise about Locke's contribution to developing human understanding:

> [...] cette philosophie que ceux qui savent la reconnaître où elle est, et où elle dirige tout secrètement, retrouvent et sentent dans toutes les pages, dans toutes les lignes, dans le choix de toutes les expressions; [...] cette philosophie trop religieuse pour vouloir expliquer le miracle des sensations, mais qui, avec ce miracle dont elle n'a pas la témérité de demander raison et compte à Dieu, développe tous les secrets de l'entendement [...].[9]

---

9   Garat, *Mémoires sur Suard*, vol. 2, p. 149.

> This philosophy which those who can see it and know where it is, a place moreover from which it directs everything in secret, can find and sense in every page, in every line, in the choice of every expression; [...] this philosophy which is too religious to wish to explain the miracle of sensation, but which, by means of that miracle which it does not have the effrontery to demand a reason or explanation of from God, develops all the secrets of the human understanding [...].

This is not merely praise of Locke, it is praise of 'cette philosophie', and a statement of its ubiquity and its secret presence and power: 'elle dirige tout secrètement' [it directs everything in secret]. Garat partly wraps this up in various imported sacred terms; thus the philosophy is *religious*, the sensations are a *miracle* which it (the philosophy) does not dare ask *God* about. Presumably these verbal fig leaves make it possible for him to deny any accusation of irreligion. But they do not hide what he is actually saying, which is that Lockean philosophy is everywhere for those readers who know how to see it, and furthermore, that it is secretly in charge. He goes on to discuss Buffon and Diderot. This book repeatedly references the great advances made in the knowledge of human understanding in the eighteenth century. And this is what the book is primarily about, where its centre of gravity is, partly because he says so, and partly because it is what he repeatedly returns to.[10]

Fontenelle (1657–1757), perpetual secretary of the French Académie royale des sciences (1699–1740), is frequently alluded to as a sort of uncontentious great man of French science.[11] Fontenelle had, of course, been the object of Garat's prize-winning *Éloge de Fontenelle* (1784), so he is familiar stamping-ground for Garat.[12] And of all the things that

---

10   Works on human understanding are repeatedly mentioned (sometimes Garat only gives the author or the title): Fontenelle, *Traité sur l'entendement humain*: 1.117–18, La Romiguière, *Leçons sur la pensée*: 2.36; Stewart: 1.185–86; Moses Mendelssohn's *Recherches sur les sentimens moraux*, I.58; Gatti: 2.198; Bonnet: 2.31; Bichat: 2.34; Condillac: 1.160–61; Helvetius: 1.125; d'Holbach: 1.207–14; Charles Georges Leroy, *Lettres philosophiques sur l'intelligence et la perfectibilité des animaux*: 1.155; Hume, *Traité de la nature humaine* and *Recherches sur l'entendement humain*: 2.153; Lavoisier (who laid out the 'principes de l'entendement' in his 'plan d'instruction publique' as skilfully as the 'principes chimiques'): 2.327. Garat, *Mémoires sur Suard*.

11   A non-exhaustive list of allusions to Fontenelle in the *Mémoires sur Suard* includes: vol. 1: 80–82; 117–22; 124–25; 212; 231.

12   Garat, *Éloge de Bernard de Fontenelle. Discours qui a remporté le prix de l'Académie Françoise, en 1784* (Paris: Démonville, Libraire-Imprimeur de l'Académie Françoise, 1784).

Fontenelle was interested in, says Garat, the thing that was 'the most intense passion of his life' was a theory of the faculties of the human mind. Here is the passage in full where he writes about it:

> Les théories de l'entendement, qui, depuis Bacon et Descartes, avaient pris dans les connaissances humaines une si grande place, et peut-être la première, avaient beaucoup occupé la jeunesse de Fontenelle; il parut long-temps y renoncer; mais la plus forte passion de sa vie, il l'eut à près de cent ans, et ce fut encore pour la métaphysique. Elle le faisait sortir de ce style fin et familier, auquel la nature probablement l'avait destiné, mais dont il se faisait aussi comme un principe du culte de la vérité. A cet âge, où toute imagination est éteinte, même dans ceux qu'elles a dominés, il peignait, par une grande image, la puissance qu'exercerait une *théorie des facultés de l'esprit humain*, tirée à la fois et de l'organisation humaine, et des chefs-d'œuvre créés déjà par la raison, déjà consacrés par cet assentiment universel qui ne s'accorde qu'à l'évidence. *Elle sera*, disait-il, *le grand luminaire suspendu entre le bon sens, commun à tous les hommes, le génie des beaux-arts et le génie des sciences; elle les rapprochera, elle les unira, en leur faisant voir comment ils sortent des mêmes sources.*
>
> Des fragments assez considérables, et très-importans, d'un Traité de la raison humaine, ont été trouves dans les papiers de Fontenelle; ils ont été publiés par l'abbé Trublet. [...] C'est dans ces fragmens qu'une main centenaire a déposé, la première fois, les germes de beaucoup d'idées très-lumineuses, développées depuis par les meilleurs métaphysiciens de l'Europe.[13]

> The theories about [human] understanding which had, since Bacon and Descartes, become such an important, perhaps even the most important, part of human knowledge, had absorbed a great deal of Fontenelle's youth; he gave up on them for a long period, but the strongest passion of his life came upon him when he was nearly one hundred years old, and it was again for metaphysics. It propelled him out of that subtle and familiar style that nature had probably destined him to have and which was also for him a sort of guiding principle in his worship of the truth. At that age, when all imagination has faded even in those whom it has dominated, he painted a great image of the power that a *theory of the faculties of the human mind* would have, one which would be drawn both from the human [bodily] organization and from the masterpieces already created by the human mind [la raison], and consecrated by that universal assent which only occurs in response to evidence. *It will be*, said he, *a great chandelier hung between the good sense every man has, the genius*

---

13 Garat, *Mémoires sur Suard*, vol. 1, pp. 117–18. Italics in the original.

> *of the fine arts and the genius of the sciences; it will bring them together, it will unite them by showing them how they share common sources.*
>
> Quite lengthy and very important fragments of a *Treatise of human reason* were found amongst Fontenelle's papers; they were published by the Reverend Trublet. [...] It is in these fragments that a hundred-year-old hand deposited the seeds of many deeply illuminating ideas, and which have since been taken forward by the best metaphysicians of Europe.

Here, in summary, are the claims Garat makes in this passage: the theories of human understanding may be the most important area of recent knowledge; Fontenelle thought about this topic a great deal when a young man; he returned to it in extreme old age; it was the strongest passion of his life; he wrote it in a less familiar ('familiar' as in 'common' or 'low' or 'oral') style than he habitually used, while still using striking imagery at an age when all imagination is extinguished even in those people whom it has dominated; important and extensive extracts of his treatise on this subject were found in his papers after his death, and have since been published; an old man wrote them; he planted in them the seeds of his luminous ideas which have since been developed by the best minds in Europe. Well now. Is Garat talking primarily about Fontenelle here?

Fontenelle did indeed write fragments on the human mind, which Nicolas-Charles-Joseph Trublet published in his grand edition of Fontenelle in ten volumes (1757–58). We find them in the seventh volume of Alain Niderst's modern edition. They consist of remarks, sketches, responses. There is a 'Fragments d'un traité de la raison humaine' [Fragments of a treatise on human reason], some pages 'Sur l'instinct' [On instinct], an 'autre fragment, la 'loi de la pensée' [Law of thought] et 'De la connoissance de l'esprit humain' [On the knowledge of the human mind], which is sub-divided into short chapters entitled 'Fragment', 'Première partie: de l'origine des idées' [First part: on the origin of ideas], and 'Analogie de la matière et de l'esprit' [Analogy of matter and spirit]. In all, they amount to 48 pages, of which the 'Fragments d'un traité de la raison humaine' make up 23 pages. In 'De l'instinct', Fontenelle considers the acts of thinking and walking, that is to say, he muses on actions of which we have no consciousness (and in fact we quoted from it in an earlier chapter).[14] In the 'Fragments d'un traité de la raison humaine', he explores why it is that not all ideas are conscious; in the 'Loi de la pensée', he differentiates the mathematical being from the physical being; he quite often seems to be replying to Leibniz. This is all serious and important work, part of and contributing to what we have described as the on-going conversation on these matters, but it does not quite live up to Garat's write-up. It feels very much more as if Garat's description of Fontenelle's work is a way of signalling Diderot's *Éléments de physiologie*, with its similar framing narrative of fragmentation and posthumous papers. What he says could certainly be applied to both Fontenelle *and* Diderot, with the main difference being that they apply *better* to Diderot than to Fontenelle. Perhaps this is the sort of passage where we are expected to see the hidden message that Garat said—in relation to Lockean philosophy—was so visible for those who knew how to see it. Of course, we cannot really pin Garat down, and that is no doubt the point.

In the following passage from the second volume of his *Mémoires sur Suard*, he again both signals and veils what he is talking about, suffusing it all with grandiose and declamatory virtue-signalling:

> Ainsi, en Angleterre et en France, et dans d'autres parties de l'Europe, la philosophie du dix-huitième siècle, c'est-à-dire, un petit nombre d'hommes qui n'avaient pour toute puissance que beaucoup de goût pour la méditation et beaucoup d'amour pour l'humanité, aspiraient à faire servir le passé, le présent, l'avenir, les tombeaux, les débris des vieux empires, les forêts et les sauvages, au perfectionnement des facultés et des destinées humaines; à fonder la raison universelle sur l'analyse, la morale sur la raison, les lois sur la morale, et le suprême bonheur de tous les êtres vivans et pensans, sur la parfaite harmonie de leurs interêts, de leurs vœux, de leurs principes d'ordre social, sur les affections et sur les actions qui rendent le plus les âmes dignes d'une immortelle félicité.[15]

> Thus, in England and France, and in some other parts of Europe, the philosophy of the eighteenth century, that is, a small number of men whose only power was in having a great deal of taste for meditation and a great deal of love for humanity, aspired to harness the past, the present, the future, tombs, the ruins of old empires, forests and savages for the improvement of human faculties and destinies, to found universal reason

---

14 See Chapter 3.
15 Garat, *Mémoires sur Suard*, vol. 2, pp. 79–80.

on analysis, morality on reason, laws on morality, and the supreme happiness of all living and thinking beings on the perfect harmonisation of their interests, their wishes, and their principles for social order, on the affections and on the actions most likely to make souls worthy of immortal felicity.

He is alternately very generalising and very precise (as well as quite difficult to quote succinctly). On the one hand, England, France, and other parts of Europe hardly limit his focus. On the other, 'un petit nombre d'hommes' [a small number of men] does, although he does not name whom he is referring to. Yet the list of what this small group of men wish to deploy for the improvement of the mind and human happiness would seem to exclude most writers and thinkers, leaving only such luminaries as Montesquieu, Voltaire, Rousseau, and Diderot; not many others have this encyclopedic range; Condillac does not, despite the Condillacian trigger word of 'analyse'. Arguably, Diderot fits the bill best as the person who did indeed write about every one of these aspects, from the *Essai sur les règnes de Claude et de Néron* to the *Supplément au voyage de Bougainville*, the *Éléments de physiologie*, and so on, not omitting his contributions to Raynal's *Histoire des deux Indes*. Interestingly, the passage we have been looking at immediately leads into this discussion of dissimulating meaning or declaring it openly:

> Ce but, tantôt ils le signalent avec la fermeté et la hauteur qui conviennent à peine à l'evidence; tantôt ils le voilent avec la défiance bien naturelle à sa grandeur et à ses difficultés; quelquefois ils l'enveloppent et le dissimulent comme si le voeu et l'espérance du bonheur du monde était une usurpation sur les puissances; mais qu'ils l'affichent ou qu'ils le cachent, jamais ils ne l'abandonnent; ils le conservent sous la hache des bourreaux, sous les traits meme du ridicule.[16]

> Sometimes they signal this goal with that resolution and authority which scarcely even do justice to what is evidently true; sometimes they veil it with that diffidence so natural given its importance and the difficulties surrounding it; sometimes they conceal and disguise it as if to wish and hope for the world's happiness were in some way to encroach on the powers that be; but whether they advertise it or hide it, they never abandon it; they keep it still when confronted with the executioner's blade, even in the face of ridicule.

---

16  Garat, *Mémoires sur Suard*, vol. 2, p. 80.

This description of how 'la philosophie du dix-huitième siècle, c'est-à-dire, un petit nombre d'hommes' [the philosophy of the eighteenth century, that is, a small number of men] alternates between open avowal and careful masking of their meaning, yet resolves into a noble declaration that whatever they do, they never abandon their purpose or commitment, be they threatened by execution or even covered in ridicule. One may wonder whether this last part refers to himself, arrested as he had been (and threatened with execution as he mentions in the fervent salvo of his opening lecture at the École normale),[17] and much vilified and ridiculed as he had also been. We will quote one such satirical poem towards the end of this section.

We can see, in any case, that whether Garat is talking about Suard, who was imprisoned in the 1740s, one of the few who could understand English, and whose most precious utterances never made it into print,[18] or Fontenelle, whose conversation was also very special, and who was interested in human understanding and worked on it at the beginning and the end of his career, leaving behind fragments of inestimable value, and whose style was full of surprises,[19] there seems to be a Diderot-shaped shadow in the background. That said, he is not only a shadow whose presence we seem to feel; Garat also discusses him explicitly, extensively, and repeatedly.[20] However, when it comes to discussing atheism, mentioning the *Interprétation de la nature*, and alluding to the *Lettre sur les aveugles* and the *Lettre sur les sourds et muets*, Diderot's name is not given, a signal of the continuing sensitivity of this topic, at least insofar as Garat is concerned.[21] At points Garat compares Suard

---

17   Garat, *Leçons d'analyse et d'entendement* [1796], ed. by G. Gengembre et al., in *L'École normale de l'an III*, ed. by J. Dhombres (Paris: Éditions ENS, 2008), vol. 4, pp. 43–160 (p. 76) (Première leçon), https://doi.org/10.4000/books.editionsulm.1445, see above.

18   On Suard in prison, see Garat, *Mémoires sur Suard*, vol. 1, p. 47 (Garat in fact makes the Diderot parallel explicit by stating that Suard wished his prison companion had been Diderot rather than the mysterious Chevalier de L***); on the English-speaking, see the 'Table analytique', vol. 1, pp. i–xliv (p. iii); conversation: 1.173; 243.

19   Fontenelle: conversation: 1.113–14; 116; 118; human understanding (see previous paragraphs): 1.117–18; style: 1.212. In Garat, *Mémoires sur Suard*.

20   Diderot is named here (probably not an exhaustive list): vol. 1: 47; 164; 207–9; 211; 213; 218; 225; 227; 235–38 (Diderot quoted on imagination); 244–45; 324; 346; vol. 2: 13–23; 157–73; 177, 197, 240; 251; 447. Garat, *Mémoires sur Suard*.

21   Diderot's *Interprétation de la nature* is discussed but Diderot's authorship is not mentioned (Garat, *Mémoires sur Suard*, 1:203).

and Diderot directly, such as when they each orate about imagination; Diderot's reported speech closes with the statement that 'Quand un philosophe a de l'imagination, je veux que l'imagination soit un peu ÉBOURIFFÉE' [When a philosopher has imagination, I want that imagination to be a bit WINDSWEPT].[22] Suard goes on to criticise Diderot for disliking order, and Garat concludes that 'M. Suard fut moins applaudi; ses idées étaient moins originales; il fut plus approuvé; elles étaient plus conformes aux oracles du goût et de la raison dans tous les siècles' [Mr Suard received less applause; his ideas were less original, but he received greater approval, because his ideas conformed more to the enduring oracles of taste and reason over the centuries].[23] Suard gets less applause; the judgement is that he is less original, and more of a conformist. Poor Suard! Elsewhere also, attention is drawn to what he does not like about Diderot; internal contrasts show Garat using Suard's lack of appreciation to highlight something particularly distinctive about Diderot. Thus, what is described as Suard's typically French taste means that he 'ne pouvait aimer ni dans Diderot, ni dans les Allemands, ces brusques voisinages d'un familier trivial et d'une inspiration trop emphatique pour être celle de la nature et des passions' [could not appreciate either in Diderot or in the Germans those abrupt juxtapositions of the over-familiar and trivial alongside passages of inspiration which are too emphatic to belong to nature or natural passions] (2.19); the description Garat then proceeds to give of this new German literature is intensely positive, and all about how well it does describe nature and passions. Furthermore, Garat later contrasts Bacon and Montaigne; Montaigne, Garat says, 'va au but par ricochets; l'autre va sans bonds et sans détours' [reaches his aim via skips and jumps; the former gets there smoothly and without detours] (2.45); the contrast between the bumpy disconcerting writer and the smooth and moderate one is similar, and although in this second comparison, the smooth thinker and the bumpy one are equally lauded, the terms in which Montaigne is described are very similar to the those used earlier about Diderot. The passage in which Diderot's 'brusques voisinages'

---

22 Garat, *Mémoires sur Suard,* vol. 1, p. 238 (italics and capitals in the original). There doesn't appear to be a separate Diderot text to confirm that he did say this, so Garat is the source for this anecdote.
23 Garat, *Mémoires sur Suard,* vol. 1, p. 242.

[abrupt juxtapositions] are evoked moves into a discussion of what Suard thought of Diderot's plays, which in turn becomes a discussion of Suard and Rousseau's opposing views of whether Diderot excelled more as a dramatist (Suard) or as a philosopher (Rousseau). This is interestingly framed, in that both Suard and Rousseau are presented as having reservations about Diderot (this is subsequent to Rousseau and Diderot's split).[24] So he is debated by two of his critics, who nonetheless praise him in strong terms. In this passage, Garat introduces, in eye-catching italics, Suard's opinion of Diderot:

> Voici, et dans les mêmes termes, si ma mémoire ne me trompe, ce que Suard, qui n'aimait pas beaucoup la personne de Diderot, pensait et disait de ses talens:
>
> *Qui sait a quel rang aurait pu se placer Diderot, s'il eût concentré toutes les forces de son esprit original et fécond et celles de sa brillante imagination sur les seuls objets propres à en exercer toute l'énergie?*[25]
>
> Here, and in the same words, if my memory is not wrong, is what Suard, who did not much like Diderot as a person, thought and said about his talents:
>
> *Who knows what level Diderot would have reached had he concentrated all the forces of his original and fertile mind as well as those of his luminous imagination on the only objects capable of bringing into play the entirety of this energy?*

Garat presents this as what Suard actually said, and claims to be recalling it from memory. We know already from a few pages earlier (and as quoted above) that Suard 'ne pouvait aimer ni dans Diderot, ni dans les Allemands, ces brusques voisinages' [could not appreciate either in Diderot or in the Germans those abrupt juxtapositions]; here, it is Diderot himself that he does not like much (we are not told why). Perhaps the idea of presenting Suard's supposed reservations about Diderot is to gain the trust of readers who might also have reservations about him, and to show by contrast that the fair-minded moderate conformist person, despite disliking his style and his personality, will still concede that he is extraordinarily important. The do-I-remember-it-correctly quotation, moreover, is a mixed compliment: how toweringly important he could have been had he only concentrated the forces of his

---

24  Garat, *Mémoires sur Suard*, vol. 2, pp. 21–22.
25  Garat, *Mémoires sur Suard*, vol. 2, p. 21. Italics in the original.

original and fertile mind and brilliant imagination on the only objects capable of deploying all their energy. This is not the first time such a view of Diderot had been expressed.[26] It is the wasted-opportunity Diderot. And yet it also promises a lot, even in the regret mode. What is especially interesting about this passage is that Garat repeats it verbatim in the closing pages. This is the only time (to my knowledge) that there is any such repetition in these two long volumes. Here the context is rather different. Garat is talking about Suard's dying years, and how he took to writing down thoughts and 'souvenirs éparpillés' [scattered memories].[27] Garat copies down in its entirety one rather longer meditation, entitled 'Du meilleur usage de l'esprit' [On the best use of the mind].[28] It is from this fragment or short essay that the not-in-fact-just-a-remembered-utterance comes. Here it is again, de-italicised this time:

> Qui sait a quel rang aurait pu se placer Diderot, s'il eût concentré toutes les forces de son esprit original et fécond et celles de sa brillante imagination sur les seuls objets propres à en exercer toute l'énergie?[29]
>
> Who knows what level Diderot would have reached if he had concentrated all the forces of his original and fertile mind as well as those of his luminous imagination on the only objects capable of bringing into play the entirety of this energy?

The framing this short essay gives is quite different from the earlier one. Here, Suard is considering how unfortunate it is to try to master 'l'universalité des connaissances' [the totality of knowledge], and the extent to which this tendency has prevented the truly great from truly realising their potential. Suard (supposing it is Suard) names four such

---

26 Even Eusèbe Salverte's brave encomium of Diderot's contribution focuses more on the genius of his spontaneous and generous *character* than on his writings, see *Éloge philosophique de Denys Diderot, lu a l'Institut National, le 7 thermidor an 8* (Paris: Chez Surosne, 1801 [an IX]), p. 67. By the time Jean-Philibert Damiron comes to write his influential assessments, Diderot has settled into being the *philosophe* who was very important and influential, but too lacking in self-discipline, too spontaneous (that is, too chatty), to be one of the greats, see Jean-Philibert Damiron, *Mémoire sur Diderot* (1852), reprinted in *Mémoires sur les Encyclopédistes* (Genève: Slatkine reprints, 1968), p. 2.
27 Garat, *Mémoires sur Suard*, vol. 2, p. 446.
28 Garat, *Mémoires sur Suard*, vol. 2, pp. 446–48.
29 Garat, *Mémoires sur Suard*, vol. 2, p. 447.

men who fell short: Leibniz, Pascal, d'Alembert, and Diderot.[30] In a way, it is amusing to contemplate this roll-call of failures; the great men who might have been. But in any case, two points need to be made. Firstly, no other of these names is so lyrically described as Diderot, or even described at all. 'Suard' simply says Leibniz would have made greater progress in mathematics had he limited himself to its study; the same can be said with respect to Pascal about physics and mathematics (who instead plunged into theological controversy); while D'Alembert would have overtaken Leonhard Euler and Pierre-Simon Laplace as a mathematician if he had not allowed himself to get involved in literary works, in which he only succeeded to a very mediocre degree. With respect to Diderot, 'Suard' does not specify the area that Diderot would have shone in if only he had not done something else instead or in addition. Secondly, extrapolating from the other examples, we see that the study of the sciences is primordial, and any other activity or controversy or glory, be it theological or literary, is a waste of time and genius. We can be fairly sure, therefore, that it is Diderot the scientist that 'Suard' is regretting the loss of, and not Diderot the dramatist, as in the first appearance of this passage. Furthermore, the contributions of Leibniz, Pascal, and D'Alembert to the fields of mathematics and physics were in fact huge. And thus, by extension, so was Diderot's, whatever area of the sciences it is that 'Suard' has in mind. We can probably assume it is something to do with the materialist investigations of nature, with the senses which Garat mentions (although without specifying Diderot's authorship), and with the human understanding, that topic which he

---

30  Mme Suard also mentions this fragment in her rival *Mémoires*, and it is interestingly similar and different. She lists Pascal, Leibtnitz [sic], and d'Alembert as the examples of men of genius who failed to focus exclusively on science and therefore the surer route to glory. There is no mention of Diderot. And she quotes an extensive passage which is (almost) identical to Garat's quotation, apart from a crucial cut, which is precisely where Garat's version of Suard mentions Leibniz, Pascal, D'Alembert, and Diderot. Instead, she moves straight to the confessional part, her cut transforming Suard's fragment into a eulogy to the happiness of those who do not aspire to glory. Mme Suard, *Essais*, pp. 105–06. The fragment itself, whose existence is confirmed at least in some details by Garat and Mme Suard's extracts, seems not ever to have been published. A later commentator and author of an *Éloge de Suard*, François Pérennès, quotes the same chunk about Suard's happy non-pursuit of glory that we find in both Garat and Mme Suard's versions, calling it simply one of Suard's 'souvenirs épars' [scattered memories]. François Pérennès, *Éloge de Suard, secrétaire perpétuel de l'Académie Française* (Besançon: Charles Deis, 1841), p. 57.

repeatedly references and claims is possibly the area in which the most important advances have been made. Perhaps therefore, he is again, as we argued before, trying to signal the existence of Diderot's unknown thought in this area, and in particular his texts the *Rêve de d'Alembert* and the *Éléments de physiologie*.

Elsewhere, we see Garat closely associating 'les noms renommés dans les lettres et dans les sciences' [the famous names of letters and sciences] who attended, along with aristocratic landowners and rich men, the salon of Diderot's friend, the financier and government administrator Jean Devaines (1735–1803);[31] Garat goes on to list not the names of these famous men of letters and science, but the areas they worked in, that is, medicine and chemistry, and more specifically the physical mechanisms of thought, physiology, life and death. He then says this same group of names renowned in letters and science also include those who wear the laurels of eloquence and poetry, and who best upheld 'la splendeur littéraire du siècle de Louis XIV' [the literary splendour of the century of Louis XIV]. It looks as if he is bringing the two seemingly distinct areas of scientific research and literary glory together. One might wish to argue that the (unnamed) names of the illustrious scientists and the illustrious men of letters are kept separate here, and technically they are; however, there is also a simultaneous effect of osmosis and association. These names are renowned 'dans les lettres et dans les sciences', not in one or the other: the syntax brings these two areas together as attributes of the same illustrious names. And the list of areas does not follow the same order of first letters, then sciences; it inverts it. Thus, there is an almost imperceptible confusion or fusion of the two areas. Garat is suggesting that those whose rhetoric and poetry best maintained 'la splendeur littéraire du siècle de Louis XIV' were those who worked on 'le mécanisme non de la pensée qui est spirituelle, mais de ses organes extérieurs, qui sont physiques' [the mechanism not of thought which is connected to the spirit, but to its external organs, which are physical], on 'la nouvelle médecine' [the new sort of medicine] which bears 'le nom de physiologie' [the name of physiology], and those 'philosophes devenus chimistes pour approcher de plus près la nature, pour lui arracher, la flamme à la main, les lois de la vie et celles de la mort'

---

31   Garat, *Mémoires sur Suard*, vol. 2, pp. 264–65.

[philosophers who became chemists in order to get closer to nature, to snatch from it, torch in hand, the laws of both life and death].³² This would be a huge claim about the importance of scientific writing, that it had inherited the mantle of Jean Racine and others. Furthermore, the specificity of Garat's list would propel Diderot's *Éléments de physiologie* to the front of the queue, seeing as it contains all these elements, with the *Rêve de d'Alembert* close behind, more poetic but less extensive in coverage. However, here as elsewhere, for all that Garat's prose allows and encourages such a reading, it also contains elements that allow total deniability. He is simultaneously hyperbolic and nebulous.

Whether Garat is using his *Mémoires sur Suard* to allude to Diderot's *Éléments de physiologie* or not is impossible to prove, because Garat suggests and signals but also masks and conceals; he will not be pinned down. It is tempting at this point to quote the poet Joseph Despaze's wicked satire of Garat in *Les Quatre Satires*, which went through five editions in two years (1799–1801). Here, he is of course referring to an earlier and more polemical stage of Garat's career, probably when Garat was defending himself against the accusation of complicity in the September massacres, and yet for those who try to wrestle with his prose, the portrait is recognizable. Apologies in advance for the translation which totally fails to capture the snarky rhymes of the original:

> Garat, toujours rempli de frayeur et d'espoir,
> A toujours le secret de dire blanc et noir:
> S'exprimer franchement lui semble trop bête:
> En sauvant son pays, il veut sauver sa tête.³³

> Garat, always full of fear and hope,
> Always knows how to explain things in both black and white:
> To express himself frankly would be, he feels, too dumb:
> While saving his country, he wants to save his head.

---

32  Garat, *Mémoires sur Suard*, vol. 2, p. 265.
33  Joseph Despaze, *Les Quatre Satires, ou la fin du XVIIIe siècle*, 3rd edn (Paris: Moller, 1799), pp. 24–25. The fifth edition (available on Gallica) has quite a number of changes, including to the section about Garat, which is much shorter, and only includes the first quatrain. We give the longer passage from the earlier edition.

Despaze waxes lyrical for another twenty-two lines on Garat's tergiversation, impersonating Garat in a pretend legal speech:

> Mais, quant à ce discours qui vous a tant déplu,
> Je ne peux le juger, car je ne l'ai pas lu.

> And as for this speech which you so disliked,
> I am unable to judge it as I haven't read it.

Whatever effect Garat hoped his *Mémoires historiques sur la vie de M. Suard, sur ses écrits, et sur le XVIIIe siècle* would have, it did not bring about his re-admission to the Académie française, it did not honour Suard, and it did not please Mme Suard. When François Pérennès wrote his *Éloge de Suard* in 1841, he did not spare Garat, criticising him for his 'détails puérils' [puerile details] and 'prolixité fatigante' [tiresome verbosity].[34] The puerile detail that Pérennès uses to exemplify this opinion is a fascinating one. Garat, describing the cell in which Suard was emprisoned, had talked about how the only light source was an arrow-slit high up in the wall. He explains how Suard learnt how to use it like a tool, to extend its reach, to see in all directions, near and far.[35] This, we may remember, is the specific point that Garat had particularly insisted on in his lectures at the École normale, the need to perfect the use of the senses, to learn to see better, to internalise the telescope somehow.[36] Yet here is this most ambitious aim of Garat's, reduced by Pérennès to the status of a puerile detail! Further bathos is introduced when we read Garat's account side by side with Mme Suard's rival version. She simply says that in order to see the sky from his miserable cell, the young and imprisoned Suard had to stand on a chair because the tiny window was too high up to look out of otherwise.[37] Ah! no

---

34 Pérennès, *Éloge de Suard*, p. 4.
35 'A force de tourner autour de la lucarne qu'il ne pouvait faire tourner, il apprit à la manier, commes les astrologues une lunette; il en étendit le champ; il parvint à regarder en tout sens, à voir, à distinguer au loin et dans toutes les dimensions' [By dint of moving around the window since he couldn't turn the thing itself, he learnt to use it, like astrologers use an eye piece; he extended its range; he learnt to look in all directions, to see, to focus on the far and near and in all dimensions] (Garat, *Mémoires sur Suard*, vol. 1, pp. 41–42).
36 See above.
37 'C'étoit un triste lieu – pour se rétablir qu'une chambre ou l'on n'apercevoit le ciel qu'à travers une lucarne élevée, encore ne pouvoit-il le voir qu'en montant sur des chaises' [It was a miserable place – for his living space nothing more than a room

curious description of how to manipulate an arrow-slit like a telescope here, no perfecting of the senses! Garat seems to have succeeded so well in his attempts to veil his embedded meaning that his readers thought he was talking gibberish, exhausting the patience of even, as Pérennès puts it, 'le lecteur le plus bienveillant' [the best-disposed reader].[38] And yet he has been an important figure in this story, and his bizarre mesh of reveals and conceals is not so much a judgement of his quality as a writer of confused intent, but of the ongoing inadmissibility of what it seems like he might have been trying to say. It is time, finally, to turn to Naigeon's *Mémoires historiques et philosophiques sur la vie et les ouvrages de Denis Diderot*.

---

from which you could only espy the sky through a small window high up, and even then he had to get up on chairs to do so] (Mme Suard, *Essais*, p. 21).

38 Pérennès, *Éloge de Suard*, p. 4.

# 12. 1823: Naigeon's *Mémoires historiques et philosophiques sur la vie et les ouvrages de Denis Diderot*

With Jacques-André Naigeon's *Mémoires historiques et philosophiques sur la vie et les ouvrages de Denis Diderot*, there is no need to make a case for the presence of the *Éléments de physiologie*, because he quotes about a thousand lines from it, completely reorganised and meshed in with about 420 lines from the *Rêve de d'Alembert*. This the interested reader will see when consulting the digital edition of Naigeon's *Mémoires historiques et philosophiques* which accompanies this monograph.[1] This is the book Naigeon had been working on so assiduously in 1792 when he wrote his article on 'Diderot', and then again in 1798 when preparing the *Œuvres de Diderot*, and each time, as we may remember, he repeatedly alludes to it, clearly planning its imminent publication, fervently advertising it, and alerting readers to its importance.[2] Central to it is his 'analyse raisonnée de celui de

---

1   See https://naigeons-diderot.mml.ox.ac.uk/index.htm. In a piece of reinforcing synchronicity, Motoichi Terada has also reproduced these pages from Naigeon's *Mémoires historiques et philosophiques* in his edition of the *Éléments de physiogie*, see 'Annexe' in Denis Diderot, *Éléments de physiologie*, ed. by Motoichi Terada (Paris: Éditions Matériologiques, 2019), pp. 513–93 [hereafter MT]. His edition was published in June 2019, when plans for this monograph's connected digital edition were already far advanced. Our digital edition allows the reader to interact with and visualise Naigeon's mosaic rewriting in a rather different way, and also restores the passages which the Brière editors censored; this is on the basis of a comparison between the printed version and the original manuscript (ms cote 2127, Bibliothèque Carnegie de Reims).

2   See above.

ces ouvrages qui m'a paru le plus profond' [an analytical account of the particular work of his that I thought most profound].³ Given that one hundred pages of Naigeon's *Mémoires historiques et philosophiques* are given over to the presentation of Diderot's philosophy of the 'opérations de l'entendement humain' [operations of the human understanding]⁴, and that of these one hundred pages no fewer than seventy-eight are made of an intricate mosaic of quotation from the *Éléments de physiologie* and the *Rêve de d'Alembert*, and that no other of Diderot's works is treated in an even remotely similar manner, there is no room to question that this is indeed 'celui de ces ouvrages qui m'a paru le plus profond' [the particular work of his that I thought most profound]. Before examining what this intricate mosaic actually looks like, let alone why Naigeon presents it as a single work rather than two separate texts, though, a rapid sketch of the *Mémoires historiques et philosophiques* as a whole is required.

Firstly, composition dates.

In Naigeon's article on 'Diderot' in the *Encyclopédie méthodique*, he states he gave over the six months following Diderot's death to the composition of the *Mémoires historiques et philosophiques*, and early in the text itself he dates that particular moment of writing to October 1784.⁵ So, he started in 1784, and he was still working on it in 1792 and in 1798, when he was obliged to interrupt writing to bring out his edition (and selection) of the *Œuvres de Diderot* in order to counter both the damaging mis-attribution of Étienne-Gabriel Morelly's *Code de la nature* and to correct the unauthorised editions of, amongst others, *Jacques le fataliste*, *La Religieuse*, and the *Supplément au voyage de Bougainville*, which all came out in 1796.⁶ This means it had an on-off

---

3   Jacques-André Naigeon, 'Diderot', in *Encyclopédie méthodique: philosophie ancienne et modern*, 3 vols (Paris: Panckoucke, 1791–94), vol. 2 (1792), p. 228; see discussion above in Chapter 6.
4   Naigeon, *Mémoires historiques et philosophiques sur la vie et les ouvrages de Denis Diderot* (Paris: J. L. L. Brière, 1821 [1823]; repr. Geneva: Slatkine Reprints, 1970), p. 207, https://naigeons-diderot.mml.ox.ac.uk/files/main/mvod.htm#page207.
5   Naigeon, 'Diderot', *Philosophie ancienne et moderne*, vol. 2 (1792), p. 153; Naigeon, *Mémoires historiques et philosophiques sur la vie et les ouvrages de Denis Diderot* (Paris: J. L. L. Brière, 1821 [1823]; repr. Geneva: Slatkine Reprints, 1970), p. 41.
6   Naigeon lambasts the edition of the first two in the *Œuvres*, discussed above. He savages the editor of the *Opuscules philosophiques et littéraires*, l'abbé Bourlet de Vauxcelles, in which the *Supplément au voyage de Bougainville* appeared, in the *Mémoires*, calling him 'un de ces écrivains obscurs, ignorés dans la république des

composition period of at least fourteen years, and almost certainly a bit more. Scholar Rudolf Brummer's careful comparison of dates and mentions leads him to surmise that it was probably finished shortly before 1800, given that in the *Mémoires historiques et philosophiques*, Naigeon refers to the *Œuvres* that he had recently published.[7] It has been suggested that the *Mémoires historiques et philosophiques* were in fact never finished, but the evidence of the text and its underlying manuscript does not support such a claim.[8]

---

lettres, et qui, sans goût, sans style, sans idées, y traînent publiquement un nom ridicule ou avili' [one of those obscure and spurned writers of the republic of letters who, devoid of style or ideas, publicly flaunt their absurd or debased name around]. And he's only just warming up to his theme (*Mémoires historiques et philosophiques*, p. 379).

[7] *Mémoires historiques et philosophiques*, p. 414; Rudolf Brummer, *Studien zur Französischen Auflärungsliteratur im Anschluss an J.-A. Naigeon*, Romanische Philologie (Breslau: Priebatsch's Buchandlung, 1932), p. 27. Interestingly, on this same page of the *Mémoires*, their publisher Brière provides a footnote (signed 'B') saying that the *Mémoires* were finished in 1795. This is contradicted by mention of the 1798 *Œuvres* only a few lines later, as well as discussion of Vauxcelles's 'Recueil' of 1796, see the previous note, and *Mémoires*, p. 377. It's not clear whether the editors have decided to fix on 1795 as the date of completion for some unknown reason or association, or whether this date is the result of an oversight.

[8] It appears to be librarian and bibliographer (and the same person who was accused of atheism at the École normale, see above) Antoine-Alexandre Barbier's entry on 'Diderot' in his *Examen critique et complément des dictionnaires historiques les plus répandus* (Paris: Rey et Gravier ; Baudouin frères, 1820), t. 1, p. 256 which leads scholars Emmanuel Boussuge and Françoise Launay to think this. Barbier, who knew the whereabouts of the manuscript before it was published, does indeed say 'Il est bon d'observer que l'ouvrage de M. Naigeon n'est pas terminé' [it is right to observe that Mr Naigeon's work is not finished], although he doesn't substantiate his 'observation'. The preface of the Brière edition of the *Mémoires* does not state that is incomplete, but rather, that *without it*, the edition of Diderot's works and knowledge of his life would be incomplete: 'C'est cet ouvrage [...] qui laissait incomplètes et les *Œuvres* et l'histoire de la vie de celui qui éleva le monument encyclopédique' [it is this work (...) which left the *Œuvres* and the story of the life of the man who built the monument of the Encyclopedia incomplete] (p. v). The version that was published was, as Maurice Tourneux observed and we show in the digital edition [https://naigeons-diderot.mml.ox.ac.uk/files/main/msmvod.htm], lightly censored by the editors of the Brière edition in order to avoid post-publication difficulties (which came anyway) and was therefore itself not complete. The fact that a censored version was published does not mean that the work itself was left unfinished. The manuscript is, as Boussuge and Launay helpfully tell us, in the Bibliothèque Carnegie de Reims. See Emmanuel Boussuge and Françoise Launay, 'Du nouveau sur Jacques André Naigeon (1735–1810) et sur ses livres et manuscrits', RDE, 53.1 (2018), 145–92, https://doi.org/10.4000/rde.5698.

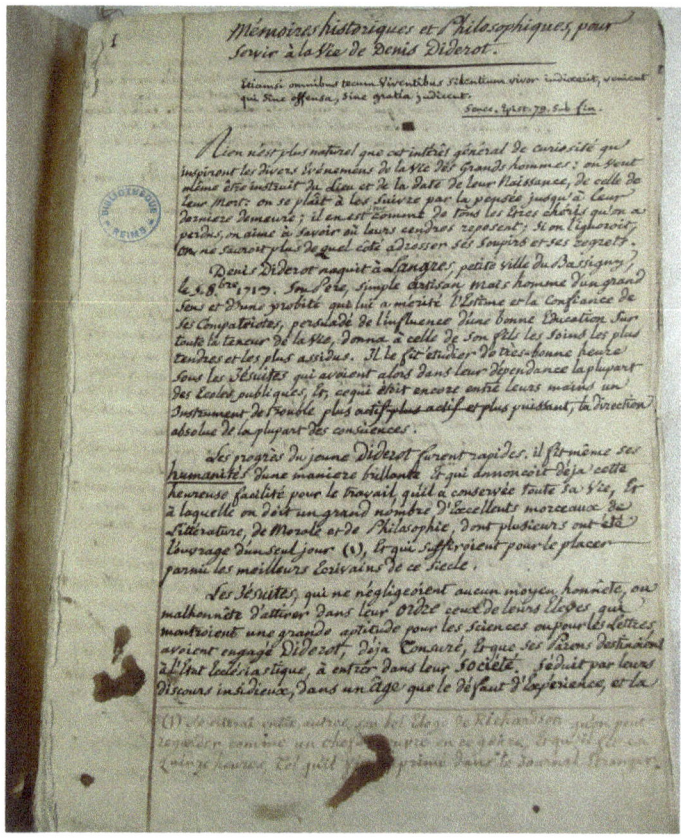

Fig. 12.1 First page of the manuscript of Naigeon's Mémoires, Bibliothèque Carnegie de Reims, MS 2127, f. 1., Jacques-André Naigeon (copyist probably his brother Charles-Claude), 1798-1800, Ink on paper, MS of Jacques-André Naigeon, Mémoires historiques et philosophiques sur la vie et les ouvrages de Denis Diderot, Bibliothèque Carnegie de Reims, CC-BY

Secondly, why was it not published during Naigeon's lifetime? He appears to have planned to publish it on completion—he repeatedly refers the reader to it, as we have seen. However, as we know, he did not publish it, and he died in 1810 with it still unpublished. We probably do not have to search far for reasons: already by 1800, Napoleon Bonaparte's censorship régime was firming up; in March 1801, the new illustrated edition of Sade's novels *Justine* and *Juliette* would be entirely destroyed; in April 1802, Naigeon's publisher Pierre Didot cut the anti-clerical preface to his edition of the Bordeaux copy of Montaigne's *Essais*; in 1805, Napoleon commanded that eminent astronomer Jérôme Lalande should no longer be allowed to publish, his atheism having become too strident.[9] Yet, it is not as if Naigeon's *Mémoires historiques et philosophiques* were censored (or not at this point); to be subject to censorship it would have needed to be published, and it did not even get that far.[10] Why would Naigeon not even *try* to publish something so important to him, something for which he had gone to such lengths to prepare an expectant space in the minds of those who read his utterances on Diderot? Rudolf Brummer, whose rather amazing research was published in 1932, shows us how indigent Naigeon was at this time. He was reliant on the French state for accommodation—granted to him as a member of the Institut national from its creation in 1795[11]—and was provided with free rooms overlooking the Louvre in the 'maison d'Angevilliers' (probably the Hôtel d'Angivillier or Angiviller, knocked down in the 1850s).[12]

In 1802, as a 'philosophe sans fortune', he was given the sum of 1,200 francs, in an order signed by Napoleon himself.[13] He did not receive any more such grants, and sold his collection of precious books to the publisher Didot in 1808, who set aside half of this amount to provide Naigeon with an annual income.[14] When Naigeon died in late February 1810, he was living with his sister, Mme Dufour de Villeneuve, in a flat on the Rue du Bac.[15] In sum, he could not afford to publish the *Mémoires historiques et philosophiques*; his financial situation was too precarious,

---

9   For Lalande, see Boussuge and Launay, 'Du nouveau sur Jacques André Naigeon', p. 166. In 1805, Lalande published a supplement to Sylvain Maréchal's *Dictionnaire des athées* which we have already had occasion to mention in connection to Sade, see above.

10  Of course, when they were finally published in 1823, they were immediately banned (David Adams, *Bibliographie des œuvres de Diderot, 1739–1900*, 2 vols (Ferney-Voltaire: Centre international d'étude du XVIIIe siècle, 2000), vol. 2, p. 141).

11  Naigeon was made a member of the Institut national, Classe des Sciences morales et politiques, but the section he was invited to be part of was 'Morale'. See above.

12  See https://bibliotheques-specialisees.paris.fr/ark:/73873/pf0001771897/0025. The Hôtel d'Angivill[i]er seems to have been on the now also non-existent Place de l'Oratoire, https://fr.wikipedia.org/wiki/Place_de_l%27Oratoire_(Paris); Brummer, *Studien*, p. 12; Brummer references the *Archives nationales*, AF III, 582, 3981, p. 64.

13  Brummer, *Studien*, p. 12; Brummer references the *Archives nationales*, AF IV, plaquette 389.

14  Boussuge and Launay, 'Du nouveau sur Jacques André Naigeon', pp. 166, 166 n. 73.

15  Boussuge and Launay, 'Du nouveau sur Jacques André Naigeon', p. 167.

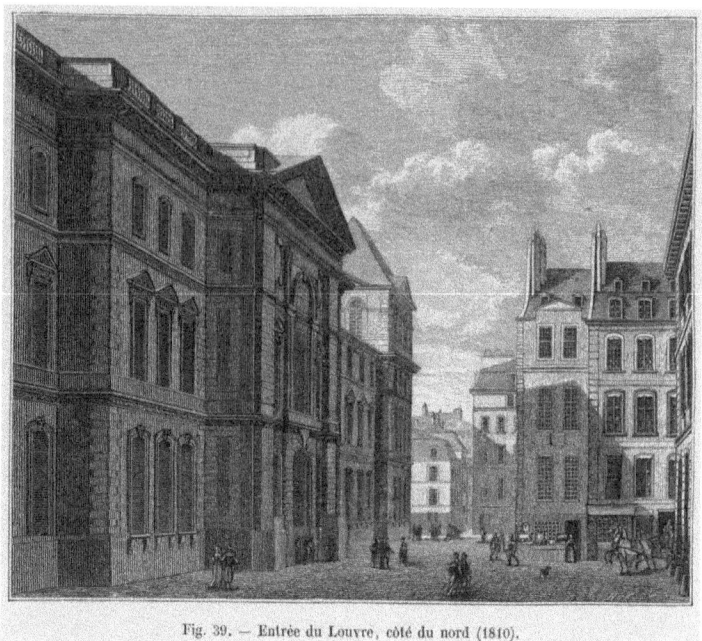

Fig. 12.2 Place de l'Oratoire, where Naigeon lived in the early 1800s, by unknown, c. 1810, Lithograph, From Fedor Hoffbauer, *Paris à travers les âges aspects successifs des monuments et quartiers historiques de Paris depuis le XIIIe siècle jusqu'à nos jours* (Paris: Firmin-Didot, 1875-1882). *Entrée du Louvre, côté du nord* (1810). Photo by Paris 16 (2013), Wikimedia, https://fr.wikipedia.org/wiki/Place_de_l%27Oratoire_(Paris)#/media/Fichier:Entr%C3%A9e_du_Louvre,_c%C3%B4t%C3%A9_du_nord,_1810.jpg, Public Domain

and he was personally indebted to Napoleon, as well as known by the Emperor to be a critic of his régime, Napoleon himself being one of the owners of the eight remaining copies of the censored Montaigne preface.[16] How the *Mémoires historiques et philosophiques* actually emerged into the world of print thirteen years later, in 1823, as the last volume in the Brière edition, is another slightly anxiety-inducing story to which we will come in due course.

As the editors of the Brière edition themselves announce in their 'Avertissement des Éditeurs', the *Mémoires historiques et philosophiques sur*

---

16   See above.

*la vie et les ouvrages de Denis Diderot* does two main things in the course of its 416 pages. Firstly, it gives 'l'histoire des ouvrages connus pour être de Diderot' [the history of the works known to be by Diderot] and secondly, it provides 'une analyse exacte de tous les manuscrits non publiés' [an accurate analysis of all his unpublished manuscripts]. In sum, it is a cross between an intellectual biography and an annotated bibliography, and its author repeatedly appeals to the 'lecteur philosophe' [philosopher reader] (pp. 164, 410), while lambasting the 'lecteurs superficiels, inattentifs et paresseux' [superficial, inattentive, and lazy readers] (p. 43), as well as those persecutors of Diderot who are as stupid as they are malevolent (p. 165). This differentiation between the philosophical and the superficial reader is one we have seen Naigeon make consistently.[17] What he does not do very much is communicate personal details about Diderot the man, as the 'Avertissement des éditeurs' also points out, and they therefore append Jacques-Henri Meister's short piece 'A la mémoire de Diderot' (1786).[18] They do not mention that they also include a three-page note in tiny font 'Extrait d'un manuscrit de M. de Vandeuil Diderot' [sic] which contains various sentimental details about his imprisonment at Vincennes, his difficulties with the *Encyclopédie*, the support he received from Catherine II of Russia, his death, what his autopsy revealed, and how Langres wished to celebrate its most famous son. This information is presumably drawn from the memoir written by Angélique Diderot, Mme de Vandeul, not by her husband; nor does his surname, Vandeul, contain the word 'deuil', *grief, mourning*, even if, in the context, the mis-spelling has a certain symbolic resonance.[19]

Naigeon, however, focuses on the writings, and discusses them chronologically, starting therefore with Diderot's first translation commission, of *L'Histoire de Grèce, de Temple Stanyan*, on page 30, to end, four hundred pages later with an almost throwaway, almost arrogant

---

17 See above.
18 'Avertissement des éditeurs', in Naigeon, *Mémoires historiques et philosophiques*, pp. v–vi. Meister's 'A la mémoire de Diderot' can be found on pp. 419–29.
19 Jules Assézat and Maurice Tourneux state that the *Mémoires pour servir à l'histoire de la vie et des ouvrages de Diderot par Mme de Vandeul, sa fille* were circulating from 1787. They were first published in 1830, in the *Mémoires, correspondance et ouvrages inédites de Diderot, publiés d'après les manuscrits confiés en mourant par l'auteur à Grimm*, also known as the *Œuvres inédites de Diderot*, 4 vols (Paris: Paulin, 1830), vol. 1, pp. 1–64. See Denis Diderot, *Œuvres complètes*, ed. by Jules Assézat and Maurice Tourneux (Paris: Garnier Frères, 1875–77), vol. 1 (1875), p. xxvi.

flourish: 'Voilà, en général, ce que j'avais à dire des manuscrits de Diderot' [That, in general, is what I had to say about Diderot's manuscripts], regretting the lack of a Pierre Bayle to assess the value of the *Œuvres de Diderot* he has brought out, and closing with a line from Montaigne.[20]

The *Mémoires historiques et philosophiques*, then, appears to be the third part of Naigeon's strategy for the publication of Diderot's works. The first part consists of the dictionary article on Diderot from 1792, in which he discussed the *Pensées philosophiques*, the *Lettre sur les aveugles* and the *Lettre sur les sourds et muets*, the *Pensées sur l'interprétation de la nature*, all works which had been published long before and were known to be by Diderot, while also publishing the *Principes philosophiques sur la matière et le mouvement* for the first time.[21] This is Diderot the philosopher, the emitter of wise aphorisms, the condensed and somewhat gnomic thinker. Secondly, in 1798, the *Œuvres de Diderot* in fifteen volumes, which presents the weighty and multi-faceted genius who is primarily a philosopher (vols 1–3), but also a dramatist (vol. 4), a historian of philosophy and encyclopedist (vols 5–6), an ancient historian and moralist (8–9), a novelist (vols 10–12), and a profound thinker about art (vols 13–15). As we see, the writer of fiction is sandwiched towards the back end of this panoply of production, detracting, so far as Naigeon is concerned, from the image he wishes to present to the (wary) public of Diderot as a serious philosopher, a virtuous moralist, someone who ponders the sublime, and is by no means the immoral monster or threat to the state whom Gracchus Babeuf and others (including Naigeon himself) had contributed to constructing.[22] Part three, then, is what we find in the *Mémoires*. Here, within the framework of the chronological account of the more-or-less virtuous and serious works Naigeon has already edited, he ever so carefully weaves in some of Diderot's unknown works and manuscripts.

Here he brings into the fold works that he had not previously mentioned: the *Promenade du Sceptique* (not published until 1830), the *Apologie de l'Abbé de Prades* (published in 1752, but often supposed to

---

20 Naigeon mentions Diderot's manuscripts: *Mémoires historiques et philosophiques*, p. 414; Bayle: p. 415; Montaigne: p. 416.
21 See above.
22 See above in Chapters 9 for Babeuf, and 10 for Naigeon's emphasis on Diderot the philosopher.

have been by the Abbé de Prades himself), the *Plan d'une Université pour le gouvernement de Russie* (first published, like Naigeon's *Mémoires*, in the Brière edition of 1821–23). These all appear as separate entries, all capitalised, in the table of contents, as indeed are all the other known and previously published works that appear there. Of the twenty-five headings, however, five are given in a little lower-case clump, separated only by the ELOGE DE RICHARDSON, and together they make up 126 pages, or more than a quarter of the book. Of these 126 pages, 100 are given over to the mesh of the *Éléments de physiologie* (which is not named) and the *Rêve de d'Alembert* (which is). The given titles of these lower-case sections are as follows: the *Suppression de l'Encyclopédie; Divers petits papiers; Danger imminent auquel Diderot se trouve exposé; Suite d'un entretien philosophique supposé, entre d'Alembert et Diderot; Le Rêve de d'Alembert*. In the first and third of these sections, Naigeon discusses the suppression of the *Encyclopédie* and the risk Diderot ran by not leaving Paris after the chevalier de la Barre's execution in 1766 when tensions ran high.[23] The second section, the 'Divers petits papiers' [various short papers], on which Naigeon bestows the grand total of three pages, refer to a trio of short pieces, the first two of which Naigeon had published in his *Œuvres*: 'Les Réflexions sur Térence' (now known as 'De Térence'), 'L'Histoire et le secret de la peinture en cire' [History and secret of painting in wax] and a 'Mémoire' [Memo] which Diderot wrote to defend the publishers of the *Encyclopédie* from the accusation—brought by Pierre-Joseph Luneau de Boisjermain (1731–1801)—that they had not fulfilled the promises laid out in their original prospectus in a lawsuit.[24] The final two of the modest lower-case headings, the *Suite d'un entretien philosophique supposé, entre d'Alembert et Diderot* and *Le Rêve de d'Alembert*, contain the core of the

---

23 François-Jean de la Barre, aged twenty, had been accused and convicted of blasphemy, impiety, and sacrilege, for having allegedly profaned a crucifix, failed to take his hat off when a religious procession passed, and owned infamous books, including Voltaire's *Dictionnaire philosophique*, a copy of which was nailed to his headless body and burned with him. Voltaire was safe in his château of Ferney on the Swiss border, but Diderot was within the instant grasp of the authorities, had they wished to seize him.

24 Naigeon, *Mémoires historiques et philosophiques*, pp. 194–95. For more on this suit, see Kate E. Tunstall, 'La fabrique du *Diderot-philosophe*, 1765-1782' , *Les Dossiers du Grihl*, 2 (2017), https://doi.org/10.4000/dossiersgrihl.6793, especially paragraphs 25–26, as discussed above.

book, and the titles would lead us to suppose that they discuss the first two parts of what we now know as *Le Rêve de d'Alembert*. *Le Rêve* would be published with all three parts in 1830.[25] As I will argue, their appearance in Naigeon's *Mémoires* constitutes the first print publication of both the *Rêve de d'Alembert* and the *Éléments de physiologie*, although as I will also show, both are considerably abridged and deformed. To consider why this is will also be my task, but no doubt the answer is partly that Naigeon is taking immense care to shepherd a very particular Diderot into the public arena, one that he hopes will survive unscathed, untainted by accusations of immorality. The anti-clerical atheist is not the Diderot Naigeon wishes to let go of; on the contrary. But he wishes to present his anti-clerical atheist as a virtuous hero of sublime nobility and seriousness. He can be atheist but not smutty or low, let alone debauched or immoral. Hence, presumably, his downplaying of Diderot the author of *Jacques le fataliste*.[26] Hence, also, one assumes, his non-inclusion of the *Neveu de Rameau*, which he only mentions in passing in a couple of sub-clauses as 'une excellente satire' (and not as anything more problematic than that); the *Paradoxe sur le comédien* is only alluded to and not even named.[27] Hence, furthermore, as we shall see, the removal from the *Rêve de d'Alembert* of all its racy aspects and its transformation into teacherly prose.

Naigeon's tripartite plan is consistent, so much so, that we should not be surprised to see a passage from the *Adresse à l'Assemblée nationale* we dwelt on at some length in an earlier section reappear at the very end of the *Mémoires historiques et philosophiques*, the part that says so forthrightly, 'quand on a quelque chose de bon à dire, il faut se presser' [when you have something good to say, you must hurry up and say it]: that entire passage is repeated here verbatim.[28] Perhaps he wrote it for the *Mémoires* first, and then re-used it in the *Adresse*. We cannot know, and it probably does not matter; the point is that what he published in

---

25  Denis Diderot, *Œuvres inédites de Diderot*, vol. 4, pp. 102–239. Followed by the *Promenade du sceptique*, pp. 241–382. The three parts are: L'Entretien entre d'Alembert; Le Rêve de d'Alembert; La Suite de l'Entretien.
26  See above.
27  Naigeon mentions the *Le Neveu de Rameau* in *Mémoires historiques et philosophiques*, p. 316; *Le Paradoxe sur le comédien* and implicitly *Neveu de Rameau* also: pp. 173–74.
28  See above; *Adresse à l'Assemblée nationale sur la liberté des opinions, sur celle de la presse*, etc. (Paris: Volland, 1790), pp. 9–10, re-used from *Mémoires historiques et philosophiques*, p. 413.

1790 and what he writes in the *Mémoires*, whether before or after, is all part of the same thing, part of the same approach, with a consistent conceptualisation and constant broadcasting of Diderot as a weighty moral atheist. The repeated cross-references across his various Diderot texts, not just forward to the unpublished and much heralded *Mémoires* but also back from them to his edition of the *Œuvres*, underscore the fact that this is a single grand design, a single weave, however complex, with repeating patterns or motifs.

Such a scheme is not surprising perhaps, given that Naigeon had been a contributor to the original *Encyclopédie*, with its extraordinary architecture of cross-references.[29] And yet the impact and very presence of the French Revolution, and the concomitant scattering and deferral of the dates of composition, completion, and publication of these different texts and editions, have made Naigeon's design rather hard to discern. However, the presence of the cross-references and the connections they make between the different parts shed some light, and in the various remarks Naigeon makes about editing in general and editing Diderot in particular, we find more. We have lifted these out for inspection wherever we have found them; it may be useful now to recall them.

In the censored Montaigne preface, Naigeon makes his most explicit statements about what an editor can and should do, perfecting the writing an author has produced, tidying the style, removing bumps that interrupt the harmony (literally *harmonising* it), and using his superior taste—his finer sense of beauty and of the proprieties—to add value to the resulting text. In his general preface to the *Œuvres de Diderot* and also in the individual introductions to *Jacques le fataliste* and *La Religieuse*, he explains what he would have removed from both of these novels, had he been the first to publish them and therefore had control over the text that appeared.[30] He returns to this theme in the *Mémoires*, and reiterates that *La Religieuse*, although an important novel, should have been shorn of some revolting and potentially morally dangerous scenes before

---

29  Naigeon contributed three articles to the *Encyclopédie*. They were: the opening section of 'Liberté', 'Richesse', and 'Unitaires'. See Franz A. Kafker and Serena L. Kafker, *The Encyclopedists as Individuals* (Oxford: Voltaire Foundation, 1988) reproduced in the online *Encyclopédie*, ed. by Robert Morrissey and Glenn Roe, https://artflsrv03.uchicago.edu/philologic4/kafker/navigate/1/97/.

30  See above.

publication, and that *Jacques le fataliste* is too long by half, being digressive and affected, often licentious and therefore (supposedly) insipid and cold.[31] It does not matter here whether Naigeon is demonstrating that he completely lacks any sense of humour or understanding of Diderot's depiction of bodies driven by desire, or whether he simply considers that such depictions are unwise given the generally hostile climate, and therefore unlikely to facilitate the acceptance of Diderot's works. His stated and restated view is that there are two Diderot tones, the sublime philosophical one which is excellent, and the low and informal one which is bad.[32] His duty, as he states it with great pride and emotion when publishing Diderot's letter to him, is to take on 'le soin d'arranger, de revoir et de publier tout ce qui lui paroîtra ne devoir nuire ni à ma mémoire, ni à la tranquillité de personne' [the duty to organize, review and publish anything which he considers will not do any damage to my memory or to anyone's security].[33] Thus, Naigeon presents himself as authorised to intervene as he sees fit, both by his general calling as an editor and also by Diderot's expressed wishes. And we can see that the likelihood is that he will suppress anything he perceives as being in bad taste, and that he may make innumerable small changes to 'harmonise' it. This much we can infer, but when it comes to his 'analyse raisonnée de celui de ces ouvrages qui m'a paru le plus profond' we also have his specific comments and framing.

Taking the specific comments first, he tells us how impossible it is to publish the substantial portfolio of manuscripts Diderot was writing between 1765 and 1779 (p. 205). This is for reasons to do with circumstances that 'il n'est point en [s]on pouvoir de changer' [it is not in [his] power to change] and which mean that 'l'épreuve pénible et dangereuse de l'impression' [the painful and dangerous ordeal of printing] cannot be thought of (p. 205). And thus he warns 'les dépositaires de ces manuscrits' [those who hold the manuscripts] not to publish these works in their entirety, because, however pure their intentions, it would damage Diderot's reputation to do so (p. 206).

---

31   Naigeon, *Mémoires historiques et philosophiques*, pp. 311–13.
32   Naigeon, *Mémoires historiques et philosophiques*, p. 206.
33   Naigeon, 'Préface de l'éditeur', in Diderot, *Œuvres* (Paris: Desray et Déterville, 1798), vol. 1, p. xxxii (for full quote, see above); Denis Diderot, *Correspondance*, ed. by Georges Roth and Jean Varloot, 15 vols (Paris: Minuit, 1955–70), vol. 12, p. 231 (3 June 1773).

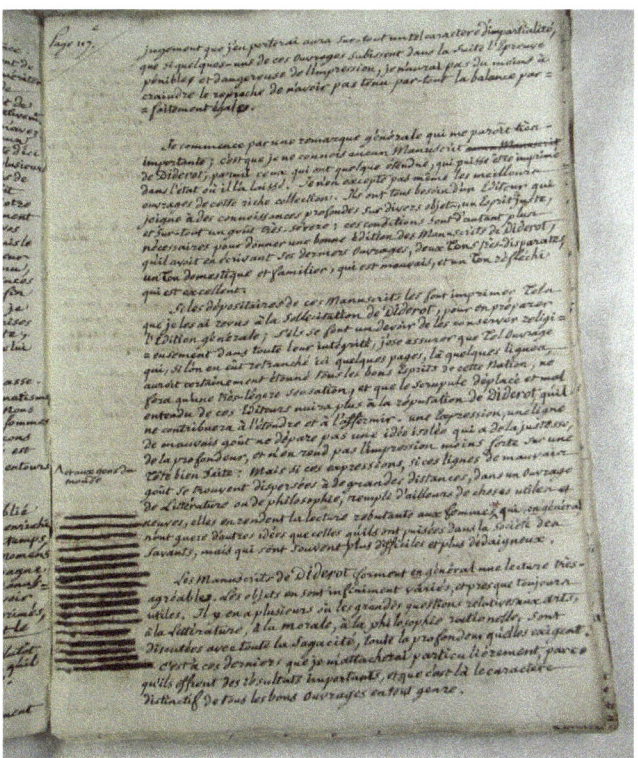

Fig. 12.3 Naigeon warns 'those who hold' Diderot's manuscripts not to publish them, Bibliothèque Carnegie de Reims, MS 2127, f. 117, Jacques-André Naigeon (copyist probably his brother Charles-Claude), 1798-1800, Ink and paper, MS of Jacques-André Naigeon, Mémoires historiques et philosophiques sur la vie et les ouvrages de Denis Diderot, Bibliothèque Carnegie de Reims, CC-BY

Here, of course, Naigeon is explicitly recalling the wording of Diderot's letter. Instead, Naigeon proposes that what is needed is 'éditeur qui joigne à des connaissances profondes sur divers objets, un esprit juste, et surtout un goût très-sévère' [an editor who combines profound knowledge across diverse subjects, a clear and accurate mind, and above all taste of the most rigorous kind] (p. 205). This knowledgeable and judicious editor with very severe tastes is, we divine, Naigeon himself. We know already that he will amend and cut where he sees fit, and so he says: he will be giving the reader 'une idée très-exacte' [an entirely accurate idea] of these works (p. 205), excising wherever required 'une expression, une ligne de mauvais goût' [an expression or a line in bad taste] specifically, he explains, to avoid provoking the hostility of women and high-society people, who, while being completely unoriginal themselves, are very hard to please and very contemptuous (p. 206). The idea of women as critics or arbiters of anything provokes almost as much of a venomous reaction in Naigeon as do priests, as his censored preface to the Montaigne edition makes rantingly explicit.[34] It is not therefore surprising that in the lines from the *Rêve de d'Alembert* in the following pages, the prominent role played by Julie de Lespinasse in the dialogue is removed, as is anything which fails to meet the 'very severe' standards of propriety whose necessity Naigeon has decreed.

These comments give us some general indication of what we can expect. Naigeon also frames the presentation of the texts quite carefully, clearly indicating start and finish, specifying what he will be focusing on at the beginning, and explaining how he has modified the texts at the end. Thus, he will particularly be looking at 'la morale' and 'la philosophie rationnelle' (p. 207).[35] Under the heading 'Suite d'un entretien philosophique supposé, entre d'Alembert et Diderot', which is very close to the title of the first dialogue in what is now known as the *Rêve de d'Alembert*, Naigeon explains that Diderot considered Locke and Condillac's writings on the workings of human understanding to be incomplete and often rather vague (p. 207). Diderot had therefore decided, Naigeon says, to:

> traiter ce sujet avec plus de précision, de philosopher sur des principes très-différents de ceux qui sont communément reçus, et de donner en quelque sorte une formule générale pour résoudre facilement toutes les questions qui concernent le phénomène identique de la sensation et de la pensée.[36]

> treat this subject with greater precision, to philosophise on the basis of principles which are completely different from those which are commonly accepted, and as it were to provide a sort of general formula for the easy resolution of all questions relating to the identical phenomenon of sensation and thought.

---

34 See above. See also Naigeon, *Mémoires historiques et philosophiques*, p. 410.
35 See https://naigeons-diderot.mml.ox.ac.uk/files/main/mvod.htm#page207.
36 Naigeon, *Mémoires historiques et philosophiques*, p. 207, and https://naigeons-diderot.mml.ox.ac.uk/files/main/mvod.htm#page207.

It seems worth drawing out how specific and yet wide-reaching this statement of Naigeon's is, even at the risk of simply paraphrasing it: Diderot planned to base his philosophy on different principles, to be much more precise, and to give some sort of general formula; this formula would henceforth resolve all questions relating to the sensation and thought, which in any case are the same thing. Naigeon's presentation of Diderot's plan seems strategically rather prudent: Locke and Condillac with the gaps filled in, plus some new and different principles (unspecified) to work from. This will make sense to the general educated reader of the time as well as to the 'lecteur philosophe' [philosopher reader], and be more or less unproblematic, and although we remember Louis-Claude de Saint-Martin's outrage that Condillac's theories should be deemed acceptable, it is clear from the publications of the Revolutionary government (the École normale, the Institut national) that Locke and Condillac's theories of thought were indeed widely accepted. What follows over the next three pages is not exactly what Naigeon will subsequently call 'le précis analytique' [analytical summary] of this imagined conversation between d'Alembert and Diderot, although with a few differences 'dans l'ordre et l'enchaînement des idées' [in the order and connection of the ideas] (p. 210). It is not a summary written by Naigeon. It is instead his selection of sentences and propositions from Diderot's text imported into this one, along with a few connectives, as consultation of the connected digital edition of these pages will demonstrate.[37] This is the first appearance of the opening section of the *Rêve de d'Alembert* in print, somewhere between a synopsis and a very harsh abridgement.[38] Naigeon does not in fact re-write the original; he cuts and he reorders. In it we find a few brief lines on sensibility as a property of matter, but the greater part of the quotation fixes on the repeated motif of the human as a musical instrument, whether as a philosophical one, as a feeling harpsichord or, different again, as merely an animal, also presented as a sensitive instrument whose strings can also be played or plucked.

He then starts working up to 'le second Dialogue', which he announces as being 'beaucoup plus varié et plus profond que le premier' [much

---

37 See https://naigeons-diderot.mml.ox.ac.uk/files/main/mvod.htm#page207.
38 Naigeon, *Mémoires historiques et philosophiques*, pp. 207–10. See https://naigeons-diderot.mml.ox.ac.uk/files/main/mvod.htm#page207.

more varied and more profound than the first] (p. 213); it is on this page, in a footnote, that he commences the quotation from the *Éléments de physiologie*. He continues to assert that the text is a dialogue, that it is called *Le Rêve de d'Alembert* (p. 213) and that what he is providing is 'une analyse' that is more or less exact (p. 219). Seventy pages later, he signals the end of his analysis of the 'second Dialogue' with a paragraph detailing his techniques and the negative consequences they may have had on the original. This is worth quoting in full, given how accurately he describes his editing technique (while concealing or disguising other aspects):

> Telle est, autant que ma mémoire et le secours de **quelques extraits très-succincts** faits autrefois sur l'original, pour ma propre utilité, peuvent m'en assurer, l'analyse de ce second Dialogue. **Si n'ayant aucune copie de ces deux manuscrits de Diderot**, il m'est arrivé quelquefois, comme cela est assez vraisemblable, **de changer l'ordre et l'enchaînement des idées de l'auteur**, c'est qu'indépendamment de cette raison qui explique et justifie assez ce renversement, cet ordre n'est pas le même pour **celui qui compose**, et pour **celui qui veut**, pour ainsi dire, **embrasser d'un coup d'œil** l'ensemble d'un ouvrage, et **indiquer rapidement les grands anneaux de la chaîne**, sans les lier entre eux par les idées intermédiaires. Je sens néanmoins que les raisonnements de Diderot, ainsi **abrégés, transposés, détachés du système** dont il font partie, et presque toujours **séparés de leurs principes généraux**, ou **des faits qui les éclaircissent et qui les confirment**, ne peuvent pas avoir pour ceux qui n'ont pas lu **son Dialogue, le même degré de force** et d'évidence qu'ils ont pour moi.[39]

> That, insofar as my memory and the help of a few **extremely short passages** copied long ago from the original for my personal use confirm, is the analysis of this second Dialogue. **If, having no copy of these two manuscripts of Diderot's**, it has sometimes occurred, as seems highly likely, that I **changed the order and connections of the author's ideas**, this is because, independently from this reason which is explanation and justification enough, the order is not the same for **the person who composes it** as it is for **the person who wishes**, so to speak, **to embrace in a single glance** the work as a whole, and **rapidly indicate the main links in the chain** without providing the intermediary ones. I sense nonetheless that Diderot's arguments, **abridged, transposed, detached**

---

39 Naigeon, *Mémoires historiques et philosophiques*, pp. 290–91 (my emphasis). See https://naigeons-diderot.mml.ox.ac.uk/files/main/mvod.htm#page290.

**from the system they were part of**, and almost always **separated from the general principles** and from the **examples which illustrate and prove them**, cannot have for those who have not read his **Dialogue, the same degree of force and evidence** that they have for me.

Taking these statements in order, let us start by dismissing the claim that 'quelques extraits très-succincts' could have supplied the range of quotation we find, either from the second part of the *Rêve de d'Alembert* or from the *Éléments de physiologie*. The 420 lines from the former and 1000 lines from the latter are from all over each text, and intricately woven together. Although the mesh of the two texts together is indisputably shorter than the two in their separate entirety, it is not made from a few very short extracts, and even less so from memory. It is implausible that he could have done this work without access to both in their manuscript form whether these were copies he himself had made, ones from the Fonds Vandeul, or yet others. The likelihood is that it is this specific piece of work that took him so many years to complete, and the term that is accurate is the plural noun 'extracts', not the misleading qualifiers.

Calling it 'ce second Dialogue', and therefore, in context, referring specifically to the text of which he has given an 'analysis' from page 213 to 290, he then claims to have no copy of either of the two manuscripts. This tells us that he is working not just with one source text but two, which is, as we know, the exact truth.

The third crucial element of this passage regards the description of his technique, which is to change the order of the author's ideas and the way they are linked together; he returns to this aspect to describe it again, stating that Diderot's arguments had been 'abrégés, transposés, détachés' [abridged, transposed, detached], and from what? From the system of which they were part, from their general principles, and from the 'facts' (or examples) which explain and demonstrate them. All these statements appear to be substantiated by the reworked text he gives us, which indeed is devoid of the starker materialist explication we find in Diderot, does explain things in a different order, and does give many fewer examples and cases. This is true whether we are talking here about the *Rêve de d'Alembert* or the *Éléments de physiologie*. Naigeon is right to fear that he has weakened the impact of the source text (or texts), but really, this is not about judging (or condemning) what he has done, but about noticing what he says: he states in perfect honesty that his version is less good than the source text (or texts), and in so doing signals the existence of the latter. Yet he also justifies his approach, thereby exemplifying his view of the editor's contribution: 'the person who composes' (the author) is not the same as 'the person who wants to see at a glance the entirety of a work and rapidly explain the main links in the chain' (the editor); we see also how 'the person who composes' is presented without any amplifying description, whereas the other (the editor) has a series of complex listed aims. The differentiation of authorial and editorial roles which we see in the censored Montaigne preface is therefore confirmed here, despite Naigeon's apologetic remarks about his account having less impact and being less persuasive.

It is at this point in the *Mémoires* that Naigeon begins to talk about fragments and scattered materials; in Chapter 2, we looked at how this passage repeats the opening 'Avertissement' of the *Éléments*, and how this particular mystification about its fragmentary and incomplete nature has been turned into the received story about it. I will not therefore return to that issue, but instead attempt to describe the version he gives us. He himself suggests, as we saw above, that what he has done is to give an overview such that the reader can see the whole at a glance, while also grasping the main links. However, as we already indicated, this is not quite right: it is not a summary of the whole of the *Éléments* and the whole of the second part of the *Rêve de d'Alembert*, also called the 'Rêve de d'Alembert'; it is a mosaic made from the two texts, and as a mosaic, it is not even very representative of its source texts. It focuses on various themes, broadly summarisable under the headings of sensation and human understanding, according to which it organises all the different Diderotian utterances. It is rather repetitive.

Before going further into our description, we should at this point remind ourselves of the different manuscript variants of the *Éléments de physiologie*, of which there are two still in existence, and one (which may or may not differ from the others) which is now lost. These are, firstly, the early draft that went with the collection of Diderot's manuscripts to Catherine II in Russia and is now in St Petersburg, secondly, the mature version that is part of the Fonds Vandeul in the Bibliothèque nationale in Paris, and thirdly, the copy recorded by Hippolyte Walferdin in 1837, along with its dedicatory letter to the Comité d'instruction publique dated 24 March 1794, and whose whereabouts are now unknown. We do not know whether Naigeon was using the early incomplete draft, the mature text, an intermediary or simply a different one. We could make arguments for all these to be the case, as there is evidence to support each supposition.[40] Without getting involved in the nitty-gritty of this particular issue at this stage, let us simply say that the most plausible solution is to suppose he had access to both the St Petersburg and the Vandeul versions, and maybe to the third (or another) one too, and that this would account for the presence of passages from each that are not in the other, and for some passages which follow the order of one manuscript, and others which follow the order of the other. This solution would also accommodate the fact that Naigeon draws on the 'Avertissement' which we find only in the mature Vandeul version.

To list the areas that Naigeon covers in the order that he covers them allows us to describe or characterise what he does while also serving to reveal the aspects he emphasises or repeats. I will not at this point look systematically at what comes from which text or version thereof, but will nonetheless signal some of the major switches between them. So, Naigeon's quotation from Diderot starts with a text from the *Éléments de physiologie* planted in a footnote on the brain (p. 213n), then gives a very condensed indication of the contents of the introduction and first two chapters ('Végéto-animal' and 'Animal', pp. 217-18), appends a note from the third chapter, 'Homme' (p. 218n), and then gives further quotation from this chapter, from the sub-section on the soul (p. 221). He then has a couple of pages on organs and sensibility (pp. 222-23). On the following page comes the explicit heading of *Le Rêve de d'Alembert*, although in fact he continues with the meshed quotation from the *Éléments de physiologie* (there has been none from the 'Rêve de d'Alembert' to this point),[41] pursuing aspects dealt

---

40   We will look at this later, and also at that point discuss Terada's view.
41   We use the italicised *Rêve de d'Alembert* to indicate the title of the work as a whole (with its three dialogues) and 'Le Rêve de d'Alembert' when we are talking about the second of these three dialogues. Naigeon only draws from this middle dialogue in these pages (*Mémoires historiques et philosophiques*, pp. 213-90), the 'Suite d'un entretien philosophique supposé, entre d'Alembert et Diderot' (the first part), having been dealt with earlier (pp. 207-10), and the third part, the 'Suite de l'entretien précédent' not even being mentioned.

with in the first section of the *Éléments*, and looking at the question of the sensitive molecule (p. 224). He moves from here to the nerve fibre as a combination of other fibres and of the animal as a bundle of fibres, to the properties of life, sensitivity and irritation being common to all life-forms (p. 225). He then turns to movement and its laws (pp. 225–26), to the ceaseless change of forms, and to how the brain and cerebellum and nerves are the first rudiments of the animal. The relationship between nerves and sensation, the health of nerves and the effect thereof on sensation follow (p. 227), along with the well-worn route from sensation to impression (p. 228), from impression to memory and thence to imagination (p. 229), to the perfecting or improvement of the senses (p. 230), and thereafter to the physiological characteristics of the nerves (p. 231). Nervous illnesses and the effects of compression on either the brain or the nerves are then mentioned (p. 232), as well as inflammation, and why pain is more intense than pleasure (p. 233). Muscle movement is discussed (p. 234) and then the different sorts of life, at the level of the molecule, the organ, and the animal as a whole; here we read about the increasingly unsociable dried-up old tendon, and learn that 'l'homme est d'abord fluide' [man is initially fluid] (p. 235).

Discussion of the organ continues, in terms of its development, aging, and relationship to the rest of the body, and we come across a further definition of man: 'l'homme est un assemblage d'animaux' [man is an assemblage of animals] (p. 236). The next few pages are given over to reproduction: these are some of the relatively few passages in which Naigeon draws on part 2 of the *Éléments de physiologie*, the 'Éléments et parties du corps humain'. This moves into a general theme of growth and transformation: 'un œil se fait comme une anémone [...], un homme se fait comme un œil' [an eye grows like an anemone (...) a man grows like an eye] (p. 239). This theme continues (pp. 240–41), and Naigeon quotes from the 'Rêve de d'Alembert' for the first time; he then places passages on the relationship of part to whole, and here we meet the famous 'grappe d'abeilles' [cluster of bees] (p. 240).[42] He returns to the *Éléments de physiologie* for further development of the relationship of part to whole; this is about the ligature of limbs and the capacity

---

42  In contradistinction to the 'Suite de l'entretien' which he quoted from in an earlier named section (Naigeon, *Mémoires historiques et philosophiques*, pp. 208–10).

of body parts to live separate from the whole (pp. 242–47): here we read that 'chaque organe a son plaisir et sa douleur particulières' [sic] [Each organ has its particular pleasure and pain] (p. 242), and that 'sur le champ de bataille les membres séparés s'agitent comme autant d'animaux' [on the field of battle, detached limbs move about like as many animals] (p. 246).

This leads to passages on the sense of self from the 'Rêve de d'Alembert' (p. 247), and we begin to see Naigeon's technique more clearly: he removes the to-and-fro of the speakers' exchange, while continuing to retain a certain oral quality; there is however, only one speaker, and that is 'Bordeu, ou Diderot dont il est ici l'interprète' [Bordeu, or rather Diderot whose mouthpiece he is] (p. 248). What is particularly striking about this is how Lespinasse is written out: this 'Bordeu, ou Diderot' is given one of her most famous passages, where she proposes the spider in its web as a way of understanding the relationship between the consciousness and the different body parts. Bordeu continues with her lines and his own, imperceptibly processed into smooth uninterrupted prose, as he considers the growth and development of the sensory organs (p. 249).

A new paragraph returns to the *Éléments de physiologie* to contemplate (again) 'la molécule sensible' [the sensitive molecule] (p. 249) and the infinite possibilities of sensation, in an oyster or a finger (p. 250). This shifts into a consideration (from 'Le Rêve') of how each strand ('brin') of living matter can be formed or deformed; these pages bring together passages from 'Le Rêve' and the *Éléments* on 'monsters', not considered as monstrous, or in later terms, as abnormalities, but as perfectly natural, part of the endless variation and production of nature, of which species themselves are part (pp. 251–52). Naigeon follows this up with sustained quotation from the bravura passages on the endless variant imperfection of human beings and on the absurdity of supposing a master craftsman could have created them, given how imperfect they are (pp. 253–54); this is from the conclusion of the *Éléments* (in the mature Vandeul version, that is).

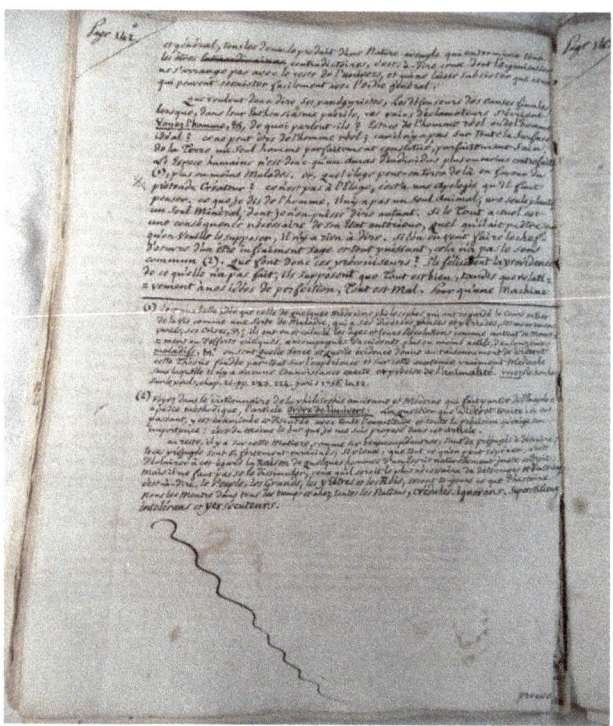

Fig. 12.4, Woven together extracts from the conclusion of the *Éléments de physiologie* and the *Rêve de d'Alembert*, Bibliothèque Carnegie de Reims, MS 2127, f. 142, Jacques-André Naigeon (copyist probably his brother Charles-Claude), 1798-1800, Pen and Paper, MS of Jacques-André Naigeon, Mémoires historiques et philosophiques sur la vie et les ouvrages de Denis Diderot, Bibliothèque Carnegie de Reims, CC-BY

This passage ends with an ellipsis of no fewer than five dots, and suddenly diverts into the theatricalised dialogue of *Le Rêve*, but with an extra twist: Naigeon introduces some rustling curtains. Thus Lespinasse and Bordeu do not just hear d'Alembert making an unspecified noise and fall quiet, as they do in Diderot's version(s); they hear him rustling the curtains round his bed. And so commences d'Alembert's grand dream monologue on shifting selfhood: 'Pourquoi suis-je tel? c'est qu'il a fallu que je fusse tel...' [Why am I this way? Because I had to be this way] (p. 255), much but not all of which is included although lightly reordered and intercut with thematically-related sentences from the *Éléments*. This is where d'Alembert contemplates change and the relationship of part to whole, concluding that flux is perpetual, and that the notion of the individual is meaningless, because not only does nothing ever stay the same, but also everything is an indivisible part of something bigger (p. 256), and furthermore that the species are also in flux (pp. 257–58). These are the pages (pp. 256–57) that Herbert Dieckmann's article of 1938 examined, when he first brought to light the presence of extensive quotation from the *Rêve de d'Alembert* and the *Éléments de physiologie*, which he at that point only knew in the incomplete early draft from St Petersburg which Assézat and Tourneux had published in 1875.[43]

Here Naigeon briefly emerges from the quotation mesh into overt commentary to declare that these ideas, merely 'systématiques' or abstract at this point in human knowledge, will come to be proven in the future, a claim which time has shown to be true, at least to some extent.[44] More locally, Naigeon also claims that d'Alembert's dreaming 'excursions' or 'trips', are very carefully placed within the system as a whole, that they are 'placées avec beaucoup d'art et de sobriété' [placed with great skill and sobriety] (p. 259). Sobriety? This seems almost comical for anyone who knows exactly what d'Alembert's trippy reveries involve. Not a chance, for example, that Naigeon will be mentioning d'Alembert's wet dream, let alone the third part of the *Rêve de d'Alembert*, the 'Suite de l'entretien précédent', where Lespinasse gives Bordeu a glass of malaga, and then asks him to tell her about miscegenation, overtly associating alcohol with dangerous freedom of thought.[45] The very mention of sobriety is like a flag signaling the opposite.

Soberly, in any case, Naigeon brings us back to theme of monsters, already touched on, and to the organisation of the organs (pp. 259–60); these sections are predominantly from the *Éléments de physiologie*, with just a few lively inserts from the 'Rêve', including Lespinasse's quip (non-attributed) on how man is the monstrous version of the woman and vice versa. The presentation of monstrosity becomes a discussion of different needs producing different organs, of how pain and pleasure

---

43 Herbert Dieckmann, 'J.-A. Naigeon's Analysis of Diderot's *Rêve de d'Alembert*', *Modern Language Notes*, 53.7 (1938), 479–86, https://doi.org/10.2307/2912683
44 See for example Phoebe von Held's experimental film, including interviews with scientists from the National Institute of Medical Research, London, 'D'Alembert's Dream', https://www.phoebevonheld.com/new-index#/dalemberts-dream, first shown at the 'State of Mind' exhibition, curated by Simon Gould and Ruth Maclennan, London School of Economics, 2005.
45 Diderot, *Le Rêve de d'Alembert*, ed. by Georges Dulac, in *Œuvres complètes*, DPV (Paris: Hermann, 1987), vol. 17, pp. 23–209 (p. 195).

drive us, and of how our vices and virtues are reliant on what our organs, understood as including the sensory organs and the imagination, are like; this then moves onto the topic of the perfectibility of organs (pp. 260–62). This organ-related material seems thematically connected, despite the fact that it is brought together from six different sections of the *Éléments* (this is the case for both draft versions), but Naigeon then, after only a semi-colon, shifts to what seems like a new topic, that of not being able to think when experiencing intense feeling (p. 262). He then returns to the brain and to Lespinasse's (unattributed) analogy of the spider (p. 263), and thence to the sense of self that arises from memory (p. 264); he meshes this with the notion that what characterises humans is their brain, returning to the previous strands on sensation without thought and on the potential faults in perception, on how a brain can misinterpret sensation (p. 265). This is developed into a political analogy (from the 'Rêve') about what happens when one or another part of the body becomes stronger than the rest (p. 266). He returns to the relationship between sensation, nerves, and thought in the brain, to the importance of memory particularly in connection to the self, to the result of imbalance and the types of character or profession produced by the various imbalances (again from the 'Rêve', pp. 267–68). He then looks at sleep and dreaming (pp. 270–71); this section draws its passages from both source texts, although the *Éléments* predominates. Then considering the sense of self during sleep, he introduces the theme of freedom or the will, or rather, in Diderot's deterministic account, the extent and influence of involuntary actions (pp. 272–73). Naigeon then provides a long counter-example, showing how instinct can misdirect. This is Diderot's proof (from the *Éléments*) that if you happen to find yourself in an out-of-control carriage, you should throw yourself out over the back wheel not the front one, because otherwise the back wheel will run you over. In a footnote, Naigeon explains how Diderot first presented this idea in a conversation with high-society people in St Petersburg, and how the mathematician Leonhard Euler, who was present, failed to back him up while knowing perfectly well that Diderot was right (pp. 274–76; the abundantly detailed footnote continues for a further couple of pages).

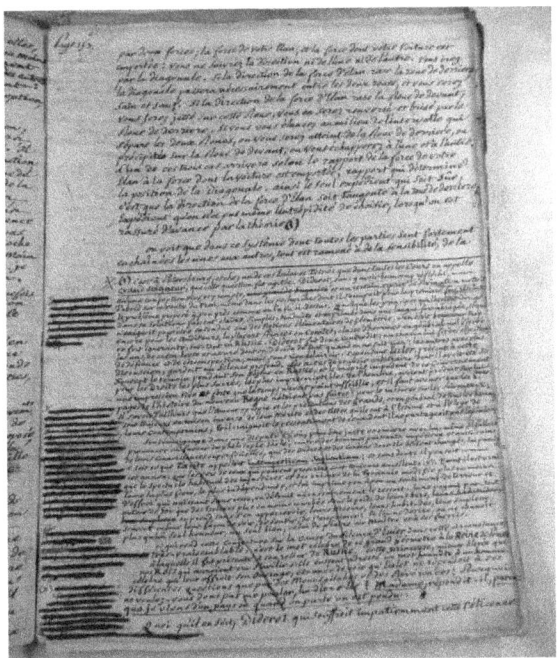

Fig. 12.5 Diderot's proof about which side of a carriage to throw yourself out of, Bibliothèque Carnegie de Reims, MS 2127, f. 153, Jacques-André Naigeon (copyist probably his brother Charles-Claude), 1798-1800, Pen and paper, MS of Jacques-André Naigeon, Mémoires historiques et philosophiques sur la vie et les ouvrages de Denis Diderot, Bibliothèque Carnegie de Reims, CC-BY

The main text then returns again to the question of the relative balance and operation of the different organs, and introduces the theme of genius (from the 'Rêve'). Naigeon then, in his own voice, paraphrases Diderot's views on the deleterious effect of excessive study, following this with a brief but intense rant about Jean-Jacques Rousseau who said something similar in the *Discours sur l'inégalité*; Naigeon calls this seminal text 'une espèce de roman métaphysique' [a sort of metaphysical novel] (pp. 278–79). Post-rant, he resumes his quotation mosaic to pursue the topic of the ill-health of the studious person, signalling the switch with a 'quoi qu'il en soit, voici l'observation de Bordeu' [in any case, this is the observation Bordeu makes], although what follows is in fact from the *Éléments*.[46]

---

46   On the deleterious effects of excessive study, see Anne C. Vila, *Suffering Scholars: Pathologies of the Intellectual in Enlightenment France* (Philadelphia, PA: University of Pennsylvania Press, 2018), https://doi.org/10.9783/9780812294804

He comes out of his quotation mosaic again to comment that because Bordeu is being harried both by the doubts or objections of d'Alembert and also by 'les questions de mademoiselle Delespinasse' [Mlle de Lespinasse's questions], he is not always as thorough as he might be. This is an interesting mark of Naigeon's hostility to the dialogue format which he systematically erases from actual quotation of the 'Rêve', while nonetheless retaining its nominal presence in the form of the frequently mentioned title, the 'second dialogue', and as part of his own framing—for example, 'voici l'observation de Bordeu' [this is the observation Bordeu makes]. Despite these claims about d'Alembert and Lespinasse, the passages that Naigeon is here introducing and excusing are taken from the *Éléments*, and what he is specifically apologising for or justifying is a certain rapidity: 'c'est ainsi qu'il explique en peu de mots, mais avec une singulière précision, les divers phénomènes du jugement, du raisonnement, de la formation des langues' [this is how he explains in few words but with striking precision, the diverse phenomena of judgement, reasoning, and the formation of languages] (p. 280). And this introduces pages of quotation, in more sustained and less re-ordered chunks than usual, from the chapter on 'Entendement' [the Understanding]: we move from sensation to idea and thence to language (pp. 280–82) and to the imagination: here the complex meshing patterns return, drawing from different parts of the *Éléments* (in either version) and also from the 'Rêve', although in smaller quantity (pp. 283–84). Naigeon then returns to the question of sensation and its functioning, and how sensation leads to judgement (p. 285). This makes way for a new topic, that of only being able to focus on one thing at a time, already implicit in the previous discussion of not being able to think when experiencing intense feeling. This also allows Naigeon to score a point against Condillac, who supposedly did not notice this aspect (p. 286); Naigeon will return to Condillac later to conduct a very thorough assault on his work (pp. 292–307). Meanwhile, he switches to the question of abstraction, using an extensive passage from the 'Rêve' that argues that 'toute abstraction n'est qu'un signe vide d'idées' [any abstraction is only ever a sign devoid of ideas] (p. 287). He has almost reached the end of the quotation mesh here, and he begins to conclude, praising 'ce profond Dialogue' [this profound Dialogue] for the way in which Diderot develops all the different parts of his system, how well it all hangs together, how enlightening it is about the operations of the human understanding, the perfecting of which, he says, can only be found in the works of those who follow the route laid out in 'these dialogues' and base their philosophy on Diderot's principles (p. 288). This claim that there are people who do follow the route laid out in 'these dialogues' is one we will return to in a few paragraphs.

Meanwhile, he gives one last passage from the *Éléments*, internally uncut, on the way in which an eye senses a tree and the soul gets an idea of it (pp. 289–90); by way of an introduction, he remarks again that Condillac failed to think of this issue (p. 288); he is beginning to prepare the way for his attack on Condillac. Placing an 'etc' to indicate the end of the quotation, Naigeon then commences his retrospective overview: 'Telle est, autant que la mémoire et le secours de quelques extraits très-succincts faits autrefois sur l'original, pour ma propre utilité, peuvent m'en assurer, l'analyse de ce second Dialogue' [That, insofar as my memory and the help of a few extremely short passages copied long ago from the original for my personal use confirm, is the analysis of this second Dialogue] (p. 290): we analysed this passage earlier.[47]

The attack on Condillac, running for many pages, is a crucial part of the presentation of the quotation mesh from the 'Rêve' and from the *Éléments de physiologie*. It is not merely a violent critique of Condillac but more importantly a comparison of Condillac's and Diderot's theories of human understanding which aims to sweep aside Condillac and give Diderot his place and prestige. His final swipe, not just at Condillac but Rousseau too, both of whom he derisively calls the 'saints du jour' [saints of the day], is also targeted at all the 'petits profonds' [tiny thinkers] who content themselves with rehearsing Condillac's views (pp. 306–07).

The nineteenth-century philosopher and historian of philosophy, Jean-Filibert Damiron (1794–1862), in his *Mémoire sur Naigeon* (1857), asks who these 'petits profonds' could be, saying that 'Je ne vois guère à citer que Gurat [sic], qui ne l'aimait pas, et auquel sans doute il le rendait' [I cannot see who to cite other than Gurat who disliked him, and whom he no doubt also disliked].[48] 'Gurat', one supposes, is a typo for Dominique-Joseph Garat. But I wonder whether Naigeon really is

---

47  See above.
48  Jean-Philibert Damiron, Mémoire sur Naigeon et accessoirement sur Sylvain Maréchal et Delalande (Paris: Durand, 1857), reprinted in *Mémoires sur les Encyclopédistes* (Geneva: Slatkine Reprints, 1968), p. 67.

Fig. 12.6 Condillac and Rousseau the "saints of the day", Bibliothèque Carnégie de Reims, MS 2127, f. 168, Jacques-André Naigeon (copyist probably his brother Charles-Claude), 1798-1800, Pen and paper, MS of Jacques-André Naigeon, Mémoires historiques et philosophiques sur la vie et les ouvrages de Denis Diderot, Bibliothèque Carnegie de Reims, CC-BY

targeting Garat or the Ideologues more generally here; it seems unlikely given their own insistent criticism of Condillac and also the presence we have traced within their work of the *Éléments de physiologie*: the particular aspects of their discussion of human understanding which I have argued came from the *Éléments* are also present in Naigeon's *Mémoires*, whether we are talking about sensation-based thought, the importance of the imagination, or the potential for the perfecting of the senses. Naigeon would have recognised these aspects when he heard or read their work, even if he had not himself been party to communicating Diderot's theories to them in the first place. Furthermore, in the *Mémoires historiques et philosophiques*, Naigeon twice mentions Diderot's 'idées mères' [mother ideas], these highly fertile ideas of his, that were so influential and whose phrasing is so recognisable (pp. 168, 412). It seems more likely that when he says that some of these 'idées mères' 'se retrouvent plus ou moins développées dans plusieurs ouvrages publiés de son temps, et dans quelques autres qui ont paru depuis, et qu'on a même beaucoup loués dans certains journaux' [can be found, more or less developed, in many works of his time and in some that have been published since, and which have received much praise in certain newspapers] (p. 412), and when he praises 'ceux qui suivent en général la route tracée de ces deux dialogues, et qui philosophent sur les principes de l'auteur' [those who in general follow in the path laid out by these two dialogues and who philosophise according to the author's principles] (p. 288), he is alluding to Garat, Cabanis, and Destutt de Tracy, and that therefore, when he attacks the disciples of Condillac, he is *not* targetting the Ideologues. However, this is what, via Damiron, has generally been supposed.

It is important, moreover, not to lose sight of what Naigeon claims here, that 'la route tracée de ces deux dialogues' [the path laid out by these two dialogues] *is being* followed by others. This is a crucial confirmatory claim for this study, that is, that the *Éléments de physiologie* were known, and were influencing the work of others. He does not say who he means, and we cannot know for sure. But it seems likely, given the common emphasis on human understanding that all these works share, that he is alluding to the work of the Ideologues. It is also possible, given the prominent position given to Bordeu, that Naigeon is thinking of vitalist doctors, such as Paul-Joseph Barthez and Paul-Victor de Sèze, both of whom he mentions as worthy of 'toute l'attention des philosophes' [all the attention of the philosophers].[49] However, it remains more likely, given the common focus on the human understanding, that he is referring primarily to the Ideologues.

Let us also linger for a moment on the title that Naigeon consistently uses, *Les deux dialogues*. These two dialogues, according to Naigeon's own internal subtitles, are the 'Suite d'un entretien philosophique supposé, entre D'Alembert et Diderot' (p. 207) and 'Le Rêve de d'Alembert' (p. 224), and as we have seen, the first is an accurate title,

---

49  Naigeon, *Mémoires historiques et philosophiques*, p. 223n for both Barthez and de Sèze; see also 233n and 245n for further extensive reference to (and quotation from) Barthez.

whereas the second is accurate to some extent, in that it does indeed introduce considerable quotation from 'Le Rêve', but also, as we know, contains concealed quotation from another, more substantial source. In fact the title of *Les deux dialogues* is not particularly mysterious. It was the title that Diderot himself gave *Le Rêve de d'Alembert* when it was freshly written; there are two instances of him referring to it by that name in his letters to Grimm from November 1769, as Georges Dulac tells us.[50] *Les deux dialogues* is also the title of a version which Diderot had copied for Catherine II in St Petersburg in 1774, with different names given for the interlocutors, and which has an opening letter to her in which he also uses a story of broken fragments.[51] This letter, however, is not quite the same as the one he will later use as the 'Avertissement' of the *Éléments de physiologie*; we have mentioned this piece, and where it fits in the narrative of the fragments, in an earlier chapter.[52] Emphasising the importance of the fragment motif, at the end of this copy of *Les deux dialogues* we find the *Fragments dont on n'a pu retrouver la véritable place*, the very first draft of the *Éléments de physiologie*.[53] Naigeon knew of the *Rêve de d'Alembert* from its very earliest versions and made a copy of it at that time, and it, along with a copy made much later, are now used to track the different draft levels of the *Rêve*.[54] So he would have known it, if not exclusively, by that title.

We have already sketched out a few suggestions for why Naigeon should have wished to mask the existence of this separate work on physiology, which are broadly that he is presenting a particular version of Diderot as the weighty philosopher of human understanding who has corrected and overtaken Locke and Condillac. Thus he minimises some of the more overt statements of materialism (they become implicit rather than explicit) and also removes anything which runs the risk of being labelled immoral. And yet, as we know, he did not completely hide this separate work. Instead, he gave it a sort of potential existence,

---

50   Georges Dulac in DPV 17, p. 76. See Denis Diderot, *Correspondance*, ed. by Roth and Varloot, vol. 9, pp. 190, 207.
51   See Dulac, 'Etablissement du texte', *Le Rêve de d'Alembert*, DPV 17, p. 76 (this manuscript is known as 'MD').
52   See Chapter 2, 'From Elements to Fragments'.
53   DPV 17, p. 225. *Le manuscrit de Pétersbourg/1774/Avertissment des deux dialogues/ Fragments dont on n'a pu trouver la véritable place*, ed. by George Dulac, DPV 17, pp. 213–60.
54   See Dulac, 'Etablissement du texte', *Le Rêve de d'Alembert*, DPV 17, p. 75 ($N^1$); 80 ($N^2$).

as a series of letters which Diderot planned to address to Naigeon and in which he was to give 'à sa manière, une nouvelle théorie, ou plutôt une histoire naturelle et expérimentale de l'homme' [in his manner, a new theory or rather a natural and experimental history of man], but which, sadly, he never got round to, leaving only disordered fragments (p. 291). This is the already-alluded-to re-evocation of the 'Avertissement' to the *Éléments de physiologie*. So he did not hide it completely.

It has also been our consistent view that Naigeon's version of this 'Second dialogue' is indeed his version, and not the reproduction of a further text by Diderot himself.[55] There are a number of reasons to support this view, starting with the commonsensical one that there exist many manuscript copies of the *Rêve de d'Alembert* (Dulac uses twelve principle ones in his DPV edition), and two extant known copies of the *Éléments de physiologie*, while there is not a single manuscript from Diderot's lifetime that meshes them. Secondly, we have Naigeon's repeated remarks on the editorial role in general, as well as his own views of what needs to be done with respect to Diderot's manuscripts and the *Deux dialogues* in particular, and indeed what he has done, reorganising and transposing Diderot's 'raisonnements' (arguments). What he claims to have done is borne out exactly by our own work tracking these reorganised and transposed arguments.[56] Furthermore, we have a precious trace of Naigeon's technique in a piece of marginalia in his copy of the *Rêve*: next to Bordeu's remark on the persistence of pain in a limb that is no longer there, Naigeon adds a passage from the *Éléments*, which he annotates as being from the 'Physiologie de Diderot'; these two passages are then sewn together in the *Mémoires* (p. 265), with the passage from the *Éléments* following the Saint Petersburg manuscript word for word (although the Vandeul version is also very close).[57]

---

55   Terada also holds this view, calling it instead 'une réécriture totale' [a complete rewriting] (MT 64–65). I would simply add that it's a *re-ordering*, not a *rewriting*.

56   Dulac, while dismissing the *Mémoires* as a useful variant text of the *Rêve*, clearly holds the same view. He writes that 'Ce ne sont cependant que des morceaux combinés dans un nouvel ensemble et il nous a pas paru possible d'en tenir compte dans l'apparat critique' [they are however nothing other than snippets of text arranged in a new order and it did not seem possible to us to include them in the critical apparatus] (Dulac, 'Etablissement du texte', *Le Rêve de d'Alembert*, DPV 17, p. 84). He refers the reader to Dieckmann's 1938 article on Naigeon: Dieckmann, 'J.-A. Naigeon's Analysis of Diderot's *Rêve de d'Alembert*'.

57   This information comes from Jean Varloot and Georges Dulac's edition. The section from *Le Rêve* is: 'on sent du mal à un membre qu'on n'a plus' [we feel pain in a

The question that remains is thus which manuscript version he was using, the early draft held in St Petersburg (hereafter SP), and published in the Assézat and Tourneux edition, or the mature draft held in the Fonds Vandeul (hereafter V) in the Bibliothèque nationale de France, as edited by Jean Mayer in DPV and subsequently by Paolo Quintili and Motoichi Terada. We said earlier that it seems most likely that he had access to both of the versions of the *Éléments de physiologie* we still have, and probably also to a third version that we no longer have access to.[58] (I am not assessing which particular manuscript or manuscripts of the *Rêve de d'Alembert* Naigeon was using.) I would now like to add some detail to this proposition, while avoiding cumbersome text comparison and commentary. The different layers and sources of the text can be instantaneously visualised in the digital edition, and I refer the reader to it for the nitty-gritty.[59] Here I want to bring together a few clear examples to show that Naigeon was using both extant manuscripts of the *Éléments*, and sometimes prefers one, sometimes the other. Starting with the mundane, I will look at a few single word variants; I will then look at the order in which Naigeon quotes chunks from the source texts to see whether we can establish which one he is following, the two

---

limb we no longer have] (*Le Rêve de d'Alembert*, DPV 17, p. 156), and in Naigeon's manuscript this passage is added: 'Lorsqu'on avait le membre, de ce membre affecté la sensation allait au cerveau; si par quelque cause la sensation est ressuscitée, alors on rapportera la sensation à son ancienne origine, et l'on aura mal au membre qu'on n'a plus. Souvent la douleur se fait sentir ailleurs qu'à la partie blessée; c'est un effet de la liaison du nerf avec un autre dont l'origine est commune à tous les deux. Physiologie de Diderot' [when we had the limb, the sensation went from the affected limb to the brain; if for some reason the sensation is restimulated, then we will associate the sensation with its old origin, and we will feel pain in a limb that we no longer have. Often the pain is felt somewhere other than in the injured part; this is an effect of the nerve being connected to another one with which it shares a common source. Diderot's Physiologie] (DPV 17, p. 156n; we find it the Saint Petersburg version, p. 312; the very close variant is Diderot, *Éléments de physiologie*, ed. by Paolo Quintili (Paris: Champion, 2004), pp. 284–85 [hereafter PQ], and DPV 17, p. 459. These two passages run on in the *Mémoires historiques et philosophiques*, pp. 265–66).

58  Motoichi Terada, whose edition of the *Éléments de physiologie* includes an appendix with the relevant pages from Naigeon's *Mémoires historiques et philosophiques*, with footnotes giving the source passages in the *Rêve de d'Alembert* and the *Éléments de physiologie*, considers that Naigeon was using SP (MT 57). He accounts for those elements in the *Mémoires* that seem closer to V by suggesting that Naigeon was developing his own analysis, one that seems to have coincidentally moved in the same direction as V (MT 66, 68).

59  See https://naigeons-diderot.mml.ox.ac.uk/index.htm.

manuscripts being organised completely differently, and I will also note the distribution of quoted passages according to the source chapters or sections; I will subsequently note where passages which are only in one of the versions of the *Éléments* are quoted by Naigeon in the *Mémoires*, and I will finally point to a passage that is to be found in neither of these extant versions, and may therefore point to a further manuscript variant. In each case, following chronological order of composition, I will take SP first and V second.

So, the words: in the *Mémoires*, we read about how the organs can be arranged in the wrong order 'depuis l'orifice de l'œsophage jusqu'à l'extrémité du canal intestinal' [from the orifice of the oesophagus to the very end of the intestinal canal] (p. 260): the word *orifice* is in SP, whereas V corrects this to *origine*.[60] This suggests that SP is the source text. However, in a passage on dreams, Naigeon mentions the disconnected dream which 'suscite une image' [provokes an image] (p. 270); *suscite* is in V, whereas SP has *surexcite* [over-excites].[61] Furthermore, when Naigeon is quoting passages about the dangers of excessive study, he writes that: 'l'homme de la nature est fait pour penser peu et agir beaucoup; la science, au contraire, pense beaucoup et se remue peu' [natural man is made to think only a little and act a lot; knowledge on the other hand thinks a lot and moves only a little] (p. 279): SP had had *l'homme de la nature* [natural man] matched by its equivalent *l'homme de la science* [the scholarly man, the mean of learning], whereas Naigeon and V miss out *l'homme de*, and simply say *la science*: this seems like a mistake, and it is common to both.[62] Thus it looks as if the particular phrasing (and probably mistake) of V is replicated in Naigeon's *Mémoires*.

Next, the order of texts: Naigeon reproduces a long passage on how violent sensation is incompatible with thought (p. 262) which we find in exactly the same form in SP (p. 356) but which is cut into two in V and placed into sections which are far apart (pp. 294, 146). Furthermore, two pages (pp. 372–73) from the section in SP entitled 'Entendement' are quoted verbatim in Naigeon (pp. 280–83), whereas

---

60 SP 420; V: Diderot, *Éléments de physiologie*, ed. by Jean Mayer, *Œuvres complètes*, DPV (Paris: Hermann, 1987), vol. 17, pp. 261–574 (p. 445) [hereafter DPV]/PQ 266/ MT 261. SP refers to the early draft now held in St Petersburg; V stands for Vandeul, the archive holding the mature version.
61 SP 362; V: DPV 482/PQ 312/MT 297.
62 SP 273; V: DPV 511/PQ 353/MT 324.

this passage is divided in V and placed in two chapters, 'Entendement' and 'Imagination' (pp. 288–89; 303–04). So this is strong evidence of SP's presence. In favour of V, we have a more complex case to present, whereby we find the source texts for a page of quotation on sensations and their variety in Naigeon in two pages from the same chapter and sub-section in V (pp. 285–86), although they are somewhat chopped about and re-ordered. However, when we look at SP, we find these same sections drawn from six pages and four different sub-sections of SP (in order of quotation: p. 358 ['*Sensations*: Effet Bizarre'], p. 356 ['*Sensations*'], pp. 355–56 ['*Sensations*'], p. 349 ['*Sens internes*: Sens en général'], pp. 350–51 ['*Sens internes*: sensations'], and as the parentheses hopefully show, from two separate main headings ('*Sens internes*' and '*Sensations*', which have their own subsections, one of which is, confusingly, 'sensations'). This seems to show that the reworked text, V, is being followed here, rather than the obviously messy and repetitive SP. Yet the picture is not clear, and one phrase we find in SP and Naigeon does not make its way into V.[63] This is why it seems likely Naigeon was consulting both draft versions, and possibly a third one as well.

There are further examples of quotation from passages we can source to only one of the versions, and again this leads us to both of them. Naigeon quotes SP on healthy nerves and free communication between the nerve and the brain (N 227; SP 311), as well as a paragraph on seminal fluid which Diderot describes as a 'folie conjecturale' [conjectural madness] (N 238; SP 403); the first statement can be found reworded in V, but the 'folie conjecturale' is not included at all.[64] However, the story Naigeon tells about Diderot's 'système particulier de physiologie' (p. 291) draws, as we have already shown, on the 'Avertissement' to V, so again, we have evidence of the presence of both draft versions. Although not conclusive, it may also be worth noting that when we plot Naigeon's quotation against the table of contents of the Vandeul version, we find that he quotes from every chapter in the first and third parts ('Des Êtres' and 'Phénomènes du cerveau' respectively), and from only seven of the twenty-five chapters from

---

63 'L'impression naît du dedans ou du dehors, selon l'organe affecté. L'impression est ou goût, ou odorat, ou vision, ou son, ou toucher' [the impression arises from inside or outside, depending on the affected organ]. Naigeon, *Mémoires historiques et philosophiques*, p. 228; SP 356.

64 DPV 458/PQ 284/MT 274.

the second part ('Éléments et parties du corps humain'). This shows a clear preference for the introductory first part considering life as an interconnected whole and for the last part focusing on sensation and the workings of the brain, to the partial exclusion of part two, with its technical physiological description, resulting, as Motoichi Terada points out, in a de-Hallerised version of the *Éléments de physiologie*.[65] We have already noted this thematic preference, and that this is also a feature of the works of Garat, Cabanis, and Destutt de Tracy.[66] This profile is much clearer to see in V. In SP, any pattern in the quotation is much harder to discern, as SP is not organised into parts, and as we have already seen, some sub-headings in one area are the same as main headings of another; this is part of its early-draft character. Thus, there are forty-seven headed sections (they often have single paragraphs that have their own sub-headings too, but they are not being counted here), and of these forty-seven, Naigeon quotes twenty-eight, with most passages coming from 'De l'homme' and 'Cerveau et cervelet' (twelve each), 'Animaux' (ten), 'âme' (eight), and 'Entendement' and 'Mouvement' (seven each), 'Organes' (six), with the following three chapters all equal—'Sens internes', 'Sommeil' and 'Nerfs' (five). Thereafter the instances of quotation are too scattered to be helpful to record.

It is difficult to pronounce clearly one way or another when surveying this evidence about the source passages, but the slight preponderance of texts from SP (both with respect to their ordering and the presence of passages absent from V), when considered alongside the relative distribution of the quotation, may suggest that Naigeon was more familiar with SP than V, and plundered it rather than V for preference, but that the re-structured mature version did nonetheless influence his understanding of it; the fact that he quotes from every chapter of the first and final parts of V tends in this direction. In favour of his also having access to a further manuscript version, we might point to a passage which is not to be found in either SP or V, and to a note which

---

65    MT 59: 'On peut ainsi constater l'absence presque totale de Haller dans le *Précis du Rêve*, malgré les nombreuses citations des *EP* [it can therefore be seen that Haller is almost completely absent from the *Summary of the Dream*, despite the numerous quotations from the *Elements of Physiology*]. Haller as in Albrecht von Haller, pre-eminent physiologist, discussed in Chapter 3.

66    See Chapters 8 and 9.

resembles passages from SP and V in different ways, and seems more likely to have been from a different version than a splicing of the two.[67]

This, then, was what Naigeon had long been referring to, his 'analyse raisonnée de celui de ces ouvrages qui m'a paru le plus profond'.[68] We can measure the distance of this piece of work from the 'quelques extraits très-succincts' [a few extremely short passages] (p. 290) which, he claims, were all he had to work from, or the 'quelques matériaux épars' [a few scattered materials] (p. 291) that Diderot had supposedly left; we see how this story is tailored to pick up on and continue Diderot's claims in the 'Avertissement' from V. It is not impossible that Naigeon may even have taken encouragement for his reordering project from this very 'Avertissement'; we saw in Chapter 10 that he was already poised to operate in that way.[69]

His *Mémoires historiques et philosophiques sur la vie et les ouvrages de Denis Diderot*, however, were not published during his lifetime. Emmanuel Boussuge and Françoise Launay trace the fate of the manuscript: left to Naigeon's brother Charles Claude, after his death in 1816, they passed to the third sibling, Mme Dufour de Villeneuve, who wrote to Diderot's daughter Angélique to offer to sell it to her; Angélique appears to have declined.[70] After Naigeon's sister died, her things were sold, and J. L. L. Brière, the publisher, bought it, planning to publish it in his edition, which indeed he did.[71] Out it came, as the twenty-second volume of that edition, in 1823, and it was banned by the Tribunal correctionnel de la Seine on 23 December 1823.[72] Decades later, Maurice Tourneux talked of a new edition of it coming out, but nothing

---

67  The passage which is in neither SP or V is here: 'On peut même dire que les nerfs' to 'qu'une même substance' (N 227); this 7-line insert sits within quotation from SP (276) and V (155). The note (N 284n) resembles SP in that it acknowledges a cut from SP with an 'etc' and uses the term 'résonnances' as SP does. However, it comes from two separate pages in SP (358; 355), whereas in V it runs on directly (283–84), with no intervening passage. V uses the term 'ressouvenances' instead of 'résonnances', and its opening clause is slightly different.
68  Naigeon, 'Diderot', *Philosophie ancienne et moderne*, vol. 2, p. 228.
69  See above.
70  Boussuge and Launay, 'Du nouveau sur Jacques André Naigeon', pp. 173, 181.
71  Boussuge and Launay, 'Du nouveau sur Jacques André Naigeon', p. 189. Its whereabouts had been known, and are mentioned in Barbier's *Examen critique et complément des dictionnaires historiques les plus répandus*; he incorrectly calls it an 'ouvrage inachevé'; we have already commented on this aspect, see above, note 8 in this chapter.
72  Boussuge and Launay, 'Du nouveau sur Jacques André Naigeon', p. 189.

came of it. However, and despite the banning, the book had already been widely bought and read; David Adams tells us it was often bought separately.[73] Its onward reception, and the reception of Diderot in the nineteenth century generally, is a new story that we do not have space to tell here.[74]

---

73   David Adams, *Bibliographie des œuvres de Diderot, 1739-1900*, vol. 2, p. 141 (see Adams' 'Commentaire', n. 3).
74   You will be relieved to hear.

# 13. Conclusion

As Jean Mayer feelingly put it when describing his difficulties with editing the *Éléments de physiologie* (for the second time), 'l'éditeur, celui de Diderot surtout, est condamné à inventer pour chaque problème des solutions spécifiques' [the editor, particularly in the case of Diderot, is condemned to come up with an individualized solution for every single problem].[1] I could not agree more, as I extend his lament about critical editions to apply also to this monograph. And the result is a rather oddly-shaped book that has developed organically from following the *Éléments de physiologie* and its fate, while simultaneously sprouting a digital edition of the relevant pages of Naigeon's *Mémoires sur Diderot*. It has become a study not only of a late work of Diderot's, but also, quite substantially, of Naigeon, Diderot's disciple and literary executor, and furthermore of the educational and research committees and institutions of the French Revolution in its swiftly revolving and ever convulsive phases.[2] It is to some extent therefore also a history of this period from a very particular point of view. It offers new readings of the Ideologues, Cabanis and Destutt de Tracy, and of their avowed influence, minister and educator Garat. Fresh materials have appeared in all these sections.

---

1   Jean Mayer, 'La composition fragmentaire des *Éléments de physiologie* (problèmes d'édition)', in *Editer Diderot*, ed. by Georges Dulac, *SVEC*, 254 (1988), pp. 253–305 (p. 255).
2   2020 is a big year for Naigeon studies! Mario Cosenza has just published his intellectual biography of Naigeon, which unfortunately came out too late for my research to benefit from it. Others will be luckier! *All'ombra dei Lumi: Jacques-André Naigeon philosophe* (Naples: FedOAPress, 2020): http://www.fedoabooks.unina.it/index.php/fedoapress/catalog/book/190.

The first part of the book contemplated the *Éléments de physiologie* itself. It offers a tour of this extraordinary work, yet bizarrely, even to make a claim so simple and basic as to say that it is extraordinary and worth taking a tour of, seems somewhat new. Our second chapter assesses the reasons for this strange state of affairs and emerges with a discussion of Pascal, having argued that the *Éléments de physiologie*, this 'Atheist's Bible', throws down the opening words about its fragmentary and incomplete state as a signal that it is accepting Pascal's challenge to the atheist to be anything other than disordered and incoherent. We muse on the irony of Pascal's own defence of his faith having remained unfinished, and also at the even greater irony implicit in Diderot's counter-defence having been thought to be fragmentary and unfinished. We don't know whether to laugh or cry.

Diderot, as a materialist philosopher writing about physiology, is directly engaging with two noisy areas—the philosophical tradition, and human physiology as it was understood in the late eighteenth century. We look at each in turn. The point we make in Chapter 3 ('Material World and Embodied Mind') is that what we find in the *Éléments de physiologie* is Diderot's ultimate iteration of the arguments to establish that man was devoid of divine parts and needed to be understood and investigated in merely material terms. *Iteration* is an important term in this context, as Diderot is repeating arguments that had been being made for more than a century prior to his composing the *Éléments de physiologie*. What is specific or original to this work is not necessarily the arguments themselves, but that he brings them all together in one place. What makes them explosive is that he frames them unapologetically and overtly within a materialist context and also demonstrates them with reference to the physiology of the human body. This makes the *Éléments de physiologie* into a book of unrivalled audacity for the period.

As an introduction to physiology, we argue that it is better than equivalent or rival introductory works for its succinct clarity, its ability to ask questions of its material, and its consistent indication of lived experience across natural forms so various—like the girl with only a stump for a tongue who still had a sense of taste, or the man who fell pregnant—that 'natural' can no longer be defined by contrast to a supposed 'unnatural'. The spare directness of its descriptions are the result of Diderot's experience as a writer of many articles for the

*Encyclopédie* (and editor of all of them) in combination with the often virtuoso ekphrastic writing of his *Salons,* and to put it bluntly, they make a whole lot more sense than the often incomprehensible and always long descriptions generated by 'real' physiologists. Diderot's physiological descriptions are set within a clear presentation of the functions of the human body as a whole, following an introduction considering natural beings and life forms more generally, and leading into an enquiry of the human mind. As the 'real' physiologist, Théophile de Bordeu, put it, and as we quoted earlier, 'Il faudroit enfin un Descartes ou un Leibniz, pour débrouiller ce qui concerne les causes, l'ordre, le rapport, les variations, l'harmonie, et les lois des fonctions de l'économie animale' [ultimately what is needed is a Descartes or a Leibniz to disentangle that which concerns the causes, the order, the relationship, the variations, the harmony, and the laws governing the functions of the animal economy].³ We argue that Diderot's response to this plea was the *Éléments de physiologie*.

Part 2 looks at what happened next. Each chapter looks at an episode of publication in which Diderot's work on physiology was being mentioned, quoted, or drawn on (each case is different), and we chart these episodes in strictly chronological order. This was the only possible approach, given that each publication event was not just attentively engaging with its immediate Revolutionary and political context, but seemingly adjusting its techniques in the light of reactions to the previous episodes. Whether we are talking about Naigeon's strident statements and structured approach to the exercise of his duties as Diderot's literary executor, about the fate of the floating manuscript of the *Éléments de physiologie,* gifted to the Comité d'instruction publique [Committee of Public Education] on 24 March 1794, or what seem to be the numerous allusions to the *Éléments* on the part of Garat, Cabanis, and Destutt de Tracy, this is an unfurling and multi-referential story in which all players are working in close proximity, unavoidably aware of what the others are doing, and of needing to take every intervention into account. During this period, what is not said and who is not mentioned are as defining as their positive opposites.

---

3   Théophile de Bordeu, *Recherches sur les glandes* (1759), in *Œuvres complètes de Bordeu: précédées d'une notice sur sa vie et sur ses ouvrages,* ed. by Anthelme Richerand, 2 vols (Paris: Caille et Ravier, 1818), vol. 1, p. 208.

Nonetheless, and despite the fact that the chronology is the only thing that helps bring clarity and readability to this complex history, it needs to be said that there are really two separate stories taking place. The first is the story of Naigeon's repeated allusions to his *Mémoires sur Diderot*, to the importance of the work he was going to discuss in it, and to the imminence of its in fact always-deferred publication. This story has involved tracking Naigeon's drum-rolling mentions of the *Mémoires* and quotations from the *Éléments de physiologie* all the way from the furore-inducing *Adresse à l'Assemblée nationale* of 1790 and the 1792 article on 'Diderot', the fifteen-volume edition of Diderot's *Œuvres* in 1798 with its selections, omissions, and statements, to the claims he makes in the *Mémoires* themselves. Here we analyse what it is that Naigeon has done with the *Éléments de physiologie* and, to a lesser extent, with the *Rêve de d'Alembert*. We look at his text in the light of his previous assertions about Diderot and about editing, not least in the censored preface to his 1802 edition of the Bordeaux copy of Montaigne's *Essais*. The immense and busy collage of interwoven snippets that he produces has to be credited for being the first publication of either of these two texts of Diderot's, given that quotation from them is exact and incessant, as the connected digital edition of these hundred pages shows immediately and comprehensively, and despite the fact that his reweaving techniques produce something completely different from either source text. Perhaps the questions of whether or not we recognise the original, and connectedly, whether or not we like what he has done, distract us from seeing something else, which is that this particular case may be providing us with invaluable details about his composition practices in earlier collaborations such as that other infamous atheist text, d'Holbach's *Système de la nature*, a collaboration, moreover, that he undertook with Diderot. Paying attention to this may indicate the route to further research on the text factory of the Encyclopédistes and in d'Holbach's circle.

Our own approach is somewhat in the style of a textual detective. We have used a metaphorical magnifying glass to compare texts and watch out for hints and traces. This is even more the case for the second of the two stories mentioned, which follows the third manuscript copy of the *Éléments de physiologie*, now lost, and the work of Garat at the École normale in 1795 and of the Ideologues at the Institut National in the late 1790s. Here we conclude on the basis of extensive comparison that they did have access to the *Éléments de physiologie* in some version, whether it was specifically by means of this third manuscript, via Naigeon, or in some other way, and that they were channelling its insights directly into their own very successful lectures. This story is a separate one from Naigeon's for one principal reason: that whereas we have incontrovertible proof of Naigeon's knowledge of the *Éléments de physiologie* in the form of his quotation of about fifty pages from it, there is nothing explicit in the cases of Garat, Cabanis, and Destutt. With them, the argument gathers force (hopefully) from the sheer weight of cumulative resonances and parallels, and although there are some striking textual resemblances, these are infrequent. The story of Garat, Cabanis, and Destutt is marked by much greater circumspection on their part. Garat indeed was famous for his circumspect style, and much mocked for it. His odd two-volume *Mémoires historiques sur la vie de M. Suard, sur ses écrits, et sur le XVIIIe siècle* of 1820 provides a perfect example of volubility and circumspection, one in which, I argue, he repeatedly alludes to Diderot's *Éléments de physiologie*.

Interwoven, these two broad strands tell a vastly different story about Diderot's influence from the one that we are used to. This new story says that there was a concerted programme on the part of those philosophers who had been close to Diderot or to his circles to disseminate his thinking on materialism, physiology, and the mind, and that the pressures operating on the public sphere during the French Revolution and in the subsequent years of reaction, first Napoleonic and then monarchical, dictated absolutely the forms that dissemination was able to take. It also tells us something about how Naigeon, Garat, Cabanis, and Destutt de Tracy related to materialist thought, something which itself resonates with what we saw in Chapter 3. This is that these people seem all to have been more committed to transmitting materialist arguments and insights than to acknowledging those who generated those arguments and insights or to preserving the characteristics or form of one particular text. Or, to put it another way, they show their commitment to Diderot, whose works they have to present very carefully (if at all), by finding new ways and forms for his thought to continue to circulate that tend to remove him from the story. This, it seems, is how unorthodox thought survived at this time and under these circumstances. As Nicholas Cronk has remarked, the re-use of texts is so extensive during this period that it could be called a defining feature of Enlightenment discourse.[4]

Ursula Le Guin wrote that 'The unread story is not a story; it is little black marks on wood pulp. The reader, reading it, makes it live: a live thing, a story.'[5] And although the *Éléments de physiologie* is not a story, this unreadness, this zombie existence as an unpublished, unread manuscript without a future, a present, or very much past, was not in fact its fate. It was a live thing. And I would argue that its reception is a story worth telling in itself.

This study is a deeply historicist one. Even the point in the previous paragraph has a historicist anchoring to it: scholars can henceforth take the *Éléments de physiologie* seriously because it was read *during the period of study* and therefore has historical value. But my final point will be a different one, an invitation not just to historians and scholars, but to those thinkers engaged with the perspectives and questions of new materialism, gender theory, and ecology, those looking with anxious urgency at the climactic and social effects of global capitalism. Might not Diderot's attention to reciprocity, equality, assemblages, his understanding of connections and relations, his up-tipping of normal hierarchies, and his view of people as vegetable, animal, and human all at once, offer ways of thinking we need to revisit?

---

4   Nicholas Cronk, 'Digitizing Enlightenment', paper delivered at the inaugural conference of The Berlin-Oxford Enlightenment Hub, St John's College, Oxford, 2 October 2019.
5   Ursula Le Guin, 'Where Do You Get Your Ideas from?', in *Dancing at the Edge of the World: Thoughts on Words, Women, Places* (London: Paladin, 1992 [1987]), pp. 192–200 (p. 198), cited by Ika Willis, *Reception* (London and New York: Routledge, 2018) p. 2.

# Acknowledgements

Thank you very much to very many people and institutions. I've been working on this project for so long that practically everybody I know is owed a thanks.

Firstly, to the Leverhulme Trust for a research fellowship in 2018-19 that allowed me to write the second half of this book, and to those many colleagues at Oxford who supported and facilitated my application to the Leverhulme. Thanks again to the Leverhulme for allowing me to divert some of my research funds into developing the connected digital edition.

Thank you to Jesus College for its general support and quite specifically for its Major Research Grant Fund that has helped publish this book and also supported the work on the digital edition. Its Postgraduate Assistant Scheme allowed me to hire Rebecca Menmuir to do essential work on the footnotes and bibliography: many thanks to her. At Jesus, I would also like to thank my close colleagues Kirstin Gwyer and Katrin Kohl, as well as Alessandra Aloisi who took charge of French at Jesus in the year that I was away. Thanks to all my students past, present, and future for their enthusiasm and engagement. You are great.

Thank you to the Faculty of Medieval and Modern Languages and the University of Oxford for their multi-facetted support, including for employing me in the first place, but also for awarding me an EHRC Fellowship in 2016-17, which allowed me to write the first draft of Chapter 4.

Thank you to OpenBook Publishers for their flexibility with respect to my work, and for their vision more generally, and in particular to

Managing Director Alessandra Tosi and Editors Adèle Kreager and Melissa Purkiss. I am proud to publish with OBP.

Thank you to the librarians of the Taylorian Institute in Oxford, particularly Joanne Ferrari, Nick Hearn, and Emma Huber, to Coline Gosciniak, conservatrice responsable de la bibliothèque Carnegie et des fonds patrimoniaux de la BMC de Reims, and to Guillaume Fau, conservateur en chef et chef du service des manuscrits modernes et contemporains of the Bibliothèque nationale de France's Département des manuscrits.

Thank you to the amazing digital editor and curator Stacey Herbert, who conceptualised and realised the digital edition of Naigeon's *Mémoires*.

Thank you Cressida Bell for your wonderful artwork.

Thank you to all those who invited me to give papers at your seminars or conferences, and thereby helped me push this work forward. Here I should particularly cite Peter Cryle and Elizabeth Stephens of the University of Queensland, John D. Lyons of the University of Virginia, Pascal Nouvel and Annie Petit of the Université de Paul-Valéry Montpellier, and, at Oxford, Nicholas Cronk and Avi Lifschitz's Enlightenment Workshop, Pietro Corsi's History of Science Seminar, and my own personal crucible, the Early Modern French Seminar, held at the Maison française d'Oxford.

Laura Mason (John Hopkins University) and Yann Robert (University of Illinois at Chicago) let me see unpublished work of theirs, and thereby helped me hugely. Fervent thanks to them: you will find their books in the bibliography.

Thanks to Colin Jones, Michael Moriarty, and François Pépin for generously agreeing to write endorsements for this book. I hope they aren't regretting it!

Thanks to all my colleagues at the British Society for Eighteenth-Century Studies, or BSECS as it's known, for keeping my feet on the eighteenth-century ground! One wouldn't have thought that co-organising a week-long International Congress of the Enlightenment for upwards of 1,500 scholars would have been conducive to finishing a book, but so it has turned out to be.

Thank you very much to my august colleague Roger Pearson for coming up with the title. I wish I could have come up with something half so nifty by myself. Mine would have been incomprehensible and probably at least 50 words long.

Thank you to the two anonymous readers of this monograph for two things: firstly and most crucially, for agreeing that it could be published, and secondly, for making some very constructive suggestions about how to improve it.

Thank you also to my two non-anonymous readers. Kate Tunstall found time to read it (how?), and made some brilliant suggestions. Even though I didn't act on all of them, I still thought they were brilliant, and I thank her for her thought and attention, this year of all years, but also, that said, over all the years I've known her. Kate, chapeau! Susannah Wilson also read the whole thing, gave it her seal of approval, and cheered me on throughout. The weekly target meetings we had during our joint Leverhulme year were the best fun. Thank you, Susannah!

Thank you to Ilya Afanasyev for his companionable and steady remote presence during the writing of this book and for introducing me to the writer Sergei Dovlatov, whose narrator's solution for connecting two otherwise disconnected parts of a narrative was a constant source of inspiration (if you're interested, see *Pushkin Hills*, trans. Katherine Dovlatov, Alma Classics, 2013, p.38). I hope Dovlatov would have found it funny that he has had such profound influence on a scholarly monograph.

Thank you to all the people, dear colleagues, friends and family, with whom I have had conversations which were crucial door-opening moments. Thank you also to all those who read sections of this book and generously gave comments, either helpfully encouraging or helpfully discouraging (both being equally important!). They may not remember when they did this or what they said (this goes back nearly 15 years), but I do, and I'm very grateful. They are Pietro Corsi, Mario Cosenza, Andrew Curran, Hugh Doherty, Alexeï Evstratov, Finn Fordham, Viola Fordham, Katherine Gerson, Matthew Grenby, Marian Hobson, Rupert McCracken, Isabelle Moreau, Neil Kenny, Richard Parish, François Pépin, Bénédicte Prot, Mariana Saad, Richard Scholar, Ruggero Sciuto, Stéphane Schmitt (via Pietro Corsi), Catriona Seth, Alain Viala, Alexandre Wenger, Richard Whatmore, and Gustav Zamore. I am looking forward to plunging into Mario Consenza's study of Naigeon, *All'ombra dei lumi* (Naples: FedOAPress, 2020) and discovering all the ways in which my own research could have benefitted from his. One of these people, and I'm not saying who, suggested that I plan the writing of this book in the same way that he would set about building a mine. I tried to use this advice.

Thank you to those people who have made it possible for me to work and function in other equally fundamental ways. Thank you Sarah Perry, thank you Hania Porucznik. Thank you Davide Antilli and Eleanor Sunley. Thank you also to my French teacher from school, Jennifer Milner. Everyone needs a good French teacher. Thank you to my family: Finn, Leo, and Viola Fordham, Christopher and Mary Warman, Elizabeth Warman, Marc Zyngier, Eric and Joyce Willcocks, Simon Birks, Max Fordham, Taddy Fordham RIP, Cato Fordham, Ann Maher, Milo Fordham. I would also like to thank Rachel Flather. Darlings, the lot of them. To my husband Finn I say: is it ok if I dedicate the next book to you? I feel a slim volume of poems coming on.

To Leo and Viola Fordham, this work is, with their permission, most respectfully dedicated by their dutiful and obedient humble servant, the author, their mother.

# Bibliography

## Archival Sources

Paris, Bibliothèque nationale de France (BnF), NAF 13720–13784, https://archivesetmanuscrits.bnf.fr/ark:/12148/cc6348h [Denis Diderot, 'Fonds Vandeul'. The *Élémens de phisiologie* is NAF 13762, https://gallica.bnf.fr/ark:/12148/btv1b10084242t.]

Reims, Bibliothèque Carnegie de Reims, MS 2127 [Jacques-André Naigeon, *Mémoires historiques et philosophiques sur la vie et les ouvrages de Denis Diderot.*]

## Primary

Aquinas, Thomas, *Quaestiones disputatae de veritate*, 3 vols (Rome: Editori di San Tommaso, 1970–76)

Babeuf, Gracchus, *Le Tribun du Peuple, ou le défenseur des droits de l'homme. An III–An IV* (Paris: Éditions d'Histoire Sociale, 1966)

Barbier, Antoine-Alexandre, 'Diderot' in *Examen critique et complément des dictionnaires historiques les plus répandus* (Paris: Rey et Gravier; Baudouin frères, 1820), t. 1, p. 256

Barruel, Abbé Augustin, *Mémoires pour servir à l'histoire du Jacobinisme*, 5 vols (Hamburg: Fauche, 1798–99)

Barthez, Paul-Joseph, *Nouveaux éléments de la science de l'homme* [1778], 2 vols, 2nd edn (Paris: Goujon et Brunot, 1806)

Bayle, Pierre, *Dictionnaire historique et critique* (Paris: Éditions Sociales, 1974)

Bichat, Xavier, *Traité d'anatomie descriptive*, 5 vols (Paris: Brosson, Babon, 1801–03)

Bonnet, Charles, *Œuvres d'histoire naturelle et de philosophie*, 18 tomes in 10 vols (Neuchâtel: chez S. Fauche, 1779–83)

Bordenave, Toussaint, *Essai sur la physiologie* (Paris: P. Al. Le Prieur, 1764)

Bordeu, Théophile de, *Œuvres complètes de Bordeu: précédées d'une notice sur sa vie et sur ses ouvrages*, ed. by Anthelme Richerand, 2 vols (Paris: Caille et Ravier, 1818)

Buffon, Georges-Louis Leclerc, Comte de, *Buffon et l'histoire naturelle*, ed. by Pietro Corsi and Thierry Hoquet (Paris: De l'Imprimerie royale, 2018), http://www.buffon.cnrs.fr/

—, *Œuvres*, ed. by Stéphane Schmitt and Cédric Crémière (Paris: Gallimard Pléiade, 2007), https://doi.org/10.5962/bhl.title.53421

Cabanis, Pierre-Jean-Georges, *Lettre, posthume et inédite de Cabanis à M. F\*\*\* sur les causes premières, avec des notes par F. Bérard* (Paris: Gabon, 1824)

—, *Œuvres philosophiques*, ed. by Claude Lehec and Jean Cazeneuve, 2 vols (Paris: Presses Universitaires de France, 1956)

—, *Rapports du physique et du moral de l'homme: introduction de Serge Nicolas suivie des commentaires de François Thurot et A.L.C. Destutt de Tracy*, 2 vols (Paris: L'Harmattan, 2005) (facsimile 1st edition of Paris: Crapart, Caille et Ravier, 1802) [N.B. For the avoidance of doubt, where the edition is not specified in footnotes, this is the one used.]

—, *Rapports du physique et du moral de l'homme* 2 vols, 2nd edn (Paris: Crapart, Caille et Ravier, 1805)

Caron, Pierre Siméon, *Collection d'anciennes facéties*, 6 vols (Paris: [n.p.], 1798–1806)

Condillac, Étienne Bonnot de, *Essai sur l'origine des connaissances humaines* [1746], ed. by Aliènor Bertrand (Paris: Vrin, 2002)

—, *Essai sur l'origine des connaissances humaines* [1746], ed. by Jean-Claude Pariente and Martine Pécharman (Paris: Vrin, 2014)

—, *Œuvres philosophiques*, ed. by Georges le Roy (Paris: Presses Universitaires de France, 1948)

—, *Traité des sensations*, ed. by Christiane Frémont (Paris: Fayard, 1984)

Crousaz, Jean-Pierre, *La Logique, ou Système de réflexions qui peuvent contribuer à la netteté et l'étendue de nos connaissances*, 2nd edn (Amsterdam: L'Honoré et Châtelain, 1720)

Damiron, Jean-Philibert, *Mémoires sur les Encyclopédistes* (Genève: Slatkine reprints, 1968 [reimpression de l'edition de Paris, 1852–57, 6 vols])

*Débats du procès, instruit par la Haute-Cour de Justice, contre Drouet, Babeuf et autres*, 6 vols (Paris: Baudouin, 1797)

Descartes, René, *Principes*, tr. Claude Picot, in *Œuvres*, ed. Charles Adam and Paul Tannery (Paris: Vrin, 1964), vol. 9: II, édition révisée

Despaze, Joseph, *Les Quatre Satires, ou la fin du XVIIIe siècle*, 3rd edn (Paris: Moller, 1799)

Destutt de Tracy, Antoine Louis Claude, *Idéologie proprement dite*, in *Œuvres complètes*, ed. by Claude Jolly (Paris: Vrin, 2012), vol. 3

—, *Mémoire sur la faculté de penser, De la métaphysique de Kant, et autres textes*, ed. by Anne and Henry Deneys (Paris: Fayard, 1992)

D'Holbach, Paul-Henri Thiry, *Système de la nature*, ed. by Josiane Boulad-Ayoub, 2 vols (Paris: Fayard, 1990),

*Dictionnaires d'autrefois*, University of Chicago: ARTFL Project, ed. by Robert Morrissey, https://artfl-project.uchicago.edu/content/dictionnaires-dautrefois

Diderot, Denis, *Correspondance*, ed. by Georges Roth and Jean Varloot, 15 vols (Paris: Minuit, 1955–70)

—, *Éléments de physiologie*, ed. by Jean Mayer (Paris: Librairie Marcel Didier, 1964)

—, *Éléments de physiologie*, ed. by Jean Mayer, *Œuvres complètes*, DPV (Paris: Hermann, 1987), vol. 17, pp. 261–574

—, *Éléments de physiologie*, ed. by Paolo Quintili (Paris: Champion, 2004)

—, *Éléments de physiologie*, ed. by Motoichi Terada (Paris: Éditions Matériologiques, 2019)

—, *Encyclopédie ou dictionnaire raisonné des sciences, des arts et des métiers, par une société de gens de lettres*: see below under Diderot and Jean le Rond d'Alembert

—, *Le manuscrit de Pétersbourg/ 1774/ Avertissement des deux dialogues/ Fragments dont on n'a pu trouver la véritable place*, ed. by George Dulac in *Œuvres complètes*, DPV (Paris: Hermann, 1987), vol. 17, pp. 213–60

—, *Lettre sur les aveugles: à l'usage de ceux qui voient; Lettre sur les sourds et muets: à l'usage de ceux qui entendent et qui parlent*, ed. by Marian Hobson and Simon Harvey (Paris: GF Flammarion, 2000)

—, *Mémoires, correspondance et ouvrages inédits de Diderot, publiés d'après les manuscrits confiés en mourant par l'auteur à Grimm*, also known as the *Œuvres inédites de Diderot*, 4 vols (Paris: Paulin, 1830)

—, *Observations sur La 'Lettre sur l'homme et ses rapports' de Hemsterhuis*, ed. by Gerhardt Stenger, in *Œuvres complètes*, DPV (Paris: Hermann, 2004), vol. 24, pp. 479-767

—, *Œuvres*, ed. by Jacques-André Naigeon, 15 vols (Paris: Desray et Déterville, 1798)

—, *Œuvres*, ed. by Laurent Versini, 5 vols (Paris: R. Laffont, 1994–97)

—, *Œuvres complètes*, ed. by Jules Assézat and Maurice Tourneux, 20 vols (Paris: Garnier Frères, 1875–77)

—, *Œuvres complètes*, ed. by Roger Lewinter, 15 vols (Paris: Club Français du Livre, 1969–73)

—, *Œuvres complètes*, ed. by H. Dieckmann, Jacques Proust, Jean Varloot (Paris: Hermann, 1975) [referred to throughout this book as DPV]

—, *Œuvres philosophiques*, ed. by Michel Delon and Barbara de Negroni (Paris: Gallimard, 2010)

—, *Pensées philosophiques, Additions aux pensées*, ed. by Jean-Claude Bourdin (Paris: GF Flammarion, 2007)

—, *Pensées sur l'interprétation de la nature*, ed. by Jean Varloot and Herbert Dieckmann, in *Œuvres complètes*, DPV (Paris: Hermann), vol. 9, pp. 1-111

—, 'Prospectus', in *Encyclopédie* (1750), ARTFL Encyclopédie Project (Autumn 2017 Edition), ed. by Robert Morrissey and Glenn Roe p. 8, http://artflsrv02.uchicago.edu/cgi-bin/extras/diderotimg.pl?0035_pg8_section3.jpg

—, *Rameau's Nephew and D'Alembert's Dream*, trans. by Leonard Tancock (London: Penguin, 1966)

—, *Rameau's Nephew – Le Neveu de Rameau, a multi-media bilingual edition*, ed. Marian Hobson, trans. K.E. Tunstall, C. Warman, music Pascal Duc (Cambridge: Open Book Publishers, 2016), https://doi.org/10.11647/OBP.0098

—, *Réfutation d'Helvétius*, ed. by Roland Desné, Didier Kahn, Annette Lorenceau and Gerhardt Stenger, in *Œuvres complètes*, DPV (Paris: Hermann, 2004), vol. 24, pp. 215-478

—, *Le Rêve de d'Alembert*, ed. by Colas Duflo (Paris: GF Flammarion, 2002)

—, *Le Rêve de d'Alembert*, ed. by Georges Dulac, in *Œuvres complètes*, DPV (Paris: Hermann, 1987), vol. 17, pp. 23–209

—, *Salon de 1767*, ed. by Else Marie Bukdhal, Michel Delon, and Annette Lorenceau (Paris: Hermann, 1995)

Diderot, Denis, and Jean le Rond d'Alembert, eds, *Encyclopédie ou dictionnaire raisonné des sciences, des arts et des métiers, par une société de gens de lettres*, 28 vols (Paris: Briasson, David, Le Breton, Durand, 1751–72), University of Chicago: ARTFL Encyclopédie Project (Autumn 2017 Edition), ed. by Robert Morrissey and Glenn Roe, http://encyclopedie.uchicago.edu/

—, *Édition numérique collaborative et critique de l'Encyclopédie* ed. by Alexandre Guilbaud, Alain Cernuschi, Marie Léca-Tsiomis and Irène Passeron, http://enccre.academie-sciences.fr/encyclopedie/

—, *The Encyclopedia of Diderot & d'Alembert Collaborative Translation Project*, https://quod.lib.umich.edu/d/did/

*Electronic Enlightenment Scholarly Edition of Correspondence*, ed. Robert McNamee et al. Vers. 3.0. University of Oxford, 2018, https://www.e-enlightenment.com/

Fabrici d'Acquapendente, Girolamo, *De formatione ovi et pulli tractatus acuratissimus* (Patavii [Padova]: A. Bencii, 1621)

Filleau de La Chaise, Jean, *Discours sur les pensées de M. Pascal où l'on essaye de faire voire quel estoit son dessein* (Paris: Guillaume Desprez, 1672)

Fontenelle, Bernard le Bovier de, *Fragments d'un traité de la raison humaine*, in *Œuvres complètes*, ed. by Alain Niderst (Paris: Fayard, 1996), vol. 7, pp. 475–98

Garat, Dominique-Joseph, 'Considérations sur la dictature et les dictateurs' in *Le conservateur, journal politique, philosophique et littéraire*, ed. by Marie-Joseph Chénier, Pierre Daunou, Dominique-Joseph Garat, Nivôse/Pluviôse an VI (January 1798).

—, *Éloge de Bernard de Fontenelle. Discours qui a remporté le prix de l'Académie Françoise, en 1784* (Paris: Démonville, Libraire-Imprimeur de l'Académie Françoise, 1784)

—, *Leçons d'analyse et d'entendement* [1796], ed. by G. Gengembre et al., in *L'École normale de l'an III*, ed. by J. Dhombres (Paris: Éditions ENS, 2008), vol. 4, pp. 43–160, https://doi.org/10.4000/books.editionsulm.1445

—, *Mémoires historiques sur la vie de M. Suard, sur ses écrits, et sur le XVIIIe siècle; par Dominique-Joseph Garat*, 2 vols (Paris: A. Belin, 1820)

—, *Mémoires sur la Révolution ou exposé de ma conduite dans les affaires et les fonctions publiques* (Paris: J.J. Smits, 1795 [erroneously recorded as 1794 in catalogues due to confusion arising from the Revolutionary calendar – an. III runs Sept 1794-Sept 1795; the *Mémoires* were published in 1795])

—, *Séances des écoles normales, recueillies par des sténographes, et revues par les professeurs*. Nouvelle édition: Débats, vols 7–8 (Paris: Cercle-social, 1800–01)

Grégoire, Henri, 'Rapport sur la bibliographie', in *Procès-verbaux du comité d'instruction publique de la convention nationale publiés et annotés*, ed. by James Guillaume (Paris: Imprimerie Nationale, 1901), vol. 4, pp. 120–29

Guillaume, James, ed., *Procès-verbaux du comité d'instruction publique de la convention nationale publiés et annotés*, 7 vols (Paris: Imprimerie Nationale, 1891–1957)

Haller, Albrecht von, *Elementa physiologiae corporis humani* ([n.p.]: Lausannae, Sumptibus M. M. Bousquet et Sociorum, 1757–66), https://catalog.hathitrust.org/Record/008593541

—, *Élémens de physiologie, ou Traité de la structure et des usages des différentes parties du corps humain*, trans. by Louis Tarin (Paris: chez Prault fils, 1752)

—, *Élémens de physiologie*, trans. by Toussaint Bordenave (Paris: chez Guillyn, 1769), https://doi.org/10.5962/bhl.title.43392

Hésine, Pierre-Nicolas, *Journal de la Haute-Cour de Justice, ou L'écho des hommes libres, vrais et sensibles* (Paris: Edhis, 1966)

Hill, Sir J., *Lucina sine concubitu* (London: M. Cooper, 1750)

*Institut national de la République française* (Paris: Baudouin, Brumaire An VI [Oct–Nov 1797])

Julia, Dominique, ed., *L'École normale de l'an III: une institution révolutionnaire et ses élèves (2). Textes fondateurs, pétitions, correspondances et autres documents (janvier–mai 1795)* (Paris: Éditions Rue d'Ulm, 2016)

La Harpe, Jean-François de, *Œuvres*, 16 vols (Paris: Verdière, 1820)

Lamarck, J.-B., *Recherches sur l'organisation des corps vivans*, ed. by J. M. Drouin (Paris: Fayard, 1986)

La Mettrie, Julien Offray de, *Machine Man and Other Writings*, trans. and ed. by Ann Thomson (Cambridge: Cambridge University Press, 1996)

—, *Œuvres philosophiques*, ed. by Francine Markovits, 2 vols (Paris: Fayard, 1987)

Lavoisier, Antoine, *Traité élémentaire de chimie, présenté dans un ordre nouveau et d'après les découvertes modernes* (Paris: Cuchet, 1789), https://doi.org/10.5962/bhl.title.67783

Leibniz, Gottfried Wilhelm, *Monadology: An Edition for Students*, ed. and trans. by Nicholas Rescher (London: Routledge, 2002)

—, *Nouveaux essais sur l'entendement humain (avant-propos et livre premier)*, ed. by Émile Boutroux (Paris: Librairie Delagrave, 1927)

—, *Principes de la nature et de la grace fondés en raison et principes de la philosophie ou monadologie*, ed. by André Robinet (Paris: Presses Universitaires de France, 1954)

Maréchal, Sylvain, *Dictionnaire des athées anciens et modernes, deuxième édition, augmentée des suppléments de J. Lalande, de plusieurs articles inédits, et d'une notice nouvelle sur Maréchal et ses ouvrages, par J.-B.-L. Germond*, 2nd edn (Bruxelles: chez l'éditeur, 1833), https://doi.org/10.1522/25051474

*Mémoires de l'Institut national des sciences et des arts: sciences morales et politiques*, 5 vols (Paris: Baudouin, An IV 1795/96–An XII 1803/04)

Mercier, L. S., *De J. J. Rousseau considéré comme l'un des premiers auteurs de la Révolution* (Paris: Buisson, 1791)

*Mercure de France* (Geneva: Slatkine Reprints, 1974), vol. 140 (1791: Jan-Jun), https://babel.hathitrust.org/cgi/pt?id=coo.31924092971732&view=1up&seq=1

Meslier, Jean, *Œuvres complètes*, ed. by Roland Desné, préface et notes par Jean Deprun, Roland Desné et Albert Soboul, 3 vols (Paris: Éditions anthropos, 1970–72)

Montaigne, Michel de, *Essais*, ed. by Denis Bjaï, Jean Céard et al. (Paris: Livre de Poche, 2001)

Naigeon, Jacques-André, *Adresse à l'Assemblée nationale sur la liberté des opinions, sur celle de la presse, etc., ou Examen philosophique de ces questions: 1 ° doit-on parler de Dieu, et en général de religion, dans une déclaration des droits de l'homme ? 2 ° la liberté des opinions, quel qu'en soit l'objet, celle du culte et la liberté de la presse peuvent-elles être légitimement circonscrites et gênées, de quelque manière que ce soit, par le législateur ?* (Paris: Volland, 1790)

—, 'Avertissement de l'éditeur', ed. by Phillipe Desan, *Montaigne Studies*, 10 (1998), 35–78

—, *Encyclopédie méthodique: Philosophie ancienne et moderne*, 3 vols (Paris: Panckoucke, 1791–94)

—, *Mémoires historiques et philosophiques sur la vie et les ouvrages de Denis Diderot* (Paris: J. L. L. Brière, 1821 [1823]; repr. Geneva: Slatkine Reprints, 1970)

—, 'Préface de l'éditeur', in Diderot, *Œuvres* (Paris: Desray et Déterville, 1798), vol. 1, pp. v–xxxiii

—, *Recueil philosophique*, 2 vols (London [Amsterdam]: Marc-Michel Rey, 1770)

Pascal, Blaise, *Éloge et Pensées de Pascal, édition établie par Condorcet et annotée par Voltaire*, ed. by Richard Parish, in *Œuvres complètes de Voltaire* (Oxford: Voltaire Foundation, 1968–), vol. 80A (2008)

—, *Œuvres*, ed. by Abbé Charles Bossut, 5 vols (The Hague [Paris]: Detune, 1779)

—, *Œuvres complètes*, ed. by Michel Le Guern, 2 vols (Paris: Gallimard, 1998)

—, *Pensées*, ed. by Léon Brunschvicg, 3 vols (Paris: Hachette, 1904)

—, *Pensées*, trans. by Roger Ariew (Indianapolis, IN: Hackett, 2005)

—, *Pensées de Monsieur Pascal sur la religion & sur quelques autres sujets: qui ont été trouvées après sa mort parmi ses papiers* (Paris: Guillaume Desprez, 1669)

—, *Pensées de M. Pascal sur la religion et sur quelques autres sujets, qui ont esté trouvées apres sa mort parmy ses papiers publiées avec une préface par* Étienne Perier (*seconde édition*) (Paris: Guillaume Desprez, 1669)

—, *Les Provinciales, Pensées, et Opuscules divers*, ed. by Gérard Ferreyrolles and Philippe Sellier (Paris: Livre de Poche 'La Pochothèque', 2004)

Pérennès, François, *Éloge de Suard, secrétaire perpétuel de l'Académie Française* (Besançon: Charles Deis, 1841)

*Procès-verbaux de la commission temporaire des arts*, ed. by Louis Tuetey (Paris: Imprimerie Nationale, 1912)

*Procès-verbaux du comité d'instruction publique de la convention nationale publiés et annotés*, ed. by James Guillaume (Paris: Imprimerie Nationale, 1901), vol. 4

Richerand, Anthelme, *Nouveaux élémens de physiologie*, 5th edn (Paris: Caille et Ravier, 1811)

Robinet, Jean-Baptiste, ed., *Supplément à l'Encyclopédie ou Dictionnaire raisonné des Sciences, des Arts & des Métiers par une Société de Gens de lettres*, 4 vols (Amsterdam: M.M. Rey, 1776–77), https://encyclopedie.uchicago.edu/node/137

Rousseau, Jean-Jacques, *Discourse on Inequality*, trans. by Franklin Philip (Oxford: Oxford University Press, 1994)

—, *Emile*, trans. by Allan Bloom (London: Penguin, 1979)

—, *Œuvres complètes*, ed. by Bernard Gagnebin and Marcel Raymond (Paris: Gallimard Pléiade, 1964)

Roussel, Pierre, *Éloge historique de M. Théophile de Bordeu* (Paris: Ruault et Mequignon, 1788)

—, *Système physique et moral de la femme* (Paris: Vincent, 1775)

Sade, Donatien Alphonse François, Marquis de, *Œuvres*, ed. by Michel Delon, 3 vols (Paris: Gallimard Pléiade, 1990–98)

Salverte, Eusèbe, *Éloge philosophique de Denys Diderot, lu a l'Institut National, le 7 thermidor an 8* (Paris: Chez Surosne, 1801 [an IX])

Spinoza, Benedict de, *Ethics*, trans. by Edwin Curley, with an introduction by Stuart Hampshire (London: Penguin, 1996)

—, *Traité de la réforme de l'entendement et de la meilleure voie à suivre pour parvenir à la vraie connaissance des choses*, ed. and trans. by A. Koyré (Paris: Vrin, 1951)

Suard, Amélie, *Essais de mémoires sur M. Suard* (Paris: Didot, 1820)

Tuetey, Louis, ed., *Procès-verbaux de la commission temporaire des arts*, 2 vols (Paris: Imprimerie nationale, 1912)

Vaumartoise, François Victor Mérat de, 'Vitalistes', in *Dictionnaire des sciences médicales*, ed. by François Pierre de Chaumeton and F. V. M. de Vaumartoise, 60 vols (Paris: Panckoucke and Plomteux, 1812–22), vol. 58, p. 281

Vicq d'Azyr, Félix, *Œuvres de Vicq d'Azyr*, ed. by J.-L. Moreau de la Sarthe, 6 vols (Paris: Duprat-Duverger, 1805), https://doi.org/10.5962/bhl.title.48727

—, *Traité d'anatomie et de physiologie: avec des planches coloriées représentant au naturel les divers organes de l'homme et des animaux* (Paris: de l'Imprimerie de Franç. Amb. Didot l'Aîné, 1786)

Voltaire, *Éléments de la philosophie de Newton*, ed. by Robert L. Walters and W.H. Barber, in *Œuvres complètes de Voltaire* (Oxford: Voltaire Foundation, 1968–), vol. 15 (1992)

—, *Lettres philosophiques*, ed. by Frédéric Deloffre (Paris: Gallimard Folio, 1986)

## Secondary Sources

Adams, David, *Bibliographie des œuvres de Diderot, 1739-1900*, 2 vols (Ferney-Voltaire: Centre international d'étude du XVIIIe siècle, 2000)

Advielle, Victor, *Histoire de Gracchus Babeuf et du babouvisme d'après de nombreux documents inédits*, 2 vols (Paris: chez l'auteur, 1884)

Albertan, Christian, and Anne-Marie Chouillet, 'Autographes et documents', *Recherches sur Diderot et sur l'Encyclopédie*, 36 (2004), https://doi.org/10.4000/rde.1892

Amiable, Louis, *Une loge maçonnique d'avant 1789: La Loge des Neuf Sœurs*, ed. by Charles Porset (Paris: Éditions maçonniques de France, 2014)

Anderson, Wilda, 'Eighteenth-Century Philosophy', in *The Cambridge History of French Literature*, ed. by William Burgwinkle, Nicholas Hammond, and Emma Wilson (Cambridge: Cambridge University Press, 2011), pp. 404–11, https://doi.org/10.1017/chol9780521897860.047

Armogathe, Jean-Robert, 'Garat et l'école normale de l'an III', *Corpus, revue de philosophie*, 14–15 (1990), 143–54

Arnaud, Sabine, *On Hysteria: The Invention of a Medical Category between 1670 & 1820* (Chicago: Chicago University Press, 2015), https://doi.org/10.7208/chicago/9780226275680.001.0001

Audidière, Sophie, Jean-Claude Bourdin, and Francine Markovits, eds, *Matérialistes français du XVIIIe siècle* (Paris: Presses Universitaires de France, 2006)

Baciocchi, Stéphane and Dominique Julia, 'La Dissolution de l'école', in *L'École normale de l'an III: une institution révolutionnaire et ses élèves* (2), ed. by Dominique Julia (Paris: Éditions Rue d'Ulm, 2016), pp. 425–62

—, 'Un hiver à Paris', in *L'École normale de l'an III: une institution révolutionnaire et ses élèves* (2), ed. by Dominique Julia (Paris: Éditions Rue d'Ulm, 2016), pp. 307–70

—, *Prosopographie des élèves nommés à l'école normale de l'an III*, ed. by Stéphane Baciocchi and Dominique Julia, http://lakanal-1795.huma-num.fr/wiki/Présentation

Ballstadt, Kurt, *Diderot: Natural Philosopher*, SVEC 2008:09 (Oxford: Voltaire Foundation, 2008)

Barbey, Nicolas, 'Comment Montaigne écrivait ses Essais: l'Exemplaire de Bordeaux', *Le Blog Gallica*, 6 July 2016, https://gallica.bnf.fr/blog/06072016/comment-montaigne-ecrivait-ses-essais-lexemplaire-de-bordeaux

Baron, Konstanze, and Robert Fajen, eds, *Diderot, le génie des Lumières: nature, normes, transgressions* (Paris: Garnier, 2019)

Barroux, Gilles, *Le Cabinet médical de Diderot: la part de la médecine dans l'élaboration d'une philosophie matérialiste* (Paris: Éditions Matériologiques, 2018)

Bernheim, Alain, 'The *Mémoire justificatif* of La Chaussée and Freemasonry in Paris until 1773', *Ars Quatuor Coronatorum*, 104 (1992), http://www.freemasons-freemasonry.com/bernheim25.html

Birchall, Ian, *The Spectre of Babeuf* (Basingstoke: Macmillan, 1997), https://doi.org/10.1007/978-1-349-25599-3

Bloch, Olivier, *Le Matérialisme* (Paris: Presses Universitaires de France, 1985)

Bonnet, Pierre, 'Évolution et structure du texte des *Essais*', in *Pour une édition critique des Essais*, ed. by Marcel Françon (Cambridge: Schoenhof's Foreign Books, 1965), p. 16

Boron, Walter F., and Emile L. Boulpaep, *Medical Physiology*, 3rd edn (Philadephia, PA: Elsevier, 2017)

Boussuge, Emmanuel, and Françoise Launay, 'Du nouveau sur Jacques André Naigeon (1735–1810) et sur ses livres et manuscrits', *RDE*, 53.1 (2018), 145–92, https://doi.org/10.4000/rde.5698

Brockliss, Laurence, and Colin Jones, *The Medical World of Early Modern France* (Oxford: Clarendon Press, 1997)

Brummer, Rudolf, *Studien zur Französischen Auflärungsliteratur im Anschluss an J.-A. Naigeon*, Romanische Philologie (Breslau: Priebatsch's Buchandlung, 1932)

Canguilhem, Georges, 'Du singulier et de la singularité en épistémologie biologique', in *Études d'histoire et de philosophie des sciences*, 2nd edn (Paris: Vrin, 1970), pp. 223–34

Caradonna, Jeremy L., *The Enlightenment in Practice: Academic Prize Contests and Intellectual Culture in France, 1670–1794* (Ithaca: Cornell University Press, 2012)

Chappey, Jean-Luc, *Ordres et désordres biographiques: dictionnaires, listes de noms, réputation des Lumières à Wikipédia* (Seyssel: Champ Vallon, 2013)

Cheung, Tobias, 'Omnis Fibra Ex Fibra: Fibre OEconomies in Bonnet's and Diderot's Models of Organic Order', *Early Science and Medicine*, 15.1–2 (2010), 66–104, https://doi.org/10.1163/138374210x12589831573108

Chottin, Marion, *Le Partage de l'empirisme: une histoire du problème de Molyneux aux XVIIe et XVIIIe siècles* (Paris: Champion, 2014)

Citton, Yves, *L'Envers de la liberté: l'invention d'un imaginaire Spinoziste dans la France des lumières* (Paris: Éditions Amsterdam, 2006)

Clark, Andrew, *Diderot's Part* (Aldershot: Ashgate, 2008), https://doi.org/10.4324/9781315257853

Cosenza, Mario, *All'ombra dei Lumi: Jacques-André Naigeon philosophe* (Naples: FedOAPress, 2020), http://www.fedoabooks.unina.it/index.php/fedoapress/catalog/book/190

Crampe-Casnabet, Martine, 'Garat à l'École normale: une entreprise de réduction du sensualisme', in *Langages de la Révolution, 1770-1815). Actes du 4<sup>e</sup> colloque international de lexicologie politique* (Paris: Klincksieck, 1995), pp. 177–84

Craveri, Benedetta, *The Age of Conversation*, trans. by Teresa Waugh (New York: New York Review of Books, 2005)

Curran, Andrew, *Sublime Disorder: Physical Monstrosity in Diderot's Universe* (Oxford: Voltaire Foundation, 2001)

Davis, Natalie Zemon, *Fiction in the Archives: Pardon Tales and Their Tellers in Sixteenth-Century France* (Cambridge: Polity Press, 1987)

Desan, Phillipe, 'Naigeon et l'"avertissement" censuré de l'édition des *Essais* de 1802', *Montaigne Studies*, 10 (1998), 7–34

Despois, Eugène, *Le Vandalisme revolutionnaire: fondations litteraires, scientifiques et artistiques de la convention* (Paris: Germer Baillière, 1868)

Dhombres, Jean, Daniel Nordman, Étienne Guyon, Béatrice Didier, eds., *L'École normale de l'an III* (Paris: Dunod 1992, 1994; Éditions ENS, 2006, 2008), 4 vols. https://doi.org/10.4000/books.editionsulm.1445

Didier, Béatrice, 'Les cours littéraires de l'an III: tradition et innovation', in *L'École normale de l'an III*, ed. by Jean Dhombres et al, vol. 4: *Leçons d'analyse de l'entendement, Art de la parole, Littérature, Morale*, ed. by Jean Dhombres and Béatrice Didier, pp. 28-35

—, 'Statut de l'Utopie chez Gracchus Babeuf', in *Présence de Babeuf: Lumières, Révolution, Communisme*, ed. by A. Maillard, Cl. Mazauric, and E. Walter (Paris: Publications de la Sorbonne, 1994), pp. 29–48

Dieckmann, Herbert, 'Diderot's Conception of Genius,' *Journal of the History of Ideas*, 2.2 (1941), 151–82, https://doi.org/10.2307/2707111

—, 'L'épopée du Fonds Vandeul', *Revue d'histoire littéraire de la France*, 85.6 (1985), 963–77

—, *Inventaire du fonds vandeul et inédits de Diderot* (Genève: TLF Droz, 1951)

—, 'J.-A. Naigeon's Analysis of Diderot's *Rêve de d'Alembert*', *Modern Language Notes*, 53.7 (1938), 479–86, https://doi.org/10.2307/2912683

Duchesneau, François, *La Physiologie des lumières: empirisme, modèles et théories*, Histoire et philosophie des sciences (Paris: Classiques Garnier, 2012)

Duflo, Colas, *Diderot philosophe* (Paris: Champion, 2003)

Dufresne, H., 'Une vocation historique: Dom Germain Poirier 1724-1803', *Bulletin des bibliothèques de France*, 11 (1956), 755–66, http://bbf.enssib.fr/consulter/bbf-1956-11-0755-001

Dupuy, Paul, 'L'École normale de l'an III', in *Le Centenaire de l'école normale, édition du Bicentenaire* [1895] (Paris: Presses de l'École normale supérieure, 1994), pp. 1–200, https://doi.org/10.4000/books.editionsulm.1538

Fellows, Otis E. 'The Theme of Genius in Diderot's Neveu de Rameau,' *Diderot Studies*, 2 (1952), 168–99

Fontenay, Elisabeth, *Le Matérialisme enchanté* (Paris: B. Grasset, 1981)

François, Étienne, 'L'École normale: une création allemande?', in *L'École normale de l'an III: une institution révolutionnaire et ses élèves (2)*, ed. by Dominique Julia (Paris: Éditions Rue d'Ulm, 2016), pp. 31–49

Gengembre, Gérard, 'Introduction', in *Leçons d'analyse et d'entendement de Garat*, ed. by G. Gengembre et al., in *L'École Normale de l'an III*, ed. by Jean Dhombres, (Paris: Éditions ENS, 2008), vol. 4, pp. 45–61, https://doi.org/10.4000/books.editionsulm.1458

Goodman, Dena, *The Republic of Letters: A Cultural History of the French Enlightenment* (Ithaca: Cornell University Press, 1994)

Guillois, Antoine, *Le Salon de Madame Helvétius: Cabanis et les idéologues* (Paris: Calmann Levy, 1894)

Hesse, Carla, *The Other Enlightenment: How French Women Became Modern* (Princeton, NJ: Princeton University Press, 2001)

Hill, Emita, *The Role of 'le monstre' in Diderot's Thought* (Banbury: Voltaire Foundation, 1972)

Hobson, Marian, 'Sensibility and Spectacle: The Medical Context for the "Paradox"', in *Diderot and Rousseau: Networks of Enlightenment*, ed. by Kate E. Tunstall and Caroline Warman (Oxford: Voltaire Foundation, 2011), pp. 65–90

Huneman, Philippe, 'Les Théories de l'économie animale et l'émergence de la psychiatrie de l'Éncyclopédie à l'aliénisme', *Psychiatrie Sciences Humaines Neurosciences*, 2.2 (2004), 47–60, https://doi.org/10.1007/BF03006001

Israel, Jonathan, *Radical Enlightenment: Philosophy and the Making of Modernity 1650-1750* (Oxford: Oxford University Press, 2001)

Jacot-Grapa, Caroline, *Dans le vif du sujet: Diderot, corps et âme* (Paris: Classiques Garnier, 2009)

—, 'Des huîtres aux grands animaux', *Dix-huitième siècle*, 42.1 (2010), 99–117, https://doi.org/10.3917/dhs.042.0099

Jacque-Lefèvre, Nicole, *Louis-Claude de Saint-Martin, le philosophe inconnu (1743-1803): un illuministe au siècle des lumières* (Paris: Dervy, 2003)

Julia, Dominique, ed., *L'École normale de l'an III: Une institution révolutionnaire et ses élèves, Introduction historique à l'édition des Leçons* (Paris: Éditions Rue d'Ulm, 2016)

Kafker, Franz A., and Serena L. Kafker, *The Encyclopedists as Individuals* (Oxford: Voltaire Foundation, 1988)

Kaitaro, Timo, *Diderot's Holism* (Frankfurt a.M.: Peter Lang, 1997)

Kennedy, Emmet, '"Ideology" from Destutt de Tracy to Marx', *Journal of the History of Ideas*, 40.3 (1979), 353–68, https://doi.org/10.2307/2709242

Kerjan, Daniel, Alain le Bihan, and Pierre Mollier, eds, *Dictionnaire du grand orient de France au XVIIIe siècle: les cadres et les loges* (Rennes: Presses Universitaires de Rennes, 2012)

Korolev, Sergeï V., *La Bibliothèque de Diderot. Vers une reconstitution* (Ferney-Voltaire: Centre international d'Études du dix-huitième siècle, 2014)

Labriolle, Marie-Rose de, 'Moët', in *Dictionnaire des journalistes, 1600-1789*, ed. by Jean Sgard (Oxford: Voltaire Foundation, 1999), http://dictionnaire-journalistes.gazettes18e.fr/journaliste/581-jean-pierre-moet

Lawlor, Krista, 'Memory', in *The Oxford Handbook of Philosophy of Mind*, ed. by Ansgar Beckermann, Brian P. McLaughlin, and Sven Walter (Oxford: Clarendon Press, 2009), pp. 663-77, https://doi.org/10.1093/oxfordhb/9780199262618.003.0039

Le Guin, Ursula, 'Where Do You Get Your Ideas from?', in *Dancing at the Edge of the World: Thoughts on Words, Women, Places* (London: Paladin, 1992 [1987]), pp. 192–200

Lehman, Christine, and François Pépin, 'La Chimie et 'l'Encyclopédie', *Corpus, revue de philosophie*, 56 (2009)

Lough, J., 'Luneau de Boisjermain v. the Publishers of the *Encyclopédie*', *SVEC*, 23 (1963), 115–77

Lovejoy, Arthur O., *The Great Chain of Being* (Cambridge, MA: Harvard University Press, 1936; repr. 2001)

Mall, Laurence, 'L'ego-philosophie à la manière de Diderot (*Réfutation d'Helvétius*)', *Littérature*, 165 (2012), 16–30, https://doi.org/10.3917/litt.165.0016

Mason, Laura, *The Last Revolutionaries: The Trial of Gracchus Babeuf and the Equals*. [submitted for publication; details forthcoming]

—, 'The "Bosom of Proof": Criminal Justice and the Renewal of Oral Culture during the French Revolution', *The Journal of Modern History*, 76.1 (2004), 29–61, https://doi.org/10.1086/421184

Mayer, Jean, *Diderot, homme de science* (Rennes: Imprimerie Bretonne, 1959)

—, 'La composition fragmentaire des *Éléments de physiologie* (problèmes d'édition)', in *Editer Diderot*, ed. by Georges Dulac, *SVEC*, 254 (1988), pp. 253-305

Mazel, H., 'La Fameuse Préface de Naigeon', *Bulletin de la société des amis de Montaigne*, 2.4 (1938), 28–29

Mee, Jon, *Conversable Worlds: Literature, Contention, & Community 1762–1830* (Oxford: Oxford University Press, 2011

Moreau, Isabelle, *'Guérir du sot': Les Stratégies d'écriture des libertins à l'âge classique* (Paris: Champion, 2007)

Mortier, Roland, 'Diderot et le problème de l'expressivité: de la pensée au dialogue heuristique', *Cahiers de l'AIEF*, 13.1 (1961), 283–97, https://doi.org/10.3406/caief.1961.2204

—, 'Naigeon critique de la déclaration des droits', *RDE*, 20 (1996), 103–13, https://doi.org/10.3406/rde.1996.1325

Murray, William, 'Garat', in *Dictionnaire des journalistes, 1600-1789*, ed. by Jean Sgard (Oxford: Voltaire Foundation, 1999), http://dictionnaire-journalistes.gazettes18e.fr/journaliste/329-dominique-garat

Norbrook, David, Stephen Harrison, and Philip Hardie, eds, *Lucretius and the Early Modern* (Oxford: Oxford University Press, 2015), https://doi.org/10.1093/acprof:oso/9780198713845.001.0001

Nouvel, Pascal, ed., *Repenser le vitalisme* (Paris: Presses Universitaires de France, 2011)

Orain, Arnaud, 'Physiocratic Arithmetic versus *Ratios*: The Analytical Economics of Jean-Joseph-Louis Graslin', in *The Economic Turn: Recasting Political Economy in Enlightenment Europe*, ed. by Steven L. Kaplan and Sophus A. Reinert (London: Anthem Press, 2019), pp. 193–220, https://doi.org/10.2307/j.ctvb1htk7.12

Ozouf, Mona, 'Liberté', in *Dictionnaire critique de la Révolution française: Idées*, ed. by François Furet, Mona Ozouf, and Bronislaw Baczko (Paris: Flammarion, 1992), pp. 253-73 (*Idées* was volume 4 of the initial 1988 *Dictionnaire critique de la Révolution française*, here published separately)

Parish, Richard, 'Blaise Pascal', *French Studies*, 71.4 (2017), 539–50, https://doi.org/10.1093/fs/knx215

Pasanek, Brad, 'The Mind as a Metaphor', http://metaphors.lib.virginia.edu/about

Paschoud, Adrien, 'Matérialisme, ordre naturel et imaginaire cosmologique dans *L'Homme-plante* (1748) de La Mettrie', in *Penser l'ordre naturel, 1680–1810*, ed. by Adrien Paschoud and Nathalie Vuillemin (Oxford: Voltaire Foundation, 2012), pp. 51-66

Paschoud, Adrien, and Barbara Selmeci Castioni, 'Le matérialisme au XVIIIe siècle en France: enjeux et perspectives', in *Matérialisme(s) en France au XVIIIe siècle. Entre littérature et philosophie*, ed. by Adrien Paschoud and Barbara Selmeci Castioni (Berlin: Frank and Timme, 2019), pp. 7–11

Pellerin, Pascale, 'Naigeon: une certaine image de Diderot sous la Révolution', in *Recherches sur Diderot et sur l'Encyclopédie*, 29.2 (2000), 25–44, https://doi.org/10.4000/rde.104

Pépin, François, 'Diderot et Leibniz face à la chimie du vivant', in *Leibniz et Diderot: rencontres et transformations*, ed. by Christian Leduc, François Pépin, Anne-Lise Rey, and Mitia Rioux-Beaulne (Paris: Vrin, 2015), pp. 211–35, https://doi.org/10.4000/books.pum.2153

—, *La Philosophie expérimentale de Diderot et la chimie: philosophie, sciences et arts* (Paris: Classiques Garnier, 2012)

Perras, Jean-Alexandre, *L'Exception exemplaire: inventions et usages du génie (XVIe-XVIIIe siècle)* (Paris: Garnier, 2015)

Pommier, Jean, 'Lueurs nouvelles sur les manuscrits de Diderot', *Bulletin du bibliophile*, 5 (1954), 201–17

Pouliquen, Yves, *Cabanis, un idéologue: de Mirabeau à Bonaparte* (Paris: Odile Jacob, 2013)

Proust, Jacques, 'Diderot et la philosophie du polype', *Revues des sciences humaines*, 182 (1981), 21–30

Quintili, Paolo, 'Diderot e la Rivoluzione francese: miti, modelli, riferimenti nel secolo XXI', *Quaderni materialisti*, 2 (2003), 81–106

Regaldo, Marc, *Un milieu intellectuel: la Décade philosophique (1794–1807)*, 5 vols (doctoral thesis, Paris-Sorbonne University, 1976)

Rey, Roselyne, *Naissance et développement du vitalisme en France de la deuxième moitié du 18e siècle à la fin du premier empire*, SVEC 381 (Oxford: Voltaire Foundation, 2000)

Roe, Shirley A., 'The Life Sciences', in *The Cambridge History of Science: Volume 4, Eighteenth-Century Science*, ed. by Roy Porter (Cambridge: Cambridge University Press, 2003), pp. 397–416, https://doi.org/10.1017/chol9780521572439.018

Roger, Jacques, *Les Sciences de la vie dans la pensée française du XVIIIe siècle: la génération des animaux de Descartes à l'Encyclopédie*, 2nd edn (Paris: A. Colin, 1971)

Rostand, Jean, 'Diderot et la biologie', *Revue d'histoire des sciences et de leurs applications*, 5.1 (1952), 5–17, https://doi.org/10.3406/rhs.1952.2892

Roussel, Jean, 'Ginguené', in *Dictionnaire des journalistes, 1600-1789*, ed. by Jean Sgard (Oxford: Voltaire Foundation, 1999), http://dictionnaire-journalistes.gazettes18e.fr/journaliste/343-pierre-ginguene

Saad, Mariana, *Cabanis, comprendre l'homme pour changer le monde* (Paris: Classiques Garnier, 2016)

Salaün, Franck, *L'Ordre des mœurs: essai sur la place du matérialisme dans la société française du XVIIIe siècle (1734–1784)* (Paris: Éditions Kimé, 1996)

Schober, Angelika, 'Aspects du génie chez Diderot et d'Alembert', *Diderot Studies*, 23 (1988), 143–49

Scholar, Richard, *The Je-Ne-Sais-Quoi in Early Modern Europe: Encounters with a Certain Something* (Oxford: Oxford University Press, 2005), https://doi.org/10.1093/acprof:oso/9780199274406.001.0001

Scholar, Richard, and Alexis Tadié, eds, *Fiction and the Frontiers of Knowledge in Europe, 1500–1800* (Farnham: Ashgate, 2010), https://doi.org/10.4324/9781315582276

Scott, John Anthony, ed. and trans., *The Defense of Gracchus Babeuf before the High Court of Vendôme with an Essay by Herbert Marcuse and Illustrations by Thomas Cornell* (Amherst: University of Massachusetts Press, 1967)

Screech, Michael, *Montaigne's Annotated Copy of Lucretius: A Transcription and Study of the Manuscript, Notes and Pen-Marks* (Geneva: Droz, 1998)

Sgard, Jean, ed., *Dictionnaire des journalistes, 1600–1789* (Oxford: Voltaire Foundation, 1999)

Spangler, May, 'Sciences, philosophie et littérature: le polype de Diderot', *RDE*, 23 (1997), 89–107, https://doi.org/10.3406/rde.1997.1391

Starobinski, Jean, *Action et réaction: vie et aventures d'un couple* (Paris: Seuil, 1999)

—, 'La Chaire, la tribune, le barreau', in *Les Lieux de mémoire. II. La Nation*, ed. by Pierre Nora (Paris: Gallimard, 1986), vol. 3, pp. 425–86

Staum, Martin, *Cabanis: Enlightenment and Medical Philosophy in the French Revolution* (Princeton, NJ: Princeton University Press, 1980)

Steinke, Hubert, 'Haller's Concept of Irritability and Sensibility and its Reception in France', *Mécanisme et vitalisme*, ed. by Mariana Saad, special issue of *La Lettre de la maison Française d'Oxford*, 14 (2001), 37–70

Stenger, Gerhardt, *Diderot, le combattant de la liberté* (Paris: Perrin, 2013).

—, 'Diderot lecteur de Heinsius: quelques éclaircissements sur la conclusion des *Éléments de physiologie*', *Revue d'histoire littéraire de la France*, 112.3 (2012), 601–12, https://doi.org/10.3917/rhlf.123.0601

Straudo, Arnoux, *La Fortune de Pascal en France au XVIIIe siècle*, SVEC 351 (Oxford: Voltaire Foundation, 1997)

Tarin, René, *Diderot et la Révolution française: controverses et polémique autour d'un philosophe* (Paris: Champion, 2001)

Thomson, Ann, *Bodies of Thought: Science, Religion, and the Soul in the Early Enlightenment* (Oxford: Oxford University Press, 2008)

Tourneux, Maurice, *Les Manuscrits de Diderot conservés en Russie* (Paris: Imprimerie nationale, 1885)

—, Review of Ernest Dupuy's edition of the *Paradoxe sur le comédien*, *Revue d'histoire littéraire de la France*, 9.3 (1902), 500–18

Trousson, Raymond, *Images de Diderot en France, 1784–1913* (Paris: Champion, 1997)

Tunstall, Kate E., *Blindness and Enlightenment: An Essay, With a New Translation of Diderot's 'Letter on the Blind' (1749) and a translation of La Mothe Le Vayer's 'Of a Man-Born-Blind' (1653)* (London: Bloomsbury, 2011)

—, 'La Fabrique du *Diderot-philosophe*, 1765–1782', *Les Dossiers du Grihl*, 2 (2017), https://doi.org/10.4000/dossiersgrihl.6793

Varloot, Jean, 'La physiologie de Diderot', *Beiträge zur Romanischen Philologie*, XXIV(2) (1985), 227-233

Vernière, Paul, *Diderot, ses manuscrits et ses copistes* (Paris: Klincksieck, 1967)

—, *Spinoza et la pensée française avant la Révolution* (Paris: Presses universitaires de France, 1954)

Vila, Anne C., *Suffering Scholars: Pathologies of the Intellectual in Enlightenment France* (Philadelphia, PA: University of Pennsylvania Press, 2018), https://doi.org/10.9783/9780812294804

Volpilhac-Auger, Catherine, *Tacite en France de Montesquieu à Chateaubriand* (Oxford: Voltaire Foundation, 1993)

Von Held, Phoebe, *D'Alembert's Dream*, 2005, 'State of Mind' Exhibition, LSE, London, curated by Simon Gould and Ruth McLennon, https://www.phoebevonheld.com/new-index#/dalemberts-dream

Warman, Caroline, '"A Little Short Fat Man, Thirty-five Years of Age, Inconceivably Vigorous, and Hairy as a Bear": The Figure of the Philosopher in Sade', in *Sade's Sensibilities*, ed. by Kate Parker and Norbert Sclippa (Lewisburg: Bucknell University Press, 2015), pp. 103–17

—, 'L'âme et la vie de l'organe dans la pensée vitaliste de Bordeu, Diderot et Bichat', in *Repenser le vitalisme*, ed. by Pascal Nouvel (Paris: Presses universitaires de France, 2011), pp. 157–65

—, '"Autre fait arrivé au château de Nicklspurg, en Moravie": Diderot and the Horrid Case Study', in *The Dark Thread: From Tragical Histories to Gothic Tales*, ed. by John D. Lyons (Newark: University of Delaware Press, 2019), pp. 149–59

—, 'Caught between Neologism and the Unmentionable: The Politics of Naming and Non-naming in 1790s France', *Romance Studies*, 31 (2013), 264–76, https://doi.org/10.1179/0263990413Z.00000000051

—, 'Charts and Signposts: Following Vitalism and Mechanism through the *Encyclopédie*, the *Encyclopédie méthodique* and the *Dictionnaire des sciences médicales*', *Mécanisme et vitalisme*, ed. by Mariana Saad, special issue of *La Lettre de la maison Française d'Oxford*, 14 (2001), 85–104

—, 'Comment écrire le vécu? Diderot et le problème matérialiste de l'abstraction', in *Matérialisme(s) en France au XVIIIe siècle. Entre littérature et philosophie*, ed. by Adrien Paschoud and Barbara Selmeci Castioni (Berlin: Frank and Timme, 2019), pp. 103–13

—, 'Garden Centres Must Become the Jacobin Clubs of the New Revolution', *Voltaire Foundation*, 20 November 2018, https://voltairefoundation.wordpress.com/2018/11/20/garden-centres-must-become-the-jacobin-clubs-of-the-new-revolution/

—, 'Naigeon, éditeur de Diderot physiologiste', *Diderot Studies*, 34 (2014), 283–302

—, '"The Revolution Is to the Human Mind What the African Sun is to Vegetation": Revolution, Heat, and the Normal School Project', *The Critical Genealogy of Normality*, ed. by Peter Cryle, special issue, *History of Human Sciences*, (2020), 1-18, https://doi.org/10.1177/0952695120946992

—, *Sade: From Materialism to Pornography* (Oxford: Voltaire Foundation, 2002)

Wenger, Alexandre, *Le Médecin et le philosophe: Théophile de Bordeu selon Diderot* (Paris: Hermann, 2012)

Whatmore, Richard, *Against War and Empire: Geneva, Britain and France in the Eighteenth Century* (New Haven: Yale University Press, 2012)

Williams, Elizabeth, *A Cultural History of Medical Vitalism in Enlightenment Montpellier* (Ashgate: Aldershot, 2003)

Williams, Wes, *Monsters and Their Meanings in Early Modern Culture* (Oxford: Oxford University Press, 2011), https://doi.org/10.1093/acprof:oso/9780199577026.001.0001

—, '"Well Said/Well Thought": How Montaigne Read His Lucretius', in *Lucretius and the Early Modern*, ed. by David Norbrook, Stephen Harrison, and Philip Hardie (Oxford: Oxford University Press, 2015), pp. 136–61, https://doi.org/10.1093/acprof:oso/9780198713845.003.0007

Willis, Ika, *Reception* (London and New York: Routledge, 2018)

Wolfe, Charles, *Monsters and Philosophy* (London: College Publications, 2005)

—, *La philosophie de la biologie avant la biologie: une histoire du vitalisme* (Paris: Classiques Garnier, 2019)

Yolton, John, *Locke and French Materialism* (Oxford: Oxford University Press, 1991), https://doi.org/10.1093/acprof:oso/9780198242741.001.0001

# Index

Académie française 73, 337
Adams, David 391
*Alice in Wonderland* 4
anemone 5, 374
animal 9, 39, 54, 91, 123, 126, 146, 169, 176, 316, 327, 369, 373–375
Aquinas, Thomas 61
Aristotle 61, 127, 203
Arnobius 108
Assemblée des quatre sections réunies d'Auxerre 239
Assemblée nationale 196
Assézat, Jules 16, 20, 22, 179, 377, 386
atom 62, 99

Babeuf, Gracchus 308, 362
  trial thereof 312
baby 108, 173
  Diderot as a 94, 97
Baciocchi, Stéphane 267
Bacon, Francis 127, 242, 341, 346
Ballstadt, Kurt 156
Barbier, Antoine-Alexandre 239
Bardel, le citoyen 220
Barère, Bertrand 235–236
Barruel, Abbé Augustin 314
Barthez, Paul-Joseph 150, 162
  *Nouveaux éléments de la science de l'homme* 151
Bayle, Pierre 200, 362
bears 88, 100, 108
Beaumarchais, Pierre-Augustin Caron de
  *Mariage de Figaro* 335

bees 374
Bergson, Henri 12, 105
Bernardin de Saint-Pierre, Jacques-Henri 238
Bible, The 339
  Book of Genesis 52
  Corinthians 44
Bichat, Xavier 148, 298, 304
bile 48
biology 142
birth, giving 109, 137, 153
blood 4, 41, 145, 158
Boerhaave, Herman 140, 144
Boindin, Nicolas 24
Boissier de Sauvages, François 150
Bonnet, Charles 10, 65, 68, 282–283
  *Analyse abrégée de l'Essai analytique sur les facultés de l'âme* 84, 129
  *Contemplation de la nature* 93, 98
  *Corps organisés* 69, 80
  *Essai analytique sur les facultés de l'âme* 110, 124, 129, 232
  *Palingénésie philosophique* 80
Bonnet, Pierre 329
book, living 73, 130
Bordenave, Toussaint 137, 155, 157, 165
  *Essai sur la physiologie* 137, 158
Bordeu, Théophile de 7, 12, 24, 148, 150, 155, 304, 395
  *Recherches sur les glandes* 149
  *Recherches sur les maladies chroniques* 149

Bossut, Charles 33
Boucher, François 24
Boucher, Mlle (daughter of François Boucher) 24
Boussuge, Emmanuel 390
boy operated for cataracts 88
boy who lived with bears 88
brain 10, 36, 56, 77, 87, 90, 113, 124, 127–131, 134, 152, 158, 160–161, 293, 373–374, 378, 389
Brière, J.L.L. 390
Brockliss, Laurence 142, 150
Brummer, Rudolf 357, 359
Buffon, Georges-Louis Leclerc, comte de 10, 65, 81, 283, 293, 340
  *Discours sur le style* 72
  *Histoire naturelle* 74, 92, 97, 106, 109

Cabanis, Pierre-Jean-Georges 162, 180, 232, 272, 319, 383, 389, 393
  *Lettre à Fauriel* 317
  *Rapports du physique et du moral* 273
Cardan, Jérôme 183, 203
Caron, le citoyen 229
Caron, Pierre-Siméon 229
Catherine II ix, 15, 21, 24, 26, 35, 179, 186, 372–373
Celsus 203
censorship 358
Cercle d'Auteuil 233, 274. *See* salon (Mme Helvétius's)
change. *See* flux
Charavay, Etienne 225
Charron, Pierre 153
Chaumette, Anaxagoras 239
chemistry 65, 144, 151, 235, 350
Cheselden, William 88
chest 164
child 37, 42, 175, 301
Clark, Andrew 153, 175
coffee 255
Comité de salut public 235
Comité de sûreté générale 268
Comité d'instruction publique 395

Commission temporaire des arts 218–220, 224
Concordat (8 April 1802) 328
Condillac, Étienne Bonnot de 11, 65, 101, 208, 264, 266, 276, 286, 292, 298, 344, 369, 380
  criticism of 283–284, 381
  *Essai sur l'origine des connaissances humaines* 72, 76, 87, 118
  *La Logique* 276
  *Traité des sensations* 102, 109, 124, 128, 276
Condorcet, Nicolas de Caritat, marquis de 33
Connor, Bernard 88
Constitution of 1793 309–310
Constitution of 1795 271, 277, 309
convalescence 84
Convention nationale 235–236, 239, 286
conversation 122, 336, 338
*Correspondance littéraire* 15, 23, 70, 195, 287
Coste, Pierre 330
crayfish 5
Crousaz, Jean-Pierre 88, 114
Curran, Andrew 81

d'Alembert, Jean le Rond 7, 14, 24, 33, 111, 349
Damiron, Jean-Filibert 381
Danton, Georges 222, 227
daughter 90
Daunou, Pierre 271, 274
  Loi Daunou 271, 303
Davis, Natalie Zemon 175
death 11, 30–31, 35–37, 84, 96, 134, 176
*Déclaration des droits de l'homme et du citoyen* 196
decline 6, 83
Delon, Michel 19
Desan, Philippe 329
Descartes, René 12, 41, 62, 66, 127, 144, 155, 341, 395

Deschamps, Léger-Marie ('Dom') 188
Desmoulins, Camille 222
Despaze, Joseph
  *Les Quatre Satires* 351
Destutt de Tracy, Antoine Louis Claude 180, 272, 319, 383, 389, 393
  *Dissertation sur quelques questions d'idéologie* 273
  *Éléments d'idéologie* 273
  *Idéologie proprement dite* 273, 275
  *Mémoire sur la faculté de penser* 273
  *Projet d'éléménts d'idéologie à l'usage des écoles centrales de la République française* 273
Devaines, Jean
  salon of 350
d'Holbach, Paul-Henri Thiry, baron 122, 179, 293
  *Système de la nature* 183, 191, 202, 396
Diderot, Angélique (Mme Caroillon de Vandeul) ix, 21, 179, 361, 390
Diderot, Denis ix
  *Additions aux pensées philosophiques* 14, 36
  *Apologie de l'Abbé de Prades* 362
  as passionate athlete of anti-propertarianism 313
  *Bijoux indiscrets, Les* 325
  *Correspondance* 183
  'De Térence' 363
  *Deux dialogues, Les* 24, 383
  *Éléments de physiologie* ix
  'Éloge de Richardson' 363
  *Essai sur les règnes de Claude et de Néron* 344
  *Fils naturel, Le* 14
  *Histoire de Grèce, de Temple Stanyan* (translation) 361
  *Jacques le fataliste* 14, 23, 109, 112, 183, 195, 325, 356, 364
  'Les Eleuthéromanes' 182
  Letter appointing Naigeon as literary executor 322
  *Lettre de M. Diderot à MM. Briasson et Le Breton* 14, 363
  *Lettre sur les aveugles* 7, 11, 23, 61, 108, 283, 287, 345
  *Lettre sur les sourds et muets* 14, 89, 108, 110, 345
  'L'Histoire et le secret de la peinture en cire' 363
  *Mélanges pour Catherine II* 186
  *Neveu de Rameau, Le* 15, 24, 190, 229, 364
  *Observations sur Hemsterhuis* 7, 20, 61, 69, 78, 93, 111, 120, 126, 132, 135, 327
  *Œuvres de Denis Diderot*, ed. Naigeon (1798) 319, 362
  *Paradoxe sur le comédien* 364
  *Pensées philosophiques* 8, 36, 61, 135, 208
  *Pensées sur l'interprétation de la nature* 14, 79, 103, 107, 208, 345
  *Père de famille, Le* 14
  *Plan d'une université pour le gouvernement de Russie* 183, 186, 363
  'Prière du sceptique' 183
  *Principes philosophiques sur la matière et le mouvement* 61, 107, 207
  *Promenade du Sceptique* 362
  *Réfutation d'Helvétius* 7, 20, 61, 69, 89, 135, 327
  *Regrets sur ma vieille robe de chambre* 14
  *Religieuse, La* 14, 23, 112, 321, 324–325, 356
  *Rêve de d'Alembert, Le* 8, 14–15, 17, 21, 24, 61, 79, 95, 111, 119, 125, 154–155, 190, 214, 287, 291, 327, 350, 355, 364, 385
  *Salons* 23, 166, 324, 395
  *Supplément au voyage de Bougainville* 23, 344, 356
Didier, Béatrice 242
Didot, Pierre 317, 329, 359–360
Dieckmann, Herbert 17, 21, 29, 377

digestion 5
dinner table, boisterous 289
Dioscorides 203
Directoire 271
dissection 145
dog 123
drunkenness 84, 377
dryness (of Condillac) 208, 246, 291
Duchesneau, François 143, 162
Dufour de Villeneuve, Mme (Naigeon's sister) 359, 390
Dumarsais, César Chesneau 24, 242
Dumont, Louis-Philippe 267
Dupuy, Paul 269

eagle 134
École des armes et des poudres (Weaponry and Gunpowder School) 223, 234
École normale 64
*Encyclopédie* 8, 14, 23, 36, 61, 107, 111, 140, 144, 166, 287, 324, 361, 363, 365, 395
  'Éléments d'une science' 280
  'Leibnitzianisme' 97
  'Machine arithmétique' 55
  'Machine arithmétique' 34
  'Observation' 154
  'Physiologie' 139
  *Supplément* 140
  'Système figuré des connoissances humaines' 141
*Encyclopédie méthodique* 228. *See* Naigeon, Jacques-André: *Philosophie ancienne et moderne*
enthusiast 37
Epicureanism 62, 134
Epicurus 62
Euler, Leonhard 349, 378
eulogy-writing 231, 242
eye 5, 41, 117, 123, 374, 381

Fabrici d'Acquapendente, Girolamo 214, 216
Favart, Charles Simon 216
feet 41, 46
fighting 42
Filleau de la Chaise, Jean 31
fingers 46, 170, 375
flecks, golden 331
flesh 41, 46, 111, 170
flux 6, 50, 79, 82, 90, 376
Fontanier, Pierre 239
Fontenay, Élisabeth de 94
Fontenelle, Bernard le Bovier de 65, 339–340
  'Loi de la pensée' 103
  'Sur l'instinct' 76, 117
Foucault, Michel 64
Fourier, Joseph 239
freedom 302
freemason. *See* Naigeon, Jacques-André: *Philosophie ancienne et moderne*
freemasonry 217
Freud, Sigmund 304
fruit 4, 170

Galen 203
Galilei, Galileo 242, 255
Garand, Jean-Baptiste 225–226, 229
Garat, Dominique-Joseph 180, 272, 316, 319, 381, 389, 393
  'Considérations' 303
  *Leçons d'analyse et d'entendement* 231–232, 241–242, 246–247, 249–253, 255–259, 263–266, 268
  *Mémoires historiques sur la vie de M. Suard, sur ses écrits, et sur le XVIIIe siècle* 335
  *Mémoires sur la Révolution ou exposé de ma conduite dans les affaires* 268
  *Mémoires sur la vie de M. Suard, sur ses écrits, et sur le dix-huitième siècle* 269
Garran de Coulon, Jean-Philippe 228–229
Garron, le citoyen 229
Gaschon, (first name unknown) 226, 229
Gassendi, Pierre 66

genius 87, 259, 298, 379
geometers (mathematicians) 104–105, 107, 111, 121
girl
  who ate her sister 109
  without a tongue 167
Goethe, Johann Wolfgang von 15
gold, flecks of 327
Grimm, Friedrich Melchior, baron von 222, 384. *See Correspondance littéraire*
growth 6, 83
Guerre, Martin 175
Guillaume, James 217
Guyomar, Pierre-Marie-Augustin 240

Haller, Albrecht von 10, 20, 27, 137, 140, 147, 155, 162, 164, 168, 298, 389
  *Elementa physiologiae* 157
  *Primae lineae physiologiae* 137, 157
hands 41, 46
happiness 6–7, 37, 48, 53–54, 133, 301
head 41
headache 89
health 87, 301
hearing, sense of 56
Helvétius, Claude Adrien 65, 197, 204, 293, 298
Helvétius, Mme (Anne-Catherine de Lignville) 232, 248. *See* salon (Mme Helvétius's)
Hemsterhuis, François 65, 78, 120
Heraclitus 82
Hill, Emita 81
Hippocrates 203
Hobbes, Thomas 66, 192, 195
Horace 200, 331
house 91
  bed 376
  building materials 91
  ceiling 90
  curtains 376
  walls 90
  wood panelling 86

*Idéologie* 299
illness 47, 49, 84, 176
imagination 87, 130, 160, 256, 259, 290
  windswept 346
individual 81, 126, 176, 377
instinct 11, 39, 76–77, 119, 121, 307, 378
Institut national des sciences et des arts 64, 270–271, 319, 328, 359
  meeting room 305
instrument 145, 148, 236, 255, 279, 369
iron 170
irritability 147

Jaucourt, Louis de 144
Jolly, Claude 282, 286
Jones, Colin 142, 150
Julia, Dominique 267

Kepler, Johannes 242

La Barre, François Jean de 363
La Harpe, Jean-François de 182, 185, 314
Lalande, Jérôme 232, 314, 359
Lamarck, Jean-Baptiste 142, 221
La Mettrie, Julien Offray de 11, 24, 65, 144, 293
  *L'Homme-machine* 54, 133
  *Traité de l'âme* 43, 87, 99, 105, 109, 114, 127
Laplace, Pierre-Simon 349
Laroche, Daniel de 293
La Rochefoucauld, François de 200
Launay, Françoise 390
Lavoisier, Antoine
  *Traité élémentaire de chimie* 78, 246
Lawlor, Krista 132
Le Camus, Antoine 293
Le Guin, Ursula 398
Leibniz, Gottfried Wilhelm 12, 65, 68, 127, 155, 343, 349, 395
  *Monadologie* 82, 97
  *Nouveaux essais sur l'entendement humain* 69, 115

Lespinasse, Julie de  7, 24, 368, 380
limb  45, 375, 385
Locke, John  62, 66, 127, 242, 264, 285, 298, 339, 369
  *Essay concerning Human Understanding*  69, 101
Loge des Neuf Sœurs  232–233, 314–315, 328
Louis, Antoine  173
Louvre  272, 359
love  3, 105, 170, 176, 244, 323
lover  172, 175
Lucretius  62, 66, 200
  *De rerum natura*  62, 82, 201
Luneau de Boisjermain, Pierre-Joseph-François  14, 363

madness  87, 89, 100
Malebranche, Nicolas  76
malformation  7
man, as monstrous version of woman  377
man, deaf, from Chartres  88
man, drowned  97–98, 298
man, gouty  85
man, miserly  86, 214, 296
man of learning  54, 330, 379
man, old  37
man or woman, surprisingly strong  85, 296
man, walking and thinking  117–118, 121, 123
Marat, Jean-Paul  215, 293
marble  111–112
Maréchal, Sylvain  314
Marmontel, Jacques-François  339
Marron, Pierre-Henri  225, 229
martyr  37
Mathieu, le citoyen  220
Maux, Jeanne-Catherine de (Mme de)  188, 190
Mayer, Jean  17, 22, 139, 153, 156, 386, 393
mechanism  144
Meister, Jacques-Henri  361

melancholy  98, 105
memory  6, 87, 121, 125–127, 130, 160, 256, 378
Ménuret de Chambaud, Jean-Joseph  154
Mérat de Vaumartoise, François Victor  163
Mercier, Louis-Sébastien  181
Meslier, Jean  65–66, 101, 182
  *Anti-Fénelon*  75, 91
  *Mémoire des pensées et sentiments*  79, 82, 90, 102, 104
midden  327
Mirabeau, Honoré Gabriel Riqueti, comte de  183
Moët, Jean-Pierre  216–217, 221, 229
molecule  99, 374–376
monstrosity  51–52, 81, 375, 377
Montaigne, Michel de  11, 66, 140, 153, 204, 332, 346, 358–359
  *Apologie de Raimond Sebond*  82
  *Essais*, Bordeaux copy, ed. Naigeon  328
Montesquieu, Charles-Louis de Secondat, baron de La Brède et de  344
Morelly, Étienne-Gabriel  309
  *Code de la nature*  309, 318–319
mother  175
music  42
mussel  99

Naigeon, Charles Claude  390
Naigeon, Jacques-André  ix, 13, 20, 22, 179, 274, 317, 319, 393
  *Adresse à l'Assemblée nationale sur la liberté des opinions, sur celle de la presse*  181, 364
  'Cardan' (*Philosophie ancienne et moderne*)  201
  'Diderot' (*Philosophie ancienne et moderne*)  207, 362
  *Mémoires historiques et philosophiques sur la vie et les ouvrages de Denis Diderot*  ix, 15, 20, 22, 32, 319, 337, 355

'Mirabeau' (*Philosophie ancienne et moderne*) 201
Montaigne's *Essais*, censored preface 181, 329, 368, 396
*Philosophie ancienne et moderne* 180
Naigeon, Jean-Claude (Naigeon l'aîné) 220
Napoleon Bonaparte 273, 316, 328–329, 337, 359–360
Negroni, Barbara de 19
Neufchâteau, François de 328
Nicolas, Serge 293
Niderst, Alain 342
Nuch, Mr (first name unknown) 173

organ 41, 45, 47, 148, 160, 374, 377–378
  memory of 295
organization 149, 301
oyster 5, 375

pain 6, 41, 46, 48, 105, 374, 377, 385
painting 42
palace 259, 290
Palissot, Charles 14
Pascal, Blaise 30, 66, 113, 153, 192, 349, 394
  Pascal's wager 57
  *Pensées*, Bossut edition 34, 38
  *Pensées*, Condorcet/Voltaire edition 33, 35, 38, 48
  *Pensées*, Port-Royal edition 30, 38
passion 84, 134, 160. *See* Naigeon, Jacques-André
  for editing texts 330
Paulin, Jean-Baptiste-Alexandre 215
Pellerin, Pascale 181
Pépin, François 151, 153
Pérennès, François 352
Périer, Étienne 31, 193
pincers 46, 170. *See* fingers
Pindar 127
Plaichard, René-François 221
plant 99, 111
Plato 127

pleasure 40, 105, 300, 374, 377
Pliny 203
Pluche, Noël-Antoine (Abbé) 80
poetry 42
Poirier, Germain (Dom) 219, 230
polyp 99
Pommier, Jean 213
Pottier, un certain 213
pregnancy 171–172, 174
Proust, Marcel 12
pulse 89, 97, 148
Pythagoras 140

Quintili, Paolo 22, 29, 139, 153, 213, 223, 293, 386

Racine, Jean 351
Raynal, Guillaume-Thomas 228, 344
reader 8, 89, 111, 131, 175, 196, 201, 204, 210–212, 217, 221, 306, 309, 324, 326, 353, 361
reproduction 96, 172
Richerand, Anthelme 304
  *Nouveaux élémens de physiologie* 162, 304
river 4, 82
Robespierre, Maximilien 222, 227, 233, 235, 239
Robinet, Jean-Baptiste 140
Roger, Jacques 18, 22
Rostand, Jean 156
Roucher, Antoine 290
Rouelle, Guillaume-François 151
Rousseau, Jean-Jacques 35, 53, 65, 147, 181, 339, 344, 347, 379, 381
  *Discours sur l'origine de l'inégalité* 53, 88, 379
  'Profession de foi du vicaire savoyard' (*Émile*) 94, 99, 125

Sade, Donatien Alphonse François, marquis de 314, 317, 358
Saint-Martin, Louis-Claude de 244, 262, 265–266, 312, 369
salon (Mme Helvétius's) 232, 248, 271, 274

salons (in general)  63, 350
sanity  87
Scaliger  204
self  6, 124, 126, 375, 378
senses, intimate (internal)  281
sex  42, 244
Sgard, Jean  216
sight, sense of  56, 254
skin  168
sleep  84, 160, 378
sleepwalking  115, 162
smell, sense of  56
societies, learned  63
soldier, bedfellow  174
soldier, drunken  109
soldier, pregnant  173
species  81, 176, 377
spider  378
Spinoza, Baruch  65
   *Ethics*  71, 75, 92, 115, 133
   *Traité de la réforme de l'entendement*  71, 101, 127
Stahl, Georg Ernst von  150, 298
Starobinski, Jean  23, 274, 304
statue  26, 109–112, 124, 128, 208, 284
stenography  237–238. *See* Babeuf, Gracchus: trial thereof; *See* École normale
Sterne, Laurence  339
stone  41, 91, 94, 121
St Paul  44
Straudo, Arnoux  34
stream  7
stupidity  87
Suard, Jean-Baptiste-Antoine  335, 347
Suard, Mme (Amélie Panckoucke)  336, 352
Swift, Jonathan  127
Sydenham, Thomas  242

Tacitus  200
Tarin, Pierre  139
Tarin, René  157, 181, 309
taste, sense of  167
telescope  254, 352
tendon  45, 374
Terada, Motoichi  22, 29, 65, 139, 153, 293, 386, 389
Theophrastus  203
tickling  42
tiredness  84
Tissot, Samuel-Auguste  54
touch, sense of  252
Tourneux, Maurice  16, 20, 179, 361, 377, 386, 390
tree  381
Trousson, Raymond  181, 222
Trublet, Nicolas-Charles-Joseph (Abbé)  341, 342

unhappiness  48, 53

Venel, Gabriel François  151
Versini, Laurent  19
Vicq d'Azyr, Félix  141, 142, 145, 146, 155, 158, 160, 161
   *Traité d'anatomie et de physiologie*  155, 160
vitalism  145, 163
vivisection  145
Volland, Sophie  195, 196
Voltaire (François Marie Arouet)  33, 35, 49, 51, 64, 79, 181, 184, 344
   *Candide*  69
   *Lettres philosophiques*  33, 185
vomiting  5, 138

Walferdin, Hippolyte  214, 215, 216, 372
Wenger, Alexandre  153, 154, 156
wife  90, 323
Wolfe, Charles  81
woman, as monstrous version of man  377
woman, hysterical  86
wood  46, 91, 170
worm  40, 134

# About the Team

Alessandra Tosi was the managing editor for this book.

Adèle Kreager and Melissa Purkiss performed the copy-editing and proofreading.

Cressida Bell designed the cover using InDesign. The cover was produced in InDesign using Fontin (titles) and Calibri (text body) fonts.

Melissa Purkiss typeset the book in InDesign and produced the paperback and hardback editions. The text font is Tex Gyre Pagella; the heading font is Californian FB.

Luca Baffa produced the EPUB, MOBI, PDF, HTML, and XML editions — the conversion is performed with open source software freely available on our GitHub page (https://github.com/OpenBookPublishers).

# This book need not end here...

## Share

All our books — including the one you have just read — are free to access online so that students, researchers and members of the public who can't afford a printed edition will have access to the same ideas. This title will be accessed online by hundreds of readers each month across the globe: why not share the link so that someone you know is one of them?

This book and additional content is available at:

https://doi.org/10.11647/OBP.0199

## Customise

Personalise your copy of this book or design new books using OBP and third-party material. Take chapters or whole books from our published list and make a special edition, a new anthology or an illuminating coursepack. Each customised edition will be produced as a paperback and a downloadable PDF.

Find out more at:

https://www.openbookpublishers.com/section/59/1

Like Open Book Publishers

Follow @OpenBookPublish

Read more at the Open Book Publishers BLOG

# You may also be interested in:

**The Idea of Europe: Enlightenment Perspectives**
*Catriona Seth and Rotraud von Kulessa*

https://doi.org/10.11647/OBP.0123

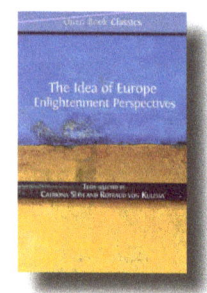

**Denis Diderot 'Rameau's Nephew' – 'Le Neveu de Rameau': A Multi-Media Bilingual Edition**
*Marian Hobson, Kate E. Tunstall and Caroline Warman*

https://doi.org/10.11647/OBP.0098

**Tolerance: The Beacon of Enlightenment**
*Caroline Warman, et al.*

https://doi.org/10.11647/OBP.0088

www.ingramcontent.com/pod-product-compliance
Lightning Source LLC
Chambersburg PA
CBHW041732300426
44116CB00019B/2959